MW01628905

Basic Drama Projects

Annotated Teacher's Edition

by Fran Averett Tanner, Ph.D.

College of Southern Idaho, Twin Falls, Idaho

Perfection Learning®

Editorial Director **Julie A. Schumacher**
Senior Editor **Gay Russell-Dempsey**
Permissions **Meghan Schumacher, Oliver Oertel**
Text Writers **Donald Abramson,** Playwright, Theatre Writer, Editor, Skokie, IL
Anthony Adler, Co-founder: The Actor's Gymnasium, Theatre Critic, Evanston, IL
Lisa Dillman, Playwright, Teacher, Education Writer, Chicago, IL
Elaine Malone, High School Drama Teacher, Atlanta, GA
Carmen McElwain, High School Drama Teacher, Plano, TX
Sheri Reda, Education Specialist, Chicago, IL
Kim Rubinstein, Artistic Associate, Long Wharf Theatre, New Haven, CT
Design **Herman Adler Design,** Evanston, Illinois

The editors would like to thank Peter Hay for permission to use material from his books *Theatrical Anecdotes* and *Broadway Anecdotes,* both published by the Oxford University Press (1987 and 1989, respectively).

Printed in the United States of America

1000 North Second Avenue
P.O. Box 500
Logan, Iowa 51546-0500
Tel: 1-800-831-4190 • Fax: 1-800-543-2745
perfectionlearning.com

3 4 5 6 7 8 RRD 12 11 10 09 08 07
ISBN-10: 0-7891-6176-1
ISBN-13: 978-0-7891-6176-5

Basic Drama Projects

Perfection Learning®

Editorial Director **Julie A. Schumacher**
Senior Editor **Gay Russell-Dempsey**
Illustrations **Mike Aspengren**
Picture Research **Lisa Lorimor**
Permissions **Meghan Schumacher, Oliver Oertel**
Text Writers **Sheri Reda,** Education Specialist, Chicago, Illinois
Lisa Dillman, Playwright, Teacher, Education Writer, Chicago, Illinois
Handbook Writer **Ric Averill,** Composer, Playwright, Drama Program Director for Lawrence Arts Center, Lawrence, Kansas
Design **Herman Adler Design,** Evanston, Illinois

Acknowledgments

Text Credits

Excerpt from "The Actor's Nightmare" by Christopher Durang from *Christopher Durang Explains It All For You.* Copyright ©1982 by Christopher Durang. Reprinted by permission of Grove/Atlantic, Inc.

Excerpt from *After Cages* by Cin Salach. Copyright ©1996 by Cin Salach. Reprinted by permission of Tia Chucha Press.

Excerpt from *Blood Wedding* by Federico Garcia Lorca. Translation by James Graham-Lujan and Richard L. O'Connell, from *Three Tragedies.* Copyright ©1947 by New Directions Publishing Corp. Reprinted by permission of New Directions Publishing Corp.

Excerpt from *Blithe Spirit* by Noel Coward. Copyright ©1941 by Noel Coward. Reprinted by permission of Alan Brodie Representation Ltd. 211 Piccadilly, London W1V 9LD.

(Acknowledgments continued on page 609)

Printed in the United States of America

1000 North Second Avenue
P.O. Box 500
Logan, Iowa 51546-0500
Tel: 1-800-831-4190 • Fax: 1-800-543-2745
perfectionlearning.com

7 8 9 10 11 12 RRD 12 11 10 09 08 07
[hardback] ISBN-13: 978-0-7569-1640-4
[hardback] ISBN-10: 0-7569-1640-2
[paperback] ISBN-13: 978-0-7891-6175-8
[paperback] ISBN-10: 0-7891-6175-3

Basic Drama Projects

8th Edition

by Fran Averett Tanner, Ph.D.
College of Southern Idaho, Twin Falls, Idaho

Perfection Learning®

Review Board

The Editors are indebted to the following teachers for their help in creating this book and for their tireless efforts on behalf of theatre students around the country.

Jeanne Averill
Drama Teacher
Lawrence High School
Lawrence, Kansas

Tracy Boylan
Drama Teacher
La Salle-Peru Township High School
LaSalle, Illinois

Deborah Clark
Drama Teacher
Hollywood Hills High School
Hollywood, Florida

Robert Kallos
Drama Teacher
The Galloway School
Atlanta, Georgia

Andrea Kidd
Drama Teacher
Dr. Michael M. Krop High School
Miami, Florida

Elaine Malone
Drama Teacher
The Galloway School
Atlanta, Georgia

Carmen McElwain
Drama Teacher
Plano, Texas

Kim Rubinstein
Professor of Theatre Arts
Northwestern University
Evanston, Illinois

Nan Zabriski
Professor of Theatre Arts
De Paul University
Chicago, Illinois

Student Actors

We would also like to thank the following student actors for their help in making the photographic images in this book lively and instructive.

Emmett Adler
Max Adler
Stephon Albert
Gail Amornpongchai
Paige Azuma
Calvin Baptiste, Jr.
Bryan D. Blaney
Peter Bloom
Elaine Coladarci
Amanda Georgantas
Alex Goode
Lauren Gray
Yasmeen Kheshgi
Christa Koskosky
Lizzie Laundy
Henry Marcus
Mghnon Martin
Tatyana Pramatarova
Alex Rosenfield
Isaac Simpson
Eileen Spangler
Hilary Ubando

Additional thanks go to Lost Era Costumes, Chicago, Illinois, for their generous help in costuming; Joe Silvestri of Lake Forest Academy for allowing use of theatre space and student models; Shauna Thieman of Western Michigan University Theatre Department, Lee Ann Bakros from the Des Moines Community Playhouse, and Christina Faison of North High in Des Moines, Iowa, for the use of photographs from their productions.

iv

Welcome to Drama Class!

We think you're going to enjoy your stay!
Basic Drama Projects offers you just what the name suggests: projects that provide an introduction to theatre basics. Basics that are engaging, challenging, creative, and fun. Here are hands-on, action-packed assignments—from improv and character development to writing and directing to creating props and planning set designs.

Success in this class will not necessarily lead to a starring role on Broadway or a career in costume design or sound engineering. Instead, it is a place where you can tap into your own creativity, gain self-confidence, and experience working collaboratively with others. You will discover that working in the theatre almost always means being part of a team.

This is a class where teamwork and dependability aren't just words—they are tools of the trade. And as you gain a broader theatre background, you will also develop other skills. You will learn to become a critical listener and viewer—qualities that will serve you well no matter where your future takes you.

v

Contents

Unit Two

Unit Three

Contents

Unit Four

Unit Five

ix

Contents

x

Contents

Unit Seven

Unit Eight

Monologues and Scenes 440

xiii

Contents

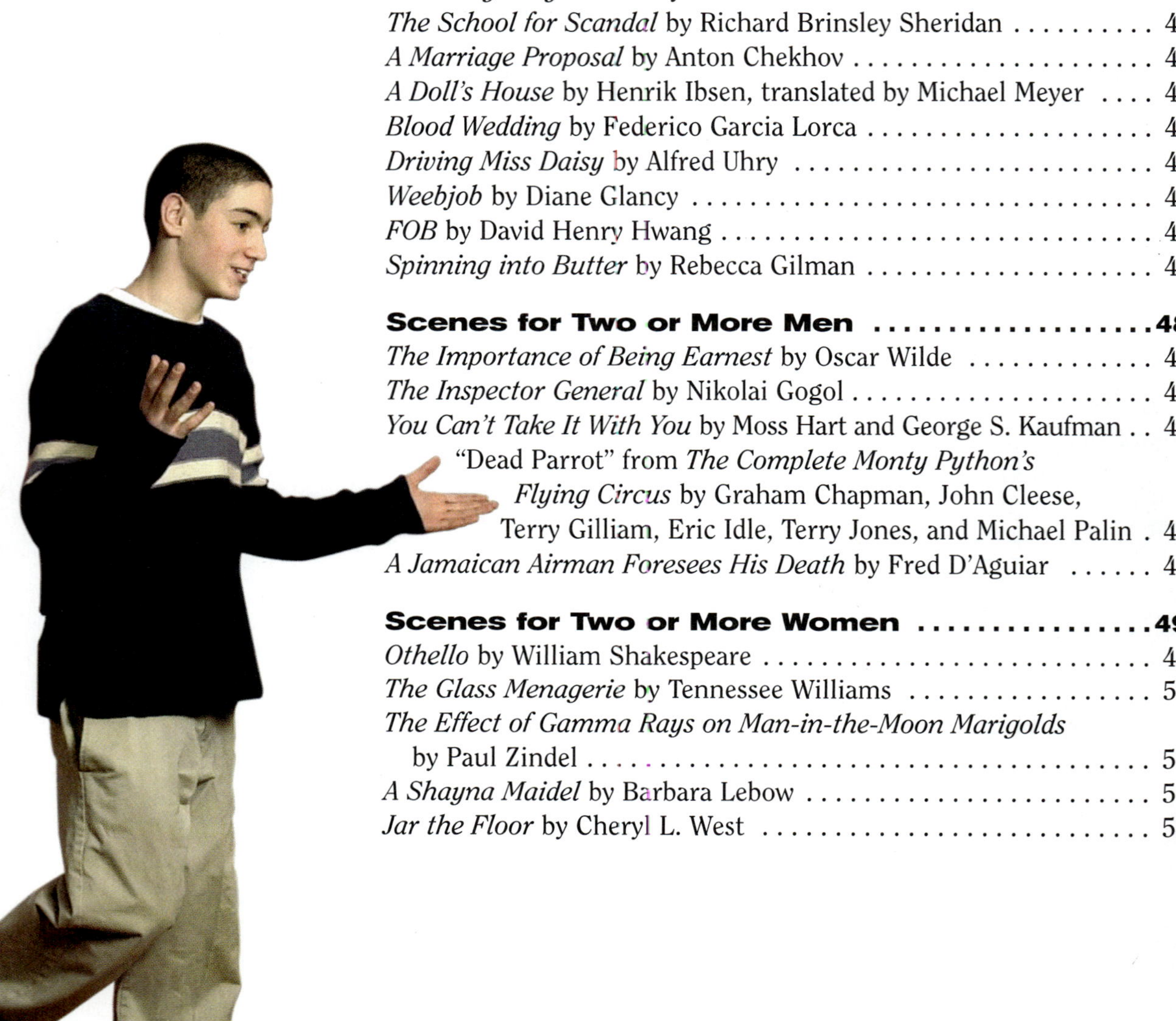

Unit One

Begin with the Basics

Unit One offers students experiential learning about the basics of performance, including warm-ups, the use of observation and experience, the elements of pantomime, and the principles of improvisation. Projects in this unit will help students learn to trust themselves and each other as performers and will introduce students to the kinds of work that underpin effective performances.

Project Preview

Chapter 1 Warm Up
Creating a warm-up routine

Chapter 2 Observation
Giving a detailed description

Chapter 3 Pantomime
Preparing a pantomime

Chapter 4 Improvisation
Performing an improvisation

Note: The Theatre Information Pack (or TIPack)

In putting together this program, the editors learned that every teacher has his or her own idea as to what material should be included in the early chapters of the student book. Teachers' varied requests demonstrated the organic nature of theatre and presented an interesting challenge.

In response to teachers' concerns, a set of thirteen blackline masters has been compiled that provide basic information for theatre students. This introductory material, which is found in the Teacher's Resource Binder, can be duplicated and taught as a preview chapter at the beginning of the year, or given to students as a reference tool.

In addition, each of the pages in the Theatre Information Pack is referenced in the appropriate chapter as a TIPack page.

Unit One

Begin with the Basics

Quotable

Use the quote below as a journal writing prompt, discussion starter, or for your own enjoyment.

On the stage you're exploring the limits of yourself. How loud and how strong and how big and how wide is the human entity? How much are we like giants and kings?

Ruby Dee, Actor

Discussion Questions

The following questions are intended to tap into students' **prior knowledge** and attitudes about the subject matter of the unit.

- What do you do to relax? How does your body feel when it is relaxed?
- Have you ever participated in an organized sport of any kind? What did you or your teammates do to prepare for a game?
- What do you think of when you hear the term *warm-up?* How do you think this phrase can be applied to theatre?
- Who is your favorite athlete or dancer? What qualities does that person display in performance?
- Some people experience the world primarily through their eyes. Others are more attuned to smells or sounds. What sense do you feel predominates in your experience of the world?
- What is the most vivid sense memory you can call up at will?
- Was there a time when someone's body language tipped you off to what they were thinking? Explain.
- What do you think your physical presence communicates about you?
- What have you experienced as the advantages and disadvantages of working with partners?

ACTivity Gather the students to pose for a group picture. First, ask them to pose for a formal shot. Then have them pose for an informal shot. You also may want to challenge the students to pose as a group of characters from a particular play.

Visual Cue

The image above shows a scene from the New York production of *Rent*. Based on the opera *La Boheme, Rent* was written by composer Jonathan Larson, who died at 35 of an aneurysm the night before the musical made its off-Broadway debut. *Rent* won both the Tony Award and the Pulitzer Prize in 1996. The following prompts can be used to exercise **critical viewing skills.**

- Describe the people in the picture. How do they seem to be interacting?
- Study the picture, then close your eyes and try to describe three of the people in it.
- How improvisational do you think this moment is? Explain.

ACTivity Have the students imitate the poses in the photograph on this page. Then invite them to improvise what various people are saying, singing, or doing.

Theatre Journal

Choose one of the characters in the photograph and write a short biography of this character. Then compare your biography to those of your classmates.

Chapter 1

Warm Up

This chapter introduces students to the basics of relaxing and warming up before rehearsing or performing. An effective performer has a flexible body and a pliable mind. The relaxation techniques and warm-up exercises students learn now will be useful throughout their lives.

Objectives

1. to learn methods of relaxing the body and mind
2. to increase flexibility and body control
3. to improve articulation
4. to create and perform a two- to three-minute warm-up routine

National Standards

Chapter 1 meets these National Theatre Standards:
Proficient 1a, 2a, 2c, 7d

Project Specs

Explain to students that most disciplines, even those as diverse as auto mechanic, weaver, and mountain climber, require the right tools and proper guidelines. These are known as *specifications,* or *specs.* In this book, the specs for each project are listed on the first page of the chapter.

Special Needs Students
Note that students who are physically challenged may need to have some exercise and warm-up routines modified for their use.

On Your Feet

Choose one of the tongue twisters and demonstrate it for the class. You may want to have a competition in which students take turns saying a tongue twister clearly as many times as possible. Students who can say a given tongue twister three times quickly without an error enter "playoffs." The winner is declared "Twister Wizard."

Chapter 1 Warm Up

Actors relax and warm up in order to be alert and responsive as they perform. Warm-ups help increase the actor's ability to direct the nervous energy that arises before going onstage. By relaxing and warming up before a performance, you too can prepare your voice and body for the strenuous work ahead.

Project Specs

Project Description You and a partner will create and perform a two- to three-minute warm-up routine using techniques and exercises learned in class.

Purpose to learn techniques that help increase flexibility, body control, relaxation, and vocal articulation

Materials loose-fitting, comfortable clothing; a list of the elements in your routine or the Warm Up Activity Sheet your teacher provides

Theatre Terms

adrenaline
articulation
pliable
professionals
routine
stage fright
vocalizing

On Your Feet

To begin exercising clear speech, or **articulation,** try to say one or more of the following tongue twisters rapidly without mispronouncing any words:

- Two teamsters tried to tag twenty-two keys.
- She makes a proper cup of coffee in a copper coffee pot.
- Red leather, yellow leather, red leather, yellow leather (repeat)
- Would Wheeler woo Wanda while Woody snoozed woozily?

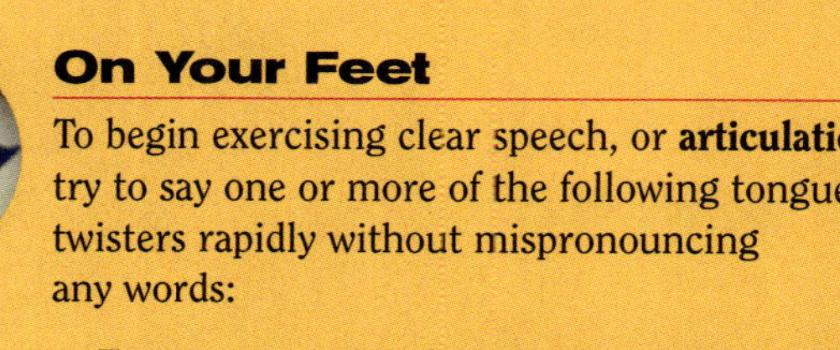

4 **Unit One** Begin with the Basics

Theatre Terms

adrenaline a hormone that produces the feeling of sudden increased energy

articulation the clear pronunciation of words

pliable supple, flexible

professionals people who make a living in their chosen line of work

routine a series of actions that may be repeated

stage fright feeling nervous before or during a performance

vocalizing singing without words

PREVIEW

The Actor Prepares

Like all disciplined **professionals,** good actors make what they do look effortless. They seem to inhabit the characters they play. Their bodies, minds, voices, and emotions are their tools, and they use them expertly to create the effects they desire. Some actors undergo rigorous physical training to maximize their capabilities onstage. Some do not. However, all serious actors warm up before rehearsals and performances. They know that they will need to be alert and responsive to stage directions, other actors, and their own physical, mental, and em otional needs.

Actors who warm up become alert and physically prepared for the demands of acting. They also direct the normal nervous energy that arises before a performance. Instead of spiraling into fright, actors who loosen up can put increased energy into the demands of their roles and of the play at hand.

Actors are often called upon to perform very vigorous movement, such as dancing, fighting, or wrestling. Singing, yelling, and other **vocalizing** may also be called for. If you learn these skills and practice them as part of your everyday **routine,** your voice and body will become strong, **pliable,** or adaptable, and disciplined. As a bonus, you will always be ready and qualified for that physically demanding, once-in-a-lifetime role.

Actors warm up before a performance.

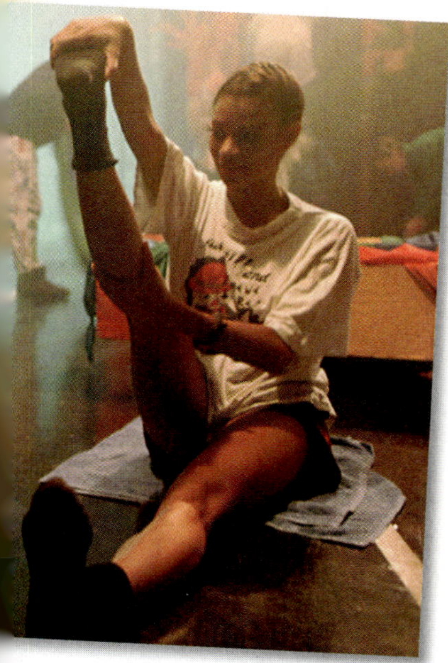

Why Warm Up?

Just as athletes do not take to the court or the field without doing warm-up exercises, neither do actors. The warm-ups help you in a number of ways: they relax you, they help clear your mind, and they prepare you to use your voice and body effectively. In other words, they take the nervous energy that arises naturally and put it to work as you portray your character on stage. Additionally, these exercises will build confidence and expand your range of communication and movement. Gaining mastery over your body's expressive ability can be exhilarating. It also helps you appreciate the work of those actors who make it look easy.

PREVIEW

The Actor Prepares

Discuss the fact that actors must rely on the body, mind, and voice as the tools and instruments of their craft. Unlike other crafts, in which a person can get a new tool whenever one is needed, the actor can only improve his or her instrument by honing personal skills.

Ask students who play a sport to demonstrate things they do to warm up before playing. Ask the same question of students who play a musical instrument or sing. Then discuss the similarities between the various warm-ups.

Why Warm Up?

Talk to students about the many injuries that athletes and dancers suffer each year. Discuss how warming up can prevent such injuries. Tell students that muscular stiffness disappears as the body is conditioned and that awkwardness subsides also.

Show, Don't Tell Because some students may think that athletic ability is required of them, demonstrate an effective stretching routine that almost anyone can do. Encourage the students to copy your moves. If you have a daily exercise routine, teach it to your students. Invite students who dance or practice yoga or the martial arts to talk about what they enjoy about these endeavors.

Use these prompts to help students exercise **critical viewing skills.**

- Where do the people in the picture appear to be?
- How close to actually performing do you think they were when photographed?
- Do you think these actors are athletic? Why or why not?

Resource Binder

- Student Contract, TIPack, p. A
- Letter to Parents, TIPack, p. B
- Dealing with Stage Fright, TIPack, p. C
- Warm Up Activity Sheet, p. 1
- Trust Exercises Worksheet, p. 2
- Critique Sheet: Warm-up Routine, p. 3
- Warm-up Test, p. 4

Handbook Connections
pages 558–559, 563, 569–570

To Have on Hand

- Extra sweatshirts and sweatpants for students who are not dressed for physical activity
- Prize for the winner of the tongue-twister challenge
- CD or tape player for those who want to put routines to music
- A large mirror students can look in when trying a new movement or position

Relaxation Techniques

If technology is available, you might want to have students perform relaxation techniques to various kinds of music.

ACTivity Encourage students to suggest names for the poses they take while performing the relaxation techniques and the warm-ups. Tell them that in yoga, particular poses are often named for animals.

ACTivity **Beginning Students** To encourage slow movements, have students perform the rag doll technique to the count of ten and the head movements to a count of five or more. Remind students that moving slowly helps avoid injuries. At the end of these movements, students should gently shake out their right wrist, left wrist, right ankle, left ankle, and so on to a count of four.

ACTivity **Advanced Students** Invite students to suggest alterations or adaptations that will help them maximize stretches safely. Mention again that some people find motivation in moving to music or naming positions so that they are easy to visualize and remember.

Warm-up Exercises

Relaxation techniques are different from warm-up exercises. Warm-up exercises are best done after putting the body into a relaxed state; therefore, they usually come after relaxation techniques. Some movement specialists recommend doing relaxation techniques both before and after warm-ups.

Show, Don't Tell Demonstrate breathing in to a count of four while swinging your arms slowly forward, then breathing out to a count of four while swinging arms slowly backward. This heightens relaxation during warm-ups by controlling the breath during the exercises.

The following warm-up routines will prepare you physically and vocally for the stage—and for the demands of everyday life.

Relaxation Techniques

- With feet apart in a comfortable balance, stretch up tall. Then bend over like a rag doll, collapsing quickly and loosely from the waist with your relaxed arms and hands dangling to the floor. Keep your arms, hands, and head completely relaxed. Slowly rise up, keeping relaxed. Repeat.
- Breathe in as your teacher or director counts to eight. Take a deep breath, bringing air in through your nose, then into your throat, your chest, and your lungs. Feel your middle expand as your breath fills your body. Then breathe out slowly through your mouth to the count of eight. Repeat several times.
- With your neck relaxed and your chin close to your chest, slowly move your head to the left, back to the front, to the right, and up. Then reverse the rotation. Be sure to move very slowly and cautiously. Keep your neck relaxed, letting your head slowly roll like a dead weight in a socket.
- Lie quietly on your back. Close your eyes and make your mind a blank slate. Chase all thoughts away, concentrating only on relaxing your body. Listen to the rhythm of your heartbeat as, one at a time, you relax every part of your body—from your toes, to your legs and arms, and up to your head. Feel your body melt into the floor. Remain in this relaxed position for a few moments before you begin your warm-up exercises.

The rag doll: Stretch and collapse gently.

Warm-up Exercises

- Swing your relaxed arms in large circles, one at a time.
- Lie on your back and tuck in your knees, holding them to your chest with your hands. Roll gently from side to side. Do this ten times.

6 **Unit One** Begin with the Basics

From the Field: Don't Look at Me!

Relaxation techniques can also be strong self-awareness tools. A few years ago I began having my students face each other for five to seven minutes and just look into one another's eyes. For many students, all the tension goes out of the body as they establish a connection to the other.

The first time I tried this exercise, though, two of my students kept clenching their fists. I thought perhaps they were nervous, but then they both said they had become increasingly angry. For them, this was not a relaxation technique at all—but a tension-builder! After some discussion, we realized that all the staring must have elicited a fight response.

It was an insightful moment in which the whole class got to explore the range of human responses.

Patti Interrante, Assistant Professor of Speech and Theatre, Oakton College, Des Plaines, Illinois

- Sit on your ankles, keeping your back straight. Stretch up, with your arms extended, as high as you can go. Keep your body straight. Do this four times.
- Use your entire body to draw huge numbers, from one to ten, in the air. Use as much space as you can. Bend, stretch, and travel around the room as you write. Do this for about three minutes.
- Play "imaginary jump rope." By yourself or with two partners (to hold the imaginary rope), jump an imaginary rope until you are tired. You might want to try using a few different rhythms, changing your jumping pattern accordingly—alternating feet together and feet apart, and so on.
- Lie on your back and then extend your entire lower body into a shoulder stand, placing your hands on your back and your elbows on the floor. Stay in this position for a count of twenty. Next, roll your legs back and over your head, letting your feet drop to the floor. Keep your legs straight. Only go back as far as is comfortable. Then unwind until you are flat on your back again. Repeat.
- Stand with your feet slightly apart. Begin to shake your hands. Shake them more and more vigorously. When your teacher yells, "Freeze!" stop all movement. Then begin to tense the same muscles in your hands. Repeat this exercise several times. Be sure you stop shaking the moment you hear, "Freeze!"
- Stretch your tongue. Try to touch the tip of your tongue to your nose. Don't be discouraged if you can't do it—only one in 1000 people can. It's the stretch, not the parlor trick, that counts. Repeat several times.

Be careful to keep your back straight as you do this exercise. Do not overdo it.

ACTivity Some students may struggle with anxiety and others may suffer from boredom while doing slow, careful movements. To keep students focused and engaged, invite volunteers to give meaning to the movements by weaving a story around them.

Vocabulary Enhancement

It can be helpful for students to understand something about anatomy in order to exercise properly. For example, those who lead theatrical warm-ups often tell actors to stretch and bend one vertebra at a time. *Vertebrae* are the individual small bones that comprise the backbone.

Similarly, voice teachers often advise actors where to place the tongue in relation to the *palate.* The palate is the roof of the mouth. The bony part is known as the *hard palate* and the soft part is known as the *soft palate.*

Chapter 1 Warm Up **7**

Here's How

Invite the entire class to join together to do the rhythm hop. If any students are having trouble with the routine, invite other students to isolate the steps and slowly repeat them. Incorporate music to help with the movement. Work on the hop until everyone can do it.

Vocal Exercises

Show, Don't Tell To encourage a sense of camaraderie, have students stand in a circle while doing these exercises. The circle shape keeps the atmosphere relaxed and the interaction intimate. Join the circle and demonstrate each vocal exercise for the students before asking them to try it.

It might help some students to do the "ahhh" and "oooo" sounds by thinking about making as big a face as possible for the "ahhh" and as small a face as possible for the "oooo."

ACTivity Challenge students to try an activity called "chewing your face." Demonstrate exaggerated stretches while going through the vowels: AAA—EEE—III—OOO—UUU.

Invite students to try these exercises with and without sound.

If your students enjoy tongue twisters, give them a few more:

- Unique New York
- Tie twine to three tree twigs.
- Four furious friends fought for the phone.

If time permits, challenge students to develop and teach the class their own tongue twisters.

Here's How
To Do the Rhythm Hop

Can't walk and chew gum at the same time? Doing the rhythm hop can help. It takes a little time, attention, and some practice to learn, but it gets easier as you do it.

- With your weight on your left foot, hop once, while pointing your right foot out front. Extend your arms out in front of you and clap your hands. Hop a second time, with your right foot extended out to the right and your arms extended out to the sides.
- Hop on your left foot a third time, and bring your right foot down to the left foot. Also put your arms down at your sides. Next, shift your weight to your right foot and repeat the process.

Do the rhythm hop 10 to 20 times rapidly. Eventually, you will be able to perform this exercise while chanting rhymes or song lyrics.

Vocal Exercises

- Smile! Smile with great exaggeration, letting your teeth show and drawing your lips as tightly as possible. Say "eeeee." Then exaggerate a pucker and say "ooooo." Repeat these two motions and sounds ten times in quick succession. Then add consonants to create sound combinations such as "me-moo," "tee-too," "bee-boo," gee-goo," and "lee-loo."
- Begin a slow yawn and make the sound "ahhhh" as you exhale. Remember the open quality of the sound you are making. Aim for it in all your speech.
- Open wide. Open your mouth as wide as possible. Say "ahhh" as you exhale. Now close your mouth, saying "oooo" as you exhale. Repeat "ahhh-oooo" several times. Take care to open your mouth as wide as possible.
- Read the rhyme below with clarity and emphasis. Start off slowly, then increase your speed as you read it two more times.

To sit in solemn silence in a dull dock
In a pestilential prison with a life long lock
Awaiting the sensation of a short sharp shock
From a cheap and chippy chopper on a big black block.

—W.S. Gilbert from *The Mikado*

Backstage Gossip: Acting 8, Basketball 3

Actor Cherry Jones once described a conversation with William Peterson about the rigors of theatrical performance, saying, "Billy Peterson, when we were doing *Night of the Iguana,* said, 'I think what we do is harder than what professional athletes do.' He said, 'Those basketball players only play three games a week. We play eight, back to back.'"

from *The Actor's Art,* edited by Jackson R. Bryer and Richard A. Davison

PREPARE

Work Out Your Warm-up Routine

Your teacher will assign you a partner or ask you to find a partner for this project. Have your partner read the various routines and exercises described on the previous pages while you follow the directions for doing them. Then you do the same for your partner. Repeat the exercises until you feel comfortable doing them all.

Together, decide whether you will use both physical and vocal elements to create your routine. Next, order the elements you will include for your two- to three-minute routine using a list or the Activity Sheet your teacher provides.

Plan how you will present the routine to the class: Will one of you instruct the class while the other demonstrates the routine? Will you both demonstrate the routine while you give instructions?

You may want to use music to accompany your routine. If you do, be sure the music has the appropriate rhythm and tune for what you are trying to achieve.

When you have completely worked out your routine, time it to be sure it is no longer than three minutes and no shorter than two minutes. Practice at least five times before you actually present your routine.

PRESENT

Be the Instructor

When your turn comes, stand still for a second with your partner and take a deep breath, bringing air into your lungs. Introduce yourselves to the class and then present your routine. Encourage your classmates to join in the routine. Have fun, smile, and harness all that nervous energy!

When you are finished, pause and then quietly leave the playing area. Remember to maintain a sense of physical and vocal control from the time you leave the playing area until you return to your seat.

Theatre Journal

Make a list of the things you do in your everyday life that could help prepare you for performing on the stage. Examples might be singing in the chorus or playing basketball. Write a short explanation of the ways in which these activities help you both physically and emotionally.

Notes

PREPARE

Work Out Your Warm-up Routine

Invite students to add music to their routines, as well as other physical elements not introduced in this book. Invite them to find additional elements through dance, yoga, martial arts, and other physical exercise programs. Have music on CDs or tape available for their use.

ACTivity Students who have access to video and/or sound equipment can use that equipment to help them develop and rehearse their routines.

PRESENT

Be the Instructor

Students who have videotaped their routines can join the class as participants in following their own routines.

ACTivity Urge students to be active teachers. After demonstrating their routines, they can break them down into movements and teach each one to the class—first performing the movement and then asking the class to perform it.

Consider using students' warm-ups throughout the year, thereby demonstrating the usefulness of the assignment and reinforcing its importance in theatre.

Theatre Journal

Use the following as an additional or substitute prompt.

Make a list of the various stretches and movements involved in achieving the everyday actions, chores, and other activities you perform regularly.

CRITIQUE

Compare Two Warm-up Routines

Hand out the Critique Sheet for this project or have students use their own paper. (You will probably want to have two Critique Sheets available, as the students are comparing two routines.) Be sure students understand that the critique activity involves several steps, including note-taking, scoring, and writing. It will be helpful to assign the two people each student will evaluate so that no one is overlooked.

Introduce students to the concept of the nonjudgmental critique. Critiquing is different from criticizing in that it is aimed at helping someone improve their performance rather than simply pointing out weaknesses. Therefore, it is a good idea for students to indicate what they like about a performance before making suggestions for improvement. Such suggestions should include ways to make a weak area as strong as the student's best work.

After you have reviewed students' critiques, trim off the evaluator's name and hand out the sheets to the subjects of the evaluations.

Spotlight on

Stage Fright Relaxation techniques and warm-ups do help alleviate stage fright, but in extreme cases students may want to try one or more of the following:

- After doing routine warm-ups, run in place for two to three minutes. The running will put some of the extra adrenaline to use.
- Some actors consciously try to exaggerate movements, such as shaking the knees or hands for a short period in order to get those movements out of their systems.
- Never lock your knees or stiffen up when nervous. If you find yourself stiff in any way, tense and relax that part of the body.

CRITIQUE

Compare Two Warm-up Routines

As you watch your classmates' warm-up routines, take notes as to how well the routines are presented. Use a scale of 1 to 5, with 5 being "outstanding" and 1 being "needs much improvement." Ask yourself questions such as those below as you evaluate the routines.

- Were the instructions clear and easy to do?
- Did the instructors speak clearly?
- Was the routine the correct length?
- Was the routine effective in warming up and relaxing the participants?
- How would you use this routine to warm up for a performance?

Compare how well two separate pairs of presenters created and presented their routines. Write a paragraph explaining the reasons for the scores you gave.

Spotlight on

Stage Fright

According to a nationwide survey, speaking in front of others is the number one fear of Americans. We experience **stage fright**–dry mouth, shaky knees, trembling hands, sweaty palms, and queasy stomach–because we suspect we won't do well. Minor stage fright can be helpful to a performer because it releases extra **adrenaline,** a chemical our bodies produce to help us deal with unfamiliar situations. The surge of adrenaline provides the performer with increased energy, enthusiasm, and animation. A heightened sense of awareness is useful to the actor, but uncontrolled stage fright can derail a performer. Below are a few tips for managing stage fright.

Be Prepared. When we are prepared we automatically feel more comfortable and confident. If you find your hands are shaky or your mouth is dry, take a moment to remind yourself that you know exactly what you're doing.

Use Good Posture. Good posture provides a strong base for movement and vocal production. Your good posture will give the audience an impression of confidence–and it just might make you feel more confident yourself!

Breathe. Don't forget to breathe! Inadequate breath can lead to a shaky voice and a feeling of physical insecurity. If necessary, take a couple of deep breaths to ground yourself before you begin speaking.

Give Yourself Time. Remember that most people who experience stage fright usually warm up after a short time. The more public speaking you do, the easier it becomes.

Backstage Gossip: The Reverse Kidnapping

It seems even college professors can succumb to stage fright. One summer Harold J. Kennedy employed a local college professor to perform in a production of *Captain Brassbound's Conversion.* He was thrilled to find that the professor was a marvelous actor. In fact, the professor had only one flaw: He had never overcome his stage fright.

On opening night, the professor entered on cue, opened his mouth, and—began shaking. He could not make words come out of his mouth. Actor Jane Cowl, who was supposed to be his kidnap victim, finally saved the day by asking, "Do you want to take me to the mountains?"

The professor nodded, dumbly, and Cowl took his hand. "Let's go!" she said, and ran with him off stage.

from *No Pickle, No Performance* by Harold J. Kennedy

Additional Projects

1 Say "ahhhhh." Sustain a comfortably pitched tone. Then create variations by increasing the volume, decreasing the volume, and bringing the volume back to start. Repeat with pitch: make the sound higher in pitch, then lower in pitch, then bring it back to start.

2 With a partner, carry on an animated conversation in gibberish or a pretend "foreign language," using only nonsense or invented words. If you find it difficult to make up words or sounds, use the syllables "da-da-shoon" repeatedly. Sincerely try to communicate through this new language.

3 Say a sentence such as "Now is the time," or "There goes the last one," in each of the following ways: sternly, eagerly, worriedly, soothingly, shyly, drowsily, angrily, sadly, and happily.

4 Blow yourself up. Imagine that you are a balloon. You can be completely inflated with three large inhalations. Expand in three stages, until you are completely expanded, like a balloon. Ask a partner or classmate to "pop" you. Then deflate as a balloon might.

5 Form a circle with seven or more classmates. Hold hands with the people on each side of you and do not let go. Begin weaving under and around the arms and legs of the other people in the circle. Once you are tangled to the point that no one can move any further, try to untangle yourselves. Do not, under any circumstances, let go of the hands you are holding, but stop the moment anyone becomes uncomfortable.

6 Memorize part of Biff's monologue from *Death of a Salesman* by Arthur Miller found in Unit Eight. Imagine that Biff is doing sit-ups or bouncing a ball during the scene. Then perform the movements of this activity while speaking the lines from the scene. Allow the words to accompany the movement. If you prefer, memorize a monologue of your own choosing and work out your own activity to accompany it.

Chapter 1 Test

The test for this chapter is available in blackline master form in the Resource Binder, page 4.

For More Information

Books

West, Edie, *210 Icebreakers*, McGraw Hill, 1997.

Other Media

Borysenko, Joan, *The Beginner's Guide to Meditation* (sound cassettes). Hay House, 1998.

Klein, Bob, *Relaxation Exercises: Chinese Chi-gung Warm-up Movements.* (one videocassette, 74 minutes), Artistic Video, Sound Beach, 1989.

Muldaur, Maria, *Developing Vocal Style and Performance* (one videocassette, one sound cassette), Homespun Tapes, Woodstock, 1990.

Webb, Tamilee, *The Teen Workout* (videorecording, 60 minutes), Graymont Enterprises, 1989.

Yee, Rodney, *The Art of Breath and Relaxation* (videocassette, 70 minutes), Healing Arts Publishing, 1999.

Substitute Teacher Activities

Here are suggestions for one or more days when you will be out of the classroom:

- Assign the Trust Exercises Worksheet on page 2 of the Resource Binder.
- Discuss the information found in the Student Handbook concerning Physical Warm-ups (p. 563), Movement (pp. 558–559), and Voice (pp. 569–570).
- Assign one or more of the Additional Projects on this page.
- **Plan a Relaxation Teach-In.** Assign the students to groups and ask each group to research and select one good relaxation tip. Have each group present their tip. The class will then gather all these tips and create a series of relaxation techniques based upon them. The entire class can then practice these techniques together.

Chapter 2

Observation

This chapter introduces students to the discipline of observation. It awakens them to the power of the senses and the importance of memory in helping to create believable characters.

Objectives

1 to improve the memory

2 to strengthen the powers of observation

3 to practice recalling observed objects through the senses

4 to give a detailed description of an object

National Standards

Chapter 2 meets these National Theatre Standards:

Proficient 2b, 6b, 7c

Advanced 2d

Project Specs

Special Needs Students
Researchers have determined that children learn in at least seven different ways. Many are predominantly visual, for example, while others are aural, tactile, or kinesthetic. The project designated for this chapter should prove rewarding for aural, tactile, or kinesthetic learners.

On Your Feet

Show, Don't Tell In order to demonstrate engagement of the senses and memory, allow students to choose an item in the room for you to observe. Have the students show you the object for one minute, then take it out of sight. Describe for the students the sights, sounds, physical sensations, smells, tastes, movements, and memories the object evokes for you.

Chapter

2 Observation

Acting is said to be the study of human behavior. So, in addition to their own memories and imaginations, actors must depend on their powers of **observation.** As an actor, you must become aware of how other people feel, move, speak, think, and behave. You must be able to recall what you observe, and use it to build believable characters.

Project Specs

Project Description For this assignment, you will give a detailed one- to three-minute description of an object.

Purpose to learn the skills of observation and recall

Materials a list of the characteristics of your chosen object or the Observation Activity Sheet provided by your teacher

Theatre Terms

conscious
observation
recall
sense memory
spontaneous
subconscious
visualize

On Your Feet

To test your powers of observation, look around the classroom and choose an object, such as a poster, and quietly observe it for one minute. Concentrate on the colors, shapes, printed words, and textures. Also pay attention to how the item makes you *feel.* Now close your eyes and try to re-create the object in your mind. Now, without looking at the object, write down every detail you remember. Compare what you have written to the object. Did you miss anything?

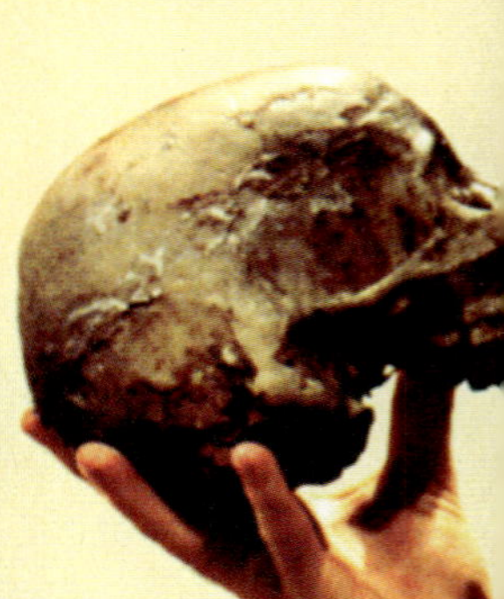

Theatre Terms

conscious aware (of in the mind)

observation the act of recognizing or noticing an object, a fact, or event

recall to remember a fact or event so as to re-create it

sense memory memory that uses all the senses to recapture an experience

spontaneous not planned

subconscious existing in the mind just below the level of consciousness

visualize picture in one's mind

PREVIEW

Getting Specific

Someone once said that only through the specific can we reveal the universal. This is true in the arts, and it is especially relevant in the theatre, where actors are called upon to create believable characters and situations in front of an audience.

As an actor you must become a keen observer—a student of the world around you. That's because to portray any character believably, you have to create a complex and specific human being made up of hundreds of key details.

That might sound difficult, but using your powers of observation can help. You can start off with something slightly less complicated than a human being—an inanimate object.

Karen Allen in a recent production of *The Glass Menagerie.*

Plays are often about people's relationship with their possessions—or their relationship with *other* people's possessions. In Tennessee Williams's play *The Glass Menagerie,* a painfully shy young woman named Laura seeks refuge from the outside world in her collection of delicate glass animals. When playing this character, an actor must have a specific *relationship* with the members of the tiny glass menagerie. After all, if the figurines mean nothing to Laura, they won't mean much to an audience either.

Alan Cumming, as Hamlet, focuses on the skull of Yorick in the 1993 London production.

PREVIEW

Getting Specific

Explain to the students that no actor has sufficient personal experience to play all types of people onstage. So, in addition to a powerful imagination, actors must depend on their powers of observation. They must become aware of how others feel, move, think, speak, behave, and experience their environments.

They must also be able to retain what they observe so that they can use it to build characters outside their own personal experience.

ACTivity To make your point, invite a volunteer to walk across the front of the classroom using his or her own natural gait. Then challenge that person to imitate your gait or the gait of a celebrity known to the class. With the class, analyze the similarities and differences between the two ways of walking.

The two images on this page show actors in relationship to inanimate objects that are central to their characters. You may want to use the following prompts to help students exercise **critical viewing skills.**

- In the top photograph, Karen Allen's character invests meaning in her glass animals. As an actor, what might you do to prepare to create this character?
- In the bottom photograph, Alan Cumming performs a scene in which Hamlet remembers his dead friend Yorick. What emotions might the actor draw upon in this scene?
- What senses are these actors using in their observation of objects?

Resource Binder

- Basic Theatre Terminology, TIPack, p. D
- Observation Activity Sheet, p. 5
- Tapping Your Inner Resources Worksheet, p. 6
- Critique Sheet: Describe an Object, p. 7
- Observation Test, p. 8

Handbook Connections
pages 559–560

To Have on Hand

Have ready a set of fairly familiar objects for display. Make sure a number of the objects have qualities or associations related to the senses of taste, hearing, and smell.

You may want to keep some objects covered with a napkin or cloth so that sounds or smells do not dissipate.

PREPARE

Your Observations and Impressions

Point out to the students that objects and events that people find memorable or remarkable often lodge themselves into the brain unconsciously. Some students will find they have very good recall abilities.

A Test Run

Beginning Students
Students with little experience might benefit from ignoring the time limit at first and simply writing as much as possible. Once they have included sufficient detail, they can pare down their description to fit the time limit. Encourage them to read their descriptions aloud.

Advanced Students
Challenge advanced students to improvise their descriptions and present them extemporaneously instead of using preparation time.

Vocabulary Enhancement

To help establish the emotional reality of a scene, actors use the principle of *recall.* When actors recall events in their own lives that provoke the same emotions their characters experience, they use what is called *emotional recall.*

Theatre Journal

Use the following as an additional or substitute prompt.

Students with a penchant for comedy or for the absurd might enjoy writing a love letter to the object, telling it what they find thrilling about it.

PREPARE

Your Observations and Impressions

In this assignment you will describe a familiar object and provide your impressions and feelings about it from your **sense memory** —in which you use all five senses to recapture an experience. You should describe the physical object in detail and also reveal to your audience what the object means to you.

Suppose, for example, that you decide upon a treasured toy from your early childhood. Using your powers of observation, you will **recall** or re-create this item in such a way that your audience will **visualize** the object you describe. But you can also share other details and memories, such as how you felt when you first saw the toy or what it meant to you at a particular time in your life. Perhaps the toy makes you feel sad that you are no longer as carefree as you once were. Or it might amuse you to think about a time when the toy was an important part of your life.

You can choose any object—but make sure it's one that means something to you or meant something to you in the past. In order to describe your object so that your audience will actually be able to see it, ask yourself the following questions and keep a list of your answers:

- What does the object look like?
- How does it smell?
- How does it feel?
- How does it/might it taste? (if applicable)
- How does it sound?
- What does it remind me of?
- What makes it important to me?

Suggestions for Objects

- a piece of jewelry
- a photograph
- an article of clothing
- a trophy or plaque
- a piece of art
- a musical instrument

A Test Run

Set a timer for three minutes. Rehearse describing your chosen object and its impact on you. This is not a scripted activity, so you do not have to memorize what you will say. Because the object has personal meaning for you, the words to describe it should be **spontaneous**. Stay within the one- to three-minute time limit.

Theatre Journal

Look at the list you have made about your chosen object. Write a paragraph about a day in your life that includes this object. Describe what the object looked like then. Be specific. Describe it in physical detail, but as you write, also pay attention to the feelings going on inside you. If you find you can go on for more than a paragraph, do so.

Backstage Gossip: Seeing Is Believing

John Gielgud often used observation to help create a character.

Once when I was rehearsing *Crime and Punishment*—it was a very hot day, I was walking through St. James Park—I saw a tramp lying down with his head buried in the dirty grass, filthy hands and everything, and he was absolutely relaxed. I thought, "This is the way that Raskolnikov must lie on the bed," and immediately it gave me a kind of line on the part.

from *Theatrical Anecdotes* by Peter Hay

Here's How
To Improve Your Sense Memory

You look at thousands of things every day without really *seeing* them. You can improve your powers of observation by using a few simple techniques.

1 **Relax.** Don't strain to focus on the details you think you're most likely to remember. Instead, try to look at the world around you with fresh eyes.

2 **Observe in segments.** For instance, if you look at an object, an ornate vase for example, you might focus on its outline, then the color, the texture, the weight, and the way it feels to the touch. Notice the associations that you make. Let your observation take in not only what your eyes tell you, but also what your other senses reveal. These associations can be very important for later recall.

3 **Use your journal** to record your impressions and observations. This gets you into the habit of paying attention to what you notice–and what you don't. Writing down what you observe can help you hold it in your **conscious** mind as well as in your **subconscious**–the part of the brain just below your awareness–so you can use it later. You can write about almost anything: what you saw on a walk, what a chocolate shake tastes like, what the air smells like after a rainstorm, and so on.

PRESENT
Describe Your Object

When your name is called, hand in your list or Activity Sheet and walk to the playing area.

Begin by telling the audience what your chosen object is. This can be a simple, objective statement, such as "I'm going to describe my trumpet."

As you begin your presentation, remember to keep your body relaxed and to breathe deeply to avoid excessive nervousness. Don't hurry. Concentrate on specifics. Don't worry that you're not including everything. Speak naturally and try to be completely truthful. After all, you are talking about something you know very well.

When you have finished, ask the audience if they have questions about the object you've just described. Set a limit of three questions. Afterward, thank your audience and return to your seat.

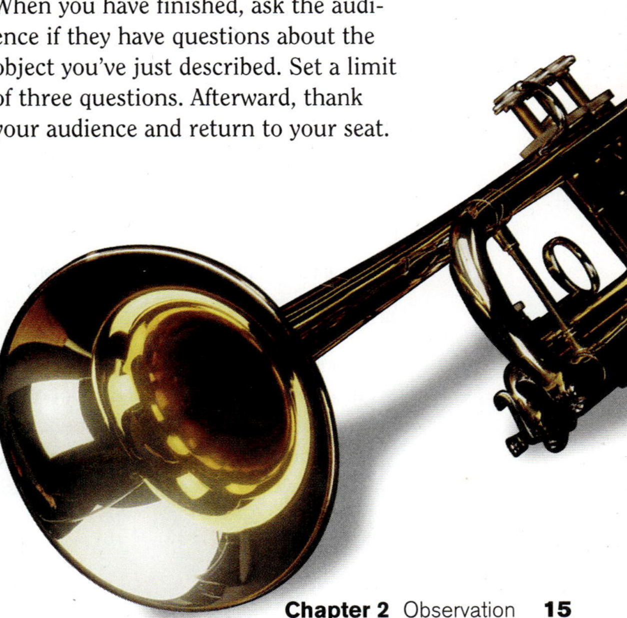

From the Field: Look at Me!

Early in the semester I advise students to start observing each other for an upcoming exercise. Then, several weeks later, I ask them to stand onstage, one at a time. The student onstage listens to what classmates have noticed about him or her. (Observers are to make only supportive, positive statements.)

At first, students find it painful to be observed. Soon, however, they become more comfortable. I tell them that they should come to expect—and that they deserve—positive attention.

The exercise has two more benefits: It builds community among the classmates, and it counteracts the tendency in performers to snipe at each other.

Kathleen Carot, Assistant Professor of Speech and Theatre, Oakton College, Des Plaines, Illinois

Here's How

Relax. Encourage students to relax by daydreaming about using an object or experiencing an event. Invite them to imagine encountering the object or event as a newcomer to this country or an alien from another planet.

Observe in segments. Unbidden associations are often the most fruitful, but students who are stuck might benefit by a conscious, formal exercise in word association. Have them state an obvious observation and then free associate around that word.

Use your journal. Encourage students to write at least one description a day in their journals. Point out that their descriptions can serve as references to enrich their acting roles.

PRESENT
Describe Your Object

Reassure students with performance anxiety by asking all students to make sure they place the emphasis on the objects they are describing, not their performance style in describing it.

Nevertheless, you may want to allow students to experiment with presentation style by speaking in the first person, as if they were the object they are describing, or by presenting their object by creating a riddle.

Show, Don't Tell Demonstrate the presentation activity by being the first to perform. To clarify and model your expectations, describe the object using one sentence for each of the five senses. Use at least one simile or metaphor. Also talk about the emotions the object evokes in you.

CRITIQUE

Evaluate a Classmate's Description

Hand out the Critique Sheet for this project or have students use their own paper.

As you evaluate presentations, let students know that you will be using the same rubrics for them as they are using for each other. In addition to their presentations, you may also wish to evaluate students on how well they assess each other's presentations.

After you have reviewed students' critiques, trim off the evaluator's name and hand each sheet to the subject of the evaluation.

ACTivity You may want to select three judges for each description to allow for more variety of response to each student's work.

Spotlight on

Peer Evaluation To be useful and effective, peer evaluation requires that each student put himself or herself in the place of the performer. Students must learn to think of themselves as collaborators on a creative project rather than competitors.

- Talk to students about "PIP," the Positive/Improvement/Positive approach to evaluation. Urge them to begin their critiques by stating something positive about the performance. Then they follow with a statement about something that can be improved. That is then followed by another positive statement about the work.
- Introduce the concept of speaking in "I" statements. Rather than making a statement about a performance as if it were an objective fact, such as "You never make eye contact," students should frame comments in terms of their own personal responses, such as "I didn't see you make eye contact."

CRITIQUE

Evaluate a Classmate's Description

Choose one of the descriptions presented in class to evaluate. Think about both the successful and unsuccessful aspects of your classmate's performance. Your evaluation should be based on a scale of 1 to 5, in which 1 is equal to "needs much improvement" and 5 is equal to "outstanding." Your evaluation should answer these questions:

- How did the person involve all five senses in the description of the object?
- Did you believe that the object meant something specific to the person?
- Could you visualize the object?
- Was any one sense emphasized while another was ignored?

Write a paragraph defending your scoring.

Spotlight on

Peer Evaluation

Peer evaluation, the act of looking critically at the work of your classmates, is beneficial to the evaluator as well as to the performers. When you critique the work of your peers, you have the opportunity to compare your work to that of others whose performance level is similar to your own. You will also participate in an exchange of ideas as you communicate your point of view, and your insights may have an impact on another's work. When your peers evaluate you, you gain worthwhile information regarding your work as well as a number of ideas for growth and improvement.

An effective peer evaluation often tells the performer what you understand to be the purpose or meaning of the work, what you enjoyed, what was especially effective or well done, and anything that confused or disturbed you. If possible, conclude with a final comment about the work as a whole.

It is very important to remember that when you are evaluating your classmates you should maintain a positive, but objective, attitude. Keep an open mind–give your classmates the benefit of any doubt–and try not to be overly critical. Remember, you are all beginners, and no performance will be perfect. State any suggestions for improvement in an even, upbeat manner, and never say anything that would unnecessarily hurt someone's feelings.

Backstage Gossip: Educating the World

Actor Julie Walters, in discussing her role in *Educating Rita,* referred to the pleasure of using recall of her own past.

"I loved . . .being able to talk about the class system, which always made me feel inadequate in life, giving voice to feelings I couldn't give voice to in life . . . oh, awful! It was wonderful playing those scenes because of the feelings I've always felt and forgotten I felt. It all came dredging out."

from *Actress to Actress* by Rita Gam

Additional Projects

1 A simple action, when analyzed in minute detail, can be hilarious. Describe a familiar action, such as eating an orange, sharpening a pencil, or washing your hair. See yourself performing the action. Describe it in as much detail as you can.

2 Write a one-page monologue in which a character uses observation and recall to describe a specific moment from the distant past.

3 Play "Who am I?" Divide into two teams. On small strips of paper, each person in the class will write down the name of a different well-known actor or musician. Put all the names in a bag or container. A member of the first team draws a name out of the hat and tries to describe that person's physical characteristics, vocal quality, and facial expressions to his or her teammates. The object is for the teammates to guess the name on the paper through descriptions and impressions—but *without* any biographical information. If a team member guesses the name within one minute, that team gets to take another turn. If no one on the team guesses correctly within the allotted time, the name goes back in the hat, and the other team takes its turn.

4 Work with a partner to play the "mirror game." Stand face to face about one foot apart. Choose which of you will be the leader. This person will initiate movements, which the other person will mirror. In other words, the follower will perform the exact same gestures as if seeing himself or herself in a mirror. If the leader's left hand goes into the air, the follower makes the same gesture but uses the right hand. Work together for several minutes. By observing each other very closely, you should be able to create a very convincing mirror image.

5 Read the scene between Nora and her husband in *A Doll's House* by Henrik Ibsen, found in Unit Eight. Consider what Nora has observed about their relationship, and write a short summary.

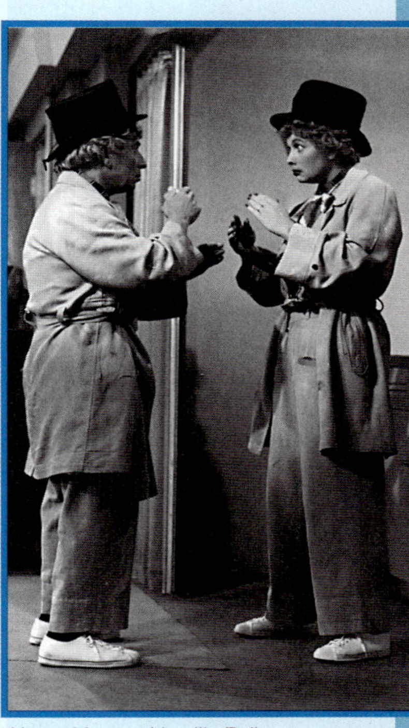

Harpo Marx and Lucille Ball play "the mirror game."

Chapter 2 Test

The test for this chapter is available in blackline master form in the Resource Binder, page 8.

For More Information

Books

Lawrence Gale, *A Field Guide to the Familiar: Learning to Observe the Natural World,* Prentice Hall, 1984.

McGaw, Charles J., *Acting Is Believing,* Wadsworth, 1995.

Other Media

Schrank, Jeffrey, *Reading People: The Unwritten Language of the Body,* VHS, Learning Seed, 1998.

Substitute Teacher Activities

Here are suggestions for one or more days when you will be out of the classroom:

- Assign the Tapping Your Inner Resources Worksheet on page 6 of the Resource Binder.
- Teach the Creating Believable Action section of the Student Handbook, pp. 559-560.
- Assign one or more of the Additional Projects on this page.
- **Plan a Shared Descriptions Session.** Using objects set out for display, have students write a thorough description of an object and then discuss the thoughts or memories it evokes. Invite students to share their descriptions, thoughts, and memories with the class. This exercise strengthens powers of observation while promoting student interaction.

Theatre Then and Now

Stanislavski and Chekhov

The work of Konstantin Stanislavski is inextricably linked with the work of Anton Chekhov, because the two helped bring out the best in each other's work. Stanislavski's Moscow Art Theatre began putting on plays in the summer of 1898, but it did not distinguish itself until it produced Chekhov's *The Seagull* in December of that year.

The play had been a miserable failure when it was performed two years earlier in St. Petersburg. Stanislavski decided to give the play another chance, however, and he put his masterful directing in the service of the play's mood and storyline. The play was a success, the unique identity of the Moscow Art Theatre was established, and Chekhov was encouraged to write more plays.

Other Cultures, Other Times

Until Stanislavski developed his system, actors paid less attention to their own inner reality than to the external requirements of a play.

In classical Greek theatre, Japanese Noh, and Kabuki, actors worked like other tradespeople in apprenticeship programs designed to teach them the proper stylized movements and expressions for individual plays and for their craft in general.

Classical European acting styles, which were popular into the 19th century, were based on presenting symbolic pictures of emotions such as grief, envy, anger, or love. Actors played a ruling emotion rather than expressing the complexity of the character. Using this system, actors specialized in "types," which could be played in much the same way from production to production. Actors often played one or two types for their entire careers.

Theatre Then and Now

Stanislavski's System/ The Actors Studio

"Live truthfully in imaginary circumstances."
—Stanislavski

The Stanislavski System

Russian actor, director, teacher, and author Konstantin Stanislavski (1863-1938) co-founded the Moscow Art Theatre, which was regarded during his lifetime as one of the world's greatest theatre companies. But he is best remembered for creating a type of theatre training that influenced generations of actors around the world, a program known as the Stanislavski System. Through experimentation he came to believe that even those who were not born with artistic genius could achieve great acting.

One of Stanislavski's main concepts was that the actor who uses imagination as well as sense memory to recall experiences will be able to substitute them for those of the character—thus achieving believability. The script's reality or truthfulness becomes secondary to the emotional reality of the actor. It all depends on what Stanislavski called the "magic if." The actor must try to answer the question "What would I do *if* I were . . ." Thus, the actor is not forced into trying to believe that he or she is the person in these actual circumstances but rather what he or she would do given the same situation.

Stanislavski's system had the following goals:

1. to make the external behavior—movement and voice—natural and convincing
2. to know and carry out the *objectives* or inner needs of a character
3. to make the life of the character onstage continuous, with a past and a future, and a life in between the scenes onstage
4. to commit to action (behaving in ways to get characters' objective) and reaction (listening and responding to the other characters)

18 Unit One Begin with the Basics

Backstage Gossip: An Abbreviated Rehearsal

When Theresa Helburn, executive director of New York's new Theatre Guild, visited Konstantin Stanislavski in Russia, she was impressed. She immediately asked Stanislavski whether he might come to the United States and direct a play for the Guild. Stanislavski was interested. So Helburn asked, "How long would you need to rehearse a play?"

"Two years," said Stanislavski.

"Two years for one play!" exclaimed Helburn. "But that's impossible!"

"Well, in that case," replied Stanislavski, "How about two weeks?"

from *Broadway Anecdotes* by Peter Hay

Stanislavski's system, based on the actor's own experience and emotions, helped create an onstage reality that revolutionized the theatre. He later cautioned against adapting his system, however, without accounting for the differences in the actors' cultural backgrounds and artistic sensibilities.

The Actors Studio

Stanislavski and his company took the American theatre world by storm when the Moscow Art Theatre performed in New York City. Among the American admirers Stanislavski won over were actors from the famed Group Theatre (1931–1941). When three members of the Group (Cheryl Crawford, Robert Lewis, and Elia Kazan) decided to create an actor training center in 1947, the basis of the program was the Stanislavski System. They called this training center the Actors Studio. In 1952, Lee Strasberg took over as head of the program, which he ran for the next thirty years. During that time Strasberg refined, developed, and branched out from Stanislavski's ideas. Strasberg's new technique would eventually become known simply as "The Method."

The Actors Studio still exists today. It is administered by the New School in New York City. It offers a three-year graduate training program in playwriting, acting, and directing. It is also the subject of the popular cable television show *Inside the Actors Studio.*

Some Distinguished Alumni of the Actors Studio

Alec Baldwin
Marlon Brando
James Dean
Robert De Niro
Shirley MacLaine
Marilyn Monroe
Paul Newman
Sidney Poitier

Vivien Leigh and Marlon Brando in the film adaptation of Tennessee Williams's *A Streetcar Named Desire.*

The Actors Studio

As Artistic Director of the Actors Studio, Lee Strasberg established the Actors Studio Theatre in the 1960s. From the start, it was plagued with difficulties, and it closed after only a year and a half. Despite the problems with the theatre, Strasberg continued to train actors in The Method at the Actors Studio. The training center turned out to be Strasberg's great contribution to theatre. Under the workshop conditions created by his program, actors could develop their craft without the pressures of a particular production. Strasberg retained his position as director until his death in 1982.

For More Information

Books

Carnicke, Sharon M., *Stanislavski in Focus,* Routledge, 1998.

Hirsh, Foster, *A Method to Their Madness: The History of the Actors Studio,* Da Capo Press, 2002.

Stanislavski, Constantine, *An Actor Prepares,* Theatre Arts Books, 2002.

Stanislavski, Constantine, *Building a Character,* Theatre Arts Books, 2002.

Stanislavski, Constantine, *Creating a Role,* Theatre Arts Books, 2002.

Strasberg, Lee, *A Dream of Passion: The Development of the Method*, New American Library Trade, 1990.

Other Media

Chekhov and the Modern Art Theatre, VHS, Insight Media, 1982.

The Group Theatre, VHS, Insight Media, 1967.

Hethmon, Robert H., ed., *Strasberg at the Actors Studio: Tape Recorded Sessions,* Theatre Communications Group, 1991.

The Stanislavski Century, VHS, Insight Media, 1993.

Visual Cue

The image on this page shows Vivien Leigh and Marlon Brando in a scene from the film *A Streetcar Named Desire.*

- Who seems to have the upper hand in this scene?
- In what ways, if any, does the scene look contrived? In what ways, if any, does the scene look real?
- How might you update this scene if you were to direct it today?

Chapter 3

Pantomime

This chapter offers students a chance to integrate relaxation, warm-up, and observation techniques to create a pantomime.

Objectives

1 to develop an awareness of body language

2 to use movement and body language as a means of communication

3 to understand the principles of pantomime

4 to pantomime an activity

National Standards

Chapter 3 meets these National Theatre Standards:

Proficient 2a, 6a, 7b
Advanced 6d

Project Specs

Special Needs Students
Physically disabled students may perform this activity to whatever extent they are able to maintain control over the body. Facial expressions alone can communicate a story.

Advanced Students
Students who are adept at movement and observation can work together to link their individual pantomimes into an episodic story.

On Your Feet

Show, Don't Tell Jumpstart this class period by letting students walk in on—and participate in—a performance in process. Pretend that you have laryngitis and that you need help getting ready for class. Using pantomime alone, request that students find particular objects or props and either put them somewhere or perform a particular task.

After the tasks are completed, tell students you'd like to discuss pantomime. Ask them what they found easy and what they found difficult about communication through pantomime.

Chapter 3 Pantomime

You face your audience with an important message, but you must communicate without words! By using **pantomime**—gestures, body movement, and facial expressions—you can get your ideas across quite well. You need not be an accomplished mime to be an actor, but training and practice in the art of pantomime will certainly help.

Project Specs

Project Description For this assignment, you will prepare a one- to three- minute pantomime of an activity.

Purpose to develop actions that are believable to both actor and audience

Materials a 50- to 100-word outline of your pantomime or the Pantomime Activity Sheet your teacher provides

Theatre Terms

body language
clown white
mime
pancake makeup
pantomime

On Your Feet

To begin your study of pantomime, think of a way you can express to a partner the following ideas without saying a word:

"Everything is OK."
"Please, help me out here."
"Don't say another word!"
"I haven't a clue."

Street mimes perform for passersby.

Theatre Terms

body language communicating thoughts and feelings through body movements (crossing arms, furrowing brow, etc.)

clown white white makeup often used by mimes and clowns

mime an actor who communicates through movements of the body and face without speaking; also, the activity of the mime

pancake makeup thick, water soluble makeup usually applied with a damp sponge

pantomime body movement and expression without dialogue

PREVIEW

Make-believe and Acting

The basis of acting is literally a matter of "make-believe." It requires the ability to pretend—an ability that nearly everyone possesses to some degree. You can probably recall the fun you had as a child playing a game in which you were a heroic astronaut or a professional athlete. Your pleasure was great because you gave yourself over completely to the game. You were believing.

The belief that a child brings to pretending is similar to the belief that an actor must bring to a part. Like children playing make-believe, actors must become the characters they play. This is a difficult task because, unlike children who enjoy the unrestrained freedom of play for its own sake, actors must communicate to an audience. In order to make an audience believe, the actor must believe!

The Basics of Pantomime

Mime is one of the oldest forms of theatre—the dramatic art of representing life through expressive movements of the body and face. The English word *mime* comes from the ancient Greek *mimos,* meaning to imitate or to mimic. *Pantomime* usually refers to the mimed dramatic sketch as a whole. The actor performing a pantomime must communicate without words, using precise gestures and exact movements to convey ideas. Like all actors, the mime's objective is to make the audience believe in the world he or she is creating. As you learn the basic techniques of mime, you will feel your body becoming your instrument. Your timing, coordination, and reflexes improve. This in turn helps you communicate better in your personal life. You will also come to appreciate the importance of nonverbal communication and **body language**—how body positioning and movement reflect thoughts and feelings.

Try It on for Size

On the following pages are just a few of the many techniques employed by students of the art of pantomime. Take the time to study the images carefully, thinking about the instructions as they relate to the pictures. Then practice these movements yourself.

Resource Binder

- Pantomime Activity Sheet, p. 9
- Mime Games Worksheet, p. 10
- Critique Sheet: Pantomime, p. 11
- Pantomime Test, p. 12

Handbook Connections
pages 560–561

To Have on Hand

- White pancake makeup
- Small sponges
- Makeup brush
- Black grease pencil or paint
- Red grease pencil or paint
- Baby powder
- White athletic sock
- Small painter's brush
- Freestanding mirror

PREVIEW

Make-believe and Acting

While some students will find freedom in omitting spoken language from their performances, others will worry about their skill level in pantomime and its implication for their abilities as actors. Make it clear that one need not be an accomplished mime to be an actor. Pantomime is a good way of training the body, but to learn it well takes more time than is available in a comprehensive drama class.

Explain that in acting, we begin with actions because of the truth in the adage "actions speak louder than words." Acting is not about what you are saying but what you are communicating. Sometimes, what a person does communicates something far more important than what he or she says.

ACTivity Invite students to relive the days of childhood by pretending that they are astronauts, cowhands, professional athletes, dancers, and so forth. Call out occupations one at a time and have students participate by wordlessly communicating that role.

The Basics of Pantomime

When discussed as forms of theatre, pantomime and mime are similar, but still distinct. Both are skilled activities that require warm-ups, especially of the wrists and ankles. But they differ in their effects. Pantomime is true to life. Mime is stylized. It often is blown up larger than life to communicate an idea, emotion, or theme. Both types of wordless performance require a clean approach to movement.

The image on this page shows street mimes whose work has a political theme.

- What do you think the issue they are addressing might be?
- How would you identify the different figures in this photograph?
- What physical details support your opinion?

The Chest

Show, Don't Tell Strut around the room with your head high and chest out and ask students to identify your prevailing attitude (pride, egotism, self-assurance, and so on). Try a few other postures and have students guess what emotions or attitudes you are conveying.

ACTivity Work with the students to create a list of emotions and the physical expressions and movements that go with them. For example, you might write *despair* on the board and ask students to stand and try to express this emotion without words, paying particular attention to the upper body and chest.

The Face and Head

Show, Don't Tell Squint your eyes and frown and say, " You are very bright students." Ask the class if they were surprised by what you said and whether they believed your words. Discuss their impressions. Then use your face and head to create a few more emotions or attitudes and have the students write sentences that say in words what your face and head convey silently.

ACTivity Ask the class to stand. Then call out various emotions at random and have students try to demonstrate them using only the head and face.

Vocabulary Enhancement

The word *mime* is pronounced MYM. The Greek word *mimos* is pronounced MEE mohs.

The Chest

The chest is an essential element in all movement in pantomime. It harbors the body's center of gravity and is often the moving force behind emotion.

This mime stands with chest expanded. This connotes pride, sophistication, nobility, or confidence.

If the chest is pushed forward more dramatically, aggressiveness and determination are suggested.

The chest is now curved inward, indicating weakness, old age, shyness, or exhaustion.

The Face and Head

The face is unique; it is what identifies us to others. We can communicate a lot with just a little effort of the facial muscles—a subtle downturn of the mouth to show displeasure or the angry flair of the nostrils. While these small facial movements speak volumes, learning how to control them may not be easy. The mime must learn to do just that, however, in order to tell his or her story. A mime often wears **clown white,** a kind of white makeup, to highlight the face and its movements.

This mime's open and upturned lips, wide eyes, arched brows, and raised head indicate happiness–or sometimes surprised delight.

Notes

A down-turned mouth, narrowed eyes, with the head thrust forward, can indicate anger or threat.

With the mouth in a straight line, eyes wide, eyebrows arched, and head raised and to the side, the mime appears to be listening, attentive, or curious.

Here's How
To Use White Makeup

Although it is not essential that you wear clown white to perform pantomime, the white, along with the black that outlines the eyes and brows, helps the audience focus on your face.

1. Dip the sponge in water, squeeze, then rub it into the white pancake makeup.
2. Apply the white over your face, excluding the lips. Gently blot the face to remove any streaks.
3. Apply red grease pencil or paint to lips.
4. Apply black grease pencil or paint to the area above eyebrows, above and below the eyes, and around eyes for emphasis.
5. Fill the sock with baby powder and tap your face to set the makeup. Brush away excess powder.

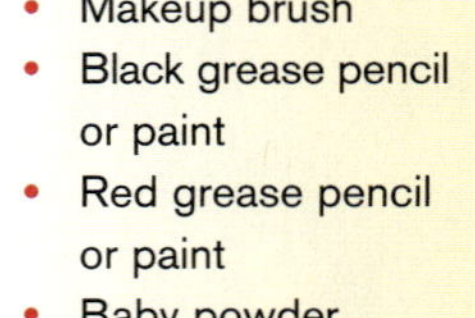

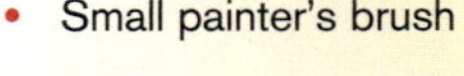

The Makeup Kit

- White **pancake makeup**
- Small sponge
- Makeup brush
- Black grease pencil or paint
- Red grease pencil or paint
- Baby powder
- White athletic sock
- Small painter's brush

Here's How

Advise students that caution is needed during every step of this process. It is always advisable to begin by using too little rather than too much of anything. Students can always add more water to the pancake makeup, but if they add too much at the beginning, the makeup will be runny and hard to use.

Similarly, if they paint too narrow or light a line above the eyebrows, they can add to it. But if they paint too broad a line, they will have to wash their faces and start over. Powder should also be applied gently so as not to collect on one area of the face.

If you decide to have students experiment with mime makeup, make sure that each person has his or her own sponge. As an alternative, you may wish to demonstrate the makeup application using one student as a model.

The Makeup Kit

Eyeliner and lipstick might replace grease pencils or paint in a pinch. Pancake makeup and baby powder are always necessary, however.

Backstage Gossip: Speak Up

In Mel Brooks's 1976 film *Silent Movie* a producer decides that the public is ready to once again embrace the silent movie. It was an interesting premise, but Brooks couldn't quite pull it off. Most viewers agree, however, that the highlight of the film is the scene in which the world-famous mime Marcel Marceau speaks the only word in the film—"Non."

The Legs and Feet

Show, Don't Tell Sit in front of the class with your legs crossed. As you discuss a subject of your choice with the students, move your leg or foot back and forth nervously. Speak in your normal tone. After a few minutes, ask the students what they noticed about you as you spoke, and what their impressions were. Discuss other ways you could relay nervousness or excitement by using your legs and feet. Ask students to demonstrate how they might do it.

ACTivity Have students use only leg and feet movements to communicate a character's personality. Class members then suggest situations for the character, and the student must assume poses that reflect the suggestions, paying particular attention to the legs and feet.

ACTivity Advanced Students Students who are ready, might carry the above exercise a bit further by adding more details to the movement. For example, you might suggest that a student who has created the body language of an angry, impatient man make a phone call to his mother. You might ask a student in a carefree toddler's pose to pour milk into a small glass. If, at any time, the volunteer forgets to remain in character, students should call out "Character" as a reminder. Allow the volunteer to complete the action in a brief demonstration or let it unfold into a story.

ACTivity Special Needs Students Invite students to duplicate the leg and feet positions of the young man in the photos on this page. If they seem ready, ask these students for other ways they might use their legs and feet to show shyness or a threatening posture.

The Legs and Feet

We walk, run, hop, jump, sit, stand, and even lie down using our legs and feet. We jiggle them when nervous or bored and stamp them when we are angry or upset. Have you ever noticed that when you are impatiently waiting for someone you tap your foot in irritation? And when you are excited or happy about something your feet almost dance? The mime can express character and personality through movement of the legs and feet just as with the face and chest. Try to imitate a few of the poses below.

One leg crossed over the other with the body leaning indicates a relaxed, casual, and sometimes, arrogant personality.

Feet turned in or one leg bent behind the other indicates a shyness or timidity.

Feet apart and legs straight show strength and confidence. Add a head held very high with the hands on the hips and you create a feeling of scorn, threat, or contempt.

Backstage Gossip: The Triumph of Mrs. Siddons

Charles Young remembers how a great actor inspired others on the stage.

I remember Mrs. Siddons coming down the stage in the triumphal entrance of her son, Coriolanus, when her dumb-show drew plaudits that shook the house. She came alone, marching and beating time to the music; rolling . . . from side to side, swelling with the triumph of her son. Such was the intoxication of joy which flashed from her eye, lit up her whole face, that the effect was irresistible. She seemed to me to reap all the glory of that procession to herself.

from *Theatrical Anecdotes* by Peter Hay

The Arms and Hands
Never underestimate the power of the arms, hands, and fingers in conveying emotion or telling a story. Mimes create invisible walls, stroke, caress, or push away using hands and arms. The joints of the elbow, wrist, and hand give the mime the flexibility to manipulate invisible objects. Practice the hand positions used in the photographs, combining them with various face, body, and leg movements.

Palms up often indicate acceptance, pleading, or sympathy.

Clenched fists indicate anger, threat, or forced control.

Palms down show rejection, demanding, denial, or fear.

Notes

The Arms and Hands

Show, Don't Tell To highlight the importance of the arms and hands, tell a story using only your arms and hands and just a few choice words. Have students continue adding to the plot, as you continue using your arms and hands to tell the main story.

ACTivity Advanced Students Direct volunteers to affect expressions and body language to define a character as in the activity on the previous page. Then extend the activity by suggesting events that change the mood or attitude of the character. Encourage the performers to go through the changes they think are appropriate to their characters.

Suggest to the students that they make their original expressions and body language the default positions for their characters.

ACTivity Special Needs Students Ask students to duplicate the arm and hand positions of the young woman in the photos on this page. If they seem ready, ask students for other ways they might use the hands and arms to indicate anger or fear.

PREPARE

Visualize and Focus on Your Pantomime

Suggest to the students that they focus on the actions and objects in their pantomimes rather than concentrating on their own movements. Point out that they don't think about the way they are moving in ordinary life; they simply move to accomplish what they want to accomplish. The same should be true of their pantomimes.

To help them focus on the object in their pantomimes, remind them that an object not only has size and shape, but texture and weight. Students can use observation and sense memory to recall the characteristics of the object. You can also supply prompts such as the following:

- How does the weight of the object feel?
- Is the object pleasant or unpleasant to the touch?
- How must I pick up and put down the object?
- What dangers are there in handling the object?

ACTivity Allow students to brainstorm a list of thirty to forty actions to pantomime. They may then use any of the actions listed or choose other actions of their own.

Theatre Journal

Use the following as an additional or substitute prompt.

Write about the ways you are similar to and different from the person you observe in the activity. How is the way you move different from the way this person moves? What gestures do you both employ?

PREPARE

Visualize and Focus on Your Pantomime

In this assignment you will need to focus all of your attention on your pantomime. This means that you must see the situation and objects in your mind's eye and work within that imaginary setting until it becomes believable to you.

Suppose that you choose bowling for your pantomime. You must "see" the alley, see where the balls are stored, and where you fill out your score sheet. You must visualize the action of bowling: wiping your hands on the towel; picking up the ball as you walk up to the starting line. Begin your approach on the proper foot. Feel the weight of the imaginary ball as you swing it back and then forward. Feel its size, shape, and texture. Then feel the release of the ball, and watch it travel down the alley or gutter. Follow through with your reaction. Make everything you do believable. Remember, in this assignment you are doing the action in your own person, not as a character in a play. Be the real you. Your teacher and classmates will be observing how true your actions are to the situation.

Suggestions for Pantomimes

- Play a computer game.
- Build a campfire.
- Row a boat.
- Go fishing.
- Eat a meal.
- Clean your room.
- Play a sport.
- Prepare a meal.
- Build something.
- Get ready for school.

Work through the following steps to prepare your pantomime.

1 **Think of an action** you want to pantomime. Choose an activity that you have performed in real life many times. Make your selection quickly. Spend your time in preparing the action rather than in choosing it. See the suggestions at the left.

2 **Outline each step** in the action. Divide each main step into smaller actions until you have a complete series of movements. Remember that your purpose is a well-planned action that is believable. Visualize your surroundings. Then think about the action and see it. If you cannot recall the exact action, perform the action or observe someone else doing it. Record the details and movement. If you need to refresh your understanding of observation, recall, and sense memory, reread Chapter 2, pages 14–15.

Theatre Journal

Observe someone participating in the activity you have chosen to pantomime. Watch carefully and record the steps in the activity in a numbered list.

Quotable

Use the quote below as a writing prompt, discussion starter, or for your own enjoyment.

If an actor can find the personal rhythm of a character, he's home free. And one of the best ways to do that is to follow a person down the street, unbeknownst to him. Pick up his walk, imitate it and continue it, even after he's out of sight. As you're doing it, observe what's happening to you. By zeroing in on a guy's personal rhythm, you'll find that you've become a different person.

Dustin Hoffman, Actor
from *The Films of Dustin Hoffman* by Douglas Brode

PRESENT

Perform Your Pantomime

Begin your presentation with a short, well-worded introduction to awaken audience curiosity. Then present your pantomime. Take your time and include each detail. If you are immersed in the task at hand, intent on doing the action in a believable way, you will not be worried about what the audience thinks of you.

At the conclusion of your scene, pause, give a slight bow, and then quietly leave the playing area. Remember, you cannot make an audience believe in something you do not believe in yourself.

CRITIQUE

Evaluate a Classmate's Pantomime

Imagine that you are a drama critic and write a short review of a classmate's pantomime. Include strong points as well as areas that could be improved. Use a scale of 1 to 5, with 5 equaling "outstanding" and 1 equaling "needs much improvement." Review Peer Evaluation on page 16 for further help.

Ask yourself these questions:

- Was the pantomime well planned?
- What important details did the actor include or leave out?
- How did the actor make you believe in the dimensions of the imaginary objects used?
- What did the actor do to help you believe that he or she was actually engaged in this action?

Write a short explanation of how you arrived at the score you gave.

To pantomime an action, first visualize it step by step.

From the Field: Well-Oiled Machines

I use many of Viola Spolin's games to get students working together. Often, I start out simple and then add elements as we go along.

For example, I might have a student go onstage and begin doing a movement a machine might do. One by one, I ask students to join the first student. After the whole group is working together, I will ask students to describe what the machine is doing.

After they come to a consensus, I ask them to keep their function in mind while I prompt the machine to speed up, slow down, or alter its movement in any number of ways. Starting slowly, they are able to use their imaginations, take direction, and work together—all at the same time.

Rick Karlin, Teacher, Chicago, Illinois

PRESENT

Perform Your Pantomime

Show, Don't Tell Describe the beginning of a great play you saw recently. Be as succinct as possible and leave a lot to the students' imaginations. When they have questions, explain that the introduction you gave was meant to whet their appetites. Similarly, their introductions should serve only to whet the audience's appetite—not to explain the scene. Point out that a pantomime, however short, is a story. To build interest in the story, they should introduce it without telling it or giving away the ending.

ACTivity If you feel your students need practice at such introductions, have them say a few words about a favorite book or movie. Encourage students to tell just enough to make others want to experience it for themselves.

CRITIQUE

Evaluate a Classmate's Pantomime

Hand out the Critique Sheet for this project or have students use their own paper.

It will be helpful to assign the person each student will evaluate so that everyone receives a peer evaluation.

Let students know that you will using the same rubrics for them as they are using for each other. In addition to their presentations, you may also wish to evaluate students on how well they assess each other's presentations.

After you have reviewed students' critiques, trim off the evaluator's name and hand out the sheets to the subjects of the evaluations.

Chapter 3 Pantomime **27**

Chapter 3 Test

The test for this chapter is available in blackline master form in the Resource Binder, page 12.

For More Information

Books

Alberts, David, *Talking About Mime*, Heinemann, 1994.

Feder, Jack, *Mime Time: A Book of Routines and Performance Tips*, Meriwether Publishing, 1992.

Kipnis, Claude, *The Mime Book*, Meriwether Publishing, 1988.

Stoltzenberg, Mark, *Exploring Mime*, Sterling Publishing, 1979.

Other Media

The Art of Mime, VHS, Insight Media, 1991.

Drama: Mime, VHS, Insight Media, 1995.

Mime Over Matter, 2 CD-ROMs, Also in VHS, Insight Media, 1988.

www.mime.info/index.html

Additional Projects

1 Using an imaginary rope, play tug-of-war. Teams of equal number should stand in front of each other in a line, facing a similarly positioned team. In your mind, see and feel the rope. Pull together as hard as you can to take the rope from the other team. Be careful that the rope does not stretch. If one side gets the advantage the other side must give. Make the game so believable to you, that at the end of it, you feel tired from the strong physical exertion.

2 In a one- to two-minute scene, make believable your efforts to escape from a place where you are trapped—perhaps a cave or an elevator. Visualize the area in which you are trapped. Then use your whole body in trying to escape. Strain, grunt, claw, climb, and dig. Make yourself and your audience believe your endeavors. Continue your efforts until your teacher calls, "Cut."

3 Play "Statues" with a group of classmates. Each person takes a turn dancing freely about the room until someone calls, "Stop!" The dancer then freezes into a statue that shows a specific emotion, such as anger, pain, fear, or joy. The others must guess the feeling being expressed. If people have trouble determining the emotion, try to discover the reason, and rework the statue until it fully captures the emotion being expressed.

4 Play the game of "changing ball toss." Make a large circle with your classmates. Toss around an imaginary ball. Start with a basketball, then switch to a tennis ball, then a bowling ball, a golf ball, a ping-pong ball, and so on. Your reactions should be very different depending on the kind of ball you are catching.

5 Read all the stage directions for *The Drummer* by Athol Fugard, found in Unit Eight. Use pantomime to tell the entire story.

28 **Unit One** Begin with the Basics

Substitute Teacher Activities

Below are suggestions for one or more days when you will be out of the classroom:

- Assign the Mime Games Worksheet on page 10 of the Resource Binder.
- Assign one or more of the Additional Projects on this page.
- Teach the Mime and Pantomime section of the Student Handbook, pp. 560-561.
- **Plan a First Meeting Pantomime.** Give students five or ten minutes to record details about the first new person they met at your school. Suggest that they consider how they felt walking into the school that day, what they were wearing, and whether they were in a hurry or not. Then have them take turns performing a pantomime of this meeting. Point out that their own expressions will be extremely important, since there will not be an actor representing the other person.

Master of the Craft

Marcel Marceau

Marcel Marceau is undoubtedly the most famous mime in the world. He usually performs on a bare stage with few or no props. The clown white makeup he wears highlights every subtle facial expression. Marceau has the ability to make his audience feel what his character is feeling and to see the imagined world that he creates.

Marceau's interest in pantomime began when he was quite young. He would imitate with gestures anything that captivated his imagination. His admiration for such silent screen artists as Charlie Chaplin and Buster Keaton inspired his pursuit of silence as a profession.

In his essay "The Poetic Halo," Marceau said this about his profession: "When the actor-mime sustains his dramatic action with the inspiration of his thought, the sensitive response he induces is the echo of his soul, and the gesture becomes a silent inner song."

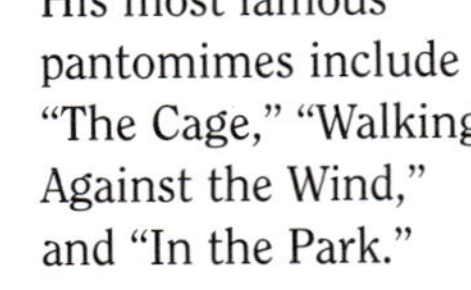

His most famous pantomimes include "The Cage," "Walking Against the Wind," and "In the Park."

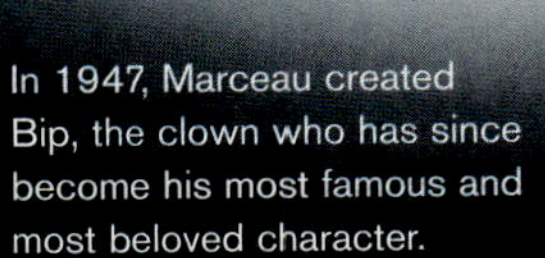

In 1947, Marceau created Bip, the clown who has since become his most famous and most beloved character.

For More Information

Books

Marceau, Marcel, *Bip in a Book,* Stewart, Tabori & Chang, 2001.

Martin, Ben, *Marcel Marceau: Master of Mime*, Viking Penguin, 1979.

Other Media

The Art of Silence: Pantomimes with Marcel Marceau, VHS, Insight Media, 1975.

Marcel Marceau Speaks, Audio CD, Times Two Audio, 2000.

The Mastery of Mimodrame, 3 VHS tapes, Insight Media.

Master of the Craft

More About Marcel Marceau

Marcel Marceau was born Marcel Mangel in Strasbourg, France, on March 22, 1923. His father died in Auschwitz during World War II, but Marceau and his brother escaped capture by the Nazis, changed their names, and joined the French Resistance.

In 1946, he enrolled as a student at the Sarah Bernhardt Theatre in Paris, where he studied with the great master of mime, Etienne Decroux. Decroux invited Marceau to join his company, casting him as Arlequin in a pantomime entitled "Baptist," which launched Marceau's career.

Marceau attracted international attention at the Berlin Festival of 1951. He then launched a tour of thirty-six countries, which made him world famous.

Today, he continues to tour. He has also founded a school, L'Ecole International de Mimodrame de Paris Marcel Marceau, to educate aspiring mimes from around the globe.

Masters Past and Present

Marceau's acclaim rests on his virtuosity and on the way he has continued a proud tradition in French pantomime. Bip, the clown character Marceau developed, is based on a touching white-faced clown created by Jean-Gaspard Deburau (1796-1846), the originator of French mime. Deburau's clown, named Pierrot, was a pale fellow, lovesick but hopeful, who became one of the most popular characters in French theatre. Deburau, in turn, is often associated with the mime of the same name in director Marcel Carné's 1946 film *Children of Paradise (Les Enfants du Paradis),* which presents a fascinating portrait of theatre folk in early 19th century France. It was a noisy, rude, haphazard theatre, with audiences often on the brink of riot; where poor and hungry actors forged friendships with thugs, and in which a sad, passionate mime could create magic from it all. This classic film is available on video and DVD.

Theatre Then and Now

Kabuki of the 1600s

Kabuki was a form of entertainment that appealed to all the classes in Japan. Samurai and ladies attended Kabuki performances along with merchants, workers, monks, and students. The higher classes sat in covered seats, while the lower classes sat out in the open air.

Government authorities in Japan looked down upon Kabuki performers and even refused them civil rights. The general public, on the other hand, idolized them. Over time, the acting profession became hereditary. Families established acting dynasties, some of which are still viable. For example, Japan's Danjuro XII, an actor born in 1946, continues a family tradition that extends back to the 17th century.

Originally, Kabuki was comprised of improvised sketches inserted into dance performances. Over time, the sketches developed into plays, and in 1670, the first important Kabuki writer emerged. By the 1800s, Kabuki was written by teams consisting of a writer and several assistants. Even so, Kabuki writing is considered to be largely a blueprint for action, rather than a form of literature in its own right.

From the mid-17th century to the mid-19th century, Kabuki performances were about twelve hours long. In 1868, they were shortened to eight hours. Since World War II, most Kabuki performances are four hours long—but most theatres offer two shows a day.

Theatre Then and Now

Kabuki of the 1600s

This male actor portrays a woman in a Kabuki play.

Probably the best known drama form of traditional Japanese theatre is Kabuki. In the early 17th century a female dancer named O-kuni is said to have developed a new form of dance and drama popular with the people. When she danced in the dry river beds of Kyoto, the capital, O-kuni caused a sensation, and soon she had many imitators. From this Kabuki was born.

Another early form of Kabuki, seldom performed today, was a simple silent performance that lasted no longer than ten minutes—much like a short pantomime. Over the years, Kabuki became more and more elaborate, stylized, and intricate. Eventually women were banned from Kabuki performance and certain men became specialists in portraying women. To this day only males perform traditional Kabuki.

Traditional Kabuki performances are distinctive for the elaborateness of their costuming, makeup, and staging. Costumes are highly stylized and colorful, and the traditional white makeup and elaborate hairstyles help create Kabuki's richness.

Actors on a traditional Kabuki stage.

30 Unit One Begin with the Basics

For More Information

Books

Ariyooshi, Sawako, trans. I. James Brandon, *The Kabuki Dance*, Kodansha International, 1994.

Leiter, Samuel L., *A Kabuki Reader: History and Performance*, Sharp, Armonk, 2001.

Other Media

Acting Techniques of the Noh Theatre of Japan, VHS, Insight Media, 1980.

The Art of Kabuki, VHS, Films for the Humanities and Sciences, 1993.

One Step in a Journey: Tadashi Suzuki, VHS, Insight Media, 1993.

The Tradition of Performing Arts in Japan, VHS, Insight Media, 1990.

Kabuki Interpretations Today

Kabuki has taken an interesting turn in the last twenty years or so in its partnership with such Western drama classics as *Macbeth* and *Medea*. Western plays with strong, universal themes lend themselves well to Kabuki interpretation. Pageantry, nobility, pride, revenge, and bloodshed are common elements.

The artist and teacher Shozo Sato earned international acclaim for producing Kabuki versions of Western classics, including *Kabuki Medea, Kabuki Faust,* and *Kabuki Othello.* He also produced the operas *Madame Butterfly* and *The Mikado* in the Kabuki style. Sato's *Kabuki Medea,* performed by the Berkeley Repertory Theatre, won the Hollywood Drama Critics Award for best theatrical production. His productions of *Macbeth* and *Medea* both received several Joseph Jefferson awards, given for Chicago theatre.

In 1991, nineteen American students toured Japan as members of Sato's production of *Achilles: A Kabuki Play*. The tour marked the first time actors from the United States had performed a Kabuki drama in Japan, where the form was born. Their two-week tour included the village of Damine, where Kabuki has been part of the religious ritual for more than three centuries.

Sato's productions have also been performed in Europe and the Middle East and continue to be popular throughout the world.

Kabuki acting is highly symbolic and rhythmic.

Kabuki Interpretations Today

One of the most interesting of recent Kabuki interpreters is Suzuki Tadashi. In a reaction against Western influence, Suzuki founded the Free Stage in 1961. There and at the Waseda Little Theatre, he began experimenting with Noh and Kabuki techniques. By 1970, he was combining Japanese and Western theatrical elements in a quest for an international form of theatre. His Suzuki Company of Toga (SCOT, for short) uses elements of both Kabuki and Noh theatre to perform what he terms intercultural plays based on Shakespeare. By combining elements of Eastern and Western theatre, Suzuki is investigating a wider range of material and appealing to a wider audience.

Visual Cue

The image on this page shows a Kabuki actor in full costume as a warrior.

- Notice the lines on the warrior's face. What impression do they create for you?
- Based on the expression and makeup the actor is wearing, what would you guess about the character's frame of mind?
- What do the actor's gestures seem to symbolize?

Notes

Chapter 4

Improvisation

This chapter introduces students to the principles of improvisation. Improvisation is a challenging activity. Students are not expected to master it at this point, but rather to understand the basics of this performance genre. We will return to improvisation in later chapters of this book.

Objectives

1. to understand the basics of improvisation
2. to understand audience etiquette
3. to work collaboratively with others
4. to use movement, voice, and body to create an improvisation

National Standards

Chapter 4 meets these National Theatre Standards:
Proficient 2c, 4c, 6c, 7c
Advanced 2d, 7f

Project Specs

ESL Students
Students who are less familiar with the English language may need to work out on paper or kinesthetically the various uses of the word *set*.

Advanced Students
For the activities in this chapter, advanced students should not be set apart in any way. In fact, advanced students may find their most significant and meaningful challenges in improvising with students who are less at home onstage.

On Your Feet

Before the students begin working with their partners on this exercise, tell them that one of them will portray a character of some kind and will have to figure out the scenario as they go along.

Chapter
4 Improvisation

One of the most demanding things an actor can be called upon to do is to **improvise**–to make up the words in the **dialogue** and the action while playing out a scene. No lines to learn, no planned movement, just you (and your fellow actors) going wherever your imagination leads you.

Project Specs

Project Description You and a partner (or partners) will perform a three- to five-minute improvisation.

Purpose to learn introductory improvisation skills in order to develop concentration and focus

Materials a 50- to 100-word sentence outline of your group improvisation or the Improvisation Activity Sheet your teacher provides

Theatre Terms

collaboration
dialogue
ensemble
etiquette
improvise
set

On Your Feet

To practice working with a partner, play a round of "Who am I?" with your classmates as the audience. Your partner will decide what kind of person he or she wants to play without telling you. For example, he or she might play a traffic cop arresting you for speeding or a babysitter looking after you, the child. Based on how your partner acts toward you, you must guess who that person is and try to respond accordingly.

Theatre Terms

collaboration working with others toward a common goal

dialogue conversation among characters

ensemble a group of actors working together to create an artistic whole rather than stressing individual players

etiquette appropriate conduct

improvise to make up the dialogue and action of a scene as you go along

set (1) establish definite movements and lines (2)* scenery used onstage

*this definition is used in another chapter

PREVIEW

Yes, and . . .

Improvisation means acting without a script. It means creating a scene on the spot that you and your fellow actors—the **ensemble**—compose together. Improvisation requires a great deal of **collaboration** and trust. You must share ideas, believe that your partners will support you, and work together to create something all your own.

Most of our actions in daily life are improvised, since real life rarely offers a script. Sometimes we have expectations about what's going to happen next, but no one ever knows for sure. In real life, those who want to make the best of things enjoy their good fortune and learn from ill luck. They embrace life's surprises. They say "yes" to life.

Successful improvisers say "yes, and. . ." They embrace a situation or comment presented to them and react to it, add to it, and make it into a character or scene. In doing this, they exercise their creativity, their mental and emotional flexibility, their trust for one another, and their capacity for concentrating on the task at hand. When they're faced with a problem onstage, they use their wits to solve it.

When actors who are adept at improvising work with a script, they know how to embrace it and make the imaginary world their own. They also know how to work with and respond to their fellow actors. An effective improviser is also an effective actor.

Basic Rules of Improv

Some improvisation scenes begin with a plot suggestion. Others begin with an idea for a character. All improvisations depend on the following rules:

- Always remain open to your partner(s), the plot, and your own ideas.
- Listen carefully and respond to your partner(s) onstage.
- Show, rather than tell how you feel.
- Take chances! Don't be afraid to fail.
- Trust yourself and your partner(s).

Members of The Second City improvise a skit suggested by an audience member.

PREVIEW

Yes, and . . .

Inform students that improvisations generally fall into two basic categories—situation centered and character centered—but that most improvisations use elements of both. As improvisers, they can begin by creating characters and putting them into situations or they can begin by developing situations and acting out a response to these situations.

ACTivity Hand out 3 x 5 cards and ask students to describe characters and situations that interest them. Collect the cards for use in scenes.

ACTivity To give students practice at responding positively and building on others' ideas, read the ideas on the 3 x 5 cards and ask students how they might go about creating a scene and characters.

Beginning Students
Call on students to add details to the situation or specific mannerisms for the characters already discussed in class.

Advanced Students
Challenge students to act out the situations presented in class and then to improvise what would happen next.

The image on this page shows a group of actors in the midst of an improvisation.

- How would you describe the characters in this photograph?
- How would you describe the situation?
- What might the standing character or the squatting characters say to begin the scene?

Resource Binder

- Audience Etiquette, TIPack, p. E
- Improvisation Activity Sheet, p. 13
- Improvisation Guidelines and Games Worksheet, p. 14
- Critique Sheet: Short Scene Improvisation, p. 15
- Improvisation Test, p. 16

Handbook Connections
pages 557–558

To Have on Hand

- Three or four chairs or cubes that can be used as chairs
- A table or a cube that can be used as a table
- Personal props such as hats, ties, scarves, purses, jackets, backpacks, and briefcases to help students get into character

PREPARE

Commit to the Reality of Improv

To increase students' comfort levels regarding improvisation, point out that they should not try to be funny. Much of the comedy that comes out of improvisation is derived from the situations the characters find themselves in. If students simply commit to finding solutions within the context of the scene, humor will come.

ACTivity Storytelling activities can offer a gentle introduction to improvisation techniques. Begin a fictional narrative of any kind. Science fiction and fantasy are good for a start. Ask students to add to the story you are telling in any way that moves the narrative forward. As students gain confidence, you can use increasingly realistic beginnings. Encourage the students to transform ordinary beginnings into fantastic or outlandish improvisations.

If time and space permit, you might want to call for volunteers to act out the story elements as they arise.

ACTivity Allow each improv group to warm up by playing "bus stop" or "movie line." In either improvisation, one person waits at a bus stop or in a movie line and is then joined by unique characters who appear one at a time.

Easing into It

Discuss with students the necessity of conveying in clear, concise, effective language any directorial information that will help the group achieve their goal.

ACTivity Expand the activity in which students try to find a new use for an everyday object. After a student finds a novel use for the object, invite other students to come on the scene with other ways to use the object. Allow students to improvise a scene based on the object and the additional characters' ways of using it.

PREPARE

Commit to the Reality of Improv

This assignment will require that you respond naturally and immediately to any suggestion that pops into your mind or the mind of your partner(s). You will need to commit to the reality of an imaginary circumstance no matter how silly or impossible it seems.

Suppose, for example, that you and your partner or team are building a fire. One of your improv partners says, "I'm getting freezer burn from this fire!" Don't argue about whether freezer burn is possible; it already has happened. Your partner said it, so it's true. Instead of denying the idea, put yourself in a world where freezer burn from a fire is possible—or even common. Respond to your partner's predicament.

This does not mean you can't ever argue in an improvisation. You can blame your partner for getting freezer burn. You can berate your partner for bringing you to Jupiter in the first place. You can claim that your injury or problem is even worse than your partner's. You must, however, buy into your partner's reality. No matter what, you must remain "in the scene."

Easing into It

Unfortunately, there's no such thing as "easing into it"! You'll have to jump in with both feet. How do you make sense out of a leap into the void? These tips can help orient you:

- Remember that trust in the team is essential. Your improv partners will enter any reality you propose. They will believe your characters are real. They will build on the plot you imagine. You are not alone.
- You can develop a character from a gesture, a voice, an expression, a piece of clothing, and so on.

Career Focus

The Improv Group

If you are an aspiring actor, improvisation can hone your skills. If you want to be a doctor, lawyer, teacher, executive, sales rep, or any other person who deals with the public, improv can help you relax, be self-confident, and have a sense of humor about yourself.

Some improv groups will accept students with little or no experience. Students and professionals alike may improvise together in workshops. Those who develop their skills may be invited onstage in a showcase, or as part of the improv cast.

Does your local improv group demand experience? Start a group of your own and rent a space when you're ready to perform.

Backstage Gossip: It's for You

Improvisation skills can come in handy even during a performance of Shakespeare. During a production of *Julius Caesar,* actors Joseph Mahar and John Tillinger had pulled out their daggers and were just about to kill Caesar when the stage manager's phone rang. The ringing phone could be heard on stage and into the house. Aware that the audience had heard the phone, Mahar turned to Tillinger and asked, "What shall we do if it's for Caesar?"

The audience roared.

from *Broadway Anecdotes* by Peter Hay

Theatre Journal

Next time you go to a restaurant, park, or mall, sit for a moment and listen to the activity around you. Then jot down interesting fragments of conversation you overhear. Such fragments can make great opening lines in an improvisation.

- You can develop an activity—and spark a plot idea—by finding a new use for an everyday object, such as turning a pot into a helmet or an umbrella into a baseball bat.
- You can open dialogue by repeating a cliché, a line from a poem, or a bit of slang.
- After you have developed a scene, or even part of a scene, you can retain, or **set,** the parts of the scene that were effective. Then you can do the scene again with your partner, letting new ideas come to the surface. Again, set the material that works. Eventually, the material that is set gives you a framework in which to perform.
- Your scene, once you set it, will have the familiarity of a memorized script. But refrain from setting the scene in stone. Go ahead and improvise words, phrases, and new moments in any scene—even one that is "finished."

PRESENT

Perform an Improvisation

When your names are called, hand in your outlines or Activity Sheets, then with your partner or partners walk to the playing area. Be aware that it is perfectly normal to be nervous. Trust your partners to help you, try to relax, and enjoy the moment. When you have finished your improvised scene, turn to the audience and ask, "What happens next?" Take a suggestion and continue the improvisation for another minute.

When you are finished, pause and then bow politely before leaving the playing area.

Two students improvise a game of baseball.

PRESENT

Perform an Improvisation

Show, Don't Tell To break the ice, ask students to call out a situation for you and a partner of your choosing to improvise. Suggest to the students how you would think through the scenario, the kinds of characters involved, and the direction the scene might take, and then do a short improv with your partner.

ACTivity When it comes time for the presenters to ask, "What happens next?" you might want to open the question to the entire class and ask volunteers to share their ideas for continuing the scene.

Theatre Journal

Use the following as an additional or substitute prompt.

Ask students to describe the people whose conversations they overhear and then to write about how they might use these characters in an improvisation.

Vocabulary Enhancement

A given character or situation in an improvisation is called a *set up.*

From the Field: Taking Risks

Improvisation is part of the acting technique I learned from Stella Adler in New York. The cornerstone of her technique is improvisation, and to develop a sense of adventure in actors, she worked hard making the theatre a place where it is safe to explore.

We did lots of exercises to build trust and a sense of community. After the exercises, we'd work with a script to explore our characters' goals and objectives. Then we'd create improvisations in which we'd go after the objectives using our own words. By using improvisation in this way, actors can use their own experience as a way of pursuing a character's goals. Then, actors can go back to the text, and bring their own experience to it.

Dameon Carot, Actor, New York, New York

CRITIQUE

Evaluate Your Classmates' Improvisation

Hand out the Critique Sheet for this project or have students use their own paper. In either case, be sure students understand that the critique activity involves several steps including note-taking, scoring, and writing.

This might be a good time to have pairs or groups of students compare, analyze, and evaluate their differing critiques in order to better understand other interpretations of similar dramatic presentations.

Spotlight on

Audience Etiquette Point out to the students that ushers are often volunteers who usher in order to see a play cheaply or for free. It is a kindness to them to avoid leaving a playbill or other material on the seat or on the floor.

CRITIQUE

Evaluate Your Classmates' Improvisation

Choose one of the improvisations presented in class and evaluate it. Use a scale of 1 to 5, with 5 being "outstanding" and 1 being "needs much improvement." Ask yourself these questions:

- In what way did the actors remain true to the improvisational principle of "yes, and. . ."?
- How did the performers display trust and acceptance?
- How did the performers build on each other's suggestions?
- How well did the performers listen and respond to each other?
- How did the partners show, rather than tell, their feelings?
- In what way did the performers keep you interested in the outcome of the scene?

Write an explanation of how you arrived at this score.

Spotlight on

Audience Etiquette

The real-time immediacy of live theatre makes it a special event. When you are in the audience, your behavior affects the enjoyment of those around you. To be a courteous audience member, follow the rules of **etiquette** below.

- Show respect for the actors and other audience members by dressing appropriately.
- Arrive early to be seated and to read your program. After the curtain is up, most theatres will not seat people until a scene break, so latecomers miss part of the show. If you are allowed to enter late, you inconvenience those already seated.
- ALWAYS turn off your cell phone and the beeper on your watch or pager. Alarms not only disturb those around you but distract the actors as well.
- Remove your hat so that those seated behind you can see.
- NEVER put your feet on the back of the seat in front of you.
- Do not talk during the performance—not even a whisper. Save it until intermission.
- Do not take food or drink into the theatre. NEVER unwrap candy or gum during a performance.
- Don't leave during the play except in an emergency, and don't leave at the end until the house lights are turned on. It is bad manners to slip out early.
- Applaud the performers at the end of the play as they take their bows, but reserve a standing ovation for the truly outstanding performance.

Backstage Gossip: If Only They'd Boo!

Modern audiences who don't like a play usually sit in stony silence. Once in a while, they boo. Audiences in the 19th century were often more forthcoming about their displeasure. Once, when Edmund Kean was touring, disaffected audience members tore out their seats and smashed the theatre lights in what came to be known as the "Boston Riot."

Additional Projects

1 Form a discussion panel with four or more classmates. Have each participant represent the line of clothes of a particular designer, a magazine in a publishing house's stable, or a piece of furniture in a housewares store. Each improviser should adopt the personality of the item represented. The teacher or a classmate can serve as the moderator, asking various panel members questions, which they must answer in character.

2 Host a party for strange and unusual superheroes, such as Yapping-Dog Man, Backwards Girl, or Bionic Bellower. The host should be a superhero, too. Have each superhero guest arrive at the party individually and reveal who he or she is. Once all the players have arrived, the host should announce that he or she needs them to solve a world problem. Have the group find a way the superheroes can collaborate to solve the problem.

3 Bring to the front of the class an everyday object, such as a tennis racket, a paper bag, or a broom. Take turns with your classmates, one by one, finding a new use for the object. Then display that use for the class. Remember that you should not be limited by the actual name or function of the object. You imagination can make it anything you want it to be.

4 Read the scene between Argan and Louison in *The Imaginary Invalid* by Molière found in Unit Eight. With a partner, improvise another scene in which Argan tries to extract information from Louison.

Chapter 4 Test

The test for this chapter is available in blackline master form in the Resource Binder, page 16.

For More Information

Books

Caruso, Sandra, *The Young Actor's Book of Improvisation: Dramatic Situations from Shakespeare to Spielberg,* Heinemann, 1998.

Cassady, Marsh, *Spontaneous Performance: Acting Through Improv,* Meriwether Publishing, 2000.

Davies, Gil, *Staging a Pantomime,* A&C Black, 1995.

Spolin, Viola, *Theatre Games for the Classroom: A Teacher's Handbook,* Northwestern University Press, 1986.

Other Media

Collins, Rives, *Introduction to Creative Drama and Improvisation* (videorecording, 110 minutes), Video Communications Design, 1990.

Substitute Teacher Activities

Below are a few suggestions for one or more days when you will be out of the classroom:

- Assign the Improvisation Guidelines and Games Worksheet on page 14 of the Resource Binder.
- Teach the Improvisation section of the Student Handbook, pp. 557-558.
- Assign one or more of the Additional Projects on this page.
- **Plan a Journal Writing Session.** Encourage students to record an event or write about a person that captured their attention. Tell them to free write imaginatively about the person or event by adding a paragraph or more that begins with the words "What if . . . ."

Theatre Then and Now

Commedia Dell'arte

Commedia was an art form popular with the common people, as opposed to the literary plays attended by nobles and royalty. It required little in the way of props or technical elements, and the professional actors who performed it played equally well on both court stages and market squares.

In *commedia,* as in later forms of European theater, actors often played one stock type their entire lives. They were completely familiar with the range of their character's expressions and thus could react quickly and creatively to any improvised circumstance.

Because *commedia* was so successful and adaptable, it spread rapidly throughout Europe. Actors simply adopted the stock characters and added their own scenarios and words.

Other Cultures, Other Times

It seems that elements of *commedia* have punctuated comedy as long as comedy has existed. Ancient Greek theatre and mime differ from classic *commedia* in that they were scripted. Nevertheless, the text of an ancient Greek mime found in Egypt has many of the elements later developed in *commedia*:

- Its text was a domestic comedy of love and adultery.
- It used stock comic characters.
- The script included gaps in which stage business could take place.
- It had outrageous plot elements that offended moralists.

Visual Cue

The images on this page show Pierrot and two players in the play *Scapin,* adapted from a Molière play.

- Describe the two figures in the photograph from *Scapin.*
- What elements identify them as stock characters?

Theatre Then and Now

Improvisation in the 1500s

Commedia Dell'arte

Developed in Italy from pantomimes that may have been remnants of ancient Roman comedy, *commedia dell'arte* (comedy of art) was flourishing in the middle 1500s. It was a highly improvised comedy performed in the streets for the masses. A company, consisting usually of seven men and three women, would improvise action, dialogue, song, and dance around a familiar plot—one that usually involved love and intrigue. Actors had to be clever and inventive to keep the plot moving, and an athletic, agile body was necessary for the fights, acrobatic stunts, and dances that were required.

Commedia dell'arte is still performed around the world with many of the stock characters that were familiar to 16th-century Italians. A few of the most famous characters are the clever, witty, and mischievous Harlequin; the flirtatious and pretty Columbine; Pantalone, the gullible father; and Pierrot, the clown.

This recent performance of *Scapin* is based on Molière's adaptation of a *commedia dell'arte* pla

Pierrot, the clown, is often lovelorn and moody.

For More Information

Books

Grantham, Barry, *Playing Commedia: A Training Guide to Commedia Techniques,* Heinemann, 2000.

Kozlowski, Rob, *The Art of Chicago Improv: Shortcuts to Long-Form Improvisation,* Heinemann, 2002.

Novelly, Maria C., et al., *Theatre Games for Young Performers: Improvisations and Exercises for Developing Acting Skills,* Meriwether Publishing, 1985.

Rudin, Jeffrey, *Commedia dell'arte: A Handbook for Troupes,* Routledge, 2001.

Sweet, Jeffrey, *Something Wonderful Right Away,* Limelight Editions, 1987.

Other Media

Aspects of the Commedia dell'arte, VHS, Insight Media, 1960

Commedia dell'arte, VHS, Insight Media, 1997.

The Green Bird, VHS, Insight Media, 1982.

Saturday Night Live, VHS, A& E Television Networks, 2002.

Improvisation Today

The Second City

In 1955, a group of students, musicians, and actors rented a storefront attached to a bar. They fashioned a house and stage that featured a few nondescript chairs. And they called themselves the Compass Players.

The Compass Players wanted to try something no one else was doing. They wanted to improvise scenes from thin air. So they walked on stage and whipped up sketches about mothers and daughters, husbands and wives, dating, taxes, social issues, and anything else that came to mind. Sometimes, they were hilarious. Sometimes they were terrible. No one—not even the actors—knew what would happen next.

Audiences loved the thrill of watching actors in process. And so, the idea caught on and led to the creation of the most successful improv group to date—The Second City, named after the city in which it was born, Chicago, Illinois.

In 1959, The Second City opened a sort of low-rent cabaret in the seedy Old Town neighborhood in the heart of Chicago. To the clink of people eating and drinking, the actors improvised dozens of scenes. Some were ideas they had worked out themselves, in advance. Others were spontaneous. Still others were based on suggestions from the audience. Thus, each evening was a brand-new collaboration. The concept was a smashing success.

The Second City today.

In the 1970s and 1980s John Belushi, Gilda Radner, Jane Curtin, Dan Akroyd, Bill Murray, and many others learned their craft at The Second City. They continued improvising on TV's "Saturday Night Live," paving the way for other TV improv shows, such as "Who's Line Is It Anyway?" The Second City is still a thriving theatrical event as well as a well-respected school in Chicago, with branches in Toronto, Cleveland, Detroit, and Los Angeles.

Backstage Gossip: Alas, Poor Del!

Del Close once played the part of Polonius in a production of *Hamlet.* He won a Joseph Jefferson award for his performance, and he was grateful, but he jokingly claimed the role he really wanted to play was Yorick. When he died, his colleagues in the theatre were startled to learn that Close had willed his own skull to the Goodman Theatre, in the hope that it would be used in future theatrical productions of *Hamlet.*

The Second City

The Second City took its name from its status as second to New York in population, size—and theatrical importance. But the success of The Second City made improvisation a theatrical industry in Chicago and elsewhere. Second City alumnus Del Close was at the forefront of many of these efforts. In the late 1960s, he helped organize an improv group known as the Committee. There, he began developing techniques for long-form improvisation, which Second City had begun exploring in 1962.

In 1970, Close established an improvisation workshop that was free and open to the public. He taught his students improv and basic acting and then worked with them on a technique that came to be known as the "Harold." The Harold is a kind of long-form improvisation that emphasizes story and plot over simple gags. Today, the Harold is well established as an improvisation art form. Companies like ImprovOlympic focus almost exclusively on teaching and performing it, and audiences go to their productions expecting to see it.

Close's only regret seems to have been the form's name. When he first introduced the form, one of his students asked what he was going to call it. Recalling that the Beatles had recently called their haircut "Arthur," he replied that he would call his technique "Harold." Later, he cheerfully rued the fact that his greatest contribution to theatre had "that stupid name."

Visual Cue

The image on this page shows improvisational actors in action.

- What do you think the second player from the left represents?
- Is this the beginning or the end of the improv?
- What might the man in the tie be about to say?

Unit One Review

PREVIEW

1 Some students may be more comfortable with techniques that involve movement, while others may find it easier to relax when relatively still. Encourage students to demonstrate the technique they describe.

2 Actors should warm up to relax, master the body, build confidence, and use up nervous energy.

3 Observation aids the imagination and the memory so that actors can play the reality of various scenes.

4 Students should demonstrate as well as explain their answers.

5 Answers may vary. Actors and children both give themselves over to the scenes they enact.

6 Answers will vary. Mimes primarily wish to communicate without words.

7 Student demonstrations should include body language such as a frown and clenched fists.

8 Answers will vary. Students should note that in real life, people adjust to new circumstances constantly and their remarks are not rehearsed.

9 Saying "Yes, and . . . " moves the action forward so that a scene can build, and advances the improvisation rather than shutting it down.

PREPARE

10 Answers will vary but should reflect an understanding of working effectively with a partner.

11 Answers will vary but should reflect collaboration.

Unit One Review

PREVIEW

Examine the following key concepts previewed in Unit One.

1 Which relaxation technique works best for you? Why?

2 Why it is important for actors to warm up before a rehearsal or performance?

3 How does observation help you as an actor?

4 If you were to play a character devoted to a pet, how would speak to, touch, and talk about that pet? Give examples.

5 How is a child's game of make-believe similar to an actor playing a role?

6 What is the mime's objective?

7 Without using words, indicate that you are angry about something.

8 How is improvisation like real life?

9 Why is it important to say "Yes, and . . ." in improvisation?

PREPARE

Assess your response to the preparation process for projects in this unit.

10 Was it easier to prepare with a partner you chose or one that your teacher chose for you? Why?

11 When working with a partner, how did you decide which tasks you would take on and which your partner would be responsible for?

12 Were you able to fully utilize all five senses when using your sense memory? Which senses seemed easier to call upon and why?

13 What techniques did you use to visualize your pantomime project?

14 Did you find it more difficult to prepare for your pantomime or your improvisation project? Why?

PRESENT

Analyze the experience of presenting your work to the class.

15 Were you able to have fun while presenting your warm-up routine? Why or why not?

16 In describing your object, were you able to help your audience see it clearly? Did you forget any important elements?

17 Were you able to become fully immersed in the pantomime you presented, or did you lose focus? What did you find distracting? How did this feel?

18 When the audience gave a suggestion for continuing your improvisation, were you able to do this to your satisfaction or would you do it differently now? If so, in what way?

CRITIQUE

Evaluate how you go about critiquing your work and the work of others.

19 What were the major stumbling blocks to remaining fair, impartial, or constructive while critiquing your classmates' presentations?

20 In what way did critiquing your classmates help you critique your own performances?

21 Did you find it easier to evaluate a performance that was closer to "outstanding" or more on the order of "needs much improvement"? Why?

EXTENSIONS

- Look at the image to the left. Use your powers of observation, sense memory, and recall to perform a short pantomime of someone eating this sundae.
- Practice standing in positions that show the following feelings, and then choose one to present to the class: impatience, sorrow, hope, delight, concern, contempt, anticipation, support.

Resource Binder

Unit One Test, p. 17

12 Answers should demonstrate an awareness of the five senses.

13 Answers should reflect the use of recall techniques.

14 Answers will vary.

PRESENT

15 Answers will vary but should reflect an analytical approach to the warm-up.

16 Answers should reflect an awareness of the use of the senses in description.

17 Answers will vary but students should describe the situation rather than blame themselves or others.

18 Answers should display thought about the student's work.

CRITIQUE

19 Answers should display self-reflection.

20 Answers should reflect an understanding of objective criteria.

21 Answers should make use of "I" statements.

EXTENSIONS

Encourage students to take chances in these extensions. Remind them that they will not know if they have worked to the extent of their abilities unless they fail once in a while.

Unit Two

Elements of Acting

Unit Two, along with Unit Three, will give students a clear picture of how actors prepare for a role and how they, along with other members of the production team, work together to create an artistic, meaningful, and unified whole. Projects in this unit will help students move comfortably on the stage and understand how they can improve their vocal production and articulation.

Project Preview

Chapter 5 Movement
Creating stage movement for a scene

Chapter 6 Stage Directions
Plotting stage crosses

Chapter 7 Voice Production and Articulation
Demonstrating a vocal exercise

Chapter 8 Ensemble Work
Performing as part of an ensemble

Unit Two Elements of Acting

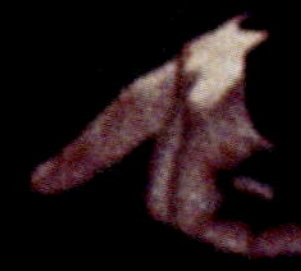

Quotables

Use the quotes below as journal writing prompts, discussion starters, or for your own enjoyment.

The performer's art is as much intellectual as physical; there is meaning in his movements; every gesture has its significance.

Lucien of Samosata, 2nd-century Greek Writer

Language springs out of the inmost parts of us. No glass renders a man's likeness so true as his speech.

Ben Jonson, 17th-century Dramatist and Poet

Discussion Questions

The following questions are intended to tap into students' **prior knowledge** and attitudes about the subject matter of this unit.

- Have you ever been on a stage for any kind of production? Describe the experience.
- How did you feel when you moved on the stage? Awkward? Comfortable? Confused?
- Who told you where to move? Did they use any special terminology such as *upstage* or *stage right*?
- Have you ever spoken to a group or an audience? Was it a class presentation? Speech? Acting role? Other?
- What happened to your voice in this speaking situation? Did you try to enunciate more clearly? Did you mumble? Did your throat tighten up? Could your audience hear you?
- As an audience member, what kinds of listening experiences have you had?
- What kind of team or group have you been a part of? Sports team? Singing group? Cooperative learning project? Debate club? Theatrical production? Family event?
- Describe your experiences in the team or group. Did you work well together or not?

Theatre Journal

Write a short monologue for the character in the photo. Consider the following: Who is he addressing? Why is he so intense? What is the reason for this tension? What is the situation?

43

Visual Cue

The image above shows Actor Matthew Lillard in Neil LaBute's play *Bash*, produced in London in 2000.

- Describe the man in the picture. What kind of character is he playing?
- What emotion might the actor be expressing? How do you know?
- How does the actor's body show this emotion?

ACTivity Have students stand and replicate the actor's stance and facial expression. On the count of three, they should assume another position that they feel shows the same emotion.

ACTivity Have groups of students work out an improvisation that begins with one of them taking on the character and stance of the actor in the picture.

Chapter 5

Movement

This chapter introduces students to the importance of natural movement on the stage and how movement communicates important information about a character.

Objectives

1 to understand how to execute natural body movements on stage
2 to learn how to incorporate stage business into a scene
3 to understand how natural, believable movement enhances characterization
4 to plan and execute a scene incorporating stage movement

National Standards

Chapter 5 meets these National Theatre Standards:
Proficient 2c, 7c, 7d, 8a
Advanced 2d, 8g

Project Specs

Special Needs Students
This project may need to be simplified. Have ready preplanned scenarios that incorporate a few easy movements.

Advanced Students
Instruct students to perform the same movement scene again, incorporating music that reflects the mood of the scene. They should determine if the music changed the way the characters moved or heightened the scene's emotion.

On Your Feet

Show, Don't Tell Choose a capable student as your partner, and demonstrate how to communicate the way in which two strangers riding in an elevator might behave.

Chapter

5 Movement

Whether you're the lead or one of the supporting players, whether you have long monologues or no lines to speak at all, the one thing you will be doing as an actor on stage is *moving*. How, when, and where to move takes some practice, so get moving!

Project Specs

Project Description You and a partner will plan and present stage movement for a two- to four-minute scene.

Purpose to practice moving naturally onstage

Materials a written scenario that details the movement needed for the scene or the Movement Activity Sheet provided by your teacher

Theatre Terms

cheating out
gestures
muscular memory
offstage
onstage
scenario
stage business
upstaging

On Your Feet

With a partner, use only movement to communicate the situations below. Stand about five feet apart. Depending on the situation you are enacting, you will move toward or away from your partner and use body language to add further texture to the moment.

- a surprise meeting between friends who haven't seen each other in a long time
- two strangers pretending not to notice one another
- friends or siblings who have just had a big argument
- friends saying good-bye knowing they will not meet again

Theatre Terms

cheating out playing toward the audience while seemingly conversing with others on stage

gestures movements of parts of the body, such as shrugging the shoulders

muscular memory having an action appear effortless and natural due to repeating the movement many times

offstage the part of the stage that the audience cannot see

onstage the part of the stage that is visible to the audience

scenario an outline of a play that includes details about the plot, movement, and gestures

stage business any small action that the actor performs without major movement

upstaging drawing the audience's attention to yourself when it should be focused on another character

PREVIEW

The Magic of Movement

In some ways, an actor is a magician who must present to the audience a world they can't help but accept and believe. The actor must persuade the audience that the small environment **onstage** is whatever the scene calls for—whether it be a ship, a living room, a faraway galaxy, or a doctor's waiting room—and that he or she is a real person interacting within that environment.

In daily life you probably don't pay all that much attention to the way you move. To be physically believable and natural onstage, however, the instruction that follows should help you.

Actors move together in a scene from *The Mikado* by the English National Opera, September 1994.

Moving on Stage

Entering

Make sure you are in position and ready to enter the stage at the appropriate time. Enter with your head up, unless your character demands otherwise. Know the exact point at which you become visible to the audience. You don't want to be seen by the audience when you think you're hidden **offstage**—it takes away from the magic of the performance.

Walking

Your normal walking movement should be rhythmical and smooth. As you walk, look ahead. To portray certain characters, however, your walk may be slow, labored, jittery, and so on.

Standing

Keep your weight on the balls of your feet. Unless you have a motivated movement to make, stand still. An actor's shuffling feet reveal nervousness and inexperience, and can make the audience uncomfortable.

Turning

When turning on stage, keep the audience in mind and turn toward them. The only exception to this rule is when such a turn would be obviously awkward because you are already in a position facing mostly away from the audience.

Sitting

If the scene calls for you to sit, place yourself in a comfortable position, but make sure you are poised to get up

PREVIEW

The Magic of Movement

"Actions speak louder than words." Write this phrase on the chalkboard and ask the students to discuss what it means. Assuming this statement is true, how a character moves must reveal just as much if not more about the character than what he or she actually says. Discuss the ways in which we communicate nonverbally with body language, facial expressions, and gestures.

ACTivity Have volunteers stand before the class and give them a specific ensemble movement to perform. Then give each individual volunteer a specific emotion to portray and ask them to express their emotion while still performing the ensemble movement.

Moving On Stage

Show, Don't Tell Demonstrate for the students the proper way to execute the stage movements of entering, walking, standing, turning, sitting, rising, gesturing, and exiting.

ACTivity Select a scene from a play that incorporates several movements. Have the students perform the scene using the stage movements discussed in the text.

The Mikado, with music by Arthur Sullivan and lyrics by W.S. Gilbert, is arguably the most popular opera ever written. This comic opera opened on March 14, 1885, and has been delighting audiences ever since. The pictured 1994 production was a controversial performance because director Jonathan Miller changed the setting from Japan to a 1920s English seaside hotel.

- How are the characters expressing their individuality while their movements remain in sync?
- What different emotions can you see portrayed by the characters in the photograph?

Resource Binder

- Movement Activity Sheet, p. 18
- Stage Business Worksheet, p. 19
- Critique Sheet: Movement, p. 20
- Movement Test, p. 21

Handbook Connections
pages 558-560

To Have on Hand

- A stopwatch to time the movement scene–for practice and performance
- A playing space and one or two chairs so that the students may incorporate the proper way to stand, sit, and rise into their movement scene presentations
- Scripts or playbooks with movement written into them for advanced extensions of the assignment
- Cards with situations on them for the On Your Feet assignment—have pairs of students draw a situation and perform

ACTivity **Beginning Students**
Divide the class into eight groups—assign each group one of the eight movements discussed in Moving on Stage. Give the groups a few minutes to practice their movement and then have one group at a time demonstrate the proper way to execute their assigned movement before the class.

ACTivity Divide the students into pairs. Instruct each student to select an emotion for his or her character to portray. Have each pair come up before the class and freeze into a portrait. Have the rest of the class discuss what emotion each character is portraying.

ACTivity **Advanced Students**
Have pairs of students write short scenes that incorporate an entrance, an exit, a turn, being seated, and two or three gestures. Have volunteers perform their scenes.

Theatre Journal

Use the following as an additional or substitute prompt.

As you watch people move in their various activities, think about what emotion each person must be feeling. Discuss possibilities as to what may have happened to the person before the moment that you began observing them, leading to the emotion they are now portraying.

The following prompts can be used to exercise critical viewing skills.

- In the bottom picture, what emotions do you think the two characters are feeling?
- Discuss the body language of the two characters. What does it tell you?

when you need to. Never slouch unless the role specifically calls for it.

If you must back up to the chair to sit down, do so until you touch it with the back of your leg, and then sit.

Rising
When getting up from your seat, anticipate the move by slowly easing forward on the chair. Keep your spine straight and rise with your weight on one foot and then shift it to the other to ensure balance.

Moving forward before rising helps you get up with ease.

Gesturing
Gestures are expressive bodily actions, such as shrugging, pointing, or raising the eyebrows. Gestures should be definite and clear. Halfhearted or extraneous gestures are the mark of an inexperienced or unfocused actor.

The gestures and the expressions of the actors below show their feelings.

Exiting
Be sure you stay in character until you are offstage and invisible to the audience.

As a student actor, you should practice these movement techniques until you can use them so effectively that they appear effortless to the audience. Only through sustained practice will you be able to move naturally onstage without having to think about it constantly. This constant repetition of motion helps you develop **"muscular memory."**

Theatre Journal

Keep notes on what you notice about the way people move when doing various things, such as getting on a bus, walking down stairs, running to catch up with friends, describing something large and impressive, walking into class late, or getting up from a sunken couch.

Backstage Gossip: The Plot Sickened

On the whole, actors like to arrive on stage on cue and leave in an orderly manner as rehearsed. It isn't always possible. George Sanders appeared in a play when he was coming down with gastric flu. In the middle of his last scene, he suddenly announced to the rest of the company that he was popping out for a breath of fresh air. He left the stage in great haste—while the other characters stayed where they were—dumbfounded—and returned less than a minute later having thrown up in the wings. He then completed his performance as usual.

from *Great Theatrical Disasters* by Gyles Brandreth

PREPARE

Working Out the Scene: Beginning, Middle, and End

With a partner, you are to perform a two- to four-minute scene that incorporates basic movement principles and action. You will have to coordinate the onstage movement between you and your partner. You will perform a scene that shows what both characters want (their intentions), a conflict, and a resolution. Your scene will have a beginning, middle, and end.

Create a Scenario

You will not need to create dialogue for this scene. You will accomplish everything through movements, gestures, and facial expressions. However, you and your partner will have to collaborate to write a detailed **scenario**—an outline that includes information about the plot, what each character wants, how their intentions conflict, and what they do about it.

You can use one of the suggestions at the right as a jumping-off point or you can create a scenario of your own. As your scenario takes shape, write down each action and each major shift in the two characters' intentions using as much detail as possible.

Add the Movement

Once you have written the scenario, add detailed notations about movement, gestures, and facial expressions. For example, if one character enters a scene in which the other character is already onstage, from what direction does the entering actor come? Where is the onstage actor standing (or sitting)? How do the actors greet each other? Do they smile or frown? Indicate movement with specific notations such as these:

Character 1 moves from left to right and opens the door. Character 2 enters.

After they exchange pleasantries, Character 1 motions for Character 2 to sit in the chair on the left side of the playing area.

Character 2 sits in the right-hand chair instead.

Character 1 looks displeased and sits opposite Character 2.

Discuss what you want to convey with each action. For example, when Character 2 doesn't sit in the recommended chair, what effect does this have on each character—and on the scene? Make sure you have a specific reason for each new movement. Take the scene as far as you can.

Possible Scenarios

- You wait for a competitive friend to come and play chess. When your friend arrives, you begin to play. Show what happens during and after the game.
- You are typing a research paper when there is a knock at the door. A pushy neighbor who wants to sell you tickets to a school carnival enters. You don't want to buy any tickets. What happens next?
- You enter a shoe store and sit down to be waited on. You tell the tired clerk the type of shoe you want. He brings three pairs. You begin trying on shoes. What does the clerk do? What do you do? Do you buy any shoes?

Notes

PREPARE

Working Out the Scene: Beginning, Middle, and End

Discuss with the students the plot structure of a play, focusing on the idea of opposing goals or intentions that create a conflict between characters.

ACTivity Using a familiar fairy tale such as *Goldilocks and the Three Bears,* break down the elements of the story. For example:

Beginning—The bears leave home and Goldilocks walks into their house.

Middle—Goldilocks proceeds to eat their food and use their house as though it were her own, finishing Little Bear's porridge and breaking his chair.

End—The bears return home to find Goldilocks in Little Bear's bed. She awakens and runs away.

Follow up by discussing the conflict and resolution of the story.

Create a Scenario

Invite students to give examples of other scenario outlines of well-known stories. Have different students describe the beginning, middle, and end of each story, followed by a discussion of various characters' goals and conflicts.

Add the Movement

ACTivity Using the example scenarios students have contributed, ask volunteers for suggestions on movement notations—how the characters move, if gestures are needed, what facial expressions might be appropriate, and so on.

Possible Scenarios

Encourage students to explore the emotions of the people in each of the possible scenarios presented. How would the person awaiting a chess match feel? How might his or her gestures and movements reveal these feelings to the audience?

Rehearse the Scene

After explaining how to rehearse the scene, hand out the Movement Activity Sheet and show the students how to use it. Give the students a time limit for completing the preparation of their presentations. Keep a stopwatch handy to help students stay within the time limit. If students are having artistic disagreements, help them work through any problems by suggesting ways to compromise and collaborate effectively.

Here's How

Have students demonstrate stage business techniques they would incorporate into these scenes:

- Reading a newspaper on a hot July evening
- Preparing a picnic by the sea
- Waiting for a long-overdue bus
- Cooking dinner at a campsite
- Walking home with a friend on a snowy day

Visual Cue

The following prompts can be used to exercise **critical viewing skills.**

- What makes this stage picture interesting?
- Discuss the various types of movement on the stage.
- What do you think is happening in this scene? What is it about the characters' body language that leads you to this conclusion?

ACTivity Have students create stage pictures like the one in the photo above. Ask a volunteer to begin by freezing into an interesting pose. Have the class study the pose and think about how they could compliment the stage picture. When students have an idea, they enter the picture and strike a new pose. Eventually, the entire class should be part of the portrait.

Each of the actors in this scene has a good sense of his motivation and position onstage.

Rehearse the Scene

Now that you've created a scenario and added the movement, practice your scene with your partner. Watch each other's movements, gestures, and facial expressions. Is everything clear? Does the scene make sense? Does the movement illustrate the characters' relationship and the situation? Make and accept suggestions for improvement. Go through the scene again. This time, make sure you are staying within the two- to four-minute time frame. When you have shaped the scene to the best of your ability, think of a title for it. Then work out the technical details of how you will set up for the scene, which of you will introduce the scene, and what you will do once you've finished performing.

Remember that no move you make will matter if the audience can't see it. Successful actors develop an innate sense of their positioning onstage in relationship to the audience.

Here's How
To Incorporate Stage Business

Any small action that the character performs without major movement is called **stage business.** Sometimes stage business is written into the script as directions, but generally it is added by the director and actor. If your character continually knits or is forever whittling a piece of wood, this reveals something about his or her nature. Stage business may communicate the time of day or the season. If you toast bread at the table, it suggests morning. Fanning yourself with a newspaper indicates a hot day in summer. Business can also create atmosphere or add interest to the play. Whatever specific business is used, it should be planned early in the rehearsals and practiced at each one. Remember, you must have a good reason for performing all stage business.

From the Field: See It with Your Elbow!

Viola Spolin's phrase "See it with your elbow!" is one I use to express to the students the importance of total body awareness. The whole body must react and feel what the character is experiencing. If the character is feeling sad, the audience must then see sadness in the way the character enters the room, in the walk, the gestures, and facial expressions. I encourage students to get their entire bodies into the scene—from head to toe.

Carmen McElwaine, Drama Instructor, Plano, Texas

Spotlight on

The Rules of Stage Movement

Become familiar with these six basic principles of stage movement.

1 Onstage, movement should always be *motivated* by the intentions of the actors in the scene. Make sure that when you move onstage you know exactly *why* you are doing so. React as though experiencing a stimulus to which you respond instinctively.

2 Movement must be *simplified*. There is no point in creating busy traffic patterns onstage. Simpler is best.

3 Movement must be *heightened* from real life. In real life you might wander into a room for no apparent reason and promptly walk back out again. In a scene onstage, however, each action counts.

4 Movement must *delineate* character. Movement tells the audience a great deal about characters and their relationship to one another. Make sure your movement is in keeping with your character.

5 Movement must be *toward the audience*. To create realistic interactions actors must have contact with the other people onstage. However, keeping an "open" position–one that turns you slightly toward the audience–works best. Often this is referred to as **cheating out.**

6 To maintain balanced and pleasing stage pictures an actor must *adjust to the movement of others*. Taking out a handkerchief on stage while another actor is the focus of the scene or angling your body so that your scene partner must turn away from the audience to speak to you is called **upstaging.** It is rude. Never do it.

Actors cheating out.

Backstage Gossip: Bad Stage Business

John Barrymore (grandfather of Drew Barrymore) once played a father who strongly disapproved of his daughter's fiancé. In one scene, as the fiancé left the stage, the daughter would ask her father what he thought of his future son-in-law. Barrymore was supposed to answer, "I think he is a dirty dog." One night, when the fiancé walked off stage, he accidentally tipped over a pitcher of water. An awkward moment of silence followed as everyone watched a puddle form. The daughter asked on cue, "What do you think of Tom, father?" To which Barrymore replied, "I think he is a dirty dog. And what's more, he isn't even housebroken!"

from the Web site *www.anecdotage.com*

Spotlight on

The Rules of Stage Movement

ACTivity To help students work on motivated intentions when moving onstage, write the following sentence on the chalkboard:

David didn't tell me you were invited to the party.

Then have students create a movement while saying this line with one of the following intentions:

- to charm the person
- to intimidate the person
- to ridicule the person
- to indicate a social error has been made
- to show surprised delight
- to show stunned outrage

Tell students they may approach the scene in a serious or humorous way, but remind them that they must move and speak naturally and convincingly—no overacting.

ACTivity Have students practice cheating out by standing together in the playing area and carrying on a conversation.

PRESENT

Perform a Scene Using Stage Movement

Before beginning the movement scenes, remind the students to hand in their Activity Sheets when their names are called. Tell students who are watching, that proper audience behavior begins as soon as the Activity Sheet is handed in. They should remain quiet and attentive for the duration of the performance. Have a stopwatch ready to time each scene.

CRITIQUE

Evaluate Classmates' Scenes

Hand out the Critique Sheet for this project or have students use their own paper. In either case be sure the students understand that the critique activity involves several steps including note-taking, scoring, and writing. It will be helpful to assign the scenes that each student will evaluate so that everyone receives a peer evaluation.

As you evaluate presentations, let the students know that you will be using the same rubrics for them as they will be using for each other. In addition to their presentations, you may also wish to evaluate students on how well they assess the other presentations.

When projects have been completed, cut off the names of the reviewers and hand the Critique Sheets back to the students being reviewed.

PRESENT

Perform a Scene Using Stage Movement

When your name is called, hand in your scenario or Activity Sheet and walk to the playing area. Deliver your introduction to the scene as you and your partner rehearsed it. Then perform your two- to four-minute scene for the class.

At the end of the scene, turn to your classmates and ask, "What just happened here?" If you have performed well, they should be able to track the plot of your scene.

Allow only two minutes for the discussion. When you are finished, thank your audience and bow politely before leaving the playing area. Remember to retain a professional demeanor until you have reached your seat.

CRITIQUE

Evaluate Classmates' Scenes

Evaluate one or two of the scenes presented in class. Begin your critique by listing all the positive aspects of the scene. Then move on to the areas that in your view needed improvement, including anything that seemed unclear in the scene. Then, using the following rating scale, give the scene a number score. "Outstanding" = 5; "well done" = 4; "fair" = 3; "needs some improvement" = 2; "needs much improvement" = 1.

To give an accurate, well-supported critique, ask yourself these questions:

- Did the scene have a beginning, middle, and end?
- How did each character make his or her intentions clear?
- Did each performer respond to what the other was doing?
- Were movements motivated by the characters' intentions?
- Did the movement seem appropriate and spontaneous or was there unnecessary business?
- Were you interested in the outcome, or resolution, of the scene?

Write a paragraph explaining why you gave the score or scores you did.

Notes

Additional Projects

1 Determine basic movement that you can use to communicate the following characters: a loudmouthed, ignorant person; a nervous, high-strung person; a vigorous athlete; an extremely weak or tired person; a timid, self-conscious person; and one other of your choice. Pay particular attention to mannerisms and gestures, the placement of your weight, and the degree of tension in your movements. If you are up for the challenge, try doing one or two of the above without any facial expression.

2 Visit a zoo, farm, wooded area, or park near your home. Select a bird or animal to observe. Note the individual movements of this creature's paws, head, eyes, tail, wings, and so on. Pay close attention to specific mannerisms. In class, portray the animal's action. Then transfer those characteristics into human action. Your human portrayal should maintain the basic movements, rhythm, and patterns of the animal.

3 Think of a situation that involves waiting—waiting in line, waiting for a bus, or waiting for a friend's arrival. Choose an age at least ten years older or younger than your current age. Then go to the playing area and portray a person of that age in your chosen situation. Make sure you incorporate the body rhythm, facial expressions, and the basic movements and attitudes of that age group. Keep your movements selective and specific.

4 Read the scene from Paula Vogel's Pulitzer Prize-winning play *How I Learned to Drive* found in Unit Eight. With several partners, work out how the characters Li'l Bit and Peck would move in the scene.

"One onstage movement can convey pages of thought and yet the same movement—overdone—has a hammy meaning all its own."

—Actor Richard Baseheart

Chapter 5 Test

The test for this chapter is available in blackline master form in the Resource Binder, page 21.

For More Information

Books

King, Nancy, *A Movement Approach to Acting,* Prentice Hall, 1981.

Kline, Peter, *Physical Movement for the Theatre,* Rosen Publishing Group, 1971.

Lecoq, Jacques, *The Moving Body: Teaching Creative Theatre*, Theatre Arts Books, 2002.

Sabatine, Jean, *Movement Training for the Stage and Screen: The Organic Connection Between Mind, Spirit, and Body,* Watson-Guptill Publishing, 1995.

Wangh, Andre Gregory, *An Acrobat at the Heart*, Vintage Books, 2000.

White, Edwin C., et al., *Acting and Stage Movements: A Complete Handbook for Amateurs and Professionals,* Meriwether Publishing, 1985.

Other Media

Body Language Skills, VHS, Insight Media, 2002.

Movement, VHS, Insight Media, 1996.

Movement for the Actor, CD-ROM, 1985; VHS, Insight Media, 1993.

Substitute Teacher Activities

Here are suggestions for one or more days when you will be out of the classroom.

- Assign the Stage Business Worksheet on page 19 of the Resource Binder.
- Teach the Motivation, Movement, and Creating Believable Action sections of the Student Handbook, pp. 558-560.
- Assign one or more of the Additional Projects on this page.
- **Play What's My Move?** On 3 x 5 cards list a number of situations, such as "You've just been cut from the team" or "You are out on a date with the most boring person on earth." Students must demonstrate the movements that would accompany the situation.

Theatre Then and Now

Ritual Dance Movement

Ritual dance was performed with the intention of influencing or controlling events important to society, such as desired rainfall, success in battle, and so on. Rituals were also performed with the intention of glorifying deities, ancestors, or an important victory. Masks, costumes, and body paint were often worn in order to call forth a higher power or to represent an animal in the hunt. These rituals contained great spectacle, and as a result became a form of entertainment to society.

A common Native American dance was the bull dance, in which the costumes consisted of actual buffalo heads as headdresses and buffalo skins.

In 1808, playwright James Nelson Barker wrote a romantic drama about Pocahontas, *The Indian Princess,* which became the first play about Native Americans to reach the stage. On the whole, American plays of the 19th century presented American Indians as "noble savages."

In 1871 a new and unfortunate trend began when Augustin Daly's play *Horizon* presented Native Americans as villains. Finally, in the middle 1900s, more realistic and historically accurate plays began to appear, such as *Black Elk Speaks*, based on the life of a Sioux holy man, written for the stage by Christopher Sergel.

Theatre Then and Now

Ritual Dance Movement

Dance and music have been important parts of human interaction since the beginning of recorded time. Sound, rhythm, and exuberant physical movement are as much a part of theatre today as they were thousands of years ago.

The theatre as we know it is believed to have evolved from shamanism and ritual dance. A shaman was a priest figure common to almost all very early cultures. Part of the shaman's job was to communicate with the gods on behalf of his community. This communication often took the form of physical imitation of animals and symbolic movements depicting weather systems or crop growth. As early as 2500 B.C., rituals merged with traditional dance to form elaborate theatrical ceremonies.

Dancing is an important part of Native American society.

Visual Cue

Have students study the image of the Native American dancer and then respond to the following questions:

- What challenges, responsibilities, and gratification would dancing in authentic costume offer the Native American dancer?
- How do costumes affect the way we move on stage? Would an actor move differently depending on the costume?

Modern Movement

In the Canadian town of Gaspe, a group of stilt walkers, jugglers, and specialty performers created a new kind of circus—a mesmerizing blend of theatre, circus techniques, street performance, high-tech lighting and sound, and eye-popping costumes. The year was 1984, and they called themselves **Cirque du Soleil** (Circus of the Sun). Their goal was nothing less than to "reinvent the circus." Pure physical movement and music form the common language that allows audiences to journey with Cirque du Soleil to a place of dreams and wonder. Cirque du Soleil has also made films of its shows for television and I-Max theatres. For more information, visit their Web site at www.cirquedusoleil.com.

Cirque du Soleil shines on.

The Blue Man Group features three bald-headed, blue-faced characters who take their audience through a fast-paced, multi-sensory experience that blends slapstick, music, art, and science into a thrilling new theatrical form. The group's award-winning theatrical productions have been described as "ground-breaking," "visually stunning," and "musically powerful." Their props include Jell-O, marshmallows, rolls and rolls of toilet paper, and cans of paint, among other things. These inventive blue fellows have a unique style of percussion music, which they play primarily on invented instruments—such as large plastic tubing, flexible fiber rods, gigantic gongs, and sheets of aluminum. Visit their entertaining Web site at www.blueman.com.

Blue Men move to the beat of their own drums.

Modern Movement

In addition to Blue Man Group and Cirque du Soleil, another exciting group found audience favor in the 1990s. The best way to describe them is to say that *Stomp* is a unique blend of percussion, movement, and visual comedy. Its creators, Luke Cresswell and Steve McNicholos, first presented the show on the streets of Brighton, England, where a group of street performers, commonly known as "buskers," tried to attract people's attention by their performances. Busking is a custom in England dating back to the Middle Ages.

Stomp contains no dialogue nor plot, but replaces it with the everyday sounds of garbage can lids, pipes, brooms, and so on, creating an incredible display of music and movement. The show premiered in England to high acclaim and eventually began its run at the Orpheum Theatre in New York in February of 1994.

ACTivity Play excerpts from various kinds of music and ask students to write a description of the movement that comes to mind as they listen. Discuss with students how music can affect the telling of a story, the expressing of an emotion, or the way characters move on stage. If there is time, have students get up and move as the music is played again.

Visual Cues

- In the top photo, what do you think is the most important physical attribute of the people on the bicycle?
- In the bottom photo, do you think the blue makeup encourages the audience to focus more on the men's faces or their movements?
- Would the visual impact be different if they were Green Man Group?

For More Information

Books

Burton, Bryan, *Moving Within the Circle, Contemporary Native American Music and Dance,* World Music Press, 1993.

Vial, Veronique, *Varekai: Cirque du Soleil,* Harry N. Abrams, 2003.

Vial, Veronique, *Wings: Backstage with Cirque du Soleil!!!,* Arena Editions, 1999.

Other Media

Cirque du Soleil—Dralion, DVD, VHS, Columbia/Tristar, 2001.

Cirque du Soleil—Quidam, DVD, VHS, Columbia/Tristar, 1999.

Dance of the Spirits: Mask Styles and Performance, VHS, Insight Media, 1988.

Finding the Circle, American Indian Dance Theatre, PBS Great Performance Series.

An Introduction to Kathakali Dance-Drama, VHS, Insight Media, 2000.

www.stomponline.com

Chapter 6

Stage Directions

This chapter introduces students to the stage areas, the effect of the actor's body position on stage, and movement across the stage.

Objectives

1 to understand and practice body positioning
2 to become familiar with the areas of the stage
3 to use movement to create expression of thought, feeling, and character
4 to plot and execute stage directions

National Standards

Chapter 6 meets these National Theatre Standards:
Proficient 2a, 3c, 4b, 7c, 7d
Advanced 2e, 3g, 4e

Project Specs

Tape or draw the floor of the playing area into nine sections representing the stage areas shown on p. 56.

Special Needs Students
Note that dyslexic students may need extra help with the "backwards" left and right stage terminology in this chapter.

Advanced Students
To complete the project, have students use a real script that combines dialogue as well as crosses.

On Your Feet

Show, Don't Tell Before the game begins, demonstrate *stage left* and *stage right* for students. You may wish to have a small prize for the last person standing.

Chapter
6 Stage Directions

Don't just stand there–do something! Theatre is all about dramatic action. The action and excitement in a play are both supported by–even created by–movement. Effective stage movement is an indispensable part of a gripping production, and the actor must know how to follow stage directions every step of the way.

Project Specs

Project Description You will plot three stage crosses for a classmate to execute and then perform a classmate's three stage crosses in two to three minutes.

Purpose to learn to create and follow stage directions and to assume body positions accurately and with confidence

Materials a drawing showing three stage crosses or the Stage Directions Activity Sheet your teacher gives you

Theatre Terms

backstage
counter-cross
cross
downstage/upstage
full back/full front
profile
quarter turn
raked
sightlines
stage left/stage right
three-quarter turn

On Your Feet

Play "Simon Says Staging!" with a small group. A "director" calls out directions in which the group must move either "stage right" or "stage left" while facing the director. For example, "Hop stage left" or "Kick stage right."

Theatre Terms

backstage behind the stage; out of view

counter-cross moving in the opposite direction of an actor making a cross

cross movement across the stage

downstage toward the audience

full back/full front facing or completely turned away from the audience

profile sideways to the audience

quarter turn halfway between full front and stage left/right

raked slanted

sightlines imaginary lines indicating visibility of stage areas

stage left/stage right the actor's left or right as he or she faces the audience

three quarter turn halfway between full back and stage left/right

upstage toward the back of the stage

PREVIEW

A Look at the Stage

The stage didn't always look the way it does today. Early on in theatre history, players found that people could see them better on a **raked,** or slanted, surface. So they built their playing areas on an incline. The back of the playing area was actually higher than the front. Thus, the back part of the stage became known as "upstage," while the front part of the stage was called "downstage." So back when the audience was on a flat level, the stage was raked. As the audience seating became raked, as it is today, the stage got flatter.

Even today, some stages have a small incline, or rake, to improve visibility, or **sightlines,** for the audience. Whether they do or not, however, the tradition remains, and actors everywhere move away from the audience to be **upstage** and toward the audience to be **downstage.**

Where Am I?

When directors and choreographers sketch an acting area, they generally divide it into nine locations, as seen on page 56.

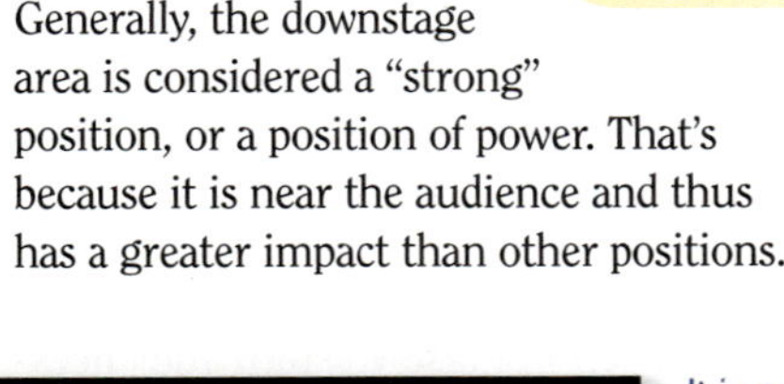

Generally, the downstage area is considered a "strong" position, or a position of power. That's because it is near the audience and thus has a greater impact than other positions.

Upstaged!

You've heard of upstaging—and you know it's NOT the thing to do, but do you know where the term originated? When actors deliver lines from upstage, they steal the focus by forcing the other actors to turn with their backs to the audience in order to speak to the upstage actors.

It is possible for a play to take place entirely in one spot, with the actor buried up to her neck in sand, as in *Happy Days* by Samuel Beckett, but it happens rarely.

PREVIEW

A Look at the Stage

Find as many images of various stages from around the world as possible. Talk to students about stage configurations. Discuss the shape, size, height, and width of each. Where are the seats in relation to the stage? Is there a curtain? What kind of play would you imagine being performed on this stage? Compare these stages to the one on page 56. Then use this image to show which part of the stage would be higher if it were raked.

Upstaged!

Show Don't Tell Use students to demonstrate how one actor can upstage another. Have students read a favorite scene in twos or threes with one actor speaking his or her lines to the others from an upstage position. Instruct the other actors to speak their lines to the upstage actor. Ask the class for their impressions of this exchange. Point out that while beginning actors often unwittingly upstage another actor, only a truly selfish performer would intentionally try to steal the focus from another.

Visual Cue

Discuss the image in the student book using the following prompts:

- What kind of challenges would face an actor who couldn't move?
- If you couldn't move, how would you develop a character?
- Would you enjoy this kind of role? Why or why not?

ACTivity Ask volunteers to portray emotions such as anger, sympathy, or excitement without moving their bodies in any way. They could improvise some lines or use an excerpt from Unit Eight.

Resource Binder

- Stage Directions Activity Sheet, p. 22
- Moving in Character Worksheet, p. 23
- Critique Sheet: Stage Crosses, p. 24
- Stage Directions Test, p. 25
- Blocking Shorthand, p. 127

Handbook Connections
pages 558-560, 567

To Have on Hand

- Tape or chalk for marking the playing area
- Prize for winner of the "Simon Says Staging" game
- Images of various types of stages
- Scripts or playbooks with stage crosses marked on them
- Cards with the eight body positions
- A box for collecting the list of students' stage crosses and diagrams or Activity Sheets

Where Am I?

ACTivity Practice body position with students by reading from various plays and asking students to demonstrate how they would position their bodies in the scene. Discuss what the actors who are not speaking would be doing while other actors are speaking. Ask students to suggest body positions for the following scenarios:

- an engaged couple planning their wedding
- a neighbor eavesdropping
- four friends planning a party
- three kids walking to school
- parents arguing with their child
- an angry teenager

Ask students to suggest other scenarios that will help them practice their body positioning.

ACTivity **Beginning Students** If you have not already done so, draw or tape a simulated stage outline on the floor. Divide the stage into nine areas. Have the students line up along a wall. One by one, call out a stage direction and have students stand on the appropriate area of the stage. Practice until the class is comfortable with each of the nine positions.

ACTivity **Advanced Students** Use the activity above, but call out the abbreviations (UR, CR, DC, CS, etc.) at a faster and faster pace. Once all the spaces are occupied, call out two positions for quick exchanges ("DR to UR!") and have those students switch spots.

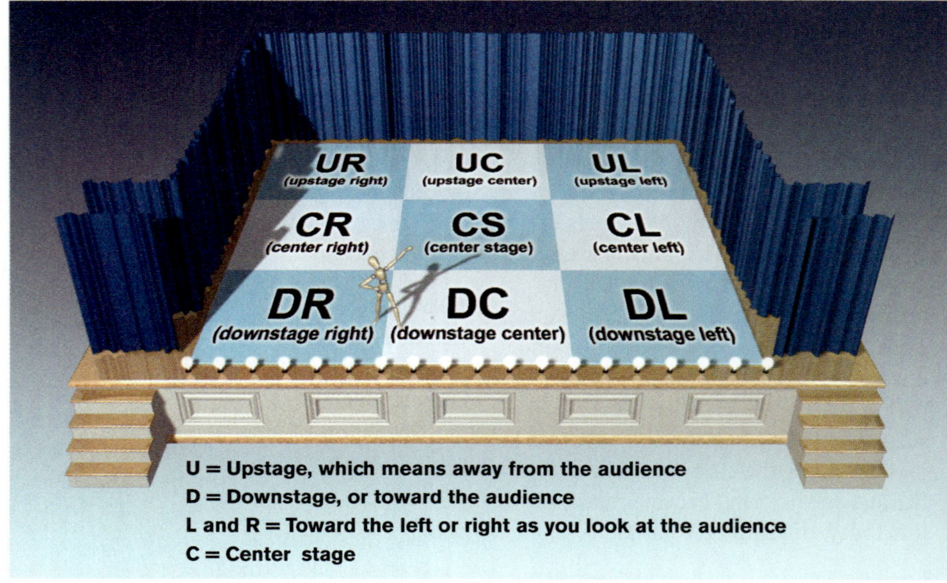

The many areas of the stage. **Backstage** is the area behind the stage that the audience cannot see.

Stage right is a stronger position than **stage left** because Western audiences are conditioned by reading to look from left to right. Thus, they tend to look stage right for the flow of action or the drama's movement. Because of the strength of downstage and stage right, important scenes will often be played there, and strong characters will tend to settle there.

The following body positions also affect the strength of one's character onstage:

1. Actors who share a scene equally often use a **quarter turn** toward each other. This places their bodies so that the audience can easily see them.
2. If a scene becomes intense, actors may turn in **profile** to the audience. This tightens their focus on each other and the audience's focus on them.
3. When one character's lines are especially important, other actors might make a **three-quarter turn** toward that actor, in order to "give" that actor focus.
4. For monologues and asides to the audience, actors often stand **full front,** facing the audience.
5. In unusual circumstances, an actor might turn his or her **full back** to the audience.

Backstage Gossip: Don't Cross Me!

Ruth Gordon once described to George Kaufman a new play in which she was appearing: "In the first scene I'm on the left side of the stage, and then the audience has to imagine I'm eating dinner in a crowded restaurant. Then in scene two I run over to the right side of the stage and the audience imagines I'm in my own drawing room." Kaufman listened, then mused: "And the second night you have to imagine there's an audience out front."

from *Theatrical Anecdotes* by Peter Hay

Getting Your Bearings

A **cross** is a movement from one stage area to another. The director will indicate a stage cross as an "X" on paper. Generally, the actor takes the shortest, most direct route, which is straight across some portion of the stage. Sometimes, however, a director will call for a complicated cross. That's because straight crosses tend to imply strength and decisiveness. A director may want to convey feelings of indecision, casualness, grace, or ease.

Following a complicated cross is not really that hard. How many times have you gone to the refrigerator for a drink, stopping first at the cabinet for a glass and then pausing to look for something to eat? Still, you will want to practice a complicated cross before performing it for an audience so that it looks natural.

The director's notations on this script indicate that Me (Meryl) stays where she is while W (Win) enters from the upper left (the porch). Win then crosses left to Meryl.

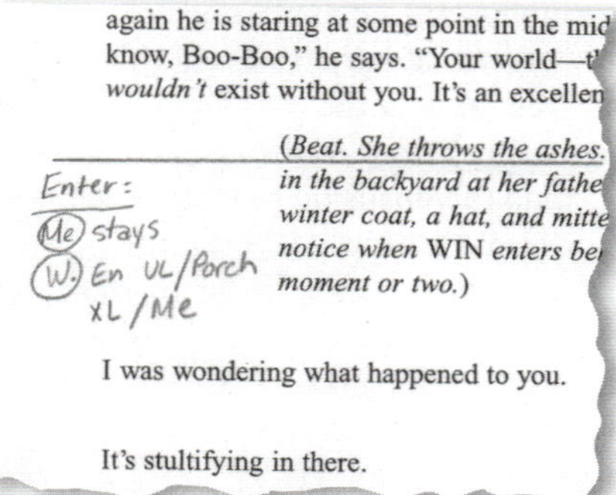
again he is staring at some point in the mid
know, Boo-Boo," he says. "Your world—t
wouldn't exist without you. It's an excellen

Enter:
Me stays
W. En UL/Porch
XL/Me

(Beat. She throws the ashes.
in the backyard at her fathe
winter coat, a hat, and mitte
notice when WIN *enters be*
moment or two.)

I was wondering what happened to you.

It's stultifying in there.

The five body positions.

Getting Your Bearings

ACTivity Practice crosses with the students by setting up a few pieces of furniture (or drawing them with chalk or using cardboard cutouts). Let students write a short script with directions such as, "Clarice saunters from the sofa to the desk and picks up the letter" or "Harvey leaps up from his chair, dances over to the door, and waltzes out of the room." Ask the students to direct one another in the crosses needed to fulfill the directions in the scripts.

Try to gather scripts or playbooks in which crosses and other directions have been marked. Talk about the marks and what they mean. Ask students to demonstrate the various crosses and other stage directions you find.

ACTivity Ask five students to stand on the simulated chalk stage in the positions shown on this page. Have large cards ready with all eight of the possible body positions written on them: "one quarter right," "three quarter left," and so on. One by one, have students pick new designated positions that they must quickly change to. When the first group has mastered all the positions, call up five new students.

Vocabulary Enhancement

Let students know that the off-stage areas on either side of the acting area are called the *wings.*

The auditorium where the audience sits is called the *house.*

From the Field: Collision Course

Well-planned crosses are not just necessary for the actor. The stage crewmembers who change scenery between scenes also need to plan their moves, especially when the change is quick and the stage is dark. We learned this the hard way when a member of our stage crew who was exiting quickly with a tray full of glasses and dishes ran into another stagehand who was entering with a heavy antique table. Both the tray and the table were dropped with a terrific crash. Fortunately the only things broken were the glasses.

Julie Nobles, Teacher, Chicago, IL

ACTivity Have students continue to practice crossing by asking them to sit in a chair, stand, and cross to a certain point on the stage or in the classroom. Check to be sure that each student rises from the chair with back straight and one foot extended. Remind students to start on the foot facing in the direction they are heading.

Add to the activity by asking several students to stand on stage while one student executes the crosses you ask for. Next, give the student who is moving a few lines of dialogue to speak while crossing. Check to be sure that the students without lines or movement stay in character but do not move or talk when the cross is going on.

Here's How

Have students practice each of the Here's How tips in order until they are very comfortable with them.

- crossing while speaking
- remaining still while another crosses
- crossing behind a speaking actor
- standing downstage while speaking more lines
- standing upstage while speaking fewer lines
- counter-crossing when someone moves toward you

across some portion of the stage. Sometimes, however, a director will call for a complicated cross. That's because straight crosses tend to imply strength and decisiveness. A director may want to convey feelings of indecision, casualness, grace, or ease.

Following a complicated cross is not really that hard. How many times have you gone to the refrigerator for a drink, stopping first at the cabinet for a glass and then pausing to look for something to eat? Still, you will want to practice a complicated cross before performing it for an audience so that it looks natural.

Here's How
To Move Without Crashing into Anyone

1. The moving figure dominates! If you are the speaking character and must cross, walk in front of the other characters.
2. If another character is talking, do not move. However, if the script calls for you to move during another character's lines, cross behind that person while staying in character.
3. If two actors cross the stage together, the one with more lines should be downstage, a short step ahead of the other actor.

It is usually necessary for actors to adjust to one another's crosses by using a **counter-cross.** If you find yourself in the direct path of another's cross you may "counter" by giving way a little and then by adjusting your position after the cross, as in the diagram.

The speaker (green arrow) crosses right in front of the listener. The listener (purple arrow) "counters" by moving in the opposite direction and turning toward the speaker. Both should finish moving at the same time.

Notes

PREPARE

Plot Three Stage Crosses

On the Activity Sheet for this chapter, which your teacher will provide, or on a separate piece of paper, list three stage crosses and body positions, and plot them on a stage diagram. You may list any combination of crosses and positions you wish. The following should serve only as an example.

Sample Directions:

- **a** X DR; stand quarter position left; raise right hand
- **b** X UC; stand in a full front position; bow
- **c** X UR; stand in a one-quarter position left; click your heels twice
- **d** X DC; stand in a profile, face left; raise both arms as high as you can
- **e** X DL; stand in a three-quarter position, face right; twist from your waist
- **f** X UL; stand in a full front position; turn right; sit down

Be sure your name appears on both the top and bottom sections of your paper. Divide the page by cutting it in two (or along the dashed lines of the Activity Sheet) and place it in a box along with your classmates' directions for stage crosses.

PRESENT

Read Aloud and Execute Three Stage Crosses

When your teacher calls your name, rise and draw at random a set of directions from the box. Be sure you do not get your own. Hand the directions to the person who wrote them. Then go to the playing area, and as your classmate calls out directions, follow them as though you were on stage. Be sure you begin each cross on the foot nearest your destination and cross to the correct stage area as directed. Finish each cross by assuming the proper body position.

When a classmate selects your set of directions from the class box and hands them to you, read each clearly. Proceed to the next direction only after your classmate has correctly followed your previous order.

Theatre Journal

Next time you're in a public place, such as a sports or cultural event, watch the unconscious movements of people in a group. Do some people in the group upstage others? Who gets the most focus? Who do the group members seem to think is their audience? Write about what you observe.

Backstage Gossip: A Starring Roll

During the rehearsal of one of his musicals, composer Jerome Kern was becoming increasingly irritated by a mannered actress who was constantly rolling her *r*'s. She had once more interrupted the rehearsal to ask:

"You want me, Mr. Kern, to cr-r-ross the stage, but I'm behind the table here. How can I get acr-r-oss?"

"It's simple," Kern suggested, "just r-r-roll over on your *r*'s."

from *Broadway Anecdotes* by Peter Hay

PREPARE

Plot Three Stage Crosses

Draw a stage diagram like the one on page 56 on the chalkboard for all the students to see. Write the directions for a stage cross on the board next to the stage diagram. For example, X DL or X DC. Indicate by drawing an X and a line to the DL position and then the DC position on the stage diagram that this is where the actor would move on the stage.

ACTivity Ask various students to come to the board. Indicate a start position for the student to place the chalk. Then ask another student to call out a cross. The student must then draw a line ending in an X to the place designated. Continue with other students, giving each a different starting position. Let all students have a turn at the chalkboard.

Finally, hand out the Stage Directions Activity Sheet and show students how to use it. Have a box ready to collect these sheets when students are done.

PRESENT

Read Aloud and Execute Three Stage Crosses

Make sure students understand that they will be picking a classmate's stage crosses from the box and executing them and not reading their own directions.

Theatre Journal

Use the following as an additional or substitute prompt.

As you observe people in a public place, try to decide what their mood is from watching how they move. Choose two or three moods and describe the kind of movements that go with them.

CRITIQUE

Evaluate a Classmate's Stage Crosses

Hand out the Critique Sheet for this project or have students use their own paper.

After you have reviewed student critiques, trim off the evaluator's name and hand out the sheets to the subjects of the evaluations.

Spotlight on

Taking Your Bows There are almost as many ways to conduct a curtain call as there are theatres, but every curtain call should be as professional as the rest of the performance.

- *Always* rehearse the curtain call.
- Some theatres have predetermined that there will be only one (or two) calls regardless of the amount of applause.
- Theatres with a strong ensemble ethic usually have the entire cast take part in each bow.
- Large cast and Broadway-type shows usually start the curtain call with the bit players and work up to the leads or "stars" who take individual bows.
- Small casts generally just line up and take simple bows. Large casts, especially musicals, may have elaborately choreographed curtain calls complete with musical reprises.

Vocabulary Enhancement

Manipulating the curtain and/or the lights to produce more clapping and curtain calls than the audience really wants to give is called *milking* the applause.

CRITIQUE

Evaluate a Classmate's Stage Crosses

Choose one of the sets of stage crosses performed by your classmates and evaluate it. Think about the impression your classmate would make if he or she were moving in ordinary life. Rate the crosses on a scale of 1 to 5, with 1 being "needs much improvement" and 5 being "outstanding." Your critique should answer these questions:

- Did the performer move to the correct locations?
- Did the performer end up in the proper body position?
- Did the performer move with confidence?
- Did the performer move with the proper foot first?
- Did the performer's movements seem natural and in character?

Write a paragraph defending your reasons for the rating you gave.

Spotlight on

Taking Your Bows

The curtain closes and the lights go up, but the show isn't over until the actors take their bows. The type of bow they perform depends on the style of the play and the particular production. Most often, actors perform a humble bow, standing straight, then bending the head and back slightly forward.

Sometimes you may be asked to perform a more genteel bow, in which you bend at the hips, keeping your back straight and your head dropped slightly.

Rarely, an actor will be asked to curtsey. To do a bob curtsey, keep your feet close together, swing one foot slightly behind the other, bend your knees quickly, and bob your head. A court curtsey is similar, but deeper and slower.

Remember to take your bows seriously. They are your way of telling the audience you are honored to perform for them and appreciate their attendance and applause.

Backstage Gossip: Philosophy Pays

Joan Rivers began her career in small off-Broadway shows, one of which led to an actor's nightmare—no applause! Rivers felt she was doing an excellent job in this show and invited every agent and show–business person she could in hopes of furthering her career. Naturally, everything that could go wrong, did. Doors stuck, props vanished, actors didn't connect, engine fumes filled the theatre, endless fire trucks went by, Rivers began to stutter, and a poor young actor whose role was to sit in a cage, shook the bars so hard they came apart in his hand. As she recalls: "Now the poor schlep had to hold the cage together and after my big speech about how this boy's spirit must go free . . . and I'm going to let him go now, the boy just handed me the bars and slunk away.

At the end . . . the cast appeared for the curtain call. Then my philosophy class at Barnard finally paid off. I understood the proposition of one hand clapping."

Additional Projects

1 Go to the stage area and make several crosses, ending with varied body positions. Challenge your classmates to identify each stage area you are in and the body position you are assuming.

2 With two partners, plot a series of crosses that might define a character type, such as a CEO at a successful board meeting, a criminal under indictment, a shy immigrant, a couple quarreling, or a child with something to hide.

3 With a partner, plot crosses for a two-person scene. You can use stage directions from an existing play or plot movements of your own. Once you have mastered the scene, try reversing the staging. What do the different crosses do to the relationship between the characters?

4 With one or more partners, plot the movement, including crosses, for the scene from *A Raisin in the Sun* by Lorraine Hansberry found in Unit Eight. Decide when to walk while speaking a line and when to walk between lines. Make sure to keep the focus on the proper actor in the scene.

The director, on the left, is helping the actor who is playing an apologetic young man cross to the actor who is playing his angry friend.

Chapter 6 Test

The test for this chapter is available in blackline master form in the Resource Binder, page 25.

For More Information

Books

Bloom, Michael, *Thinking Like a Director,* Faber & Faber, 2001.

King, Nancy, *A Movement Approach to Acting,* Prentice Hall, 1981.

Kline, Peter, *Physical Movement for the Theatre,* Rosen Publishing Group, 1971.

White, Edwin C., et al., *Acting and Stage Movements: A Complete Handbook for Amateurs and Professionals,* Meriwether Publishing, 1985.

Other Media

Blocking a Scene: Basic Staging with Actors, VHS, Insight Media, 1990.

Body Language Skills, VHS, Insight Media, 2002.

Movement, VHS, Insight Media, 1996.

Substitute Teacher Activities

- Assign the Moving in Character Worksheet on page 23 of the Resource Binder.
- Teach the Movement section, pp. 558-560, and/or the Storytelling section, p. 567, of the Student Handbook.
- Assign one or more of the Additional Projects on this page.
- **Plan a Fairy Tale Festival.** Divide the class into small groups and assign a well-known fairy tale to each group. "Cinderella," "The Three Pigs," "Little Red Riding Hood," "Goldilocks and the Three Bears," and "Hansel and Gretel" are all good candidates. Have the group choose a narrator and then work together to plan how the narrator should move as she or she tells the story.

Theatre Then and Now

The Actor Onstage

The Theatre of Dionysus was created in honor of Dionysus, the fertility god. It contained two performance areas: the dancing circle (or orchestra) and the area backed by the scene building (or *skene*). The chorus performed in the dancing circle. Statues were used to decorate such theatres, often glorifying a ruler or important battle.

Other Cultures, Other Times

There were two types of Medieval stages, the *fixed stage* and the *movable* stage. The most well known fixed stage was constructed in 1547, at Valenciennes in northern France, and contained a rectangular platform with two areas. One area contained huts, which served as the plays' different locations, and the other was the *platea*, an extended playing space. The actor went from hut to hut to show change of location as there were no set changes.

The most famous of Elizabethan theatres was the Globe Theatre, built in 1599, which consisted of an open-air building with a platform stage in the middle surrounded on three sides by open standing room. A large enclosed balcony covered by small roofed galleries surrounded the theatre, offering seating for those that could afford the fee. The back of the stage contained a multi-level façade. The stage was covered by a roof supported by two columns. The underside, called the heavens, was painted with moons, stars, and planets. For more about the Globe, see pages 424-425.

ACTivity Gather pictures of playbills and posters that depict characters from theatrical productions. Using the pictures, discuss what the posture, mannerisms, and facial expressions of the characters portray about them. Make comparisons between the way the Romans integrated the arts and how we integrate the arts today.

Theatre Then and Now

The Actor Onstage

With flexibility, creativity, and a good concept, theatre can be performed almost anywhere. In ancient times, outdoor theatre was the norm. Excavations in ancient Crete and the mainland nearby have uncovered evidence of early outdoor performance spaces that consisted of a rectangular area flanked by rows of stone seats.

Ancient Arenas

The Theatre of Dionysus in Athens was the West's first public *theatron,* or seeing-place. It was situated on a hillside below the Acropolis. Originally people simply sat or stood on the hillside to watch choral performances. As time went on and choral performances turned into full-length tragedies, terraces were built into the hillsides. Wooden seats were added, and when those deteriorated, stone seats were built. The stone auditorium completed some time around 330 B.C. could seat 14,000 to 17,000 people. Some historians believe stages were built into the theatres; others do not.

Nevertheless, historians agree that the audience–and the performances–remained outdoors. Music and dancing were an integral part of productions. And as time went on, spectacle became increasingly important. Indeed, some productions after the Romans conquered the Greeks became little more than loud and gory spectacle.

Under these conditions, actors relied heavily on pantomime and large gestures. Roman actors studied great orators and made extensive use of stylized movements, including stock placement of the head, hands, and feet, along with special intonations to signal specific emotions. Tragic acting involved slow, stately movements befitting the dignity of the characters and subject matter. Comic plays always included running, fighting, beatings, and physical humor. These acting conventions persisted through the Elizabethan age and into the 19th century.

This Roman statuette of a comic actor is from around the 1st century. It is from the collection of The Newark Museum.

Visual Cues

The following prompts can be used to discuss the Roman statuette and the photo from *Tony 'n Tina's Wedding.*

- How does the facial expression of the statuette show a comedic role rather than a dramatic one?
- As an audience member or actor, would you enjoy being a part of *Tony 'n Tina's Wedding* or would you be uncomfortable?

Today's Intimate Spaces
Today, arenas are reserved for sporting events and large scale entertainment such as rock concerts. Big musicals like *Stomp, Rent,* or *The Lion King* might play to houses that seat 2000 to 3000 people. But most commercial theatre takes place in smaller, indoor houses that seat 200–1200. Off-Broadway and off-off-Broadway shows might take place in storefronts that seat 50 or fewer audience members.

As a result, stages have been scaled back. So have conventions in movement, gesture, and intonation. Actors in most plays today don't seek to impress the audience. Their movements tend to be smaller, realistic, even intimate.

Tragedy might include simple stillness or tears. Comedy might include the broad physical humor of an earlier burlesque, but it might rely instead upon quick, witty wordplay such as that perfected by playwrights David Mamet or Tom Stoppard.

Today it is not uncommon for actors who are entering or exiting to wind their way through the house. And sometimes audience members are invited to become part of the play, as in *Tony 'n Tina's Wedding,* shown below.

The audience joins the conga line during the play *Tony 'n Tina's Wedding.*

Today's Intimate Spaces

The most popular type of stage, the proscenium stage, developed during the Italian Renaissance of the early 17th century. The proscenium arch is designed to frame the stage and hide what is going on backstage, separating the audience from the actors, creating the illusion of a self-contained world on the stage. The advantage of the "picture-frame stage" is that it allows for large scenery. The disadvantage is that it keeps the audience at a distance.

The arena stage, also called theatre in the round, can locate audiences on all four sides of the stage, allowing for an intimate setting, but restricting scenery to minimal sets. Margo Jones pioneered the arena stage in 1947 by establishing Theatre 47 in Dallas, Texas.

The thrust stage, a variation of the proscenium, emerged in America after WWII. The actors perform on a platform that thrusts out into the audience.

The black box stage is a type of minimal performance space emerging from the 1960s. Usually painted black and containing complex overhead lighting and moveable audience seating, the black box theatre is very flexible. The audience may be placed on one, two, three, or even all four sides of the playing area, while entrances and exits can be placed on either side of the stage space or through the audience.

For More Information

Books

Arnott, Peter D., *The Ancient Greek and Roman Theatre,* Random House.

Ball, James, *The Greek Theatre,* Old Vicarage Publications, 1983.

Elder, Eldon, *Will It Make a Theatre? Find, Renovate, and Finance the Non-Traditional Performance Space,* Allworth Press, 1997.

McAuley, Gay, *Space in Performance: Making Meaning in the Theatre,* University of Michigan Press, 2000.

Other Media

The Design of the Modern Theatre: Adolphe Appia's Innovations, VHS, Insight Media, 1993.

The Role of Theatre in Ancient Greece, DVD, VHS, Films for the Humanities and Sciences, 1989.

Stages of Theatre: From the Greeks to Shakespeare, CD-Rom, Films for the Humanities and Sciences, 2002.

Proper Breathing

Breathing is the basis of the voice. The actor's goal is to breath "normally" while under the pressure of a performance. The actor's breath must originate from the abdomen, not from the diaphragm. Deep breaths give the voice the support it needs for the stage.

ACTivity Have students recite the poem "Jack and Jill," as follows:

Jack and Jill went up the hill
To fetch a pail of water.
Jack fell down and broke his crown
And Jill came tumbling after.

The poem should be recited in one slow breath. Instruct students to maintain a volume and rate appropriate to the poem and to articulate each word carefully.

Here's How To Protect Your Voice

Vocal training begins by taking care of the voice you have. After all, you can *improve* your voice, but you can't *exchange* it. Prevent vocal problems by following these simple rules.

- Eat well, get enough sleep, and exercise regularly. This should help you avoid colds and other respiratory illnesses; they present a serious threat to your voice.
- Don't smoke or drink alcohol. While there are many reasons to avoid these substances, the chemicals and toxins in them are exceptionally harmful to the voice.
- Never strain your voice by shouting when you have a cold or by singing in an improper range.
- Never shout yourself hoarse at a ball game. Such strain makes throat membranes sore and invites infection that can lead to permanent damage. When in doubt, don't shout.

The sound produced is modified by the resonators (throat, nose, mouth, and sinuses) and formed into vowels and consonants by the articulators (tongue, jaw, teeth, cheeks, lips, and hard and soft palates).

When exercising your voice you will be working to achieve controlled breathing and **resonance,** or a rich, warm sound quality. In addition, variety in **pitch,** volume, **inflection,** and **rate** is important. Clear articulation, or way of speaking, and proper pronunciation round out the important elements of voice production. The diagram on page 65 shows all the areas of your body that contribute to the sound of your voice.

Proper Breathing

Actors and singers know that to have the necessary air control for a performance they must breathe from the diaphragm. This means that the chest cavity stays relatively still, while the waist expands and contracts, and the lower ribs rise and fall slightly. Once you have mastered diaphragmatic breathing, you will notice that it requires less effort than chest breathing, allows you to breathe more deeply, and provides the control you need to project long passages without running out of breath. That said, breathing from your diaphragm might feel strange at first. To get comfortable with this type of breathing, practice daily.

Notes

Richer Tone

Tone depends on many factors, including the shape and size of your vocal mechanism, which you will not be able to change. However, you can learn to make the most of what you've got by keeping your throat open and controlling your breath. If your voice sounds harsh or raspy, it is usually the result of a closed throat. If your voice sounds breathy, you are probably using more breath than you need.

To relax your throat and improve your tone, try this exercise:

Yawn exaggeratedly. Take a deep breath, stretch, and then yawn again. With your throat open and relaxed, quietly, and slowly say the following while prolonging the vowel sounds "Ma-a-ah, blo-o-oh, fla-a-aw, pla-a-ay, be-e-e, t-o-o." Yawn again to relax, then

Try This

1 Lie flat on your back with one hand on your abdomen and the other on your chest. Keep your chest still. The abdomen should move up when you inhale and down when you exhale. Now stand up and try the identical action. Gradually speed up your breathing until you are panting like a dog. Remember to use only your abdomen–try to keep your chest still.

2 Using your diaphragm, take a deep breath and see how far you can count as you exhale. Do not force or speed up the count. If you start to get tense, breathe normally, and start again. Practice this until you can exhale to a count of sixty.

Karita Mattila performs in a Royal Opera production of *Lohengrin.*

Backstage Gossip: A Violet Velvet Voice

When Laurence Olivier played Othello in 1964, he felt his natural voice was inadequate for the task.

"I did go through a long period of vocal training especially for it, to increase the depth of my voice, and I actually managed to attain about six more notes in the bass. I never used to be able to sing below D, but now, after a little exercising, I can get down to A, through all the semitones; and that helps at the beginning of the play, it helps the violet velvet that I felt was necessary in the timbre of the voice."

from *Theatrical Anecdotes* by Peter Hay

Richer Tone

The yawn is the perfect form of breath because it comes from a relaxed body. Most of the time when people yawn, they breathe in air from the abdomen, not from the chest, exactly where the actor's breath must come from. When an actor is feeling nervous and experiencing stage fright, breathing becomes shorter and shallower. Therefore, actors must train themselves to take deep breaths—allowing good vocal support and ensuring a relaxed speaking voice.

Try This

ACTivity After performing the first two exercises, instruct students to walk around the room, making sure their arms, shoulders, and necks are loose, breathing in deep breaths, and being conscious not to breathe from the chest but from the abdomen.

ACTivity Have students loosen their facial and vocal muscles by using the following exercises:

1 Open the mouth and eyes as wide as possible and then close them as tightly as possible.

2 Slowly and silently count to ten, exaggerating the mouth, using the tongue and lips. Add sound.

3 Silently speak the scale (do, re, me, fa, so, la, ti, do), exaggerating the mouth, using the tongue and the lips. Add sound.

Visual Cue

Lohengrin, the most popular of Richard Wagner's operas, was first performed in 1850. You may find the synopsis of Wagner's *Lohengrin* at *www.metopera.org/synopses/lohengri.html.*

- Does Ms. Mattila appear to be singing with a relaxed and open throat?
- What emotion do you think she is portraying? What leads you to this conclusion?

Show, Don't Tell For this experiment in tone techniques, model one of the words for the students. Say "Oh" in a sarcastic tone and have students tell you what emotion they think you are conveying, and so on.

Pitch, Inflection, Volume, and Rate

Actors can take the same line and change its meaning simply by where they choose to place the inflection. It is important for actors to understand inflection and to use it to convey meaning.

Try This

Have two candles at the front of the room and ask students to come forward two at a time to test their breath control. Depending on the fire codes in your school, you may have to go outside the building.

Inflection Marks

Show Don't Tell Draw a chart with the three headings below on the chalkboard and model for students under which head one of the emotions listed should be placed. Then write on the board a sentence that reveals this emotion, adding the proper inflection mark. Finally, say the sentence using the correct inflection.

- Rising Inflection
- Lowering Inflection
- Sustained Inflection

Nervousness	*Boredom*
Calm	*Despair*
Excitement	*Disgust*
Anger	*Sarcasm*
Fear	*Doubt*

Continue working on inflection using the rest of the list.

continue with other vowel sounds. Read a passage from your literature book, prolonging the vowels.

Tone is the vocal element you use to create different emotional colors when you speak or sing. Try these simple techniques to experiment with tone:

1 Say each of these words—*oh, yes, well, really, possibly*—to convey each of these emotions or states of being: happiness, pride, fatigue, fright, anger, suspicion, innocence, pleading, and sorrow.

2 Reproduce the tone color of these words by making your voice sound like the word's meaning: *bang, crackle, swish, grunt, tinkle, roar, coo, thin, wheeze, bubble, buzzy, splash, clang, gurgle.*

Try This

Test yourself for breathlessness. Light a candle and hold it about five or six inches away from your face. Speak directly toward the flame. If the candle flickers or goes out, you are using too much breath. When you produce a clear tone, you actually use very little breath–the candle flame will move only a tiny bit, if at all.

Pitch, Inflection, Volume, and Rate

Pitch is the relative highness or lowness of your voice. You can produce a medium pitch by relaxing your throat. This is the easiest pitch to project and the easiest for an audience to listen to. In acting, high pitch indicates nervousness, excitement, anger, or fear. A low pitch conveys despair or disgust.

Inflection, in combination with pitch, allows you to glide from high to low on a single word, syllable, or phrase. Rising inflection connotes questioning. Falling inflection signifies finality. **Circumflex** is a combination of the two, expressing sarcasm, doubt, and innuendo.

Inflection Marks

Laura:
Oh, Jack! What are you doing?
[rising inflection]

Damon:
Jack always has a reason.
[sustained inflection]

Lateefa:
Stay out of this, Jack.
[falling inflection]

Volume is the relative loudness of your voice. To send, or **project,** their voices to all areas of the theatre, performers often must speak very loudly, yet they must seem to the audience to be speaking at a normal volume. Breathing from the diaphragm is the key to vocal projection.

Rate is the speed at which you speak. Rate of speech can indicate many things about a person or a character. For example, a slow rate usually indicates old age, important ideas, and/or a state of sorrow or exhaustion. A faster rate indicates youth and/or the emotions of excitement, happiness, and anger.

Notes

PREPARE

Articulation and Pronunciation

Proper breathing technique, great tone, and perfect pitch will make no difference at all if you have poor articulation. After all, the audience has to understand what you're saying. Poor articulation is generally the result of carelessness and sluggish speech; it can make you sound as if you're talking through a mouthful of oatmeal. People can get by with this type of speech in real life; but on the stage, where every word counts, it can cause real problems.

Using proper pronunciation means making sure you know how to say each word you speak. If you do not know the meaning of a word you read, or you are unsure of its pronunciation, look it up *before* you say it in front of an audience! There is no excuse for mispronouncing a word in performance.

On pages 4 and 8 of Chapter 1, you tried a few tongue twisters to practice articulation. Repeat those once again and then try the additional phrases below. Remember to open your mouth wide as you say each one. Pick up speed as you gain control.

- Six slim sleek saplings stood silently.
- She sells seashells by the seashore.
- A big black bug bit a big black bear.
- Fill the sieve with thistles; then sift the thistles through the sieve.
- Better buy the bigger rubber baby buggy bumpers.

Choose Your Exercise

Choose one of the exercises suggested below and on the following page to perform in front of the class. Write down your ideas for presenting this exercise or use the Activity Sheet your teacher provides. Practice your selection several times using proper breathing, a medium pitch, sufficient volume, and clear articulation. Remember that your presentation should not exceed two minutes.

Feel free to adapt any of the suggestions in an imaginative way.

- Choose a favorite childhood poem or song lyrics such as "My Shadow" or "She'll Be Comin' 'Round the Mountain" to recite.

Practice articulation and pronunciation so that you are prepared when you go onstage.

Articulation and Pronunciation

Special Needs and ESL Students Allow these students to say either simplified tongue twisters or tongue twisters in their native languages.

Show, Don't Tell Write a few lines from one of Shakespeare's plays on the board. Begin by modeling *scansion*, the analysis of the verse for emphasis. When scanning, look for things such as *glottal sounds* (consonants caused by air held back, such as in *g* and *k*), *alliteration* (repetitive consonants), and *sibilants* (hissing sounds). Read the passage to the students and have them discuss your articulation and pronunciation.

ACTivity Write the following from *Macbeth* on the chalkboard:

If it were done when 'tis done, then 'twere well
It were done quickly. If th' assassination
Could trammel up the consequence and catch
With his surcease, success that but this blow
Might be the be-all and the end-all here,
But here, upon this bank and shoal of time,
We'd jump the life to come.

Have a volunteer scan for glottal sounds, alliteration, and sibilants, marking them on the board. Then give the class a few minutes to practice the passage silently, being careful to stress the things they found during scansion. Ask volunteers to perform the passage aloud.

Backstage Gossip: Isn't He a Scream?

Dustin Hoffman, an actor who likes to totally transform himself into a character and to hide his own personality traits as much as possible, actually locked himself in a room and screamed for more than five hours . . . in order to make his voice sound like the 121-year-old man in the film *Little Big Man.*

from *Introducing Theatre* by Joy H. Reilly and M. Scott Phillips

PREPARE

Choose Your Exercise

Remind the students of the importance of using proper breathing, pitch, volume, and articulation.

Show, Don't Tell Model for the students how you would choose and prepare one of the suggested exercises.

Special Needs Students
Have a simple poem or paragraph available for students who might have a difficult time finding one of their own.

PRESENT

Perform Your Vocal Exercise

Before students begin presenting their vocal exercises, remind them to hand in their Activity Sheet or description when their name is called. Also remind the students who are watching that proper audience behavior begins as soon as the Activity Sheet is handed in. The audience should remain quiet and attentive for the duration of the performance. Have a stopwatch ready to time each scene.

Theatre Journal

Use the following as an additional or substitute prompt.

As you listen to yourself on the tape recorder and analyze what you hear, try to immediately record any corrections you feel you need to make. Listen to your corrected recordings and practice speaking in that manner.

Breathe from your diaphragm as you practice saying the lines from memory. Work toward saying the poem or lyric with expression. Try to finish one stanza on a single exhalation. Try to control your breath so that you don't run out of air in the middle of a phrase or sentence.

- Choose a dramatic paragraph from the text of your literature book or from your personal reading. Alternatively, you may write a paragraph of your own. Practice reading the paragraph aloud varying your pitch, volume, and rate to convey meaning and feeling. Remember to use proper breathing technique. Keep your throat relaxed and open to achieve the best tone possible, and read with feeling.
- Select an excerpt from one of Shakespeare's monologues or scenes found in Unit Eight of this book. Read it over, and then read it aloud for the class. You will need a partner for the scene.
- Create a new tongue twister consisting of two to four lines. Use the tongue twisters on pages 4, 8, and 69 as a guide. Share the tongue twister you create with the class.

PRESENT

Perform Your Vocal Exercise

When your name is called, hand your description of your vocal exercise or Activity Sheet to your teacher, and then proceed to the playing area. Perform your exercise for the class. Remember to take your time. Every word and breath counts.

When you have finished your presentation, try not to make faces or shrug your shoulders if you feel you didn't do as well as you would have liked. Remember that your presentation doesn't truly end until you sit down.

Theatre Journal

To some extent, improving your voice is based on listening. So listen to the way others speak. Listen to recordings by famous actors and orators. Listen to yourself on a tape recorder. Then write down an analysis of what you hear. Use the inflection marks on page 68 to help you remember the sounds of people speaking.

From the Field: Voice, Movement, Gesture

I have my theatre arts students take positions throughout the auditorium. Once an order has been determined in a criss cross pattern, the first actor calls out the name of the person who is next, accompanied by a sweeping gesture toward the person, followed by a resounding "Hah." The order can be changed and eventually lines from scenes they are working on can be substituted for the vocalized "Hah." Moving the students outdoors to work on this exercise adds additional space between them and requires greater movement and a louder voice.

Richard Steggerda, Teacher, Bristol, VT

CRITIQUE

Evaluate Classmates' Vocal Exercises

Take notes as you watch your classmates' vocal presentations. Use a scale of 1 to 5, with 5 being "outstanding," 4 being "very good," 3 being "good," 2 being "needs some improvement," and 1 being "needs much improvement." Ask yourself the questions below as you evaluate.

- Did the performer use proper breathing?
- How audible was the performer's presentation?
- How clearly did he or she articulate?
- Did the performer speak at the proper rate—neither too fast nor too slow?
- If the performer stumbled over a word, did he or she move on gracefully?

Choose two of the presentations you have already critiqued and write a paragraph explaining why you gave each the score you did. Use the answers you wrote to the questions above to help in your evaluation.

Career Focus

Voice-over Actor

Many stage actors supplement their theatre careers by working as voice-over performers. Though you may never have seen a voice-over actor, you hear them all the time. Typical voice-overs are radio spots, television commercials, corporate training films, documentary and educational film narration, and so on. Some actors make their livings entirely from this type of work. Most live in larger urban areas where talent agents aid them in their search for work.

Agents take ten percent or more of a voice-over actor's pay in exchange for getting the actor auditions with companies who are hiring for voice-over jobs. A career in voice-over requires a strong, supple voice; a personable, professional demeanor; and the ability to do dialects and/or impressions. A musical background can also be very helpful. To showcase their talents, most voice-over actors have a professional CD made. Created in a sound studio, this type of CD features multiple short samples of the actor's voice from commercials, films, or other recordings. A good voice-over CD gives a well-rounded idea of the actor's overall voice and versatility.

Being able to convey a strong personality is an asset to the voice-over actor.

Notes

CRITIQUE

Evaluate Classmates' Vocal Exercises

Hand out Critique Sheets for this project or have students use their own paper. You might prefer to assign two exercises for each student to evaluate in order to insure that everyone gets evaluated.

Career Focus

There are many different areas where the voice-over actor can find work. In addition to those mentioned in the pupil book, sports teams announcers and voice-overs for movie trailers are other examples. Web sites, such as *voiceovers.com* and *voiceovers.co.uk* are available to support the actor in finding work. A very popular type of voice-over work is animation, where actors become the voices of cartoon characters. *Shrek,* a popular 2001 animated film based on the children's book by William Steig, featured the voices of Mike Myers, Eddie Murphy, Cameron Diaz, and John Lithgow. *Shrek 2* is set to be released in 2004 with the same popular voices as well as such stars as Julie Andrews, Antonio Banderas, and Rupert Everett.

The following prompts can be used to begin a discussion about the photo on this page.

- What are the challenges an actor would face when totally dependent on the voice?
- Do you think this voice-over actor has made an attempt to memorize his lines? Why would he do this?

Chapter 7 Test

The test for this chapter is available in blackline master form in the Resource Binder, page 29.

For More Information

Books

Alburger, James, *The Art of Voice Acting: The Craft and Business of Performing for Voice-Over,* Focal Press, 1998.

Berry, Cicely, *Voice and the Actor,* John Wiley & Sons, 1991.

Cohen, Robert, *Acting One,* McGraw-Hill, 2001.

Hogan, Harlan, *VO: Tales and Techniques of a Voice-Over Actor,* Palgrave Macmillan, 2002.

Jones, Chuck, *Make Your Voice Heard: An Actor's Guide to Increased Dramatic Range Through Vocal Training,* Back Stage Books, 1996.

Other Media

Articulation, CD-ROM, Insight Media, 1998.

Save Your Voice, VHS, Insight Media, 1995.

Voice Skills, VHS, Insight Media, 2002.

Voice Workout for the Actor, VHS, Insight Media.

Additional Projects

1 With a partner, select a two- to four-minute scene in which two characters exchange dialogue. In reading the scenes, employ the various vocal techniques you have learned. Try to go further with a particular element than you have gone before.

2 Say the following lines aloud, using the inflection indicated in brackets.

- I'm sorry, but I must decline your invitation. [falling inflection]
- What's the big idea? [rising inflection]
- So you took my new sweater! [rising inflection]
- I think I've solved the problem. [sustained inflection]

3 Read aloud two poems that feature contrasting emotional content. Imagine that you are delivering these poems in a large crowded auditorium. Experiment with your volume, articulation, inflection, tone, and the flexibility of your voice.

4 Practice projecting your voice to the last row in the classroom. Stand up and focus your eyes on the back wall. Say your name, the name of your street, and the name of your favorite song. Repeat all of this information using only vowels; then do the same using only consonants. Finally, repeat your name, street name, and favorite song articulating and projecting to the best of your ability.

5 Rehearse the monologue from *Clear Glass Marbles* by Jane Martin found in Unit Eight. Use all the techniques you have learned in this chapter to give your reading as much emotional color as possible. Experiment with a number of different accents. Time yourself to make sure the monologue will fit within a four-minute time period.

"Speech finely framed delighteth the ears."

—2 Maccabees.II, 39

Substitute Teacher Activities

- Assign the Vocal Exercises Worksheet on page 27 of the Resource Binder.
- Teach the Voice section of the Student Handbook, pp. 569-570.
- Assign one or more of the Additional Projects on this page.
- **Play a Twist of the Tongue.** Repeat a few of the tongue twisters on page 69 for students. Then, divide the class into groups of four and have each group write two tongue twisters. Ask each group to present its tongue twisters to the class. Have the class stand and repeat the tongue twisters with the originators.

Master of the Craft

John Leguizamo: Man of Many Voices

"I see the new Latin artist as a pioneer, opening up doors for others to follow. And when they don't open, we crowbar our way in . . . . "

—John Leguizamo

As it turns out, John Leguizamo doesn't need a crowbar. Instead, he has become a major star by way of his talent and ambition. Born in Bogota, Colombia, in 1964 and raised in New York City, he was voted Most Talkative in his high school class. But this charming chatterbox went on to become a respected comedian and serious actor, writer, and director. No matter what the role, he has won fans with his sharply observed takes on the life and times of Latinos; he pokes fun at stereotypes as he merrily shatters them.

Leguizamo studied acting at New York University where he was the only Latino in his class. Opting for further professional training, he enrolled in the Lee Strasberg Institute. Leguizamo only studied with Strasberg for one day, however, before the legendary teacher died. (Leguizamo, never one to ignore the potential for a dark joke, later said of his teacher's unexpected death: "I have that effect on people.") He began his stand-up comedy career in clubs in and around New York City. From there he began getting small roles in movies.

In 1991 his first one-man show, *Mambo Mouth,* premiered off Broadway and became a runaway hit. He received multiple awards for his renditions of seven different Latino characters. He has since premiered several more one-man shows with great success. In each of these shows he has used his stamina, razor-sharp timing, versatile voice, and one-of-kind storytelling to create multifaceted characters that move audiences to both tears and laughter.

In 2001 he played Toulouse-Lautrec in Baz Luhrmann's film *Moulin Rouge* alongside Nicole Kidman.

John Leguizamo in his one-man show.

For More Information

Books

Leguizamo, John, *Freak: A Semi-Demi-Quasi-Pseudo Autobiography,* Riverhead Books, 1997.

Leguizamo, John, *Mambo Mouth: A Savage Comedy,* Bantam Doubleday Dell, 1993.

Leguizamo, John, *Spic-O-Rama: A Dysfunctional Family,* Bantam Doubleday Dell, 1994.

Other Media

Live, [Explicit Lyrics] John Leguizamo, CD, RCA, 2001.

Mambo Mouth, VHS, Uni/Polar, 1992.

Master of the Craft

More About John Leguizamo

John Leguizamo grew up in what he calls "the big melting pot of America" where every accent was at his "beck and call." This explains why he became a fine mimic with a great ear for the nuances of human speech and interaction. Leguizamo can transform instantly into a 65-year-old man, an unruly teenager, a small child, or even a young woman. Since winning the film role of Chi Chi Rodriguez in the film *To Wong Foo: Thanks for Everything, Julie Newmar,* he has continued to score bigger and better roles. In 1996 he played Tybalt in Baz Luhrmann's film adaptation of William Shakespeare's *Romeo and Juliet* with Leonardo DiCaprio and Claire Danes. A favorite starring role was in Spike Lee's *Summer of Sam* in 1999. A recent role was as a voice-over actor in the 2002 animated film *Ice Age,* in which he was the voice of Sid the Sloth. In 1999, he won the Emmy for Outstanding Performance in a Variety or Music Performance for his role in *Freak*. Leguizamo is married to Justine Maurer, an estate planner and economist, and has two children.

Masters Past and Present

Ray Romano began his career at sixteen when he formed a comedy troupe titled *No Talent*. After attending Queens College, he began performing in the late-night comedy circuit while holding a day job. Finally in 1987, Romano decided to pursue work in the entertainment industry full time. In 1991, Romano's dream was realized when he performed on the *Tonight Show* with the legendary host Johnny Carson. His 1995 appearance on *Late Night With David Letterman* prompted the idea of developing a sitcom. The comic's offbeat domestic observations struck a chord with audiences and critics alike in the hit television series *Everybody Loves Raymond*, and the series is still running. Romano's most recent adventure was his vocal role in the animated film *Ice Age.*

Theatre Then and Now

Storytellers Across Time

The word *story* comes from the Latin word *historia*, meaning *history*. Before written history, people told stories in order to understand the past and the present. Many people believe that storytelling played an important part in the birth of theatre. Men would go off to hunt for food or to battle an enemy and then come back to those anxiously awaiting to hear what had happened. Storytelling was the means for passing history down from generation to generation.

ACTivity Have the students select a short story to read to the class. Instruct the students to also select music that will enhance the mood and spirit of the story. Remind the students that not only do they need to incorporate the vocal techniques learned in this chapter in their presentation, but they also need to use facial expressions and body language.

The Griot

A popular griot school is located in Gambia, a small country in West Africa. The man in the photo, Dembo Jobarteh, is the general manager and main teacher of the school. He is also a master at the kora and the drums. The Web site of the Gambian Griot School of Music and Dance contains a wealth of information for those interested in the griot: *home01.wxs.nl/~verka067/*

Theatre Then and Now

Storytellers Across Time

The Griot

The ancient griots were native West African storytellers. They fulfilled a wide variety of roles in African society, serving not only as the keepers of a community's oral tradition, but also as genealogists, teachers, masters of ceremonies, and advisors. Some historians believe that through their efforts to mediate conflicts and take part in ceremonials, griots became a form of social glue, which worked to keep African societies united. Griots were present at births, weddings, sports events, and governmental meetings, and also spread the word to others. In short, they played a vital part in every aspect of society. No other profession in any part of the world comes close to the intricate and intimate ties the griots had to their people.

The griot is not simply a cultural and historical oddity. Modern-day griots have become extremely popular, thanks in part to the 1970s television miniseries "Roots." In it, author Alex Haley authenticated the story of his ancestry by listening to village history told to him by an African griot. Over the past twenty-five years, African griots, weaving a spellbinding collage of spoken word, song, and movement, have played to packed houses in New York, London, and elsewhere around the world.

Gambian griot Dembo Jobarteh tuning his kora. The instrument's body is made from a gourd that is cut in half and partially covered with cow skin. Fishing line is used for the twenty-one strings.

Visual Cues

Use the prompts below to discuss the images on this and the next page.

- How do you think Dembo Jobarteh uses his kora when telling a story?
- What instruments might storytellers from other nations use to tell their stories?
- What emotion do you think the Moth storyteller is trying to convey? What leads you to this conclusion?
- What advantages and disadvantages would a storyteller have if he or she were to use a microphone on a stand during a presentation?

The Moth

Of course, storytelling has played a key part in almost every culture. In the United States, the American Indians had an extensive oral tradition. The immigrants who came to America from all over the world brought their oral traditions with them. And storytelling in the United States today? It's alive and well. In fact, there are a number of organizations that are completely devoted to the fine art of storytelling. One such organization is The Moth.

The brainchild of poet and novelist George Dawes Green, The Moth started small. Green thought back to his Georgia childhood, where some of his fondest memories were of sitting in any one of many backyards in the evening and listening to his friends telling amazing stories. He even told a few of his own. Often these stories focused on a tale of woe about some unlucky character, which drew the listeners in like moths to a flame. Green wanted to re-create these evenings of storytelling in an urban environment. He started in 1997 with just a few friends in his living room. But The Moth, as he called it, quickly developed a following. Soon the event moved to Joe's Pub at New York's Joseph Papp Public Theatre and later to the Brooklyn Academy of Music and the Players Club. The Moth often moves from location to location, drawing a wide audience of approving spectators and storytellers. It is usually presented in a comfortable lounge environment. Each evening features a specific theme, such as "A Savage Mood" or "Gigs Gone Bad." Each event features five to seven storytellers, each of whom has about ten minutes to tell a story.

Because the storytellers at The Moth usually are not professional performers, and because most of them tell stories from their own lives, audiences find the stories exhilarating, fresh, and unique. You can learn more about The Moth by visiting www.themoth.org.

Moth storyteller Jason Kordelos responds to the theme "Love and War."

The Moth

The goal of the storytellers at the Moth is twofold: to entertain and to spark a story in people watching. The Moth believes that everyone has a story to tell. The show usually runs about ninety minutes. The best way to be invited to perform at the Moth is by participating in the StorySLAM. You can e-mail a synopsis of your story to submit@themoth.org or send a cassette tape of the story to The Moth, PO Box 1708, New York, NY 10013.

ACTivity Instruct the students to read or remember a story from childhood. They should use the vocal techniques learned in this chapter to present the story to the class.

Advanced Students

Encourage students to tell a story they make up themselves. A story of creation or an important event would be good choices. Suggest that they visit the Moth Web site for more information.

For More Information

Books

Geisler, Harlynne, *Storytelling Professionally,* Libraries Unlimited, 1997.

Hale, Thomas A., *Griots and Griottes: Masters of Words and Music,* Indiana University Press, 1999.

Walsh, John, *The Art of Storytelling: Easy Steps to Presenting an Unforgettable Story,* Moody Publishing, 2003.

Other Media

By Word of Mouth: Storytelling in America, VHS, Insight Media, 1984.

Distant Voices, Thunder Words, VHS, Insight Media, 2001.

Jay O'Callahan: A Master Class in Storytelling, VHS, Insight Media, 1983.

Shared Visions: The Art of Storytelling, VHS, Insight Media, 1999.

Chapter 8

Ensemble Work

This chapter will teach students the importance of working together as an ensemble. Students will learn how to enhance their characters by developing concentration and listening skills, learning how to react and how to play off the other characters in the scene.

Objectives

1. to understand the importance of ensemble acting
2. to develop the concentration, skill, trust, teamwork, and courtesy necessary to work in an ensemble
3. to perform an improvised ensemble scene with several partners

National Standards

Chapter 8 meets these National Theatre Standards:

Proficient 2a, 2c, 7c, 7d, 8a, 8c
Advanced 2d, 2e, 8g

Project Specs

Advanced Students
Have students use a real script that combines movement and planned dialogue as well as ensemble acting.

On Your Feet

Show, Don't Tell Demonstrate with student volunteers how to perform a short improvised scene. Encourage students to look again at the rules of improvisation found on page 33.

Advanced Students
Have students use the suggested situations but give each character a physical obstacle (sick to one's stomach, waiting to sneeze, an uncontrollable itch, etc.) that occurs every time the character tries to achieve the goal. Have the students discuss the challenge of trying to achieve a goal with the added physical difficulty.

Chapter 8 Ensemble Work

What if every night of your life were a one-person show? What if every conversation ended in a monologue? Life would be quite dull. Human beings are social creatures. We want to know all about the nooks and crannies of one another's lives. We want to be involved in those lives too—not as helpers or onlookers, but as participants—as part of the ensemble.

Project Specs

Project Description For this assignment, you and several partners will perform a three- to five-minute improvised ensemble scene.

Purpose to develop the concentration, skill, teamwork, and courtesy necessary to work in an ensemble

Materials an annotated list of your character's relationship with other characters in a scene or the Ensemble Work Activity Sheet your teacher provides

Theatre Terms

emoting
ensemble ethic
fall
going up
illusion of the first time
interplay
step on
supporting roles

On Your Feet

With one to three partners, improvise one of the scenes below:

- Four of you are in the family room at home. Two of you want to clean up the clutter; the other two try to find ways out of the job.
- A boy attempts to make a date with a girl he just met. She likes him, but doesn't think she should accept. He is determined, however.
- One of you is packing a suitcase, determined to take a trip. Two friends try to keep you from packing.

Theatre Terms

emoting expressing oneself emotionally

ensemble ethic working for the good of the group rather than for the individual

fall when an actor does not stay in character

going up forgetting ones lines or actions

illusion of the first time a mental technique that allows performers to repeat their scenes again and again with freshness and spontaneity

interplay interaction between characters

step on to cut off or interrupt another character by speaking over his or her lines

supporting roles roles that support main characters

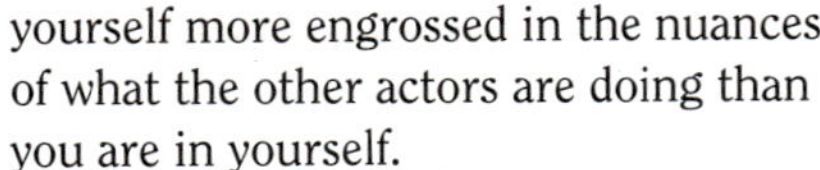

PREVIEW

Ensemble Acting

Acting demands **interplay,** or interaction, between all of the characters. To be realistic, characters must play off one another in an interactive way. They must pay attention to everything going on around them. Every time an actor speaks, his or her words should seem new and interesting to the others onstage. The actor must communicate the **illusion of the first time,** which means that the action must seem spontaneous and fresh even after hours and hours of practice. When your character is not speaking, you must react as though you are hearing the other characters for the first time. It takes practice, but it's not hard. Watch carefully as the other actors speak and move. You'll find yourself more engrossed in the nuances of what the other actors are doing than you are in yourself.

When you interact purposefully with your fellow actors, you begin to develop a working relationship based on trust and respect. You become not just an individual, but an important part of the whole. That's what the **ensemble ethic** is all about.

The Ensemble Actor's Safety Net

It is empowering to be part of a mutually supportive group onstage. Interacting wholeheartedly with others offers the ensemble actor the benefits below.

- Your close ties to the other characters won't let you **"fall"** out of character or forget your lines.
- You won't have time for your own private speculations or fears.
- If you have learned your lines well, the reality of your situation won't allow you to forget them.

In the play *Experiment with an Airpump,* each member of the ensemble contributes a unique individual interpretation that impacts on the dynamics of the entire group.

PREVIEW

Ensemble Acting

Discuss the importance of the *illusion of the first time* to the believability of a performance.

The Ensemble Actor's Safety Net

Discuss the importance of developing trust among an ensemble. The students must trust each other and feel the environment is "safe" before they will feel truly comfortable. Remind students that trust builds slowly and is destroyed quickly.

ACTivity Have ten to twelve students at a time stand in a tight circle facing inward. One person stands in the center with his or her arms crossed in front of the chest. Students comprising the circle face the person in the middle, palms up, ready to catch the person. When everyone is ready, the center student falls backward and is caught by the other students. Slowly, the center student is passed around the circle. No one student in the circle should ever have the weight of the center student alone. Everyone should have a chance to be in the center.

An Experiment with an Airpump, by Shelagh Stephenson, explores the issue and moral questions behind scientific research. The setting of the play shifts back and forth from 1799 to 1999, between two families who occupy the same house two hundred years apart.

- What do you think is happening in the picture? What leads you to this conclusion?
- Pick one character in the group and write a short description of his or her life. Read it for the class.

Resource Binder

- Performers' Etiquette, TIPack, p. G
- Crew Etiquette, TIPack, p. H
- Safety Rules and Reminders, TIPack, p. I
- Ensemble Work Activity Sheet, p. 30
- Guidelines for the Ensemble Worksheet, p. 31
- Critique Sheet: Ensemble Work p. 32
- Ensemble Work Test, p. 33

Handbook Connections
page 565

To Have on Hand

- A stopwatch to time the ensemble scene presentations for practice and performance
- A playing space and possibly one or two chairs to help the students have different levels in their ensemble
- Scripts or playbooks for several actors with movement and dialogue for advanced extensions of the assignment

Chapter 8 Ensemble Work **77**

PREPARE

Choose Your Situation

Discuss with the students the plot structure of a play and what should be incorporated in the beginning, middle and end of a scene. Review the rules and guidelines of improvisation. If you wish, divide the students into groups in advance, or you can allow the students to pick their own groups.

Special Needs and ESL Students
These students may need help with this project. You may want to discuss with them in advance the characters they choose and the characters' objectives. Additionally, try to pair these students with advanced students who are willing to help them develop their characters and the characters' objectives as they work on their scene.

ACTivity Select two students to begin a "Freeze-n'-go" improv activity. Give the actors a situation and a location in which to begin their scene. As the actors begin their improvisation, the audience should watch for interesting body positions to spark an idea in which to start a new improv. When an audience member has an idea, he should call "Freeze" and then go onstage and tap the person he would like to replace. He should then assume the exact body position of the frozen actor and begin the scene establishing a new situation and location.

Beginning Students
Perform the same exercise, but instead the instructor will call "Freeze" and the name of a student to replace an actor on stage. It might be necessary to help the student think of a new situation and location to begin the new scene. Have the class offer ideas.

PREPARE

Choose Your Situation

Divide into mixed groups of five. (Your teacher may wish to assign groups, scenes, and roles.) With your partners, choose a group of characters and situations from the following chart, or invent a detailed situation with characters of your own.

Location	Character	Objective/Intention/Need
A spring garage sale in an empty building downtown	Antique dealer	Hopes to find something of value
	Old woman	Has to crochet 50 booties for bazaar
	Theatre prop person	Looking for a cane
	Real estate salesman	Needs a commission
	Young man	Has no place to live
An airport in which a boarding flight has been delayed	Ticket agent	Trying to help customers
	Business executive	Has to keep an important appointment
	Orphan	Going to meet new foster family
	College student	Heading back to school
	Foreign visitor	Anxious to get back home
A living room on prom night	Young man	Just meeting his date's parents
	Young woman	Anxious about her parents' reaction to her date
	Mother	Anxious about her daughter
	Father	Not impressed with his daughter's date
	Younger brother	Getting in the way
A lakeside resort full of vacationers	Older woman	Wealthy, concerned with social position
	Personal assistant	Works for the wealthy woman
	Reporter	Looking for a scoop
	Competitive swimmer	Training for the next Olympics
	Manager of the resort	Trying to keep everyone happy
A drawing room in a Victorian mansion where a murder has just occurred	Detective questioning those assembled	Wants to solve this murder before dinner
	Butler	Named in the will
	Business partner of the deceased	Was being sued by the deceased
	Brother of the deceased	Argued with the deceased recently
	Neighbor	Disliked the deceased

From the Field: Building Trust

Arthur Bartow, author of *The Director's Voice,* approached Gordon Davidson, a celebrated but controversial director, and asked, "How do you build trust?" Davidson replied, "I really do believe that the work is a collaboration, that it is not a judgmental situation, that the actors absolutely have the right to experiment and fail. I feel that there is as much chance that they are going to teach me something about the event or the character as there is that I'm going to be able to teach them."

from *The Director's Voice* by Arthur Bartow

Developing Relationships

In an ensemble, all the parts are **supporting roles,** or roles that support another role. When working on any of your group projects in drama, make a point of encouraging everyone to contribute. Respect everyone's ideas, even if they differ markedly from your own. Strong discussions and disagreements over various points of view are to be expected—this is a healthy and productive way of working within the group. Getting angry in order to convince others you are right or insulting others' opinions is not acceptable.

Working with the Group

With the others in your group, decide on the situation you are going to improvise together. Choose your parts and decide what your various objectives will be. Throughout this project you should each be keeping a list of your own character's relationship to the other characters in the scene (or using the Activity Sheet provided by your teacher). Briefly discuss your characters' relationships, being sure to consider carefully what your partners have to say.

Working Alone

On your own, quickly sketch out in more detail what your character thinks of the other characters in your scene, as well as how your character sees himself or herself. Think about the kind of person your character will be and how your character might move, speak, and gesture.

Back with the Group

When you all think you have a fairly good understanding of your characters, meet again as a group. Decide upon the opening line in your scene. To ensure that all characters play a part in the

Even with such a large cast, everyone's role is equally important.

Theatre Journal

Next time you sit down to a meal, watch and listen to the people around the table. Who starts most of the conversations? Who is the joker at the table? Who's the rebel? Keep an eye on the way body language conveys people's roles and attitudes. You can make use of the same attitudes and habits in your acting roles.

Backstage Gossip: Ghost on Strike

A company of players producing a Shakespearean repertoire were in desperate straits when they one day announced a performance of *Hamlet* in a small town. Salaries had been unpaid for many weeks, and there was much dissatisfaction in the company. All went well with the performance until Hamlet's line about his father's ghost: "Perchance 'twill walk again." Here the ghost broke into the scene from off-stage with the loudly-voiced answer: "Nay, 'twill walk no more until its salary is paid."

from *Theatrical Anecdotes* by Peter Hay

Developing Relationships

ACTivity Divide the class into groups of five. Each group will be assigned a task to perform without verbal communication. Tasks might range from moving an imaginary sofa to preparing an invisible enchilada. Give each group time to discuss strategy. When performing, the group must rely on nonverbal skills to communicate to the audience what they are doing.

Working with the Group

Help students decide which character they will play and how to map out their objectives. Encourage students to think about which roles they would be best suited for or which roles might offer a new challenge.

ACTivity Divide the class into two circles. Have each group create a pattern by throwing a ball to someone in the group until everyone has received the ball just once. When the ball gets back to the person who began the activity, they repeat the pattern until they have it down smoothly. Next, they reverse the pattern. Once the reversed pattern is smooth, a second ball is added, maintaining the same pattern. Continue to add balls. The object is to see how many balls the group can add and still maintain the pattern.

Theatre Journal

Use the following as additional or substitute prompts.

Take a look inward. What is your own role at the family dinner table? How do you react to different members of your family?

When you observe people in public, notice how different families relate to each other. Create a scenario about what you think is happening between them.

Back with the Group

After explaining how to develop and rehearse the scene, hand out the Ensemble Work Activity Sheets and show the students how to use them. Give the students a time limit to go through the steps to complete the preparation of their presentations. Time students as they practice to see that they stay within the three- to five-minute time limit.

ACTivity Have several actors line up on one end of the stage. Ask them to walk as a character completely different from themselves—someone much older or younger, or someone of the opposite sex. Ask the students to use recall or actual observation as they practice at home. Remind students that the goal is to master an accurate portrayal, not necessarily a comic portrayal, though the walk could naturally be amusing.

Career Focus

Entertainment papers and resources can be found best by searching the Web. Listed below are helpful Web sites.

New York
www.backstage.com

Los Angeles
www.variety.com
www.backstage.com

Dallas
www.dallasobserver.com
www.stage-online.org

Chicago
www.performink.com
www.studioz.org/chicago/actors.htm

Unions
www.actorsequity.org
www.aftra.org
www.sag.org

Audition Material
www.stageplays.com

General Information
www.onlinetalentdirectory.com

scene, sketch out a sequence of events that includes dialogue for each of the characters. Decide as a group how the scene will develop and what the outcome will be.

If you feel confident with what you have established this far, continue by working on how each of your characters will move throughout the scene. When you have created a scene to your satisfaction, practice it a few times, making sure you do not exceed five minutes. Remember, this project is improvisational. Don't go over it so often that you memorize it. You are now ready to present your ensemble scene.

Dominic West rises to the actor's ultimate challenge: playing a character of the opposite sex (in Caryl Churchill's *Cloud Nine*).

Career Focus

Stage Actor

The best way to become an actor is to act! Of course, Broadway might not want you just yet, but you can begin by acting in school plays, teen acting classes, community theatres, and small professional companies. These are ways to build skills and a resume.

Some actors join with others to form scene study groups. They choose a scene from a play they like or one that offers challenges. Then they work on the scene together. Members of the group take turns acting and critiquing one another's work.

Once you feel adept at acting, memorize and bring to performance level a monologue or two. Look for audition calls in the local newspaper or entertainment paper. Then get ready for rejection! One rule of thumb states that an actor must endure 50 auditions before getting a role.

And remember, Broadway isn't the only place where a serious actor can find his or her place on the stage. All over the country, from La Jolla, California, to Provincetown, Massachusetts, regional theatre is alive and well and drawing audiences. Many actors earn a good living in cities with a strong cultural and theatrical base. You might become a star of the stage without ever going near Broadway.

Visual Cue

In 1979 Caryl Churchill received wide notice for *Cloud Nine,* a satirical play involving farcical moments in the relationships between characters cast in a cross-gender fashion.

- What challenges would an actor face when trying to play someone of the opposite sex?
- Can you think of a greater challenge than playing this kind of role?

Backstage Gossip: Show Me the $$$

When Tom Cruise was starting out, he was told by a TV executive, "You're too intense and you're not pretty enough for television. You should try features." Shortly thereafter Cruise announced his plan to move to New York to seek his fortune as an actor. His concerned stepfather asked a question which later became the source of amusement—"How much is this gonna cost me?"

from the Web site *anecdotage.com*

Spotlight on

Stage Etiquette

Understanding and respecting the roles, responsibilities, and efforts of all those you work with on stage is an important part of theatre work. Whether you are a beginner or a seasoned professional, you can go a long way toward winning the respect of your colleagues by simply being courteous and following the rules below.

Actor

- Be on time for rehearsals and performances–don't make others wait for you.
- Know your lines.
- Pick up your cues on time. Don't miss your lines or say them too late.
- Don't **step on** another actor's lines (cut them off) or upstage another actor.
- Avoid stealing focus by moving, gesturing, or **emoting** too much (overacting) while another actor is speaking.
- Find ways to cover for an actor who gets lost in a scene or goes blank, called **"going up."**

Director

- Whenever possible, set the schedule more than one week in advance, and stick to it.
- Listen respectfully to the thoughts and opinions of the actor, as well as the design and tech crews.
- Use positive and encouraging words.

Designer

- Talk to the cast and crew before finalizing your concept.
- Alter your design according to cast and crew feedback.

Technical Professionals

- Always keep tools in their proper location when not in use.
- Maintain respect for the needs of other professionals at work.
- Be very careful with tools while working around others (see Safety Rules on pages 220 and 244).

Backstage Gossip: Line Going Up!

John Barrymore used to tell of the confusion that prevailed in an old stock company with which he had once played in repertory. The vast number of plays and the frequency and inconsistency with which they were performed, rendered confusion more or less inevitable. One evening Barrymore found himself unable to remember his lines. Faking a piece of business, he sidled over into the wings and hastily called to the director, "What's the line, what's the line?" The director sighed wearily and asked, "What's the play?"

from *Theatrical Anecdotes* by Peter Hay

Spotlight on

Stage Etiquette An important part of ensuring that a play's rehearsals and performances run smoothly is setting up an atmosphere of professionalism and communication. It is important that everyone involved in the show arrives at rehearsal prepared and ready to work. Actors must listen to the director and be ready to take and use constructive criticism. Actors must also listen and respond to the other actors in the scene so as not to miss cues or step on lines.

Vocabulary Enhancement

"To do nothing" refers to a situation where an actor is expected to look as though he belongs in the scene, but to not steal the focus of the scene away from where it belongs. The challenge for the actor is to find ways to make the audience accept his or her presence as a part of the scene, but not become guilty of scene stealing. This is a very important technique to master for the ensemble actor.

PRESENT

Perform Your Ensemble Scene

Before they begin their ensemble scenes, remind students to hand in their Activity Sheets when their group is called. Once they have handed in their sheets, they should stand before the class in a professional manner. One group member should introduce the scene, briefly describing the location, the situation, and the characters, as well as who will be playing them.

Remind the audience that as soon as the Activity Sheets are in and the group enters the playing area, the audience should remain quiet and attentive for the duration of the performance. Have a stopwatch ready to time each scene.

CRITIQUE

Evaluate Your Classmates' Scenes

Hand out the Critique Sheet for this project or have students use their own paper. In addition to their presentations, you may also wish to evaluate students on how well they critique others. Later, discuss with them any problems you see with their critiques.

Here's How

Show Don't Tell Use student volunteers to set up an example situation of a scene gone off track. Then show the students how you would use the techniques in that situation to get the scene back on the right track.

PRESENT

Perform Your Ensemble Scene

Before your name or the name of someone in your group is called, decide which member of the group will introduce the scene. Give your lists or Activity Sheets to your teacher. The group member who has agreed to do the introduction should briefly describe the location of the scene, the characters and the situation, as well as indicating who plays which character. Perform your scene for the class. Remember that trust is an important part of the ensemble. When you have finished, bow politely.

Here's How To Keep Your Ensemble on Track

If you think a scene is going off track, remind yourself or the other actors of your relationship in one of the following ways:

1. **State the relationship outright.** Say something such as, "You may be my boss, but . . ." or "I know you are angry about my being five hours late, Dad, and . . . ."
2. **Use a gesture or action** that reinforces your relationship to a character. Hug or strong-arm someone, flirt, or shoot a glance of withering scorn.
3. **Pause.** Take a breath. It's better than rushing headlong out of control.

CRITIQUE

Evaluate Your Classmates' Scene

Choose one of the ensemble scenes presented in class to critique. As you watch and take notes, ask yourself the following questions:

- Could I describe each character's objective in the scene and the tactics used to get what he or she wanted?
- Could I outline each character's relationship to the other characters in the scene?
- Could I describe each character's attitude toward the other characters in the scene?
- Did any one character stand out among the others? Why?
- Did all the characters have some action, event, relationship, or motivation in common?

Use a scale of 1 to 5 to rate the scene, with 5 being "outstanding" and 1 being "needs much improvement." After you have rated the scene, write a short paragraph explaining why you gave the rating you did.

Backstage Gossip: One Night Stand

A road company at the end of the 19th century and its financial resources arrived in Waco, Texas, hoping to stay for a while and recoup. They failed to take the town by storm, which was put into perspective the next morning in the local paper: "Rainstorm in Galveston, lasted twenty minutes. Hail storm in Beaumont, ten minutes. Wind-storm in Langtry, two days. Barnstorm in Opera House, one night."

from *Theatrical Anecdotes* by Peter Hay

82 **Unit Two** Elements of Acting

Additional Projects

1 Choose a partner and wait onstage for your partner to enter the scene. Based on the way in which your partner acts toward you and responds to you, try to determine what your relationship is. When you respond correctly, your partner should let you know and end the scene.

2 Choose a three-person scene and rehearse it with your partners. Then, at the moment of performance, switch characters and perform one another's parts.

3 Work with a group to make a simple task into an ensemble job. For example, make use of six actors to build a birdhouse, make a stew, or get someone a job. Make sure each group member has an equally important role.

4 To enhance your teamwork and listening skills, play the following alphabet game in a large group. Starting with *A*, each player names a person, place, and object—always repeating everything said previously. So, for example, player number four would say, "*Anna* lives in the *attic* with an *apple, Bob* lives in a *boat* with a *bicycle, Carl* lives in a *cabin* with a *cat,*" and might add, "*Doris* lives in a *dungeon* with a *duck*." As you continue through the alphabet, try to be dramatic and expressive, and don't forget anything you've heard!

5 Perform a staged reading of the scene from *Blithe Spirit* by Noel Coward found in Unit Eight. Take into account the way the comedy depends upon listening and precise responses between each actor in the scene.

"We were never cute, I think that still holds true. Everyone always liked everyone's work, and that's what also kept it together. There was very much a shared sensibility . . . but also a respect for one another's work."

—John Malkovich, discussing his work as a member of Chicago's Steppenwolf Theatre Company

Chapter 8 Test

The test for this chapter is available in blackline master form in the Resource Binder, page 33.

For More Information

Books

Gwinn, Peter Campbell, and Charna Halpern, *Group Improvisation: The Manual of Ensemble Improv Games,* Meriwether Publishing, 2003.

Kozlowski, Rob, *The Art of Chicago Improv: Short Cuts to Long-Form Improvisation,* Heinemann, 2002.

Wilk, John R., *The Creation of an Ensemble: The First Years of the American Conservatory Theatre,* Southern Illinois University Press, 1986.

Other Media

Ensemble Performance, VHS, Insight Media, 1993.

Stage for a Nation, VHS, Films for the Humanities and Sciences.

Substitute Teacher Activities

Here are suggestions for one or more days when you will be out of the classroom.

- Assign the Guidelines for the Ensemble Worksheet on page 31 of the Resource Binder.
- Teach the Group Readings section of the Student Handbook, p. 565.
- Assign one or more of the Additional Projects on this page.
- Divide the class into groups of four or five to **Present a Play called** *Trapped.*

Members of the group will be trapped somewhere, and they must decide Who, What, When, and Where. Who are the characters, What happened to cause them to become trapped, How do they manage to get out, When does the scene occur (time period, time of day, time span), and Where does it occur. The plot should have a *beginning* that shows the action as they become trapped, a *middle* that shows them trying to get out, and an *end* that shows how they escape.

Theatre Then and Now

Ensembles of Old

Anton Chekhov lived from 1860 to 1904. He began his career with short stories and then went on to writing plays. His play *The Sea Gull* opened in 1896, but was a failure because the actors neither understood their roles nor learned their lines. In later years, he provided the Moscow Art Theatre with *Uncle Vanya* in 1899, *The Three Sisters* in 1901, and *The Cherry Orchard* in 1904. All four plays reveal the monotonous and frustrating life of Russian characters who hope for a more meaningful life but don't know how to obtain it.

Some found Chekhov's plays dark and obscure, but the great director Konstantin Stanislavski worked hard to illuminate Chekhov's work. He would carefully study each play before rehearsals began, often visiting the locale of the play. He and the Moscow Art Theatre were the perfect match for Anton Chekhov.

Other Cultures, Other Times

The longest continuously running professional theatre in Australia, the *Ensemble Theatre* of Sydney, has strived to entertain as well as challenge its audiences for over forty years. Founded in a north Sydney location in the 1950s, it moved to its current location on Sydney Harbor's Careening Cove in 1960. This location was converted into Australia's first theatre-in-the-round stage, where fine theatre continues to be produced.

Visual Cue

- By studying the picture of *The Three Sisters* performance, what conclusions do you come to about what is going on in the scene?
- What is it about the stage picture that makes the scene visually interesting?
- Does any one character stand out more than another? Why?

Theatre Then and Now

Ensembles of Old

Elizabethan Actors

Elizabethan England saw theatre grow from an occasional, itinerant art form to a commercial enterprise complete with permanent playhouses and professional acting companies. These early companies embraced a star system, by which the most celebrated actors won leading, sympathetic roles, while other actors specialized in playing particular types. Leading Elizabethan actors like Richard Burbage learned more than 50 plays and performed about 70 roles in rotation—over and over again—during a typical three-year period. This system encouraged actors to think in terms of generalized types and to play to the audience rather than to each other.

19th-Century Actors

In the 19th century, however, things began to change. New playwrights like George Buchner in Germany and Anton Chekhov in Russia began experimenting with naturalistic and expressionistic plays. Directors like Duke George II of Meiningen and Stanislavski of the Moscow Art Theatre began asking actors to work closely together to create a unified, realistic picture onstage. Companies began working together for weeks, even months on end, to develop a unified approach to a single play. Stars still emerged, but they gave themselves over to each production's social or artistic ideals.

Chekhov's *The Three Sisters,* one of the earliest ensemble productions, has been produced continually since its debut in 1901.

For More Information

Books

Dauphin, Sue, *Houston by Stages: A History of Theatre in Houston,* Eakin Publications, 1981.

Grote, David, *The Best Actors in the World: Shakespeare and His Acting Company,* Greenwood Publishing Group, 2002.

Peterson, Bernard L., *The African American Theatre Directory 1816-1960: A Comprehensive Guide to Early Black Theatre Organizations, Companies, Theatres, and Performing Groups,* Greenwood Press, 1997.

Skrebneski, Victor, *Steppenwolf Theatre Company: Twenty-Five Years of an Actor's Theatre,* Sourcebooks Trade, 2000.

Other Media

A Day at the Globe, VHS, Insight Media, 1977.

The Negro Ensemble Company, VHS, Films for the Humanities and Sciences, 1987.

Theatre in Shakespeare's Time, VHS, Insight Media, 1973.

Ensembles of Today

Steppenwolf Theatre Company
There are many theatre companies today who work entirely as ensembles, such as Steppenwolf Theatre in Chicago. At Steppenwolf, plays are chosen that will reflect the artistic vision and theatrical values that the company members hold. Steppenwolf is famous for being an ensemble of very strong, determined actors willing to "look the fool" and take on unusual roles and offbeat characters. The actors have made names for themselves not only as stage actors, but as directors and producers, and in many cases, as movie actors also. The plays that Steppenwolf has become known for are often contemporary and cutting-edge, even raw. This is a company that is not averse to controversy.

Ensemble Theatre of Houston
The Ensemble Theatre of Houston strives to promote collaboration among theatre professionals of all races, genders, and ethnicities. Too often in the past, Black actors, directors, and crew members had trouble finding a place in the theatre. Over the years, however, this ensemble has helped to encourage and preserve African-American artistic expression. The company brings its mission to both classics and contemporary plays, international and local work, and even children's productions. The core troupe is African American, but the ensemble is committed to maintaining a "color-blind" approach to casting, as well as to hiring directors, designers, and playwrights. They are unified in their theatrical values, their social vision, and their artistic mission. They invite visiting stars to join them on occasion, but the ensemble itself is the star of its shows.

Top: The Ensemble Theatre of Houston offers family entertainment. Bottom: The 1994 Steppenwolf Theatre Company's production *Of Mice and Men.*

Steppenwolf Theatre Company

The nationally acclaimed not-for-profit Steppenwolf Theatre Company first performed in a church basement in 1974. It began under the leadership of Terry Kinney, Jeff Perry, and Gary Sinise, but has grown into an ensemble that includes thirty-five artists. Among them are John Malkovich of *Being John Malkovich*, Gary Sinise of *Forrest Gump* and *The Green Mile*, John Mahoney of the TV sitcom *Frazier*, and Laurie Metcalf of the sitcom *Roseanne*. The company is committed to ensemble collaboration and taking artistic risks. Located in Chicago's Lincoln Park area and in its third decade, the company has performed over 200 works and continues to thrive.

Ensemble Theatre of Houston

One of the oldest and most distinguished professional theater companies, the Ensemble Theatre in Houston, Texas, is dedicated to the African American experience. Financing the theatre with his own money, George Hawkins, an accomplished stage and film actor, founded the theatre in 1976. Beginning as a touring company, the Ensemble Theatre now proudly resides in two theaters, a 200-seat main stage and a black box theatre located in downtown Houston. Ruby Dee, Avery Brooks, and Louis Gossett, Jr., have attended the Board's annual galas. Though Hawkins died in 1990, the theatre remains dedicated to giving artists a place to work and grow.

Visual Cue

The novel *Of Mice and Men* was written in 1937 by John Steinbeck. It was adapted into play form by Horton Foote, among others.

- By looking at the facial expressions of the men in *Of Mice and Men*, what conclusions can you draw about what might be happening?
- What about the stage picture makes it visually interesting? Would it change if the actors were all sitting together?

Unit Two Review

PREVIEW

1 When standing naturally, you should put your weight on the balls of your feet.

2 **scenario** an outline of a play that includes details about the plot, movement, and gestures

cheating out playing toward the audience while seemingly conversing with others on stage

stage business any small action that the character performs without major movement

upstaging drawing the audience's attention to yourself when it should be focused on another character

3 The strongest stage positions are *downstage,* because it is close to the audience, and *stage right,* because we are trained to read from left to right, and so the audience's eye will look left first.

4 The person is standing in a *full front* body position.

5 X DL means *cross down left.*

6 Emoting is NOT essential to voice production. Emoting means to overact.

7 Ask students to say these sentences aloud in class and discuss the results.

8 The most import thing an ensemble actor must learn is the *ensemble ethic,* developing a working relationship based on trust and respect.

9 Discipline is what drives the actor to take care of his "instrument" and improve his skills. It is also what drives the actor back to another audition when he has been rejected. Trust and courtesy are vital components of a successful ensemble. It is NOT important for the actor to have good looks.

Unit Two Review

PREVIEW

Examine the following key concepts previewed in Unit Two.

1 Where should you put your weight when you stand naturally?

2 Define the terms below.
a. scenario b. stage business c. cheating out d. upstaging

3 Of the following, which are the stronger positions, and why?
upstage or downstage stage right or stage left

4 In what body position is the person below standing?

5 What does X DL mean?

6 Which of the following is NOT essential to voice production and articulation?
pitch volume articulation emoting inflection

7 Say this sentence using rising inflection, falling inflection, and sustained inflection: *You always go for a run in the park before you eat breakfast.*

8 What would you say is the most important thing an ensemble actor must learn?

9 Which of these are important qualities for a good actor, and why?
discipline trust good looks courtesy

PREPARE

Assess your response to the preparation process for projects in this unit.

10 How did you and your partner work together to create the scenario and add the movement to your stage movement project?

11 When working on voice and articulation, which aspect of the process did you find most difficult and why?

12 What advice would you give to others learning about stage crosses?

13 Were you able to fully trust the people in your ensemble? Why or why not?

14 Were you and your partner or partners able to work together smoothly and efficiently to prepare your ensemble improvisation?

PRESENT

Analyze the experience of presenting your work to the class.

15 Which project did you find the most rewarding? Why?

16 Did you find it easier to write the three stage crosses or to execute them? Why?

17 Were you happy with the vocal exercise you chose to do, or do you now wish you'd chosen another one? Explain your feelings.

18 Were you able to present your ensemble improvisation in an atmosphere of trust and support?

CRITIQUE

Evaluate how you go about critiquing your work and the work of others.

19 Did you find it easier to critique your classmates in terms of movement, vocal presentation, or ensemble work?

20 Ask a classmate who critiqued one of your presentations to share the critique with you. How balanced and insightful do you find it to be?

21 Evaluate the critiques you wrote in this unit. In what way could they have been more balanced and helpful?

EXTENSIONS

- Read each group of letters below until you understand their meaning. Then play with pitch and inflection as you say them aloud.

  I C U R A Q T   I N V U   G U R O K   P T S N X T C

- Create gestures for the following sentiments:

  I'm really tired and need to get some sleep.
  This is one mighty boring conversation.
  Stop lecturing me, please.
  This guy is definitely not telling the truth.
  The dog needs to go for a walk, and I'm not in the mood to do it.
  These dirty dishes have been sitting on the counter for five days!

PREPARE

10-14 These questions should be answered honestly and thoughtfully by students. Discuss with students any answers that are not satisfactory.

PRESENT

15-18 Discuss with students their feelings about the presentation process: What did they enjoy about, what they would do differently, and what they learned.

CRITIQUE

19-21 Talk to students about their impressions of the critique process. Have them share both positive and negative experiences.

EXTENSIONS

- I SEE YOU ARE A CUTIE.
  I ENVY YOU.
  GEE, YOU ARE OK or GEE, YOU ROCK!
  PETE'S IN ECSTASY. or PETEY IS IN ECSTASY.
- Have students present their gestures to the class. Ask them to discuss the ones that they found the most inventive and effective.

Resource Binder

Unit Two Test, p. 34

Unit Three

Creating a Character

Unit Three teaches students to analyze characters from clues in the play's text and gives students tools to use in the development of characters in a variety of comic and dramatic roles.

Project Preview

Chapter 9 Character Analysis
Creating distinct characters in an improvised scene

Chapter 10 Character Development
Developing characters and performing a scene

Chapter 11 Dramatic Roles
Writing and performing a dramatic scene

Chapter 12 Comic Roles
Writing and performing a comic scene

Unit Three

Creating a Character

Quotable

Use the quote below for a journal writing prompt, discussion starter, or creating a class lesson.

Observation (of human behavior) is like breathing . . . I believe we have a camera lens inside our heads and when something is required in a character that I haven't personally experienced, I find that at some time I have observed a similar characteristic in another person which remains in my subconscious . . . .

Judi Dench, Actor

Discussion Questions

The following questions are intended to tap into students' **prior knowledge** and stimulate ideas about what it means to create a character for a play.

- Who are your favorite dramatic actors? Why do you admire their work?
- List five traits about yourself that you feel define who you are at present. Choose a character from a play and do the same. Is it easier to create a list about yourself or a character? Why?
- What would you do to discover the important details about a character's circumstances if you have never experienced them?
- Do you think it is more difficult to play a character very similar to you or very different? Why?
- Create two lists: one titled COMIC and the other DRAMATIC. What qualities and abilities are necessary to play each kind of role? Write them on the list.
- Do you think it is more challenging to play a comic or a dramatic role. Why?
- Faye Dunaway said on the PBS television program *Inside the Actor's Studio* that to be an actor one needs "to be willing to excavate your mind and soul." What do you think she meant by that? Do you think you would be willing to do that to create a character? Why or why not?

Theatre Journal

Search through magazines to find images of people that represent either a comic or dramatic point of view. Make a collage of comic characters and one of dramatic characters. Compare their qualities, physical mannerisms, and other characteristics.

Visual Cue

The above image shows a performance of the comic opera *Platee* at Covent Garden in London, England.

- Do you think the characters in this production are comic or dramatic characters? What visual clues give you this impression?
- What do the actors' body positions, gestures, expressions, and costumes tell you about their characters?
- Which characters seem to have the highest and lowest status? How can you tell?

ACTivity Ask students to write a short speech for the froglike character at the left of the photo. Have volunteers read their speeches using the voice, gestures, and movement as they envision it for the character.

Chapter 9

Character Analysis

In this chapter students will learn to use the text to uncover a character's circumstances, characteristics, and objectives. They will create distinct characters with articulated goals.

Objectives

1 to detect clues about character from the dramatic text, including physical and emotional traits

2 to delineate and specify emotional, mental, and spiritual aspects of character

3 to articulate with precision character motivation, objective, and obstacle

4 to prepare and perform a scene involving distinct characters

National Standards

Chapter 9 meets these National Theatre Standards:

Proficient 2a, 2c, 5a, 7c, 7d, 8a
Advanced 2d, 5b, 7g, 7h

Project Specs

Explain to students that analyzing a character can be as involved, challenging, rigorous, and enjoyable as they make it. Many actors do outside research to gather information on a character's background, historical period, psychological underpinnings, and so on. Other actors just take the script and go from there.

On Your Feet

ACTivity After the interview, have each student write a character description of himself or herself for a dramatic or comic play based on the partner's interview notes. Tell students to use vivid language that will stimulate the imagination of the actor playing the role. Have the class mix up the descriptions and read them aloud, guessing whom each description is based upon.

Chapter

9 Character Analysis

To be a good actor, you must become a student of humanity. Your knowledge of people is one of the most valuable assets you have when it comes to creating a believable character. As you analyze and develop a role, you will draw upon the text of the play, your own experiences, and remembered observations of people you meet, read about, or see on film.

Project Specs

Project Description You and a partner will each create distinct characters with specific goals in a three- to five-minute improvised scene.

Purpose to analyze a character in terms of internal and external traits, motivation, objectives, and stakes

Materials a list of shared information between your own and your partner's character, a list of your character's internal and external traits, or the Character Analysis Activity Sheet provided by your teacher

Theatre Terms

artistic selectivity
conflict
dual role
external traits
internal traits
motivation
objectives
obstacle
outcome
stakes

On Your Feet

Spend two minutes interviewing a partner. Ask questions about his or her background, family, friends, personal preferences, hobbies, accomplishments, and so on. Take notes and try to create a composite of the person. At the end of two minutes, look over your notes and tell your partner about himself or herself. Then switch roles.

Theatre Terms

artistic selectivity selecting the optimum amount of information necessary to portray a character

conflict dramatic opposition of the protagonist with society, peers, or himself/herself

dual role the two aspects of acting: the actor-as-character and the actor-as-actor

external traits characteristics that make up physical appearance

internal traits characteristics that make up personality

motivation reason for a behavior or action

objectives goals or needs

obstacle anything that gets in the way of reaching an objective

outcome result

stakes level or degree of importance in getting objectives met

PREVIEW

The Actor and the Character

As an actor in a play you have a **dual role.** You are both the actor-as-character and the actor-as-actor. If you are to be convincing onstage, you must use your imagination—and the work you've done analyzing and developing your character—to maintain your belief in what you as the character are doing, feeling, and saying. You should think as the character thinks and concentrate on fulfilling his or her goals, or **objectives.** On the other hand, as an actor you must maintain technical control and a professional attitude at all times. None of your performing will matter if the audience has trouble seeing or hearing you. You the actor and you the character must work as a unit to create the delicate balance of believable characterization.

This may sound like a demanding job—and it is. But characterization shouldn't be a strain. Relax and enjoy the process as you create a believable individual onstage.

Developing the Character

To be an effective onstage presence you will need to know hundreds of things about your character—much more than you will actually be able to portray onstage. Your job then becomes one of **artistic selectivity.** What are the really important aspects of this character? How can you effectively communicate the essentials of the character? At the same time, remember that none of the work you do while developing your character is wasted. The more you know about the character, the more textured your performance will be.

And you must harness your character's emotions and avoid overacting, which offends both the audience and your fellow actors.

Julian Glover and Alan Doble create distinctive characters in the Piccadilly Theatre production of *Waiting for Godot.*

PREVIEW

The Actor and the Character

Actors have a unique artistic advantage over many other artists: They require no canvas, paint, paper, or other tools of the trade. All an actor really needs is his or her own body—and the ability to move, speak, and think. Let students know from the start that acting is certainly gratifying and exciting work, but it is also very demanding— and often difficult. Acting requires hours of hard physical and emotional dedication and a great deal of discipline—the result of which, ironically, should be conveyed in a relaxed and seemingly effortless way. What separates the good actor from the great actor is how well he or she can use the imagination to make a character live and breathe.

Developing the Character

Suggest to students that instead of asking how much they can do with their parts to decide how *little* they can do and still communicate the necessary ideas and emotions. Instill in them the belief that as artists creating a role, they must:

- Select
- Combine
- Discard

Vocabulary Enhancement

Theatre-goers and critics alike often speak of a fine actor's *stage presence*, which is the ability to seem perfectly at ease onstage, as if he or she belonged there.

Resource Binder

- Character Analysis Activity Sheet, p. 35
- Finding Your Motivation Worksheet, p. 36
- Critique Sheet: High-Stakes Scene, p. 37
- Character Analysis Test, p. 38
- Actor's Script Analysis, p. 128

Handbook Connections
pages 551-553

To Have on Hand

Have examples of well-written scenarios from various sources on hand, including some written by high school students.

Motivation and Conflict

Draw three columns on the chalkboard and write the words *WHAT* and *WHY* at the top of the first two. Then ask students to think about times in the last week when they had a strong need to do something. Ask them to tell you what it was as you write it on the board. Next ask them to explain why they wanted what they did. Write that on the board also. Explain that WHAT is the goal, or OBJECTIVE, and WHY indicates the MOTIVATION. Discuss the motivations and objectives that the students expressed.

Now add the last title, *HOW,* to the third column, and ask students what they did to achieve their goals. Tell them that the means they used to achieve their objectives are called *tactics.* Write down the tactics that they used. Discuss other tactics that might have been used to achieve the same objectives.

ACTivity Make a list of objectives with the class using verbs that stimulate an emotional response. Examples: to *incite* a riot, to *seize* power, to *hypnotize* into submission, to *abscond* with funds, etc. Once the list is complete, one student at a time acts out a movement or short scene using one verb and its objective.

The Character Inside and Out

ACTivity Suggest to students that they create a character notebook for a specific character from a play. This can be done as a project over several days. Have them create a biography of the character that describes the character's history, occupation, family status, and any other circumstances.

Some of this information will come directly from the text, some will come from research, and some will come from the imagination.

The hundreds of things you understand about your character will reveal themselves through the various layers and colors you are able to bring to the role.

Motivation and Conflict

In real life people often do and say things for no apparent reason. A character in a play, however, needs a specific reason, or **motivation,** for doing or saying anything. Motivation determines your character's objectives. Whatever is standing in the way of your character's objectives is an **obstacle.**

This is the essence of **conflict,** which in turn is the basis of drama. The **outcome** of a conflict is the result of the steps the characters take to overcome their obstacles. What the characters may gain or lose as a result of the outcome are the **stakes.** The higher the stakes are in a play, the greater the character's motivation; the more powerful the conflict, the more important the outcome.

The Character Inside and Out

To find your way into the mind and body of a character, you must know the role inside and out. That means you must understand both the character's internal and external traits.

To determine a character's **internal traits,** challenge yourself to discover what he or she is like inside. Find out the character's background—that is his or her family circumstances, environment, occupation, level of education, hobbies, and so on—and his or her emotional reactions to all of these circumstances. You can break internal traits into three basic categories.

1. **Mental characteristics** Is the character intelligent, clever, dull, slow, or average?
2. **Spiritual qualities** What are the character's ideals, ethical code, and beliefs? What is his or her attitude toward other people and toward life in general?
3. **Emotional characteristics** Is the character confident, outgoing, happy, and poised or sullen, confused, nervous, cynical, and timid? What are his or her likes and dislikes? How does he or she respond to others? (One good technique when analyzing emotional characteristics is to ask yourself how a character's temperament is similar to and different from your own.)

Answering all these questions should give you a good idea of your character's personality. Now it's time to get even more specific. You will have to determine your character's motivating desire within the play or scene. In other words, what does your character *want*? You may have to do the additional work of imagining the circumstances that led to the events of the play or scene.

92 **Unit Three** Creating a Character

Quotable

Acting is the life of the human soul receiving its birth through art.

from *Acting: The First Six Lessons* by Richard Boleslavski

To play the title role in *Mary Stuart* convincingly, actor Jenny Bacon must convey the motivation and obstacles faced by the Scottish queen.

A character's **external traits** have to do with outward appearance and what that appearance says about him or her. Here are some external traits to think about.

1 **Posture** Does the way the character sits and stands suggest confidence, timidity, awkwardness, or grace?

2 **Movement and gestures** Does the character's movement and gait reveal poise, nervousness, weakness, or strength? What does the character's movement reveal about his or her age, health, or general attitude?

3 **Mannerism** Does the character have any tics or little habits that provide keys to his or her personality? Examples might be nail biting, gum chewing, head scratching, or table tapping.

4 **Voice** Does the character have a specific regional dialect or any vocal mannerisms?

5 **Mode of dress** Is the character's appearance neat, casual, prim, or sloppy? Are the clothes clean or dirty? Are they in good taste?

Visual Cue

Friedrich Schiller's 19th-century play, *Mary Stuart,* brings to the stage the last three days of the life of Mary, Queen of Scots. Imprisoned for eighteen years in England, she was finally beheaded for her supposed involvement in an attempt on the life of Queen Elizabeth I. The play revolves around Mary and Elizabeth and their followers, who exhibit different perspectives on almost every important idea of their age.

- In what way does the character's attire suggest who she is?
- Does the character exhibit the bearing of a queen? Explain.
- What does the actress's posture suggest about the queen's circumstances?
- Imagine that you are Queen Elizabeth I standing before Mary Stuart. How would you approach her? What might you say?

Suggest also that they answer the questions below about the character.

- What is your character's deepest fear?
- What is your character's deepest desire?
- What is the biggest obstacle in the way of your character getting his or her desire?
- Does your character have any odd habits?
- What songs or poems remind you of this character?
- Is there an aspect of your character that you know nothing about? Research this information and include it in your notebook.

Also have students include any photographs, artwork, lyrics, or poetry that suggest their character's traits—external and internal.

ACTivity Place five chairs in a row in the playing area and ask five students to sit down. Ask them to experiment with different postures that reveal character. Have the class suggest what each posture tells them about the person.

ACTivity Invite other students to be seated, and add an environment and circumstances to the mix, such as waiting in a hospital waiting room or a police station. Each person in a chair creates the posture based on one sentence that represents his or her character, i.e. "I'm very worried about these headaches" or "Keep clear, I'm tough."

ACTivity **Advanced Students** Add more dimensions to the seated characters. Two are from the South, one is from England, one has a peculiar habit, and so on. Continue to challenge advanced students to create characters whose actions reveal both internal and external characteristics.

ACTivity **Advanced Students** Ask students to choose two or three gestures they have seen people make and memorize them so that they have a "choreography of gestures." When they are ready, ask these students to show their choreography of gestures to the class. Discuss the characters created by these gestures.

Chapter 9 Character Analysis **93**

PREPARE

Create a High-Stakes Scenario

Show, Don't Tell As you discuss some aspect of the work involved for this chapter, incorporate a mannerism of some kind, such as biting a lip or wrinkling your nose. Do not indicate that you are upset in words but by gesture or manner alone. Continue until students indicate in some way that they are aware of this physical tic. Ask them to discuss what they thought as you repeated this movement. What did it reveal about you and what you might be feeling or thinking?

Discuss with the class the scenario for two siblings presented on this page. Does it have a familiar ring? Which sibling do they think should realistically come out on top, and why? Suggest ways in which disagreements over the outcome of this scenario might be resolved, including tossing a coin, asking an arbitrator, compromising on the time each uses the line, or giving up use of the phone line altogether. Have students suggest other possibilities. Encourage them to be willing collaborators as they exchange ideas with their partners for their own scenarios.

ACTivity Have pairs of students face one another. Ask them to choose two opposite words, such as summer/winter or big/small. Each of them has one minute to describe to the other all the positive aspects of one of these words. Then each has two minutes to explain to the class why their word is a better one. Students should use as many tactics as possible to win.

Theatre Journal

Use the following as an additional or substitute prompt.

Ask students to use their character studies to present a short scene in which their character introduces himself or herself.

Mannerisms can tell a lot about your character.

When analyzing and developing a character's external qualities, you'll want to avoid stereotypes. For example, you don't necessarily want to choose a cartoonlike drawling "hick" voice simply because your character is supposed to be uneducated. Try to make the more interesting, less obvious choice.

Theatre Journal

Go to a public place such as a museum, a park, or a mall. Sit down on a bench and do a bit of people watching. Take note of the way people walk and the expressions on their faces. Imagine what the lives of these people might be like. Choose one passerby to use as the basis for a character. Write a history for this character. Use what you see and your imagination to create a rich character study.

PREPARE

Create a High-Stakes Scenario

You are now going to work with a partner to improvise a scenario in which the stakes are high for each of your characters. You will need to think of a situation in which two characters come into conflict over a physical object of some kind (perhaps a bag of money, a legal document, or a treasured family heirloom). Decide when and where your scene takes place and what the relationship between your characters should be. Then nail down a bit of their shared history (if any). Write down everything you decide upon. Here's an example:

Scenario for Two Siblings

Characters: Rita and Joe
Relationship: Sister and Brother
Ages: Rita is 15; Joe is 14
Situation: Rita desperately needs to use the telephone; Joe is searching an online Web site and has been tying up the phone line for an hour.
Time of year: Just after Thanksgiving
Time of day: 10 P.M.

Decide which character will ultimately achieve his or her objectives. This will serve as the outcome of the scene. DO NOT determine what your characters will say and do in the scene ahead of time—you are to improvise your actual exchange.

Visual Cue

Have students look at the picture at the top of the page. Use the following prompts.

- What does the mannerism of the student on the left tell you about him?
- What does the posture of the student on the right indicate about her?
- What other habit might someone have involving glasses?

After you have come up with your shared situation and history, take some time to work independently. Both of you should come up with external and internal traits for your character, as well as motivations (Rita: Why does she need to use the phone? Joe: Why does he have to be online?), objectives (Rita: How will she get Joe offline? Joe: How will he distract Rita until he can finish what he is doing?), and stakes (Rita: What will happen if she doesn't make her phone call? Joe: What will happen if he doesn't finish what he is doing?).

At the right are a few other possible scenarios. You can use one of them or create your own. The important thing is to be specific about your shared history and your character's internal and external traits, motivation, and objectives. Rehearse your scene so that you know only the basic shape of the improvisation. Don't write down specific lines you want to say; keep this improvisation spontaneous. Time yourselves to make sure you will come within the three- to five-minute time frame.

Suggestions for Scenarios

- Two students compete for a school award.
- Two siblings both want a particular item that belonged to their dead grandfather.
- Two bank robbers want to be in charge of divvying up the loot.
- Two people at a library want to use the only available computer.
- Two people bid on a priceless object at an auction.

Two characters clash over a high-stakes real estate deal in David Mamet's *Glengarry Glen Ross.*

As the students work independently on their scenarios, continue to use the example of the two siblings to help them along. They should, at this point, know enough about their partner's character to be able to explore how they will continue with their encounter and what will happen next.

As the students begin to rehearse their scenarios, remind them to remain open to new ideas—their own and their partner's. They should not be using any specific words, but they should have a specific direction.

Suggestions for Scenarios

If students choose any of these scenarios, instruct them to put themselves into the place of the character and try to imagine how they would feel and to what lengths they would go to reach their objective in the scene.

Glengarry Glen Ross remains one of David Mamet's most admired plays. It was made into a film in 1992, starring Jack Lemmon, Al Pacino, Ed Harris, Alan Arkin, Kevin Spacey, and Alec Baldwin, among others.

- What do their postures say about how these two men are relating to one another?
- Which man appears to have the upper hand?
- Judging by the set, what might have happened in this real estate office?

Backstage Gossip: The Greatest Motivator

Early in 1962 Noel [Coward] was the guest of honor one Sunday at a dinner given by the Gallery First-Nighter's Club. Beginning his speech, "Desperately accustomed as I am to public speaking," he continued, "you ask my advice about acting? Speak clearly, don't bump into people, and if you must have motivation think of your pay packet on Friday."

from *Theatrical Anecdotes* by Peter Hay

PRESENT

Perform Your High-Stakes Scene

It always helps to add a time limit to a scene in order to heighten the stakes and the feeling of urgency. You might want to watch the presentations with watch in hand, letting the actors know when they have four, three, two, and then one minute left to achieve their goals. Tell students to create for themselves a motivation for the time limit, for example, in the scenario on page 94 it might be that the siblings have only a few minutes until their parents get home and end their confrontation.

It might also be helpful to coach students into trying different tactics or working harder to reach their objective as they work through their scenes. Remind them also to be sure they respond to the other character's demands, and so on.

CRITIQUE

Evaluate Your Classmates' Scene

Hand out the Critique Sheet for this activity or have students use their own paper. If you have counted down the time for the students, ask how they think this affected their work on the scene.

If you have focused on tactics, you might want to add an additional question about what tactics were used by each of the partners and which ones were successful and why.

PRESENT

Perform Your High-Stakes Scene

When your or your partner's name is called, give your lists or Activity Sheets to your teacher. Then take a few moments to set up your scene (arrange chairs if you need them, for example). Do not rush.

Remember to keep the stakes high with the choices your character makes during the scene. If one method doesn't work, try another. Each character must work hard to achieve the goal. When you perform your scene, you will no doubt find out things about the other character that you didn't know. You must respond to these things in the moment. Try to make everything clear within the scene. You will not be using an introduction for this activity.

Remember to keep yourself open to the audience, both physically and emotionally as you perform your scene. When you have finished your scene, turn to the audience and bow politely before returning to your seat.

CRITIQUE

Evaluate Your Classmates' Scene

Choose one of the scenes presented and evaluate it on a scale of 1 to 5, with 5 being "outstanding" and 1 being "needs much improvement." Your critique should answer these questions:

- How old were these two characters?
- What was their relationship to one another?
- What was each character's objective?
- How high were the stakes for each character?
- What did each character do to get what he or she wanted?
- Which character got what he or she wanted—and how was this achieved?
- Did one character appear stronger than the other? If so, in what way?

Write a paragraph detailing the reasons for the score you gave.

96 **Unit Three** Creating a Character

Quotable

The actor is an artist, not a critic. His job is not to explain a text, but to bring a character to life. To understand as an intelligent man and to understand as an artist are two completely different things . . . .

Paul Claudel, French Poet and Playwright

Additional Projects

1 Select newspaper human-interest stories to analyze. In groups, supply the necessary characters for the action of the story. Establish the characters' physical, emotional, and social dimensions. Then improvise a scene built around them.

2 In groups, build a scene around a historical event, such as Lewis and Clark's first meeting with Sacajawea, General Lee's surrender to Ulysses S. Grant at Appomattox Courthouse, the Lincoln/ Douglas debates, and so on. Be sure your story has characters in conflict, high stakes, a clear outcome, and is historically correct.

3 Choose a hand prop or costume accessory such as a pair of long white gloves, an oversized umbrella, a colorful silk handkerchief, a pocket watch, or a stuffed bird. Create a brief scene in which you portray a character who is wearing this costume or holding this prop.

4 Work with a partner to create a scene. Character A goes on stage and waits for Character B to enter. A decides upon a definite character relationship with B, but does not tell B what it is. B must discover who he or she is strictly through the way A talks and behaves toward him or her. B responds as sensibly as possible until his or her identity becomes clear.

5 Read the scene from *A Marriage Proposal* by Anton Chekhov found in Unit Eight of this book. With a partner, choose a part and read the scene through together. As you read, be aware of each character's motivation, obstacles, and stakes in this particular scene.

This image might help you build a scene around one of the debates between Abraham Lincoln and Stephen A. Douglas that took place throughout Illinois in 1858. It is possible to find transcripts of these debates at your library or on the Internet.

Substitute Teacher Activities

Here are some suggestions for the days that you will be out of the classroom.

- Assign the Finding Your Motivation Worksheet on page 36 of the Resource Binder.
- Discuss the information concerning Characterization found on pages 551–553 in the Student Handbook.
- Assign one or more of the Additional Projects on this page.
- **Play Who Am I?** Students give pertinent internal and external characteristics of a famous person in fiction, film, or television without revealing the character's name in any way. Classmates must guess the person's name.

Chapter 9 Test

The test for this chapter is available in blackline master form in the Resource Binder, page 38.

For More Information

Books

Adler, Stella, *The Techniques of Acting,* Bantam Books, 1992.

Boleslavski, Richard, *Acting: The First Six Lessons,* Routledge, 2003.

Cohen, Robert, *Acting One,* McGraw-Hill, 2001.

Meisner, Sanford, *Acting,* Vintage Books, 1987.

Stanislavski, Constantine, *Creating a Role,* Theatre Art Books, 2002.

Other Media

Character and Actors: Plot and Conflict, VHS, Insight Media, 1992.

What's the Score? Text Analysis for the Actor, VHS, Insight Media, 1989.

Theatre Then and Now

Henrik Ibsen

When Ibsen's *A Doll's House* was first performed in Norway, it was said that when Nora leaves her husband and children at the end of the play and slams the door it was "a slam heard around the world." No one in a play had ever left her family before and it shocked the world.

Many theatre experts believe that the last scene in the play is one of the most perfectly crafted scenes in theatre. They believe that when Nora asks her husband Torvald to "sit down and talk" that naturalism and realism were born in the theatre. For the first time, people sat down and discussed their problems.

For More Information

Books

Adler, Stella, Barry Paris, ed. *Stella Adler on Ibsen, Strindberg, and Chekhov,* Knopf, 1999.

Gosse, Edmund, *Henrik Ibsen,* University Press of the Pacific, 2003.

Shaw, George Bernard, *The Quintessence of Ibsenism,* Dover Publications, 1994.

Templeton, Joan, *Ibsen's Women,* Cambridge University Press, 2001.

Other Media

The Wild Duck, VHS, Insight Media, 1978.

Theatre Then and Now

Ibsen and Miller—Appointment with Humanity

Amira Casar and Marie Adam in a recent production of *Hedda Gabler.*

Henrik Ibsen and Arthur Miller both wrote plays with universal themes about the human condition. They created flesh-and-blood, flawed characters on desperate quests for meaning and fulfillment. A testimony to this universality is the fact that much of Ibsen's work is still produced more than 110 years after it was written, and *Death of a Salesman,* a play that celebrated its fifty-fourth birthday in 2003, remains one of the world's most produced plays.

Henrik Ibsen (1828–1906)

Throughout history, playwrights have struggled to define and illustrate what it means to be human. The Greeks gave the world classical tragedy, a form that depicted a noble-born person who, through a flaw in his own character, brings about his own ruin. William Shakespeare's dramas also focused on highborn individuals whose character flaws brought them down.

In the mid- to late-1800s the Norwegian writer Henrik Ibsen created a series of social dramas about middle-class people. These were plays of such psychological depth that Ibsen later became known as the "Freud of the theatre," a reference to the famous psychoanalyst Sigmund Freud. Ibsen wrote about characters who struggled with the often negative forces in their own minds. And he slammed these tortured souls up against conventional society in ways that revealed much about both the characters and the social order of the day.

In his 1890 play *Hedda Gabler,* the formidable but desperately unhappy title character sets about changing and destroying the lives of those around her as a way of fulfilling her own dreams of freedom and independence. Hedda is a strong, intelligent woman who is trapped by the role society has created for her.

Ibsen created characters whose desperate need to live differently drove them to self-destruction while also ruining the lives of others.

98 Unit Three Creating a Character

Backstage Gossip: Ibsen's Open Drain

When Henrik Ibsen's play *Ghosts* was first produced in 1881, the fact that it dealt with hereditary venereal disease and took the view that the social conventions of the day laid personal happiness to waste caused the *Daily Telegraph* in London to label it "an open drain; a loathsome sore unbandaged" and a "a dirty act done publicly . . . ."

"I think now that the great thing is not so much the formulation of an answer for myself, the theatre, or the play—but rather the most accurate possible statement of the problem."

—Arthur Miller

Arthur Miller (1915–)

Nearly sixty years after *Hedda Gabler* was written, playwright Arthur Miller's 1949 masterpiece, *Death of a Salesman,* took the American theatre by storm. The play focuses on Willy Loman, a salesman long past his prime, who is still waiting in vain for his small corner of the American Dream. Like Ibsen, Miller was interested in how society affects the individual. Willy Loman is a complex blend of desperation and bravado. At his core, he knows he is a failure, but he spends much of the play trying to convince himself and those around him that he is just about to make a comeback as the great salesman he once was.

As the play progresses, it becomes clear that Willy is reinventing his past and that in fact he was never a great salesman. He has always been an average man with unreachable dreams. Toward the end of the play, Willy realizes that his failure as a salesman is mirrored in his failure as a husband and father. The American dream has escaped his grasp, and like Hedda Gabler, Willy Loman makes a desperate final statement.

The role of Willy Loman has tempted many fine actors over the years, including Dustin Hoffman, above.

"My main goal has been to depict people, human moods and human fates, on the basis of certain predominant social conditions and perceptions."

—Henrik Ibsen

Backstage Gossip: But What About Marilyn?

When David Merrick was first introduced to Arthur Miller, who had been an idol to him, the playwright was accompanied by Marilyn Monroe, then at the height of her glamorous fame. It says something about the stature of both men that the producer forever remembered the impact of this meeting: "I just couldn't stop staring at Arthur Miller."

from *Broadway Anecdotes* by Peter Hay

Arthur Miller

Arthur Miller won the Pulitzer Prize in 1949 for *Death of a Salesman,* which has come to be regarded as one of the great dramas of American theatre. His plays, particularly the early ones, are produced throughout the world.

When it was first performed, however, the play caused heated arguments as to its status as a tragedy. Some critics believed that Willy Loman was too ordinary and petty to cause the pity and fear instilled in audiences of great tragic drama. Willy's small life and sorry aspirations could not stand up against such tragic heroes as Antigone or Oedipus, they argued. Miller defended his work by saying that any character willing to sacrifice his life to secure his own dignity was a worthy successor to the tragic tradition.

Visual Cue

In the *Death of a Salesman* photograph, all three characters seem to have strong objectives.

- Describe the relationships of these three men based on their body postures and shapes?
- How high do the stakes seem and how can you tell?

For More Information

Books

Gottfried, Martin, *Arthur Miller,* DaCapo Press, 2003.

Miller, Arthur, et.al., *Echoes Down the Corridor: Collected Essays, 1994-2000,* Viking Press, 2000.

Miller, Arthur, *On Politics and the Art of Acting,* Viking Press, 2001.

Other Media

Arthur Miller, VHS, Insight Media, 1991.

Private Conversations on the Set of Death of a Salesman, VHS, Insight Media, 1986.

Plot and Structure

Draw the bell-shaped outline of the basic structure of a traditional play on the chalkboard so that all students can see it. Write the words *Turning Point, Rising Action, Resolution, Falling Action,* and *Conflict* on the board and have students come to the board and label the diagram appropriately, starting with *Conflict* and ending with *Resolution*. Discuss each element in turn with students and then break down these elements in a short story they are familiar with, such as *The Lottery* by Shirley Jackson or *To Build a Fire* by Jack London.

Note that while the bell-shaped diagram reflects the structure of traditional plays, some modern works do not follow this pattern.

ACTivity Use the plot of *The Wizard of Oz* or *Harry Potter and the Sorcerer's Stone* and call on various students to identify the plot elements in order, from conflict to resolution. If there is time, ask students to suggest additional stories.

Surreal scenic elements and lighting reveal the mood of David Saar's play *The Yellow Boat*, about Saar's real-life son's death from AIDS.

Plot and Structure

To analyze your character effectively, you must analyze the play's plot and structure. Like any good work of literature, a play's plot is made up of a series of incidents linked by a theme. It involves conflict (struggle) that is revealed through action, which leads to the dramatic turning point, or climax, and then to a logical conclusion, or resolution.

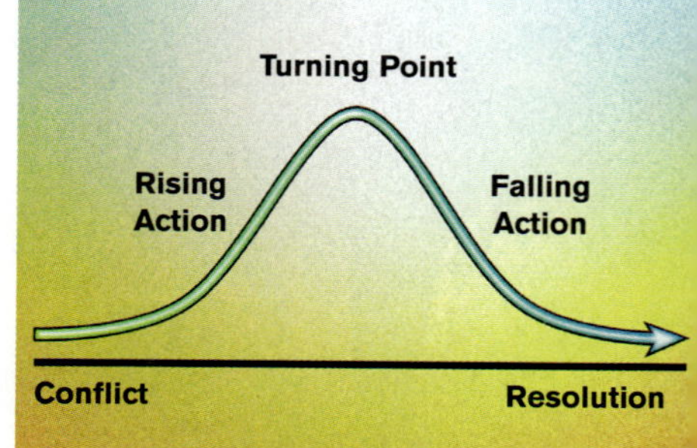

The basic structure of most plays includes these five elements.

Visual Cue

The Yellow Boat was written as an affirmation of a child's life and of the courage and wonder of all children. Benjamin Saar, the son of David and Sonja Saar, was eight years old when he died in 1987 of complications of AIDS. While he lived, Benjamin's imagination and artistic gifts transformed his physical and emotional pain into beautiful, deftly colored drawings.

- Do you think this scene reflects the son's or the parents' point of view?
- Why do you think a playwright's story of his son's life and death would contain surreal elements?

The Actor and the Traditional Play Structure

In order to really understand drama, an actor must understand the importance of a play's structure. The structure of a play is what holds together the characters' actions and words. By analyzing the elements of a story's structure, the actor has important insight into the plot, the theme, and his character's motivations. Study the elements that follow as they relate to the actor.

1. **Conflict** As you know, in most plays, the plot is built around a conflict, a problem or struggle of some sort. The conflict may be between characters, between a character and some object or event, or between a character and the character's inner self. It is your job as an actor to assess your character's role in the conflict and to determine how your character should act and react as the conflict intensifies.
2. **Rising Action** (or complications) Any additional events that stem from the conflict are important elements for you to be aware of and to think about in terms of the forward movement of the play and your character's role in it.
3. **Turning Point** This is the highest point of emotional intensity in the drama. It usually occurs near the end of the play. Here, the main character will most likely take an action to end the conflict. All the play's action leads to this point, and again, as an actor, you must be aware of the momentum that has been generated to this point and adjust your performance intensity accordingly.
4. **Falling Action** (also called the **denouement**) These are the events that happen after the turning point. As an actor, you must adjust your performance to the atmosphere of the denouement.
5. **Resolution** Here is where the complications are worked out. And, although the play is at this point winding toward its conclusion, be careful not to lose your energy as an actor or to slide into sluggish line delivery or posture. Stay with the rhythm and flow of the play, but keep your performance energy high.

Keep in mind that some contemporary playwrights do not adhere to this traditional structure and may omit one or more of these elements.

Mood

The mood of a play is its emotional texture. The audience should sense the play's mood early on—during the rising action. Nearly every aspect of the play contributes to the mood—from the characters to the plot to the design elements.

Quotable

When in doubt, make a fool of yourself. There is a microscopically thin line between being brilliantly creative and acting like the most gigantic idiot on earth.

Cynthia Heimel, Actor

The Actor and the Traditional Play Structure

ACTivity It will be helpful to use a play the group is familiar with or a play you are working on in class as you discuss play structure with students. *Romeo and Juliet* is a good choice because most students are familiar with the story.

Together, isolate, analyze, and discuss each element of the traditional play structure within the text you chose. Then follow one character, Juliet for example, through the play's structure and analyze how her character is revealed through her actions during the rising action, the turning point, and so on. Example: What is Juliet's *conflict* and what does she do to solve it during the *rising action*?

Beginning or ESL Students
You can help any student who is not familiar with *Romeo and Juliet* or any other play under discussion to understand plot structure by using a familiar movie instead. Help the student understand the conflict in the story, the actions that lead to a decisive moment, the turning point, and the resolution of the story.

Mood

Ask students to make a list of three pervasive moods that alter all they see and everything they may do. Under each mood ask them to describe its tempo, rhythm, colors, sounds, music, weather, or temperature. Advise them that when they are working on their scene, they should use the mood that underlies the scene and incorporate this into the development of their characters.

ACTivity Sound is a strong way to affect mood. Have groups of students create silent improvisations within a specific environment and situation (who, what, where) using sound effects or music. Example: Use music and improvisation to depict a city bar at 2 A.M. after the city's team has won a big game. Each actor chooses a character with a motivation and objective for the scene. During the silent scene, use different sound effects and music to alter the mood. Body language and movement should change with the changing mood created by the sound.

Characterization

Share with students a few of the techniques below and on the following page, which are helpful when working through a script.

- Ask a friend to record your cue lines on a tape recorder. Leave the right amount of empty space on the recorder for you to speak your lines before the next cue line. Practice your lines using the tape recorder for the cues. You can also ask your friend to cue you in person as you practice your lines.
- Do a physical activity while reading the script out loud: jog, bounce a ball, do situps, and so on. Let the words travel through the physical activity and out your mouth. Let the activity naturally change the way you say the lines. By memorizing lines this way, you are learning them deep into your system.

Theatre Journal

Use the following as an additional or substitute prompt.

Write a short scene in which you use the impressions you gathered about a familiar person you re-examined. Have this person exhibit the new characteristics you uncovered.

When you have studied the plot, mood, and structure of the play or scene in which you've been cast, you can at last begin to focus on your particular character and how he or she fits into the play.

Light, setting, and the actor's body language all create a mood of defeat in this scene from *Death of a Salesman.*

After you have read the play once to understand all of its elements, read it again to identify with your specific role. Visualize the action through your character's eyes. Understand your character's behavior and dialogue in view of his or her motivation.

Characterization

In previous chapters, you've learned that making observations, drawing upon your own experience, using your imagination, and investigating the character's internal and external traits all help you understand a given character. To concentrate on knowing your character through and through, use the steps below as you memorize your script.

- Concentrate on your character's internal and external traits via the clues the script provides you. (See Chapter 9, pages 92–93 for more on internal and external traits). Think about people you know who remind you of your character. Discover ways in which your character is like you, and determine how the character is unlike you. Research aspects of your character that are unknown to you.

Theatre Journal

When you create a character, you build a whole new world for yourself. And that means you must learn to look at the world from a different point of view. As an exercise, try to re-examine a very familiar person in your life. Try to see this person in a fresh, new way, then write about what you notice.

Visual Cue

In this scene from Arthur Miller's classic drama, Willy Loman has arrived home after a sales trip. Ask students to use their **critical viewing skills** to answer the following questions:

- How does the lighting affect the impression given in this scene?
- What do you imagine the character to be thinking?
- What do you think the actor will do once he is inside the house?

- Have a clear sense of what happened to your character before the events depicted in the play. Some actors make complete histories of their character's family life, employment, friendships and alliances, and so on as a way of delving as deeply as possible into the person they are playing.
- Ask yourself what your character wants and what he or she does to get it. Does the character want different things from different people?
- Figure out whose side your character is on. Is yours the central character? Or, does your character oppose the central character in some way? Or, does your character assist the central character? Most characters fall into one of these categories.
- In addition to the dialogue (what your character *says*), you should pay close attention to the stage directions to figure out what your character *does*—and why.
- Pay attention to what the other characters say about your character and how they behave toward him or her.
- Think about how your character *changes* over the course of the play. Does the character experience a major shift—a change of attitude or circumstance? How will you convey this?
- Remember that plays, like real life, are mostly about what *isn't* said. The dialogue of a play can be compared to the tip of an iceberg. What's said represents only a part of the whole story. The information that is implied but not stated by a character is called the **subtext.** For example, consider the character who tells another character, "I hate you! I'm leaving!" but proceeds to stay onstage. What the character *does* contradicts what he or she says—so you can be fairly certain the character is experiencing something besides hatred—perhaps even its exact opposite! The subtext a character conveys is often much more important than what the character actually says.
- Pay special attention to your character's rhythms. Does he or she speak in a staccato manner (short, choppy sentences and fragments) or in long fluid sentences? The way the character speaks is likely to reflect the way the character moves.

Love Your Character!

Acting teachers often tell their students they must "love" their characters. By this they mean that you must respect, understand, and empathize with a character in order to bring life to the role. This does not mean that you as a person would make the same choices the character does, nor does it mean you necessarily approve of the character's actions. But you must attempt to live inside the character's skin–and that's impossible to do if you stand outside and judge him or her. Above all, remember that if you're not fascinated by your character, no one else will be either.

From the Field: Death by the Spoonful

We enjoy warming up in class with a game we like to call "The Spoon of Death." The class passes a spoon around until I call either "Poison!", "Swordfight!", or "Heart Attack!" The person left holding the spoon must die the appropriate death, in a tragic or comic manner. The designated student may use dialogue—and subtext is encouraged.

Kay Jacobs, Drama Instructor, San Francisco, California

- Practice your lines with your scene partner while doing a shared activity such as throwing a ball back and forth or arm wrestling. Again, allow the lines to be connected to and fall out of the action.

Share the following questions that actors should ask when creating a character:

- Who am I?
- What is my goal and what will I do to achieve it?
- What are my obstacles?
- What are my circumstances?
- What are my relationships?

ACTivity Advanced Students
Have students create a silent improvisation in groups of six to eight. Give them the circumstances of a scene, such as "It is Paris in the spring at midday in a romantic café." The actors choose the characters' circumstances—why they are at the café and what they want to have happen while they are there (objectives). Play music to create mood. At different moments throughout the improv, freeze the group and ask one character to speak his or her subtext or inner monologue out loud. Return to the group action for a while, then repeat with another actor.

In order to listen well onstage, it is important to know what you are listening for. When you know your character's motivation and objective, you must relate them to what the other character(s) onstage do or say or feel.

Love Your Character!

Discuss with students how they would go about trying to "love" despicable characters such as Shakespeare's *Richard III* or Beatrice in Paul Zindel's *The Effect of Gamma Rays on Man-in-the-Moon Marigolds*. Talk about the rich depth of character to be discovered in villains and the necessity not to overdo their evil ways.

Spotlight on

Cues and Cue Pickup Picking up cues takes a bit of practice. Demonstrate cue pickup with a volunteer. Then have students pair off and read a two-character scene of their own choosing. After they have worked on their scenes for a time, ask volunteers to share their readings with the class.

Visual Cue

Anton Chekhov's play *The Good Doctor* is a riotous romp in which a woman demands that a bank manager pay compensation for her husband's disability. The play involves a great deal of physical humor.

- Who seems to be in control of this situation?
- If you were playing the man, what tone of voice might you be using?

Spotlight on

Cues and Cue Pickup

Cues are the last few words of the speech that precedes yours. Sometimes a sound or movement will be your cue, but generally you take your cue from someone else's lines. A **cue pickup** occurs the minute you begin saying your lines. To pick up your cues at the correct time, you should learn to take a breath before the other actor has finished speaking, so that you are ready to come in with your line.

Most plays call for quick cue pickup, a tempo that holds audience interest and simulates real-life conversation. Quick cue pickup does *not* mean you should race through your lines. Vary each line according to the ideas and emotions it expresses.

Never anticipate your cue. Picking up the phone before it rings or bursting into tears before you hear a piece of bad news can render your acting ridiculous.

If the script indicates an interrupted sentence—in other words, one actor cutting off another actor's line—give special attention to this timing. If someone is to cut in on your speech, make sure that you have concocted a completion for the line, just in case your scene partner doesn't come in right on cue!

In this scene from *The Good Doctor,* the actors must pick up their cues even in unusual body positions.

Backstage Gossip: She's the Top!

Famed teacher Alvina Krause of Northwestern University hated extra pausing in a scene, which she felt killed the pacing of a play. She used the concept of "topping in" as a way to pick up one's cues. The concept involves starting to speak your line on the last word of the cue lines that come right before yours. Many of her students thought it was quite exciting, but some were perhaps less pleased when Krause would stop a play in performance by standing up in the audience and screaming "TOP IN!"

106 **Unit Three** Creating a Character

PREPARE

Choose a Play and a Character

Get together with several classmates and choose a ten-minute play, a scene from a one-act play, or a scene from a full-length play (your teacher may wish to assign a scene to you). Try to read the entire play to understand its general structure and approach. With your group, discuss the mood, basic action, and climax of the play. DO NOT concentrate on your specific role at this time. Work to understand the play as a whole. Then analyze the characters together. Decide how the scene you have chosen relates to the play as a whole.

Next, each of you should study your individual role in the scene. Identify your character's actions, feelings, and words. Work hard to create a vivid character.

Rehearse the Scene

The next step is to come together again to rehearse the scene. As a group, create basic movements and stage business for the scene. When you are not speaking your lines, listen in character to your fellow actors.

After you have read the scene together a few times, have someone time it to be sure you are not exceeding the ten-minute limit.

Memorize Your Lines

Finally, you must memorize your dialogue in the scene. It's impossible to achieve complete character concentration when you still have the script in your hand. When you and your partners have memorized the scene to the point where it runs smoothly, you are ready to perform.

Listening closely to others helps actors remain in character while allowing the audience to focus on the speaker.

PREPARE

Choose a Play and a Character

Help students decide which plays would be appropriate for them based on their skill level and degree of sophistication. Discuss with students the need to be sensitive to others in their selections. Advise them to avoid choosing plays that some students would consider offensive.

Go over the tips for evaluating the script and the characters in it. Have students break into groups to choose the play and the scene they will present.

As students study their individual roles, be available to answer any questions as to characterization, author's intent, background history, and so on.

Rehearse the Scene

Students may need extra time in or after class to rehearse their scenes. Be available to help them time their scene as well as to discuss any questions regarding interpretation or stage business.

Memorize Your Lines

Remind students to use a tape recorder or ask for a friend or family member's help in memorizing their lines. Then be sure that all members of the group have a place to rehearse their scene together.

Visual Cue

Chief Inspector Foot (of the Yard) tries to crack the case in Tom Stoppard's play *After Magritte* at the Bridewell Theatre in London.

- Which character do you think is Inspector Foot?
- Who seems to be the focal point of this scene, and how do you think he feels about it?
- Who do you think is about to speak next? Why?

PRESENT

Perform Your Group Scene

Give any students who would like to dress in costume the time needed to do so. Be sure that each group has any props they may need ready in the playing area before they begin their scene.

CRITIQUE

Evaluate Your Classmates' Scene

Hand out the Critique Sheet for this project or have students use their own paper. (You may want to use two Critique Sheets, as the students are evaluating both the scene and a particular actor from the scene.)

Go over the questions that students should ask for the group presentation and the individual actor. Note that the critique for the group focuses on how well the actors worked together, picked up cues, and maintained relationships. The questions about the actor's performance focus more on goals and character representation.

PRESENT

Perform Your Group Scene

Choose one person to introduce your scene. This person will also set the scene by providing a bit of background about how this section fits into the larger play. This need not be long; just make sure the audience has enough information to know what's going on. Make sure you have all the necessary props. Once the designated person has introduced the play and given the audience a bit of background, play the scene as you rehearsed it. Stay focused and remain in character throughout.

CRITIQUE

Evaluate Your Classmates' Scene

Evaluate a presentation by one group of classmates. Because the scene represents a team effort, you should evaluate the ensemble as well as the individual performances. Your critique should answer these questions about the group:

- Did the actors work together as an ensemble?
- How did they develop and maintain viable characters?
- What did the actors do to make their characters' motivations and intentions clear?
- Did the actors pick up their cues?
- In what way did the actors establish a consistent mood in the scene?
- Were the relationships between the characters clear?
- Did the actors maintain a consistent style and tone?

Then choose one actor from the scene and evaluate his or her performance using a rating of 1 to 5, with 5 representing "outstanding," 4 representing "very good," 3 representing "good," 2 representing "needs some improvement," and 1 representing "needs much improvement." Use the criteria below to help in your evaluation.

Did the actor

- have a specific goal within the scene?
- listen and respond in character?
- embody the character both physically and vocally?
- have clearly established external traits?
- provide information as to the scene's subtext?

Write a short paragraph explaining why you gave this particular actor the score you did.

Quotable

Acting is not about dressing up.
Acting is about stripping bare.
The whole essence of learning lines is to forget them so you can make them sound like you thought of them that instant.

Glenda Jackson, Actor

Additional Projects

1 Write a prose biography of the character you portrayed in the class project. Include as many facets of the character as possible; for example, you might include family background, level of education, leisure activities, employment status, favorite food, favorite color, most memorable experience, greatest disappointment, and so on. Base your writing on your interpretation of your character within the play.

2 Read a full-length play and write a review of its style, mood, characters, plot, and structure.

3 It is sometimes said that a majority of plots are about one of two things: either a stranger coming to town or a character going on a journey. Write a scene in which three distinctive characters take part in one of these basic plots.

4 Attend a full-length play staged by a professional or amateur group. Write a critique of the play answering the following questions:

- Did the play's theme convey an important idea?
- Did the plot consist of related events that rose to an exciting climax and created a logical conclusion?
- Were the characters true to life? Were they interesting?
- Did the dialogue reveal the characters and enhance the story?
- Was the author's style distinctive?
- Did the audience respond to the play the way you think the author intended them to?
- Did you enjoy the play? Why or why not?

5 Read the scene from *Macbeth* by William Shakespeare found in Unit Eight. Get together with two classmates and choose different parts. Discuss the subtext of this short scene and the emotions and motivations of the characters, as well as its realism and romanticism. Work on the scene together.

Chapter 10 Test

The test for this chapter is available in blackline master form in the Resource Binder, page 42.

For More Information

Books

Harrop, John, and Sabin Epstein, *Acting with Style,* Pearson Allyn & Bacon, 1999.

Jones, Brie, *Improve with Improv: A Guide to Improvisation and Character Development,* Meriwether Publishing, 1993.

Perry, John, *The Encyclopedia of Acting Techniques,* Betterway Publications, 1997.

Stanislavski, Constantine, *Building a Character,* Theatre Arts Books, 2002.

Other Media

Building a Character, VHS, Insight Media, 1988.

Drama: Creating a Character, VHS, Insight Media, 1999.

Substitute Teacher Activities

- Assign the Finding the Subtext Worksheet on page 40 of the Resource Binder.
- Discuss the information concerning Acting Types and Characterization found on pages 551–553 in the Student Handbook.
- Assign one or more of the Additional Projects on this page.
- **Play What's My Subtext?** Students are given written copies of various sentences, such as "Hello, dear, I see you've been shopping again." or "Is that a new tie? What color would you call that?" The actor must pick a sentence and then quickly say the line and convey the subtext. Students must guess what the actor is really saying.

Theatre Then and Now

William Shakespeare and the Elizabethan Drama

William Shakespeare was born in 1564 in Stratford-upon-Avon, England. He married Anne Hathaway, with whom he had three children. He decided to pursue a professional career in the theatre, which prompted his move to London between the years of 1587 and 1588. While in London he became a member of an acting troupe called The Lord Chamberlain's Men. He was part owner of two famous theatres, The Blackfriar's Theatre and the original Globe Theatre. Shakespeare wrote thirty-seven plays, two long poems, and many sonnets. His plays are classified as historical, comedic, and tragic.

The back of the stage of the Globe Theatre contained a tiring house on top for the actors and a multi-leveled façade that was part of the tiring house. The stage was covered by a roof supported by two columns, the underside, called the heavens, was painted with moons, stars, and planets.

Theatre Then and Now

Elizabethan Drama to Epic Theatre

William Shakespeare and the Elizabethan Drama

The Elizabethan period began in 1558 with the coronation of Queen Elizabeth I of England. The period ended with her death in 1602. Although many people think of William Shakespeare (1564–1616) as *the* Elizabethan dramatist, there were a number of other fine playwrights creating work during this period, such as Christopher Marlowe and Ben Johnson. Marlowe (1564–1593) was considered by many of his contemporaries to be Shakespeare's equal. Unfortunately, Marlowe died in a barroom knife fight at the age of twenty-nine.

Because there was no artificial lighting, performances were often held outdoors in the afternoon. Performances that took place at night were lit by huge standing torches. No women were allowed to perform in the plays. Young boys often played female roles as it was thought they could better assume the character and movement of a woman. They would speak in lighter voices and use exaggerated feminine gestures.

Shakespeare's plays featured many highborn or noble characters. The language is rich and layered with images. Low-born characters were often used for comic relief or as the hero's sidekick.

William Shakespeare

The style of acting during Shakespeare's time was much more overblown than actors use today. Actors were not much concerned with rendering subtle emotions. They tended to shout their lines, which in fact was usually necessary given the size of the theatre. The actors concentrated on getting the play's words and ideas across. After all, as Hamlet says, "The play's the thing . . . ."

Many of Shakespeare's plays were first seen in the original Globe Theatre.

For More Information

Books

Bradley, David, *From Text to Performance in the Elizabethan Theatre: Preparing the Play for the Stage,* Cambridge University Press, 1992.

Day, Barry, and John Gielgud, *This Wooden 'O,' Shakespeare's Globe Reborn: Achieving an American Dream,* Limelight Editions, 1998.

Dillon, Janette, *Theatre, Court and City 1595-1610: Drama and Social Space in London,* Cambridge University Press, 2002.

Hodges Walter C., *Globe Restored: Study of the Elizabethan Theatre,* Native American Books, 1990.

Other Media

Performing Shakespeare, VHS, Insight Media, 1990.

Shakespearean Stage Production, VHS, Insight Media, 1966.

Bertolt Brecht and the Epic Theatre

Bertolt Brecht (1898–1956) was a German poet and playwright. His plays were openly political and usually addressed issues such as poverty, war, and class struggle. He rejected the principles of classical drama and realism and did not believe a play needed a dramatic climax. He often employed direct address to the audience as well as songs to comment on the play's action. His theory of drama came to be known as epic theatre. It is best illustrated in his plays *Mother Courage, The Good Woman of Setzuan,* and *The Caucasian Chalk Circle.* Above all, Brecht believed that drama should not try to create the illusion of reality, but should exist on its own terms. Rather than attempting to persuade the audience of a play's *reality,* Brecht tried to distance viewers. In this way, he thought that the audience would think for themselves.

Achieving this type of alienation effect, as it came to be called, required a highly stylized performance method. Brecht believed in the idea of argument as opposed to plot. Traditional plots, Brecht believed, attempted to implicate the viewer in the action as opposed to allowing the viewer to remain an outside spectator. In Brecht's view, the epic theatre's detached methods aroused the viewer to take action—to take a side in the argument. Brecht's views on characterization are perhaps best illustrated by this quote: "The actor has to discard whatever means he has learnt of getting the audience to identify itself with the characters which he plays . . . . At no moment must he go so far as to be wholly transformed into the character played . . . ."

Bertolt Brecht

A classic of epic theatre, Brecht's *Mother Courage* depicts the lengths to which people will go to survive during wartime.

Chapter 10 Character Development 111

Bertolt Brecht and the Epic Theatre

Author, director, teacher, and performer, Paul Sills is the creator of Story Theatre, a storytelling venue that has appeared on and off Broadway. Story Theatre is a descendent of Brecht's Epic Theatre. Sills applied the concept of stepping out of the play and speaking directly to the audience.

ACTivity Have the students repeat their group scene. At any time, one of the actors can step out of the scene, face the audience and speak directly to them about what is going to happen next in story-theatre style. Or add a third actor who narrates the scene as a commentator might narrate a sporting event.

For More Information

Books

Brecht, Bertolt, Tom Kuhn, ed., *Brecht on Art and Politics,* Methuen Publishing, 2003.

Brecht, Bertolt, John Willett, trans., *Brecht on Theatre: The Development of an Aesthetic,* Hill & Wang, 1994.

Ewen, Frederic, *Bertolt Brecht: His Life, His Art and His Times,* Citadel Press, 1992.

Sills, Paul, *Story Theatre: Four Shows,* Applause Books, 2000.

Other Media

Bertolt Brecht, VHS, Insight Media, 1996.

Brecht Practice Pieces, VHS, Insight Media, 1964.

Brecht on Stage, VHS, Insight Media, 1992.

Galileo: Bertolt Brecht, VHS, Insight Media, 1985.

Chapter 11

Dramatic Roles

In this chapter students will be introduced to a brief history of dramatic literature and how to prepare for a role in a dramatic scene.

Objectives

1 to learn something of the history and range of dramatic roles

2 to understand three types of dramatic literature

3 to use imagination and memory to stimulate the emotional responses necessary to play a dramatic scene

4 to write a short dramatic scene with detailed characters

National Standards

Chapter 11 meets these National Theatre Standards:

Proficient 1a, 2a, 2b, 7c, 7d

Advanced 2d, 2e, 7f, 7g, 7h

Project Specs

For this chapter it is important that you choose whether to guide your students towards using personal stories to create their short dramatic plays, or whether you want them to create more from fiction or imagination.

On Your Feet

Show, Don't Tell Demonstrate how you would capture the emotion of a tragic event, such as the destruction of the World Trade Center in New York, using only one line. Ask students to comment on your posture and facial expression.

Chapter 11 Dramatic Roles

Many actors believe that dramatic roles are the real "meat" of acting. Plays that treat their subject seriously are placed into three broadly defined categories—tragedy, social drama, and melodrama. While exploring each of these dramatic forms, you will acquire the tools to take on serious dramatic roles yourself.

Project Specs

Project Description For this assignment, you and a classmate will write and perform a three- to five-minute dramatic scene.

Purpose to use strong characterization and controlled emotional intensity

Materials an outline of your scene or the Dramatic Roles Activity Sheet your teacher provides

Theatre Terms

antagonist
catharsis
melodrama
protagonist
regional accent
social drama
tragedy
tragic flaw

On Your Feet

Think about a difficult, sad, or dramatic event that happened to a friend or family member. Capture the emotions that event holds for you in one sentence. Practice saying the sentence out loud, taking on the character of your friend or family member. Create a specific posture and facial expression for the character, and then repeat the line until you can "hear" the person on whom you based the character.

Donald Sinden creates one of the most dramatic roles of all time as the title character in *Othello*.

Theatre Terms

antagonist the character who is the opposing force to the protagonist, or main character

catharsis the sense of calm that comes after experiencing intense emotions

melodrama a play that focuses more on cliff-hanging action and intense emotions than on character development

protagonist the main character in a work of literature

regional accent the sound of speech from a particular region

social drama a play that focuses on serious, real-life problems of ordinary people

tragedy a drama in which a protagonist struggles against some force, usually making a sacrifice before going down in defeat

tragic flaw a weakness of personality that ultimately causes a character's destruction

PREVIEW

The Elements of Drama

Dramatic productions are categorized in three ways: as tragedy, social (or serious) drama, or melodrama. Each type has its own unique characteristics and each requires its own set of acting skills.

Greek Tragedy

Considered to be the highest form of drama, **tragedy** magnifies the intensity of profound human emotions to tell the story of a person who achieves a sense of nobility by means of unswerving sacrifice and/or suffering. In classic Greek tragedy, the **protagonist** (or main character) struggles with a particular problem or an opposing force (the **antagonist**) and eventually goes down in defeat—usually death—but not before achieving an aura of dignity. Because of the depth of a tragedy's emotion, the audience tends to experience horror, pity, and deep sadness, which are typically followed by a **catharsis,** the sense of calm that comes from purging such emotions.

Also typical in Greek tragedies is a tragic hero who comes into conflict with the gods. The audience always knew the plot of these classic myths, but was eager to see how a particular playwright would handle the relationship between the gods and the hero. Violence, as such, was never witnessed by the audience in these tragedies. The chorus or a messenger would report the violent action. The tragedies of Sophocles (c. 495-406 B.C.), such as *Oedipus Rex* and *Antigone,* are perfect examples of classic Greek tragedy.

Shakespeare's Tragedies

The Elizabethan playwrights ignored the classical tragic form, for the most part. The tragedies of William Shakespeare (1564-1616) often focused on a protagonist at odds with himself. This often highborn hero has a **tragic flaw,** a weakness of character, which ultimately brings about his or her own destruction. Shakespeare and his contemporaries often mixed comedy into their tragedies; and music, song,

PREVIEW

The Elements of Drama

ACTivity Ask various students to read pivotal soliloquies from *Hamlet, Othello, Julius Caesar, Macbeth,* or other of Shakespeare's tragedies. Discuss the students' interpretations of the scenes as they relate to each character's tragic flaw.

In Shakespeare's *Othello,* a powerful man is lead astray by an insidious friend and his own false pride. Ask students to use their critical viewing skills to answer the questions below.

- What does the actor's expression tell you about the character?
- How would you describe the actor's costume?

Resource Binder

- Dramatic Roles Activity Sheet, p. 43
- Using Dialects Worksheet, p. 44
- Critique Sheet: Dramatic Scene, p. 45
- Dramatic Roles Test, p. 46

Handbook Connections
pages 551-554, 559-560, 569-570

To Have on Hand

- One-act plays for the students to use as inspiration or guides for the plays they write, such as the ten-minute plays published by Smith and Kraus, Inc. under the title *Humana Festival Plays*
- Recording device
- Stopwatch to time student performances
- Soliloquies from Shakespeare's tragedies
- Scenes from social dramas

Serious Drama Today

Read scenes from contemporary social dramas of the last fifty years, including *All My Sons, Look Back in Anger, Spinning into Butter*, and *Angels in America.* Discuss the issues raised in these plays with students.

ACTivity Advanced Students Have pairs or groups of students choose a scene from a social drama they admire and perform the scene for the class. Ask the class to discuss the social issues addressed in the scene.

Building a Dramatic Character

Discuss with students how they would order the four elements in terms of difficulty. Is it harder for an actor to convey motivation than emotional intensity? Why or why not?

Visual Cue

Arthur Miller's *The Crucible* was written in 1953, during the time of the McCarthy hearings, in which many Americans were accused of and tried for being Communists. The play follows events during the famous witch hunts in 17th-century Salem, Massachusetts.

- These two people are husband and wife. What do their costumes tell you about them?
- What do their postures and expressions tell you about their relationship?

and dance were sometimes part of a scene as well. Dialogue that was intellectual or meaningful would be presented in iambic pentameter (ten syllables with five stresses to the line); the uneducated or foolish often spoke in prose. The tragic universe of Shakespeare's plays often highlights a disrupted life that seeks to regain order within a spiritual context. *Hamlet, Macbeth,* and *King Lear* are fine examples of Shakespearean tragedy.

Liam Neeson plays the flawed but courageous John Proctor in Arthur Miller's *The Crucible.*

Serious Drama Today

Of course, actors are still taking on the plays of the Greeks and Elizabethans, but there are many contemporary plays that investigate issues similar to those in the tragedies of the past. This serious drama, also called **social drama,** tackles subjects that do not fall strictly into the category of tragedy—the everyday struggles and failures of ordinary folk in the hard-edged landscape of the 20th and 21st centuries. Arthur Miller's heroes, in such plays as *All My Sons* and *Death of a Salesman,* struggle to maintain their dignity and humanity while acting in immoral ways. Lawrence and Lee's *Inherit the Wind* and Rebecca Gilman's *Boy Gets Girl* also explore important contemporary issues. In *Waiting for Godot* and *Endgame,* Samuel Beckett's antiheroes come to realize the modern world is meaningless and chaotic.

All of these dramatists point out the problems people face today, without necessarily suggesting solutions to them.

Building a Dramatic Character

There are four essential elements when it comes to acting in a tragedy or a serious drama.

The actor must convey:

1. strong characterization
2. emotional intensity
3. simplicity of objective
4. motivation

Backstage Gossip: You're Not Serious!

Having written a string of hit comedies, Philip Barry tried his hand at serious, socially significant dramas. After one of these failed, director and critic Harold Clurman said to drama critic Brooks Atkinson: "We should encourage him to remain superficial."

from *Broadway Anecdotes* by Peter Hay

In serious and tragic plays, the characters are usually fully drawn individuals who have one dominant trait that the actor must project. Hamlet is indecisive; Othello is jealous; Anne Sullivan in *The Miracle Worker* is stubborn and determined. The protagonist of just about any tragedy or serious play is in some definable way very impressive. This is the result of not only the character's indomitable spirit but also because he or she has the courage to stand up against a great obstacle. It should go without saying that the antagonist must also be played with strength to provide an adequate conflict for the protagonist. Keep this in mind as you prepare to write your scene.

Gay Nineties melodramas such as *Lily, the Felon's Daughter* feature stock characters such as Lord Monty, played by Kent Streed, a suitor with slicked-down hair and an offering of roses.

Using Emotion

The intense emotions called for in dramatic roles must be portrayed with utter conviction and sincerity while maintaining the poise necessary to put the play across. To create these emotions, you may need to use emotional recall. This is the process by which you use the memory of emotional incidents from your own past and transfer them to the similarly emotional situation your character is in. To do this, you must focus on the details of the past event and try to visualize and feel the emotion all over again. Then try to create that same emotion in the character. (See Chapter 2 for more on recall.)

Melodrama

Melodrama is a type of play that focuses more on cliff-hanging action and tugs on the heartstrings than on character development or society's real problems. The purpose of a **melodrama** is to create great suspense and excitement in

Visual Cue

Tom Taggart's play *Lily, the Felon's Daughter* is a classic American melodrama of the Victorian era. Even today audiences continue to boo the villain and cheer the hero while the piano plays a rollicking tune.

- How would you describe Lord Monty?
- Do you think Monty is a hero or a villain?

Using Emotion

You may want to have students reread pages 14–15 in which recall is discussed. Then ask them to re-create an emotion in their minds. Suggest that students imagine how they would feel in similar circumstances and go from there. Volunteers may wish to share this emotion with the class.

Melodrama

Though melodrama is not as popular as it once was, many contemporary plays are in some ways derived from this early form. Read excerpts from the melodrama *The Bad Seed* to the students. Then compare it to the Gay Nineties melodrama *Lily, the Felon's Daughter.* Discuss the heightened emotions, simple plots, and one-dimensional characters.

If it is difficult for the students to grasp the idea of the melodrama, show them a silent film video or DVD with dramatic content such a D. W. Griffith's *Broken Blossoms*, Erich von Stroheim's *Greed*, or F. W. Murnau's *Sunrise*. Be sure you discuss the fact that from our contemporary perspective these films may seem highly melodramatic, but give proper credit to the fact that in the hands of these skilled early directors, the stories are still very moving and the film work quite compelling.

ACTivity **Advanced Students**
Ask these students to analyze and write a short dramatic scene in all three styles of drama: tragedy (Greek or Shakespearean), social drama, and melodrama.

ACTivity What contemporary music sounds might be associated with the three types of drama? An example might be Janis Joplin as Greek drama, Tom Waits or Eminem as social drama, and Loretta Lynn as melodrama. Ask students to bring in music that they feel has the sound, feel, and texture of each type and share it with the class.

Using Regional Accents

Discuss with the class the variations in how English is spoken in America. Consider the South, the East, the West, and the Midwest, as well as differences between city speakers and rural speakers. Suggest that, in general, urban dwellers speak with a quicker pace and rural speakers may have a more nasal twang. Note the drawl, and the light, lingering *AH* instead of long *I* used in the South, and the loss of the *r* sound in certain areas, such as Boston (where *car* is pronounced *cAH*). Tell them to resist any temptation to fall back on stereotypes when creating a character from a region with which they have limited knowledge.

ACTivity Have the class work on their British accents by practicing the broader vowel range and higher pitch of the typical speaker of British English. Ask students to practice Eliza Doolittle's "The rain in Spain falls mainly in the plain. In Hampshire hurricanes hardly happen." And then add "I know you are right, Sir Henry," first in standard English, then in Cockney English. The chart below should help.

Standard Sound
face pronounced fAs
slow pronounced slO
ice pronounced Is
right pronounced rIt
help pronounced help

Cockney Sound
face pronounced fIs
slow pronounced sLOU
ice pronounced OIs
right pronounced roYIt
help pronounced elp

the audience. It was very popular in the United States in the early 1800s and is still performed by small theatre groups and high school drama groups across the country. Most melodramas have a happy ending. Examples of contemporary melodramas include Frederick Knott's *Dial M for Murder,* Agatha Christie's *The Mousetrap,* and Maxwell Anderson's *The Bad Seed.*

A subcategory of melodrama are the Gay Nineties melodramas (meaning they were written and first performed during the 1890s). These plays have exaggerated values of right and wrong. They feature such stock types as the mustachioed villain and the sweet, innocent heroine. Though modern audiences find these plays humorous, in their time such works also aroused tears.

Using Regional Accents

A **regional accent** is the particular sound of speech of a region. Inexperienced actors are not usually cast in roles for which an accent is necessary, but even actors with plenty of experience can be frustrated by tricky speech patterns associated with particular places.

If you are cast in a role that requires you to speak with an accent of a certain region, you can, of course, get a book on the subject, but a better choice would be to listen to a native speaker, either in person or on tape.

To do a credible accent, you will need to develop your ear. For example, imagine that you have been cast as the cockney flower girl, Eliza Doolittle, in *Pygmalion* by George Bernard Shaw (or the musical version of that play, *My Fair Lady*). You might get a videotape of the play, or you might find a tape that includes a lower-class urban English accent. Listen for specific sounds in the accent and think about how they differ from your normal speech. You will need to figure out the phonetic differences so that you can recreate them consistently. In fact, consistency is the most crucial element when it comes to developing a believable accent. When you perform, it's important to give the suggestion of the accent rather than concerning yourself with making every sound recognizable as being from a particular place. The important thing is that you be clearly understood.

Most actors take on the acquisition of an accent privately, not during rehearsal time. However, professional theatres sometimes employ coaches to help the actors in this regard. These experts work with the cast to hone and perfect their speech and create the kind of consistent accents that audiences expect.

Notes

Here's How
To Stay in Control

When acting in an intense dramatic play, you may feel the need to drain yourself completely during the climactic scene. Resist this impulse! To present the strongest characterization possible, you need to maintain control. Always hold something in reserve. Some acting teachers suggest that you "give it ninety percent–and hold back ten percent." If you do this, the audience will think you're acting with abandon, when in reality you will be in complete control–able to stay focused and aware.

And don't turn on those water works, either. Many young actors feel that they must work themselves up to tears to get the audience to feel the emotion of a sad scene. But good actors know that succumbing completely to tears can have a distancing effect on the audience. Uncontrolled tears can also lead to inaudibility. The better choice for an actor is almost always to work against breaking into tears. An actor struggling against falling apart creates tension; that tension draws the audience in.

PREPARE

Ready, Set, Write!

What would you consider to be one of the most tragic events that could happen to someone? You will have the chance to dramatize your idea in this presentation.

First you will work with a partner to brainstorm your scene. The suggestions on the following page may help you. Then improvise back and forth, and outline the scene and some of the dialogue for both characters. You may wish to use a tape recorder so that you can remember your best lines. When you have completed the outline of your scene, go over it and reshape it so that each moment is clear and distinct.

Ready, Set, Act!

Now rehearse your scene. Create basic movement, and critique each other's performance as you go through the script. You may find that some of the lines you wrote do not sound quite right as you rehearse. Edit these lines accordingly.

Remember to employ emotional recall and sense memory to help you fully realize the situation. Concentrate on what your character *does,* rather than on the specific emotional content. Stay in character, focus on the objectives, and respond to your partner. Time your scene to be sure it remains within the three- to five-minute time range.

Backstage Gossip: Sense Memory

Stella Adler's teaching method was Stanislavian but it led her to major differences with Lee Strasberg and the method as practiced at the Actors Studio. When he died in 1982 she spoke to her class.... "A man of the theatre died last night," she intoned, having asked her class to stand for a moment of silence. "It will take a hundred years before the harm that man has done to the art of acting can be corrected."

from *Ned Sherrin's Theatrical Anecdotes*

PREPARE

Ready, Set, Write

Encourage students to use their own ideas to find a subject for their dramatic scene, but ask them to go over it with you before they proceed. Try to have some type of recording device available for students who wish to use one.

Here's How

To really understand control, this might be a good time to have interested students experience the dramatic equivalent of being out of control by taking on a bit of Shakespeare. Ask students to read the lines below from *A Midsummer Night's Dream.* These lines are spoken in full bombast by Bottom, who is acting the character Pyramus in the play *Pyramus and Thisbe.* His approach knows not the word *control.*

Approach ye Furies fell!
O Fates, come, come
Cut thread and thrum;
Quail, crush, conclude, and quell. . .

[Tell students to read this line with an awareness of the force of the alliteration.]

Thus die I, thus, thus, thus.
Now am I dead.
Now am I fled;
My soul is in the sky.
Tongue lose thy light;
Moon take thy flight.
Now die, die, die, die, die.

[Advise students that as they perform the death to remember that Bottom, as Pyramus, would not hold back in any way. This death would involve lots of swooning, falling, getting up, dropping again, writhing, jerking, and so on.]

When students have performed this short scene, discuss the process, the outcomes, and the limitations of this type of acting.

PRESENT

Act in a Dramatic Scene

Remind the students presenting their scenes that the "moment before" not only allows them to focus and relax before they begin, it also gives the audience a chance to settle down and focus. Tell them that they should not begin a presentation until they have the attention of the entire audience.

CRITIQUE

Evaluate Your Classmates' Dramatic Scene

Before they begin their evaluations, let the students in the audience discuss each scene. How did the presentation make them feel? Did the scene elicit in them feelings of empathy, catharsis, or agitation? Was this what the playwright intended to elicit? Encourage give-and-take between the audience and the writers/presenters.

Theatre Journal

Use the following as an additional or substitute prompt.

Turn your short account of a newspaper event into a monologue. Act out the part of a witness to the event telling the audience the important details about what happened.

PRESENT

Act in a Dramatic Scene

When either your own or your partner's name is called, give the outline of your scene or the Dramatic Roles Activity Sheet to your teacher before you begin your presentation. Then introduce your scene briefly. You only need to give the audience enough information to allow them to understand the basic situation.

Take a moment before you begin. This "moment before" is a handy tool for actors. It allows you to focus more completely before you launch into a scene, and it allows the audience time to settle down.

Perform your scene. Stay focused and remain in character throughout. When you are finished, take a brief bow and return to your seat.

Suggestions for Dramatic Scenes

- A mother learns that her only child is critically injured.
- A brilliant painter finds that she is going blind.
- A young man about to be married finds out he has a terminal disease.
- A father is sentenced to life in prison for a crime he did not commit.
- A woman with a proud family background discovers that her brother has committed a serious crime.

CRITIQUE

Evaluate Your Classmates' Scene

Evaluate a presentation by one pair of your classmates using a scale of 1 to 5, with 5 being "outstanding" and 1 being "needs much improvement." Your evaluation should be confined to the performance, not the writing. Ask yourself these questions:

- How were the presenters able to convey the drama of the scene?
- How well did the actors convey their characters' objectives?
- In what way did the actors' movements and gestures impact the scene?
- Did the actors stay in character, listen to each other, and respond throughout the scene?

Write a short paragraph explaining why you gave this pair the score you did.

Theatre Journal

Skim through the daily newspaper. Find a story that has serious elements, such as a fire, a car accident, or some other life-or-death incident. In your journal, write a short account of the event from the point of view of someone either directly or peripherally involved. Try to think about the events as they might seem to that person.

From the Field: Just Do It

The playwright Maria Irene Fornes teaches young playwrights to write their plays in a "trance state." Giving them meditation exercises first, with suggestions of what to be thinking about that will help create the play, she then asks them to sit down and write for twenty minutes without any pauses to evaluate or think. Just write. She has written her plays this way.

Spotlight on

The Worst Romeo Ever

Over the course of history, plenty of actors have made a mess of Shakespeare's lines. But many theatre historians agree that Robert Coates was perhaps the worst offender. Coates (1772–1848) had no talent but plenty of money—enough to finance vanity productions to star in. He produced *Romeo and Juliet* often and, to the utter despair of his various Juliets, he always played Romeo. Audiences loved Coates or, more accurately, they loved to use him for target practice by lobbing rotten fruits and vegetables at him during the show. In the scene in which Romeo discovers that Juliet has killed herself, audiences would jeer at Coates and yell such comments as "Why don't YOU die?" The critics weren't kind to Coates either. Reviews of his performances were often descriptions of the rioting audience and the flying foodstuffs.

Robert Coates

Notes

Spotlight on

The Worst Romeo Ever In his 1995-1996 diary, *My Name Escapes Me*, Alec Guinness uses his eye for observation as well as his own reflections to describe a life well lived. In the book, Guinness, who died in 2000, writes of enjoying Baz Luhrmann's film adaptation of William Shakespeare's *Romeo and Juliet*, adding ruefully that the worst Romeo ever was, in fact, "none other than me."

John Gielgud also struggled with the part of Romeo when he and Laurence Olivier alternated the roles of Mercutio and Romeo. Says Gielgud, "I was directing and I bullied him a great deal about his verse-speaking, which he admitted himself, he wasn't happy about. I was rather showy about mine, and fancied myself very much a verse-speaker, and I became very mannered in consequence. But I was so jealous, because not only did he play Romeo with tremendous energy, but he knew just how to cope with it and select. I remember Ralph Richardson saying to me, 'But you see, when Larry leans against the balcony and looks up, then you have the whole scene immediately.'

"Because he had this wonderful plastique, which is absolutely unselfconscious, like a lithe panther or something. I had been draping myself around the stage for weeks, thinking myself very romantic as Romeo, and I was rather baffled and dismayed that I couldn't achieve the same effect at all."

Chapter 11 Test

The test for this chapter is available in blackline master form in the Resource Binder, page 46.

For More Information

Books

Blumenfield, Robert H., *Accents: A Manual for Actors,* Limelight Editions, 2002.

Brook, Peter, *The Open Door,* Theatre Communications Group, 1995.

Perry, John, *The Encyclopedia of Acting Techniques,* Betterway Publications, 1997.

O'Neill, Cecily, and Alan Lambert, *Drama Structures: A Practical Handbook for Teachers,* Heinemann, 1990.

Shapiro, Mel, *An Actor Performs,* Wadsworth Publishing, 1996.

Waxberg, Charles, *The Actor's Script: Script Analysis for Performers,* Heinemann, 1998.

Zucker, Carole, ed., *In the Company of Actors: Reflections on the Craft of Acting,* Routledge, 2000.

Other Media

Acting with Accent, Audio, Insight Media, 1979.

Acting in Tragedy with Brian Cox, VHS, Insight Media, 1992.

Additional Projects

1. Dramatize a dramatic event from your life or from your family history.
2. Improvise serious group scenes that build to a climax. Your scenes should include classical, contemporary, realistic, and nonrealistic elements. Here are some suggestions for sample scenes:
   - A group of miners working underground senses something is wrong. As they prepare to go up, rocks begin to cave in on them.
   - A group of striking workers are demonstrating outside an office building. They see that other workers have arrived and are crossing the picket line. Shouting ensues.
   - A political speaker is heckled at an outdoor rally until bedlam breaks loose.
   - A bus driver picks up various passengers. One woman appears to have wings. A man is able to read the minds of other passengers.
3. Write a short dramatic monologue (a long speech given by one character) and present it to the class.
4. Memorize either the monologue from *Saint Joan* by George Bernard Shaw or the monologue from *The Janitor* by August Wilson found in Unit Eight. Present the monologue to the class. Think about the accent you might use to convey your character.

Substitute Teacher Activities

Here are some suggestions for the days that you will be out of the classroom.

- Assign the Using Dialects Worksheet on page 44 of the Resource Binder.
- Discuss the information concerning Acting Types and Characterization found on pages 551–553 and Accents found on page 569 in the Student Handbook.
- Assign one or more of the Additional Projects on this page.
- **Play Name that Character.** Students act out a character in fiction, film, or television by moving, gesturing, and speaking like that character. Classmates must guess who the person is.

Master of the Craft

Kenneth Branagh

Born in 1960 in Belfast, Ireland, actor Kenneth Branagh was the second of three children born to a working-class family. When he was still a boy, his family moved to England. At the age of fifteen, a crucial event took place in Branagh's life: He saw English theatre legend Derek Jacobi play Hamlet. From then on, he knew he wanted to be an actor.

At eighteen he was accepted into one of the best theatre schools in the world—the Royal Academy of Dramatic Art. Once out of school he was immediately cast in a play on the West End (London's version of Broadway). The Royal Shakespeare Company subsequently hired him into its repertory company, and at the age of twenty-three, he took on the pivotal role of Prince Hal in Shakespeare's *Henry V.* He became an immediate sensation, winning many awards for his performance.

Kenneth Branagh, as Hamlet, with Kate Winslet.

In 1987, Branagh and a friend started a theatre company of their own, the Renaissance Theatre Company. Branagh's productions of the Shakespeare plays *Twelfth Night* and *Much Ado About Nothing* won rave reviews. Then Branagh fulfilled one of his many ambitions by playing Hamlet. Shortly thereafter, in 1989, he directed and starred in a film version of *Henry V.* The success of the film brought Branagh unexpected international fame.

He was quickly scooped up to make several more films.

Kenneth Branagh has, of course, had some failures along the way, but he is an artist whose ambition is evenly balanced with his great talent. He continues to challenge himself as an artist, acting in and directing film, television, and theatre. In 2001, he directed a West End hit, *The Play What I Wrote,* which won multiple Olivier Awards (the English equivalent of the Tony Award). The play opened on Broadway in 2003.

Branagh as Prince Hal in *Henry V.*

Quotable

I said I'm a kid from Brooklyn, and I'm not supposed to be able to do this [Othello]. Then Kenneth Branagh said, 'I'm an Irish kid from Belfast, and I'm not supposed to be able to do this either.' But Shakespeare was an actor first. Those words were written to be spoken. And once you do that a couple of times, you think, 'That's pretty! I want to say that again! Where can I get more?'

Laurence Fishburne, Actor

Master of the Craft

Masters Past and Present

ACTivity Make a large class collage of masters of the craft of acting. Students bring in pictures of actors and actresses they feel are masters at dramatic acting. They can be cut from magazines, photocopied from books, or printed from online sources. Ask them to also cut out or bring in typed words that describe qualities that make these people masters. On a large piece of cardboard, create a collage with the pictures and quotes.

For More Information

Books

Branagh, Kenneth, *Beginning,* Chatto & Windus, 1989.

Crowl, Samuel, *Shakespeare at the Cineplex: The Kenneth Branagh Era,* Ohio University Press, 2003.

Shuttleworth, Ian, and Shuttan Leworth, *Ken & Em: A Biography of Kenneth Branagh and Emma Thompson,* St. Martin's Press, 1995.

Theatre Then and Now

A Role for All Eras

Other actors who have played Hamlet through the ages include John Gielgud, Richard Burton, David Wagner, and even Sarah Bernhard. Film stars who have played the role include Mel Gibson and Leonardo DiCaprio.

For More Information

Books

Proctor, Bryan W., *The Life of Edmund Kean,* Arno Press, 1970.

Shakespeare, William, *Hamlet: A Parallel Text Edition,* Perfection Learning, 2003.

Shakespeare, William, Harold Jenkins, ed., *Hamlet: Playgoer's Edition,* Arden, 1997.

Shattuck, Charles Harlen, *The Hamlet of Edwin Booth,* University of Illinois Press, 1969.

Smith, Gene A., *American Gothic: The Story of America's Legendary Theatrical Family: Junius, Edwin, and John Wilkes Booth,* Touchstone Books, 1993.

Other Media

Hamlet C/WIN/US, CD-ROM, Shakespeare Interact, AAA, 1997.

Hamlet: Film and Stage Scenes, VHS, Insight Media, 2001.

Theatre Then and Now

A Role for All Eras: Hamlet, Prince of Denmark

For more than 300 years, actors have coveted the role of Hamlet, the brilliant, angry, indecisive title character of Shakespeare's tragedy. The role's richness, humor, and emotional depth have challenged generations of actors.

Edmund Kean (1787–1833) was the leading English actor of the early 1800s. He specialized in tragic roles and was best known for his many portrayals of Hamlet. He had many opportunities to sharpen his skills in this role—he first played it when he was only fourteen years old. Extremely charismatic, Kean brought romanticism to every role. His acting was once described by a critic as "quietly imploding before his audience." The great poet Coleridge said of Kean, "Seeing him act was like reading Shakespeare by flashes of lightning." Kean's reputation as a great interpreter of Shakespeare was assured. His excessive drinking and wild lifestyle earned him quite another reputation, however, and eventually it took its toll. He died in his mid-forties.

Edwin Booth (1833–1893) "An actor is a sculptor who carves in snow." So said Edwin Booth with regard to the fleeting nature of the theatre: Once a scene is played, it is gone forever.

Edwin Booth played the role of Hamlet for a remarkable 100 consecutive nights. The melancholy Dane was a role for which Booth's appearance, voice, and bearing were ideally suited. Slender and darkly handsome, Booth possessed a voice that was both musical and tempered with a natural air of reserve. His acting style, quieter than most other actors of his day, became increasingly sensitive and subdued.

His career was tarnished in 1865 when his brother, John Wilkes Booth, assassinated President Lincoln. After that, Edwin did not reappear onstage until January 1866, when he again played Hamlet. The audience's applause after this performance showed their conviction that the glory of one Booth brother had not been eclipsed by the infamy of the other. Edwin Booth's final stage appearance was in Brooklyn, New York, as Hamlet in 1891.

Backstage Gossip: Who's in Charge?

William Macready (1793-1873) was an actor with a notoriously violent temper. During rehearsals for *Hamlet*, he angered the actor playing King Claudius, and, on opening night, the latter chose to die in the same spot on stage that the Prince of Denmark had selected as his own. "Die farther upstage!" Macready whispered. No answer. "Die farther upstage, sir!" Macready demanded more loudly. The corpse sat up and, to the audience's delight, said, "I'm King here, and I'll die where I damned well please!"

Sir Laurence Olivier (1907–1989). "If I wasn't an actor, I think I'd have gone mad. You have to have extra voltage, some extra temperament to reach certain heights. Art is a little bit larger than life, and I think you probably need a little touch of madness." These are the words of legendary English actor Laurence Olivier. He began his career in 1926 as a member of the Birmingham Repertory Theatre. He was known for his physical athleticism and his dazzling vocal ability and range—particularly in Shakespearean roles. There is a famous story that shines a light on Olivier's acting technique. While making the 1976 film *Marathon Man,* Olivier found out that his costar, American actor Dustin Hoffman, had been preparing for his role by going without food and sleep. Hoffman wanted to look and feel just like the character he was playing—a torture victim. Olivier, mystified, asked Hoffman, "My dear boy, why don't you just *act*?" Olivier's film version of *Hamlet,* which he starred in and directed, is available on videotape.

Laurence Olivier as Hamlet in 1948.

It won Oscars for Best Picture and Best Actor in 1948. In 1970, Olivier was made a lord, the first member of the theatrical profession to receive such an honor. Olivier's extraordinary ability to illuminate the words and ideas of Shakespeare won him a well-deserved place in theatre and film history.

Edwin Booth as Hamlet, the "Melancholy Dane."

Sir Laurence Olivier

It has been said that to prepare to play Hamlet every night Sir Laurence Olivier would try to push down the walls of the theatre with all of his might. When he was at the height of physical and emotional frustration, he would enter the stage as Hamlet.

Other Cultures, Other Times

A Hamlet for Russia

In 1971, at Moscow's Taganka Theater, a production of *Hamlet* premiered that ran for over ten years, ending with the early death of Vladimir Vysotsky, the poet-singer-actor who played Hamlet. This production was innovative in its use of film montage as well as the ever-present image of a moving curtain. More important was the spiritual and cultural influence Vysotsky's performance gave the play.

Before playing Hamlet, Vysotsky was already a popular proponent of conscience and freedom, and he was much loved throughout the country. When he died, many of his countrymen participated in a spontaneous memorial service.

For More Information

Books

Lewis, Roger, *The Real Life of Laurence Olivier,* Applause Books, 2000.

Mer, Nathan, *Vladimir Vysotsky: 1938–1980,* International University Press, 1991.

Olivier, Laurence, *On Acting,* Simon & Schuster, 1986.

Olivier, Laurence, *Confessions of an Actor: Laurence Olivier, an Autobiography,* Simon & Schuster, 1985.

Spoto, Donald, *Laurence Olivier: A Biography,* Harper, 1993.

Other Media

For an audio file of Vladimir Vysotsky singing go to *www.pnpi.spb.ru/art/vys.wav.*

Backstage Gossip: A Peripheral Actor

Laurence Olivier talks about creating the role of Richard III.

I began to build up a character, a characterization. I'm afraid I do work mostly from the outside in. I usually collect a lot of details, a lot of characteristics, and find a creature swimming about somewhere in the middle of them . . . . Some people start from the inside, some people start from the periphery. I would say, at a guess, that Alec Guinness is what we would call a peripheral actor. I think I'm the same. The actor who starts from the inside is more likely to find himself in the parts he plays, than to find the parts in himself.

from *Theatrical Anecdotes* by Peter Hay

Chapter 11 Dramatic Roles **123**

Chapter 12

Comic Roles

In this chapter students will learn about several different comedy genres and some proven comedy techniques for the stage. They will practice writing and performing their own comic monologue.

Objectives

1 to recognize and perform different genres of theatrical comedy

2 to experiment with age-old comic techniques for the stage and try out their effectiveness

3 to understand the difference between playing comedy and drama

4 to create a comic character and then write and perform a monologue for that character

National Standards

Chapter 12 meets these National Theatre Standards:

Proficient 1a, 2a, 7b, 7c, 7d, 8a, 8d
Advanced 1b, 7e, 7h, 8g

Project Specs

Talk to students about the quote from Lynn Fontanne on page 127. Would they agree?

Show, Don't Tell Pick a selection that you think would illustrate how a passage can be played for drama or for laughs. Read the passage with dramatic intent and ask students to comment. Then read the same passage in a comedic way and discuss the result with students.

On Your Feet

Ask volunteers to read their funny stories to the class before your work on this chapter begins. Return to these stories later and ask students how they might change them in light of what they have learned.

Chapter
12 Comic Roles

It is said that tragedy is when you fall down the stairs and comedy is when someone else does. It's not that we enjoy seeing others suffer–it's that we know how to laugh at ourselves–after it stops hurting. Good comedy requires perspective: The comic actor presents a character's misfortune while providing just enough emotional distance to let us laugh. It's a juggling act, but when it works, it's magic.

Project Specs

Project Description You will write and perform a comic monologue of three to five minutes in length.

Purpose to develop a sense of comic presentation and timing

Materials a list of character traits that describe your character or the Comic Roles Activity Sheet your teacher provides

Theatre Terms

burlesque
comedy of manners
farce
high comedy
hold
low comedy
middlebrow comedy
parody
rule of three
satire
travesty

On Your Feet

Think of a funny story from your childhood. It can be an actual experience or something funny you once read or saw. Practice telling the story, then tell it to a friend and ask for feedback as to what the friend found funny.

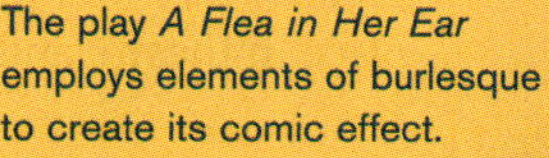

The play *A Flea in Her Ear* employs elements of burlesque to create its comic effect.

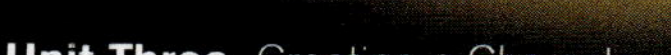

Theatre Terms

burlesque physical comedy that uses exaggeration

comedy of manners comedy that makes fun of upper-class pretentiousness

farce physical comedy that exaggerates situations until they are hardly believable

high comedy comedy that pokes fun at political situations and social standards

hold the pause required after a character delivers a funny line

low comedy comedy that is physical and sometimes vulgar

middlebrow comedy comedy based on plot and sentimental situations

parody to imitate in a humorous way

rule of three the belief that comedic routines designed to make the audience laugh are only funny three times in a row

satire comedy that makes fun of people to try to change their foolish behavior

travesty a humorous imitation

PREVIEW

What's So Funny?

No two people have funny bones in exactly the same spot. What some people find hilarious, others find painful or sad. What sends you rolling on the floor might only nudge a smile out of the person next to you. In fact, humor varies so greatly that it can be classified in several different genres.

Low comedy, which is physical and sometimes vulgar, includes outlandish, exaggerated forms of humor such as **farce** and **burlesque.** Both genres make use of oddly harmless violence. Farce stretches common plots to the very edge of believability through exaggeration and surprise. Burlesque uses a great deal of exaggeration too—but it's directed at a person, custom, artifact, or event. A burlesque can take the form of a **travesty** and poke fun at respected subjects. It can **parody** a famous work by imitating the author's style in a humorous way. The loftier the subject, the more likely it will become a target for burlesque. As you may have guessed, burlesque and farcical characters tend to be fairly extreme in their appearance, movements, and reactions. They often don't think they are being funny, but their circumstance and habits are laughable.

Arsenic and Old Lace is an example of a middlebrow situation comedy.

Middlebrow comedy includes more plot-based, sentimental genres, such as romantic comedy, situation comedy, and sentimental comedy. These genres may provoke chuckles and smiles, but they also encourage weeping and other emotional responses. Characters in these comedies are more realistic, though their situations and responses can still be quite broad.

High comedy includes **satire** and **comedy of manners.** Satire makes fun of individual people and their follies in an attempt to change their foolish behavior. A comedy of manners, such as Sheridan's *The School for Scandal,* often makes fun of upper-class pretentiousness and the accepted standards of

Resource Binder

- Comic Roles Activity Sheet, p. 47
- Analyzing Humor Worksheet, p. 48
- Critique Sheet: Comic Monologue, p. 49
- Comic Roles Test, p. 50

Handbook Connections
pages 551-554, 559-560, 569-570

To Have on Hand

It is always a good idea to have a collection of good examples of the different kinds of comedy you will be studying in the form of videos, cassettes or CDs, and DVDs. Spalding Gray's video *The Slippery Slope* is a fine example of a comedy monologue. Films of some of the great teams such as the Marx Brothers and George Burns and Gracie Allen, along with the performances of stand-up comics such as Robin Williams, Richard Pryor, and Ellen DeGeneres are good ways to see how comic timing operates.

PREVIEW

What's So Funny?

Discuss with students what makes them laugh and why other people laugh at things that don't seem funny to the observer.

Show, Don't Tell Show the students part or all of a Charlie Chaplin or Buster Keaton silent film. Then show them part or all of a Jim Carrey film or Mike Myers as Austin Powers. Ask students to compare and contrast these comedies, and to talk about what they found funny in each. Discuss how elements of these films could be categorized as farce, parody, or satire.

ACTivity Play a storytelling game. In turn, have students sit at the head of the class. Each one tells a comic story that is either true or invented. The audience votes whether they have told a true or fictitious story. Tabulate the votes, then ask the teller to reveal whether it was truth or fiction. Ask the class to discuss whether the teller's behaviors seem truthful. Did storytellers seem more comfortable telling a true or a made up story?

Beginning Students
To accomplish the activity above, you may want to give students a theme to base their stories on, such as "Tell about your most embarrassing moment."

A Flea in Her Ear, Georges Feydeau's classic French farce is a mad romp in which a wife tries to trap her innocent husband in a love tryst. A film version, starring Rex Harrison and Rosemary Harris, is also available.

- Describe two of the people in the photo.
- Look at the man in the striped costume at the left. Imitate the way he would move and speak.

The Rule of Three

Show, Don't Tell Watch videos of one of the films mentioned previously, such as one of the Marx Brothers' popular movies or clips from the Burns and Allen TV show and try to catch them using the rule of three.

Advanced Students
Ask students to write and perform the two forms of comedy below.

- **Stand-up Comedy in a Comic Persona** You might want to set up a "comedy club" in the classroom with an audience stage and perhaps a live drummer.
- **Comic Parody** Have students write and perform a comic parody that imitates some other theatrical form.

Engaging the Audience

Discuss with the students how the comic actor engages an audience. How might an actor walk the fine line between making the audience feel superior to the character while at the same time identifying with the character?

Vocabulary Enhancement

Commedia dell'arte, the popular comedy born in 16th-century Italy that has been discussed in previous chapters, often contained improvisations called *lazzi.* These comic routines incorporated acrobatics, slapstick, and repetition. *Lazzi* are the ancestors of *schtick.*

Visual Cue

Oscar Wilde's *The Importance of Being Earnest* is just as popular today as it was in the 1890s. Indeed, a film version starring Reese Witherspoon, Judi Dench, and Colin Firth is available on video and DVD.

- When you look at this photo, how can you tell it's a comedy?
- How would you read a book in a comic way?
- Would you rather play a comic or dramatic role?

The Rule of Three

If there is one thing comic writers and comedians hold sacred, it's the **rule of three.** It goes like this: Pratfalls, accidents, misunderstandings, and similar "schticks" are funny only three times in a row. After that, they tend to fall flat. No one knows why exactly; they just know that fourth time won't get a laugh.

What's the exception to the rule? The rule of three times three. Sometimes, a play offers an opportunity to use the rule of three on three separate occasions. On the third occasion, you might get away with adding a fourth surprise–repetition. After the third set of three, you may actually go for a fourth time. The schtick is funny the fourth time, because it's not expected.

Oscar Wilde's *The Importance of Being Earnest* is a perfect example of a comedy of manners.

the wealthy. Both these genres appeal to the intelligence of their audience. They poke fun at political situations, cultural habits, and entrenched attitudes. The more you know about the subject of a satire and how these comedies approach this subject, the more you can appreciate the characters' sly and subtle sarcasm. Characters in these genres must be fairly realistic and restrained, yet quirky and witty enough to provoke laughter.

What do almost all comic actors have in common? Commitment. No matter how ridiculous their situation. . . they take their acting seriously!

Engaging the Audience

Obviously, drama and comedy have some things in common. However, some necessary techniques are particular to comedy. A comic writer and performer must engage an audience in the comic character, employing at least some of the elements below.

- Be sure that the audience identifies with your character.
- The audience should feel that it knows something your character doesn't.
- Help the audience feel superior to your character.
- Throw in the unexpected just when the audience is least expecting it.
- Invert the logic of a situation by doing what seems illogical. For example, two enemies might hug in the middle of an argument.

Quotable

So why do we laugh at comic situations? Because laughter comes from a feeling of superiority. Whether we laugh at danger, weakness, inadequacy, meanness, deformity, or simply because we feel good, laughter is an indication that we are not intimidated by life.

from *Introducing Theatre* by Joy Reilly and M. Scott Phillips

126 **Unit Three** Creating a Character

- Juxtapose two opposite things to heighten confusion. For example, pair a short, fat person with a tall thin one, or create a character who loves kittens but is full of rage.
- Use rapid-fire dialogue and movement.
- Remember the Rule of Three.

Once an audience starts to respond, the actor must remember to **hold** for laughs. This means you must pause a bit to wait until the laughing dies down. If you speak and act over the laughing, the audience will start to restrain their laughter in order to follow the action, or they may lose an important point in the dialogue. If, however, you freeze—while staying in character and focusing on the situation at hand—you can continue when the laughter subsides. This allows the laughter to build and, perhaps, fill the house.

PREPARE

The Comic Edge

Comic playwrights such as Oscar Wilde and Tom Stoppard have created characters full of wit, charm, and snappy dialogue to comment on the social pretensions of their times. While making fun of his characters in *The Importance of Being Earnest,* Wilde also imbued them with such charm and grace that the audience couldn't help but be fond of them. Stoppard's brilliant use of language in *Rosencrantz and Guildenstern Are Dead* also endears the audience to this pair of rogues.

It is very important that comedy stays on the edge of what is considered safe and polite. Too polite equals boring, and too edgy may offend the audience. The comic character must hold the audience in a tenuous balance between the two. A good comedy makes fun of the foibles and pretensions of the audience while also recognizing that we all share these faults.

Gary Oldman, Tim Roth, and Richard Dreyfus in *Rosencrantz and Guildenstern Are Dead.*

ACTivity Have students practice using rapid-fire comic dialogue by reading in pairs from Molière's *The Imaginary Invalid* or Chekhov's *A Marriage Proposal* in Unit Eight of their text. Have them reread the tips on cues and cue pickup on page 106 in preparation.

Remind them that when performing comedy, actors must know how to hold for laughs. The standard rule is to hold only until the laugh has reached its peak. When the actor hears the laugh begin to subside, he or she should begin—or continue—speaking at a slightly increased volume. This gets easier with experience.

Advanced Students
Have capable students throw in gestures and movement as they practice their rapid-fire comic readings.

Vocabulary Enhancement

Comic timing refers, in part, to the ability of actors to speak in rapid-fire dialogue, often in one breath. At the ends of each line they lift the last word and then pause with some kind of take or gesture that releases the joke. This is also called *"serving up the joke."*

If students watch *Whose Line Is It Anyway?* or *The Gilmore Girls* on television they will probably understand the effectiveness of the juxtaposition of opposite character types and dialogue that incorporates fast-paced give-and-take to create a comic effect. If you can tape examples from these two shows, share them with the students.

Quotable

I think comedy is more difficult to play . . . If you are capable of playing tragedy it means you have a great well of emotion in you—and you just push yourself off and roll downhill . . . Comedy—you really have to have that ear out and that eye on yourself. You have to be very up and brilliant . . .

Lynn Fontanne, Actor

PREPARE

The Comic Edge

As students prepare to create their comic characters, recap what they have learned about types of comedy, how to engage an audience, and how laughs are created and sustained.

Find Your Comic Character

Help students as they first find their characters and then create lists and outlines of their characters' traits. Urge them to be as specific as they can be in their descriptions. Share first drafts with students after they have read them to family members and friends. Encourage them to rework their drafts as many times as needed.

Special Needs Students

These students may be best at oral comic storytelling in which they practice their story orally without having to write it down. You might also want to start these students with a comic story from their own lives told in first person before asking them to create a comic character.

ACTivity Play the "Hidden Problem Game." Students choose a physical problem that they must hide. Examples are bad breath, a huge pimple, having to go to the washroom, cramps, etc. They then improvise a scene in which they are being interviewed for a job while having to hide their problem from the audience. Ask them to first do this in a realistic way and then in a very exaggerated and comic way.

Theatre Journal

Use the following as additional or substitute prompts.

In tragedies, the protagonist often has a "tragic flaw." In comedies the protagonist often has a "comic foible." Comic foibles are character traits that we recognize in ourselves and exaggerate. Write about your comic foible and how it affects your life. Or write about the comic foibles of two other people you know. Then write a comic foible for the character you are working on for your comic monologue.

Find Your Comic Character

You too must try to create in your comic character someone who is flawed in some way—silly, vain, snobbish, gossipy, for example—but someone who also draws the audience in and arouses their interest. At the left are a few suggestions to help you find your character and create your monologue.

Think about yourself as the character in your monologue. How is your character different from the other characters that might be in this situation? How can you emphasize the uniqueness of your character? What surprises can you inject into your character's speech or actions?

Make a list of your character's traits or use the Comic Roles Activity Sheet provided by your teacher. Refer to these notes as you write a rough description of your character's activities in the scene. You can write this first draft more as an outline than a monologue. Then read your first draft aloud to a family member, friend, or even the mirror. Based on what was funny and what was not funny, write a new draft with specific lines and stage directions. Don't give up. It may take several drafts to get the comic monologue you are happy with.

Rehearse your monologue until you are sure of your character, actions, and lines. Your audience will enjoy the scene only if they can relax—confident that you are well prepared. Do not exceed the five-minute time limit.

Suggestions for Comedy Characters

- a prim person visiting a tattoo or piercing parlor
- Beethoven at a rave
- a sedate man buying women's lingerie in an exclusive store
- a parent with four children, arms full of bundles, trying to find change for the bus
- a tourist in Hawaii eager to learn the hula
- a parent teaching a sixteen-year-old to drive the family car
- a person trying to build a bookcase using directions in a foreign language

Theatre Journal

Next time you embarrass yourself, stop as soon as you are able and make a note of the event. Analyze what it was that made the event funny to others. Think about the kinds of characters who might find themselves in such a situation and the circumstances in which it might occur. Consider ways to make the event funnier and then rehearse it as a comic bit!

Notes

PRESENT

Perform a Comic Monologue

When your name is called, give your list of character traits or the Activity Sheet to your teacher and walk quietly to the playing area.

Present your comic scene to the class. Remember the importance of engaging your audience. When you have finished your monologue, pause, and then bow politely before leaving the playing area.

Here's How To Deal with the Giggles

Of course, if you remain focused, you will not get the giggles during a comic performance. But momentary lapses happen to everyone. If it happens to you, bring yourself back into your character using any of the following methods:

1. Tell yourself the situation is laughable. Let your character be overtaken by disbelief.
2. As the character, tell yourself–and communicate by your actions or gestures–that you simply cannot believe the circumstances. If you must, repeat them to yourself, in order to bring your character's situation back to the center of your awareness.
3. Turn your laughter into a character trait. Become a character who laughs, cries, and reacts uncontrollably.

CRITIQUE

Evaluate a Classmate's Monologue

Choose one of the monologues presented in class and evaluate your classmate's comedy performance. Use a rating system based on 5 points in your evaluation, with "outstanding" being a 5; "well done" being a 4; "fair" being a 3; "needs some improvement" being a 2; and "needs much improvement" being a 1. To give an accurate, well-supported critique, ask yourself these questions:

- Was this a performance of a low, middlebrow, or high comedy?
- What genre or genres of comedy could I identify in this performance?
- What elements of humor did the performer use (for example, the rule of three, sarcasm, and so on)?
- Was one moment particularly funny? Which one, and why?

Write an explanation of how you arrived at the score you gave.

Backstage Gossip: Rx for Giggles

Laurence Olivier's stage career almost ended before it began because he could not stop giggling onstage. He was finally cured by Noel Coward during a seven-month run of *Private Lives.* Every night during performance, Coward and co-star Gertrude Lawrence would think up another way to try and break Olivier up until he was finally able to control himself.

PRESENT

Perform a Comic Monologue

Before they begin, discuss with students the fact that their comic monologue should reflect all aspects of their character— the words, the voice, the gestures, the movements, and so on, should all play into their comic intent.

ACTivity Before each student presents his or her comic monologue, have the student make a funny face just as the character might do.

Here's How

Discuss with students the possibility that in some situations breaking up in front of an audience may serve to heighten the fun. The idea being that the comedy must be good if it cracks up the comedian.

CRITIQUE

Evaluate a Classmate's Monologue

Hand out the Critique Sheet for this project or have students use their own paper. Quickly go over the elements of humor and what to look for in a strong comic monologue.

After you have reviewed student critiques, discuss with the subjects of the evaluations any recurrent suggestions for improvement.

Chapter 12 Test

The test for this chapter is available in blackline master form in the Resource Binder, page 50.

For More Information

Books

Aitken, Maria, *Style: Acting in High Comedy,* Applause Books, 1996.

Helitzer, Mel, *Comedy Writing Secrets,* Writers Digest Books, 1992.

Perret, Gene, and Carol Burnett, *Comedy Writing Step by Step,* Samuel French, 1990.

Robinson, Davis Rider, *The Physical Comedy Handbook,* Heinemann, 1999.

Roche, Jenny, *Comedy Writing,* McGraw-Hill, 1999.

Seyler, Athene, *The Craft of Comedy,* Theatre Arts Books, 1990.

Vorhaus, John, *The Comic Toolbox: How to Be Funny Even if You're Not,* Silman-James Press, 1994.

Other Media

Comedy, VHS, Insight Media, 1998.

Comedy Through the Ages, VHS, Insight Media, 2000.

Drama/Comedy, VHS, Insight Media, 1975.

Satire, VHS, Insight Media, 1999.

Additional Projects

1 Translate the funny story you told at the beginning of this lesson—or some other funny experience—into a humorous scene.

2 With a partner, research an audio library in order to find and learn a classic comedy routine. Rehearse it thoroughly and then perform it for the class.

3 In a group with two or three others, read a classic farce such as *Tartuffe* by Molière or *What the Butler Saw* by Joe Orton and discuss the humorous elements it contains. Work on a scene you find particularly funny, and then present it to the class.

4 Read a comedy of manners. Then memorize and present a humorous two- to three-minute monologue from it. The following plays are possible sources for monologues: *The Women* by Clare Boothe Luce, *Blithe Spirit* by Noel Coward, *The Importance of Being Earnest* by Oscar Wilde, or *The School for Scandal* by Richard Brinsley Sheridan.

5 Read the scene from *The Importance of Being Earnest* by Oscar Wilde or the scene from *The Imaginary Invalid* by Molière found in Unit Eight. Choose a character, and then write a short description of how you would play this character. Include physical details.

"Laughter seems like a trifle, yet it has a power… that is well-nigh irresistible; it often changes the tendency of the greatest affairs, as it very often dissipates hatred and anger."

–Quintilian, Roman orator

130 **Unit Three** Creating a Character

Substitute Teacher Activities

- Assign the Analyzing Humor Worksheet on page 48 of the Resource Binder.
- Assign one or more of the Additional Projects on this page.
- **Create a Comedy Club.** Rearrange the space so that it looks like a club with a small stage and mike in the center or front. An emcee should be designated, and the students can work on the following acts to perform at the Club:

1 Stand-up comedy, either as self or in character
2 Improv scenes as in Second City or "Saturday Night Live"
3 Comic storytelling from a life story
4 Parodies or satires of songs, TV shows, or life events
5 Political satires
6 Burlesque show that uses song, dance, pratfalls, slapstick, and other schtick

You can even serve refreshments!

Master of the Craft

Lily Tomlin

"All my life, I always wanted to be somebody. Now I see that I should have been more specific."

–Lily Tomlin

Mary Jean Tomlin didn't know she wanted to be a famous comedian when she was growing up in Detroit, Michigan, but she did enjoy gags. In fact, when she ordered gag items from the back of a comic book and couldn't pay for them, her mother paid for the package and made her do odd jobs until she could pay the money back. Such is the price of comedy.

When she got older, Tomlin didn't try acting until her second year of college at Michigan's Wayne State University. She appeared in student productions, including a variety show, where she presented a character called "The Tasteful Lady," which she still plays today.

Tomlin left Wayne State after her junior year and moved to New York. Beginning in 1960, she worked during the day at temporary jobs and performed in cabarets at night. Tomlin's career caught fire in 1969, when she was cast in the television comedy revue *Laugh-In.* There, she developed some of her classic characters, including Ernestine, the obnoxious telephone operator, and Edith Ann, the precocious child who tells outlandish stories ending with "And that's the truth!"

Tomlin has appeared in comic and dramatic roles in movies and television for more than thirty years. She has a recurring role on TV's *The West Wing*, and she continues to tour and perform onstage. Her most celebrated work is her one-woman show entitled *The Search for Signs of Intelligent Life in the Universe,* which was written for her by Jane Wagner.

If flexibility and creativity are keys to a successful life, then Lily Tomlin has a pocketful of keys. But she is not overly impressed with success. "The trouble with the rat race," says Tomlin, "is that even if you win, you're still a rat!"

Lily Tomlin as Ernestine.

Notes

Master of the Craft

More About Lily Tomlin

Lily Tomlin cut her teeth on the television comedy-variety show *Rowan & Martin's Laugh-In*, which ran from 1968 to early 1973.

Other regulars included Flip Wilson, Sammy Davis Jr., Goldie Hawn, Arte Johnson, Henry Gibson, and Jo Anne Worley. On *Laugh-In*, Tomlin developed her sarcastic, nasal-voiced telephone operator, Ernestine, as well as Edith Anne, a child philosopher whose monologues always ended in the phrase "and that's the truth," followed by raspberries.

Tomlin's charming Web site, *www.lilytomlin.com/intro.htm* gives just about all the information you could possibly want concerning the versatile Lily.

For More Information

Books

Sorensen, Jeff, *Lily Tomlin: Woman of a Thousand Faces*, St. Martin's Press, 1989.

Wagner, Jane, *The Search for Intelligent Life in the Universe*, Perennial Press, 1991.

Other Media

Lily Tomlin: This Is a Recording, audio CD, laugh.com.

Theatre Then and Now

Great Comic Playwrights

William Shakespeare is thought to be the greatest playwright of all time, and with good reason. Not only did he write elegant, thrilling drama and create memorable characters in his tragedies and histories, he also fashioned fascinating characters and inventive, witty dialogue in a number of comedies. Many of these comedies have a dusting of fairy folk and fools who have been beloved by audiences from his time to ours. No fool is more hilarious than Nick Bottom and no fairy so wry and mischievous than Puck in *A Midsummer Night's Dream.* Puck finds delight in playing tricks on mortals and Bottom is inept enough to fall victim to Puck's spell.

A Midsummer Night's Dream, thought to have been written for a wedding couple, is perhaps Shakespeare's most sparkling comedy. In addition to the fools and fairies, there are two pairs of scrambled lovers, the wedding of a duke, and a hilarious play-within-a-play. It all that takes place on the night before Midsummer Day, a night often associated with a crazed, albeit temporary, state of mind. The witty dialogue, frantic pace, and matrimonial mix-ups all come together to bring us a play that has had audiences laughing for hundreds of years.

Theatre Then and Now

Great Comic Playwrights

Molière at work.

Molière (1622–1673)
Jean-Baptiste Poquelin's father was a well-respected court upholsterer. His mother was aristocratic and devout in her religion. Poquelin was well on his way to a comfortable life at court—except for one thing. He was smitten by theatre.

He was also smitten by Madeleine Bejart, who was an actress. So he changed his name to Molière, probably to avoid embarrassing his family, and founded a theatre troupe called The Illustrious Theatre.

Unfortunately, The Illustrious Theatre was not very good. Fortunately, the troupe decided to do something about it. They left their failures behind in Paris and traveled from town to town for twelve years, honing their skills.

Molière began writing plays for the company, and the plays began to find success. Then, in 1658, Molière and his company were invited to perform for King Louis XIV in Paris. Molière asked if the company might present a play of his own. That play, *The Love-Sick Doctor,* so delighted the king that he gave the company the title of Troupe de Monsieur and granted them the use of the Hotel du Petit Bourbon, one of the most important theatres in Paris.

Over the next twenty-four years, Molière's plays included such classics as *The Imaginary Invalid, The Misanthrope, The School for Wives,* and *Tartuffe.* They ridiculed powerful courtiers, clergymen, and tragedians of the time. But as the plays ripened from clever satirical farces into comedies of manners, they came to have a lasting impact on theatre and on society as a whole. Molière's work earned him powerful enemies who tried to destroy his career. But his enemies were unsuccessful, and his controversial plays are still performed today.

"The more we love our friends, the less we flatter them. It is by excusing nothing that pure love shows itself."

—Molière

132 Unit Three Creating a Character

For More Information

Books

Beaudin, Beth, *Molière,* Chelsea House, 2003.

Fernandez, Ramon, *Molière: The Man Seen Through the Plays,* Octagon Books, 1980.

Knutson, Harold C., *The Triumph of Wit: Molière and Restoration Comedy,* Ohio State University Press, 1988.

McCarthy, Gerry, *The Theatres of Molière,* Routledge, 2002.

Scott, Virginia, *Molière: A Theatrical Life,* Cambridge University Press, 2002.

Other Media

Le Bourgeois Gentilhomme, VHS, Insight Media, 1958.

Molière and the Comédie Française, VHS, Insight Media, 1982.

Tartuffe: An Analysis, VHS, Insight Media, 1994.

Neil Simon (1927–)

Neil Simon has always been devoted to comedy. He got his first major childhood injury by laughing so hard he fell off a stone wall. He earned his childhood nickname, Doc, through his accurate imitation of the family doctor. In the 1940s, he co-founded a comedy team with his brother Danny and began writing comedy sketches for radio and television personalities.

In 1961, Simon opened his first play, *Come Blow Your Horn,* on Broadway. He followed up the first play with *Barefoot in the Park* and *The Odd Couple,* both of which became popular hits. In 1966, when Simon's *The Star-Spangled Girl* opened at the Plymouth Theatre, he had four plays running on Broadway at the same time.

Audience members loved Simon's plays from the start, but critics complained that Simon's characters were not as developed as they might be. So, over the years, Neil Simon deepened his work. Once, he says, he tried to figure out what kinds of things were funny. Now he tries to think about serious things he can write about in a humorous way.

Neil Simon

"It was my [low] SAT scores that led me into my present vocation in life, comedy."
—Neil Simon

This approach has been successful. Simon's *Biloxi Blues* won a Tony award for Best Drama in 1985. In 1991, he won both a Pulitzer and a Tony award for *Lost in Yonkers.* Today, Simon enjoys double good fortune: popularity and professional respect. Even so, he won't rest on his laurels. He continues to write at least five days a week, almost every week of the year.

Richard Dreyfus and Marsha Mason in Neil Simon's play *The Prisoner of Second Avenue.*

Along with Neil Simon, David Ives is one of the most brilliantly comic playwrights living today. He is well known for the series of imaginative, delightful, and often loony one-act comedies that have been entertaining playgoers for years. *All in the Timing,* which ran over 600 performances during the 1995-96 off-Broadway season, was described by *The New York Times* as ". . . one-act plays that percolate with comic brio." The plays from this collection are said to be the most performed plays in the country (not counting the works of Shakespeare).

One of the selections from *All in the Timing,* "Words, Words, Words," deals with three monkeys sitting at typewriters who are called upon to prove the theory that, if given long enough, one of them will write *Hamlet*. A silly theory, surely, but sillier still are the words that the monkeys actually do type as well as their conversations concerning their task.

Lives of the Saints and *Mere Mortals* are two other popular collections of Ives's plays. David Ives was awarded a Guggenheim Fellowship in playwriting in 1995.

For More Information

Books

Simon, Neil, *The Play Goes On: A Memoir,* Simon & Schuster, 2002.

Simon, Neil, *REWRITES: A Memoir,* Simon & Schuster, 1998.

Backstage Gossip: On Second Thought

Harold Clurman was introduced at a party to Neil Simon's business manager. Clurman told him that he had just written an article called "In Defense of Neil Simon."

"That's wonderful," said the manager, "I look forward to reading it." They went their separate ways, but a little while later, the man came back to ask Clurman:

"I don't quite understand why a man who earns forty thousand dollars a week needs a defense."

from *Broadway Anecdotes* by Peter Hay

Chapter 12 Comic Roles **133**

Unit Three Review

PREVIEW

Examine the following key concepts previewed in Unit Three.

1. Describe an actor's "dual role."
2. Which of the following are a character's external traits?
   a. posture
   b. spiritual qualities
   c. mode of dress
   d. mental characteristics
   e. voice
3. What is the fourth wall?
4. Name the five elements of plot structure.
5. What do we call information that is implied but not stated by a character?
   a. subculture b. subtext c. secret script d. innuendo e. gossip
6. Explain how a protagonist differs from an antagonist.
7. Compare social drama to melodrama.
8. What is the difference between low and middlebrow comedies?
9. Which of the following is NOT important when engaging an audience in a comedy?
   a. the audience feels superior to your character
   b. the character can be easily identified with
   c. the character has a tragic flaw
   d. something happens when least expected

PREPARE

Assess your response to the preparation process for projects in this unit.

10. In analyzing your character for the high-stakes scenario, was it easier to determine the character's traits or motivation? Explain why.
11. As you prepared a scene from a play, was it easier to work out the character's actions, words, or feelings? Why?
12. How did you go about finding your comic character while preparing for your comic monologue?
13. Was it easier to prepare your dramatic scene or your comic monologue? Why?
14. Did you find it more satisfying to work out a character on paper or onstage?

Unit Three Review

PREVIEW

1. An actor's "dual role" means that the actor is the character while also being the actor.
2. External traits are: a) posture, c) mode of dress, and e) voice.
3. The fourth wall is the space between the actors on stage and the audience, which the audience looks through as if it were a window to the scene.
4. The five elements of plot structure are conflict, rising action, turning point (or climax), falling action (or denouement), and resolution.
5. Implied information is b) subtext.
6. The protagonist is the person the audience cares about, often a hero, but not always. The antagonist is any force, often a person, that opposes the protagonist.
7. Social drama is serious drama that focuses on the hopes and struggles of ordinary people, while melodrama is much less realistic in its attempt to create excitement and suspense.
8. Lowbrow comedies use outlandish and sometimes vulgar humor to elicit laughs while middlebrow comedies are more refined, sentimental, and plot-based.
9. Characters in a comedy do not have c) a tragic flaw.

PREPARE

10. Answers will vary, but students should support their reasons for choosing character traits or motivation as the most difficult part of analyzing a character.
11. Most students will probably say it was easier to work out the feelings than the actions and easier to work out the actions than the words in the scene.

PRESENT

Analyze the experience of presenting your work to the class.

15 When you performed your high-stakes scenario, could you feel the audience responding to your situation? How were you able to keep the audience interested?

16 Was it difficult to remain in character while presenting a dramatic scene?

17 Which presentation in this unit did you find the most challenging? Why?

18 Which was more satisfying: acting in a scene you wrote yourself or acting in a scene written by another? Explain why.

CRITIQUE

Evaluate how you go about critiquing your work and the work of others.

19 Did you find it easier to evaluate a comedy or a dramatic work? Why?

20 Describe an insightful critique you received from your teacher or classmate and how it helped your performance.

21 What one thing did most performers have trouble with in creating a character, and what could they do to improve their performance?

EXTENSIONS

- Based on what you learned in this unit, write a short paper entitled: "How I Create a Character." It can be as serious or humorous as you would like.
- Look at the photograph at the right. Write a list of all the things you know about this character just from her appearance.

Resource Binder

Unit Three Test, p. 51

12 Answers will vary but should show an understanding of the preparation process in putting together a comic monologue.

13 Most students will probably agree that it was easier to prepare a dramatic scene than to prepare a comic monologue.

14 Answers will vary. Actors will probably say the onstage work was more satisfying; writers will say the writing was more satisfying.

PRESENT

15 Answers will vary, but most students will probably say that they could feel the audience responding, and that they worked harder if they thought they were losing the audience.

16 Some students may admit to difficulty in staying in character; others will have no problem.

17 Answers will vary.

18 Most students will probably say that acting in a scene they wrote themselves was more satisfying.

CRITIQUE

19 Most students will say the comedy was harder to evaluate.

20 Descriptions will vary.

21 For most students staying fresh and giving the illusion of the first time causes the most problems. Continuing to practice helps.

EXTENSIONS

- Students' papers should be thoughtfully and carefully written.
- She is elderly and probably wealthy. She has a strong sense of herself. She likes to dress with style and flair. She doesn't mind overdoing it a bit. She has good posture and probably lots of confidence. She likes to strike a pose, and so on.

Unit Four

The Play: From Vision to Reality

Unit Four will allow students to explore what it takes to get a play from the page to the stage. Projects in this unit will help students analyze and understand the elements of drama, the personnel involved in a typical production, the ways in which directors orchestrate physical action onstage, and the experience of actually attending a play.

Project Preview

Chapter 13 The Playwright
Creating a scenario

Chapter 14 The Director and Producer
Analyzing a play as a director would

Chapter 15 The Cast
Creating a rehearsal schedule

Chapter 16 Blocking
Blocking a scene with more than one actor

Chapter 17 Attend a Play
Presenting a talk show about a play you attend

Unit Four

The Play: From Vision to Reality

136 Unit Four The Play: From Vision to Reality

Quotables

Use the quotes below as writing prompts, discussion starters, or for your own enjoyment.

Speak the speech, I pray you, as I pronounced it to you, trippingly on the tongue. But if you mouth it, as many of our players do, I had as lief the town crier spoke my lines . . . .

from *Hamlet* by William Shakespeare

Don't tell me anything's impossible. Let's try it first.

Joseph Papp, Director and Producer

Discussion Questions

The following questions are intended to tap into students' **prior knowledge** and attitudes about the subject matter of the unit.

- Have you ever seen a play or film and thought you might want to write one yourself someday? What was it that inspired you?
- Have you ever been cast in a play or worked as a member of a stage crew? Describe the experience.
- To whom did you report in your capacity as an actor or crewmember? What kinds of responsibilities did you have?
- Have you ever been in charge of a group of people? What was it like?
- Have you ever worked as a member of a team? How did that experience make you feel about yourself and the other team members?
- Have you ever had to learn specific physical movements, such as dance steps? Who taught you? What techniques helped you learn the movements?
- Have you ever been to a theatre production? What was the experience like?

Theatre Journal

Write a short two-character scene that evokes an emotional state similar to the one in the photograph.

Visual Cue

The image above shows Luz Marabel and Ted Castellanos in a production of *Parece Blanca* at Cuba's Havana National Theatre. The following prompts can be used to exercise students' **critical viewing skills.**

- What is a possible relationship between the two characters in the picture?
- What do the actors' positions reveal about their emotional states?
- How would you describe to another person the moment portrayed in this photo?

ACTivity Have students improvise three or four lines of a monologue for one of these two characters.

ACTivity Have two students at a time simulate the positions of the people in the photograph. Then ask them to assume positions that show the opposite of those in the photo.

Chapter 13

The Playwright

This chapter introduces students to Aristotle's *Poetics* and the structural components of a play. Students will learn how to create a scenario for an original play.

Objectives

1. to understand the six elements of drama
2. to learn and recognize the structural components of a drama
3. to understand theatre as a collaborative storytelling process
4. to create a dramatic scenario based on standard play structure

National Standards

Chapter 13 meets these National Theatre Standards:

Proficient 1a, 7c, 8a, 8b
Advanced 1b, 8e, 8g

Project Specs

Have students pair off to act out the sample scene on p. 142 to solidify their understanding of conflict.

Special Needs Students
Students with visual or developmental impairments may be unable to complete this assignment as written. Be sensitive to these students by allowing them to work with a partner to tape-record their scenarios instead of writing them and presenting them aloud.

Advanced Students
Have students create an entire act from their scenario.

On Your Feet

Some students may confuse what happens in the play (plot) with what the play is about (theme). Help students determine the play's theme, if it seems vague or confusing to them.

Chapter 13 The Playwright

Theatre requires more collaboration than any other art form. The playwright, director, designers, actors, and crew must combine their talents to create a final production. The script is the blueprint for the work. In this chapter you will take on the role of playwright.

Project Specs

Project Description You will write and present a five- to ten-minute scenario for a play—complete with theme, plot, and characters in conflict.

Purpose to understand basic dramatic concepts and the structural elements of a play

Materials a one- or two-page scenario for an original play or The Playwright Activity Sheet your teacher provides

Theatre Terms

archetype
climax or turning point
crisis
diction
epic
exposition
inciting incident
plot
resolution
spectacle
staged readings
theme
workshop

On Your Feet

Think about a play you have seen or read. Ask yourself what happened in the play. (What was the plot?) Now ask yourself what the play was about. (What was the main idea, or theme?) Discuss the play's plot and theme with your classmates.

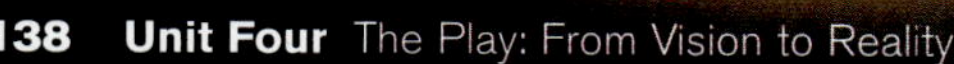

Theatre Terms

archetype a character who represents a certain type or idea

climax or **turning point** the high point of the play, when a decision is made

crisis an event that occurs just when it seems things could either resolve or worsen

diction the vocal style, dialect, rhythm, and words of the characters

epic a long narrative poem about a hero

exposition the information telling the *who, what, when, where,* and *why* of a play

inciting incident the event to which all other actions in the play can be traced

plot the story of the play

resolution the end of the story when the conflict is resolved

spectacle everything the audience sees

staged readings readings that are roughly blocked

theme the underlying meaning of a play

workshop to discuss, analyze, and revise a play in collaboration with others

PREVIEW

Writing a Drama

Theatre is as old as humankind itself. The earliest forms of theatre emerged from religion and ritual. Ancient people used to act out the success of a hunt or a harvest as well as rituals having to do with life events such as birth, coming of age, and death. Many of these accounts were handed down orally and didn't achieve written form until around 500 B.C., the beginning of the classical age of Greek drama.

The Greeks developed a written body of work, including the **epic** (a long narrative poem that told the story of legendary heroes and their travels and exploits), all of which originated with the oral tradition. The Greeks then developed ways of dramatizing some of these stories for performance. The great

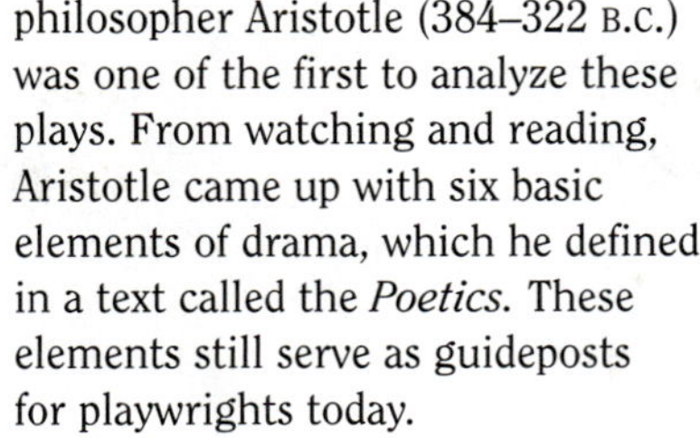

philosopher Aristotle (384–322 B.C.) was one of the first to analyze these plays. From watching and reading, Aristotle came up with six basic elements of drama, which he defined in a text called the *Poetics.* These elements still serve as guideposts for playwrights today.

Aristotle's Elements of Drama

Thought This is the central idea the playwright is exploring, which embodies a truth about life. Today, this is usually referred to as the **theme.**

Plot The **plot** is the story of the play, or the progression of the main character, called the *protagonist,* which includes his or her conflict with an opposing force. The manner in which the protagonist deals with this force is what illuminates the play's theme.

Action The central action is the pivotal dramatic moment when the issues and progression of the play become clear through a decision made and carried out by the protagonist.

Diction The language, or the **diction** as Aristotle called it, includes the style, dialect, rhythm, and the actual words of the characters.

American playwright Arthur Miller shares his ideas about the theatre.

PREVIEW

Writing a Drama

Students might be interested to know that one of the early Greek playwrights, **Sophocles** (406-496 B.C.), began his career as an actor and performed in many of his own plays. However, his voice was relatively weak, and eventually he gave up acting to focus on playwriting and other artistic pursuits. His most famous works, *Oedipus the King, Antigone,* and *Electra,* are still performed today.

Aristotle's Elements of Drama

Although the *protagonist* is the play's main character, he or she need not be a heroic or admirable person. Remind students that, personality aside, the protagonist is the character who changes, and is changed by, the course of the play's action because of the way he or she deals with the conflict.

Show, Don't Tell With a very capable student, read a two-person scene from *Glengarry Glen Ross* by David Mamet for the students and ask them to think about the diction—including Mamet's staccato style, the overlapping rhythm of the interchange, and the precise word choices. You may want to choose a passage that is free of language that might be offensive to some students.

ACTivity Have students discuss plays they have read or seen in which the language seemed unusual or particularly effective. Have them discuss the rhythm, dialect, and word choices of the play.

Discuss with students the photograph of Arthur Miller.

- What special insights might the playwright bring to the rehearsal process?
- As a cast member, what sorts of questions might you ask of the playwright?
- As an actor, would you appreciate the playwright being on hand during play rehearsal? Explain.

Resource Binder

- The Playwright Activity Sheet, p. 52
- Aristotle's Elements of Drama Worksheet, p. 53
- Critique Sheet: Write a Scenario for a Play, p. 54
- Playwright Test, p. 55

Handbook Connections
pages 575-576

To Have on Hand

- Photos of and biographical information on great American playwrights, directors, and producers
- A full rehearsal schedule from a professional or community theatre
- Flash cards with the elements of drama listed on one side and the definitions on the other, which can be used by students to quiz one another
- A list of local or regional theatres students might attend

ACTivity **Advanced Students**
Have students read the opening scene of Tennessee Williams' *A Streetcar Named Desire* and jot down each sound effect the author specifies. Then give them a few minutes to think about what additional sound elements (including music) might work in the scene and add these to their lists.

Why Is It Called a Play?

Discuss the concept of the *archetype* with students. Together, name archetypal characters in books, movies, and television shows. What do each of these characters represent?

ACTivity Have students write short monologues incorporating an archetypal character and then exchange their work with a partner. Each student reads his or her partner's monologue aloud, trying to capture the essence of the archetype.

Theatre Journal

Use the following to further enhance the prompt.

Before you begin the Theatre Journal activity, brainstorm possible topics with your classmates. Then choose the one that you find most intriguing and relevant.

Vocabulary Enhancement

Share with students that playwrights are also called *dramatists.*

Visual Cue

- What kind of atmosphere is depicted in this picture?
- What sounds might you expect to hear in the environment?

The spectacle of the play *Camino Reál* is a treat for the eyes.

Sound Everything the audience hears in the play—from the words to the music to the sound effects—is included in the sound.

Spectacle Everything the audience sees—including scenery, costuming, dance, pantomime, and swordplay—is included in the **spectacle.**

Note that the first four elements are also found in other literary forms, such as novels and short stories. The last two elements, however, are unique to the theatre.

Why Is It Called a Play?

The answer is simple. A play is exactly that—an event carried out with the spontaneity, intense concentration, and commitment of children at play.

But *writing* a play requires planning the entire course of action—what happens and why. The play will involve a central character who becomes involved in a conflict. As in other literary genres, a play's conflict and the progress of the central character can include an **archetype** or two—a character who represents a certain type. An archetype can symbolize universal ideas about human behavior.

There are lots of different ways to write a play. But every playwright must discover a plot (characters in conflict); choose a central course of action that illuminates the theme; select diction appropriate to the desired time period and style; and use sound, scenery, and spectacle to bring the play to vibrant life.

Theatre Journal

As a playwright, you are a student of human nature—and what better human can you practice on than yourself? Spend some time analyzing an incident from your life. Perhaps it was a comment someone made to you that bothered or confused you. Maybe you did something that made you proud or that you regret. In your journal, write about the incident until you feel that you have a handle on why it happened and what it means to you.

Backstage Gossip: August Wilson Interviews Himself

In May 2003 August Wilson, a preeminent American playwright and two-time Pulitzer Prize winner, took to the Seattle Repertory stage to present a one-man show called *How I Learned What I Learned.* In this autobiographical work, Wilson more or less interviewed himself, presenting an in-depth look at his past and present, and his thoughts on everything from race to family to music.

You might want to have your students use a self-interview process to find elements of their own lives on which to base a play.

PREPARE

Gather Ideas for Your Scenario

Many playwrights claim that they do not choose what to write about—instead, they say, ideas and subject matter choose them! You may find the same thing yourself. However, to jump-start your process, try the following writing exercises to develop an idea for a play.

1 **Find a Subject.** Think of a starting point for your play—a challenging question, an interesting character, or a problem to solve—and write it at the top of a sheet of paper. You may take your idea from a newspaper article, a person you know, an incident from your own life, a story you heard, and so on. Once you have chosen your starting point, take five to ten minutes to freewrite about everything you can think of that might be included in the play. For example, if your idea has to do with a robbery, ask and answer questions for yourself about the perpetrators, the victims, the bystanders, and so on. Where did the robbery take place? Why? What time of year? What time of day? How might personal circumstances drive a person to commit a robbery? What are the consequences of such an action—both legally and morally? Be specific, and include every detail and question you think you might be able to use later.

2 **Create a Character.** Using the information you've created about the subject, think of a character to represent a part of the idea. In the example of the robbery, you might choose the robber, the victim, a relative of either of these, a bystander, and so on. Take five minutes to write a short monologue from this character's point of view. This should open up other areas of thought. It may lead you in any number of directions. For example, you may decide that your play is about how witnessing a crime affects a bystander's life. Or you might decide that it's about the events that led up to the robbery or made it seem necessary. You can write a play about almost anything, as long as your characters and your situation are specific and meaningful to you.

3 **Develop a Conflict.** This is a simple exercise based on the same principles used in many improvisations. Your job here is to let the audience know the "Ws." *Who* is in the scene? *Where* are they? *What* are they doing? The *What* should be the conflict, which creates a problem to be solved. Remember that conflict results when one character's objective, or goal, bumps into an obstacle.

From the Field: The Passive Playwright

In his book *The Dramatist's Toolkit,* playwright Jeffrey Sweet claims that autobiographical characters—those based upon the writer's own life—tend to be the most passive characters in a play. They often comment wryly or stand off to the side of the action rather than taking an active role in the play's conflict.

Remind students that drama is based on conflict. If they put themselves into their own play they need to explore what that character wants within the context of the scene.

PREPARE

Gather Ideas for Your Scenario

Before students begin to write about their ideas for a play, share with them that many playwriting teachers advocate writing in groups. They claim that the energy generated by a room full of writers can stimulate the entire group's process even though no words are exchanged. After your students have written for the allotted time, discuss whether anyone felt the group energy as they worked.

Find a Subject. If students are having trouble finding a subject, have them look through current newspapers or back over their journals for ideas.

Create a Character. Have students close their eyes and try to visualize their characters. Then ask them to write a short description of the character.

Develop a Conflict. To help them develop a conflict, ask students to think about the kinds of situations this particular character would get into. What problems might result for the character, his or her family, or society as a whole?

ACTivity Assign students a situation for their character, such as waiting for a bus, sitting at a counter in a diner, or attending a family reunion. Each student improvises a short scene in which his or her character assesses what is happening in the situation. This short monologue can help to bring out interesting character traits.

Sample Scene

Review with students that a character's *objective* is his or her *goal*—the thing this character wants more than anything else. The *obstacle* is a person or situation that gets in the way of the character's objective and does everything possible to thwart it. In the sample scene, Ray's objective is to get the car keys from Molly. Molly's refusal is Ray's obstacle.

ACTivity Beginning Students
Have pairs of students read through the sample scene. Encourage them to make strong vocal and physical choices. Then allow them to discuss their reasons for making the choices they did. Ask, "What clues did the script give you about the characters?"

ACTivity Advanced Students
Most students will interpret the scene as one in which Molly tries to help her son Ray. Ask students to think about the scene in another way. What if Molly's motivations weren't quite so selfless? Have them play the scene using this new interpretation.

Add to the activity by allowing students to improvise what happens next in the scene.

Sample Scene

(A small, cluttered kitchen [where]. MOLLY [who] sits at the table clipping coupons. RAY [who] enters suddenly from outside. He has a cut on his forehead and is very agitated.)

RAY. Ma, I gotta use the car *[what/objective]*.

MOLLY. Raymond.

RAY. I got no time to talk, Ma. Give me the keys.

MOLLY. What's happened?

RAY. Listen, I gotta get out of town for a couple days *[what/objective]*. I'll call you. Keys?

(A silence. RAY shifts uncomfortably under his mother's steady gaze.)

MOLLY. You're not taking my car. You're not going anywhere till you tell me what's going on here, Raymond Joseph *[what/obstacle]*.

(A siren sounds in the distance.)

RAY. You want me to go to jail?! Is that it?

MOLLY. No.

RAY. Then give me the keys.

(He spies the keys on the table and makes a grab for them. MOLLY snatches them away and puts them in her pocket.) [what/obstacle]

MOLLY. Talk to me, Raymond . . . You know I am trying to help you. Please . . .

Read the sample scene above. Notice how much information the scene provides in a small amount of space. Also notice how the tension between the characters is heightened by Molly's refusal to give up the keys and by the sound of the approaching police siren.

Create a one- to two-page scene of your own using the subject, main character, and conflict you devised in the three steps just discussed. Then add a second or third character. Make sure that your situation is driven by conflict between the characters or between a character and some obstacle.

From the Field: Points for Participation

I give my students ten points each day for participation. They learn that these points average in to have a significant impact on their grades. This ensures student involvement in the day's activities.

Tanya Dean Hoyle, Drama Teacher, Tuscumbia, AL

Think About a Scenario

Where will your play go from here? That depends on the statement you are trying to make and the story you want to tell. Now that you have a basic situation, two or more characters, and the conflict or obstacles they must face, you are ready to think about a whole play that might stem from them.

You and a partner were asked to create a scenario for your project in Chapter 5, Movement. For the project in this unit, you will create a more detailed scenario that applies Aristotle's elements of drama. First, you will need to develop the theme. Based on the example of a robbery given previously, the theme might be that crime doesn't pay. Or it might be that desperate situations call for desperate solutions. It could be both of these—and more. Above all, the theme you choose should contain ideas that you care about and are interested in.

Then you must decide who your characters are and what they are trying to do in the play. No matter what your theme is, you must tell a story in which the characters are believable or interesting enough to draw the audience into the play.

You will need a plot, the beginning of which you have already created while developing the play's conflicts. What happens next? What happens after that?

Your scenario must show that the action arises logically from the conflict and leads to a crisis and climax. You have probably discovered the characters' ways of speaking while exploring the theme, the characters themselves, and their conflicts. Also keep in mind the spectacle and sound of your play—in other words, what it will look and sound like.

Keeping all these principles in mind will help you create a scenario that structures the progression of your idea for a play. In Chapter 10, you learned about play structure from the perspective of an actor working on character development. Now we will add a few more elements and look at the play from the perspective of the playwright creating a new work.

As you write your scenario, think about all of the elements on the following page.

From the Field: To Right (and Write) a Wrong

Lisa Loomer, discussing her play *The Waiting Room,* once said: "I definitely write from a need to try, in my own two hours, to right a wrong. My little play is inconsequential in terms of whether or not we have health care, but it may affect the way people who see the play think about the issue."

Think About a Scenario

Ask students to think about how to categorize the play they would like to write. Is it

- personal?
- political?
- sociological?
- comic?
- tragic?

ACTivity Have students write a brief paragraph that reveals the thematic statement they want their play to make.

Show, Don't Tell On the chalkboard, draw a plot structure diagram like the one on page 145 labeled *Exposition, Inciting Incident, Rising Action, Crisis, Climax, Falling Action,* and *Resolution.* Have students take turns coming to the board and plotting each of the seven structural elements of a play with which they are all familiar. Then create a flow chart together that tells in sentence form each of these important elements of the play.

ACTivity Have students create flow charts that depict the important elements they plan for their plays using the seven structural components you have listed on the chalkboard (a complete list is also available on page 144).

Have students use the sample script from page 142 and the Plot Structure diagram on page 145 to continue plotting out the short scenario involving Molly and Ray. Students may come up with ideas similar to the ones below.

1 **Exposition:** Ray has committed armed robbery. Though no one was hurt, the police are after him.

2 **Inciting Incident:** He goes to see his mother, who refuses to give him the keys to her car.

3 **Rising Action:** The police arrive at the door and Ray hides.

4 **Crisis:** The police believe Molly is withholding information about Ray and they threaten to take her down to the station for questioning.

5 **Climax:** Ray enters with a gun. It turns out to be a squirt gun. His mother points this out and Ray surrenders to the police.

6 **Falling Action:** The police take Ray away in handcuffs.

7 **Resolution:** Molly puts on her coat and hat calling, "Don't worry, Ray. I'm coming too. You know I want to help you."

Encourage students to be imaginative in getting to the resolution. Remind them that the characters do not have to be heroic or even good-hearted. Above all the characters must work hard to fulfill their objectives. Whether they accomplish these objectives or not is another matter.

Write Your Scenario

Remind students that the rules of playwriting structure can be applied to a great many, but not all, plays.

1 **Exposition** This is the setup of the play. You learned about the three Ws of exposition previously (Who, Where, and What), and it is important that as a playwright you have a clear idea what your characters' lives were all about before the events of your play begin. In the sample scene on page 142 the **exposition** informs us that Molly is Ray's mother. The scene takes place in her house. It also allows us to see that Ray has committed a crime. This is not stated, but it is strongly implied by the playwright's dialogue and by the actions created in the stage directions for Ray.

2 **Inciting Incident** The event that sets the action on its course is called the **inciting incident.** In the example, the inciting incident is Molly's refusal to give Ray her car keys. Here is where the conflict begins. The playwright must be sure that this conflict has enough dramatic impetus to carry the scene forward, because the rest of the play will spin out from it.

3 **Rising Action** The playwright must carefully build the dramatic tension as characters encounter obstacles to their goals. It is important for the playwright to keep the drama tight and to give the characters ways to help the audience understand how they rationalize their feelings and actions.

4 **Crisis** As the play continues, the playwright must create an event that occurs just at the moment when it seems things could either resolve or get much worse. This is the **crisis.** The playwright must be sure not to infuse in the crisis too much emotional intensity, as this could make the climax to follow seem anticlimactic.

5 **Climax** In the **climax,** which is the high point of the play, the playwright creates a situation in which the protagonist makes an irrevocable decision. The playwright must strive to convince the audience that this highly emotional event will either result in victory or in some way bring an end to the conflict. The climax is also called the *turning point.*

6 **Falling Action** The events after the climax must seem logical and true to the play. This is where the playwright wraps up any loose ends and moves toward the outcome of the play.

7 **Resolution** The end of the story, in which the conflicts are resolved, is called the **resolution.** It takes a light touch in terms of writing. At this point, the playwright must be sure that the audience can see clearly the result of the choice or action of the protagonist.

Write Your Scenario

You are now ready to write your scenario. Go back to your seed idea, then begin to make choices. There is

Quotable

Use the quote below as a prompt, discussion starter, or for your own enjoyment.

Usually you can't write ten lines without someone wanting something. Even if you don't know it.

Lanford Wilson, Playwright

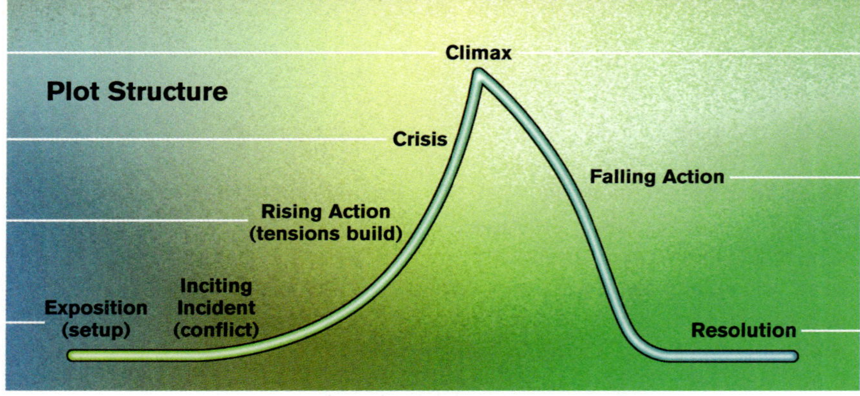

Your scenario should include these plot elements. Be aware that not all plays contain all elements.

a benefit to restricting yourself by making strong choices. Each time you make a decision about the play, you rid yourself of other elements that you no longer have to deal with. For example, once you decide that your play takes place in a kitchen, you need no longer worry about other scenic considerations. If your play features only two characters, you know who's going to be doing the talking and when. Once you have boxed in the essential ideas of the play, you have effectively boxed out other nonessential ideas—you've given your play a direction. Your goal is to set the play's structure up so effectively that it will have a logical, effective, and satisfying ending—the seeds of which were planted in the beginning.

You will need to make the following choices:

- **Who is in the play?**
- **Where does it take place?**
- **Who is the protagonist?**
- **Who or what is the antagonistic force?**
- **Where do these two meet?** (the inciting incident)
- **What does the protagonist decide to do** about it?
- **What is the response of the antagonistic force?**
- **What is the critical choice or action of the protagonist** that brings the play to its logical conclusion?
- **What happens after the play ends?** (This should be clear from what happens within the play.)

Your scenario should be a scene-by-scene telling of the story in narrative form. Be sure to come up with a title.

When you have completed your writing, exchange your scenario with a classmate. Discuss each other's work in terms of the progression of the story and the clarity of the theme. Make any necessary changes and create a clean copy.

Practice reading your scenario aloud, and time yourself to be sure it is between five- and ten- minutes long.

In such great plays as Samuel Beckett's *Waiting for Godot* and Eugene Ionesco's absurdist classic *The Bald Soprano* there are no clearcut answers to the question of who is the protagonist and who or what is the antagonistic force. Harold Pinter rose to fame by eliminating any semblance of exposition in such plays as *The Caretaker* and *The Birthday Party*. It is very difficult to tell the players without exposition; we find it hard to tell the villains from the heroes in these plays. This was one of the points Pinter probably wanted to make.

Remind students that as in most endeavors, it is important to *know* the rules before making the decision to diverge from them.

ACTivity Have pairs of students exchange their scenarios while the work is still evolving. Have them determine how well the scenario follows the elements of good plot structure. Remind students that collaboration should consist of constructive feedback presented in a positive manner. They should respond to the work they read, not the work they would like to have written themselves or the work they feel should have been written.

Vocabulary Enhancement

The resolution is also referred to as the *denouement* (day new MAH), which comes from a French word meaning "to untie."

Backstage Gossip: Earache

When Mr. Boaden had read his unsuccessful drama *Aurelio and Miranda* in the green room, he observed that he knew nothing so terrible as reading a piece before such a critical audience. The actress Mrs. Powell who was present said she knew one thing much more terrible. "What can that be?" demanded the author. "To be obliged," said she, "to sit and hear it."

from *Theatrical Anecdotes* by Peter Hay

Chapter 13 The Playwright **145**

PRESENT

Share Your Drama Scenario

Help students understand that they can use their voices to build excitement as they share their scenarios. They may wish to review some of the techniques discussed in Chapter 7, Voice Production and Articulation.

ACTivity Many larger communities have theatre companies that workshop new plays. Call your local theatre. You may be able to set up a time for your students to see a staged reading. Or you might be able to obtain a copy of a script in development. Workshops and readings are very different from productions and would provide students with an entirely different view of the playwriting process.

CRITIQUE

Evaluate a Classmate's Scenario

Hand out the Critique Sheet for this project or have students use their own paper. Quickly go over the elements to look for in a strong scenario and leave the plot structure diagram on the chalkboard.

After you have reviewed student critiques, discuss with the subjects of the evaluations any recurrent suggestions for improvement.

PRESENT

Share Your Drama Scenario

When your name is called, hand in a copy of your scenario or the Activity Sheet and walk to the playing area. As always, take a moment to gather yourself by drawing a deep relaxing breath before you begin.

Begin by telling the audience the title of your play. Then read through your scenario. Rhythm and pacing are important when you're reading aloud. Avoid speaking in a monotone! Remember that you are telling a story. Vocally emphasize the most important or interesting parts of that story. It's important to establish a connection with the audience, so make eye contact with your listeners periodically.

When you have finished, thank your audience, and return to your seat.

CRITIQUE

Evaluate a Classmate's Scenario

Choose one of the scenarios presented in class and evaluate it on a scale of 1 to 5, with 5 being "outstanding" and 1 being "needs much improvement." Ask yourself the questions below to help focus your evaluation.

- What details did the playwright use to make the plot clear?
- How would you describe the theme (or themes) of the play?
- What was the conflict, and was it strong enough?
- What changes to the play would you suggest based on this scenario?
- In what way did the speaker's manner of presentation impact your appreciation of the scenario?

Write a paragraph that details your evaluation and explains the rating you gave.

Quotable

When you go to the theatre you want know who the main character is, and you want to be able see what they want, see what's against them, and see whether they get it or not. Then you want to go home.

Marsha Norman, Playwright

Spotlight on

Collaboration

Unlike the novelist or the poet—who can work alone—playwrights are dependent upon the artistic vision of others to bring their work to life. Collaboration is a vital aspect of a playwright's job. First-time playwrights should seek out directors who enjoy working on new plays and actors who are eager to create a role for the very first time. These collaborators can often help the playwright create more vibrant and believable scenes. Above all, plays are meant to be seen and heard. They can be developed and refined through private and public readings and through productions.

"The Eugene O'Neill Center National Playwrights Conference is dedicated to the development of new work for the theatre . . . ." So begins the mission statement of one of the most prestigious theatre organizations in the United States. Founded in 1964, the Eugene O'Neill Theatre Center has set a high standard for new play development. Named after one of America's greatest playwrights, the O'Neill Center is a haven where playwrights can develop their craft free from the pressures of the marketplace. It offers many different programs, but perhaps the most famous is the annual summer workshop known as the National Playwrights Conference. Each year, playwrights from all over the country compete for a workshop slot there. Located in Waterford, Connecticut, the conference typically receives 650 play submissions annually. Of these, only 12 to 15 are selected for participation. Each selected play is assigned a director and a group of actors. Together with the playwright, these artists **workshop** the play—discussing, analyzing, and reading it aloud many times over the course of one month. The playwright has the opportunity to revise and rewrite the play. The process, culminating in two public **staged readings,** is designed to take a good script and make it stronger and more producible.

Over the years, many of the country's most distinguished writers have developed their plays at the O'Neill—including John Guare, August Wilson (see the Master of the Craft on page 149), Edwin Sanchez, and Kia Corthron.

Three artists collaborate on a play at the Eugene O'Neill Theatre Center.

Spotlight on

Collaboration In addition to the O'Neill Theatre Center, there are a number of other organizations devoted to new-play development around the country. Here are just a few of them:

- Humana Festival of New Plays, Actors Theatre of Louisville, KY (actorstheatre.org)
- Minneapolis Playwrights' Center, Minneapolis, MN (pwcenter.org)
- New Dramatists, New York, NY (newdramatists.org)
- Chicago Dramatists, Chicago, IL (chicagodramatists.org)
- Sundance Institute Theatre Program, Sundance, UT (*http://institute.sundance.org*)

Visit these Web sites yourself and encourage students to visit them as well to find out more about the collaborative process of each organization.

Vocabulary Enhancement

Tell students that staged readings and workshops fall under the general heading of *development,* the process through which many new plays must go before they are deemed ready for full production.

Visual Cue

The following prompts can be used to help students exercise **critical viewing skills.**

- What do you think the interpersonal dynamic is like among these three artists?
- Which one do you think is the playwright? What makes you think so?
- If you had to describe this scene using only one sentence, what would you say?

Chapter 13 Test

The test for this chapter is available in blackline master form in the Resource Binder, page 55.

For More Information

Books

Here are some excellent text resources on playwriting fundamentals:

Garrison, Gary, *Perfect 10: Writing and Producing the 10-Minute Play,* Heinemann, 2001.

Hatcher, Jeffrey, *The Art and Craft of Playwrighting,* Heinemann, 2001.

McLaughlin, Buzz, *The Playwright's Process: Learning the Craft from Today's Leading Dramatists,* Back Stage Books, 1997.

Sweet, Jeffrey, *Solving Your Script: Tools and Techniques for the Playwright,* Heinemann, 2001.

Sweet, Jeffrey, *The Dramatist's Toolkit: The Craft of the Working Playwright,* Heinemann, 1993.

Other Media

Links to playwriting opportunities for young people can be found at:

www.aate.com

http://liberalarts.iupui.edu/bonderman

www.youngplaywrights.org

Dramatists Play Service, Inc. recommends The 52nd Street Project Kid Theatre Kit. Call (212) 683-8960 for information.

Additional Projects

1 Write a one-act play from the scenario you created. When you have finished it, collaborate with a small group of classmates to refine and act out the script. You may wish to perform your new play for the entire class.

2 Read a full-length play and then write a two-page scenario for it. Include a statement of the play's theme, a summary of its plot and conflict, and brief sketches of each character.

3 Put on a playreading for your classmates. You can read something you've written or select a published work. Perform the play as a sit-down reading. Cast the reading and make sure you have someone to read the stage directions. Remember that a committed reading can sometimes almost fool the audience into thinking they've watched a full-fledged production.

4 Take a current news story and create a scenario for it. Describe the story's exposition, inciting incident, plot, characters, conflict, and resolution (if any). Try to come up with a theme that pertains to the story.

5 If you have written a play, enter it in a playwriting contest. You can find a wealth of information about writing contests on the Internet. You might start with the Young Playwrights Inc.'s National Playwriting Contest (see Theatre Then and Now on page 151).

6 Read *The Drummer* by Athol Fugard, which can be found in Unit Eight. Re-create this simple pantomime as a two-character scene with dialogue that motivates the action.

Substitute Teacher Activities

Here are ideas for the substitute teacher when you are out of the classroom.

- Assign the Aristotle's Elements of Drama Worksheet on page 53 of the Resource Binder.
- Assign one or more additional projects on this page.
- Teach The Script on pages 575-576 of the Student Handbook.
- **Have a Class Discussion About Play Structure** by comparing theatre and film. Ask students which aspects of playwriting structure are common to both plays and movies. Create a Venn diagram illustrating the similarities and differences.

Master of the Craft

August Wilson: Master Playwright

Frederick August Kittel was born in Pittsburgh, Pennsylvania, in 1945. At an early age, he knew he wanted to be a poet. He dropped out of school in the tenth grade, but went on to educate himself—at the library and on the street. His father essentially abandoned the family, and in 1965 the young August changed his last name to Wilson—his mother's maiden name.

In 1978, Wilson took a job in St. Paul, writing scripts for the Science Museum of Minnesota. The move put him in close proximity to The Playwrights' Center, a Minneapolis-based play development organization, which granted Wilson a fellowship in 1980. In 1982, Wilson's play *Ma Rainey's Black Bottom* was selected for participation in the O'Neill Theatre Center's National Playwrights Conference. There Wilson met the center's artistic director, Lloyd Richards. It was a fruitful alliance. Richards went on to direct six of Wilson's plays on Broadway.

In an interview with the *New York Times* in 1984, Wilson said, "My generation of blacks knew very little about the past of our parents. They shielded us from the indignities they suffered." Wilson began to throw light on that shadowy past with an ambitious series of plays, each set in a different decade of the 20th century and focused specifically on black issues. *Fences, Joe Turner's Come and Gone, Two Trains Running,* and *Seven Guitars* are some of these plays.

His roots as a poet are evident in each of Wilson's dramas. His work is explosive and fiercely beautiful—the language is alive and real, yet lyrical. In a 1990 review of *The Piano Lesson, New York Post* critic Clive Barnes stated, "This is a play in which to lose yourself—to give yourself up . . . to August Wilson's thoughts, humors and thrills, always talking the same language of humanity."

Two-time Pulitzer Prize-winner August Wilson.

Backstage Gossip: Wilson Versus Brustein

In 1997 a feud sprang up between playwright August Wilson and director, writer, and critic Robert Brustein. Their disagreement over matters such as colorblind casting and funding for African American writers led to a public debate between the two men.

Wilson said in part: "We reject any attempt to blot us out, to reinvent history and ignore our presence . . . . We want you to see us. We are black and beautiful. We have an honorable history in the world of men . . . . We do not need colorblind casting; we need some theaters to develop our playwrights."

Brustein responded by questioning whether there should perhaps be "some kind of statute of limitations on white guilt and white reparations." He further berated Wilson for having "fallen into a monotonous tone of victimization."

Master of the Craft

More About August Wilson

Wilson has said that he is fiercely opposed to colorblind casting—casting that does not take race into account, or that uses racial casting dynamics other than those called for in the script. He finds the idea of an all-black *Death of a Salesman* "an assault on our presence, an insult to our [African American] intelligence."

Encourage a class discussion on what might be the pros and cons of colorblind casting as well as the social and artistic impact of under-representing certain ethnic and racial groups.

ACTivity August Wilson honed his craft at development organizations such as the Minneapolis Playwrights' Center and the Eugene O'Neill Center. As a long-term project, encourage your students to write one-act plays and workshop them in small groups. Students should offer constructive feedback and suggestions about character, plot, and structure.

Masters Past and Present

August Wilson's plays are set in past decades, but their themes resonate with modern viewers. When writing a play set in the past, there must be a connection between the events of the play and the world we live in today.

Below are playwrights who have also worked from historical perspectives.

- William Shakespeare, despite a lack of both formal education and world travel, wrote many plays set in ancient times and exotic places, including *Antony and Cleopatra, Julius Caesar,* and *Titus Andronicus.*
- In *Life of Galileo,* Bertolt Brecht (1898-1956) wrote about the famous 16th-century Italian astronomer Galileo Galilei.
- Jean Anouilh (1910-1987) wrote a version of *Antigone,* an ancient play by Sophocles.
- Caryl Churchill (1938-) wrote about English colonial Africa during the time of Queen Victoria in her play *Cloud Nine.*

Theatre Then and Now

The plays presented at festivals to honor Dionysus included the Great Dionysia at Athens, held in the spring; the Rural Dionysia, held in the winter; and the Lenaea, which followed the Rural Dionysia and was also held in the winter. Every year the festival held three competitions for playwriting. One was for comedy; another for dithyramb, an elaborate choral form that typically featured fifty or more singers; and one for tragic plays. From these ancient contests sprang some of the world's greatest drama.

The oldest existing comedies are by Aristophanes. His writing is a mixture of satirical attacks on public figures of the time and bawdy jokes.

Other Cultures, Other Times

Among the most famous of the early 20th-century Indian playwrights was **Rabindranath Tagore** (1861-1941). Born into a wealthy and artistically inclined Calcutta family, Tagore wrote plays, poems, and songs, most of which were originally performed by the many talented members of his immediate family. In 1913 Tagore won the Nobel Prize for literature. He also wrote the Indian national anthem. Tagore's best-known play is *The Post Office,* written in 1931. This poignant play, about a dying boy who is restricted to his home and denied the joys of the outdoors by a rigid-minded doctor, is still performed throughout the world. The child longs to enter life and believes that the king will send him a message through the post office opposite his window. When a message finally comes, it is blank.

ACTivity Obtain a copy of *The Post Office* and have a group of students perform it as a staged reading. You can download a copy of the play from *www.abacci.com.*

Theatre Then and Now

Sophocles

Playwriting Contests of Old: Greek Goat Songs

Written drama as we know it began in Greece around 500 B.C. A playwriting competition was held at a yearly festival in honor of the patron of Greek theatre, Dionysus, god of wine, agriculture, and fertility. The festival featured choruses of goatskin-clad men who played satyrs (the half-man/half-goat creatures devoted to Dionysus). In fact, the word *tragedy* originated from the idea of these goat costumes, *tragos* ("goat"), and the words and music of the chorus, *ode* ("song"), or "goatsong."

Originally, tragedies were in the form of spoken song performed by a leader and a chorus. But in 534 B.C., at the Athenian festival, Thespis starred in a tragedy he'd written himself. He impersonated a character who engaged the traditional Greek chorus in dialogue. Thespis won first prize and became history's first known actor and its first true playwright. The word *thespian,* which means "actor," is derived from this ancient innovator.

From these ancient contests sprang some of the world's greatest drama. Many of the winning playwrights are thought to have been extremely prolific, yet only a few of their works survive. Euripides (484–406 B.C.) holds the record. Of the 90 plays he wrote, 18 remain, including *Medea.* His plays mine the deep sorrow of the human condition. Aeschylus (525–456 B.C.) is believed to have written 90 tragedies. Of these, only 7 remain, including the Oresteia trilogy. Sophocles (496–406 B.C.) wrote perhaps 125 tragedies, of which only 7 survive, including *Antigone* and *Oedipus Rex.* These great classical tragedies continue to influence generations of playwrights.

Tara Fitzgerald plays the title role in *Antigone* at the Old Vic Theatre in London.

Visual Cue

Use the questions that follow to help students use **critical viewing skills** to analyze this scene from *Antigone.*

- What does the expression on the face of Tara Fitzgerald tell you about this scene?
- What does her body language reveal?

Playwriting Contests Today: Up-and-Coming Playwrights

"If you want to say you knew them when, you have to see them now." That's the philosophy of Young Playwrights Inc.'s annual playwriting contest for young writers. Young Playwrights Inc. began in 1981, the brainchild of composer Stephen Sondheim, who made it his mission to foster new American writers. Today Young Playwrights Inc. has grown to be a major force in American theatre.

Each year the contest receives approximately 1100 submissions from all over the United States. The judges select only seven winners. These young writers attend a nine-day summer workshop of their plays. During that time they work with a professional director and actors, peers, and mentor playwrights. At night they attend Broadway and off-Broadway shows. At the end of the workshop process, each playwright has a public reading. Some of the plays are selected for full off-Broadway production by Young Playwrights Inc. in a festival the following season.

Professional writers who got their start at Young Playwrights Inc.'s annual contest include Rebecca Gilman *(Spinning into Butter, Boy Gets Girl)* and Kenneth Lonergan *(You Can Count on Me, This Is Our Youth, Lobby Hero).* If you're interested in becoming a playwright, start now! This contest offers amazing opportunities for talented young people—but it's only open to writers under the age of eighteen. For more information, write to Young Playwrights Inc. Dept. WEB, 306 W. 38th Street #300, New York, NY 10018. Or visit the Web site at www.youngplaywrights.org.

World-renowned composer Stephen Sondheim began Young Playwrights Inc. in 1981.

From the Field: Write What You Know

When I work with student playwrights, I begin with the idea that they must write about what they know and, more importantly, what they have experienced.

I have found that the biggest problems kids have with writing scenes (or stories) is finding the material. I feel that if I can get them to look at their own lives and believe that it is a great (possibly the greatest) source for their writing, they can then truly begin to work and explore.

It is a lesson that really sticks with them because it tells them right away that they must be emotionally connected to their writing or it has little real value.

Joel Drake Johnson, Playwright and Teacher, Chicago, IL

Playwriting Newsletter

Insight for Playwrights is a monthly marketing newsletter with the latest submission information for theatres, contests, fellowships, residencies, and other development programs for dramatic writers. *Insight* offers sixteen pages a month of important submission information: "We scour the trades and the Internet for playwriting opportunities . . . so you can concentrate on your writing." Write to *Insight for Playwrights,* P.O. Box 127778, San Diego, CA 92112-7778.

For More Information

Here are some more contest opportunities for high school-age playwrights.

Baker's Plays High School Playwriting Contest. Write to Baker's Plays, 100 Chauncy St., Boston, MA 02111.

California Young Playwrights Contest (California residents under the age of nineteen). Write to The Playwrights Project, P.O. Box 2068, San Diego, CA 92112.

Chicago Young Playwrights Festival (Chicago residents, eighth grade through age nineteen). Write to Artistic Director, Pegasus Players, 1145 W. Wilson Avenue, Chicago, IL 60640.

Chapter 14

The Director and Producer

This chapter helps students to understand the personnel and the team effort that go into producing a play. Students will learn how to analyze a play as a director would.

Objectives

1. to understand the specific duties of the director and the producer
2. to understand the role of other members of the production team
3. to use analytical skills to make casting and staging decisions
4. to use the structural elements of drama to analyze a play

National Standards

Chapter 14 meets these National Theatre Standards:

Proficient 4a, 4b, 7a, 7b, 7c, 8a, 8b, 8c
Advanced 4e, 4f, 7e, 7h, 8e, 8g

Project Specs

For this chapter, encourage students to use their imaginations to visualize a performance of their selected play as they read it.

ESL Students
Note that ESL students may need extra help with some of this chapter's vocabulary.

Advanced Students
For extra credit, students may wish to contact a local or regional theatre and interview a director, producer, or house manager.

On Your Feet

Instead of a list, students may want to create a graphic showing the responsibilities and duties of each member of the production team they can think of. They can leave some blank space where they can add personnel when they complete this chapter.

Chapter 14 The Director and Producer

The production of a play represents the talent and commitment of many people. Whether on the stage or in the wings, you should have an understanding of all phases of the production process. This chapter will give you more information about each job—focusing particularly on the work of the director and the producer.

Project Specs

Project Description For this assignment, you will analyze a play as a director would and give a three- to five-minute presentation.

Purpose to hone your skills at play analysis and interpretation and to understand some of the basic elements of directing a play

Materials a written breakdown or a graphic representation of the important elements of a play you would like to direct or the Director and Producer Activity Sheet your teacher provides

Theatre Terms

director
dramaturg
general admission
producer
prompt book
royalties
strike
symbol

On Your Feet

With a classmate, discuss what you think the director and producer do to make a play happen. Who else is necessary for the production of a play? Make a list of who does what on a play. When you finish working on this chapter, compare your list to what you have learned.

Director Jean-Pierre Vincent, right, and actor Daniel Auteuil discuss the leading role in Molière's *That Scoundrel Scapin* for the annual theatre festival in Avignon, France.

Theatre Terms

director a person who interprets a play, casts, blocks, and helps actors create their roles

dramaturg a person who performs a variety of tasks to assist with the production of a play, such as script evaluation and historical research

general admission when seating is not assigned and audience members can sit where they like

producer a person who finds financing for a play, chooses the director, and oversees the day-to-day business activities

prompt book a three-ring binder or other notebook that holds the annotated script along with the director's ideas

royalties the money paid to the rights holder of a play

strike disassembling of the set

symbol a concrete image that is used to represent an abstract concept or principal

152 **Unit Four** The Play: From Vision to Reality

PREVIEW

The Director

It is the responsibility of the **director** to create a cohesive group that will work together to accomplish a successful dramatic presentation. In high school, the director is often the drama teacher, but students should also have the opportunity to try out their directing skills. A good director has a keen sense of the play and the playwright's intentions as well as the ability to encourage actors and designers in interpreting the play. The director helps the actors use their skills and intuition to create meaningful characters. A director must also be able to see trouble coming among the cast and/or crew and figure out ways to circumvent it, pinpoint areas that need improvement, and come up with plans to overcome any weaknesses in the staff—and communicate solutions to all these problems in a diplomatic way. A director must be insightful, dependable, responsible, and able to take on many tasks at once. It is a job that demands a very special individual.

The Producer

Most high school drama groups do not have a **producer,** but they are very common in the legitimate theatre. The producer finds the people who are willing to invest money in the show and creates a budget. The producer also hires the director and the staff who will work on the production. And while the producer will have help from members of the crew in running the advertising campaign, he is responsible for its direction. In many high schools, the producer is also the director.

If you're interested in directing or producing plays, you'll need to familiarize yourself with every aspect of the theatre. Involvement in a production means you will deal with actors, design staff, stage managers, technical crew members, and much more.

A Short List of the Director's Duties

If you choose to be a director, you have a big job ahead of you. On the following page are just a few responsibilities of the director.

PREVIEW

The Director

The best stage directors, through their creative vision, inspire the people on a production to do their best, most imaginative work. Remind students that it is hard to inspire others if you are not inspired and excited yourself. Good directors bring an infectious enthusiasm to all phases of the production process.

ACTivity Have students work in pairs on a directing activity. One student reads a passage from a play, novel, or poem. The other student offers suggestions on how to present the material more expressively. The "director" may suggest movements or vocal adjustments, changes of rhythm and volume, and so on. After the "actor" has rehearsed the material with the director, the two students switch places.

The Producer

A good way for a student to learn about all aspects of the theatre, is to assist a producer. At the high school level, you might do well to select one or two students to assist you as you direct and produce a play. If there are good non-profit or community theatre groups in your area, contact them about having students job-shadow various theatre personnel for a week or two.

A Short List of the Director's Duties

Reading and Research Tell students that while reading and rereading the script, the director may enlist the aid of any number of other resources to gain a thorough understanding of the world of the play.

Resource Binder

- Who's Who: Flow Chart, TIPack, p. J
- Who's Who: Job Descriptions, TIPack, p. K
- The Director and Producer Activity Sheet, p. 56
- Profiles of Management Personnel Worksheet, p. 57
- Critique Sheet: Director's Presentation, p. 58
- Director and Producer Test, p. 59
- Director's Script Analysis: Plot/Theme, p. 129 and Character/Setting, p. 130
- Production Budget Form, p. 131

To Have on Hand

- Books or magazine articles with information about well-known theatre directors and producers
- Anthologies from which students may select their plays

Handbook Connections
pages 571-576

The director will probably also research the characters' professions, religions, ethnic customs, and so on.

Assembling the Team In addition, the director must be able to project his or her vision of the play to the design team and the actors, for they are the ones who will be bringing that vision to life.

Assembling the Tools Many plays can be obtained through the Samuel French Catalogue. French publishes Broadway and off-Broadway hits as well as plays from London's West End and original scripts submitted by untested authors. The catalogue is available for $3.50, including postage. Contact Samuel French, Inc., 45 West 25th Street, Dept. W, New York, NY 10010; (212) 206-8990 or fax (212) 206-1429.

A Short List of Producer's Duties

Tell students that in the professional theatre, particularly for Broadway-scale musicals, there is often a team of producers who work together to either invest the money themselves or to find a larger group of investors willing to take on the risk. Remind them that producing theatre on any level is a risk in terms of finding an audience, winning critical praise, and making a profit. Therefore, producers must be more than just money people. They should also have a deep belief in the artistic product and the creative team.

Vocabulary Enhancement

Casting an actor who has very similar characteristics to those of the character is called *typecasting.* The term *typecast* is often used to describe an actor who is constantly cast in similar and/or stereotypical roles, e.g., the smirking lawyer; the lusty girlfriend; the crusty old-timer with a bad temper, etc.

1 **Getting Started** The director selects the play, sets the dates for auditions, rehearsals, and the performance, and develops the artistic vision for the play. The chosen script should be well written and of high artistic quality, and the director should connect with it strongly. The theme should truthfully reveal some important element of the human experience. The play should feature strong characters, cohesive dialogue, and an interesting plot. It should be suitable to the school and community audience as well as the available talent pool and the school's technical capabilities. The fact is, if you don't have the necessary casting pool and facilities, you can't use the play.

2 **Reading and Researching** The director studies the play through multiple readings. If the play takes place in a different historical period, the director should also check a number of references to learn more about how people who lived during that time looked, spoke, worked, and so on. Often the director gets help from a **dramaturg** (see the box on page 157).

3 **Assembling the Team** The director enlists the aid of the production team to establish both continuity of design and a production schedule.

4 **Assembling the Tools** The director prepares a **prompt book** using a three-ring loose-leaf binder. Each page of the prompt book contains a page of the script, glued onto a piece of paper. The wide margins allow the director to write detailed notations about movement, technical cues, and so on. Think of the prompt book as the entire production written down on paper.

5 **Getting Down to It** The director conducts auditions, casts the play, and schedules and conducts rehearsals.

A Short List of the Producer's Duties

While the director is analyzing the script, creating the preliminary prompt book, and thinking about all the other onstage aspects of the production, the producer is hard at work on the business end. He or she finds investors, pays bills, oversees the budget, and works closely with a variety of different production crews. Here are some of the production areas for which the producer is ultimately responsible.

1 **Getting Permission** The producer must figure out a budget that takes into consideration the costs of producing the play, including the payment of **royalties,** money paid to the author for the use of the script. The box office receipts should help to pay

Backstage Gossip: New Play, Anyone?

When actor Sidney Poitier brought Lorraine Hansberry's brand new script *A Raisin in the Sun* to fledgling director Lloyd Richards, Richards fell in love with it. But for a long time neither he nor producer Phil Rose could find a theatre willing to take a chance on staging it. *A Raisin in the Sun* finally premiered at the Ethel Barrymore Theatre in New York in February 1959 to great critical and popular acclaim. It has had hundreds of productions since then and is widely regarded as one of the best American plays of the 20th century.

the royalties, which can sometimes involve a great deal of money. Be sure to check the royalty fees before committing to any play. (It should go without saying that even schools *must* pay the necessary royalties. Failure to do so is a criminal offense.) To secure the royalties, the producer must contact the play's publisher by mail or fax. Rights cannot be secured by telephone. Information the producer gives to the publisher includes performance dates, number of seats, ticket price, and type of theatre (in the case of a school, nonprofessional/educational).

2 **Getting an Audience** Of course there's no point in producing a play if you don't have an audience. A large part of the producer's job is to bring in a crowd—in other words, to let the school and community know about the production and to get them excited about attending. This involves:

- Creating and distributing posters/flyers advertising the show. Posters should be put up at least two or three weeks before opening night.
- Writing public service announcements (PSAs) for local radio and TV stations. These brief announcements are typically made free of charge.
- Sending press releases to local newspapers. With planning and imagination, a producer can sometimes wrangle a feature story from the newspaper or a public radio station.
- Running an ad in the paper or on the radio (if the school's budget allows for this). The ad must be turned in far enough in advance so that it will do some good. The approved copy should be submitted at least two weeks before opening night. The copy should be edited and proofread to make sure all the information a potential ticket-buyer will need is included.
- Selling program ads. The money from these ads goes to pay for the program printing and to fund other areas of the production.

3 **The Program** The producer is also in charge of creating the program. There should be artistic continuity between the program and the advertising, posters, and flyers. Per the royalties agreement, the program must credit the playwright. Each publisher provides the guidelines for this credit, so check the agreement carefully. The program recognizes each cast and production team member. Programs may include a "Special Thanks To" section in which people

Quotable

What a playwright needs most is a director, because a good director lifts the play off the page into radiant life. The playwrights who've succeeded have had that director. To my mind, it's the most important collaboration in the theatre.

Tina Howe, Playwright

Sometimes shows are funded through corporate sponsorship. A theatre's marketing personnel often try to find a link between a particular play and a sponsor's product or service. For example, a play about a food critic might receive funding from a national food-services corporation or even a local restaurant.

Remind students that the closer the show gets to opening night, the more the producer may have to fill in for the director with regard to offstage production details both large and small.

ACTivity Have students choose a play and write a brief public service announcement (PSA) about a production of it. Specify a length of 150 words or less. Then have students exchange their PSAs with a partner and read them aloud.

ACTivity **ESL Students** These students can create a PSA in their native language if they wish.

ACTivity **Advanced Students** These students may wish to create both a PSA and a radio ad. Encourage them to record their ads using background music. Play the finished tapes for the class.

ACTivity **Special Needs Students** Have students read or watch a play and discuss the type of sponsor who might be interested in providing financial backing for it.

Show, Don't Tell If possible, bring in programs from various theatre productions (professional, community, school) and compare the different elements of each. Discuss with students which ones they think have the most impact and why. Discuss the importance of including all the necessary information in a program.

ACTivity Have students choose a well-known play and create their own program for the play.

The Production Team

Tell students that the set, lighting, sound, makeup, and costume designers' ideas are carried out during production by the various production crews. Each designer creates drawings and or models of his or her designs. These are then built and maintained by the assigned crew members. For example, the set designer creates plans, drawings, and a scale model of the set for the play. The set crew then builds the set based on these specifications.

In the professional theatre and at many schools, the stage manager serves as the prompter during rehearsals, but during performances professional theatres (and most schools) do not use a prompter at all. If an actor forgets a line, he or she—sometimes with the help of other cast members—is responsible for getting the show back on track.

ACTivity Advanced Students Obtain a copy of *Stage Design: A Practical Guide* by Gary Thorne (Crowood Press, 1999). It contains information on how to create scale models. Have interested students choose a play from which to create a scale model of a set design.

Vocabulary Enhancement

Let students know that forgetting one's lines is called *going up.* An actor might say, for example, "I completely went up in scene one!"

Have students look at the photo of the production team. Then use the following prompts to exercise their **critical viewing skills.**

- What skills do you think are necessary for the work these members of the production team are doing?
- What seems to be the attitude of these crew members?

The production team works to prepare for an upcoming play.

and organizations that have made contributions to the production are credited. Depending on the budget, the program may be anything from a single sheet of paper folded in half that lists the names and roles of the cast and crew to an elaborate document that includes biographies (and sometimes photographs).

4 **Running Interference** The duties of the director and the producer overlap at times. The producer's role often expands as the director gets deeper into the rehearsal process. A good producer stays in very close contact with the director—and picks up the slack when needed!

The Production Team

It takes a lot of people to put on a play. The director, producer, designers, and actors may have the jobs with the highest profiles, but they wouldn't get far without the production team. Following is a list of backstage and offstage personnel and their duties.

The *assistant director* helps the director in conducting rehearsals, making phone calls, and sometimes doing research or taking on the role of a dramaturg (see the box at the right).

The *stage manager* is in charge of all stage crews. He or she also assists the director. During rehearsals, the stage manager takes notes, informs the production team as to the director's needs, and helps with scheduling. During final rehearsals and performances, the stage manager has complete supervision of the stage. He or she gives warning calls for lights, special effects, and curtains. After the play has closed, the stage manager assists with the **strike** (disassembling) of the set.

The *prompter* must attend every rehearsal to become completely familiar with the script and all its cues and pauses. The prompter is responsible for feeding actors their lines should they forget them. The prompter also makes sure the rehearsal room or theatre is ready, and during rehearsals he or she holds the prompt book, noting all

Backstage Gossip: Whose Line Is It Anyway?

Kenneth Tynan, in *Persona Grata,* tells of an occasion during a London production of a Lunt-Fontanne vehicle when that wonderfully proficient team suddenly stopped in mid-scene. The prompter, after a first astonished moment, threw the next line to them, and Mr. Lunt responded charmingly, "It's not that we don't know the line, old boy. We just can't remember which one of us says it."

movements assigned by the director. (For more on prompting and the rehearsal process, see Chapter 15.)

Stage crews build, paint, and set up stage scenery. *Running crews* shift scenery during the performance. After each performance, the running crew sets up for Act I of the next night's show. They also help with strike after the final performance. (See Chapter 18 for more on set design and the stage crew.)

The *light crew* uses the lighting charts and cue sheets to properly hang and focus the lights. The crew then runs the lights during the show. The light crew assists with strike. (See Chapter 19 for more about lighting design and the light crew.)

The *sound effects* crew works on the sound cue sheet and provides the necessary sound effects. Under the direction of the sound designer, they may help select music to enhance the scene transitions and the mood of the play. (See Chapter 20 for more about sound design.)

The *costume crew* supplies the costumes and assigns dressing rooms. During the run of the play, the costume crew keeps the costumes clean, organized, mended, and pressed. (See Chapter 21 for more about costuming.)

Spotlight on

The Dramaturg

What is a dramaturg? You may not have heard this word before, but a dramaturg plays a vital part in many production teams. He or she may serve as a script reader in the theatre's literary department, evaluating plays that are under consideration for production. The dramaturg often does research into the historical or societal issues of a play and shares that information with the director and cast. Most dramaturgs know a great deal about playwriting structure, so they are particularly useful during productions of world premiere plays.

Although dramaturgs have been a part of the theatre scene since the 1800s, it has only been relatively recently that their place within the American production process has been clearly defined. Twenty or so years ago, most American theatres did not work with a dramaturg. Now these multifaceted professionals represent a strong creative component in theatre productions large and small.

Spotlight on

The Dramaturg Many schools do not use dramaturgs. For those that do, the dramaturg is often a history teacher. He or she generally prepares a presentation for the cast and crew about the playwright, the time period, and the issues the play deals with. Ask teachers at your school with expertise on the subject or time period of a play you are working on (or the play or playwright) to come to a rehearsal to make a presentation to your students. List this person's name in the program as the production dramaturg.

A good dramaturg functions as a third set of eyes for the playwright and the director. When working on a new play, the dramaturg asks questions about character, structure, and plot in order to help create a tightly molded concept of the work. For the actors, designers, and director, a good dramaturg provides historical/religious/political/socio-cultural research to help put the play into a proper context, all the while remaining focused on the text.

From the Field: Mallaturgy

I've found that the best dramaturgy occurs through what I call "mallaturgy"—the time when another theatre artist and a dramaturg can spend some time together outside the theatre setting—perhaps in the mall—talking about the piece and its background in more universal terms.

Michele Volansky, Dramaturg, Philadelphia Theatre Company

Chapter 14 The Director and Producer **157**

ACTivity Ask students to create publicity items for a play of their choice. They might write a human-interest story using research about the play or the playwright. Or they might create a large poster or ad. Encourage them to use their imaginations and to think of visual and textual ways to get potential audience members interested in attending the show.

ACTivity When ushers must tell audience members they cannot be seated during the performance, it is helpful for them to have a polite but firm statement in mind. Ask students to imagine that they are ushers and that several audience members have arrived five minutes after the start of the play. Students may wish to write down their statement and memorize it before they present it to the class.

The *makeup crew* plans makeup for each actor, obtains necessary supplies, and arranges for a separate makeup room if possible. During the final rehearsals and the run of the show, the makeup crew assists the actors in applying their makeup. (See Chapter 22 for more about makeup design and the makeup crew.)

The *properties (props) crew* prepares detailed props lists for each scene and locates all props and furniture, including those props that will not be used in performance but are used during rehearsal. The head of the props crew assigns each crew member specific props to set and strike for each act. The crew organizes the props, keeping those for each scene in a separate basket or on a separate table. Although actors are expected to check their individual props, the props crew is responsible for making sure the props are in the correct spot for the actor to check. (See Chapter 23 for more about props.)

The *business manager* is in charge of the money. In a school setting, this person is often a faculty member. He or she serves as public relations officer and supervises the publicity, ticket sales, and program issues.

The *publicity crew* advertises the show by giving the school and local papers various news stories concerning performance dates, people involved, and information about the play, the playwright, and so on. This crew remains alert for possible feature stories engendered by the rehearsal process and arranges for photographers or arts and community reporters to have access to the cast. The crew puts up posters in the community and sends out postcards and flyers. The work of the publicity crew is crucial when it comes to attracting an audience.

The *house manager* is responsible for the seating and comfort of the audience during performances. The house manager sees to it that the auditorium is cool enough or warm enough, that the doors open on time, and that there are plenty of programs for distribution. He or she also supervises the ushers.

Ushers escort the audience members to their seats. If the performance is **general admission** (meaning that no seats are assigned and audience members can sit where they like), the ushers' main duty is to hand out programs and present an upbeat and courteous attitude. Ushers ask latecomers to wait in the lobby until the next scene change to avoid disturbing others (including the actors who are performing onstage). After the audience has left the auditorium, the ushers are responsible for picking up any trash or programs that may have been left behind.

Backstage Gossip: A Brilliant Publicity Move

When Murray Mednick's *The Coyote Cycle* premiered at Santa Fe, New Mexico's Theatre in the Red in 1984, the producers needed a way to entice the public into coming to an epic outdoor show—one that had never before been produced. During the months leading up to the opening, the savvy producers hung flyers all over town that simply read "Coyote is Coming."

As a result of this low-cost advertising ploy, by the time the show opened, Santa Fe was abuzz with the question, "What the heck *is* Coyote?"

PREPARE

Symbolic Elements of Drama

In previous chapters, we have looked at characters in conflict and analyzed the elements of plot. But to direct a play, you must also understand its theme (or themes) and the symbols it employs. A **symbol** is a concrete image that is used to represent an abstract concept or principle. In Arthur Miller's *Death of a Salesman,* Willy Loman's vegetable patch represents the old way of life with its opportunities for growth and renewal. In Jane Martin's *Clear Glass Marbles,* a bowl of marbles represents the waning days of a dying mother's life. In August Wilson's *The Piano Lesson,* a piano symbolizes for one character the need to remember the past; for another character, it represents the key to a new future.

A play's setting can often be symbolic as well. Think about what the following settings might convey.

- cemetery
- dining room
- train
- corporate boardroom
- museum
- Las Vegas

Theatre Journal

Think about the jobs in theatre production that do not involve acting, and choose one that interests you. Think about why this position interests you, and write about it in your journal.

Put on Your Director's Hat

In order to fulfill your assignment, you will first have to look at a play the way a director would. Follow the steps below.

1. Select a play you think you will like and read through it carefully. Pay close attention to what the characters say and do.
2. Once you have become familiar with the play's plot and characters, read the play a second time. Look for its themes and symbols. Remember that very often a play's theme is not explicitly stated. Complex plots have a major or central theme and an array of secondary ideas. Ask yourself questions as you go along. If you notice a recurring idea, track that idea all the way through to the end of the play. Take notes. Be sure this is a play you are excited about directing.
3. When you have finished analyzing the play, you should be able to
   - Name the protagonist.
   - Name the antagonistic force.
   - Explain the major plot line. (This should not take more than five sentences.)
   - Specify the conflict.
   - Define the play's theme.
   - List one or more symbols.
   - Explain why this play is the one you want to direct.

Next, you may either write a one- or two-page paper that illuminates all the

Symbolic Elements of Drama

ACTivity Ask students to think about the symbolism in some of the plays they have read. Then have them choose one play and make a list of its symbols. Before they begin, remind them that very often a prop or a place has special symbolic significance. For example, Belle Reeve, the family plantation Blanche speaks of in *A Streetcar Named Desire,* is a symbol of Blanche's loss, not only of her home, but also of her youth and the promise of love.

Theatre Journal

Use the following as an additional or substitute prompt.

Think about the choice you made of theatre-related jobs. What jobs outside the theatre might employ the same basic skills? For example, a stage manager must be organized and detail oriented, must be able to work efficiently with many different people, and must wield authority when necessary to keep things on track. Describe other jobs that require these skills.

PREPARE

Put on Your Director's Hat

Remind students that directing a play is hard work. There is no point in a director working on a play that doesn't excite him or her deeply. Ask students to analyze what it is about their chosen play that they find so intriguing. Is it hilarious, frightening, uplifting, or disturbing? Does it relate to their own life issues? At some point early in the rehearsal process, directors usually share their vision of the play with the actors and crew. The more personal the play is to the director, the more capable he or she will be of stimulating the cast and the other members of the production team.

Quotable

Use the quote below as a writing prompt or discussion starter.

I regard the theatre as the greatest of all art forms, the most immediate way in which a human being can share with another the sense of what it is to be a human being.

Oscar Wilde, Playwright

Rehearse Your Presentation

Get together with students who are using visual aids before the time assigned for their presentations and go over with them how they will proceed. Let them practice using overhead projector materials, slide-show carriages, and any other audio-video equipment they plan to employ. Help them run through their presentations until all elements flow together seamlessly.

Career Focus

Contact your local professional or community theatre and invite a stage director to come and speak to your class or to give students a tour of the theatre facility. If possible, ask your visitor to provide a short presentation (similar to the one students are working on) about a play he or she recently directed.

The following prompts can be used to help students build their **critical viewing skills.**

- What interpersonal skills do you think this director might be using to get a point across to the actor?
- What does the actor's body language tell you about how the director's words are being received?
- How important do you think openness is to the rehearsal process?

points on the previous page or create one or more visual aids that illustrate your points graphically. Your teacher may supply a Director and Producer Activity Sheet, which you may also use to work through this assignment. Whichever way you decide to handle your preparation, be sure that you cover each of the elements listed in the previous paragraph.

Rehearse Your Presentation

If you have written a paper, practice reading it aloud a few times, making sure you have covered each of the assignment's points and that you don't go over three minutes. Be sure to include time for about two minutes of questions from the audience. You should be familiar enough with the material that questions about theme, symbolism, plot, character, and your vision of the play will not throw you.

If you choose to present your project by means of visual aids, make sure you can explain each element and how it is linked to the other elements. Cover the same elements you would cover in a written essay. If you need an easel or a small table to show your work, arrange this with your teacher ahead of time. Make sure your presentation does not exceed five minutes, including questions from the audience.

Career Focus

Stage Director

As is the case in so many areas of the theatre, becoming a successful stage director takes more than just talent. Directors must have the drive to succeed. They must educate themselves in all areas of the theatre, read and analyze both new plays and classics, and be comfortable in the rehearsal room.

Many professional directors begin learning their craft in high school and college and go on to obtain master of fine arts degrees in directing. Some directors begin their careers as actors and gradually shift their focus to directing. The time they spent as actors is not wasted, however—in fact, having been an actor can prove very helpful for a director in terms of understanding the collaborative process.

If you are interested in becoming a director, you will need to read as much as you can. Read plays, read books on directing, and read magazines with articles about directors and their process. For that all-important real-world experience, you might apply to apprentice at a local theatre as an assistant director.

The stage director discusses a scene with a lead actor while other actors rehearse.

Notes

PRESENT

Share Your Director's Vision

When your name is called, step to the playing area and either arrange your graphics or make certain your written information is in order. Hand in any written material or the Activity Sheet to your teacher. Take a moment before introducing your presentation to breathe and focus. Tell the class the name of the play and its author before you begin. Once you begin, keep up the pace, but make sure you cover each point.

When you have finished, ask the audience if they have questions. Set a limit of three questions. If someone asks you a question for which you simply have no answer, admit that you don't know, but try to suggest ways that one might find the answer. After you have answered the third question, thank your audience and return to your seat.

CRITIQUE

Evaluate a Classmate's Presentation

Choose one of the class presentations to review. Evaluate the presenter using a scale from 1 to 5, with 5 being "outstanding," and 1 being "needs much improvement." To begin, ask yourself the questions below.

For verbal presentations:

- Was the presenter's overall vision of the play clear and insightful?
- Did the presenter cover the play's theme adequately?
- How well did the presenter convey an understanding of the play's symbols?
- Was the statement of the conflict clear?
- How did the presenter handle the plot description?
- In what way did the presenter answer the questions from the audience?

For graphic presentations:

- How did the graphics convey the play's plot and theme?
- In what way did the presenter involve conflict, symbols, and character?
- Were you able to get a good sense of the play?
- How comfortable did the presenter appear while answering questions?

Write a paragraph explaining why you gave the presenter the rating you did.

PRESENT

Share Your Director's Vision

Before students begin to share their work, remind them that their presentations start the moment their names are called. Approaching the playing area with a calm but confident gait and expression will go a long way toward keeping the presenter focused and will set the tone for the presentation.

CRITIQUE

Evaluate a Classmate's Presentation

Hand out the Critique Sheet for this project or have students use their own paper. Be sure the students understand what they will be looking for in the verbal presentations, including what theme entails, what symbols in a play encompass, and the seven elements of a plot. You might want to have information on these points written on the chalkboard for the students.

With regard to the graphic presentation, remind students that they are evaluating how well any charts, graphs, or other aids convey the presenter's points. Are the graphics easy to understand and helpful to the presentation?

After you have read the critiques, share them with students, allowing them to analyze and evaluate the critical comments. Discuss with students any points that they feel will help the further development of their work.

Quotable

It's not a field, I think, for people who need to have success every day: If you can't live with a nightly sort of disaster, you should get out. I wouldn't describe myself as lacking in confidence, but I would just say that the ghosts you chase you never catch.

John Malkovich, Actor and Director

Chapter 14 Test

The test for this chapter is available in blackline master form in the Resource Binder, page 59.

For More Information

Books

Bogart, Anne, *A Director Prepares: Seven Essays on Art in Theatre,* Routledge, 2001.

Botto, Louis, and Robert Viagas, *At This Theatre: 100 Years of Broadway Shows, Stories and Stars,* Applause Theatre Book Publishers, 2002.

Brook, Peter, *The Empty Space: A Book about Theater,* Simon & Schuster, 1995.

Frick, John W., editor, and Stephen Valliool, editor, *Theatrical Directors: A Biographical Dictionary,* Greenwood Press, 1994.

Gallaway, Marian, *The Director in the Theatre,* E. P. Waggener & Sons, 1963.

Grippo, Charles, *The Stage Producer's Business and Legal Guide,* Allworth Press, 2002.

Vaughn, Stuart, *A Possible Theatre: the Experiences of a Pioneer Director in America's Resident Theatre,* McGraw-Hill, 1969.

Other Media

Basics of Directing for the Stage, VHS, Insight Media, 1999.

Blocking a Scene: Basic Staging with Actors, VHS, Insight Media 1990.

The Creative Team, VHS, Insight Media, 1994.

The Directing Process, VHS or CD-ROM, Insight Media, 1990.

Additional Projects

1 Coach a classmate in the performance of a monologue. Encourage your classmate to read through the monologue silently several times before reading it aloud. Once he or she has delivered the monologue aloud, work together to clarify its theme. Give your classmate notes on character and physical/vocal presentation. When the two of you have rehearsed the monologue to your satisfaction, present it to the class.

2 Use the Internet, interviews, or other resources to research one small element of a play that interests you but you know little about. This element could be the occupation of one of the characters, a pasttime enjoyed by the characters, or some other specific item found in the play. Write a short description based on your research.

3 Write character sketches for each character in the play you worked on for this chapter's project. Analyze the play thoroughly to create the most detailed sketches you can.

4 Select a full-length period play to research. Your research should focus on a wide-ranging issue, such as the politics of the time, the social issues, or some other issue inherent to the play. Write a paper outlining your dramaturgic findings.

5 Select one of the longer excerpts from the monologues and scenes in Unit Eight. Discuss the excerpt in terms of how you might direct the scene. Think about the play's theme, plot, symbols, major conflict, and the classmates you would cast to play the various parts.

Substitute Teacher Activities

Below are a few ideas that will help the substitute teacher.

- Assign the Profiles of Management Personnel Worksheet on page 57 of the Resource Binder.
- Teach portions of the Directing and Producing section of the Student Handbook found on pages 571-576.
- Assign one or more of the Additional Projects on this page.
- **Create a Production Checklist.** Encourage students to discuss the various duties of the production team. Assume that *The Little Foxes* by Lillian Hellman has been selected for production. Students must create a list of all the things that must be done to prepare the play, including obtaining performance rights, casting the play, assembling the production team, advertising the play, scheduling rehearsals, and so on.

Master of the Craft

Peter Brook (1925–)

Peter Brook is an English theatrical producer and director who became known in the 1950s for his experimental productions with London's Royal Shakespeare Company. As a young man, he directed a startling variety of plays—from Shakespeare to musical comedy—with skill and ingenuity.

His early work was inspired by the theories of experimental theatre; these plays and theatrical events defied the notions of realistic and naturalistic acting and pushed the boundaries of the stage. In one memorable Brook production of Shakespeare's *Titus Andronicus,* actress Vivien Leigh spouted a seemingly endless length of bright red ribbon in a scene in which her character's tongue was cut out. Such visual touches would influence a generation of theatre practitioners.

Over the course of his nearly sixty years in the theatre, Brook has acquired a well-deserved reputation as the greatest living inventor of the modern stage. But by his own admission, he has never lost his sense of being an apprentice to his craft. "I think you can't lose this, because a craft has no end. A craft is a ladder. There always has to be another level to everything . . ."

Brook's work is challenging, physical, electrifying, and visually alive. He values the audience's intelligence. "In being aware of what holds an audience and what loses them, you develop more and more the awareness that rhythm, space, all the physical sides of theatre are playing on the audience, and it is in this way you develop your tools."

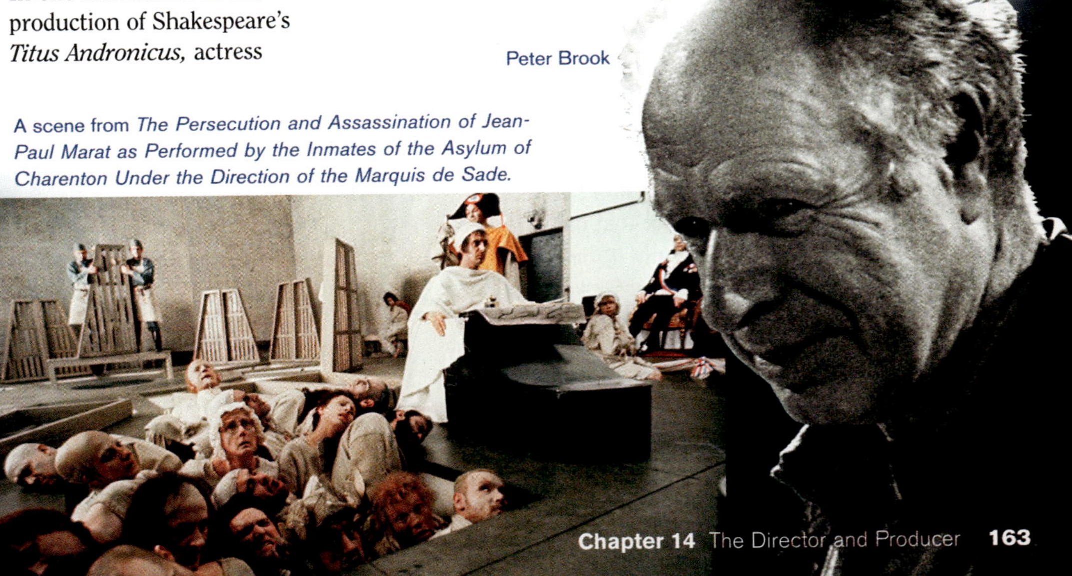

Peter Brook

A scene from *The Persecution and Assassination of Jean-Paul Marat as Performed by the Inmates of the Asylum of Charenton Under the Direction of the Marquis de Sade.*

Backstage Gossip: Sheer Terror

Peter Brook is known for spending weeks of rehearsals with improvisations. One of the best-known theatrical stories concerns his production of Seneca's *Oedipus . . .* Brook had made the distinguished cast go through many days of primal screaming, imitating various animals—everything except work on the text. One day he asked the actors to prepare a short improvisation based on the most terrifying experience they could possibly imagine. When it came to Sir John Gielgud's turn, he did nothing . . . . Brook asked whether there was nothing terrifying that he could think of. "Actually, Peter, there is," replied Sir John quietly: "we open in two weeks."

from *Theatrical Anecdotes* by Peter Hay

Master of the Craft

More About Peter Brook

Peter Brook often tests new work, particularly his re-imaginings of Shakespeare's texts, on student audiences. About two-thirds of the way through a rehearsal process, when his actors have learned all their lines, he has them improvise a segment of the text for students. This puts the emphasis on the storytelling aspects of the play and lets him know if the progression is clear. Brook claims that students are honest in their reactions and if they're bored, they usually don't try to hide it. He listens to the "quality of their silences" during the performance, as well as to what they tell him afterward.

Tell your students that many artists who are considered geniuses in their particular art form claim that they, like Peter Brook, maintain a lifelong sense of being a student. Lead a class discussion about this idea. Ask individual students if they have anyone in their lives who has remained a student of life, of human nature, or of an art form. What other traits do these people have?

Masters Past and Present

Eva Le Gallienne (1899-1991) was a stage actress whose versatility made her one of the biggest Broadway stars of the early 1920s. But in 1926, tired of the male-dominated theatre scene, she established the first classical repertory theatre in the United States, the Civic Repertory Theatre (1926-1935). She offered the classics in rotating repertory at one-third the regular Broadway ticket price. As the Civic's producer and director, she demanded absolute loyalty from the actors she worked with. She had a sharp eye for new talent. Among her many "discoveries" were Peter Falk and Burgess Meredith.

Theatre Then and Now

Zeami Motokiro was born into a theatrical family in the 14th century. Here are some modern-day theatrical families:

- English actresses Vanessa and Lynn Redgrave are the daughters of the late Sir Michael Redgrave.
- Gwynneth Paltrow is the daughter of actress Blythe Danner and director Bruce Paltrow.
- English playwright Amy Rosenthal is the daughter of actress Maureen Lipman and playwright Jack Rosenthal.
- Performers Liza Minelli and Lorna Luft are the daughters of the late singer/actress Judy Garland.
- Film director Rebecca Miller is the daughter of playwright Arthur Miller.

See if your students can think of more.

Other Cultures, Other Times

Up until the end of the 19th century, there really was no such position as that embodied by the directors of today. Actors performed roles in the way they wanted to. A "director" might stand by to fulfill duties—such as choreographing entrances and exits, organizing scenic arrangements, and even coordinating costumes. But as plays became more and more psychologically complex, it became clear that an overall artistic eye was needed in the process. Here are some directors who had a major influence on the directing profession as we know it:

Konstantin Stanislavski, Russia (1863-1938)

Vsevolod Meyerhold, Russia (1874-1940)

Eva Le Gallienne, England and the United States (1899-1991)

Jerzy Grotowski, Poland (1933-1999)

Theatre Then and Now

The Evolution of the "Director"

The role of the director as a creative force in the artistic process is a relatively recent phenomenon. Only over the course of the past 120 years has the director become an active, vital component in the production of the play. Prior to that time, the "director" of a theatre troupe was typically either a kind of business manager or an actor or playwright who assumed extra responsibilities. Following are two theatre luminaries: the Japanese playwright Zeami and the Broadway director Hal Prince.

Zeami: The Father of Japanese Noh Drama

Zeami Motokiro (1363–1443) was the son of an itinerant actor. This familial connection naturally led Zeami into the world of the theatre at an early age. When he was eleven, he performed with his father's company at a shrine in Kyoto. His audience that day included Yoshimitsu, the ruler of Japan. Yoshimitsu was so taken with the performance of young Zeami that he set the troupe up in his palace and thereby became their financial protector. Over the course of his life, Zeami's fortunes tended to change with the political climate. But along the way, he became an accomplished playwright, penning more than one hundred plays that would form the basis of Noh drama.

What this 14th-century pioneer created was a dramatic form written in the upper-class language of the time that based its stories on people and situations of an earlier period. The result was a series of plays of poetic richness and universality. Many of these works are regularly performed today. In 1423, Zeami documented the skills and methods of the Noh actor; his teachings are still studied by young actors.

Noh drama is still performed in much the same way it was over six hundred years ago.

Visual Cue

The following prompts can be used to exercise students' **critical viewing skills.**

- What can you tell about the Noh actor just from looking at the picture on this page?
- What do the picture on this page and the inset photo from *Sweeney Todd* on page 165 have in common?

164 **Unit Four** The Play: From Vision to Reality

Hal Prince: Broadway Innovator

The *New York Times* once said that director/producer Hal Prince "may be one of the most innovative directors on Broadway. He may be the one most obsessed with craft as well . . . ."

According to Prince, he owes his success to theatrical legend George Abbott. Prince was apprenticed to Abbott at the age of twenty-five as a stage manager. But what belies Prince's modesty is the fact that, at the age of twenty-six, he co-directed a new musical called *The Pajama Game.* It became the hottest ticket in town and instantly made Prince one of the top names on Broadway.

Since that time, Hal Prince has directed more than fifty Broadway musicals. Among his hits are *Cabaret, Evita,* and *Phantom of the Opera.* His most artistically daring and groundbreaking productions, however, were the result of collaborations with composer Stephen Sondheim. Beginning in the early 1970s, these two theatre pros brought a new notion to the stage—the "concept musical," a musical play in which theme takes precedence over plot. Prince's productions of the Sondheim musicals *Company, Pacific Overtures, Sweeney Todd,* and others took the American musical into brand-new territory. Each was different from the one before—and each challenged the notions of standard musicals to that point. Along the way, Prince picked up twenty Tony Awards.

Hal Prince approaches his craft from an intensely personal standpoint.

Mrs. Lovett sharpens her knife in a production of *Sweeney Todd.*

Visual Cue

Sweeney Todd tells the supposedly true story of a barber in London who, instead of shaving his clients' faces, slit their throats. If that tale isn't gory enough, he is additionally said to have chopped up the bodies for use in his wife's homemade meat pies. It's hard to imagine that this would be the stuff of a popular Broadway musical, but Stephen Sondheim's musical rendition is touching, funny, cautionary, and infinitely melodious.

- How would you describe Mrs. Lovett in *Sweeney Todd*?
- What do you think she is about to say? Use your best Cockney accent and say it for the class.

For More Information

Books

Brockett, Oscar G., *History of the Theatre,* Prentice Hall, 1998.

Brown, John Russell, *The Oxford Illustrated History of Theatre,* Oxford University Press, 2001.

Mamet, David, *On Directing*, Penguin Putnam, 1991.

Phillips, M. Scott, and Joy H. Reilly, *Introducing Theatre*, Forbes, 1999.

Prince, Hal, *Contradictions: Notes on Twenty-six Years in the Theatre,* Dodd, Mead & Co., 1974.

Other Media

American Theatre magazine, Theatre Communications Group, *tcg@tcg.org* (1-212-609-5900)

Chapter 15

The Cast

This chapter introduces various aspects of the rehearsal process. Students will learn how to make up a rehearsal schedule based on a two-act play of their own choosing.

Objectives

1 to understand what the cast of a play does—from the audition process through opening night and beyond

2 to become familiar with the casting process

3 to understand audition etiquette

4 to organize information into a viable rehearsal schedule

National Standards

Chapter 15 meets these National Theatre Standards:

Proficient 2b, 7b, 7c, 8b

Advanced 2d, 2e, 8e, 8f, 8g

Project Specs

Special Needs Students
Students with visual impairment may need to work in a larger format than the one offered on The Cast Activity Sheet. Help these students create larger-sized schedules.

Advanced Students
In addition to the chapter project, assign the Casting a Play Worksheet, p. 61, of the Resource Binder. To complete the project, have students create a rehearsal schedule for *Death of a Salesman.*

On Your Feet

Ask students whether they think it would be better to engage their fellow auditioners in conversation while waiting to audition or to remain silent. Tell them there are no specific rules about this, but that it is a good idea to be sensitive to another performer's preference, especially if he or she wants to be left alone to concentrate.

Chapter 15 The Cast

The process of selecting actors for various roles, called **casting,** can make or break a show. Some directors consider casting to be ninety percent of their job! It's important to find the best actor for each role so that the performance will be as effective as possible. This chapter will focus on the cast as they audition and rehearse in preparation for opening night.

Project Specs

Project Description For this project, you will create and discuss for no more than six minutes a rehearsal schedule for a production of a two-act play.

Purpose to learn how to create a real-world rehearsal schedule using information from a particular play

Materials a sheet listing various personnel and duties for six weeks of rehearsal or The Cast Activity Sheet provided by your teacher; colored pens or pencils; an overhead projector and the appropriate transparency sheets

Theatre Terms

auditions
callbacks
cameo
casting
casting call
casting director
cold reading
double cast
offbook
rehearsals
spiking
understudy

On Your Feet

With a partner, improvise a very short scene in which you both play actors waiting in line for the opportunity to audition for a play.

The casting director of *Martin Guerre* had to find actors who could look, speak, and move according to the parts played—from farmer to war hero.

Theatre Terms

auditions events at which actors try out for a role in a play

callbacks when actors are called back for a second audition

cameo a one-scene part

casting selecting actors for various roles

casting call an audition notice

casting director the person in charge of selecting actors for various roles

cold reading when an actor auditions for a role without having read the script

double cast selecting two actors for each role; the casts then split the performances

off book having one's lines memorized

rehearsals practices of the play in preparation for performance

spiking marking with tape where furniture will be placed onstage

understudy an actor who learns a role in case the lead actor cannot perform

PREVIEW

Assembling the Cast

Casting is usually accomplished through a series of tryouts or **auditions.** The audition time, place, and specific procedures for community tryouts are often published in local newspapers. The **casting call** for your school auditions might appear in the school paper, be announced over the PA system, or be posted in the school building. Scripts often may be found in the school or local library, where those who are interested in auditioning may read them and prepare scenes.

Some theatres employ a **casting director** to find actors for particular parts (see page 175). Directors may sometimes prefer a **cold reading** at auditions. This means the performer is probably unfamiliar with the script, and is reading the lines of the scene for the first time.

If you audition, you will usually start by filling out a casting sheet similar to the one on page 168. You will then read a scene or scenes in combination with others. The director will announce the first audition scene and assign two or more actors to perform it.

After the preliminary auditions, the director selects those actors who seem best suited to the parts. Sometimes there are as many as four people chosen

Chapter 15 The Cast 167

PREVIEW

Assembling the Cast

Tell students that some auditions require the actors to present one- to two-minute prepared monologues. Most professional actors have several monologues memorized so that if they are asked to present a monologue they can do a contemporary or a classical reading, or a comic or dramatic one, and so on.

To find the right cast, a director may have to look at a great many actors. And although directors take notes about most of the people who audition for them, to a large extent they must rely on their memories when deciding which actors to call back. Tell students that professional actors often wear the same clothes to both their first audition and their callback. This is thought to jar the auditor's memory of the audition that earned the actor the callback.

The following prompts can be used to help students exercise their **critical viewing skills.**

- In what time period and in what part of the world might *Martin Guerre* be set?
- What type of characters make up the chorus of this musical? Are they rich? Poor? Do they live in the city or the country?
- What kind of challenges would you face if you were performing in such a large group?

Resource Binder

- The Cast Activity Sheet, p. 60
- Casting a Play Worksheet, p. 61
- Critique Sheet: Rehearsal Schedule, p. 62
- Cast Test, p. 63
- Resume Form, p. 132
- Casting Sheet, p. 133
- Audition Evaluation Form, p. 134

Handbook Connections
page 592

To Have on Hand

- Colored pens and pencils
- Scripts or anthologies for students from which to choose their plays

The Casting Sheet

Some casting sheets ask actors to list their weight. However, with the currently rampant problem of eating disorders in young women, it's a good idea to leave the issue of weight out of the casting process. There are plenty of stressors involved in auditioning and performing. Worrying about weight and other body-image issues shouldn't be among them. You may want to find other samples of casting sheets to show the students, so they are aware of other points of view, however. Discuss the items on the casting sheet on this page, and make students aware they will be expected to fill them out legibly.

Show, Don't Tell Model for your students the correct way to introduce yourself at an audition. Show them the difference between a slumping posture and a confident one, a quavering voice and one that is supported from the diaphragm, a firm handshake and a weak one.

ACTivity Advanced Students Have students choose a monologue that they would like to present as an audition piece. Remind them to look for something that fits their age range. The monologue should be less than one page long and should run no more than two minutes. Students may either memorize their monologue or read it aloud for the class.

ACTivity ESL Students Ask students to prepare a monologue in their primary language. As students present their monologues, the rest of the class can take notes and analyze the types of emotional content being expressed.

Vocabulary Enhancement

The largest or most important roles in the show are called the *leads.* Smaller parts are *supporting roles.* Actors sometimes refer to a large or particularly juicy part as a *plum role.*

as possible candidates for a particular role. When this happens, the director will hold **callbacks,** a second audition in which only those who are under serious consideration for the roles are called in. At the callbacks, the director may give you suggestions as to how to perform a particular scene. He or she might also direct you in terms of how and where to move. You may be asked to memorize a scene or speech or to improvise a scene.

When casting the play, the director takes into account your physical appearance, personality, level of acting, and the chemistry between you and other possible cast members. Singing or dancing skills may also be noted. In drama class, performers are cast according to what skills they need to develop. For public presentation, however, the director casts the actors best suited to the roles.

The director will be looking for people with expressive, supple voices; good physical presences; and emotional intensity. In short, the director wants to find a group of actors who can engage

When auditioning for a part, you may be asked to fill out a form similar to this one.

Casting Sheet

Name ______ **Height** ______ **Year in School** ______
Address ______ **Female** ______ **Male** ______
Phone ______ **E-mail** ______ **Hair Color** ______
Special Talents (sing, dance, play musical instrument, etc.) ______

Check what you would like to work on:

______ **Costumes** ______ **Makeup** ______ **Publicity**
______ **Director's Assistant** ______ **Prompter** ______ **Stage Manager**
______ **Lighting & Sound** ______ **Props**

On back of page, please list:

1. Previous acting experience (include play, role, place)
2. Hours when you can rehearse
3. Other commitments (orchestra, sports, work, religious schedule, etc.)

Director's comments:

Appearance ______ Ability to take direction ______
Voice ______ Personality ______
Speech ______ Possible for role of ______
Interpretation ______
Movement ______

Notes

Spotlight on

The Audition

As a beginning actor, you may not get many chances to perform for a paying audience. But you can perform for theatrical peers or professionals every time you audition.

Most auditions begin with a notice, to which you must respond by calling to make an appointment or by appearing at an open call. The notice will probably indicate whether actors will be expected to read a scene from the play, perform a serious or comic monologue from memory, sing, dance, or do any combination of these things.

In any case, it is a good idea to read the play and make note of the characters it calls for. The better you know the play, the better you will be able to concentrate on acting in the scene, rather than reading or, worse, finding your place!

Once you have read the play or a description of the play, ask yourself:

- Which of these characters would I like to play?
- As which character am I likely to be cast?

Then prepare yourself for the audition by thinking about the character in the context of the play. Get a sense of the character's history and circumstances, hopes and fears, and loves and hates. Incorporate them as best you can into your monologue or scene.

As you wait for your audition, do so quietly. If you are allowed to, listen to the other readers. You may learn something that will help you in a later reading.

When you are called onstage, assume the role of a professional. Focus on the character's objective. Remember to breathe. And remember that the director wants you to do well–he or she is on your side. As you perform, be open to any acting advice the director may have. And have fun–isn't that the point?

Being relaxed and well prepared is important when auditioning.

Spotlight on

The Audition There are plenty of do's and don'ts when it comes to auditioning. Here are just a few.

- Many theatres do not allow waiting actors to listen in on other people's auditions. Instead they will ask you to wait outside the auditorium or audition space until someone summons you.
- In the Special Talents section of the casting sheet, never list a skill you do not possess. It can be very embarrassing if a director calls upon you to perform that skill at the audition or after you have been cast.
- During your audition, you may be called upon to deliver a monologue or play a scene a second time to implement an instruction from the director. If this happens, listen closely to the director's instructions, and do your best. Directors look for actors who are both flexible and able to take direction.
- No matter how you feel about your audition performance, you should thank the director and the other auditors at the end. Professionalism demands a friendly and polite presentation from beginning to end. You are not finished auditioning until you are out of the auditors' sight.

Backstage Gossip: Standing Out from the Crowd

An aspiring singer auditions for a Broadway show. She is young and chatters nervously to the auditors. She's a mess; her shoes don't match and to make matters worse she's chewing gum. When it comes time for her to perform, she pulls the wad of gum out of her mouth and sticks it to the bottom of her chair. Then she begins to sing. The power of her voice and the confidence of her performance stun the auditors. After the young singer leaves, one of the auditors plays a hunch and checks the bottom of the chair—where there is no gum to be found.

Who was that memorable singer with the big-time voice? None other than Barbra Streisand.

Chapter 15 The Cast **169**

"Leave your dirty shoes at the door!"

Another quote along these lines comes not from a theatre professional, but from Albert Einstein, who once said, " If A equals success, then the formula is:
A = X + Y + Z.
X is work.
Y is play.
Z is keep your mouth shut.

Tell students that in addition to studying a major role, the understudy often has a smaller role in the show. For example, a chorus member might understudy the lead. The understudy's part is then sometimes covered by a crewmember who is familiar with the show or by doubling up the chorus.

ACTivity Read Albert Einstein's quote to the class. Then have students compare it to the one in their books. How are the two quotes similar? Does one appeal to them more than the other? Why?

Rehearsals

Russian director and acting teacher Konstantin Stanislavski believed that "There are no small parts, only small actors." He believed that even cameo roles were important to a production, and the actor with the small, or bit, part had an obligation just as compelling as the star of the show.

ACTivity Read Stanislavski's quote above to students, and ask them to rephrase the sentiment in their own words. Ask them whether they think it holds true today.

an audience's attention and imagination, have a variety of physiques and voices, and seem to work well together.

The director will either phone the actors he or she has chosen or post the cast list on a bulletin board. Not getting a part you wanted can be hard, but just remember that no actor—whether famous or not—has ever gotten all the roles he or she wanted. Learning to face disappointment is part of being an actor.

"Leave your dirty shoes at the door!"

Thus states an old rehearsal adage. It means that no matter what your mood or current situation, you must come to each rehearsal fresh and ready to do your best. Leave your worries at home.

To provide acting opportunities for a larger number of students, some schools **double cast.** With a double cast, two groups split the performances. However, this process takes a lot of extra rehearsal time, sometimes at the expense of a polished performance. Another choice is to select a single cast with understudies for the main roles. An **understudy** attends all rehearsals and learns a role thoroughly. If an actor becomes ill or can't perform, the understudy is able to go on in his or her place.

Rehearsals

Once the play is cast, the director must organize **rehearsals,** various run-throughs of the play. A rehearsal schedule makes the best possible use of everyone's time. To this end, the director should group together scenes that feature the same characters. With proper attention to detail, only the necessary actors need be called for each rehearsal. This avoids the long waits that can lead to boredom and inattention. At the beginning of the rehearsal process, the director hands out a rehearsal schedule to the cast and the crew. One copy of the schedule is tacked to a board where the rehearsals take place. Often this schedule cannot be altered, so all the cast involved must meet it! Even if a role is a small **cameo,** a brief one-scene part, the actor is expected to show up to every rehearsal to which he or she is called. Being prompt and maintaining the highest standards of behavior are very important. Rehearsals are hard work, but if everyone cooperates and works as a team, the time spent will be not only fun, but also productive. After all, each member of the cast is working toward the same goal: a great show.

Rehearsal schedules vary according to the difficulty of the play, the experience of the actors, and the time available. Full-length school plays typically require at least a five- or six-week rehearsal period. That means committing five or six days a week of two to three hours each to rehearsal time. One-act plays obviously take less rehearsal time. For these shows,

Backstage Gossip: A Major Understudy

At Chicago's Goodman Theatre, when a cast member became ill and couldn't go on in the major role of Hecuba in the 2003 production of *The Trojan Women,* chorus member Laura T. Fisher stepped into the role. That left Fisher's role empty, so the production's director, Tony Award winner and MacArthur "Genius" Grant recipient Mary Zimmerman, went on in her place until a replacement could be hired.

rehearsal generally lasts only three to four weeks with three to four sessions per week. It's important to schedule as many rehearsals as possible to maintain the highest performance standards. Some casts practice after school and some in the evenings. Cast members should count on at least two long Saturday rehearsals at some point in the schedule. The director (or teacher) may ask for a personal pledge that cast members will attend all rehearsals required of them.

The Rehearsal Sequence

The director typically provides specific goals for each rehearsal session. The following illustrates a standard rehearsal sequence.

Reading rehearsals begin right after casting is complete. Actors and designers work as a group to gain an overall understanding of the play. The director discusses his or her concept for the show—including specifics about characters, plot, and theme. The actors read through the script, after which the director may ask them questions about the play or their specific characters. Actors should also take this opportunity to ask questions about motivation and character relationships.

Blocking rehearsals are conducted onstage or in a large room where the floor plan of the set is taped onto the floor. Blocking rehearsals work out the actors' onstage movements. You will read more about blocking in Chapter 16.

Developing rehearsals begin on each act once the blocking is set. When the actors have memorized their lines, which is called being **off book,** they can fully concentrate on projecting emotion and relating to others onstage. During this stage of rehearsal, you will begin to work with rehearsal props and certain costume pieces. These rehearsals may be tailored to specific situations within the script, for example, love scenes, fights, or crowd scenes.

An Actor's Credo

Never accept a role unless you are also willing to accept the responsibility of attending each rehearsal to which you're called.

Polishing rehearsals are all about the little touches that make a good production great. In polishing, the director works on the actors' projection and

Theatre Journal

Think of a character from a play you have read or seen. Looking around the classroom, think about which of your classmates might play the role in a school production. Write a short entry explaining your choice.

Quotables

Below are two quotes from many attributed to the great Russian director Konstantin Stanislavski. They were written in 1897.

Today Hamlet, tomorrow an extra, but even as an extra the actor must be an artist.

Arriving late at the theatre, laziness, capriciousness, hysteria, ignorance of parts, the necessity of repeating the same thing twice, are all equally harmful and must be rooted out.

The Rehearsal Sequence

Students might think that actors learn their lines during rehearsal. They might be surprised to find out that most actors study their lines outside of rehearsal. They use rehearsal time to figure out important details of their character.

A typical rehearsal period for a full-length play is about 100 hours. This includes all the phases of rehearsal discussed on pages 171 through 173.

Tell students that when working on a play, the only stupid question is the one that goes unasked.

As soon as the actors are off book, the stage manager (or prompter) goes *on book* during rehearsals. If an actor loses a line, he or she calls "Line," and the stage manager says the missing line aloud to get the actor back on track. If an actor simply misses lines and keeps on going, the stage manager makes note of the missing text and reminds the actor about it later. If the actor's dropped lines cause other actors in the scene to flounder, however, the stage manager will generally clear up the problem on the spot by stopping the action.

ACTivity Have students choose a play they are familiar with and imagine that they have been cast in a production of this play. They are at the very first rehearsal. Ask them to write a list of questions—about the play, the production, or the director's vision—they might have.

Theatre Journal

Use the following as an additional or substitute prompt.

Remind students that their casting ideas should be positively phrased. Also suggest that they think about typecasting and make an effort to avoid it. They should also avoid casting friends in major roles just because they are friends.

Tell students that, particularly in period dramas, actors often begin to simulate their costumes or costume pieces early in rehearsal to get used to, for example, a long skirt, a corset, high-heeled shoes, knee-length boots, and so on. They do this so that when the actual costumes are provided they will make the transition more comfortably.

ACTivity Have your students read a short play, such as *The Actor's Nightmare* by Christopher Durang. Ask them to make notes about the play for a possible photo call as they read. Then have them make a list of five to ten setup shots to be taken in reverse order of the play.

Vocabulary Enhancement

If an actor must be replaced once the play has opened, the understudy is trained into the role during what is called a *put-in rehearsal* or an *understudy rehearsal.*

emphasis. Murky moments between actors are cleaned up and strengthened. The pacing and rhythm of the play are perfected. Any extraneous movements are eliminated at this point, and group scenes are tightened to allow for stronger ensemble playing. Polishing rehearsals are very important. Rehearsal schedules should be planned to allow for sufficient polishing before the show opens. Including enough time to polish the production is very important.

Technical rehearsals must be held onstage. The purpose of the technical rehearsal is to synchronize technical and performance aspects of the production. The first technical rehearsal can be long and arduous. It is often referred to as a "dry tech," meaning a rehearsal specifically to set technical cues, without actors. Also at this point, scenery shifts are choreographed and curtains are hung.

The next technical rehearsal is with the whole cast. The director asks only for those scenes requiring scene shifts, light and sound, or major prop changes. Crews now mark the furniture positions on the stage floor with masking tape, a process called **spiking.** If the schedule allows, actors do a dress parade. This means that they put on their costumes and walk across the stage under the proper lighting. This is done so that the costume crew can make any necessary adjustments.

Three dress rehearsals should be conducted in full costume. Prior to the first dress rehearsal, the director gives the cast and crew instructions—usually in writing—about the time, procedure, and requirements of each dress rehearsal and performance. Dress rehearsals begin on time, whether the

Actors rehearse on a spiked stage in order to practice moving around furniture that will be positioned onstage.

From the Field: The Actor's Instrument

For the theatre artist, a vital part of his instrument is the voice; therefore careful consideration must be taken to protect and train it.

In his book *Acting One*, Robert Cohen writes of the importance of training; "for the actor is both the player and the instrument played; the actor therefore plays upon herself or himself in much the same way that a violinist plays upon a violin; an actor, like the violinist, can be no better than the instrument."

172 **Unit Four** The Play: From Vision to Reality

cast and crew are ready or not! The purpose of dress rehearsal is to get the show to performance level. There is an old saying that "A bad dress rehearsal means a great opening night." Don't fall for this. A bad dress rehearsal usually only creates opening night jitters. Dress rehearsals should go smoothly, however, if everyone works efficiently.

The first dress rehearsal is the most hectic, as it coordinates sound, lights, scenery, and props. The cast wears full costumes. The director sits in the audience and watches the entire show. The prompter times the show and each scene shift. (Scene shifts should be executed within a matter of seconds.) Intermissions should be no longer than ten minutes. The only time a dress rehearsal should be interrupted is if someone is injured or a major technical problem occurs. The director gives notes on the performance at the end of the rehearsal.

The second dress rehearsal adds make-up and other technical requirements. The director also stages the curtain call—or actors' bows—at the end of the show. (See the Spotlight on Taking Your Bows on page 60 for more on this.) After this dress rehearsal, most productions have a photo call. The director usually selects the setups in advance and hands out copies of the sequence of photos. Because the cast will be in costume for the end of the show, the photographer usually shoots the photos in reverse order. Sometimes the director will give notes after the second dress rehearsal, but many directors withhold the critique until just prior to the final dress rehearsal.

The third or final dress rehearsal should run exactly like a performance. There should be absolutely no interruptions, and every detail should be in place. Some directors make this an *invited dress,* meaning that there will be some guests in the audience. This is particularly important when the production is a comedy because the cast will need practice holding for laughs. Before this final rehearsal, there is generally a full cast-and-crew meeting backstage. At this point, the cast gives the crews a round of applause for all their hard work.

The Performance

At last the opening night arrives. Now all the hard work on the part of the cast, crews, director, and producer will pay off in a memorable performance. Here are some final thoughts to help you prepare to create the best show possible.

Before and During the Performance

- Only those with specific jobs are allowed backstage.

During dress rehearsals, many directors move from seat to seat to watch and listen to the play from various spots around the theatre. In this way they can check to make sure that all the blocking is smooth and that the actors are visible and audible at all times.

The Performance

Tell students that in the professional theatre, stage managers rarely take roll call. Instead the actors sign a call sheet when they arrive for each performance. The stage manager checks the call sheet periodically to ensure that all the actors are on hand in plenty of time for the curtain. If an actor does not make his or her scheduled call time, the stage manager must then try to locate the missing actor. Remind students that, as actors, it is their duty to be on time. If they are going to be even a few minutes late, they should call in.

Vocabulary Enhancement

Tell students that because actors and crewmembers must often maneuver scene changes in the dark, *glow tape*—tape that glows in the dark—is often used to mark sharp corners, steps, and the edge of the stage. This helps production personnel get their bearings when they are unable to see clearly.

Quotable

Use the quote below as a writing prompt or discussion starter.

We respond to a drama to that extent to which it corresponds to our dreamlife.

David Mamet, Playwright and Director

After the Performance

- You might want to assign the task of tidying dressing rooms to a small group of energetic students who can complete the task quickly and efficiently.
- Personally check to see that the set is completely struck the day after the final performance.
- Go over the list of borrowed items two days after the performance to be sure they have all been returned.
- Assign various duties to all the cast and crew for bringing food and beverages to the cast party and let everyone know when it will be.

- Crews should arrive early enough to have the stage set up two hours before show time.
- The cast should arrive at least one hour before curtain time to warm up, put on makeup and costumes, and check personal props. When these duties are completed, each cast member should remain quietly in the dressing room getting into character.
- The stage manager calls roll about fifteen minutes before curtain time. Then the director talks to the cast and crew. This is generally a pep talk, but most directors also remind the cast not to change anything regardless of what their friends and family members may have to say about the show.
- Remember that when you're onstage, small errors usually go unnoticed by the audience. If you make a mistake, such as calling another character by the wrong name, do not call attention to your error. Go on. If another character fails to enter on time, create inconsequential talk to fill the gap. Do not check your watch and say, "I wonder where [the missing character] is."
- As in dress rehearsal, during the production the stage manager has charge of the performance. The director sits out front and takes notes or observes the audience reaction.
- The show should always begin on time. Prompt curtain times ensure that the audience will arrive on time.

After the Performance

- The actors remove their makeup and costumes and tidy the dressing rooms. Actors should never leave a mess for the crews.
- After the final show, the crews should immediately strike the set and props.
- Borrowed items should be returned on the day following the last performance.
- Return any missing pages to the prompt book.
- Have a cast party. This is a theatre tradition; everyone is invited—cast, crews, and director. It is often held onstage after strike. If the strike is expected to go late, the party sometimes is scheduled for another night.

Notes

PREPARE

Create Your Rehearsal Schedule

Imagine that you are a director about to begin rehearsals for a two-act play. You may have a particular play in mind, or you can find one at the library. You may choose from plays listed in Unit Eight or you may be assigned a play by your teacher. Your assignment is to create a complete six-week rehearsal schedule. You may create your own calendar or list or use the Activity Sheet your teacher gives you. You may wish to make a larger copy of the Activity Sheet so that you can include all the relevant information on your rehearsal schedule. If an overhead projector is available for this project, be prepared to transfer the schedule you create to transparency sheets.

On the following page is a sample rehearsal schedule. Note that it does not include which actors are called for each rehearsal or the hours during which the rehearsal will take place.

Career Focus

Casting Director

If you're a "people person," you might consider a career as a casting director. These consultants contact and secure suitable actors to audition for various projects. They are the conduit that connects actors and their agents to the people and organizations that do the hiring.

Many professional theatre companies have full-time casting directors. But casting directors may also work on a freelance basis to cast for film, radio, and television. Some casting directors work for advertising agencies to find the right actors for television and radio spots, print ads, and voice-overs. Through a blend of experience, intuition, and savvy, the casting director brings the best possible group of actors into the audition process.

In general, the casting director prescreens possible actors. He or she secures actors to audition but does not make final casting decisions, which are typically left to the director or producer. Once casting is complete, however, it is often the casting director who negotiates money and scheduling with the actor's agent.

Most professional casting directors are located in large cities such as Los Angeles, New York, and Chicago. They are familiar with a vast number of actors within their home city, but they also create and maintain connections with other casting services and talent agencies to secure the largest possible actor list. In fact, many casting directors began their careers as actors or directors. Some have worked in stage management or as other behind-the-scenes theatre personnel. Others may have begun working as assistants to film or theatre producers. Firsthand theatre, film, or television experience is vital for the successful casting director.

PREPARE

Create Your Rehearsal Schedule

Good examples of two-act plays students might like to work on are:

- *How I Learned to Drive* by Paula Vogel
- *Collected Stories* by Donald Margulies
- *Spinning into Butter* by Rebecca Gilman
- *Holes* by Louis Sachar
- *Jar the Floor* by Cheryl West
- *Two Trains Running* by August Wilson

Tell students that there is no specific format for creating a rehearsal schedule. They can set it up however they like; but remind them that their goal is for the schedule to be as easy to read as possible.

Vocabulary Enhancement

Let students know that when an actor accidentally leaves out a sequence of lines and picks up at a point further on in the script, he or she is said to have *jumped lines* or *jumped the cue.*

Career Focus: Casting Director

ACTivity **Advanced Students**
Have students do Internet research to find out more about casting directors and, if possible, arrange an online or telephone interview. They can use the casting Web sites or contact large regional theatres that have full-time casting directors on staff.

Backstage Gossip: A Very Young Fan

After a performance one evening, Bill Cosby was visited back stage by an aide who asked him to autograph a baby book for a young couple who had recently had their first child. The book was soon returned to the couple, who excitedly searched for Cosby's signature. Unable to find it, they left the theater rather disappointed. While looking through the book some time later, the mother saw a page entitled "Baby's first sentence." The Cos had written: "I like Bill Cosby!"

from the Web site *anecdotage.com*

Here are some tips you can share with students to help them create the most effective schedules possible.

- To fit all the information on your rehearsal schedule you'll need to write small. Use pencil first. Then you can go over your work in pen once you've figured out the whole schedule.
- Remember to be consistent with your color coding. For example, if the color blue indicates actors, don't also use blue for designers.

Mark each rehearsal's specific goals with a star or an asterisk.

Copy the Schedule and Rehearse Your Talk

Before students copy their schedules, remind them to double-check their work against an actual calendar. In a real-life rehearsal situation, errors in the days of the week or month can be both embarrassing and problematic.

Make sure students have access to a copier, or copy the rehearsal schedules for them.

You will create a schedule that includes the date of each rehearsal, the specific actors called for each rehearsal, the hours of the rehearsal, and the location where the rehearsal will take place (auditorium, rehearsal room, and so on). Remember that rehearsals close to opening night, especially technical and dress rehearsals, always take place on the stage where the performance will be.

Remember to schedule only those actors you will need for each rehearsal. For example, if you are only rehearsing the first half of Act I, don't call in actors who appear only in the second half of Act I. Your job is to make the most efficient use of everyone's time. Write schedule information pertaining to cast members in one color. For crew members, use a different color. For scheduling that involves both cast and crew, use a third color.

Remember that Saturday rehearsals can be longer and can take place during the day. Also bear in mind what you have learned about technical rehearsals and performances. Have a specific goal for each rehearsal on your schedule.

You will need a calendar of the current year so you can write accurate dates next to each rehearsal day.

You may decide that your schedule is for the fall or the spring production. Choose your dates accordingly. Note that on the first day of rehearsal all cast and crew members are called. For subsequent rehearsals, you may either schedule by act and scene numbers or (for smaller cast shows) by character names.

Copy the Schedule and Rehearse Your Talk

Make a copy of your schedule for use on an overhead projector or try to make an oversized copy on a copier. Rehearse your presentation. Allow about a minute to address comments or answer questions about the play or your rehearsal schedule after your talk. The talk itself should not exceed five minutes.

This schedule calls for five rehearsals a week, two Saturday rehearsals, and three performances. Adjust your schedule to fit the needs of the play you chose.

Sample Rehearsal Schedule for a Two-Act Play

1st week:	
Monday	Read complete play with all cast and crew.
Tuesday	Read first half; discussion and analysis.
Wednesday	Read second half; discussion and analysis.
Thursday	Act I: block first half; repeat to set.
Friday	Act I; block remainder; repeat to set.

Notes

176 Unit Four The Play: From Vision to Reality

Sample Rehearsal Schedule for a Two-Act Play (Continued)	
2nd week:	
Monday	Act I; characterization and motivation.
Tuesday	Act II; block first half; repeat to set.
Wednesday	Act II; block remainder; repeat to set.
Thursday	Run through Acts I and II; adjust groupings if necessary.
Friday	Act II; characterization and motivation.
Saturday	Special private rehearsals for love scenes, fight scenes, etc.
3rd week:	
Monday	Act I memorized; no books; work on detailed business.
Tuesday	Run through Act I (no books).
Wednesday	Act II; work on belief and response; actors should look at each other and listen to each other.
Thursday	Act II memorized; no books; work on business detail.
Friday	Run through Act II memorized; clarify business detail; use hand props.
4th week:	
Monday	Run through Acts I and II memorized; work on detailed business.
Tuesday	Run through Acts I and II; work on audibility, groupings, characterization.
Wednesday	Polish Act I; business, lines, tempo, climax, props.
Thursday	Polish Act II; business, lines, tempo, climax, props.
Friday	Run through Acts I and II; concentrate on minor roles.
Saturday	Polish Acts I and II.
5th week:	
Monday	Run through Acts I and II; work on audibility, unity, tempo, climax, line pickup, transitions, ensemble playing. Check for spontaneity. Actors must not anticipate lines or mouth the lines of others.
Tuesday	Polish difficult scenes, climaxes, etc.
Wednesday	Technical rehearsal without actors. Set up scenery, furniture, lights, etc. Practice shifts. Actors may run a line rehearsal with the prompter. No movement; just say lines and pick up cues readily.
Thursday	Technical rehearsal with actors. Repeat scenes needed for technical changes. Do costume review.
Friday	Run through complete show with set, lights, props.
6th week:	
Monday	First dress; full costume, lights, sound, props, scenery, and shifts.
Tuesday	Second dress; as Monday, plus makeup. Plan curtain calls; take pictures.
Wednesday	Invitational dress; performance level.
Thursday	Opening night performance.
Friday	Performance.
Saturday	Performance, strike, and cast party.

Sample Rehearsal Schedule

Go through the sample schedule with your students. Ask:

- What kind of rehearsals are taking place during week one? (reading and blocking)
- During week two? (blocking and developing)
- During week three? (developing)
- During week four? (developing and polishing)
- During week five? (polishing and technical)
- During week six? (technical and performances)

Quotable

Somewhere in talking and rehearsing, there is a magical moment where actors catch a current; they're on the right road. If they really catch it, then whatever they do from then on is correct and it all comes out of them from that point on.

David Lynch, Director

PRESENT

Display and Explain Your Rehearsal Schedule

Tell students not to get too caught up in explaining the plot and other details of the play. Their project should remain focused on the schedule itself.

Remind students that they will have no more than six minutes to complete their presentations, including one minute for questions. However, if a student completes the presentation in less than a minute or two, you might step in and ask a few more questions to encourage further sharing.

CRITIQUE

Evaluate a Schedule

Prompt students to ask each presenter specific questions about details of the schedule. They should take particular note of any areas of the schedule that do not seem clear or easy to follow.

Let students know that you will be using the same rubrics for them as they are using for each other. In addition to their presentations, you may also wish to evaluate students on how well they assess each other's presentation.

Collect the student evaluations. You might wish to read a few of their evaluation paragraphs aloud.

PRESENT

Display and Explain Your Rehearsal Schedule

When your name is called, bring your rehearsal schedule or Activity Sheet to the front of the classroom. If your teacher has arranged for the use of an overhead projector, place the transparency containing your schedule on the projector and display it.

Your presentation will include a very brief description of the play you chose. Then take about five minutes to talk about your schedule. Be sure to mention any special rehearsal considerations the play warranted. You may wish to discuss why you broke the schedule down the way you did. Your entire presentation (with comments and questions) should not exceed six minutes. When you are finished, remove the schedule and hand it to your teacher. Then return to your seat.

CRITIQUE

Evaluate a Schedule

Select one classmate's rehearsal schedule to evaluate. Imagine that you are an actor in the play. Listen carefully to what your classmate says about the schedule. Look carefully at the way the schedule is set up and organized. You will not have time to do an in-depth analysis. You will mainly be judging this schedule on legibility, clarity of organization, color coding, and consistency. Rate the schedule on a scale of 1 to 5, with 5 being "outstanding," and 1 being "needs much improvement."

After you have rated the schedule based on the qualities suggested above, write a short paragraph explaining your evaluation.

Backstage Gossip: Department of Nightmare Auditions

Actor/singer Brian Duguay landed an audition for a production at a small theatre in Florida. They sent him two scenes to work on. When he got to the theatre, the person holding the audition said, "I don't have a reader for you today. I don't want to read it, so you read your part, and when it's time for the other character to speak, just leave space there and I'll imagine what it sounds like. We'll just pretend we hear the lines." The startled actor did the dialogue all alone.

Additional Projects

1 Read one of the following plays, and create a list of suitable actors you might cast. You can use well-known theatre, television, or film actors.
- *Medea* by Euripides
- *The Seagull* by Anton Chekhov
- *The Crucible* by Arthur Miller
- *The Heidi Chronicles* by Wendy Wasserstein
- *Arcadia* by Tom Stoppard
- *Cloud Nine* by Caryl Churchill

2 Watch a video of a play and write a review of the performance based on the casting of three characters.

3 Create two or three pages for the playbill that will accompany a play of your choice. Include interesting biographies of all the cast members.

4 Read the excerpt found in Unit Eight of *A Jamaican Airman Foresees His Death* by Fred D'Aguiar. Write a short rehearsal schedule for this scene, along with the names of classmates and the roles they would play. Try to cast both males and females.

Scene from *Arcadia* by Tom Stoppard

Chapter 15 Test

The test for this chapter is available in blackline master form in the Resource Binder, page 63.

Use the following prompts to help students exercise **critical viewing skills.**
- What can you tell about the time period in which *Arcadia* is set?
- If you had to provide a physical description of these actors on a casting sheet, what would you write?

For More Information

Books

Cohen, Robert, *Acting One,* McGraw-Hill, 2001.

Kohlhaas, Karen, *Monologue Audition: A Practical Guide for Actors,* Limelight, 2000.

Kondazian, Karen, *The Actors Encyclopedia of Casting Directors: Conversations with Over 100 Casting Directors on How to Get the Job*, Lone Eagle, 2000.

Shurtleff, Michael, *Audition: Everything an Actor Needs to Know to Get the Part*, Walker and Co., 1984. (This text, originally published in 1978, remains a highly regarded handbook for auditioning actors.)

Substitute Teacher Activities

- Assign the Casting a Play Worksheet on page 61 of the Resource Binder.
- Assign one or more of the Additional Projects on this page.
- Teach the Auditions section of the Student Handbook on page 592.
- **Hold a Mock Audition** for a play the class will choose. Have four or five students be the co-directors (auditors). They will decide whether they want those auditioning to prepare monologues or to read from the script. The remainder of the class then either selects monologues to present or chooses a scene from the play to prepare with a partner (or partners). This activity may take several days.

  Make sure that each student has a chance to audition and that as many as possible take the position of auditor.

Theatre Then and Now

Talk to students about the fact that directors sometimes use *gender-blind casting.* This means that men can be cast in women's roles and vice versa. On occasion, a playwright will do a bit of gender-bending also, as Caryl Churchill did in her play *Cloud Nine.*

In 1979, Churchill received a great deal of attention for this play, in which a female actor plays a sensitive schoolboy and a male actor plays an unfulfilled wife. The result is comic and thought-provoking. The play illustrates one of Churchill's recurrent themes—shedding light on gender distinctions.

ACTivity Ask students to find or create scenes for one male and one female actor. Then have pairs of students play the scenes with the roles reversed and discuss their experience.

Other Cultures, Other Times

- Hrotsvitha of Gandersheim, a Benedictine nun writing in the 10th century, is the fist recorded female playwright. Six of her plays still survive.
- The first recorded woman playwright to write in English was Katherine of Sutton. Between 1363 and 1376 she wrote entertaining adaptations of liturgical plays.
- Mary Sidney Herbert, Countess of Pembroke, became the first woman in England to publish a play (*Antonie,* 1592).

Theatre Then and Now

A Leading Lady of His Time: Edward Kynaston

Edward Kynaston

Some of the greatest women's roles of all time were first played by . . . men. That's right, toward the middle of the 17th century, the most beautiful woman on the London stage was not a woman at all. And that didn't bother audiences one bit. The "leading lady" in question was actor Edward Kynaston (1619–1687), and he would go on to play an interesting role in theatre history.

At that time in England, women weren't allowed to set foot on the stage for any reason—and that included playing female characters in the plays of William Shakespeare and others. These roles were instead taken by smooth-faced, fair-skinned young men. And Kynaston was one of the best of these—he was much admired for the naturalness of his delivery, not to mention his physical beauty, in roles such as Desdemona in Shakespeare's tragedy *Othello.*

In 1660, Charles II took the throne as king of England, and with him came a new era of tolerance and religious and social reforms. In 1662, he decreed that from then on women would be allowed to play female roles in the theatre. But King Charles wasn't content to leave it at that. He also enacted a law forbidding men to play women.

And so it was that poor Edward Kynaston became the last of the great male players of women. He went from being a popular leading player to an often out-of-work actor unable to make a successful transition to male roles. In building his celebrity by playing only female roles, Kynaston effectively shut himself out of his own profession.

Contemporary playwright Jeffrey Hatcher chronicles and re-envisions the life and times of Edward Kynaston in a play called *Compleat Female Stage Beauty.*

Visual Cue

Use the prompts below to help students broaden their **visual learning skills.**

- What physical attributes do you think Edward Kynaston might have possessed that made him the top-rated performer of women's roles?
- Do you think it would be difficult to play someone of the opposite gender? Why or why not?

A Leading Lady of Our Time: Cherry Jones

In his review of the 1995 Broadway revival of *The Heiress, New York Times* critic Vincent Canby called Cherry Jones "a splendid young actress who's new to me." This is a somewhat ironic quote in view of the fact that at the time Jones had more than fifty productions under her belt, a Tony nomination for *Our Country's Good* (1991), and a 1992 OBIE Award for her performance in Paula Vogel's play *The Baltimore Waltz.*

Before landing the lead role in the Lincoln Center's production of *The Heiress,* Jones had played characters both far younger and far older than her actual age. In fact, when she was called in to audition for *The Heiress,* she believed it was for the role of the play's older character, Aunt Penniman. Jones did not realize she'd been called in for the lead role of Catherine Sloper until she came to the audition and informed the director that she was unwilling to play the aunt.

Cherry Jones has a unique ability to disappear into a role by completely changing her voice and physical bearing. She's had plenty of opportunity to perfect this versatility. She trained at Carnegie-Mellon University and spent a year at the Brooklyn Academy of Music (BAM) before joining the American Repertory Company (Cambridge, MA) in 1980. There she performed in twenty-five plays in six seasons. She developed a reputation as a risk-taker, playing roles in everything from Shakespeare to Brecht.

Over the years, Cherry Jones has gone from a nearly anonymous actor to a major theatrical star. Her celebrity is easy to explain: She is completely dedicated to the craft of acting.

Cherry Jones

Quotable

This is such a lark. I can be sexy. I can be goofy. I can be an old yenta. I can be young. I can be whatever I need to be at the moment and decide what that is as I go. I have done so much grim theater for so long. I love hard theater, but it is just so nice for once to get to go to work where the object is to be stupid and funny and dear and innocent — and driven to save Greece.

Cherry Jones, on her role in *Lysistrata*

- In Italy in the 16th through 18th centuries women were closely involved with the *commedia dell'arte* not only as actresses, but also as *capocomico,* running companies and producing their own material.

ACTivity Encourage students to do library or Internet research on these leading ladies of the 19th and 20th centuries.

Sarah Bernhardt (1844-1923)

Ellen Terry (1847-1928)

Eleanora Duse (1859-1924)

Uta Hagen (1919-)

Marian Seldes (1928-)

Meryl Streep (1949-)

The Women's Project is a New York-based theatre devoted solely to plays written by women. The site *www.womensproject.org* contains information on female innovators throughout the history of theatre as well as links to other theatre-related sites. You might also find tips related to the chapter at *www.geocities.com/Broadway/Alley/5379.*

Visual Cues

Have students look at the two images of Cherry Jones as she appears as Lysistrata (left) and as Josie in *Moon for the Misbegotten* (top). Ask the questions below.

- What kind of person do you think Jones has created as Josie in *Moon for the Misbegotten*?
- As Lysistrata, does Jones appear sexy, goofy, or one of the others of her descriptions in the quote at the left? How would you describe her?

Chapter 16

Blocking

Students build their understanding of stage movement through the use of areas, levels, focus, and balance, and create and direct movement onstage. Because this involves both directing a scene and acting in one, you might want to schedule two or more class periods.

Objectives

1. to discover levels of meaning in movement
2. to understand the differences between functional and artistic movement
3. to create powerful stage pictures using stage positions
4. to effectively block and execute a scene with more than one actor

National Standards

Chapter 16 meets these National Theatre Standards:

Proficient 2a, 2c, 7c, 8a

Advanced 2d, 7e, 7f, 8e, 8f, 8g

Project Specs

For this chapter, tape the floor of the playing area to represent the various stage areas (See page 56.)

Special Needs Students Students who have limited or impaired movement may need alternate versions of the movement exercises. Students who are unable to walk should use their hands, arms, and heads to create character-based and artistic movement.

Advanced Students These students may wish to move beyond basic movements to more highly choreographed work.

On Your Feet

Show, Don't Tell Before students begin this exercise, use the board to demonstrate the activity by drawing a stick figure kicking a soccer ball.

Chapter 16 Blocking

The actor is here . . . and then there . . . and then here again—all the while speaking, gesturing, and doing odd bits of stage business. What helps the actor keep all this together? Blocking!

Project Specs

Project Description For this assignment, you will block a scene of from four to six minutes long involving more than one actor.

Purpose to understand blocking and to apply techniques for handling complex movement onstage

Materials pencil and paper; a ground plan or the Blocking Activity Sheet your teacher provides

Theatre Terms

aesthetic balance
asymmetrical balance
blocking
counter-focus
direct focus
floor plan or ground plan
open stance
symmetrical balance
unity

On Your Feet

With a partner, discuss how you might break down the elements of playing a particular sport. One of you should slowly pantomime the action "frame by frame," while the other draws each step in the sequence. Then change roles. You don't have to draw well; creating stick figures will do.

Theatre Terms

aesthetic balance when the placement of actors onstage appears equally balanced

asymmetrical balance when position is used to balance characters on either side of the stage

blocking the planned movements and arrangements of actors

counter-focus when actors look from one to another, to another, and so on

direct focus when several actors look at one specific actor

floor plan or ground plan a diagram that shows the walls, doors, windows, furniture, and other architectural details onstage

open stance when an actor faces the audience directly; full front

symmetrical balance when there is an equal number of characters on each side of the stage, equidistant from the center

unity a balance in the variety and kinds of movement in a play

PREVIEW

Blocking: Skills in Action

Theatre is a composite art. As you have begun to learn, it is not a particular skill, but a combination of technical, verbal, and visual skills. One very important element is the **blocking,** or planning of the movement and arrangement of the actors within scenes and from one scene to the next. Blocking tells the actor how to get his character from one place to another on the stage. It also supports communication between the characters within the play. And it creates a visual picture that affects the experience of performing and watching the play. Thus, effective blocking creates meaningful, functional, and artistic movement.

Meaningful Movement

Of course, movement in a play must carry out the plot. Juliet must swallow the sleeping potion and Hamlet must stab Polonius if their stories are to follow the playwright's intent. But movement can also be engineered to carry information about the characters' motivations, emotional states, and relationships. What a character does is often more important than what he or she says!

The way in which a character places a prop can telegraph his or her feelings. The way a character primps in a mirror, thumbs through a magazine, or buttons a coat may suggest details about his or her emotional life. An arrangement of characters on a sofa can reveal a wealth of details about their relationships.

The Flying Karamazov Brothers must carefully plan the blocking of their action-packed stage productions.

PREVIEW

Blocking: Skills in Action

Tell students that blocking done well usually goes unnoticed by the audience. However, clumsy or inappropriate blocking can cause problems within a scene and within the play itself.

Although some directors allow the actors to discover their own blocking, most plot out the movement in advance and tell the actors where to move during rehearsals set aside for blocking. However, many directors allow actors to collaborate in the process. If an actor feels uncomfortable moving at a certain point—or wants to move when there is no specific blocking—the director should find out why.

Meaningful Movement

ACTivity Have students take turns miming a simple series of movements such as going to a mailbox, removing letters, and looking through them. Then give individual students a motivating statement such as, "You're waiting for a letter telling you whether or not you got into the college you've always wanted to attend. The letter has just arrived." Get them to think about how this piece of information might affect their blocking.

The following prompts can be used to exercise **critical viewing skills.**

- What might go wrong if the movement shown in this photo weren't well blocked?
- What do you think the lines on the floor might contribute to the blocking?
- How important do you think eye contact is in this scene? Why?

ACTivity Have pairs of students face each other. Each of them tosses a tennis ball simultaneously. The other must catch it. Tell them to take their time, throw gently, and maintain eye contact. When they have perfected this, have them add one and then two more balls.

Resource Binder

- Blocking Activity Sheet, p. 64
- Stage Pictures Worksheet, p. 65
- Critique Sheet: Blocked Scene, p. 66
- Blocking Test, p. 67
- Blocking Shorthand, p. 127

Handbook Connections
pages 572-573

To Have on Hand

- Tape for spiking the floor of the playing area
- Images of various forms of movement expression–from disciplines such as dance, performance art, and theatre
- Scripts or anthologies from which students can select plays

Chapter 16 Blocking 183

PREPARE

Functional Movement

Draw a large ground plan on the chalkboard. Then ask students to help position a wall, doors, windows, and furniture for a scene from a play they are all familiar with—perhaps *The Diary of Anne Frank* or *Romeo and Juliet*.

ACTivity Using the classroom as the available area, have three or four students collaborate to create a ground plan of a scene from a play of their own choosing.

Show, Don't Tell Demonstrate for students open, one-quarter, profile, three-quarter, and full back positions. Then model the difference between erect and slouched posture.

ACTivity Have students review the body positions by playing a game similar to "Simon Says." Students stand in a relaxed fashion while you call out various body positions—full front to full back—and they must assume these positions quickly and with good posture.

Functional Movement

In order to fully communicate a play's meaning to the audience, you must be sure that the blocking emphasizes important characters, moments, and even objects in the play. In order to facilitate the blocking, a **ground plan,** or **floor plan,** must be created. This plan is a diagram on paper that shows the walls, doors, windows, furniture, and other important architectural details of the stage drawn to scale. The director should create a blocking plan well in advance. This saves rehearsal time and helps to keep the movement organized and unified. Even with this plan, however, changes will always be made during the evolution of the play.

A ground plan of a very symmetrical set. The ground plan is drawn as though looking down from a place high above the stage.

Creating a center of interest that catches and holds the audience's attention is important onstage. Usually the actor who is speaking important lines receives the emphasis. Sometimes audience attention is drawn to an inanimate object, an important line of dialogue, or significant movements that show feelings or desires. A center of interest is achieved in subtle ways so that the audience members give their attention effortlessly. The following are the director's tools for creating emphasis.

The Actor As you learned in Chapter 6, an actor will face the audience, full front, to convey important dialogue. This is called an **open stance,** and it draws attention to the character. When blocking a scene, remember that standing full front is the most emphatic stance, followed by one-quarter, profile, three-quarter, and full back stances. (See page 57 for a photograph of these.) A standing position is usually more dominant than a sitting position; sitting is more emphatic than lying down. An erect posture generally commands more attention than a slouched posture.

Stage Areas The diagram on page 185 shows the relative strength of stage areas, with number 1 being the strongest and 6 the weakest. The exception to area strength occurs when a downstage character assumes a three-quarter position in order to face an upstage character who is then emphasized.

From the Field: Mad Libs Mix-Ups

I start by having students fill out Mad Libs® together in class. Then the students act out the goofy scene they have created. Not only is this an excellent drama activity, but it is also a great review of the parts of speech.

LeAnn Gausman, Theatre Teacher, Westlake, OH

See For More Information on page 194 for a few Mad Lib® titles.

A stage mapped out with areas of strength.

The director must choose the playing area according to the scene's importance. If it is a climactic scene, a strong area may be chosen. Or to weaken a strong action, such as a gory stabbing, the scene can be softened by playing it in a weaker stage area.

Some directors subscribe to the theory that each stage area has an emotional value that lends itself to certain types of scenes. You can see these connections in the following list:

Area 1 Climactic scenes
Area 2 Dignified scenes
Area 3 Love scenes
Area 4 Scenes that build tension
Area 5 Eavesdropping or foreshadowing events
Area 6 Horror and unrealistic scenes

While the link between acting area and scene can be helpful when working out a blocking plan, remember that these connections are only suggestions, not hard and fast rules.

Stage Levels The higher the level, the more attention a character receives. Not only is this because the audience can readily see raised figures, but there is also a psychological aspect of height dominating a scene. For example, the tall person dominates the short person. Elevation can be varied by using platforms and stairs, as well as by having some figures stand, sit, and kneel.

Eye Focus People look where others look, so if characters A and B are looking directly at C, the audience will look at C also. This is called **direct focus.** To add variety, a director sometimes employs **counter-focus,** where A focuses on B who looks at C who looks at the speaking figure D. The audience will follow the pattern from A to B to C and finally to D. The most effective stage arrangement is the triangle, because the eyes of the audience travel along either side and focus on the figure in the middle. Generally the middle person is upstage with the downstage characters turned in three-quarter positions.

In discussing the psychology behind raised stage levels, tell students that politicians and other public speakers often speak to the public from a raised platform for the same reason important characters or scenes are played on the higher stage levels.

Draw the stage with its areas of strength labels 1 to 6 as on this page. Discuss various scenes from plays the students are familiar with in terms of where on the stage the characters would be positioned. For example, a soliloquy from Hamlet would probably be staged in area 1.

ACTivity **Advanced Students** Have interested students choose from among the six stage areas to position characters in scenes from *Julius Caesar, A Streetcar Named Desire,* or *Death of a Salesman.* They can create floor plans with actors' positions labeled. They should write a caption telling which scene they are depicting and why they chose the stage area they did.

Show, Don't Tell Use four actors to model an example of counterfocus. A looks at B; B looks at C; C looks at D.

ACTivity Tell students to bring in images or ads from magazines that reflect the stage picture concepts depicted in this chapter. Have students work together to analyze the pictures.

Although blocking can add dimension and visual interest to talky scenes, students should be aware that "busy" blocking can detract from the scene's overall effectiveness.

Notes

Show, Don't Tell Ask groups of students to come up to the playing area. Arrange them in various ways that indicate who is receiving the emphasis on the stage. Start with an arrangement similar to the one at the bottom of this page and proceed from there.

ACTivity Have students work together in groups of five to create a balanced stage picture, freeze, and then have one person take the focus using space, speech, or movement.

Try to bring in color photographs from actual theatrical productions to share with students. Discuss how light and color affect the scene.

Show, Don't Tell Recite a bit of dialogue from a play or a short poem for the students while standing still. Recite the same dialogue or poem again, but this time add movement that enhances what you are saying.

Alert students that movement on stage is probably one of the most challenging things they will be learning in drama class and that you will revisit creating meaningful movement again.

A Clockwork Orange is based on a book by Anthony Burgess. It tells of the violent rampages of a young criminal and his gang. He is finally caught and subjected to extreme behavior modification techniques. The following prompts can be used to exercise **critical viewing skills** as students study the photo at the top of the page:

- Which actor has the primary focus? Why?
- How do you think the character in the middle is feeling? What adds to this impression?
- Who are the other people in the picture? How can you tell?
- In what way does the furniture add visual focus to the scene?

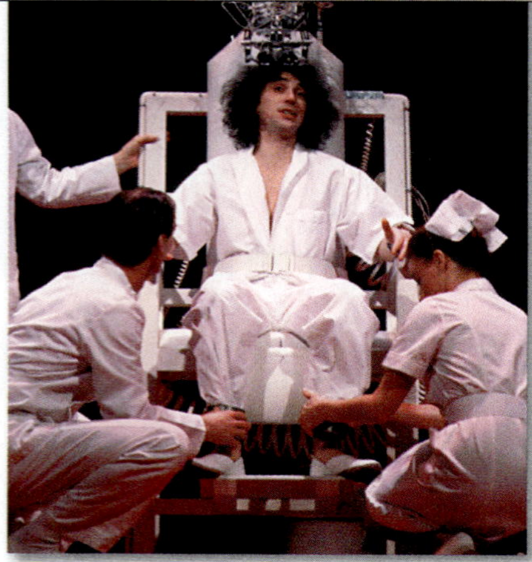

In the triangle arrangement seen here in *A Clockwork Orange,* we focus on the character in the center. While effective, avoid overusing the triangle.

Space and Contrast A character surrounded by space draws attention because of being easily seen, and the audience wonders about the isolation from the group. The more space between the character and the group, the more emphasis on the character. In the diagram below, character A receives emphasis. If one actor is different from all the rest, dominance is achieved through contrast. A person who sits while others stand, who is in a full back position while others are full front, or who is dressed in one color while others are all dressed in another color will be accented through contrast.

Because she is set apart spatially from the group, character A receives the attention of the audience.

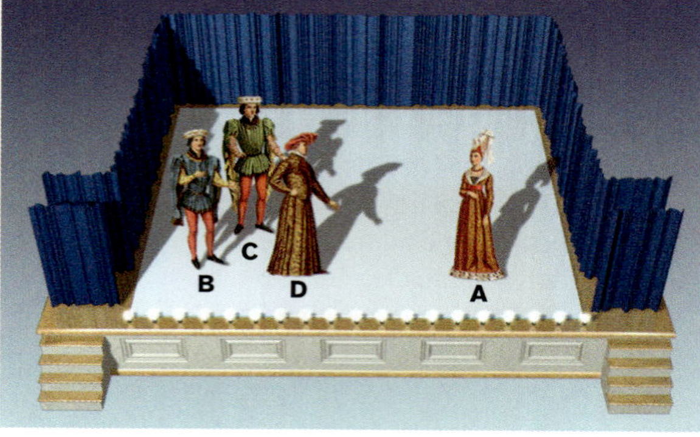

Light and Color A character in a strong pool of light dominates those in a dim light.

The more brilliant the costume color, the more emphasis on the actor. Depending on the costume design for the play as a whole, of course, it is generally assumed that only principal characters should wear red or white, and these colors should be used with care, since they easily attract audience attention.

Speech and Movement The speaker dominates unless there is movement on stage. The moving figure always achieves emphasis. Remember that forward movement is strong; retreating movement is weak.

"Talky" scenes can be made more interesting if you add movement. To accent certain words in the dialogue, move before the line or phrase. Movement after the line stresses the action, not the words. Movement during the line weakens the words, and so is often used when the lines are to be subordinated or "thrown away."

Notes

Reinforcement Any major figure who is reinforced or backed up by minor figures achieves attention. A business executive with three secretaries hovering behind is more emphatic than one without any secretaries. The queen with her attendants or the gang leader with thugs behind him are impressive because of the reinforcement. Also, a character can be emphasized with scenery, such as being framed by an arch, a column, or a tree; or a person can be emphasized with furniture such as a high-backed chair.

Artistic Movement

Artistry in blocking means that the stage picture you create with your actors' movement is pleasing to the mind and senses. For stage movement to become satisfying, it must employ the three qualities below.

Variety By presenting various levels of emphasis and changes of mood, a play maintains variety and avoids monotony. Variety helps the audience stay focused on the elements of the plot and follow the progression of the story.

Unity There must be **unity** in the variety and kind of movement the play requires. Unity provides continuity so that a play's disparate elements come together as a whole.

Balance The elements on either side of the playing area should seem to be equal. The aim is to move from one balanced picture to another during most scenes.

The Balanced Stage Picture

Of course, it's impossible to keep the stage balanced constantly, but the ideal is to attempt to do so. Following are three balance formats to keep in mind:

Symmetrical balance is achieved when there is an equal number of figures on each side of the stage, and all are placed

This scene from *Twelfth Night* creates an artistic picture.

Arrange students in the playing area in such a way as to illustrate scenes that show the reinforcement discussed on this page—a business executive with three secretaries, a queen and her attendants, and a gang leader with his or her thugs. Once the students get a feel for the characters and how they interact, have them move as the characters, always being aware of the need to maintain the reinforcement.

ACTivity Have students work in groups of six to create entrances that use the idea of reinforcement to highlight a specific character.

Artistic Movement

Particularly in period pieces, actors must be trained to move in ways that amplify aspects of the time and place. Sometimes directors hire a movement coach to work with the cast to ensure unity of physical presentation.

The Balanced Stage Picture

Clumsy blocking often features clumps of actors hovering on one side of the playing area or the other while a large area remains unused. To create balance, the director should aim for stage pictures that do not create too much weight on one side or the other.

Show, Don't Tell Arrange a group of students in the playing area in ways that DO NOT show balance. Discuss what is wrong with the picture and ask other students to rearrange the group to achieve a more pleasing balance.

Visual Cue

Shakespeare's *Twelfth Night* offers the director and actors a wealth of inspiration for achieving artistic movement and a balanced stage picture. The following prompts can be used to help students **think critically** about what they see.

- What elements make this scene pleasing to the eye? Describe them.
- Is the picture symmetrically balanced? If so, how?
- Is there an element of contrast in the picture? Describe it.

Lead a group discussion of the blocking in plays or other performances in which students may have taken part. For example, mention that the school marching band uses a form of blocking to create individual and group effects. Cheerleading, debate, and other programs may also use a form of blocking to create exciting visual pictures for an audience.

Show, Don't Tell Re-create the images on this page and the next by asking students to move about in the playing area maintaining the arrangements pictured. After students have moved in groups in an asymmetrically and symmetrically balanced group, ask them to create characters that relate to one another and move as those characters would in these same arrangements.

Vocabulary Enhancement

As students learned in Chapter 5, when an actor *cheats out,* he or she turns toward the audience. In actuality, making any action onstage look realistic without actually doing what you seem to be doing is called *cheating.* When blocking a scene, a director may also call out phrases such as "Cheat left" or "Cheat right," meaning the actor should angle his or her body more to the left or to the right.

equidistant from the center. This composition is usually artificial and stylized, and it is extremely formal. It is sometimes used to indicate church, state, or courtroom scenes or with certain period plays that demand stylized acting such as Oscar Wilde's *The Importance of Being Earnest.*

Asymmetrical balance is informal. It employs the teeter-totter principle. A lighter figure on one side balances a heavier figure on the other side if the lighter figure is farther from the center. Or a character on one side can balance a group on the other side.

Aesthetic balance is sometimes called psychological balance. It gives the impression of equal weight on both sides of the center, even though the actual weight is not equal. For instance, one major character in the play gives the impression of outweighing several less important characters. A standing figure can balance several seated people. A speaker has more weight than a listener, and a character reinforced by scenery can balance a large group. Strong movement and bright colors also balance large masses.

No matter how you balance your stage area, one curiosity remains: If only one stage area is used for a scene and that area is balanced, the audience will be oblivious to the empty portion of the stage.

These two symmetrically balanced groups present a stylized, formal picture.

Quotable

Any smoothly functioning technology will have the appearance of magic.

Arthur C. Clarke, Science Fiction Writer

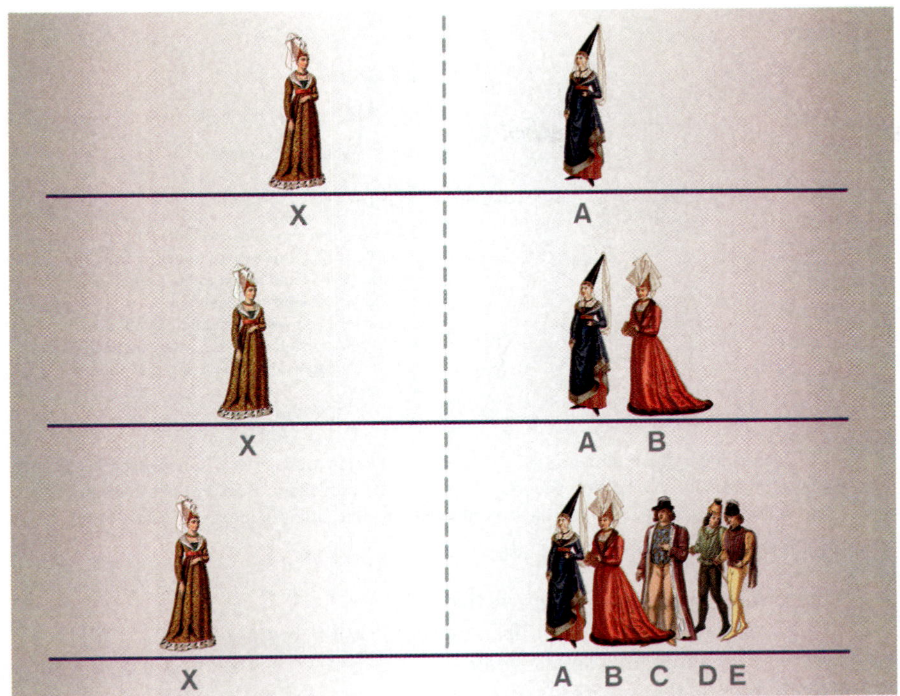

Examples of asymmetrical balance. X and A are in balance, but in order to remain in balance with A and B, X must take one step toward the side. To balance A, B, C, D, E, or more, X must take two steps to the side.

The Director Plots the Blocking

Using the ground or floor plan of the set, the director will place the furniture, being sure to keep important entrances and exits free. Furniture grouping should provide a variety of playing areas. While there should be ample space on stage for movement, there should be enough furniture to prevent the stage from looking bare, unless that is the desired effect.

Next, the director will go through each scene, recording the basic crosses of each character in the margins of the prompt book. He or she will usually block the climactic scenes first to prevent repetition of the climax pictures in earlier, less important scenes. To work out the blocking, some directors use chess pieces, buttons, or inverted golf tees for characters, moving them in various positions on the floor plan.

Quotable

When asked how he handled rehearsals, this was the response from director Arvin Brown:

I get the actors on their feet almost immediately. I feel that that is how their instrument gets operating.

The Director Plots the Blocking

Tell students that there has long been a debate among professional directors concerning the use of a script's stage directions. Some directors admit to deleting the playwright's stage directions entirely, while others rely on the playwright's blueprint for the blocking and tend not to change it unless it does not make sense with the parameters of the performance space and/or the set specifications.

ACTivity Have individual students block the rest of the group to illustrate such activities as waiting in a long line, cheering in the stands at a football game, watching from the ground as something amazing happens far above, and so on. Remind students to create the most intriguing stage pictures they can while still conveying the basic action of the scene. Construct the activity so that students feel free to improvise dialogue.

ACTivity **Advanced Students** The park bench is a setting that has long been popular with playwrights. Ask students to think about possible staging problems such a setting might present. Then have them read one of these plays set on a park bench and create interesting blocking for it.

The Zoo Story by Edward Albee

A Talk in the Park by Alan Ayckbourn

The Loveliest Afternoon of the Year by John Guare

Whisper Into My Good Ear by William Hanley

Discuss with students the relationship between the script on this page and the movements indicated in the drawing. Ask three students to play the parts of Carl, Bob, and Alice and to create the scene using the dialogue and the blocking indicated. (You might want to spike the floor to indicate where the tables, desk, and chairs will be placed.)

ACTivity Give a number of groups of students the chance to combine the movement and dialogue in the script. Discuss their impressions of the blocking of this short scene.

ACTivity **Advanced Students** Challenge three students to memorize the lines of the script on this page and then perform the scene using the blocking called for. You could assign the role of Alice to an advanced student and encourage a beginning, ESL, or Special Needs student to take the part of Bob.

Theatre Journal

Use the following to elaborate the journal prompt.

Lead students in a group discussion of what they discovered during the journal activity.

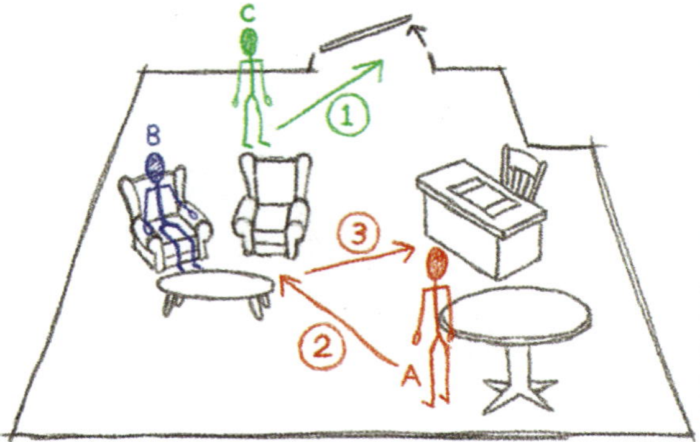

The doorbell rings.

CARL: Well, I guess I had better get that! [He exits.] (1)

BOB: So, what do you propose we do about this?

ALICE: I propose that you do nothing. I will handle it in my own way. It is obvious to me that you have no real understanding of the situation, and I feel that I can handle it. Look, Bob, (2) I don't mean to embarrass or confuse you, I am just determined to get to the bottom of things. I want to show you something that I found yesterday. I think once you see this, you will understand my concern. (3) Here, take a look at this and tell me what you think. Surely, you can't now imagine that I am being picky about this situation.

Alice (A) is standing by the round table. Bob (B) is sitting in a chair. Carl (C) is UR. For the first move (1), Carl exits UC. For the second move (2), Alice crosses to Bob. For the third move (3), Alice moves to the desk. All three movements are indicated at the appropriate place in the script.

When a movement seems effective, the director notes it in the prompt book by drawing in the margin a small rough draft of the stage floor with its furniture placement. Using a different colored pencil for each character, the character's position is labeled, and an arrow is drawn to indicate new movement. Each move is numbered using a corresponding number notated in the script at the exact place in the dialogue where the movement is to be made. Dots or crosses may be used to indicate characters. Sometimes stick figures are used to better visualize the picture and to show characters standing, sitting, and facing in certain directions.

Theatre Journal

When you next find yourself at a large dinner or the school lunchroom, sketch the seating arrangement at a table that holds your interest. Then answer these questions: Who appears to be drawing the most attention at the table? Who appears to be drawing the least attention? What effect does closeness to the center of attention have upon the dynamics of the conversations and behaviors at the table?

Backstage Gossip: Seeing the Written Action

Many playwrights feel that the stage directions they write should be given as much consideration as the dialogue. Others write very few stage directions (or none at all) and leave the blocking entirely to the director.

Emily Mann, a well-known playwright as well as a respected director, has this to say on the subject of stage directions: "Directorial ideas are very vivid images for me, and I consider them part of the writing so that people can see it as they are reading it."

PREPARE

Plot the Blocking of Your Scene

You are to assume the director's duties by choosing and analyzing a scene and then blocking it on paper. Your teacher may provide a Blocking Activity Sheet to help you in this. After you have planned the blocking of the scene, you will direct classmates in the scene until the movement is believable, appropriate to the dialogue, and well executed. Follow the steps below as you work on this project:

1. Select a favorite one-act play that has literary merit and that has meaning for you.
2. Consider the theme, style, mood, and structure of the play as well as the motivations and relationships of the characters.
3. Choose a four- to six-minute scene from the play, preferably one with only two or three characters in it. Copy the scene in such a way that you have wide margins for your blocking notations. Make as many copies as there are characters so that each of your actors will have a script from which to read. On a piece of paper or the Activity Sheet, complete a master floor plan using your classroom playing area as the stage size. Draw the necessary furniture, doors, and windows as near to scale as you can approximate.
4. Visualize the scene. Then, on your copy of the script, pencil in blocking notes in the margins by drawing a small, rough floor plan, labeling the characters, and indicating with arrows and lines each cross you want them to make. If the scene you have chosen is "talky," break up the speeches with motivated movement. Remember to consider the meaning, function, and artistic effect of the movements you employ.
5. Set up makeshift furniture, and provide your actors with their scene copies. As they read the scene aloud, direct them according to the blocking you have plotted on your script. As you direct, call each actor by the character's name. Ask the actors to write down their crosses on their scripts. This will enable them to remember the blocking accurately. If necessary, explain your reasons for wanting certain movements. While your directions should be concrete, your aim is to guide, not dictate. Be pleasant, patient, and willing to listen and make changes based on the actors' ideas.
6. Work out your planned movements with the cast. Change and refine them until they work smoothly onstage. Rehearse several times until the actors feel sure of the movement. Time them to be certain the scene does not exceed six minutes.

PREPARE

Plot the Blocking of Your Scene

Provide students with a variety of colored pens and pencils to use while they work on the Blocking Activity Sheet. Remind them that not all movement is interesting and that overly busy blocking can be distracting. The blocking should enhance the scene.

Tell students that often in the professional theatre an actor may come up with an idea that solves a tricky blocking problem. Good directors listen to their actors. In the end, the blocking remains the director's decision, but remind students that theatre is a collaborative art and that the people carrying out the blocking may very well make valid contributions to the blocking process.

Allow students plenty of time to rehearse their scenes.

From the Field: Go with the Flow

When I direct a student production, I have an idea in my head how to block most scenes, but I encourage students to let movement evolve from their characters as well as the relationships among the characters in the play. With this approach, the patterns of movement are fairly well set after only a few rehearsals.

P. Yeary, Drama Coach and Choral Director, Orlando, FL

PRESENT

Introduce and Enjoy Your Blocked Scene

Tell students to simulate only the furniture that is necessary for the scene. In other words, if the scene is set in a living room but the only furniture needed is a couch and a coffee table, students should set up three or four chairs side by side (the couch) and an overturned box (the coffee table). They need not bother setting up other chairs, a simulated television set, etc. Students may wish to point out the exit areas before they begin their presentations.

Remind students that as directors their work is done once the presentation begins.

CRITIQUE

Evaluate Your Classmate's Blocked Scene

Hand out the Critique Sheet for this project or have students use their own paper. Remind students that evaluating others involves taking good notes, scoring using the rubric, and writing an explanation of the scoring.

It will be helpful to assign the person each student will evaluate so that everyone receives a peer evaluation.

You might want to help students who had obvious trouble with blocking by going over their scene with them once again, making suggestions, and showing them the movements you believe would have been more effective.

PRESENT

Introduce and Enjoy Your Blocked Scene

In order for you to present your scene and act in someone else's, this project will probably take several class periods to complete. When your teacher calls for your scene, hand in a copy of your script and ground plan or the Activity Sheet. Set up any furniture that will be needed in the playing area.

Briefly discuss which of the principles provided in the Preview section you used to block this scene. Then introduce your cast and announce the play's title. Finally, join the audience, watching your scene objectively.

Your instructor may offer to show more effective movement for your scene. Accept any suggestions cheerfully.

CRITIQUE

Evaluate Your Classmate's Blocked Scene

Choose one of the scenes presented in class, and evaluate the blocking. Your evaluation should be based on a scale of 1 to 5, in which 1 is equal to "needs much improvement" and 5 is equal to "outstanding." Your evaluation should answer these questions:

- Which character was made to seem most important to the action of the scene, and why?
- How did the blocking help focus attention on the character emphasized in the scene?
- Did you feel that this emphasis was true to the script?
- In what way was the stage picture balanced?
- What did the blocking tell you about the emotional states and relationships of the characters?

Write a short explanation for the rating you gave this scene.

Notes

Spotlight on

Stage Combat

Actors in a play that involves violence must perform realistic movements safely. Through the use of stage combat, they can make it appear that they are dueling, hitting, punching, pulling hair, or even throwing each other around a room. What they are actually doing is more like dancing than fighting, however. Because it makes use of quick, sharp movements and near misses, stage combat can be dangerous. *Do not attempt stage combat without special training and careful preparation.*

Stage combat is choreographed much like a dance. Like dance, it requires a good deal of rehearsal to get the moves just right.

Hair Pulling One actor grasps the other actor's hair. The second actor hangs on to the wrists of the first and shouts as if hair is being pulled.

Slaps and Punches One actor aims a slap or punch near the victim. The other performs a hidden clap to simulate contact, then reels backward as if hit.

Stabbing An actor shows a knife, dagger, or sword, then turns so that it is hidden to the audience. He or she then plunges forward, thrusting the weapon under the armpit or in some other spot near, not on, the victim. The victim recoils as if stabbed. The weapon is withdrawn with more force than it took to plunge it in and is then disposed of so the audience won't notice the lack of blood.

Falling The secret of falling is to stay relaxed. To lessen the shock, actors break their falls a little at a time—knees, torso, arms, and then head. Whenever possible, they land on soft furniture!

Dying A person who's been shot, stabbed, or beaten tenses immediately, inhales, and doubles toward the wound. The dying person who speaks is generally short of breath, speaking in broken lines with a voice that suggests weakness.

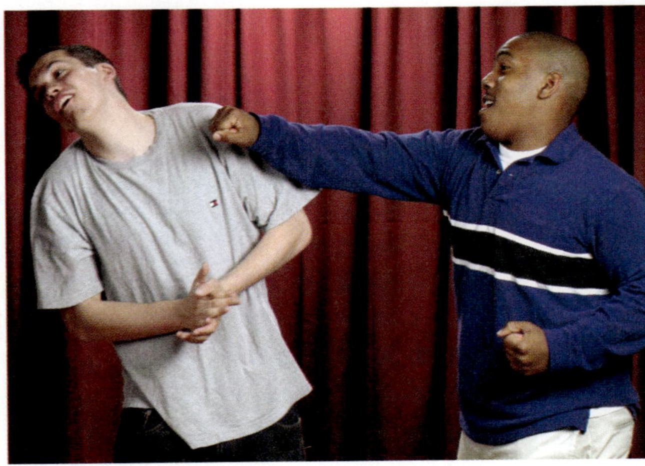

Spotlight on

Stage Combat Share these tips about stage combat with your students.

- **Look your scene partner in the eye.** Eye contact is very important in stage combat.
- **Keep in constant communication.** There is an unspoken communication between actors involved in stage combat. Counting and using physical signals is how many actors continually check in with one another to achieve the most realistic looking combat possible.
- **Make noise.** Much of the realistic look and sound of stage combat comes from the noises the actors make. They gasp and grunt and scream and bellow as the fight progresses. These sounds also make up for the sounds that might be present in a real fight (cracking bones, the thud of a head against a wall, and so on).
- **Never change the fight choreography** without first rehearsing the change with your partner.
- Always remember, **safety first!**

Backstage Gossip: A Little Too Real

The 1991 Broadway production of Paul Rudnick's *I Hate Hamlet* starred eccentric British actor Nicol Williamson as the ghost of legendary thespian John Barrymore. The play featured a scene in which the ghost duels with his young protégé, played by Evan Handler. One night Williamson, who had already been ad-libbing up a storm during that performance, changed the choreography during the swordfight and wound up nicking Handler and drawing blood. Outraged, Handler promptly stormed offstage in mid-performance.

Chapter 16 Blocking **193**

Chapter 16 Test

The test for this chapter is available in blackline master form in the Resource Binder, page 67.

For More Information

Books

Barranger, Milly S., *Theatre: A Way of Seeing,* Wadsworth Publishing Company, 1991.

Price, Roger, and Leonard Stern, *The Original #1 Mad Libs,* Price Stern Sloan, 1974.

Price, Roger, and Leonard Stern, *Cool Mad Libs,* Price Stern Sloan, 2001.

Price, Roger, and Leonard Stern, *Straight "A" Mad Libs,* Price Stern Sloan, 2003.

Rubin, Lucille S., *Movement for the Actor,* Drama Book Specialists Publications, 1980.

Wright, Edwin C., and Marguerite Battye, *Acting and Stage Movement,* Meriwether Publishing, Ltd., 1985.

Other Media

Basic Stage Combat (one videocassette, 20 minutes), Insight Media,1997.

Blocking a Scene: Basic Staging With Actors (one videocassette, 90 minutes), Insight Media,1990.

The Stage Fight Director (one videocassette, 33 minutes), Insight Media, 1990.

Combat for the Stage (one videocassette, 96 minutes), Insight Media, 1988.

Movement for the Actor (one videocassette, 75 minutes), Insight Media,1993.

Movement for Period Plays (one videocassette, 25 minutes), Insight Media, 1985.

Movement (one videocassette, 30 minutes), Insight Media, New York, NY, 1996.

For more information about blocking and stage combat, visit:

www.safd.org
www.geocities.com/Broadway/Stage/2203/SMhandbook4.html

Additional Projects

1 Using one big sofa or overstuffed armchair, see how many varied groupings you can achieve with two characters.

2 Block scenes which reveal the following situations:

- three people whispering
- two people quarreling
- four people looking for something
- a messenger bringing good news to a group
- three people shopping
- five people showing surprise
- three people telling a story to four others

3 Study famous paintings, and identify the artist's use of balance and emphasis. Write a short essay relating this technique to the theatre. Suggested paintings for study:

- Cézanne's *Card Players*
- De Hooch's *A Dutch Courtyard*
- da Vinci's *The Last Supper*
- Hopper's *Nighthawks*

4 Ask your teacher for help in performing an element of stage combat. Practice the technique, under supervision, until you can execute it well. Then demonstrate your technique for the class.

5 Block a scene from a period play such as *MacBeth* by William Shakespeare or a stylized play such as *A Waitress in Yellowstone* by David Mamet. You can find scenes from these plays in Unit Eight of this book.

Cézanne's *Card Players*

Substitute Teacher Activities

Here are suggestions for one or more days when you will be out of the classroom.

- Assign the Stage Pictures Worksheet on page 65 of the Resource Binder.
- Assign one or more of the Additional Projects on this page.
- Teach the Blocking and Stage Composition section of the Student Handbook, pp. 572-573.
- **Create Stage Movement** based on animals. Have students look at pictures of animals in motion. Then have each student choose an animal and create stage movement to depict it. The movement may be highly choreographed and stylized or it may be a more realistic simulation of the animal's movement patterns. Students can present one-minute interpretations of their chosen animal. The rest of the class tries to guess what animal is being portrayed.

Master of the Craft

Anne Bogart

Method actors are generally directed to first find meaning in a script and let that meaning direct their movements. "Viewpoints," a technique developed by Mary Overlie and made famous by director Anne Bogart, begins with actions and gestures, using them to stimulate emotion and meaning. In intensely physical, expressive stage productions such as "Bob" and "Going, Going, Gone," Bogart has created a radical and influential new way of putting together a play.

Drawing on Overlie's influences as well as Martha Graham, the pioneer of modern dance, and Japanese director Tadashi Suzuki, Bogart has created a distinctive body of work. She once told *American Theatre* magazine that "Viewpoints is a way to practice creating fiction using time and space." It allows actors to create as they rehearse. Thus, they collaborate rather than simply follow directions.

In her actor training workshops, Bogart has actors use Viewpoints to develop a common language of movement. The technique calls for actors to relate to time and space in nine different ways. The four time elements are: tempo, duration, kinesthetic response, and repetition of a movement. The five elements of space are shape, gesture, architecture, topography, and spatial relationships. The technique unifies the actors and the production. The movements that emerge become part of the play's choreography, so that the physical, mental, and emotional components develop at the same time.

Bogart declares that Viewpoints is not THE way to produce a play, it is ONE way. She is committed to letting every actor—and every production—develop in its own unique way.

"Depending on the point of view, Anne Bogart is either an innovator or a provocateur assaulting a script."

–Mel Gussow, *New York Times*

A scene from Bogart's *Dispute*

Anne Bogart

Master of the Craft

More About Anne Bogart

For complete information about Anne Bogart's SITI Company, visit www.siti.org. This site provides not only a history of the company and biographies of its members, but also links to other interesting sites related to movement for the stage.

Masters Past and Present

Theatre originally sprang from religious festivals involving dance. It therefore makes sense that some of the greatest innovators in movement for the stage were dancers.

- O-kuni (exact dates unknown, although some sources claim she died in 1613 at the age of 87), performed at Kitano shrine in Kyoto, Japan. The dances she and her companions performed, a mixture of folk and religious movements, were the beginning of the Kabuki theatre tradition. (For more on O-kuni and Kabuki, see page 30.)
- Isadora Duncan (1878-1927) was a dancer whose style and methods ushered in the era of modern dance and signaled a revolution in contemporary stage movement. (For more on Isadora Duncan read her autobiography, *My Life,* published by Sphere Books, 1969.)

Quotables

Share with your students these quotes from Isadora Duncan, the first lady of modern dance.

Movement is life.

The dancer of the future will be one whose body and soul have grown so harmoniously together that the natural language of that soul will have become the movement of the body.

If I could say it, I wouldn't have to dance it.

Theatre Then and Now

The Ancient Greek Chorus

The Greek chorus represented a unique blend of empathy and aloofness. On the one hand, the chorus rejoiced in human good and flailed in sorrow at the flaws of humankind and the fickleness of the gods. On the other hand, it stood apart, somewhat removed from both triumph and tragedy, commenting on the action rather than taking part in it. In a sense, the chorus showed the audience how to respond to the events of the play.

Other Cultures, Other Times

Around 1485, Italian rulers began to finance productions of ancient Roman plays. These productions used a fifteen-member chorus, the same number the ancient Romans used.

Theatre Then and Now

The Ancient Greek Chorus

In ancient Greece, being a member of the chorus was an important role. Early Greek tragedies featured only one actor, who often exited to change costumes, leaving the chorus to continue the story until he returned. The chorus learned about half the lines in the play, all the songs, and all the dances. And every play included dances.

Most often, the Greek chorus made its entrance on stage in a stately march. Chorus members sang and danced in unison and recited their lines together. Occasionally, the chorus would be split into groups. The groups would enter separately and take turns performing.

This Greek chorus in the National Theatre of London's production of the Oresteia trilogy was made up entirely of men.

Once in a while, a second chorus stood mute onstage, except for a few lines. Rarely did individual chorus members have more than a line of their own.

The reason for all this togetherness? The lines, the songs, and the movement of the chorus represented the voice, the sentiment, and the action of society. Greek theatre was about the common good.

196 Unit Four The Play: From Vision to Reality

Visual Cue

A Chorus Line began when a group of dancers were tape recorded as they talked about their personal and professional lives. A musical libretto was pieced together from their stories. Marvin Hamlisch composed the music, and Edward Kleban wrote the lyrics. Michael Bennett then choreographed the show, resulting in staging, songs, dialogue, and dance that segued beautifully one into the other.

Ask students to look at the image from *A Chorus Line* and respond to the following prompts.

- Although this is obviously a chorus number, which performer or performers have the focus?
- Is the stage picture balanced?
- Is there unity?

Spotlight on

Audience Participation

Some shows, particularly those with an improvisatory component, use the audience as part of the act. Many improv troupes, for example, ask audience members to shout out ideas for the improvisers to use as the basis for sketches.

Audience participation is a big part of the fun at the Chicago-based performance phenomenon known as *Too Much Light Makes the Baby Go Blind.* For this show, a small group of improvisers, the Neofuturists, performs "thirty plays in sixty minutes." The material changes from week to week; the performers spend the days in between performances writing batches of new, extremely short plays. During the show the company performs the plays at breakneck speed. The numbers 1 through 30 are pinned onto a clothesline. The audience shouts out a number and the actors rip it down and perform the sketch to which that number was assigned. The Neofuturists also ask questions of the audience, sometimes demanding feedback, sometimes bringing members of the audience onto the stage to participate.

As a special audience-participation bonus, after every sold-out performance, the cast members order pizza for the audience.

By means of a unique blend of performance velocity, improvisation, and sharp writing, the Neofuturists and their ever-changing show *Too Much Light Makes the Baby Go Blind* have become an international phenomenon.

Notes

Spotlight on

Audience Participation

Theatres are finding that audience-participation shows are popular. *Tony 'n Tina's Wedding* has enjoyed long runs and sold-out houses, and the fun lies in the fact that the audience is part of the show—as wedding guests. They eat and drink and interact with each other and the cast as the play progresses.

For more information on the Neofuturists, including examples of some of the show's recurring playlets, visit *www.neofuturists.org.*

ACTivity Play an audience participation game with the students. Divide them into four groups. Each group is assigned a particular line to speak. As you read the story, pause so that players can make appropriate responses.

The Players	Their Lines
Bold Knights	"Clankety-clank"
Fair Maidens	"Help, Help"
Cruel Monarchs	"Gr-r-r-r, Gr-r-r-r"
Wicked Witches	"Cackle, Cackle"
Fierce Dragons	"Roar-r-r-r-r-r"

The Story begins: *Back in the days of bold knights ______ and fair maidens ______, there lived two cruel monarchs ______ who had two daughters. These fair maidens ______ were the kindest in all the land. Those who passed by the castle would see the fair maidens ______ high in the castle, leaning out the window, longing for freedom. It was told about the land that these fair maidens ______ had a curse placed upon them by a covey of wicked witches ______. Only six fierce dragons ______ that lived in the woods could set them free. Should the fierce dragons ______ look upon the fair maidens ______, the fair maidens ______ would have the superior strength to escape their confinement. That is why the cruel monarchs ______ enlisted two bold knights ______ to slay the fierce dragons ______.* Have a student volunteer to continue telling the story.

PREPARE

Attend the Play of Your Choice

Monitor the students' preparation for this project. A trip outside of the school grounds can be problematic in terms of travel and safety. Make certain that adequate transportation has been arranged— perhaps students' parents or guardians might volunteer to coordinate car pools.

Tell students that many people volunteer as ushers at their local theatre. They take tickets, hand out programs, and escort audience members to their seats. In exchange for these services they usually are allowed to see the show for free. Have students look into the possibility of ushering at a community or professional theatre in your area.

Depending on where your school is located, this chapter's project may be difficult, if not impossible, to carry out. If there are no theatres in your area, you can have student groups do the talk-show presentation about a play they have all read. Tell them to take notes on:

- structure
- plot
- characters
- theme

They should also think about whether the play would be producible at the school level and what kind of marketing it might need to gain an audience.

Vocabulary Enhancement

A great review is called a *rave.*
A terrible review is called a *pan.*

Theatres often provide critics with *press kits,* packets of photos and text materials full of information about the theatre, the production, the playwright, the actors, and so on.

PREPARE

Attend the Play of Your Choice

When we attend a play, we are offered a look into our lives. Sometimes we feel an affirmation as we laugh at situations and characters that encourage us to loosen up. Other times we are pulled into life's serious issues that demand deep thinking and genuine emotional investment. For example, Henrik Ibsen's *An Enemy of the People* addresses environmental issues; Edward Albee's *Three Tall Women* reveals female generational relationships; and Tony Kushner's *Angels in America* focuses on the social, political, and personal ramifications of the AIDS crisis. While many plays do not carry the heavy messages of those named above, most plays give us the opportunity to examine ourselves and our values.

Sometimes as audience members we are not aware of a play's theme until we analyze the play later. At other times the theme is clear throughout the performance.

With a group of friends, you will attend a play. As part of the experience, you will monitor your own, your companions', and the rest of the audience's experience.

Before You Go

To prepare for your theatre-going experience, you and your companions should:

- Buy your tickets in advance.
- Dress appropriately.
- Arrive at the theatre at least fifteen minutes prior to curtain time.
- Consider and discuss your responsibilities as thoughtful and responsive audience members.

While You're There

Before the play begins, observe the audience as they take their seats and settle in. Do they seem excited and happy to be there? Take notes on their behavior before and after the play and during the intermission. You can generally tell by body language, facial expressions, and the amount of shifting or coughing going on whether the audience as a whole is engaged. During the intermission you might even ask your companions and a few of the other audience members what they think about the performance so far. Be aware of your own response as well.

Try to track the play's theme or guiding statement. Remember that the theme is usually found in the way the protagonist handles the play's central conflict. Check in with yourself periodically as you watch the play. When you believe you have become aware of the play's theme, jot it down using as few words as possible. You can always adjust your analysis later on.

When You Leave the Theatre

After the play, make sure you still have your program. Look through it for any

Backstage Gossip: Is Kate Aging Badly?

In Shakespeare's day his comedy *The Taming of the Shrew* was both a box-office draw and a crowd-pleaser. But in the 20th century, some critics and audiences began to feel uncomfortable about *Shrew.* The play is about an ill-tempered, independent-minded woman named Kate and the man who "tames" her, Petruchio. First through cruelty and later through rewards, Petruchio turns Kate into a "fitting wife." Some argue that the play is anti-woman, a blatant example of male chauvinism. Apart from the anti-feminist point, critics have argued about the play's artistic merits. However, many Shakespeare fans still respond favorably to the play's physical comedy and clever wordplay.

202 **Unit Four** The Play: From Vision to Reality

director's notes or playwright's notes that might give you further insights into the play. Keep the program. Later, you will turn it in to your teacher.

Sometimes the most enjoyable part of a theatre outing is talking about the play afterward, so try to discuss the play for at least a few minutes with your companions.

When you get home, take some private time to think about your experience at the theatre. Then, with the aid of your notes, write a two-page paper describing that experience. Include the following:

- a summary of the play's theme
- any particularly intriguing performances or memorable lines
- your emotional reaction to the play or to a particular character
- a description in your own words of how attending a play differs from attending a movie or watching television
- at least one paragraph in which you describe the audience response

You will not be reading from your paper. Instead, you will use it as the basis for a panel discussion in which you and the people with whom you attended the play will talk about the experience. You should be familiar enough with the points discussed in your paper that you can easily chat about each.

The Talk Show Format

You will be presenting a live talk show based on your experience of attending the play. Choose a discussion leader (the talk show host) to help focus your group's discussion. This person will introduce each of you and tell the name of the play you attended together. He or she will then ask questions and give each participant a chance to respond. The talk show host must take part in the discussion as well, giving his or her point of view for each question. Questions should be loosely based on the notes each of you took before, during, and after the play. Panel members must answer the questions informally without reading from their notes.

As a group, decide in advance the order of the questions and which topics you will deal with. The talk show host will keep track of the time and make sure your group doesn't go on longer than the ten-minute limit.

Try This

To practice answering questions and giving opinions spontaneously, ask a friend or relative to write down four or five questions for you. The questions can range from serious to silly, but they should require some thought on your part. Sit in a chair, read the questions aloud, and practice answering them. This should help prepare you for your talk show participation.

Notes

If students are reading the play instead of attending it, they can use these criteria as the basis of their two-page paper:

- a summary of the play's theme
- any particularly intriguing characters or lines
- their own emotional reaction to the writing or to character descriptions
- their own visualization of the set and lighting
- thoughts about how various audiences (under twelve, young adult, middle aged, elderly) might respond to the play's subject matter

The Talk Show Format

Suggest that students ask if any member of their group would like to be the discussion leader. However, if you think a particular student needs a chance to work on leadership qualities, ask that student to lead the group.

Suggest also that they may wish to watch a television talk show to get a clearer idea of the style and format. Remind the group leader, that he or she must do more than ask pertinent and probing questions, however. The leader of this presentation is also responsible for contributing ideas and opinions.

Give each discussion leader in turn your stopwatch to use during the group's presentation. Be sure it is returned to you when each talk show is over.

Try This

Tell students that the questions can be about any subject with which they have some familiarity. The key is to be relaxed and spontaneous.

PRESENT

Put on Your Talk Show

Remind students that their goal is to be objective and well informed, not simply opinionated. Tell them that a critic is not someone who merely criticizes, but a person who studies, analyzes, and renders an informed opinion. Students should bear in mind that tone is important—sometimes it's not what one says but rather the way one says it.

Visual Cue

- Which person in the photo do you think is the host? What makes you think so?
- Does this remind you of a talk show you have seen on television? What are the similarities? How is it different?
- What might be some of the benefits of having more than two people take part in a talk show? What might be some of the disadvantages?

CRITIQUE

Evaluate a Panelist's Performance

Hand out the Critique Sheet for this project or have students use their own paper. Remind students that they are critiquing only one person in the talk show panel—it can be either the discussion leader or one of the panelists.

Discuss with students the rubrics they will be using to evaluate this person. Let them know that you will be assessing each of them in the much the same way, and that you will also evaluate how well they assess others.

If you feel that a student had a particularly difficult time with the talk-show format, talk to the student about his or her impressions of the process. Suggest techniques the student can use to become more comfortable in the setting.

PRESENT

Put on Your Talk Show

When your name or another group member's name is called, give all of your papers or Activity Sheets to your teacher, along with the program for the play. Step into the performance area and set up your chairs in a talk show arrangement, side by side in a straight line or a semicircle.

The talk show host will introduce each of you and begin the discussion by asking a question. When it is your turn to answer, try to present as clear a picture of your experience as you can. For example, if you felt excitement during the performance convey that to the class. Make sure you discuss both your own reaction and your perception of the audience's reaction to the play.

When nine minutes have passed, the host should start to wrap things up by asking the group for any final thoughts. At the end of the ten minutes, stop the discussion, shake hands with your fellow participants, and return to your seat.

Students present a talk show.

CRITIQUE

Evaluate a Panelist's Performance

There is a difference between playing a part and playing yourself. Some people have a much more difficult time being themselves in front of an audience than they do playing a character.

Remaining relaxed and comfortable in front of an audience without notes or a script can be nerve-wracking. You will see that some of your classmates are better at it than others. Select one classmate from a talk show panel who struck you as the most effective speaker in the group, the student you would rate as "outstanding." Write a paper explaining why. Ask yourself the questions below as you evaluate the outstanding individual in the talk show panel.

- What did the panelist do to appear physically comfortable?
- What elements (humor, enthusiasm, storytelling, etc.) did this person use to engage the audience?
- What aspects of the panelist's behavior particularly engaged you?
- How did the other participants in the presentation react to this panelist?
- What insights into the theatre-going experience impressed you in the panelist's remarks?
- What insights brought you to a higher level of understanding?

Backstage Gossip: Cell Phones in Traffic

Celebrated playwright and actor Sam Shepard was performing in Chicago as part of the Steppenwolf Theatre Company's Traffic series–programming that features live music and the spoken word. Early in the performance an audience member's cell phone began to ring. Shepard looked out, found the woman whose phone was ringing, and said fiercely, "Turn that thing off!" The mortified patron did.

Additional Projects

1 Attend a play, or watch a filmed version of a play of your choice. Choose a particular actor to focus on throughout the play. Keep a list of questions you would ask this actor about the performance.

2 Imagine that you are the house manager and you have been asked to deliver a curtain speech before the beginning of the current play. Your goal is to make the audience feel welcome and to give them a few pre-show instructions. Confine your speech to ninety seconds but make sure you include the following elements.

- Greet the audience and thank them for coming.
- Warn them not to take photographs during the show.
- Tell them to turn off their beepers and cell phones.
- Tell them to unwrap their candy before the show begins.
- Thank them again, and tell them to enjoy the show.

3 A good audience is often a knowledgeable audience. Write an outline with as much detail as you can find about the theatre of a particular country or era.

4 Read the scene from *The Actor's Nightmare* by Christopher Durang, found in Unit Eight of this book, and think about the nightmare aspect of this scene. Write a short scene of your own entitled *The Student's Nightmare.*

Think of a few questions you might ask the actor playing Charlotte in *Charlotte's Web.*

Chapter 17 Test

The test for this chapter is available in blackline master form in the Resource Binder, page 71.

For More Information

For tips on audience etiquette, visit *www.wcupa.edu/oca/EKA/etiquette.htm.*

For more on what it takes to be a good audience member visit *http://search.centerstage.net/theatre/articles/etiquette.html.*

For an interesting talk-show alternative, tune in to National Public Radio for interview programming such as Terry Gross's popular "Fresh Air."

Visual Cue

Questions the students might ask the actress in the photo could include:

- Is it necessary to be athletic or physically strong to play the part of Charlotte?
- How do you go about identifying with your character when it's a spider?
- Does your voice have to have a particular pitch or tone in this role?
- How do you move to give the audience a sense of your character?

Substitute Teacher Activities

The suggestions below are intended for the substitute teacher when you are out of the classroom for a day or two.

- Assign the Be a Theatre Critic Worksheet on page 69 of the Resource Binder, and have students write a review of a play, film, or television show.
- Assign one or more of the additional projects on this page.
- Go over the Audience Etiquette rules on page 36 of the student book.
- **Conduct a Current Events Talk Show.** Have students use the talk-show format to work in groups to discuss current events, important school activities, or other timely topics. Have each group choose a "host," who introduces and asks questions of the "guests."

Theatre Then and Now

Other Cultures, Other Times

Many theatres throughout the centuries have presented outdoor plays, especially those written by William Shakespeare, during the summer months. The most famous of the outdoor Elizabethan theatres was the Globe Theatre, built in London in 1599 by Richard Burbage. It consisted of an open-air building with a platform stage in the middle surrounded on three sides by open standing room. A large enclosed balcony covered by small roofed galleries surrounded the theatre, offering seating for the few who could afford it. You might want to gather images of the old and new Globe theatres to show students. There are also models of the Globe available that can be fairly easily assembled.

Invite a director or administrator from a local theatre that presents outdoor performances to visit the class. Ask him or her what adjustments must be made when presenting plays outside, including the technical requirements, and so on.

Bertolt Brecht (1898-1956) believed in abolishing anything artificial that separated the audience from the performers. This belief extended to the performance space. Brecht did not believe in the use of realistic sets; he preferred environmental staging, often working without even a stage.

Theatre Then and Now

The Roman Audience in 200 A.D.

Imagine that you are attending a play at the imposing Roman theatre at Sabratha, around 200 A.D. You are one of thousands of people lucky enough to get a seat in the largest theatre in North Africa. By this time Roman theatres have been constructed all over Italy, Spain, and France, as well as North Africa.

Imagine the noise all these people are making. Then consider the fact that the performance is held outdoors and the performers onstage have no microphones or other artificial amplification.

In such a large performance space, subtlety won't be the first order of business. In fact, most of the actors wear masks painted with characteristic facial expressions that can be seen by audience members seated great distances away.

If you picture yourself sitting high in the stands at a football stadium watching a play going on down there on the 50-yard line, you'll have some idea of the dimensions. You should also consider that your seat is made of stone. There are no artificial lights of course, so the play is performed using that most natural of lighting systems—the sun.

For your theatre comfort, there are awnings, fruit vendors, and if it gets particularly hot, showers of perfumed water. More likely than not, you are watching a bawdy farce full of greed, horseplay, infidelities, and women in scanty costumes. Here you are, centuries in the past, watching a performance not unlike the TV situation comedies of today!

In the theatre at Sabratha, the audience sat on the tiered stone seats at the left while the actors performed on the dark street-like area to the right.

Visual Cue

Use the following prompts about the theatre at Sabratha to help students exercise their **critical viewing skills**.

- How might the shape of the theatre add to the sound quality?
- What type of modern-day facility does this amphitheatre remind you of?
- What might be the disadvantages of performing an entire play during daylight hours? Can you think of any benefits?

An Off-Broadway Audience Today

Flash forward to a typical off-Broadway theatre in the early 21st century. There are anywhere from 150 to 300 seats in a performance space that seems almost intimate. You sit down on a soft cushioned seat in a room that, no matter what the weather outdoors, is temperature-controlled for maximum comfort. You and your fellow audience members are cautioned via a high-tech sound system to turn off your cell phones, beepers, and other noisemakers for the duration of the performance.

The lights go to black. Then they rise again, and the actors begin to perform. They could be in your living room—that's how well you can hear them, thanks to that same high-tech sound system, which has tiny powerful microphones placed on, around, or above the stage. You have no problem seeing the actors, partly because they're not all that far away from you and partly because of an offstage light board, which is run by computer. The lights create subtle effects that allow you to enjoy a very realistic setting.

The acting is very natural, and the play's subject speaks to the issues of our day and the concerns of our hearts. When the play ends, the actors take their bows. You can see the pride in each of their faces.

This off-Broadway experience bears little resemblance to watching a sitcom—it is much more real and immediate. And while we may sometimes choose the farce and fantasy of TV, there's so much more being offered in live theatre.

The Culture Project on Bleecker Street in New York City performs *Rev. Billy and the Church of Stop Shopping.*

Chapter 17 Attend a Play 207

Off-Broadway Venues

Tell students that the actors union, Actor's Equity Association (AEA), lists a special showcase code, which is available in many areas, for theatres with ninety-nine seats or less. The code usually states that actors can forgo payment in order to showcase themselves for possible future (paying) work. This allows producers to use union actors at a minimal production cost. The code generally stipulates a low ticket price and a limited run. In larger cities such as New York and Los Angeles there are many of these ninety-nine-seat houses.

In the 1960s, avant-garde theatre folk began performing in a number of unusual locations—an abandoned factory, a loft, a city bus, or the city streets—anywhere but in an actual theatre. The idea was to bring people together in unexpected and provocative ways. In this context, the play often seemed far less important than the "in-your-face" performers and the spectacle they offered. This type of theatre, sometimes called Guerilla Theatre, began to taper off toward the end of the 1960s, but it earned a place in theatre history.

For More Information

Books

Beacham, Richard C., *The Roman Theatre and Its Audience,* Harvard University Press, 1996.

Chase, Ramond G., *Ancient Hellenistic and Roman Amphitheatres, Stadiums, and Theatres: The Way They Look Now,* Peter Randall, 2003.

Farber, Donald C., *From Option to Opening: A Guide to Producing Plays Off-Broadway,* Limelight Editions, 1989.

Other Media

The Renaissance Stage (one videocassette, 30 minutes), Insight Media, 1990.

The Restoration Theater: From Tennis Court to Playhouse (one videocassette, 45 minutes), Insight Media, 1996.

Stages of Theatre: from the Greeks to Shakespeare (one CD-ROM), Films for the Humanities and Sciences, 2002.

Shakespeare's Language (one videocassette, 45 minutes), Insight Media, 1994.

Unit Four Review

PREVIEW

1 Aristotle's six basic elements of drama are thought, plot, action, diction, spectacle, and sound.

2 1) Exposition
2) Inciting Incident
3) Rising Action
4) Crisis
5) Climax
6) Falling Action
7) Resolution

3 The director selects the play.

4 Royalties are payments made to the author for the right to produce the play.

5 An audition is the actor's initial tryout. The callback is the final tryout to get the role.

6 The most important thing a casting director looks for in an actor is that he or she is best suited to role.

7 If you agree to perform in a full-length play, you can expect to be in rehearsal approximately 100 hours.

8 A ground plan allows the director to see the stage graphically and to envision the actors in motion.

9 The area where these scenes would most likely be presented are:

a scene in which two lovers kiss
Area 3

a fantasy scene
Area 6

a scene in which two nobles meet
Area 2

a scene that is the play's dramatic high point
Area 1

a scene where someone listens in
Area 5

10 Answers will vary, but students should note that theatre is ephemeral, that a theatre audience has a more complex relationship with the performance—a give-and-take of energy passing from the actors into the audience, etc.

Unit Four Review

PREVIEW

Examine the following key concepts previewed in Unit Four.

1 What are Aristotle's six basic elements of drama?

2 Put the following plot elements in the order they should occur.

Climax	Falling Action	Exposition	Inciting Incident
Crisis	Resolution	Rising Action	

3 Who selects the play, the producer or the director?

4 What are royalties?

5 What is the difference between an audition and a callback?

6 The most important thing a casting director looks for in an actor is:
a. enthusiasm b. intensity c. best suited to role d. a supple voice

7 If you agree to perform in a full-length play, how long can you expect to be in rehearsal?

8 How does a ground plan help block a play?

9 Match the scenes described below to the area where they would most likely be presented onstage.

a scene in which two lovers kiss	Area 1
a fantasy scene	Area 2
a scene in which two nobles meet	Area 3
a scene that is the play's dramatic high point	Area 4
a scene where someone listens in	Area 5
	Area 6

10 Compare watching a movie to attending live theatre.

PREPARE

Assess your response to the preparation process for projects in this unit.

11 Explain which of the following was the most difficult for you in preparing your drama scenario: finding the subject, creating the characters, or developing a conflict.

12 What was the most difficult aspect of creating a rehearsal schedule?

13 Which of the steps in blocking your scene did you find most challenging?

14 Which do you find most satisfying: writing scenes, blocking scenes, discussing scenes, or acting in scenes? Explain why.

PRESENT

Analyze the experience of presenting your work to the class.

15 In sharing your drama scenario, did you feel that you were connecting with the audience?

16 Do you find question-and-answer sessions after giving a presentation interesting and informative or nerve-wracking and embarrassing? Explain.

17 In your talk show discussion, did all members have an equal chance to describe their theatre-going experience?

CRITIQUE

Evaluate how you go about critiquing your work and the work of others.

18 Did you find it easier to assess a classmate's drama scenario, play analysis, blocking, or talk show contribution? Why?

19 Did you feel that the presenters were asked meaningful questions during question-and-answer periods? Give two examples.

20 How did evaluating the work of others help you approach your own?

EXTENSIONS

- With a partner, block a short scene in which you play a game of imaginary darts and discuss the wonders (and flaws) of the opposite sex.
- Research and discuss additional elements of stage combat.

Resource Binder

Unit Four Test, p. 72

PREPARE

11 Answers will vary. Many students will say that developing the conflict was the most challenging. Answers should be well supported.

12 Answers will vary but should reveal an understanding of each phase of the rehearsal process.

13 Answers will vary.

14 Students' answers will depend on individual preferences. Students who enjoy acting will probably indicate that acting in or blocking the scene was the most satisfying, while student writers will indicate that writing was the most satisfying.

PRESENT

15 Answers will vary depending on the audience and the presenters.

16 Question-and-answer periods can be nerve-wracking and embarrassing to even experienced presenters. Students will probably indicate that while they can be informative, they are difficult.

17 Answers will vary but should show some insight into the group dynamics of the presentation.

CRITIQUE

18 Answers will vary but students will probably indicate that the play analysis was easier to assess, particularly a familiar play.

19 Answers will vary but students should present two well-documented examples.

20 Answers will vary.

EXTENSIONS

- The short scene should show an understanding of effective blocking while also presenting a realistic dialogue about the opposite sex.
- Invite students to demonstrate stage combat under your supervision.

Unit Five

Technical Theatre

Unit Five will give the students an overview of all the technical elements that go into the making of a successful production. The students will learn how to work as a part of a team to design, create, and build the lighting, the sets, the costumes, the sound, the makeup, and the props for a play. Students will learn to create the environment in which a play resides.

Project Preview

Chapter 18 Set Design and Construction
Creating a set design for a scene or a one-act play

Chapter 19 Lighting
Creating a light design for a scene from a play

Chapter 20 Sound
Making a cue sheet and sound effects tape

Chapter 21 Costumes
Preparing three to five costume designs for a character in a play

Chapter 22 Makeup
Applying character makeup

Chapter 23 Props
Preparing a prop plot for a full-length play

Unit Five

Technical Theatre

210 Unit Five Technical Theatre

Quotables

I am enough of an artist to draw freely upon my imagination. Imagination is more important than knowledge. Knowledge is limited. Imagination encircles the world.

Albert Einstein, Physicist

Any smoothly functioning technology will have the appearance of magic.

Arthur C. Clarke, Science Fiction Author

Discussion Questions

The following questions should tap into students' **prior knowledge** and encourage reflection on the topics discussed in this unit.

- Have you ever designed or built anything, such as a table, a box to hold your keepsakes, or a bookcase to organize your room?
- Have you ever taken an art class?
- Do you enjoy painting, drawing, or sculpting works of art?
- Is clothes-shopping high on your list of fun things to do? Do you enjoy matching garments, fabrics, and colors?
- Have you wondered how the lighting effects are created at a concert? Do you ever look toward the lights as they shift and change color?
- Are you competent with computers or other technology?
- What kind of music do you enjoy?
- Have you ever made a tape recording or a CD of your favorite songs?
- Are you good at organizing things, helping others, and working as part of a team?
- Did you write and perform back-yard or basement plays when you were younger? What did you use to create your imaginary play places? What kind of "sets" did you create?

Theatre Journal

Write about one of the characters in the picture. Why did he catch your eye? What made him stand apart from the others? Did his costume reflect his character as you see it in the picture? Does his costume tell you something about his social class, age, or what the climate, setting, or time period is?

Visual Cue

The image above shows the original London cast of *Les Misérables*. The following prompts can be used to help the student **identify and analyze** scenic elements.

- Describe the wooden structure (the "barricade"). What might this scenic element tell you about the play? Does the set seem heavy or light, strong or weak, organized or chaotic? What might your answer tell you about the play?
- Would you feel safe on this set? What does thinking about that question tell you must be an integral part of all set design and construction?
- What are the predominate props in this picture? What might be happening in this scene that relates to the props?
- How does the lighting affect your emotional response to the scene?

Chapter 18

Set Design and Construction

This chapter introduces students to stage terminology, the construction of basic scenic elements, and the supplies needed to build a set. Students will learn how to design a set for a play.

Objectives

1. to learn about production concepts and the different types of sets
2. to learn the basic tools and principles of set construction
3. to create a set design for a one-act play or scene

National Standards

Chapter 18 meets these National Theatre Standards:
Proficient 3a, 3b, 3c
Advanced 3f

Project Specs

It would be helpful for students to have an outline of your own stage on which to draw their designs. Give students a hands-on demonstration of the tools, makeup, lights, and props they will be using on activities in this unit.

ESL Students
Different cultures interpret colors differently. Ask students from diverse backgrounds to talk about how people in their culture respond to specific colors. For example, in China, red is the color of good luck; in Russia, red means beautiful; and in South Africa, red is the color of mourning.

On Your Feet

Giving students a handout with the outline of the school's stage and/or taping the floor to indicate the stage space might help students to visualize their designs.

Chapter
18 Set Design and Construction

The magic of theatre, like the genius of invention, is as much a matter of sweat as inspiration. Set designers and construction experts use hard work and imagination in order to help realize a play's vision.

Project Specs

Project Description You will create a set design for a one-act play or a scene from a longer work. Then you will present your work in a five- to ten-minute talk.

Purpose to understand the basics of set design and the connection between stage design and the effectiveness of a production

Materials a hand-drawn, computer-generated, or three-dimensional design for a stage plan and/or the Set Design and Construction Activity Sheet provided by your teacher

Theatre Terms

arena stage
box set
curtain set
cyclorama (stage curtain)
drops
elevation sketch
flats
minimal set
permanent set
prism set
proscenium stage
scrim
set pieces
teaser
thrust stage
unit set

On Your Feet

Using the materials available in the room, design a space that is especially suited to one of the following functions: a business meeting, a friendly lunch, a therapy session, a flea market. Test your design by inviting two or more students to improvise a short scene in the space you have created.

The set design for *Phantom of the Opera* is suitably atmospheric and elaborate.

Theatre Terms

arena stage a stage with seating on all four sides

box set a set that consists of two or three walls and a ceiling

curtain set a set that uses a wall or drapery at the back of the set

cyclorama a curtain that covers the back wall and sides of the stage

drops decorated canvas or muslin curtains that form part of the scenery

elevation sketch a drawing that shows how the stage will look from the perspective of the audience

flats canvas stretched over wooden frames, painted, and used for scenery

minimal set a set made of two- or three-fold flats that create walls

PREVIEW

Principles of Design

The same skills that help you match your wardrobe, decorate your room, and fulfill art projects can be put into play for stage design. Learning set design and construction principles can take you a long way toward understanding the play's meaning. Scenery is often the first thing that shows the audience something about the time, the setting, and the even the purpose of the play.

Some sets tell you immediately about the people who live in these surroundings. Others tell you more about their environment, their psychological states, or conditions under which they live. For example, *Our Town* is a very powerful play about human emotion that uses very little scenery. Instead, the imagination of the audience, and the strong interpretations of the actors set the scene.

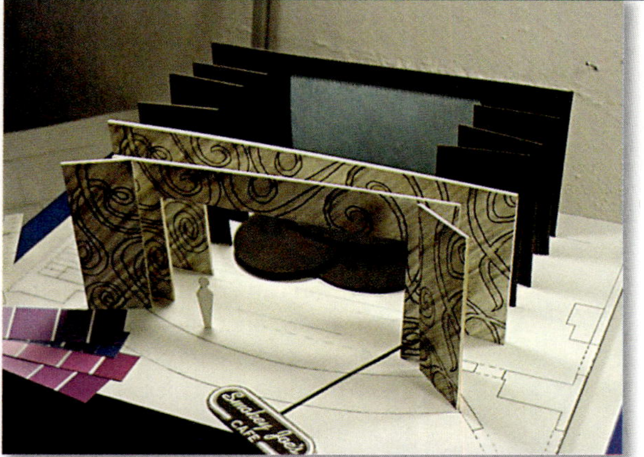

Some designers create a model of the proposed set, such as this one for *Smokey Joe's Cafe.*

When designing scenery, the director, set designer, and technical director study the play to determine the style, atmosphere, and color they want to create. In Chapter 16, you learned how important a ground plan (or floor plan) is to blocking the play. This bird's-eye view of the set—showing doors, windows, walls, stairs, platforms, ramps, and furniture placement—is also important to the people working on the design and construction of the set. The ground plan should be as detailed as possible so that that the stage crew can build the set to the necessary specifications.

The designer also does an **elevation sketch,** which shows how the stage will look from the audience, and a color rendering of the set. These sketches and the ground plan will go into the prompt book. Some scene designers also construct a three-dimensional model that is an accurate miniature reproduction of the set, showing construction, furniture, and so on.

permanent set a set that remains in place throughout the production

prism set a set made of triangles of flats mounted on wheels

proscenium stage a stage in which the audience looks through the "fourth wall" to see the play

scrim a gauzelike curtain used as a drop

set pieces furniture and other three-dimensional objects

teaser a heavy curtain or frame that adjusts the height of the proscenium

thrust stage a low platform stage that juts out into the audience

unit set a set made of pieces that can be rearranged

PREVIEW

Principles of Design

Bring in copies of several scenes from *Our Town.* Engage the students in a short rehearsal of a scene or two. After the students have a feel for the play, engage them in a discussion about set design. What do they think is the purpose of scenery? What is the job of the set designer? Students will then discuss the "minimal" sets used in productions of *Our Town.*

Bring several sketches of different ground plans, elevation sketches, and color renderings. Compare and contrast the designs based on the play and the director's concept. Can the students tell from the design what that concept is? Engage the students in a discussion about design, style, color, and atmosphere on the stage. Bring in fine art books or images to stimulate analysis. Show the pictures and ask the students what the style is or how the color affects their emotional reaction to the picture.

Show, Don't Tell Make simple shapes—cylinders, square boxes, rectangular boxes, wedges, etc.—from card stock and clear tape. Define a small space in the classroom as a performance space, a desktop perhaps. Use the shapes you made in different ways inside the stage space. Ask students to describe what the different shapes do to the space. How does the stage change as the shapes are moved around?

Phantom of the Opera employs many inventive set designs. The following prompts can be used to exercise critical viewing skills.

- How does the set design in this scene contribute to the atmosphere of the play?
- How does the set help the actors convey the style and mood of the play to the audience?
- Research the use of "fog" onstage.

Types of Stages

ACTivity Draw or tape the outline of the different types of stages on the floor. Divide the class into three groups. Each group will take a turn as actors and then as audience members. Give each group a funny poem to perform (Shel Silverstein's poetry works well) and tell each group which type of stage—proscenium, thrust, or arena—they will sit in to watch a performance. Assign each performance group to a specific audience configuration. Remind them that the actors must be blocked so that the audience can see the action. Give the students time to discuss the advantages and disadvantages in performing and watching a performance from each type of stage. Discuss the use of scenery and set pieces for each type.

Vocabulary Enhancement

The word proscenium (Pro SEE nee um) is from the Greek *proskenion,* which is from *pro* meaning "before" and *skene* meaning "building at the back of the stage" or the "scene" house. Our word *scene* comes from the Greek word *skene.*

The word *orchestra* (OR kes trah) is from the Greek word *orkheisthai,* meaning "to dance." The *orkheisthai* was the area in front of the stage where the Greek chorus performed. Today, it is the area where the orchestra sits during a musical.

Types of Stages

The kind of stage available for your production influences the kind of set design you can create. You must know your performance space very well—its challenges and its potential. Get to know the different types of stages and what they can offer a production.

The Proscenium Stage The **proscenium stage** is like a picture frame. The audience sits looking into the frame to see the play. It is separated from the audience by three stage walls and an invisible "fourth wall," which the audience looks through. Proscenium productions generally require the most elaborate set designs since they cover three sides of the performance space.

The Thrust Stage A low platform stage that juts (or "thrusts") out into the audience, with seating on three sides, is called a **thrust stage.** This kind of stage offers opportunities to create several distinct acting areas. Set designs are usually minimal.

The Arena Stage Arena staging, sometimes called "theatre-in-the-round," seats the audience entirely around the playing area. An **arena stage** encourages actor-audience interaction, but it requires a set that allows for continuous movement onstage and one that does not block audience viewing from any side of the house. Due to the closeness of the audience, props and scenery must look authentic.

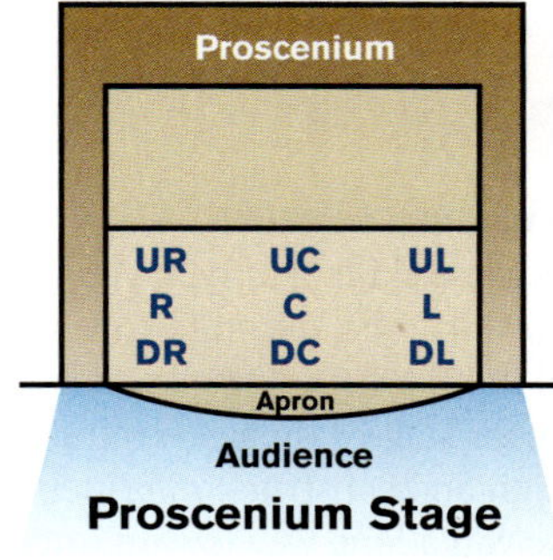

The proscenium stage, with its grand frame, is the most common of all types of stages.

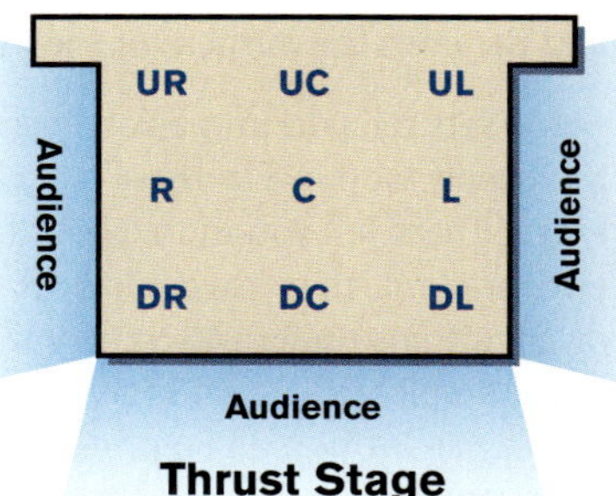

The thrust stage comes in many different shapes, but always juts out into the audience. The Globe Theatre is a thrust stage.

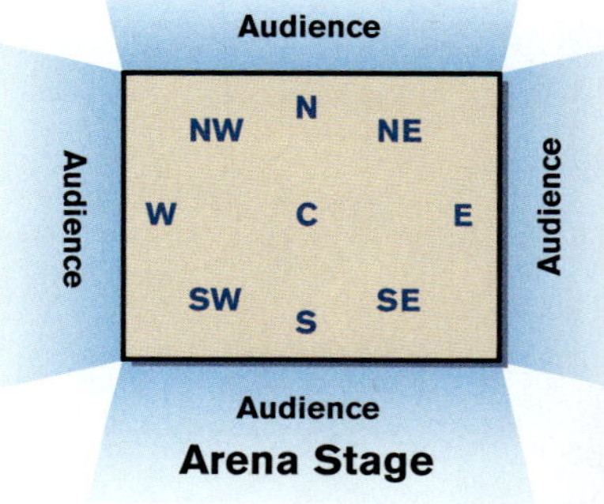

The arena stage, in which only the center of the stage corresponds to traditional stage positions. Here the points of the compass are often used instead.

Resource Binder

- Stage Configurations, TIPack, p. L
- Stage Diagram, TIPack, p. M
- Set Design and Construction Activity Sheet, p. 73
- Painting Techniques Worksheet, p. 74
- Critique Sheet: Create a Set Design, p. 75
- Set Design and Construction Test, p. 76
- Set Designer's Script Analysis, p. 135
- Master Production Schedule, p. 136

Handbook Connections
pages 585-589

To Have on Hand

- Scripts or scenes from various plays
- Images of various types of sets
- Fine art books
- Cutting tools
- Tape measure and graph paper
- Pre-stretched, commercially framed canvas
- Pencils, erasers, colored pencils, rulers, scissors, stapler
- Color charts
- Paint and brushes
- Project board, foam core, shoe boxes

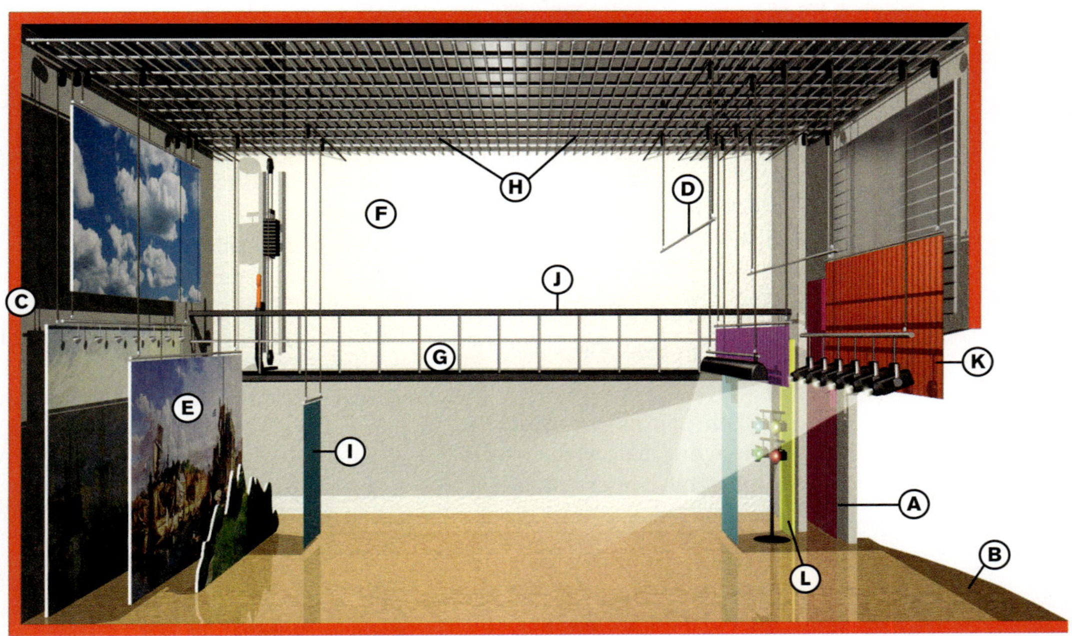

Stage Elements

Knowing, understanding, and using the terms that follow will help you as you learn about designing and constructing stage sets. Take time to read the definitions. Some of their counterparts can be seen on the accompanying diagram.

Act Curtain (A) Curtain that masks the acting area from the audience. Sometimes called the front or grand curtain, it is opened at the beginning of the play and closed between acts or scenes. It usually parts in the middle.

Apron (B) Acting area between the front edge of the stage and the front curtain.

Back Wall (C) Opposite the proscenium opening; it can be used as a background for exterior sets.

Battens (D) Long pipes or poles from which curtains, lights, or flats are hung.

Cyclorama or **Cyc** Background curtain covering stage back and sides.

Drop or **backdrop (E)** A canvas or muslin curtain, usually painted, that forms part of the scenery.

Stage Elements

If the cutaway stage on this page is not like the one at your school, try to find one at another school, college, or professional theatre in your community that is. Make arrangements for the students to visit this stage. If this is not possible, try to relate the stage at your school to this cutaway drawing as best you can.

There are many schools that do not have stages this sophisticated, but the drama instructors and students create wonderful productions nonetheless. Ask the students to compare their performance space to the one pictured here. Use the vocabulary list as the focus of the discussion. Does your school use a cyc? Does your school have a fly loft? How do you adapt your sets to use the space you have to full advantage?

Even if your school doesn't have some of these elements, the students should learn about them. They may one day be in a position to work on a state-of-the-art stage and should be familiar with the terminology.

ACTivity Make several game boards out of the illustration of the stage on this page using blackline master M, the labeled Stage Diagram, from the TIPack Section of the Resource Binder. Put the vocabulary words (*Act Curtain, Wings, Pin Rail,* and so on) on heavy card stock and have students make their own game pieces. Students pull one card from the deck, give the definition of the word, and place the game piece on the matching area of the diagram.

Quotable

It's better to do the design work upfront. Wood, Styrofoam, paint, and canvas can't be changed as easily as the written word. You can't put those in a word processor and play around with them. They are expensive.

Marjorie Kellogg, Set Designer

Chapter 18 Set Design and Construction **215**

ACTivity Divide the students into small groups. They will need to have the use of several 12' to 25' tape measures and graph paper. Using the scale of 1"= 4' (1 inch of the scale drawing represents 4 feet of the real stage), the students will measure, plot out, and draw the dimensions of the stage they usually work on. If the stage is unavailable, they can measure and draw the drama classroom. Students will gain practice in measuring and drawing stage plans.

ACTivity Working further on the activity above, students will use the stage plan they measured and graphed and build a three dimensional, accurate scale model of the stage. One of the best materials for this model is heavy project board or foam core board which can be found at a craft store or a discount retailer. Have students work on this activity before and after school hours and at home, if time does not permit working during class.

Constructing the Sets

Bring a commercial framed canvas to class. This would be a pre-stretched frame from a craft store that is intended for an artist to paint on. It will not be constructed exactly the way a flat needs to be—it might not have toggle rails or braces, for instance—but it will be a starting point for discussing the construction of a flat. If you have the budget, the students can make miniature flats from balsa wood (or some other very lightweight wood), glue, and inexpensive white cotton fabric.

Twine or heavy thread could be used as lash lines. The students can then paint their "flats" to be a backdrop for a play of their choosing. The students might create these flats to the same scale as the model of the stage they created previously. Then they could use the flats on the model of the stage to see how their sets would look.

Flies (F) Area above the stage where scenery is hung out of view.

Fly Gallery (G) Narrow platform about halfway up the backstage side wall from which the lines for flying scenery are worked. Without a fly gallery, you may work fly lines from the backstage floor. For a close-up of the rigging for flying flats, see page 219.

Gridiron or **Grid (H)** Framework of beams above the stage that supports riggings for flying scenery.

Ground Cloth Canvas that covers the floor of the acting area, which may be painted to resemble bricks, stones, carpet, and so forth.

Leg (I) One of a pair of drapes hung stage right and left behind the tormentors to mask the backstage.

Pin Rail (J) Rail on the fly gallery or backstage wall to which lines are pulled and tied off. (See page 219.)

Proscenium Arch Frame or opening of a proscenium stage through which the audience views the play.

Teaser (K) Heavy curtain or canvas-covered wooden frame hung above the proscenium opening to adjust the height of the opening. Shorter curtains hung at intervals to mask lights and unused scenery are called *borders.*

Tormentors (L) Curtain or flat at each side of the proscenium opening used to regulate the width of the opening.

Trap Opening in the stage floor.

Wings The offstage area to the left and right of the stage.

Constructing the Sets

When the ground plan, sketch, and model are complete, the scene construction and painting crews begin their work. Most sets are built using **flats,** which are wooden frames covered by canvas, muslin, or lightweight wood and painted. Flats can be lashed together to create walls and doorways. They can be painted in realistic or symbolic styles. They can become the backdrop for the furniture or **set pieces** (three-dimensional objects such as rocks, trees, or ramps).

Building Flats

Basic Construction

With adequate equipment and knowledge, and with assistance from the school's shop director, technical director, or other knowledgeable adult, you can create flats—wooden frames made from 1-inch x 4-inch white pine. Most flats are 12 feet high and no wider than 5 feet, 9 inches. Wider flats won't fit through doors and are hard to handle. Most flats are covered with eight-ounce flameproof canvas or six-ounce muslin, but some use a hard lightweight sheet of wood (often lauan) that is glued and stapled to the frame. Hard-cover flats

Backstage Gossip: Seeing the Sea

They don't make oceans the way they used to. That way was to cover the floor of the stage with painted canvas and to place under this a sizable number of boy [extras] whose wrigglings simulated the motion of the sea. In a naval melodrama in a Paris theatre. . . one of these extras exerted himself too strenuously and his head came bobbing through a tear in the canvas. With great presence of mind, the actor playing a pirate captain shouted "Man overboard!" and his crew hauled the youngster over the ship's side.

from *All Wrong on the Night* by Maurice Dolbier

are more expensive but easier to make. Muslin is cheaper, but it is not as durable as canvas and must be made flameproof. All flats must be made ready for painting. Follow the instructions that follow and refer to the illustrations to build a canvas-covered flat.

1. **Cut the frame**
   - To use a butt joint, which is the most common way to join pieces of the frame, cut the two horizontal pieces, the rails, the width you want the finished flat to be. Measure carefully: Lumber sizes are not exact. Lumber marked 1 x 4 inches will actually measure 3/4 x 3 1/2 inches.
   - Cut the two vertical pieces, the stiles, the required height less the width of the two rails.
   - Cut the toggle rails the width of the flat minus the width of the two stiles. Use one toggle rail about every 5 feet.
   - Cut the keystones and corner blocks out of 1/4-inch plywood. Keystones are 6 inches long; corner blocks have 8-inch legs.

2. **Assemble the frame**
   - Place the ends of the stiles against the edges of the rails. Using a framing square to ensure square corners, nail the corner blocks over the butt joints, setting them 3/4 inch inside all outer edges. (This border allows two flats to be placed tightly together at right angles.)

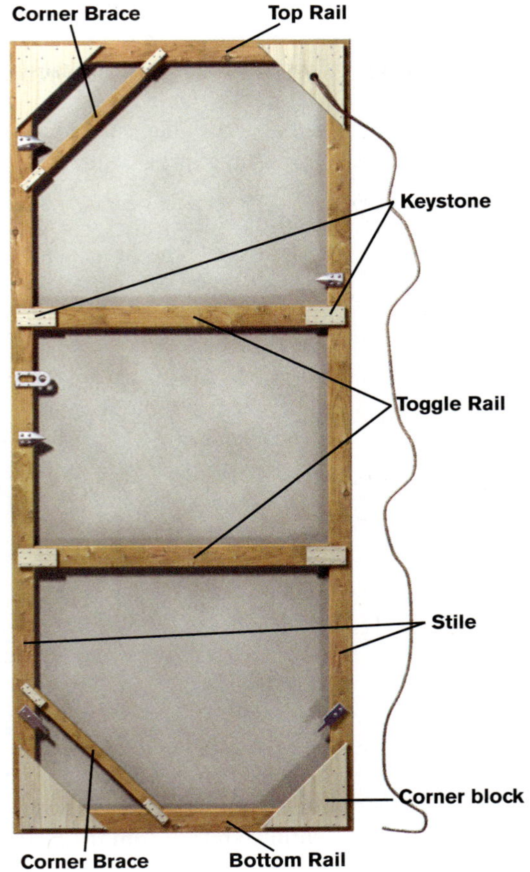

   - Set in the toggle rails and nail them between the stiles with keystone blocks.
   - Attach the two corner braces (cut approximately the length of the rail) on the same side to prevent the flat from twisting.

Building Flats

Go over the four steps of flat construction outlined on pages 216 through 218 with the students. If appropriate, demonstrate the assembly process using one of the student's miniature flats. Share the vocabulary words below with students. You may want to write the definitions on the chalkboard.

Vocabulary Enhancement

Stile the two long, vertical side pieces of lumber.

Toggle rail one of the two or three (depending on the height of your flat) horizontal center pieces of lumber.

Keystone a small piece of lumber that covers each joint where the toggles touch the stiles. The keystone provides extra support at the joints.

Sizing Sizing is frequently a mixture of glue and water, but you can use a coat of thinned white paint as your sizing. It will cause the muslin to shrink and become tighter on the frame, and will cover the holes in the fabric. This will give you a smoother surface for painting your scenery.

Backstage Gossip: Flat Flats

Moss Hart was often asked to critique shows during their out-of-town tryouts. In Baltimore on one of these occasions, the curtain opened to show a set made of a series of green flats. Suddenly, an actor dressed as an elf came flying out on a wire and crashed into the set knocking over several flats. The curtain closed immediately in order to repair the damage. Hart's review? "It's short, but I like it!"

Ask a student to explain what is going on in the three images on this page. Then ask another student to use the pre-stretched framed canvas and a piece of fabric that will cover the frame to show how one would go about stapling, gluing, and trimming the fabric onto the flat. An ordinary staple, a dry brush, and a pair of scissors will do for illustration purposes.

3 Cover the flat

- Turn the frame over so that it rests on the corner blocks.
- Cut a piece of flameproof canvas or muslin 4 inches wider than the frame.
- Starting at the center of a stile, tack or staple the fabric along the side of the stile closest to the opening of the frame every 4 or 5 inches.
- Lift the fabric and spread glue along the top of the stiles and rails. Then bring the muslin over the glued surface, smoothing it with a wooden block. The muslin should sag a bit because it will shrink when painted.
- Tack or staple the fabric to the outer edges of the stiles, spacing tacks to fall between the staples already placed.
- Paint the flat with sizing (a mixture that seals and provides a good painting surface).
- When the fabric has dried, use a utility knife to trim the fabric 1/8 inch from the edge.

4 Join the flats

- Screw in both the lash-line cleats for connecting flats as a wall and the tie-off cleat about two feet from the floor.
- Attach the lash-line cord.
- Drill a hole in the upper right corner block.

Staple the fabric to the inner edge of the stile.

Be careful not to glue the braces or the toggle rail.

Cutting 1/8" from the edge avoids having loose threads hanging over the edge.

From the Field: Set to Go

Building a set is challenging, exacting, and fulfilling. First the set has to be conceptualized, then it must be designed. Once the design is down on paper, the director has to approve it. Then I step in—the designer has to get busy figuring out the best way to build the set—always keeping in mind building standards. The sets must be safe for cast and crew and yet serve the message of the play. The actual physical construction of a set can take several weeks.

Stephen Nathan, Set Designer

Lashed flats

Drops and Set Pieces

Drops can be painted on muslin or **scrim** (theatrical gauze). You hang these above the **teaser,** a curtain or other flat piece hung behind the act curtain, so that the audience cannot see them until they are dropped. Many theatres use a counterweight system to make drops easy to raise and lower. Set pieces are usually rolled in from the wings. Sets should be finished at least one week before production, to allow technicians and actors to have several "tech rehearsals," in which all technical elements are polished before opening night.

- Thread a 1/4-inch cotton sash cord through the hole and knot it. Pull the cord tight, and cut it off 6 inches longer than the flat.
- Apply dutchman, 4-inch strips of muslin, to cover the cracks between the flats.

The dutchman being applied.

Close-up of a drop with a counterweight. Lines or cables run through pulleys and are tied off at the pin rail.

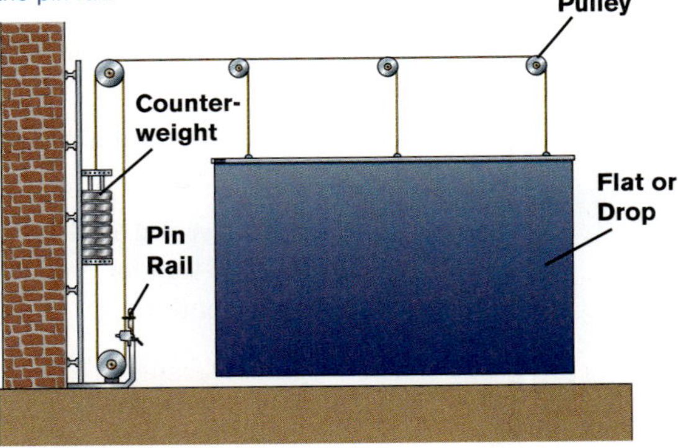

When lit from the front, a scrim will look like a solid backdrop. When lit from behind, it allows you to see what's behind the scrim. Many special effects use the scrim. If you want to hide something from the audience, front light your scrim. Then light behind it and voila! Like magic, the actor (or anything else) behind a scrim suddenly appears.

Vocabulary Enhancement

A dutchman covers the gap between two flats. Where do you think the term *dutchman* comes from? Could it be from the story of the Dutch boy who saved his village by covering the gap in the dike to prevent a flood?

Notes

Construction Safety Tips

After students have read the safety tips on this page, have them open their journals or get out a piece of paper and choose one of the suggestions below to work on.

- Think back to the last show at your school or another school. Were all of the safety rules followed? If not, create a poster containing the necessary precautions and hang it backstage.
- Prepare a checklist of what each crew member, actor, and director should do if an emergency occurs during a rehearsal or a show at your school.
- Draw a plan of your theatre building. Locate the fire extinguishers, fire exits, and nearest phone. Do you know and can you plot on your plan the proper fire evacuation routes? Write a paragraph about how you would take charge and direct people to the nearest safe exit in an emergency.

Construction Safety Tips

Scene shops and stages abound with potential hazards. People are working simultaneously at different jobs—sawing, nailing, painting, and moving sets. Ropes and cables are hung overhead to suspend heavy instruments that, if accidentally dropped, could cause severe injury. Often actors need to walk backstage in the dark amid furniture, properties, and lighting cable. To prevent people from getting hurt, observe these safety rules—and make up more if the situation demands!

General Safety Tips

- Keep all working areas clean and organized.
- Be alert to what others are doing. As in driving, construction safety requires a defensive approach.
- Know the location of fire extinguishers on the stage, in the shop, and in the control booth, and know how to use them.
- Know the location of a well-equipped first-aid kit.
- Report all injuries or potential hazards to your instructor.
- Before raising or lowering a batten yell "Heads up!" and wait for everyone to respond before continuing.

Shop Safety Tips

- Wear protective clothing, including long pants, long sleeves, and hard-toed, rubber-soled shoes. Avoid loose clothing or jewelry that could get caught in power tools.
- Tie back long hair to prevent its being caught in power tools.
- Wear protective gear when necessary. Depending on the job, you might need goggles, earplugs, a dust mask, or a mask that filters out fumes.
- Know how to use your tools. Obey any warnings on tools. If you don't know what you are doing, don't do it!
- Pay attention. Don't talk and become distracted.
- Unplug all power tools immediately after using them.
- Look for and correct any potential hazard, such as nails sticking out of boards.
- Watch where you are going. Look up if people are working above you. Also, don't work on the floor when someone is overhead on a ladder, as tools can fall.
- Keep the shop well ventilated when dust and fumes are around.
- Use tools only as they were designed to be used. Do not improvise.

Backstage Gossip: Wrong Number?

Two Broadway actors found themselves in a fix at the very beginning of their scene together. It should have opened with a telephone ringing and would have if the phone had been set. As it was, there was no phone and the two actors stood looking panic-stricken into the wings until the stage manager appeared on stage with the phone under his arm, saying he was from the phone company and asking if he could install it.

from *Great Theatrical Disasters* by Gyles Brandreth

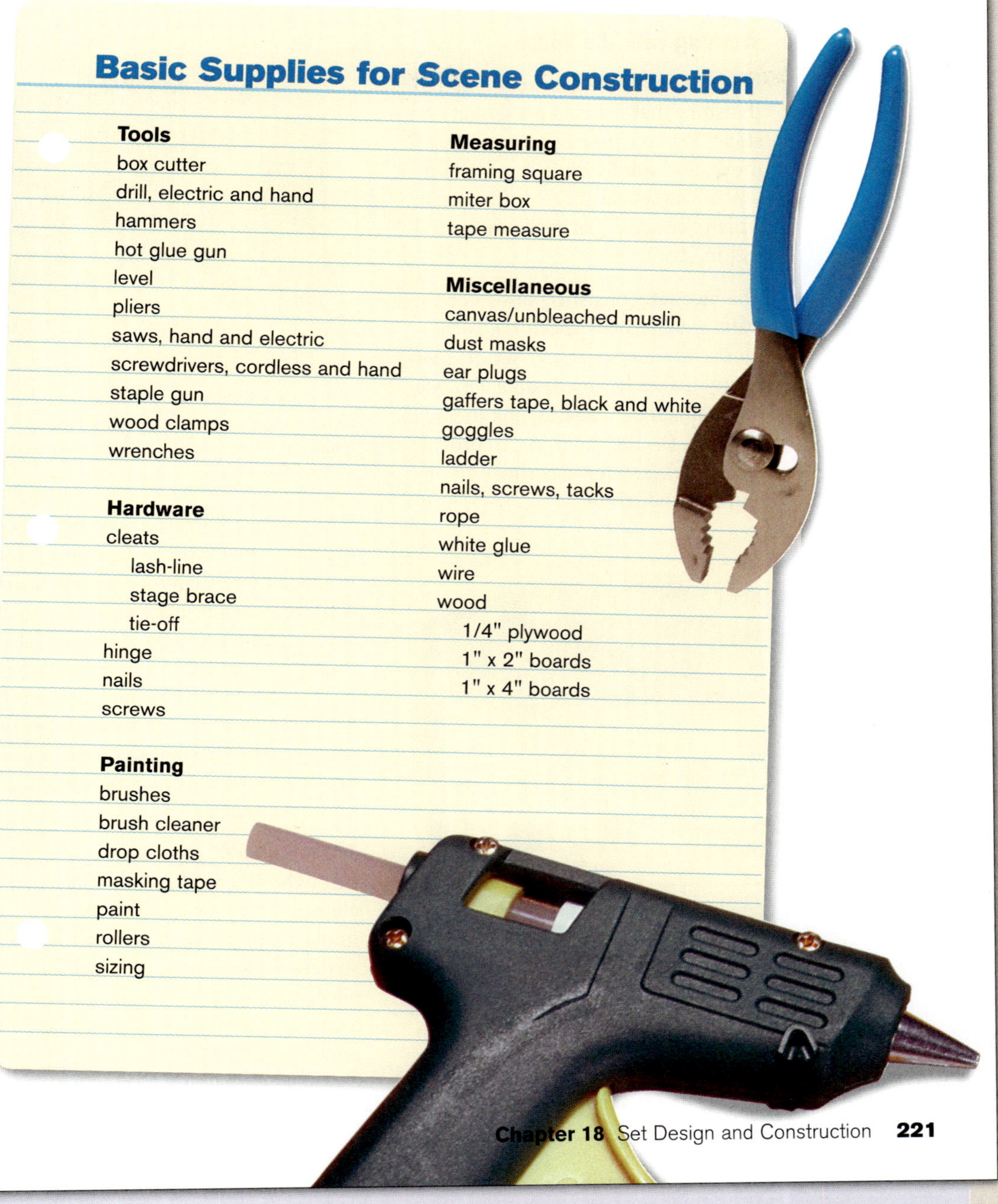

Basic Supplies for Scene Construction

Tools
box cutter
drill, electric and hand
hammers
hot glue gun
level
pliers
saws, hand and electric
screwdrivers, cordless and hand
staple gun
wood clamps
wrenches

Hardware
cleats
lash-line
stage brace
tie-off
hinge
nails
screws

Painting
brushes
brush cleaner
drop cloths
masking tape
paint
rollers
sizing

Measuring
framing square
miter box
tape measure

Miscellaneous
canvas/unbleached muslin
dust masks
ear plugs
gaffers tape, black and white
goggles
ladder
nails, screws, tacks
rope
white glue
wire
wood
1/4" plywood
1" x 2" boards
1" x 4" boards

Basic Supplies for Scene Construction

Plan some time for a safety discussion. In an emergency, each student should feel confident that he or she knows where the first aid kit is located, and how to follow the procedures you have set in place if an accident occurs.

For your convenience, the Safety Rules and Reminders blackline master I can be found in the Teacher's Resource Binder TIPack.

From the Field: Be Prepared

Be sure that each student knows the proper way to use all of the tools in your shop. After each student has been trained on the use of a particular tool, prepare a badge with a picture of that tool on it for that student to wear each time he or she is working in the scene shop. This will give you a quick visual reference to know that the student has been checked out on the piece of equipment he or she is currently using. You should also keep a record in your files to show which students have received training on which tools.

Elaine Malone, Drama Teacher, Atlanta, GA

Working with the Space

Talk to students about the various sets discussed on this and the following page. Ask students to describe a theatre production they worked on or attended that used a box set. Ask how the set conveyed the style and atmosphere of the play and how color was used on the set. Was the overall design effective?

You can continue in this same way with the unit, permanent, minimal, prism, and curtain set.

ACTivity Have students make a set from a shoebox. The unit set or the prism set would be good examples to try. Use pieces of cardboard so that the set can be changed either from one unit set to another or from one prism set to another. Ask students to show how the use of the unit or prism set allows one to change the elements of the design.

Working with the Space

Like the actor, the set must help tell the story that is being presented on stage. Sets must be effective, easy to move, and solidly built. Most importantly, the set must create a space in which the actor can easily move and feel in character.

The **box set,** consisting of two or three walls and, perhaps, a ceiling, is the most common theatrical set. Its simplicity makes it very flexible. On one hand, it can be made to look incredibly realistic. On the other, it can provide a bland backdrop for experimental or surreal productions.

To change this unit set, the balcony may be removed and a small porch added to the house, while apples or fall leaves may be attached to the tree.

This box set contains a number of windows and a door. Using *backing*, flats that mask the backstage area from view, makes the set seem more realistic.

The **unit set** is made of several pieces, or units, which can be rearranged to produce more than one setting. Unit sets are useful in plays requiring many scene changes. One kind of unit set is made of many individual flats that can be moved or struck completely to form a different setting. Another kind of unit set uses generic openings that can be dressed to represent doors, windows, or other elements.

The **permanent set** remains in place throughout a production. Additional elements may be added to the set to imply a change in scene, but the basic structure always remains. Some permanent sets have many playing areas, and so they are sometimes known as *multiple sets.*

222 **Unit Five** Technical Theatre

Notes

Changes to the permanent set will probably involve lighting and props.

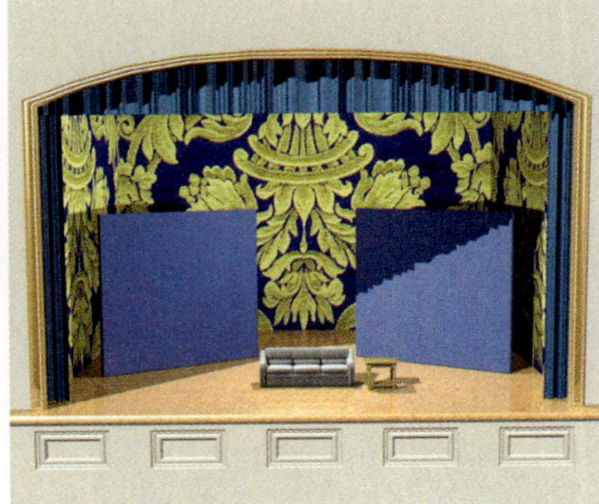

A dramatic statement can be made in a minimal set with the use of bold pattern and color.

The **minimal set,** which is sometimes called the profile set, is usually made of two-fold or three-fold flats that can be used to represent walls or hide and reveal furniture.

The **prism set** uses prisms, or *periaktoi,* three-sided flats mounted on a wheeled carriage. They can be moved or pivoted, and individual flats can be inserted between prisms to create scenic elements.

The **curtain set** makes use of the **cyclorama,** or **stage curtain,** at the back of the stage, as part of the background. A few additional flats can highlight doors, fireplaces, or architectural elements, and set pieces can be arranged as if the curtains were walls and drapes.

A prism set showing one possible arrangement.

The same prism set with the flats rearranged.

Show Don't Tell Bring in pictures or go to *www.siue.edu/ITDA* (the International Theatre Design Archive) where you will find many pictures of set designs from many designers and many shows. Share the designs with the students. Discuss each type of set represented in the pictures. Can the students tell what type of set is used in each picture? Discuss what types of plays would appear more dynamic on which type of set? Would *Les Misérables* be as powerful on a box set or a prism set?

Backstage Gossip: No Whistling Backstage

Whistling backstage is considered bad luck because, the superstition goes, it means danger. This superstition probably began years ago when sailors were hired to operate the fly system because of their experience raising and lowering the sails on boats. The sailors would raise and lower the batten on the ship upon hearing a specific whistle. Therefore, the superstition arose that if an actor or crew member whistled backstage it might cause the lowering of a batten at the wrong time, causing injury to anyone standing below.

Design Requirements

Discuss the six design requirements one at a time with the students. Note that two concern freedom of movement and safety issues while the others are concerned with artistry. Ask students which of the six they think is the most important. List the six requirements on the board as a majority of class members agree on the order of importance.

ACTivity Help students make a "set inspiration" bulletin board of pictures that communicate different times of the year, times of the day, and locations. Include both indoor and outdoor pictures. Ask them to search decorating magazines and the home section of newspapers for pictures that represent different moods and styles. Encourage them to bring in pictures that have different styles of architecture, furniture, and wallpaper of varying textures, interesting landscapes, and colorful decorations. Have students arrange these pictures on the board under various headings. The students can use the images as a reference when it comes time to work on their design project.

Show, Don't Tell Select a short scene from a video or DVD and show it to the class. Then draw two sets on the board for the scene you just watched. Make one a realistic set and one a symbolic set. Discuss with the students the concepts of *realism* and *symbolism*. Brainstorm all the different ways the designer can use symbolism in a set design.

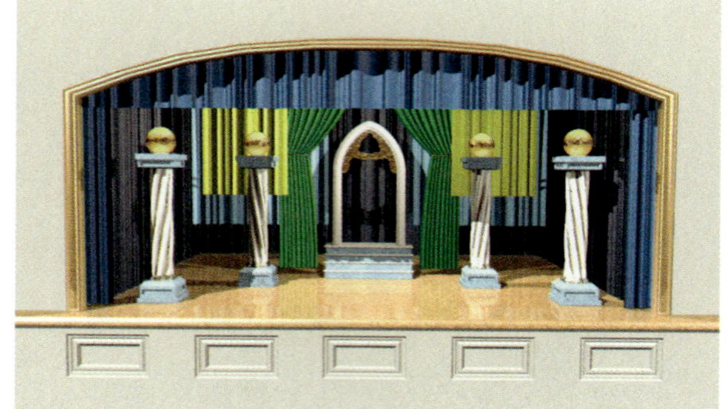

The curtain set makes use of the cyclorama as well as other curtains to create a formal setting.

Design Requirements

Though your play's scenery will depend upon the stage facilities, available crew, and your budgeted time and money, your design should meet the following requirements.

- The design and setting should provide adequate space for movement, including several acting areas or levels to provide variety and interest and to motivate the actors into using the whole stage in the course of the play.
- The design and setting should communicate the time and place in which the action occurs and the cultural, social, and economic status of the characters.
- From observing the scenery with its particular color and design, the audience should immediately be able to judge the mood and style of the play.
- The design and setting must be technically usable and safe. Doors and windows must open if they are to be used. Stairs, platforms, and ramps must be built firmly if they are to bear the actor's weight. If there are set changes, scenery must be planned for quick shifts carried out safely.

What mood does this set, used in the play *Broken Sleep*, create?

224 Unit Five Technical Theatre

Backstage Gossip: The Real Thing

Producer David Belasco was famous for his insistence on realistic sets. For the play *The Easiest Way* he needed a cheap, boardinghouse bedroom. "We tried to build the scene in my shops, but, somehow, we could not make it look shabby enough. So I went to the meanest theatrical lodging house I could find . . . and bought the entire interior of one of its most dilapidated rooms—patched furniture, threadbare carpet, tarnished and broken gas fixtures . . . even the faded paper on the walls."

- The design and setting should be pleasing to the eye. It should be unified, balanced, and varied, and it should allow for the actors' faces to be readily seen. Most of all, it should be unobtrusive—except in the rare case when the characters are in conflict with their environment.
- The design should include set pieces that are functional and that contribute to the overall design of the set.

Setting the Mood

Your set can help establish the mood of your production by its angularity or softness, its luxury or sparseness, its complexity or simplicity. None of these elements will have as immediate an effect, however, as the colors you use in your design. Scientists who have studied color have learned that various colors have specific emotional effects. Reds, oranges, and yellows, for example, are considered warm tones. They tend to be stimulating and exciting. Blues, greens, and violets are cool colors that tend to be relaxing or sobering. Of course, too much of any one tone or set of tones can be simply annoying. But careful use of color can help establish the character and overall mood in a play and influence the audience's response.

Certain colors arouse specific emotions. The set designer is always aware of this.

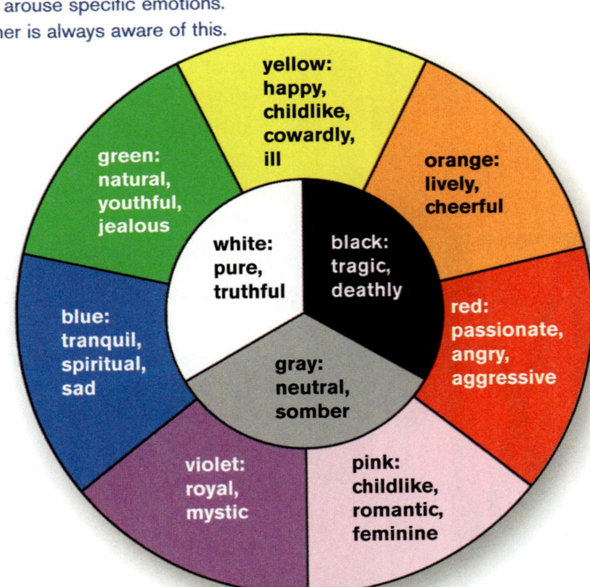

Setting the Mood

Talk to the class about color. Do they have a favorite color? What is it? What emotions does this color call forth and why?

Ask them to close their eyes and envision this color. Then have them visualize a color that feels opposite to the one they favor in emotional tone. What can they say about the "tension" they see or feel between the two colors? Have they seen a play or movie where opposite colors indicated opposite emotions? Have them explain.

ACTivity Write the names of familiar people or characters on cards – Bugs Bunny, Julia Roberts, J Lo, Whoopie Goldberg, and Homer Simpson are a few suggestions. Based on the type of person or character that is chosen, the student will assign a color that the person or character evokes. Ask the student to explain why he or she selected that particular color. Is Ben Affleck light blue, gold, or fire engine red? Why?

ACTivity Make a list of emotions or feelings. Put them on individual cards. Have the students select an emotion card and then respond to the emotion with a color. Ask the students to explain why the emotion is associated with a specific color. Is BORED blue? Is CONFUSED, green? Is SILLY, purple? Why or why not?

ESL Students

Using both English and the student's language, make a list of specific locations— the beach, the mall, in the kitchen, under the sofa, etc. Ask the student what color they equate with each location and why.

Notes

PREPARE

Work on Your Set Design

Select a play for each student (or group of students) or approve the play selected by the students. It might be interesting to use the same play for each group to see what different ideas each student or group can generate.

Go over each of the five steps, in order, with the students. You might want to give them a list of plays or make copies of the plays available to them. Note that there are lists of plays at the back of this Teacher's Edition. Be sure to hand out the Set Design and Construction Activity Sheet from page 73 of the Resource Binder at this time. Encourage students to rehearse their talks with a partner who can time the length and suggest areas for improvement.

PREPARE

Work on Your Set Design

In order to create a set design, you will first have to determine the type and size of stage you will be working on (or perhaps the size and layout of your classroom playing area). Measure the stage or acting space and draw a ground plan using either the Activity Sheet your teacher provides, a computer program, or pencil and paper. A good scale of measure might be 1 foot equals 1/4 inch. If you have access to graph paper, this might be very helpful in drawing your ground plan. Follow the step-by-step instructions at right to continue working on your set design.

1. **Read a play.** (Your instructor may wish to assign you one.) Determine the kind of design, style, and color you think will best communicate the play's intent.
2. **Make a list of your ground plan needs,** such as all necessary doors, windows, furniture, set pieces, and stairs.
3. **Fill in the Activity Sheet** or create your drawn or computer-generated ground plan, always keeping in mind your understanding of the play's theme, mood, period, and locale.
4. **Prepare a five- to ten-minute talk** explaining your set design in terms of its colors, style, sets, and scenery and furniture placement. Tell how your set meets both the intent of the play and the design requirements discussed in this chapter. If possible, prepare copies of your ground plan for each member of the class or make a transparency to be used on an overhead projector as a visual aid.
5. **Rehearse and time your report** until you can give it in a smooth and interesting manner in no more than ten minutes.

A very minimal set can make a strong statement.

226 Unit Five Technical Theatre

Quotable

What is necessary ... is ... a design that has clarity without rigidity; one that could be called "open" as against "shut." This is the essence of theatrical thinking: a true theatre designer will think of his designs as being all the time in motion, in action, in relation to what the actor brings to a scene as it unfolds. In other words, unlike the easel painter, in two dimensions, or the sculptor in three, the designer thinks in terms of the fourth dimension, the passage of time—not the stage picture, but the stage moving picture.

from *The Empty Space* by Peter Brook, Producer and Director

PRESENT

Unveil Your Design

When your name is called, hand in your Activity Sheet or ground plan and walk to the playing area. Be sure to hand out copies of your ground plan to the class before you begin your talk. If you have prepared a transparency, place it on the overhead projector before you begin. Remember, if you show interest and enthusiasm in what you are saying, your listeners will be interested and alert also.

Theatre Journal

Write a description of one or more of the spaces you frequent. Examine the design elements of the space. See if you can figure out how the designers achieved or failed to achieve a desired mood. Try to determine how the appealing elements would be translated to the stage.

CRITIQUE

Evaluate Your Classmate's Set Design and Presentation

Choose one of the designs presented in class and evaluate it using a scale from 1 to 5. A rating of 5 equals "outstanding," while a rating of 1 equals "needs much improvement." As you prepare your critique, think about the following questions.

- How easy to read and understand was the set design?
- What elements necessary for a production of the play were incorporated in the ground plan?
- In what ways did the set design plan fulfill the needs of the play's theme?
- Did the set design cover all the important design requirements?
- How did the speaker go about convincing you that this design would enhance the play?
- What were the strengths and weaknesses of the speaker's presentation style?

Write a paragraph explaining why you gave this presentation the score you did.

PRESENT

Unveil Your Design

Establish with each student beforehand how he or she will be presenting the ground plan. Advise students that if they want to use the drawing they have created on the Activity Sheet, they can simply redraw it in a larger form on the chalkboard. Have the overhead projector ready for those students who have created a transparency of their ground plan. It might be a good idea to allow students using the overhead projector to use it while rehearsing their talk.

Theatre Journal

Use the following as an additional or substitute prompt.

Write a description of the colors that you associate with each season: summer, fall, winter, and spring. Include the kinds of light that is reflected in these colors. Then write a short description of an outdoor set for one of these seasons.

Critique

Evaluate Your Classmate's Set Design and Presentation

Go over the evaluation rubric with the students before they begin their presentations so that they will know the criteria on which the evaluation will be based. Talk about the rating system—1 through 5.

Remind the students that they will be evaluated using the same rubric that they are using to evaluate their classmates. Also tell them to evaluate the work and not the personality. An appropriate phrase to use before the students tackle peer evaluation is "Do unto others . . . " And let them know if you will be evaluating them on how well they evaluate each other.

Notes

Chapter 18 Test

The test for this chapter is available in blackline master form in the Resource Binder, page 76.

For More Information

Books

Campbell, Drew, *Technical Theater for Nontechnical People*, Allworth Press, 1998.

Carter, Paul, *The Backstage Handbook*, Broadway Press, 1994.

Craig, Gordon, *On the Art of Theatre*, Heinemann, 1993.

Ingham, Rosemary, *From Page to Stage: How Theatre Designers Make Connections Between Scripts and Images*, Heinemann, 1998.

Ionazzi, Daniel A., *The Stage Craft Handbook*, Betterway Books, 1996.

Jones, Inigo, *Designs by Inigo Jones for Masques and Plays at Court*, Russell & Russell, 1966.

Miller, James Hull, *James Hull Miller's Self-supporting Scenery for Children's Theater and Grown-ups Too*, Meriwether Publishing, 1993.

Raoul, Bill, *Stock Scenery Construction: A Handbook*, Broadway Press, 1991.

Other Media

Basic Design, VHS, Insight Media, 1988.

Design: The Elements, VHS, Insight Media, 2001.

Fundamentals of Scenic Painting, VHS, Insight Media, 1989.

How Do I Paint It?, VHS or CD-ROM, Insight Media, 1988.

Theatre Fundamentals: Backstage–Is It Safe?, VHS, Insight Media, 1983.

Set Construction: Where Do I Start?, VHS or CD-Rom, Insight Media, 1987.

www.usitt.org (United States Institute for Theatre Technology)

www.siue.edu/TDA (the International Theatre Design Archive)

Additional Projects

1 Construct a model of a set you have designed.

2 Research one of the following subjects and give a report or demonstration on it:

- a Painting special effects
- b Constructing a practical rock, tree, and/or column
- c Using materials to make masks and/or props

3 Choose a musical such as *Stomp* or *Rent* and design on paper or computer a backdrop for the set.

4 Indicate the kinds of color, design approach, kind of set, and kind of stage you would ideally use for two of the books listed below if they were brought to the stage. Explain your choices in a few sentences.

Lord of the Rings
Catcher in the Rye
The Joy Luck Club
Hatchet
Native Son

5 On paper or a computer, create a set design for *The School for Scandal* by Richard Brinsley Sheridan based on the scene found in Unit Eight of this book. Keep in mind the time period and tone of the scene, as well as set elements such as screens, curtains, set pieces, furniture, and a background.

Substitute Teacher Activities

Here are a few suggestions for one or more days when you will be out of the classroom:

- Assign the Painting Techniques Worksheet on page 74 of the Resource Binder and allow students to try out these techniques.
- Assign one or more of the Additional Projects on this page.
- Teach the appropriate sections of Part Seven, Sets, from pages 585-589 of the Student Handbook.
- **Create a Fairy Tale Set.** Divide students into several small groups and have them select a favorite fairy tale—*Jack in the Beanstalk* or *Little Red Riding Hood*, for example. The students will then design a set and draw a color rendering for their fairy tale. Provide the students a supply of colored pencils and paper. After they have finished the design, ask each group to explain their design to the class.

Master of the Craft

G. W. "Skip" Mercier

One day, when he was an English major at the University of California at Berkeley, G. W. "Skip" Mercier walked into Henry May's office. May was a set designer who took great joy in his work and who won awards no set designer had ever won before. May's office was covered with photos and drawings, and Mercier studied them for more than an hour. He fell in love with the "visual magic" he saw on May's walls, and from that moment, his career was decided.

Mercier went on to design numerous plays on and off Broadway. Over the years, he's been nominated for a Tony Award and several Drama Desk Awards for his set design. And he's in constant demand, working on Broadway and for major regional theatres throughout the country, including Arena Stage, Alliance Theatre, and Lincoln Center. He has also taught design at the National Theatre Institute for the past 18 years.

Mercier says that his mentor, May, "showed me that being a good designer was in direct proportion to being a good man." If that's true, Mercier must be an impressive person. His set designs are creative, effective, and true to the productions they support.

G.W. Mercier

A 1" scale model set was created by Mercier for Shakespeare's *The Taming of the Shrew,* directed by Julie Taymor.

Mercier created this elegant set for *Dead Guilty,* presented at Studio Arena Theatre and directed by Jane Page.

Master of the Craft

More About G. W. "Skip" Mercier

G. W. Mercier studied at Yale University and has seen over 280 of his designs come to life on stage. In 1997, the year Mercier received his Tony nomination for scenic design for *Juan Darien: A Carnival Mass,* Stewart Laing took home the award for *Titanic.*

Masters Past and Present

Inigo Jones (1573-1652) was an accomplished classical architect who built homes for royalty that embodied classical proportions and the Palladian tradition. At the English courts of James I and Charles I, Jones designed costumes and sets for fanciful masques, many of which he wrote himself. He studied in Italy and brought to England scene design that included the proscenium arch, the moveable set, and painted perspective scenery.

Gordon Craig (1872-1966) has been called by some the greatest creative genius of British theatre. Craig gained fame in the early 1900s. His designs were focused on creating mood and atmosphere rather than realistic settings. He designed productions for The Abbey Theatre in Ireland and the Moscow Art Theatre, where his "white" *Hamlet* made theatre history in 1912. His conception of the play was to have Hamlet, all in black, move relentlessly through an all white set.

Ming Cho Lee (1939-) was born and grew up in Shanghai, China. He is considered one of the leading set designers in the United States today, and many of the students he taught at Yale University during his 25-year career there have gone on to become noted designers also. Lee has designed sets for Broadway, off-Broadway, regional theatre, dance, and opera. In his set designs, which are presentational rather than representational, Lee attempts to discover the essence of the play and use iconographic symbols to represent this on the stage. Lee has said of theatre design that "the bottom line is that the set has to look good . . . If the set looks bad, all bets are off."

Quotable

I hope that going to the theatre will be a national activity for all ages, one that we cannot live without. I hope that theatre and the arts will eventually take their rightful place in this country, like elections to preserve our freedom and education to nurture our minds. Art is our connection to our past and the heritage for our future. . . it provokes, it questions, it celebrates. In joy and outrage, it is the true expression of our time.

Ming Cho Lee, in his introduction to Ronn Smith's *American Set Design 2*

Theatre Then and Now

Other Cultures, Other Times

The first use of painted perspective on stage was during the Italian Renaissance. Sebastiano Serlio designed three perspectives for stage scenery, one for each of the three types of play—tragedy, comedy, and satyr plays.

During Shakespeare's time, there was very little use of scenery or props. Elizabethan theatre-goers would remark that they were going to "hear" a play, not "see" a play. The language of the theatre was one of the most important elements of the theatre experience to Shakespeare's audiences. Today we frequently rely on elaborate special effects to entertain us.

In the 20th century, experiments in nontraditional production methods were developed by directors and designers such as V. E. Meyerhold (1874-1940) in Russia and Max Reinhardt (1873-1943) in Germany. Both of them explored theatre by moving outside the confines of the proscenium arch with its traditional scenery and lighting systems. Meyerhold brought his running crew out in front of the audience, who watched while the sets were shifted. His actors performed on multi-level scenery which was often extremely abstract and mechanical looking. While not uncommon today, these devices were not the usual practice in the early to middle 1900s.

Theatre Then and Now

Staging Through the Ages

Early Mechanics

Although staging in ancient Greece was simple, it did include the use of a large crane, which could lower and raise characters above the playing area. Since these "flying" characters were often gods who arrived in time to resolve a problem, the apparatus was named *deus ex machina,* or "god in the machine." The Greeks also used the three-sided *periaktoi,* discussed previously on page 223.

The Romans, whose appetite for spectacle knew no bounds, developed more elaborate special effects. In their productions, forests filled with exotic animals appeared from nowhere, and fountains spouting wine rose up from under the stage or arena floor.

Theatre died out during Europe's Dark Ages, but plays based on biblical themes began to be performed in churches during the second half of the 11th century. Large audiences and increasingly bawdy subject matter forced drama out of the churches and into the streets.

In the Middle Ages, plays were mounted on pageant wagons that traveled throughout Europe. Each scene of the play might be set on a separate wagon, with machinery and costumes stored below and the playing area above. Guilds, or groups of tradesmen, sponsored these wagons and competed with each other to create elaborate effects. One device, called Hell's Mouth, resembled the jaws of a fire-breathing dragon, complete with smoke and flames.

The pageant wagon rolls into town.

The Renaissance, which began in Italy in the 14th century, brought a rebirth of interest in art, including theatre, and spectacular effects continued to play an important part. In England, where the Renaissance was slower to take hold, dramas were performed on simple stages with little or no scenery, but by the 17th century, England too began to experiment with trapdoors, "flying" characters, raked stages, and movable scenery.

Notes

Current Technology

The Industrial Age that spread through Europe and the United States in the late 18th and 19th centuries brought new technology to the theatre. Crews needed technical help to move heavy furniture, roll flats on and off the stage, and handle more complex scenery and theatrical effects.

Today, it is not uncommon for entire stages to rotate and for scenery to move by an unseen hand. Many professionally staged musicals include spectacular technical effects. *The Phantom of the Opera,* for example, features a computerized chandelier that swings out over the audience as well as a gondola that floats through misty, candlelit waters. (See pages 212–213.) *Les Misérables* uses massive wooden barricades that pivot in from each side of the stage and connect to become a "practical" unit onto which the actors can climb. (See page 211.) The staging for *Starlight Express* includes multiple tracks on which actors skate around the audience area and uses a double-decker railroad trestle bridge on stage that moves into place as the audience watches.

Technology is still a handmaiden to the play, but it is an increasingly capable servant, providing ever more impressive effects.

Wiring helps the descending angel in Tony Kushner's play *Angels in America.*

For More Information

Books

Carnaby, Ann J., *A Guidebook for Creating Three-Dimensional Theatre Art*, Reed Elsevier Incorporated, 1997.

Forrest, Tim, *The Bulfinch Anatomy of Antique Furniture*, Bulfinch Press, 1996.

Larson, Orville K., *Scene Design in the American Theatre from 1915 to 1960*, University of Arkansas Press, 1990.

Porter, Tom, and Sue Goldman, *Designer Primer*, Butterworth-Heinemann, 1989.

Summerson, John, *Inigo Jones*, Yale University Press, 2000.

Walton, J. Michael, editor, *Craig on Theatre*, Heinemann, 1988.

Visual Cues

Use the following prompts to generate discussion of the two images on these pages. Note that additional information on pageant wagons can be found on pages 416–418.

- From what you can see in the picture on page 230, describe how pageant wagons were used.
- How might the concept of pageant wagons be utilized in today's theatre productions? In what other forms of entertainment might they be used?
- Describe the image from *Angels in America* on page 231.
- Can you think of other plays where characters "fly"?
- What other unique staging have you seen or heard about?

Chapter 19

Lighting

This chapter introduces the student to the tools and equipment of the lighting designer. The function of lighting, the types of lighting instruments, and the fundamentals of safety will be covered. Students will create a lighting plot for a scene.

Objectives

1. to understand the effect that lighting has on interpretation, mood, and emphasis
2. to understand the safety issues involved in lighting
3. to analyze a scene in a play to determine the light design requirements
4. to use the tools of the designer to create a lighting plot

National Standards

Chapter 19 meets these National Standards:

Proficient 3a, 3b, 3c, 3d
Advanced 3f

Project Specs

For this chapter you will need a scene or several scenes from a play. If the students have completed their set designs, you might want to have them design the lights for that set.

Beginning Students
Discuss the safety issues when working with electricity and working from heights. Let students know that if they are afraid of heights, you need to know it now, not when they are up on the ladder. Excuse any student who is uncomfortable.

On Your Feet

After students have discussed the lighting for a play or television show they saw, have them draw the scene.

Chapter

19 Lighting

You are sitting in a theatre as the house lights slowly dim. There is a hush as the audience waits in anticipation. The curtain opens and the lights rise on the scene. It's a different world up there on the stage—both magical and recognizable. The lighting is a key factor in its creation.

Project Specs

Project Description You will create a lighting plot for one scene in a play and present it to the class in a five- to ten-minute talk.

Purpose to understand the basics of stage lighting and to implement principles of visibility, mood, and color

Materials a lighting plot on paper (showing color, type, intensity, and beam of lighting) for a scene from a play or the Lighting Activity Sheet your teacher provides

On Your Feet

Think back to a play or television show you saw recently. Discuss with a partner anything you can remember about the lighting. Your discussion might consist of statements such as, "The kitchen was lighted with warm lights, including a lamp the actors could turn on and off" or "There was dim light outside the windows of the office building, which made it look like a winter afternoon."

Theatre Terms

barn doors
batten or teaser batten
border lights or strip lights
cross light
dimmers
ERS (ellipsoidal reflector spotlight)
floodlights
followspots
Fresnel
gelatins (gels)
gobo
roundels
scoops
spill
spotlights
tableau

Theatre Terms

barn doors light accessories that have moveable flaps to control the light beam

batten (or teaser batten) a pipe above the stage to hold lights or scenery

border lights (or strip lights) long, narrow, strip of lamps and reflectors

cross light when two spotlights are placed on opposite sides of the stage at a 45-degree angle

dimmers controls that change the level of lighting intensity

ERS an ellipsoidal spotlight with a strong beam that can be precisely focused

floodlights lights that illuminate broad areas of the stage

followspots spotlights that produce strong beams of light that follow an actor as he or she moves across the stage

PREVIEW

The Functions of Lighting

Among other things, effective stage lighting provides visibility, establishes emphasis and mood, and provides logical light sources.

1 First, the audience has to be able to see the onstage action. Visibility is the number one requirement of stage lighting. If there is too much light, the result will be a glare. If there is too little, the audience must strain to see. The goal for a lighting designer is to create a balance of intensity that allows the audience to see without being overly aware of the lights. Even if a scene is to be played "in darkness," it should start with extremely dim lighting that rises very gradually as the scene progresses.

2 Lighting also creates emphasis and mood. Bright lights tend to dominate while dim lights subordinate, so stage areas that carry the most important action usually need brighter and more dramatic lighting. The mood of the play serves as a guide for how the lights will be blended. Comedies generally require a mix of bright lights in mostly warm colors. A tragedy or serious drama usually calls for a blend of medium to low tones, shadows, and cool colors.

3 Finally, lighting should be "logical." It should accurately reproduce obvious light sources such as the sun, moon, a fireplace, lamps, and so on. By suggesting the light source, you can often imply the time of day and the weather. A cool blue apparently coming in through a window can suggest early morning. A bright, warm amber light may indicate late afternoon on a warm, sunny day.

The Williamstown Theatre Festival's production of Arthur Miller's *All My Sons* uses evocative lighting.

Fresnel a spotlight whose beams create soft-edged light pools

gelatins (gels) transparent color sheets

gobo a metal sheet with a punched-out design that produces a patterned effect

roundels colored glass disks

scoops lights that illuminate broad areas

spill unwanted light leakage

spotlights lights that produce concentrated illumination

tableau a visual effect in which actors stand in a frozen position

PREVIEW

The Functions of Lighting

Engage the students in a discussion of the *purpose* of lighting, using a scene from a play they have read in class. Read over the scene together. Then ask the following questions:

- How might lighting define the environment in this scene?
- What emphasis or mood should the lighting create?
- Will lighting be used to create a climate, location, time of day, or year also?
- Will the light source be from a lamp, the sun through a window, or the glow of a fireplace?
- What color should predominate in the lighting?
- Will the lights reflect an abstract concept such as the mood of the play, a specific design, or an emotion?

ACTivity Choose two students to go to the board and act as class recorders or secretaries for this exercise. Divide the rest of the class into two groups. One group is called "mood." The other is called "emphasis." Using the pictures from magazines or art books, show one picture at a time. Have the group of "mood" students call out the words they would use to describe the mood of the picture. One of the students at the board will write the words on the board. Repeat the process with the students who are called "emphasis." After going through the exercise, you will have a list of descriptive words generated by the students that they can use when they begin their lighting project.

ESL Students

Discuss with students the meaning of the words *mood* and *emphasis*. Allow them to use words in their primary language to describe the images.

ACTivity Assign students to work in groups to take an inventory of your school's lighting instruments. Have one group determine how many Fresnels, ERS's, border lights, and followspots the theatre department has. Ask another group to start a file of this inventory, being responsible for updating it as new instruments are added and old ones are retired. A third group will keep track of instruments that need repair and will arrange to have this done, with your assistance. A fourth group might research any new lighting instruments your school needs and try to come up with ways to earn the money to buy them.

Equipment and Accessories for Lighting

Piece of Equipment	Description	
ERS (ellipsoidal reflector spotlight), sometimes called a Leko	throws strong, focused light from long distance	
Fresnel spotlight	throws softer light on larger area from shorter distance	
scoop floodlight	lights large areas in strong light	
followspot	throws bright focused light on a moving actor	
border lights/strip lights	washes light over a large area	
lighting control board	the unit that controls the operation of lights and dimmer board	

Resource Binder

- Lighting Activity Sheet, p. 77
- Script Analysis for Lighting Worksheet, p. 78
- Critique Sheet: Create a Lighting Plan, p. 79
- Lighting Test, p. 80
- Lighting Plot, p. 137
- Lighting Cue Sheet, p. 138
- Instrument Schedule, p. 139

Handbook Connections
pages 580-582

To Have on Hand

- Art books and magazines
- Play scripts
- Stage plan showing electrical batten locations
- Gel swatch books (available from theatrical supply houses)
- Instrument symbols templates
- Pens, erasers, large paper
- Flashlights or several desk lamps
- Color charts
- Paint
- White fabric
- Scissors
- Rubber bands

Accessory Piece	Description
batten	metal pipe that holds lights
gelatins or gels	color filters for creating colored light
twist-lock connectors	connect lights to source of power
pin connectors	connect lights to source of power
gobos	metal disks with cutouts for creating patterns of light, sometimes called cookies
roundels	colored glass disks used in strip lights to create color onstage

From the Field: Organizing Those Gobos and Gels

Make an inventory of how many and what types of gobos your theatre has. Label a file folder with the type, manufacturer, and number of the gobo. Put each gobo in either a file drawer or designated container. Keeping the gobos stored in a logical order will make locating them each time you need them a simple matter.

Organize the gels in your inventory in the same manner. Label the color, manufacturer, and the number of each gel on the file folder. Keep the folders in a file drawer or other container. The next light hang and focus will be much easier if you can easily locate the correct gel.

Robert Kallos, Teacher, Atlanta, Georgia

There are computer software programs that enable the designer to create a light design on his or her computer. CADD (Computer Assisted Design and Drafting) programs are expensive, so your school may not have this capability. Many colleges, universities, and professional designers have these programs. Current light design software programs can actually model and demonstrate your light design on a "virtual stage"—thus the light designer can change the design and instantly see the effect of the changes.

ACTivity Ask students to design their own gobos by creating a design on a round sheet of paper. Have students talk about their patterns and what atmosphere they intend them to create when used.

Advanced Students
These students may want to measure an actual gobo, find the correct metal stock, and create their pattern on a metal disk that will fit an ERS owned by your school.

Vocabulary Enhancement

Lighting that illuminates the actors from the front is called *frontlight,* while lighting that illuminates the actor from above and behind is called *backlight.* Backlight separates the actor from the background. *Sidelight,* lighting that illuminates the actor from the side, is often used to light dance shows and the ballet, and *downlight,* which comes from above, is used to form a pool of light. The distance between the instrument and the object to be illuminated is called the *throw.*

A good book that provides the throw distance and the beam spread for most manufacturer's lighting instruments is the *Photometrics Handbook* by the Broadway Press of Louisville, Kentucky.

The Types and Elements of Lighting Instruments

Set up a light lab in your classroom or workshop or even on your stage. You can hang an ERS or two and Fresnels and then experiment with different gel colors and the different throws. A Fresnel will give a wider, softer focus, while an ERS will give a longer throw with a sharp edge.

If you have access to barn doors, the students can try controlling the light on the Fresnel with the barn door flaps. Likewise, the students can experiment with the shutters on the ERS. Remind the students never to plug in and turn on an ERS unless the shutters are in the open position.

If you do not have access to theatrical instruments, you can conduct a light color lab with several desk lamps or even flashlights. Small, high-intensity flashlights are best. Many theatrical supply houses will provide you, free of charge, with gel color swatch books. Give one to each student. Let them experiment with the small rectangles of colored gel. Also bring different fabric swatches to class to further investigate how light, color, and costume interact.

ACTivity Using gel colors, ask students to work in pairs to experiment with different effects. What do a warm color and a cool color do if they are held in front of two separate light sources and focused on a single object below? How does the effect change if they use a more saturated color? What impression does a saturated green give that light blue doesn't? How do the colors change where they overlap?

ACTivity Have the students experiment with different colored gels and different colored fabrics. How do gel colors in the light affect the fabric color?

The Types and Elements of Lighting Instruments

There are four main types of stage lights. **Spotlights** produce focused illumination, while **floodlights** illuminate, or flood, broad areas of the stage. **Strip,** or **border, lights** provide a wide, uniform wash of light; **followspots** produce a strong beam of light that follows an actor while he or she moves about the stage. These instruments and their accessories are pictured on pages 234–235.

The main elements of these lighting instruments are:

1 a bulb, referred to as a *lamp,* which produces the light

2 a *reflector,* which reflects the light and throws it forward onto the area to be lighted

3 the *lens,* which focuses and shapes the light

4 the *housing,* or metal framework, which encloses the unit and holds the gels

5 shutters, used in the housing of some lights to shape the beam of light.

Spotlights One very efficient spotlight is the **Fresnel,** which has a ridged lens, tubular lamp, and a parabolic mirror reflector. Beams from the Fresnel cast diffused or soft-edged light pools, which blend easily with other lighted areas. **Barn doors** are usually used with Fresnels to control the beam of light with their movable flaps.

Another type of spotlight is the **ERS (ellipsoidal reflector spot).** It features a plano-convex lens, a tubular lamp, and an oval-shaped reflector. Spots such as these are excellent for situations in which the light must be thrown a great distance, as the beam is strong and can be focused with extreme precision. This instrument is ideal for lighting an area without **spill,** or unwanted light leakage. The beam can be narrowed or widened to provide either a harsh or

The logical light in this scene comes from the fire pit.

236 Unit Five Technical Theatre

Backstage Gossip: Playing with Fire

Queen Elizabeth I almost always saw plays at night. The performances started about ten o'clock and did not end until well after midnight, which meant the use of artificial light. . . . Elizabeth was content with a general blaze from huge candelabra, tall candle-sticks, and flaming torches which illuminated her as well as the players and helped warm the draughty spaces of the palace.

from *Theatrical Anecdotes* by Peter Hay

The starlight pattern for this scene from *Space* by Tina Landau was created using a gobo.

a soft edge. As a rule, ellipsoidals are hung out in the house, while Fresnels are used onstage. A **gobo,** which is a metal sheet with a punched out design, can be placed inside the ERS to produce a patterned or textured effect.

Border lights or **strip lights** are long narrow metal enclosures that house a row of lamps and reflectors. These lights provide general illumination; they tone the lighted areas without changing the contrast or emphasis provided by the specific spotlighting.

Floodlights, known as **scoops,** are large lamps—500 to 1000 watts—that are mounted in an open-faced housing. Floodlights differ from spots in that they have no lens. They provide soft, widely diffused light, which is perfect for backdrops and the background behind doors and windows. These instruments are equipped with yokes for hanging the units.

Colored Light: Glass, Gels, and Plastics

Three media are used to provide colored light on stage: gelatins, plastics, and glass.

Gelatins (or **gels**) are transparent color sheets inserted into a frame that mounts in front of spotlights and floods. Gelatin is popular because it comes in a wide variety of colors and it is inexpensive. However, it must be replaced often because it becomes brittle and fades with use. Plastic costs more than gelatin but it also lasts longer. Both gelatin and plastic sheets are available in a variety of colors from most theatrical or lighting supply houses.

Strip lights usually have a standard color combination of red, blue, and amber or green lights. When amber and blue are mixed, they produce a nearly white light that illuminates without drastically changing costume and makeup colors. Colored glass disks called **roundels** are used in some strip lights instead of gels or plastic. However, because of their intense color, they tend to lower the illumination and make blending more difficult.

Colored Light: Glass, Gels, and Plastics

Have a grease pencil or china marker handy for the days you are hanging lights. After the student has cut the gel from the sheet to fit the gel holder, have the student write the name of the gel manufacturer and the gel number on the gel before he or she puts the gel into the gel frame. This will make replacing the gel or locating its storage file much easier.

Gobos add texture to light, creating mood and atmosphere. They can also supply information (the name of the show) or be a part of the scenic design. If you have access to different types of gobos, bring them to class. A theatrical supply house can give you catalogues from the manufacturers that show pictures of each type of gobo they manufacture. Examples might include tree branches, flowers, windows, doors, clouds, stars, and city skylines.

ACTivity Ask the students to look through a theatrical lighting supply catalogue and choose several patterns for gobos they find interesting. Then have them write a short scene indicating the gobos they would use and why.

Special Needs Students
Have students choose a gobo and then draw a scene that shows the effect of the gobo.

Vocabulary Enhancement

A light that actually works onstage—such as a lamp, a lantern, or a candle—is called *practical.*

Visual Cue

Writer/director Tina Landau is notable for her innovative use of visual as well as physical space on stage. Ask students to use the gobos available to them as they use their **creative thinking skills** to answer the following questions.

- What other gobo might be used just as effectively in this scene?
- If these two characters were to next visit Paris, France, what gobos might you use?

Ask the students to describe how they would use light and color to create the atmosphere and mood for the following situations:

- the throne room of an evil emperor
- the forest glen of an elf in a fairy tale
- the captain's bridge of an alien spaceship
- the secret caves of the mountain ice dwellers

ACTivity If you have access to computers, ask the students to create a PowerPoint® slide of each one of the locations above and share the designs with the class. How did each design represent the topic? What colors and moods emerged?

Talk to students about the terms *saturated* color, which is a pure color or hue, and *intensity,* the brightness of the light on the stage or the amount of color. Then look at the color swatches on this page and discuss each one in terms of its intensity and whether or not it seems saturated.

ACTivity Have students keep a lighting diary for two weeks or use a section of their journals. Tell them to sit quietly for ten minutes each day and record their observations about light. They can sit on a front porch, in the backyard, in their living room, in the library, or any place that has interesting light. Ask them to write down a description of each kind of light. They might describe the color tones of a particular light. Advise them to really pay attention to what light looks like and what it does, and then to use a variety of descriptors.

In preparing your lighting plot, your choice of lighting colors will depend on the mood of the play and its setting (location, time of day, season). Experiment with colors until you obtain the effect you're looking for. As you experiment you may wish to try the following combinations of gel colors to see how they look with the scenery and costumes. Your teacher may have sets of color samples for you to use. The popular colors seen below can create many different effects.

Be aware that these colors may appear slightly different in this textbook than they do in real life.

This scene from Eugene O'Neill's *Moon for the Misbegotten* suggests late afternoon by using blue lighting.

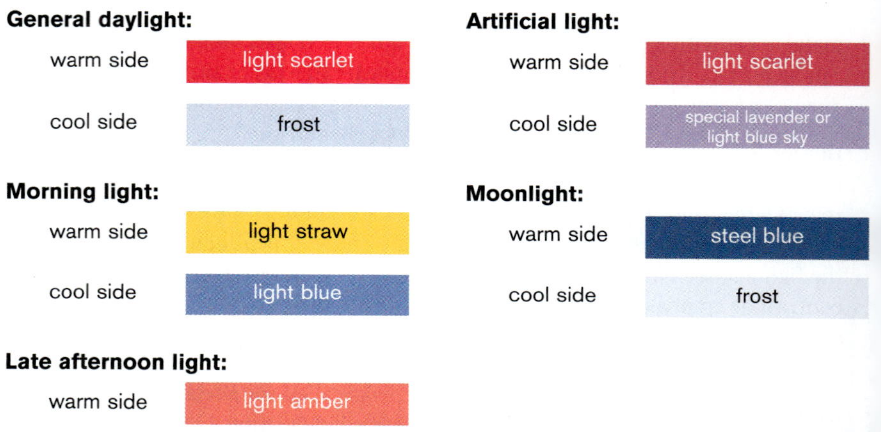

Quotable

Lights are to drama what music is to the lyrics of a song. The greatest part of my success in the theatre I attribute to my feeling for colors, translated into effects of light.

David Belasco, Theatrical Producer

238 **Unit Five** Technical Theatre

Here's How
To Create Special Lighting Effects

Special effects usually require a bit of experimentation if they are to be convincing. Try the following techniques, and refer to a specialized lighting text for additional ideas.

- *Burning logs.* Well-positioned lights can make the audience think they're seeing logs burning in a fireplace. Place an amber or orange light at the back of the logs. Attach a small tin pinwheel in front of the light. The hot air rising from the lamp will turn the pinwheel and provide the necessary flicker. You can also achieve this effect by screwing different colored lamps into flicker sockets (often used for holiday lights) that are attached to a board and placed behind the logs. A small orange or amber flood will provide a warm glow while the other lights give off a flicker.
- *Burning coals.* To simulate burning coals, place small pieces of broken amber-colored glass or crumpled orange and red gelatins over an amber lamp placed in the bottom of the grate.
- *Lighted floor lamps and table lamps.* On the stage, all floor and table lamps should only use low-wattage globes. The actual light should come from stage spots focused on the area. If floor lighting is used, be sure it is clear of all flammable materials, such as curtains.

Connections and Controls

Lighting instruments are connected to the electric current by special stage connectors and cables. Some schools use twist-lock connectors, which provide a safe connection without the worry of accidentally pulling the connectors apart. Others prefer the more expensive pin connectors. While pin connectors must be tied with an overhand knot to ensure the connection, they are much more durable than twist locks. In many states, electrical codes require that schools use a grounded plug for all connections.

Use heavy three-conductor grade cable for theatre lighting; it can carry a larger load than ordinary household cord. For school use, you should have #140-gauge cable that carries 15 amperes or #12-gauge that carries 20 amperes. Be careful not to overload the circuit. Wires can safely handle only the stated wattage.

The control board contains switches for the various lights. It also houses the **dimmers** that change the level of lighting intensity. If possible, all instruments should be connected to dimmers. Dimmers can be controlled manually or electronically. Electronic systems are operated by remote control with preset scene devices. School lighting control boards vary greatly. In some, each dimmer is wired to a specific light or group

Notes

Here's How

Following are a few additional suggestions for creating special lighting techniques:

- To project a rotating image onto a wall, use a roto gobo.
- To make an image move across the stage from right to left, use gobo scanners.
- To simulate candlelight, acquire electronic candles that flicker.
- Use blacklights to make any white object, including costumes, glow in the dark.
- Aquasplash is a device used to create the effect of bright, rippling water.
- Use strobe lights to create the effect of actors moving in slow motion.
- A mirror ball (using a motor) and pin spots give the effect of a disco dance floor.
- Use a police beacon and siren to simulate the approach of a police car.

Connections and Controls

Another way to ensure the connection of a pin connector is to tape the connection with gaffer's tape, readily available at theatrical supply houses.

Use the following phrases as starting points of a discussion about color and atmosphere. Ask the students to describe how they believe a lighting designer might respond to these phrases in a script and how he or she would use imagination to make them come alive onstage. Encourage students to refer to the colors on page 238 for help.

- Bright, summer morning
- Foggy afternoon
- Burnished by the sun
- Dark and stormy night
- Icy, crisp winter's morning
- Not a cloud in the sky
- Arid, dry, parched desert
- Humid, sun-drenched forest

Chapter 19 Lighting **239**

Lighting Plots, Charts, and Cue Sheets

Go over the diagrams on this page, referring back to page 234 and 235 to see images of the spots indicated. Discuss the areas of the stage being lighted and the kinds and positioning of the spotlights used.

Then have your students design a moon box. You will need paint, white fabric, large paper or plastic cups, rubber bands, scissors, and flashlights. Using thin, white fabric, have them draw the "face" of the moon's surface on the fabric as realistically as possible. Cut the bottom out of the paper cup. Stretch the fabric across the large end of the paper cup, securing it with a rubber band. Shine a flashlight through the small end of the cup, creating a moon image.

ACTivity Ask students to get into groups and improvise a short scene that utilizes the moon box that they have created.

Help students create lighting stencils, plastic that has cutouts in the shape of theatrical lighting instruments, which they can use to trace the outline of each instrument onto their lighting plot.

of lights. In others, a special panel gangs lights together according to certain areas of the stage. Every board has a master dimmer that can turn off all the stage lights for a blackout.

Lighting Plots, Charts, and Cue Sheets

A lighting designer must be familiar with the script so that he or she knows the play's mood, setting, time of day, season, weather, and any necessary special effects. The lighting designer consults with the director and views the floor plan to figure out the number and location of doors and windows, the light sources, such as a fireplace or table lamps, and the color of scenery and costumes. The lighting designer also works closely with the set and costume designers to create an overall effect.

The lighting designer determines the light plot by tracing over the ground plan of the set and applying to this copy the position of each light that will be used for each scene. He or she then numbers each light and indicates its

This partial lighting plot shows which spotlights light which areas of the stage.

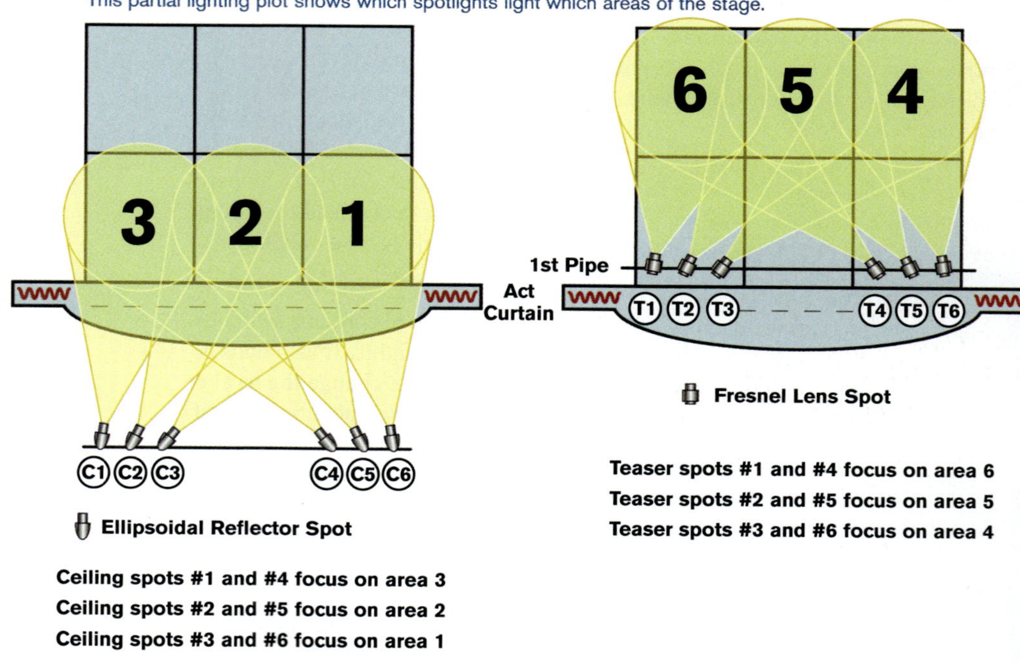

Quotable

How far that little candle throws his beams! So shines a good deed in a naughty world.

William Shakespeare

240 **Unit Five** Technical Theatre

color. The light plot shows all the light units, including foots, strips, spots, backing lights, and special lighting effects, as well as the throw of the spot beams.

Finally, the lighting designer makes a light chart or instrument schedule, listing each light, its number, type, watt, color, and dimmer connection. A light cue sheet is also prepared that tells the light level and the changes needed at exact places in the script.

INSTRUMENT SCHEDULE

Number	Instrument Type	Wattage	Color	Dimmer
T1	Fresnel	500	#4 Pink	A4
T2	"	"	"	A7
T3	"	"	"	A5
T4	"	"	#17 Lau	A3
T5	"	"	"	A2
T6	"	"	"	A1
C1	ERS	1000	Frost	B1
C2	"	"	"	B2
C3	"	"	"	

An instrument schedule lets the light crew know which lights are being used in the production.

With the cue sheet, the light crew can see at a glance when to use which lights.

CUE SHEET	Act 1 Scene 1
CUE 1	House Lights Full
CUE 2	Stage Lights – On
	C1 & C2 – full
	C2 & C5 – full
	C3 & C6 – up 2/3
	Teaser Spots – full
	Border – up 2/3
CUE 3	Slowly dim house
CUE 4	Foots – up 2/3
CUE 5	Harry "I'm Tired"
	teasers on dimmers 4 & 6 – dim 1/2
CUE 6	

Go over the instrument schedule and cue sheet on this page with students. Note how the instrument schedule and the cue sheet both correspond to the lighting plot on the previous page.

Discuss how light can come from different directions—the front, the back, either side, and from below. Have students name specific scenes in plays where they might use light from different directions and why. Ask them to be aware of the effects they would be trying to achieve as well. Would this scene work best with backlight, frontlight, sidelight, or downlight?

Vocabulary Enhancement

A *magic sheet* is a picture of your light plan usually drawn on the ground plan of the stage. It uses simple symbols to show where the instruments are hung, what the focus of the light is, in what direction the light is going, and the color used in the instruments. It helps the designer to conceptualize the plot by creating a picture of the design. Sometimes the magic sheet also tells the designer which dimmer controls which instrument.

Backstage Gossip: Let There Be Light

Before gas and electric lighting, candles lit the stage.

The use of candles involved the employment of candlesnuffers, who came on at certain pauses in the performance to tend and rectify the lighting on the stage . . . . The duties of a candlesnuffer were somewhat arduous. It was the custom of the audience, especially among those frequenting the galleries, to regard him as a butt with whom to amuse themselves during the pauses between the acts, hurling missiles at the unfortunate candlesnuffer.

from *Theatrical Anecdotes* by Peter Hay

Positioning Lighting Instruments

Show Don't Tell Go over with students how to hang ERS lights and Fresnels. If you have a well-equipped stage, show them the battens where Fresnels should be hung and the beams or stands that will support the ERS lights. Point out the strip lights, if your school has them. Show the students where cross lights would be placed on each side of the stage and demonstrate a 45-degree angle.

ACTivity Have students take turns practicing cross lighting two actors standing center stage. Have actors vary their positions in order for the students to work on adjusting their cross lighting.

Encourage students to make a lighting scrapbook made up of their own designs as well as pictures from magazines. They can find interesting pictures that show various examples of light. Pictures of rooms with lamps turned on, landscape pictures with the light playing through the trees, and pictures of moonlight on a field are just a few examples. Find pictures that represent different moods and atmospheres, different climates, different directions of the light source, and different times of day. Remind students that their scrapbooks can be used as a reference when it comes time to work on their design project.

This set is identical in each photo above, but the different lighting used in each changes the effect.

Positioning Lighting Instruments

To provide adequate visibility, emphasis, and mood, lights must be properly positioned. To some extent the lighting will depend on the size of the performance space, but here are some general rules.

ERS lights, with their capacity to throw light over long distances, should be hung from beams in the auditorium ceiling or on stands in the balcony. Large stages generally require 1000-watt ERS's, but smaller stages can use 500-watt lamps. ERS's should be carefully focused to light the downstage area while avoiding spill onto either the audience or the proscenium arch. To light the upstage area, hang Fresnels by clamping them to the teaser batten. **Battens** are metal pipes hung above the stage. The batten directly behind the teaser curtain is called the **teaser batten.** Strip, or border, lights are also attached to the overhead battens. While some school stages have the luxury of many border strips, two are essential. There should be a teaser unit of six or more compartments hung just upstage of the teaser curtain. It is best placed in the center of the batten, with spots filling out the rest of the batten on either side. The second border strip should be placed upstage to light the top of the backdrop. Each color in the border should be wired to a separate circuit so that they can be adjusted individually.

To prevent the actors' faces from being in shadow, **cross light** each stage area with two spots placed on opposite sides of the stage at a 45-degree angle. To focus these spots, position an actor in each lighting area and aim the center of the light pool at his or her face. Do not

Visual Cues

- Compare and contrast the two pictures at the top of the page. How do they look alike, how are they different?
- Where is the light coming from in each picture?
- Why do you think the designer chose the specific light directions for each scene?
- How would you describe the mood and the atmosphere in each picture? Why do you think the designer used these lights to define the mood and atmosphere?

aim at the floor or the scenery. The set will be adequately lit by the spill. Cross lighting can also be used to enhance natural shadows and highlights. For this type of effect, the spots on one side of the stage should have a warmer color than those on the other side. For example, if the spots on stage right are warm light pink, those on stage left may be cool, pale lavender. The actor's face will then have a very natural, three-dimensional appearance, as this arrangement of colors provides subtle highlights on the warm side and shadows on the cool side. To create an interesting visual effect called a **tableau,** in which a group of characters form a silent frozen picture, light the actors from overhead.

A Basic Lighting System

Few schools have what a professional theatre would consider an adequate lighting system. But by making smart choices, your drama department can create a system that fulfills at least the most basic lighting needs. What equipment will you need to effectively light a play? Ideally you should have at least

- ten Fresnels for the lights on the teaser batten
- six ellipsoidals for auditorium spots
- two floods
- two strip lights (one teaser strip and one for lighting the backdrop)
- an adequate dimmer system

If money is available for lighting supplies, instead of buying small spotlights, you are better off putting it toward the eventual purchase of ellipsoidal reflective spotlights and Fresnels.

From the Field: A.M. to P.M.

These days, with computer boards, it's easier for the lighting designer to stay on top of script changes . . . A lighting plot has a certain amount of built-in flexibility. A plot should be specific enough that it is designed for that particular show, but general enough so that you can deal with changes. You have to deal with moving a morning scene to nighttime without rehanging all the instruments.

Allen Lee Hughes, Lighting Designer

Arrange for students to tour a nearby professional theatre or college theatre and meet with one of the lighting designers. Allow your class to ask questions about their lighting system—the types of instruments they have, the number of channels they work with, where they store and how they access their instruments. If possible arrange for your students to see a show there. Then discuss the following questions: How effective was the lighting design? Do you think the designer captured the mood of the show?

Show, Don't Tell Select a short scene from a movie and show it to the class. Find small objects within the classroom to replicate the furnishings—a paperback book as a sofa, an eraser as a table, and so forth. Use the desk lamps from earlier in the chapter and try to replicate the light design in your scene. Ask the students for their input. Does it change the mood of the scene if you move the lamps? Does it affect the mood if you change the color?

Vocabulary Enhancement

The main source of light focused on an acting area is called the *key light.* When a *fill light* is used with the key light, it fills in the shadows and helps to blend the lights. A fill light that gives general illumination to the stage, as opposed to light that is aimed at a specific area, is called a *wash.*

Hanging Lighting Instruments

Before any light hang, take the time to go over all the safety rules with the students. Remind them that the "buddy system" is always in effect. They must always have a buddy with them when climbing a ladder or when they are on a scaffold or lift. Light hang and focus should only occur when a knowledgeable adult is present and supervising the work. The fly system is a dangerous and complicated system and requires that safety instructions be followed to the letter. This system is probably best left to professionals or knowledgeable adults.

Remind students that technical rehearsals are allotted to the technical crew so that they may rehearse the set changes, light cues, sound cues, or any other tasks that the crew performs to make the show run smoothly. This is the time when the actor and the tech crew practice their timing. The tech person works to turn on the light switch just as the actor's hand flips the switch and the lights come up—all with precision timing.

Lighting Crew Safety Tips

Here are a few tools that you might want to have handy when hanging the lights:

- Crescent wrench or light hang tool
- Safety cord (to attach the tool to a belt)
- Black cotton rope
- Black gaffer's tape
- The light plot

NOTE: All lighting instruments must be safety cabled to the batten.

Use a *safety cable,* a wire cable with a loop at one end and a clip fastener at the other end. Put the wire through the yolk of the instrument and around the pipe batten, attaching the clip fastener to the loop end of the cable.

Hanging Lighting Instruments

The lighting crew mounts and connects the lights for the play at least 10 days before performance, working when the stage is not in use. At least a week before production, the director will call a special lighting session during which the lights are focused and set. Each light cue will be rehearsed at this time. The lighting crew must make sure that all connections are securely fastened, that circuits are not overloaded, and that there is no glare from the stage into the audience. If there are unwanted shadows on the back wall, the crew will lower the intensity of the border strips a bit.

During the week of dress rehearsal, complete stage lighting is used, and all the cues are carefully rehearsed so that the action and the lights are perfectly synchronized. The cue sheet should always be close at hand. (See page 241 for a sample cue sheet.)

At the right are a few safety tips to keep in mind when working with lighting components.

Lighting Crew Safety Tips

- Wear cotton gloves to protect your hands from heat. With tungsten-halogen lamps, grease or fingerprints on the lamp could cause it to explode when it reaches a high temperature.
- Mark the handle of each instrument with its wattage and the type of light it is to ensure proper connections.
- Make sure that you have your tools safely pocketed or attached by clips to your clothing or tool belt. When you are working above the stage, a dropped tool could injure someone down below.
- Using a piece of tape, mark each cable to show the number of the instrument and its circuit. That way, even if the cables are ganged together, you will be able to see where each must go. It's also handy to write down the cable's length.
- Check cables periodically and replace any that are worn.
- Disconnect a plug by pulling the connector body—not the cord.
- Always wear closed-toe shoes—steel-tipped, if possible.

Notes

Visual Cue

- Describe the different lighting instruments in this picture. What is the function of the different lights?
- What kind of lights are along the front edge of the stage? What purpose do they serve?
- Why would the designer want to light the performers from below?

Chapter 19 Lighting 245

Backstage Gossip: Temper Tantrum

John Barrymore once took drastic action when a spotlight misbehaved. During a scene between him and Constance Collier in *Peter Ibbetson*, the light lit their feet instead of their faces. Mr. Barrymore left the love scene abruptly, went offstage, and knocked the lightman down. (He later had to pay damages . . .).

from *All Wrong on the Night* by Maurice Dolbier

Career Focus

Engage the students in a discussion of possible jobs outside the theatre in which lighting design is important. Some possible jobs are lighting industrial shows; lighting concerts, museums and exhibition halls; and lighting furniture showrooms and hotel lobbies.

Some colleges are now requiring a portfolio of student work. Much as the acting students are required to audition, technical students are required to show and discuss their portfolios. Remind your students to save copies of all of their work. In lighting design they should have copies of the light plots, instrument schedules, magic sheets, cue sheets, and any research they did. The students should also take photographs of all the shows they design and put copies in their portfolios.

Career Focus

Lighting Designer

A lighting designer can work in a variety of media, including theatre, dance, opera, television, and film. He or she might also be hired to light museum exhibits or public spaces. No matter what the media, the designer's first task is to meet with the director, or whoever is in charge of the project, to discuss the mood and action of each scene or event. The designer then develops a lighting plan that charts changes in tone and mood.

Lighting designers often do double duty as technicians–they design the lights placement, then hang and operate the lights. This naturally requires quite a bit of technical skill. A designer/ technician must be comfortable working the rigging–in other words he or she must be unafraid to work at great heights.

Some designers thrive on the excitement of a career in the theatre, film, or television. Others prefer to work in the architectural realm, lighting building exteriors as well as residential and commercial interiors. A lighting designer who works architecturally may design task lighting for a modern kitchen, accent lighting for the art in an office building, as well as landscape lighting for gardens of all kinds.

Until recently, most theatrical lighting designers received their training on the job. Beginning as an apprentice and then as an assistant technician, the budding professional gradually moved up through the ranks to become a chief electrician and then a full-fledged designer. However, with more and more universities offering degrees in lighting design, a new breed of designer has emerged. When these designers hit the marketplace in their early twenties, they often have had a great deal of training and experience not only in university theatres, but also in associated professional theatres.

No matter which path a person takes into the business, he or she must be organized and work well with others. Designers who work in the theatre must read and analyze scripts, perform research if necessary, and often work long and inconsistent hours. An architectural lighting designer must know how to please the client.

If you are beginning to tackle lighting design, be sure to start a portfolio showing your work.

Notes

PREPARE

Work Out Your Lighting Plan

In this project, you are going to assume the initial duties of a lighting designer by planning a light plot for a designated scene or play. Employ your school's lighting equipment and any additional homemade spots that you wish to indicate.

1. Choose a play appropriate to your school's lighting capabilities. As you read the play, picture the scenes and imagine the lighting you would use. You may want to draw upon the lighting in a play you have seen. Try to remember the lighting used and decide if you want to create a similar effect.
2. Keeping your school's lighting equipment in mind, plan your light plot. Decide the position of each light, its identifying number, its color, and the type of beam. Indicate all the lighting instruments you plan to use. Remember that your cross beams should be placed at approximately 45-degree angles. Be sure the important acting areas are well lighted. Choose colors that will establish the proper mood, light source, weather, time of day, and visibility (refer to the color chart on page 238). Provide highlighting and shadows with warm colors on one side and cool colors on the other.
3. Trace the ground plan of the set and overlay the lighting plot you planned in step two. Be sure you show each light and its number and color. For example, you may number your lights by the abbreviation C1—standing for ceiling spot number one; T1—for teaser spot number one; and so on. Be sure the lights overlap for proper light blending. Provide lighting for the complete scene, including any special effects lighting.
4. When your plan is finished, ask your teacher to either help you make enough copies for everyone in your class or create a copy on a transparency to be used on an overhead projector.
5. Practice your presentation so that you are comfortable talking about the choices you made in devising this plan. Be sure you do not exceed ten minutes.

Theatre Journal

Think about a room in your house—a bedroom, a family room, or a kitchen. Describe how the lighting changes in this room over the course of a day—in the morning, at noon, and at night. Write some notes about what kinds of theatrical lighting you might use to represent this room onstage.

Quotable

There are two ways of spreading light: to be the candle or the mirror that reflects it.

Edith Wharton, Writer

PREPARE

Work Out Your Lighting Plan

Go over with the class your expectations for this project step by step.

- Help them select the scene for their design or suggest the same scene they used for the set design.
- Give them an inventory of light instruments to use. This can be based on the inventory your theatre program uses, if you wish.
- Hand out copies of the Lighting Plot on page 137 of the Resource Binder or have students draw their own.
- Give them the design tools they need, such as lighting templates and gel color swatches.

Theatre Journal

Use the following as an additional or substitute prompt.

The next time you attend a play or view a film, be aware of the lighting used to help tell the story. When you get home, write about what you saw and how the lighting design influenced the experience.

PRESENT

Explain Your Lighting Plan

Help students who have enlarged any of their presentation materials or augmented their designs in any way to secure and use any necessary display tools.

Discuss the evaluation rubric with the students before they begin their presentations so that they are clear about all the criteria on which their evaluations will be based. Remind them that the rating system—1 through 5—gives 5 the highest, or "outstanding," rating.

CRITIQUE

Evaluate a Classmate's Lighting Plan Presentation

Tell students that all presentations will be evaluated using the same 1 to 5 rubric. If there is time, invite them to add another criterion they agree, as a class, should be added to the list of considerations for this presentation. Then make it clear that the class's additional evaluation question must be added to the five that are listed in their books.

Vocabulary Enhancement

The phrase "Let there be light" is a popular one in many languages, such as:

Latin Lux fiat
French Que la lumiére brille!
Spanish ¡Qué brille la luz!

PRESENT

Explain Your Lighting Plan

When your name is called, step to the front of the room and pass out copies of your plan or use the overhead to project it. Give the name of the play and tell something about the scene your plan reflects. Discuss your lighting plan in terms of how it relates to the plot, the theme, and the characters. Explain the effects you want to create in this scene. Invite your classmates to ask questions and make comments on your work. Answer any questions they might have about the decisions you made, taking care not to exceed the allotted ten minute time limit.

CRITIQUE

Evaluate a Classmate's Lighting Plan Presentation

Evaluate the work of a classmate. Rate the work on a scale of 1 to 5, with 1 being "needs much improvement" and 5 being "outstanding." Ask yourself the following questions:

- Was the presentation well organized and easy to understand?
- Did the speaker display a good understanding of lighting?
- How well did the speaker answer questions?
- How well did the speaker's lighting plan successfully reflect the play's intent?
- How clear and easy would it be to use the lighting plot?

Then write a few sentences to explain why you gave this rating. Include in your paragraph suggestions for any alternative creative choices.

Backstage Gossip: Very Funny

In a University of Minnesota production of *Daniel Boone*, when the actor playing the title role called out "The sky is red tonight" the electricians gave him a green sky, and when he urged "On to Boonesville!" a number of Indian tepees, with mischievous stagehands inside them, rose and scurried off in the opposite direction.

from *All Wrong on the Night* by Maurice Dolbier

Additional Projects

1 Make an instrument chart and cue sheet for the same play or scene you selected for this chapter's project.

2 On a computer, design a lighting plot for a contemporary play. Discuss your design with the class.

3 Demonstrate the effect of colored lights on costumes made of different fabrics, colors, and textures or on a made-up face. Refer to pages 238 and 294 for color information.

4 Research and report on the principles of electricity, explaining such terms as *watt, ampere, volt, circuit, direct current,* and *alternating current.* Create a graphic organizer to help explain your research.

5 Interview a local lighting designer or technician about his or her early career. What did this person do to break into the field? Tape-record your interview and play it for the class.

6 Read the excerpt from *Icarus* by Edwin Sánchez found in Unit Eight, and create a cue sheet for it.

"Theater is magical and evanescent; examine it closely and it turns into tricks of lighting . . ."

Robertson Davies, Canadian novelist

Substitute Teacher Activities

Below are a few suggestions for days when you will be out of the classroom:

- Assign the Script Analysis for Lighting Worksheet, p. 78
- Discuss the information found in the Student Handbook concerning Lighting on pages 580-582.
- Assign one or more of the Additional Projects on this page.
- Divide the students into groups and play **Rhyme Light.** Students select rhymes such as "Little Jack Horner," "Humpty Dumpty," "Old King Cole," "Little Miss Muffet," and so on. Have them work together to define the mood, the environment, the emphasis, and the emotional context of the rhyme. Have them decide the kind, color, direction, and focus of the lighting for the rhyme and then describe to the class how they would light a performance of it.

Chapter 19 Test

The test for this chapter is available in blackline master form in the Resource Binder on page 80.

For More Information

Books

Essing, Linda, *The Speed of Light: Dialogues on Lighting Design and Technological Change*, Heinemann, 2002.

Fitt, Brian, *A–Z of Lighting Terms*, Focal Press, 1999.

Keller, Max, *Light Fantastic: The Art and Design of Stage Lighting*, Prestel Publishing, 2000.

Parker, Oren W., *Scene Design and Stage Lighting with Infotrac*, International Thomson Publishing, 2003.

Pilbrow, Richard, and Hal Prince, *Stage Lighting Design: The Art, the Craft, the Life*, By Design Press, 2000.

Reid, Francis, *The Stage Lighting Handbook*, Theatre Arts Books, 2001.

Shelley, Steven Louis, *A Practical Guide to Stage Lighting*, Focal Press, 1999.

Other Media

Conducting Light, VHS (2 tapes), Insight Media, 1998.

Conducting Light on a Shoestring, VHS, Insight Media, 2000.

Designing with Gobos, VHS, Insight Media, 1999.

Lighting, VHS, Insight Media, 1991.

Stage Lighting, VHS and CD-ROM, Insight Media, 1988.

Theatrical Lighting, VHS, Insight Media, 1995.

Theatre **Then** and Now

Let There Be Light

Shakespeare's Globe Theatre used no artificial light of any kind. The plays took place in the afternoon with only natural daylight. No special lighting effects were used.

Vocabulary Enhancement

Limelight n. 1: a focus of public attention; "he enjoyed being in the limelight" [syn: *spotlight, public eye*] 2: a lamp consisting of a flame directed at a cylinder of lime with a lens to concentrate the light; formerly used for stage lighting [syn: *calcium light*]

Theatre **Then** and Now

Let There Be Light: From Candles to Computers

Up until the late 1700s, theatres such as the old Covent Garden in London were lit by candles.

Theatre by Candlelight

Lighting has come a long way since the ancient Greeks first took to the stage. They performed only in daylight; the plays were designed to take full advantage of the sun, and performance spaces were chosen to gain the best possible natural light.

Most historians believe that the ancient Romans were the first to use torches in theatrical presentations. This allowed them to present evening performances. Medieval lighting consisted primarily of stationary torches, but there were also some that could be moved by torch-bearers. Although these illumination sources created a fair amount of smoke and odor, they also produced some exciting lighting effects.

In the 18th century, stage lighting was problematic for theatres located in enclosed buildings since the smoke, odor, and flammability of open-flame light sources presented both discomfort and danger. Theatre fires were not uncommon. Later in the century, chandeliers and huge candelabras came into fashion. It was also common to use carefully placed reflectors to bounce the available light onto the stage. Toward the end of the century, theatres began to use scrims, gauze drops that become transparent when a light is shined from behind but that appear opaque when lit from the front.

It wasn't until the middle of the 19th century that a new invention, the gaslight, effectively snuffed out the lamps, candles, and torches that had served as standard lighting elements for hundreds of years. Gaslight was first developed in England in 1817. By 1849 it could be centrally controlled—although it also caused some major fires over the years. The first spotlight, called a limelight because a flame was directed on a cylinder of lime, was introduced in 1816.

250 **Unit Five** Technical Theatre

For More Information

Books

Graves, Robert, *Lighting the Shakespearean Stage, 1567–1642*, Southern Illinois University Press, 1979.

McCandless, Stanley, *A Method of Lighting the Stage*, Theatre Arts Books, 1958.

McCandless, Stanley, *Syllabus of Stage Lighting*, Drama Publishers, 1968.

Penzel, Frederick, *Theatre Lighting Before Electricity*, Wesleyan University Press, 1979.

Rees, Terrence, *Theatre Lighting in the Age of Gas*, Society for Theatre Research, 1978.

Lights Up on the 20th Century

It was the invention of the incandescent bulb in 1879 and its rapid-fire use in the 20th century that brought lighting into the modern age. Perhaps the person most directly credited for creating modern stage lighting was a Swiss designer named Adolphe Appia (1862–1928). Hired to create the sets for Richard Wagner's operas, Appia rejected the tradition of the painted backdrop and instead opted for a three-dimensional set. According to his theory, shadow was as important as light as a way of creating a link between the actor and the setting. Appia's use of lighting with varying degrees of intensity, color, and mobility created a revolution in lighting and stage design.

Today, stage lighting effects are typically run by a computerized dimmer board that can transform a stage from sunlight to moonlight to a lightning storm in seconds. Lighting has become not simply a tool but a high-tech art form all its own. With a small arsenal of scoops, ERS's, and Fresnels, a trained lighting designer can add layers of visual and atmospheric magic to any production. And although the basic principles of lighting have not changed much in recent years, the technology of illumination continues to evolve, and design trends come and go. It's impossible to know just what the stage lighting of tomorrow will bring.

This scene from the play *Corners* uses computerized lighting effects to create a dramatic mood.

Adolphe Appia is considered the father of modern stage lighting.

Lights Up on the 20th Century

Stanley McCandless

Stanley McCandless has been called "the founder of lighting design in the United States." McCandless was a professor at Yale University and one of the first to teach a class on stage lighting. He wrote a book, published in 1930, called *A Method of Lighting the Stage.* McCandless devised a system of lighting the stage that gave the actor a more natural look. He suggested positioning the lighting instruments on either side of the actor at a 45-degree angle and using a warm color in one instrument and a cool color in the other. The warm color became the key light; the cool color became the fill light. The McCandless system of primary source and reflected source, warm and cool tone mixed together, became the underpinning of modern light design.

Tharon Musser

Tharon Musser began her lighting design career in 1956 with the original production of *Long Day's Journey Into Night.* She subsequently received Tony Awards for Best Lighting Design for the Broadway shows *Follies, A Chorus Line,* and *Dreamgirls.* She was nominated for her work on *Applause, A Little Night Music, The Good Doctor, Pacific Overtures, The Act, Ballroom,* and *42nd Street.* Tharon Musser was honored in June of 2003 by the League of Professional Theatre Women for her distinguished career as a lighting designer.

Quotable

Twenty years ago lighting design was low man on the totem pole. Barely five percent of the programs you picked up had a credit for lighting other than "Sets and Lights by Whomever." Now, you won't pick up more than five percent of the programs that don't have 'Lighting designed by . . . . It's been very exciting to see that happen. It's exciting to see that lighting is becoming known as an art form . . . .

Tharon Musser, Lighting Designer

Chapter 20

Sound Design

This chapter will introduce the student to the techniques used by the sound designer to define mood, amplify voices, and provide sound effects for a stage production. Students will learn how to use basic sound recording and playback equipment.

Objectives

1 to understand the role and the equipment of the sound designer

2 to analyze a play to determine the needs and uses of sound for that script

3 to make a sound cue sheet and a sound effects tape

National Standards

Chapter 20 meets the following National Standards:

Proficient 3a, 3b, 3c, 3d

Advanced 3f, 3h

Project Specs

For this chapter you will need to have several sound effects tapes or CDs. The students will need access to a tape recorder or a CD burner, cassette tapes, CDs, and a microphone to record live sound.

Because this project involves creating appropriate sound, it should prove rewarding for the aural learner, as well as for students who learn best doing hands-on activities.

On Your Feet

To extend this listening activity, walk with your students around the school. They will need to bring a notebook and a pencil. They must maintain silence throughout the walk. Go through several hallways, past the library, the gym, and the music rooms. Be sure to go outside as well. When you return to your classroom, have the students share with the class three sounds they heard on their trip.

Chapter 20 Sound

Somewhere up there in the back of the house, maybe behind the last distant row of balcony seats, there's a small booth from which all the sound effects and music for a play are controlled. Inside this booth, a sound operator manipulates all the electronic equipment that will ensure the audience's listening pleasure.

Project Specs

Project Description With a partner, you will make and present a detailed cue sheet and sound effects tape for a scene that is no longer than fifteen minutes.

Purpose to understand the role and production of sound for theatrical presentations

Materials paper or the Sound Activity Sheet your teacher provides; a tape recorder with a seconds counter and a sensitive microphone

Theatre Terms

amplifier
body mic or lavalier mic
CD-R (compact disk, recordable)
crash box
DAT (digital audiotape)
digital audio software
equalizer
minidisks
public domain
sound board, console, or mixer
transmitter

On Your Feet

Sit quietly for a few moments and listen to the sounds going on all around you. As your teacher points to individuals, each person will name a sound that he or she can hear, such as a ticking clock or people talking in the hall. List the sounds as they are named. This would be an excellent starting point for the sound design of a play set in a classroom.

Theatre Terms

amplifier a device that provides the power supply for the speakers
body mic a small microphone that can be hidden in the performer's clothing
CD-R a compact disk used for recording and playing back sound
crash box a heavy box filled with glass or broken shards, used for sound effects
DAT a small tape used for recording audiotape
digital audio software computer software that allows the user to mix sounds together
equalizer a device that balances the high, medium, and low frequencies from each sound source to achieve a desired blend
minidisks fairly small disks that contain digital recordings that can be played back
public domain a work that belongs to the public; free for anyone to use
sound board the device that controls all incoming sounds and allows them to be mixed or manipulated as desired
transmitter a device that sends a signal from the microphone to the receiver

PREVIEW

Sound and the Play

Sound design has become an increasingly important element in the theatre. Advances in audio technology and computerized electronic mixing of sounds and music greatly enhance the quality of productions.

In theatrical performances, the main purpose of sound design is to support the mood and purpose of each scene. To achieve this end, sound is used:

1 To amplify the actors' voices.

2 To supply incidental or dramatic music and underscoring.

3 To provide special, realistic sound effects (crickets chirping, dogs barking, car doors slamming, children playing, and so on).

The sounds that are generally used in a play are prerecorded music and sound effects from special CDs, **minidisks,** or cassette tapes; sounds using compiled live music and/or sound effects; and environmental sounds recorded by the stage crew in locations such as beaches, shopping malls, or city streets. A show's sound design, like its other technical elements, should not be intrusive in any way. If the sound designer does the job right, what the audience hears will be experienced as an integral part of the world of the play.

Stomp uses sound, rhythm, and movement to create an exciting evening of theatre.

PREVIEW

Sound and the Play

ACTivity So the students begin to develop a sound designer's vocabulary, brainstorm a list of words that have specific "sound" meaning. This will help the students as they discuss their sound design plot with their partners —or with a play director later on. The list might include *thump, crash, zing, boom, roar, snarl, bash, clang, clunk, ding, hoot,* etc. Ask the students to describe these sounds. Are they high-pitched sounds, or low-pitched sounds? Are they long or short sounds? Are they happy sounds? Scary sounds? Write the list on the board as the students call them out.

With its blend of percussion, movement, and visual humor, the high-energy group that comprises *Stomp* has played to rave reviews around the world.

- What objects are the cast members of *Stomp* using to create sound?
- What other objects do you think such a cast might use to produce percussive sound?
- Do you think, based on this picture, that this show uses sound as amplification, underscore, or a sound effect? Explain your ideas.

ACTivity If your classroom location permits, divide the students into groups of four or five. Using classroom items, have students improvise a two-minute piece that uses sound, rhythm, and movement as if they were the actors/musicians in *Stomp*.

Resource Binder

- Sound Activity Sheet, p. 81
- Creating a Sound Library Worksheet, p. 82
- Critique Sheet: Create a Sound Effects Tape, p. 83
- Sound Test, p. 84
- Sound Cue Sheet, p. 140

Handbook Connections
pages 590-591

To Have on Hand

- Various electronic devices
- Hand drum, bells, a whistle, sticks, a triangle, etc.
- "Found" objects such as key rings and a box of pencils

The Sound Production Process

ACTivity Brainstorm with the students many different outdoor and indoor sounds. The list for outdoor sounds might include rain, the rustle of leaves, birds chirping, traffic, crickets, and so on. Indoor sounds might be a pot boiling on the stove, the washing machine, the garage door opening, water running in the shower, and the like.

Be sure that all students have access to some type of recording device. Then, have them go home and make a recording of two different sounds—one obtained indoors and one obtained outdoors. Have the students play their recording for the class.

Vocabulary Enhancement

Sound crews often use an electronic instrument called a *synthesizer*, usually played with a keyboard. The synthesizer generates and modifies sounds electronically and can imitate a variety of musical instruments. It allows the person playing it to compose music or devise sound effects for a play.

Theatre Journal

Use the following as an additional or substitute prompt.

If tape recorders are available in your classroom, take one along when you go to the mall or supermarket and record selected sounds throughout the area. Then think of a scene from a play that would be able to use these sounds.

The Sound Production Process

The sound designer's first job is to become familiar with the script. To effectively analyze a script, the designer must read it more than once. The first reading should be for understanding; the second should be dedicated to finding the obvious places where sound effects, voice-overs, or music will be required. A third reading will typically show the designer even more areas of sound possibility and should lead to a preliminary plan for the show. After researching the music of the play's time period and consulting with the director and other technical designers about the mood and purpose of the play, the sound design is created.

The sound crew has a variety of responsibilities both before and after the show opens. Before the production goes into final rehearsals, the sound crew must put together a detailed list of cues and then find or create the necessary sounds. If recorded music is used in the show, the sound crew must either obtain the rights to the music or ascertain that the music can be used without payment of royalties because it is in the **public domain,** in other words, it belongs to the public.

During tech crew sessions, technical rehearsals, and performances, the sound crew is responsible for setting up, checking, and maintaining the microphones, speakers, recorders, and all other sound equipment used in the show.

During performances, the sound crew sees and hears everything the audience does because, for the most part, the crew must take their real-time cues from the performance in progress.

Theatre Journal

Go to a shopping mall or supermarket. Stop and listen for three minutes. Write an entry on what you heard. What sound effects might you record if you were the sound designer for a play set in one of these environments?

From the Field: Sounding Out the Play

I do research. It tends to be generalized research—research that has a kind of emotional value, that somehow gives a sense of the place . . . the sound you might hear in the place . . . if you can't hear the play, you really can't see the play.

Ming Cho Lee, Chairman, Yale School of Drama, Department of Design

A Basic Sound System

A workable sound system consists of equipment to produce and control sound elements. A well-equipped sound crew will need:

The **sound board,** also referred to as a **mixer** or **console,** is the heart of the sound system. It controls input from mics, tape recorders, DAT and CD players; allows levels and equalization to be set; adds effects such as reverberation, and sends all this to the amplifier.

Equalizers balance the high, medium, and low frequencies from each sound source (e.g. the microphones) to achieve the desired blending of the sounds.

The **amplifier** provides the power supply for the speakers.

Speakers project the sound. They are typically hung at the front of the house near the proscenium arch, facing toward the audience.

Headphones allow the crew to establish levels, check the quality of the sound, and cue up sounds.

CD-R player/recorder, cassette deck, digital audiotape (DAT) can be used for recording and playing back sound.

Microphones are used for recording and amplifying sound. Hardwired mics are directly connected to the sound board. A **body,** or **lavaliere,** mic is small enough to be hidden on the performer and has a small battery-powered **transmitter** that sends a signal to a receiver unit attached to the sound board. Handheld mics and body mics provide excellent mobility for the performer.

A **crew intercom system** allows the sound operators and other crew members to communicate with each other. It is totally separate from the main sound system.

Also used, but not usually tied into the sound system, is the computer-driven **digital audio software** that allows for the mixing of a wide variety of sound sources and effects on a personal computer. Once the desired mix is obtained, it can be downloaded from the PC to a CD-R for playback on the sound board's CD or minidisk player.

You will also need a variety of smaller supplies including cassettes, CDs or minidisks, and batteries.

Notes

A Basic Sound System

Have students do an inventory to see if your drama department has the items listed for a basic sound system. If there are any items lacking, discuss what options you may have for substituting another device or going without the item altogether.

Each sound we hear can be interpreted on a different emotional plane. The very same sound could be interpreted very differently by individuals in the audience. To some it might sound exciting and intriguing; to others, it might seem threatening or foreboding. It is the job of the sound designer to select the sound effect that will be interpreted by the majority of the audience in the manner the script and the director intend.

ACTivity Divide the class into groups. Assign each group a category such as water, traffic, or wind. Have the students generate as many different types of sound for each category as they can. For instance, under *water* they might list *babbling brook, whitewater, waterfall, splashing fountain,* and so on. Have the students search the Internet for these sounds and write down the site addresses for possible use in their projects.

Crew Intercom Rules

Following are rules to give to students who are using an intercom system:

- Keep it clean and appropriate.
- Do not use the headsets to carry on personal conversations. Stay on the topic of the show or rehearsal.
- Be professional at all times.
- If you must leave your position and take off your headset, let the stage manager or others on the crew know by saying that you are going "off headset."

PREPARE

Think About Your Sound Design

Have students pair up or assign every student a partner. Supply a good number of scripts for the students to look through. If the students have enjoyed the work of particular playwrights, see that there are other plays available by these same people. Most students find David Ives not only very amusing but fairly accessible. Paula Vogel's work is darker and may be troubling to some students. *The Actor's Nightmare* is very funny but contains allusions that beginning students may not understand.

Discuss the mood of a scene that most of the students are familiar with—perhaps the scene from *A Christmas Carol* in which Scrooge is visited by the first ghost. What sound effects music would create the mood of this scene?

ACTivity Write "mood" words on individual cards. Words such as *mournful, intense, frightened, silly, restless,* and *joyful* might be included. The students will select a mood card from the deck and suggest a type or a piece of music that conveys the mood of that word. Write all the words on the board. If there is time, ask students to record a sound that represents one of those moods and share it with the class. The other students will guess what mood the designer has recorded.

The Sounds of the Scene

Continue using the first ghost scene from *A Christmas Carol* to discuss sound. Ask students to think about the sounds that would be heard during this encounter. Would the wind howl, would the clock tick loudly, would you hear the clinking of the chains worn by Marley's ghost? Tell students to consider all aspects of the scene they have chosen when working on the sound elements.

PREPARE

Think About Your Sound Design

You are now ready to create a simple sound design. As a sound designer you would ordinarily work closely with the director when making decisions about the show's music, voice-overs, and sound effects. For this project, you will work with a partner to analyze a one-act play or a scene from a full-length play for sound possibilities.

With your partner, choose a script that offers a number of opportunities to use sound. Examples from Unit Eight of this book might include Paula Vogel's *How I Learned to Drive* or Christopher Durang's *The Actor's Nightmare.* Other possibilities might include something from David Ives's collection *All in the Timing* or one of the plays from the collection *Plays in One Act* edited by Daniel Halpern. If you prefer, you can use a short scene of your own that incorporates a number of sound effects and music. Make sure your scene or play will take no longer than 15 minutes to perform.

As you read your selected scene, think about the mood it creates. You will want to select music to reflect and enhance that mood. Almost all contemporary music is subject to copyright laws, which means you must get permission from the music publisher to use it for a theatre performance. For classroom use, however, you can feel free to use any music you like. If your selected scene does not take place in the present, try to find music that is reflective of the time period of the setting.

The Sounds of the Scene

Next, you and your partner should analyze the script. What information must be conveyed by sound? Think about where the play is set, and the sounds you would hear in this location. For example, let's say your scene takes place

In this scene from *Sky Girls,* the only sound accompanying the dialogue is the lonely drone of an antique airplane engine.

Quotable

Human beings, vegetables, or cosmic dust, we all dance to a mysterious tune intoned in the distance by an invisible player.

Albert Einstein

at night on the porch of a house out in the country. First look for any sounds that are specifically called for in the script. Make a list, complete with page numbers. Then try to imagine yourself in the scene. What do you hear? Crickets? The wind? A distant train whistle? The television from inside the house? Remember that your goal is to enhance the scene with sound, not to turn it into a scene *about* sound. Add the new sounds to your list. Also include ideas for music, either as background for some part of the scene and/or as introductory music that plays before the scene begins and that fades out as the house lights dim.

Create the Sound Effects

You are now ready to create sound effects for each cue in the scene or play. Although most common sounds are available on CD, you may wish to create "live" sound effects. Many schools have a doorbell unit—a board with a button that can be pushed to activate a buzzer or other ringer. A ringing telephone can be handled the same way.

You will probably have to experiment a bit to create your sound effects. Slamming or creaking doors, falling rain, and other effects can have a variety of "tones," and you will need to figure out how best to achieve the one that works best for your scene.

You may wish to listen to some sound tapes or CDs to decide whether you want to use any prerecorded effects.

Record Your Scene

The CD, cassette, or minidisk contains all the music and sound you will use in the scene in the order they will be used. Record all your sounds and set up any manual cues (such as a handheld doorbell that will be rung by a technician, and so on). Although your recording equipment will not be as sophisticated as a theatre system, try to record as pure a sound as possible. Record only the sound and not yourself breathing, moving the microphone, or rattling papers, all of which break the mood of the scene. Allow a bit of silence in between each cue so that you will have some space to set up for the next one.

Remember, you must record the sounds and the music in the order they are presented in the script. You cannot change the order of cues or add new ones once they are recorded. Note also that if you plan on using two sounds at the same time or a series of sounds that occur one right after the other, you will probably need two separate recordings and two players.

Backstage Gossip: Wondervoice

Bobby McFerrin is a performer who makes incredible vocal sounds. In his early days, McFerrin sang multiple vocal parts without any musical backing, and when he needed rhythmic accompaniment, he created it himself with his voice or body. People in Germany took to calling him "Stimmwunder," or "Wondervoice." He is now collaborating with Tony Kushner, author of *Angels in America*, on a new opera.

Create the Sound Effects

Have students who have captured sounds from the Internet share them with the class. Have sound tapes or CDs available for student use. Make available recording devices for students to borrow when creating their sound effects and help them if they have trouble operating them.

ACTivity Divide the students into "Decade Groups." Have the groups research a different decade's historical phone rings. They will locate the ring pattern and tone for a typical phone of the 1950s, the 1960s, the 1970s, and so on. How has the sound changed throughout time? How is a cell phone ring different from the ring on a phone at home? Have them make a recording of their assigned ring and play it for the class.

Rent or purchase the video or DVD of *The Best of Victor Borge Act I and II* (available from *www.amazon.com*). Victor Borge was a comedian and classical musician from Denmark who developed a system of sounds that took the place of punctuation when he read stories to his audiences. He called his verbal punctuation marks Phonetic Punctuation.

Record Your Scene

You might want to ask students to bring in their tapes for you to preview before their presentations. That way, you can make any recommendations for re-recording sounds that are distorted or difficult to hear.

Go over the script while listening to the tape with the student to be sure that each sound or piece of music occurs in the proper order. Help any students who are having trouble chart the script according to the sound.

Make a Sound Cue Sheet

ACTivity Have the students research music associated with specific time periods. What music was popular in the 1600s, 1890s, 1920s, 1940s, and so on. What instruments predominated in each time period? Harpsichord? Guitar? Lute? Trumpet? Schedule a decade dance in your classroom. Have the students bring in examples of the music of their assigned time period and make up a dance that they think would go with each type of music.

Vocabulary Enhancement

Some theatrical productions have music playing as the audience enters. This is called *pre-show music*. It is used to set the mood before the show begins and tells the audience something about the subject or style of the show.

It's easy to create your own sound if you have the right equipment and an imagination.

Make a Sound Cue Sheet

To guide you in operating the sound, create a cue sheet like the one below on a piece of paper or on the Sound Activity Sheet that your teacher provides. For each sound cue, you will fill in a cue number, the number of the page of the script on which it appears, the sound cue, the tape recorder's counter number or the CD or minidisk player's track number, the spoken line or when the sound cue begins, the volume level, and the line when the sound cue ends. If you use a cassette recorder, cue up the sound using headphones because counters aren't exact. Tape can stretch, and you may have to back up to find the exact spot.

Be sure to write a cue for every sound in your scene.

Sound Cue Sheet

Name of Play *Wonder of Wonders*

Crew Members *Darlene and Calvin*

Cue No.	Script Pg.	Sound	Counter or Track No.	Cue	Level	Cue to End
1	1	doorbell	005	He's 15 minutes late.	7	Finally!
2	3	crash	78	Oh, my gosh!	9	Are you OK?
3	5	music	94	Let's have some fun.	8	I'm not in the mood!
4	8	dog bark	208	Something strange is going on.	8	But we don't have a dog!

Notes

PRESENT

Cast and Rehearse the Scene

Choose members of the class to perform in your scene, and ask them to read it through aloud. Stop the actors from speaking every time you come to a sound cue. Then, play the sound for them. You will need to go over each cue several times to get the timing right.

If you have music or sound cues that are to play underneath the scene, make sure the actors are projecting enough to be heard over the sound.

Time your presentation to make sure you remain under the fifteen-minute time limit. Rehearse the scene at least three or four times with the sounds in place. If you need to rehearse the scene more than this to be sure that everything goes smoothly, by all means do so.

Here's How
To Create a Crash Box

Have you ever seen a play that featured a loud offstage crashing sound—perhaps to sound as if a person is falling down the stairs or tripping over a pile of junk? This sound effect is most often created by a **crash box,** a wooden or metal box weighted at the bottom and filled with broken dishes or glass. The box is securely taped or fastened at the top. When the box is dropped on the floor it makes a loud crashing sound that can be very convincing!

Play the Scene with Sound Effects

When your name is called, gather your tape recorder, CD player, or minidisk player and other materials, and walk with your partner and actors to the playing area. Place chairs so that the actors can sit down to read. Set your own chair off to the side near a desk or table to hold your equipment. Introduce your presentation by announcing the title and author of your play. You may wish to say a few words about why you selected this particular scene and the sound challenges it presented.

Make sure your equipment is properly cued up and that your other sound tools are close at hand.

Go through your presentation exactly as you rehearsed it. If you miss a cue, do not try to go back. Instead, check your cue sheet and move ahead to the next cue. When you have finished your presentation, allow the actors to take a bow. Then hand your paper or Activity Sheet to your teacher and return to your seat.

Cast and Rehearse the Scene

Allow class time for students to cast classmates to perform in their scenes, play the sound cues, and rehearse with the sound and music. You may want to time the final rehearsals for the students yourself.

ACTivity Have the students rescore a short scene (between two and three minutes) from an existing film on video or DVD. They will need to time the scene carefully, and be sure that it is a scene with a good bit of movement and facial reaction from the actors. They will turn off the sound on the film and watch the scene in silence. Then they will decide what music or sound effects they would put in place of the existing sound and record those effects or the music. Remind them to pay attention to the timing. Action must match the sound. Have them bring the film and their new score to share with the class.

Here's How

Have students work on making a crash box together. Have one bring in the wooden or tin box and others bring in cracked plates, marbles, and other odds and ends.

PRESENT

Play the Scene with Sound Effects

You may want to go over with the students the directions for presenting their project as well as doing a sound check of the equipment.

Quotable

[In sound design] the silences—as well as the dog barks or musical underscoring—are determined by specific aesthetic decisions. Meaning and purpose are attached to everything you do as a sound designer…your choices for underscoring and ambience are the "sound scenery" within which the production moves.

from *Sound and Music for the Theatre* by Deena Kaye and James LeBrecht

CRITIQUE

Evaluate the Sound Effects in the Presentation

Remind students that the evaluation rubric for the sound project is in their book. Talk about the rating system from the lowest (1) to the highest (5).

Originality is sometimes difficult for young people to judge. You might want to talk about the concept before the evaluating begins.

CRITIQUE

Evaluate the Sound Effects in the Presentation

You will be evaluating how well your classmates integrated their sound effects into the scenes they presented. The presentations will be rated on a scale of 1 to 5, with 5 being "outstanding" and 1 being "needs much improvement." As you listen to the presentations, ask yourself the following questions:

- How could the technical execution (volume, recording, etc.) be improved?
- In what way did the music and other effects fit the theme and mood of the scene?
- How good was the quality of the sound effects?
- Was the timing of sound cues appropriate to the scene?
- How original was the presentation?

Choose one of the presentations and give it a rating from 1 to 5, explaining in a few sentences your reasons for giving this score.

Career Focus

Sound Technician

A good sound technician should

- have a "good ear" for subtle sound differences.
- enjoy working with electronic equipment.
- be detail oriented.
- work well under pressure.
- be able to make split-second decisions.

There are plenty of options for a person with these qualities who chooses a career as a sound technician, or sound operator. These professionals can work in a variety of settings where live performances are staged, either as an employee of the facility or production team or as part of an entertainer's road crew. They may also find work in radio, television, in a recording studio, or in businesses that specialize in the sale and rental of sound equipment.

Sound techs must be able to determine sound requirements, build and install sound systems, set up and test equipment, service and maintain audio and recording equipment, and dub and edit tapes. In addition, they must be able to operate the controls to maintain proper sound levels.

For the right individual, the job of sound technician can be rewarding. But because many of the available jobs are oriented toward live performances, sound technicians must be willing to travel and work long hours—including evenings and weekends. They often work under difficult conditions with tight deadlines.

260 **Unit Five** Technical Theatre

Notes

Additional Projects

1 Create a radio play using two or more tape recorders or other recording equipment.

2 Create a movement-based performance that uses sound rather than dialogue to tell a story.

3 Interview a sound technician or sound designer at a local theatre. Ask about the various pros and cons of the job. Tape your interview, and play it for the class.

4 Make an audio documentary of your class. Pick a theme—for example, first love, family relationships, or money—and create a brief series of questions. Tape-record the members of your class as they answer one or more of these questions. Then compile their remarks and your own into the documentary.

5 Read the "Dead Parrot" excerpt from *Monty Python's Flying Circus* found in Unit Eight, and create a sound cue sheet for the scene.

John Cleese in the "Dead Parrot" episode from *Monty Python's Flying Circus.*

Chapter 20 Test

The test for this chapter is available in blackline master form in the Resource Binder, page 84.

ACTivity If students are familiar with *Monty Python and the Holy Grail,* ask them what those coconut shells smacking together were supposed to sound like. (Horses galloping down the lane.) Then ask if they can think of any other movies in which the sound effects were used in so obvious and silly a manner?

For More Information

Books

Bracewell, John L., *Sound Design in the Theatre*, New Jersey, 1996.

Ionazzi, Daniel A., *The Stagecraft Handbook*, Betterway Books, 1996.

Kaye, Deena, and James LeBrecht, *Sound and Music for the Theatre*, Second Edition, Focal Press, 1999.

Moscal, Tony, *Sound Check: The Basics of Sound and Sound Systems*, Hal Leonard Corp., 1994.

White, Glenn D., *The Audio Dictionary*, Second Edition, University of Washington Press, 1999.

Other Media

Shaping Your Sound with Microphones, Mixers, and Analog Multi-Track Recording, DVD, Insight Media, 2002.

Shaping Your Sound with Reverb, Delay, Equalizers, Compressors, and Gates, DVD, Insight Media, 2002.

Wireless Microphone Operation, CD-ROM, Insight Media, 2001.

www.soundfx.com

www.ProSoundWeb.com

www.sound-effects-library.com

Substitute Teacher Activities

Here are a few suggestions for one or more days when you will be out of the classroom:

- Assign the Creating a Sound Library Worksheet on page 82 of the Resource Binder.
- Assign one or more of the Additional Projects on this page.
- Teach Part Eight, Sound, pages 590-591 of the Student Handbook.
- **Act Out Familiar Folk Tales.** Divide students into groups of four or five. Ask them to act out a folk or fairy tale. Two or three students will be the actors, and the remaining students will be the live sound effects. For example, in *The Three Little Pigs,* the sound effects will include the fire under the pot in the pig's fireplace, the crumbling of the straw house, and the sound of running feet as the pigs scurry to the next house.

Theatre Then and Now

Other Cultures, Other Times

Religious rituals and ceremonies were the very first theatrical happenings. These ceremonies were filled with sound. Most rituals and ceremonies were accompanied by chanting, primitive musical instruments, and dance.

Commedia dell'arte used music before, during, and after the plays. The *commedia* is responsible for the first use of the sound effect producing "slapstick" which, when slapped together, provided a comic effect to accompany the humorous stage slaps and punches. This is the same stick still used by Punch in Punch and Judy puppet shows.

Theatre Then and Now

Sound Effects Through Time

Early Thunder

Theatre has been using sound effects for hundreds of years. In ancient times, when a play called for thunder, for example, the sound was created by bouncing balls of lead onto stretched leather. During Shakespeare's time, the same sound came from the practice of rolling a cannon ball down a wooden chute and allowing it to hit a large drum.

In later years, another popular source of theatrical thunder was the rumble cart. This contraption consisted of a large wooden box mounted on irregularly shaped wheels and filled with heavy objects. When pulled along the floor or ground, the cart lurched along, displacing the objects inside and causing them to rumble and crash into one another.

In 1708, a playwright named John Dennis came up with yet another way to produce a thunderous sound for the stage. For one of his plays, he strung a copper sheet from wires and put a handle at one end. When the time came for the thunder effect, a stagehand would shake the copper sheet, which produced a very natural thunder effect. Soon, other theatre practitioners began using this technique themselves. It is said that Dennis, upset by the callous appropriation of his invention, routinely chided his imitators that they were "stealing his thunder." Today that phrase is used to describe situations in which someone who should be getting credit is eclipsed by the actions of another.

The rumble cart and the thunder sheet were very effective ways of producing thunderous sound.

262 Unit Five Technical Theatre

Backstage Gossip: The Roar of Cannons

A production of *King Lear* in Washington D.C., during the nineteenth century made use of a surplus of cannonballs in the capital to provide sound effects in the storm scene. While Lear and his companions listened to the winds blowing and cracking their cheeks, one of the stagehands pushed a wheelbarrow of cannonballs over a special uneven surface to simulate the roar of thunder. At one performance the stagehand became over-confident and, striving for a truly deafening rumble, upset the barrow. Canon balls burst through the flats and rolled down the stage towards the floodlights. The sight of the aged king leaping for his life with new-found agility provoked its own uncalled for storm of audience laughter.

from *Great Theatrical Disasters* by Gyles Brandreth

Sound designer Rob Milburn recorded multiple thunderstorms and the felling of twenty trees to create just the right sound for this scene from Frank Galati's production of *The Grapes of Wrath.*

The Sound of Curly's Knuckles

Musical instruments have been a popular source of sound effects through the ages. From the 1930s through the 1940s, the Three Stooges perfected the use of the musical sound effect. Perhaps you've seen old films of the Stooges gouging and poking one another, and, when knocked unconscious, sliding down walls. Among the sound effects these film buffoons used were:

- cracking the shells of nuts to simulate crunched knuckles
- the plucking of a violin string for eye pokes
- a bang on a bass drum for a belly thump
- ratchets for twisting limbs, ears, or noses
- a slide whistle for a slide down the wall after an injury

The Three Stooges crack a nut.

The Sounds of Today

Today, theatrical sound designers have access to a wide variety of prerecorded sound effects—or the means of producing their own. If a designer wants to simulate the sound of a waterfall, for example, he or she will have to decide just how much rushing water the effect calls for. Is it water trickling over rocks or Niagara Falls? Is the play's rainstorm a summer shower or a typhoon? Many libraries and larger professional theatres have collections of recorded sound effects that can be rerecorded onto a CD-R and so on. If you have a minidisk system, you can find and record sound effects from the Internet, usually for a fee.

Sound effects have always played an important part in our theatre enjoyment—and theatres today have more sophisticated sound effects than ever before—whether we notice them or not.

The Sounds of Today

The Foley Artist

When the credits roll after a movie, have you ever wondered what a "Foley Artist" does? The name comes from Jack Foley (1891-1967), who created sound effects for movies. Foley sounds are those sounds created to accompany the onscreen creaks, thumps, and crunches that you hear when the door opens, the cabinet shuts, or the actor walks across the gravel driveway. To provide the sound of a squeak on a stairway, Jack Foley watched the film, and as the actor descended the stars, he recorded the sound of himself, sitting in an old rocking chair, slowly rocking back. This effect was then added to the movie soundtrack.

www.marblehead.net/foley/jack.html

Quotable

[Foley is] the art of recreating incidental sound effects (such as footsteps) in synchronization with the visual component of a movie. Named after an early practitioner, foley artists sometimes use bizarre objects and methods to achieve sound effects, e.g., snapping celery to mimic bones being broken. The sounds are often exaggerated for extra effect—fight sequences are almost always accompanied by loud foley added thuds and slaps.

from www.imdb.com/Glossary/F

Chapter 21

Costumes

This chapter introduces students to the methods and tools used by the costume designer. It allows the student to practice designing a costume plot for a play and offers many options for costuming a show.

Objectives

1 to understand the job of the costume designer

2 to know and utilize the tools of the costume designer

3 to analyze a play for time period, style, mood, and design

4 to create and present costume designs for a character

National Standards

Chapter 21 meets the following National Standards:

Proficient 3a, 3b, 3c, 3d

Advanced 3f, 3g

Project Specs

This project involves drawing costumes for a character in a play. Some students may feel uncomfortable with this assignment. Remind students that not everyone is a visual artist, but that most of us can draw well enough to convey our ideas. In this class you are not concerned with students' drawing skills, but with their concepts. Tell students you are looking for:

- careful, diligent work
- creativity
- attention to detail
- an understanding of the needs of the play

On Your Feet

Once students have brainstormed the design features from each period, ask volunteers to draw examples on the board to illustrate each one.

Chapter

21 Costumes

Do clothes really make the man or woman? Probably not. But in the theatre, they add a visual element that enhances the audience's understanding of the character, the period, and even the theme.

Project Specs

Project Description You will prepare a set of three to five costume designs for one character from an existing play, then in a five- to ten-minute presentation, you will show your designs to the class.

Purpose to learn the basics of costume design

Materials hand-drawn or computer-based costume designs or the Costumes Activity Sheet provided by your teacher; fabric swatches, colored pencils, and appropriate paper

Theatre Terms

building
costume parade
costume plot
crinolines
modified authenticity
notions
pinking shears
silhouette
swatches
trim

On Your Feet

What do you already know about historical styles? Four classmates should go to the chalkboard and write one of these years: 1776, 1850, 1920, 1950. The rest of the class brainstorms design features from each period, which are recorded under the appropriate heading. Consider clothing, hairstyles, and footwear for both men and women.

Paul Freeman and Joanne Pierce wear costumes that reflect their characters' personalities in the Royal Shakespeare Company's production of *Cymbeline*.

Theatre Terms

building making a costume by hand

costume parade walking onstage in full costume to determine comfort, movement, and proper lighting

costume plot a list of every character and costume for each scene

crinolines full, stiff underskirts

modified authenticity the idea that clothing must give the impression of a certain time period, but need not be absolutely authentic

notions the needles, threads, pins, and so on used in sewing

pinking shears scissors with zig-zags along the blades so that cut cloth doesn't ravel

silhouette the outline of an item

swatches small samples of fabric

trim decorative items such as buttons, lace, hats, shoes, and jewelry

PREVIEW

Costume Design Meets Stage Design
Costume designers are an important part of the design team. Their work, like that of set, lighting, and sound designers, supports the mood, the style, and the message of a play. This requires more than a flair for fashion; it requires careful study and planning. Before you design costumes for a play, you must first research the time period, the setting, and any relevant social situations. When you understand why the fashions of a certain period developed as they did, you will also begin to understand the manners and beliefs of the time. Research can take many forms, but good sources include paintings, books, photos, and illustrations from the period, as well as costume design books.

After a few careful readings of the play and researching the period, the costume designer meets with the director and other technical designers. Together, they discuss the theme and style of the production and decide on an approach to color, scenery, and lighting. Then, with this and the production budget in mind, the costume designer begins to develop design concepts and sketches.

Pull, Rent, Borrow, Buy, or Build?
Once the designer has a concept in mind, he or she must decide how the costuming will be achieved. There are generally five ways to get the costumes needed, and all of the methods will probably have to be used at some point.

PREVIEW

Costume Design Meets Stage Design

Show, Don't Tell Show students various images from costume books, theatre books, or the Internet. Focus on the types of clothing from different time periods and cultures. Have students discuss what they observe about the changes clothes have undergone throughout the ages. Ask the students if they can surmise why specific clothing was used at specific times in specific locales. Examples would be the wearing of light, cool clothing in dry, hot regions and heavy fur in cold, icy climates or the fact that at one time only people above a certain station were allowed to wear the color purple.

After a careful reading of the play that the students are using for their costume design project, ask the students to respond to the following questions:

- Where does the play take place?
- What is the time of year, time of day, and climate?
- What is this play about?
- Is this play realistic or fanciful?
- What adjectives best describe each character?
- What is the scenic design for the play?
- What gel colors will be used in the lighting design?

Shakespeare's *Cymbeline* is a very complex comedy, involving a banished husband, a faithful wife, kidnapped infants, an invented infidelity, a treacherous queen, and several murderous plots . . . all in good fun.

Use the following prompts to exercise students' **critical viewing skills.**

- What can you tell about the time period of this scene?
- What might the color choices say about the characters?

Resource Binder

- Costumes Activity Sheet, p. 85
- Create Your Own Costumes Worksheet, p. 86
- Critique Sheet: Create Costumes, p. 87
- Costumes Test, p. 88
- Costume Designer's Script Analysis, p. 141
- Pull/Rent/Buy/Borrow/Build List: Costumes, p. 142
- Female Figure Outline, p. 143
- Male Figure Outline, p. 144
- Costume Plot, p. 145

To Have on Hand

- Costume books with various costume examples
- Paper, pencils, colored pencils, erasers
- Fabric swatches
- Box full of fabric remnants
- Tracing paper
- Thread, needles, scissors, patterns, sewing machines
- Templates from fashion Web sites

Handbook Connections
pages 577-579

ACTivity Have the names of various time periods or styles labeled on individual index cards. Select a play that the students have read. A good choice might be *Antigone* by Sophocles. The students select two characters from the play and one card from the periods/style stack, then design two costumes based on the period/style chosen. For example, Character: Creon/Antigone; Period/Style: Early 20th century. Hand out copies of the Female and Male Outline forms (pages 143 and 144) from the Resource Binder and supply extra paper and colored pencils. Have on hand the books *Historic Costumes in Pictures* or *What People Wore* for reference. (See page 276 for more information on these books.) Students might also visit sites such as *www.costumes.org*.

Pull, Rent, Borrow, Buy, or Build?

Go over each of these terms with students until you are satisfied that they understand what each one means. Discuss productions you have worked on in terms of the costumes you pulled, rented, or borrowed for each.

Show, Don't Tell Take a little field trip to the wardrobe area or costume storage room in your school. Let the students look at the selections. Point out design elements and sewing techniques that may be of interest. Discuss color and fabric types. If you have pictures of the shows the costumes were used in, show them to the students to demonstrate the costumes under the lights and on the set.

If you have a costume rental house in your area, call to ask if you can take your class to tour the facility and to meet with the designers and seamstresses or tailors. Brainstorm with the students a list of questions that they will ask as they tour, such as "How many costumes do you have here?" or "How do you know which costumes will fit which actors?"

Pull Some schools and theatres are fortunate enough to have their own wardrobe of costumes from previous productions. This is the first place the designer looks—not only for appropriate costumes, but also for any items that could be modified to meet current needs.

Rent Renting can be both expensive and disappointing. Rented costumes are often ill-fitting, not available in the size and color required, or in poor condition. In addition, since rented costumes are usually available for only dress rehearsal and production, actors have little time to become used to wearing them. Still, there are times when renting is the only option. If a costume must be rented, it is best to deal with a large company with a good reputation, or better still, a local company with costumes on display.

Borrow While it is tempting to borrow costume items from friends, relatives, and neighbors, it is a risky idea. No matter how careful the costume crew and the actors are, costumes take a beating onstage. Actors perspire under the lights, and it is almost impossible to avoid getting makeup on clothing. Plus, borrowed items are often fragile and easily snagged or torn. If a costume is borrowed, it must be returned promptly and in good, clean condition.

An Egyptian costume from about 3000 B.C.

A Roman gladiator's attire from around 500 B.C.

What an upper-class lady might have worn in the 1300s.

This Elizabethan costume could be that of a pirate or a nobleman.

Medieval servant presents the meal.

Quotable

Sure this robe of mine does change my disposition.

William Shakespeare, *The Winter's Tale*

Buy It is rare to actually buy a complete costume, however, parts of costumes such as shoes, boots, shawls, and hats can often be found at secondhand stores, flea markets, and garage sales—places haunted by savvy designers. These locations, plus discount stores, are also good sources for costume jewelry, clothing that can be modified, and draperies and bed linens that can be used as fabric for making costumes.

Build Making a costume, or **building** one as it is referred to in the theatre, is the most difficult, but probably the most satisfying method of costuming. When costumes are built from scratch, the designer can get the exact look he or she has envisioned and has more creative control over color and harmony among all costumes. Costumes should not war with each other or with the scenery—unless their disharmony is part of the director's message.

After the director has approved the costume design, but before costumes are actually built, a wise costume designer gathers **swatches,** or samples, of fabric for various costumes and tries them under the lighting in which they will be seen. Colors and patterns are also checked to make sure they work together—and with the scenic elements onstage.

What a typical beggar might wear to plead for "alms."

Ben Franklin himself might have worn this American outfit from the 1700s.

An elegant lady of the 1800s would have worn a gown like this to a formal gathering.

This costume suits a Victorian chap of the 1890s.

A simple homespun dress suits this American prairie girl.

Backstage Gossip: Fashion Casualty

Dorothy Parker, known for her caustic reviews, had this to say about an actress in The Silent Witness

Miss Strozzi . . . had the temerity to wear as truly a horrible gown as ever I have seen on the American stage. There was a flowing skirt of pale chiffon . . . a bodice of rose-colored taffeta, the sleeves of which ended shortly below her shoulder. Then there was an expanse of naked arms, and then, around the wrists, taffeta frills such as are fastened about the unfortunate necks of beaten while poodle-dogs in animal acts. Had she not luckily been strangled by a member of the cast while disporting this garment, I should have fought my way to the stage and done her in myself.

Continue discussing the costuming of various productions in which you have participated, particularly in regards to buying and building. Share any personal insights regarding either.

Alert students that when buying costume elements they should try to find bargains on fabric at local discount or fabric stores. Most fabric stores have sale tables and some fabric stores offer teachers discounts on fabric.

ACTivity With scraps of about two yards each, students can practice designing and making a simple vest or scarf. If you don't sew, see if a colleague or parent who does is willing to help the students. In addition to the fabric, students will need thread, needles, scissors, and patterns. If you can borrow five or six sewing machines, things will move along faster.

If you have a community theatre or college theatre near by, call to see if the resident costume designer or teacher will make a presentation about building a costume to your class. Ask them to bring their portfolio to show and discuss with your students.

ESL Students
Your ESL students may find it confusing that in the theatre sewing a costume is referred to as "building." Tell them that the word is used more in the sense of "construct" or "create."

ACTivity Keep a collection of assorted costume pieces in a box in your room. This can include gloves, hats, scarves, an old sweater, a bandana, a tie, a few vests, and some assorted pieces of costume jewelry. Divide the students into small groups. Let the students select an item from the costume box. Each group of students will improvise a scene based around the wearing of their particular costume selection.

Modified Authenticity

Use the Web site *www.freepapertoys.com* to find a variety of fashionable paper dolls from different time periods. Use white paper to trace their silhouettes for the students to identify. Then ask students to use colored pencils to enhance the silhouettes.

ACTivity Have a costume contest in your room. The students will create simple costumes made of found items to wear in class. Ask colleagues to come in to act as judges. Select unusual categories for prizes. Some suggestions for titles of prizes might be: Best Costume Use of the Color Red, Most Creative Use of a Hat, Best Design Using Beads and Feathers, Best Costume for a Future World.

Elements of Style

Bring in old family photos and ask students to do the same. Look them over together. How has clothing changed over the years? What did our grandparents wear to school or on outings? How did people dress when traveling? What did they wear when having a portrait taken?

ACTivity Have students interview parents, grandparents, or other older relatives or neighbors about what they wore when they were teenagers. What fashion changes have occurred over the years, and what in our society do they think caused these changes? Have students share their information with the class.

Modified Authenticity

No matter how you acquire them, note that period costumes require only **"modified authenticity."** That is, the fashions do not have to be replicated stitch by stitch, as long as prominent design elements and the basic **silhouette,** or line of the garment, that identifies the era are in place. Lines can be simplified, and elements such as hats and collars can be modified so that the audience can see the stage and the actors' faces clearly. Most accessories can be eliminated—just a few important, symbolic pieces such as a cane or fan may be necessary.

Oddly, underwear often becomes important to a period costume. Greek robes require long slips to prevent "see-through" under the lights. The skirts of the Elizabethan era need special frames underneath to produce the proper shape and fullness. A dress from the Civil War period needs a hoop and plenty of **crinolines,** full stiff underskirts. A "Gay Nineties" dress must have a corseted form for the smooth, snug waist and midriff.

Elements of Style

As designers build or gather costumes, these are the elements they keep in mind.

The poodle skirt was popular with teenagers in the 1950s.

What the typical flapper wore in the 1920s.

A zoot suit of the 1940s.

This fellow from the 1970s is ready for the disco.

A typical tribal costume of Nigeria, Africa.

268 Unit Five Technical Theatre

Backstage Gossip: Your Shift is Showing

In 1907, John Synge's comedy of rural Ireland *The Playboy of the Western World* caused a riot at the Abbey Theatre in Dublin. The play's use of such words as *shift* had the audience enraged. Five hundred police were brought in to calm the situation. And what is a *shift* anyway? It's a slip or petticoat.

In *Romeo and Juliet,* the Montagues often wear gradations of one color, while the Capulets wear another.

Fabric Textures and types of fabric communicate a great deal about characters. Unfortunately, most theatres are on a limited budget. Fortunately, substitutes can often stand in well for expensive fabrics. For example, instead of brocade, you can stencil designs on muslin. Unbleached muslin has another advantage too—it looks like linen at a distance. Burlap, monk's cloth, and terry cloth can substitute for wool. Instead of velvet, use heavy cotton flannel or corduroy. Silks can be made from cheesecloth and nylon chiffon. For lace collars and cuffs, use paper or plastic doilies.

Color Colors can help identify and define characters and also establish a tone for the play as a whole. Costume colors must harmonize or contrast with the set; if the costume is the same color as the background, the audience "loses" the actor. Costumes and sets must also play off each other. Especially in plays with large casts, costuming characters in different tones helps audience members identify and remember relationships between the characters.

Proper choice of color will help establish the play's mood. For example, blues and greens are restful; red conveys danger, power, or anger; black denotes tragedy or elegance; purple suggests royalty; and white is associated with purity and innocence. Principal characters should wear the more dominant colors in a show—either the brightest or the darkest on stage. Sometimes groups of characters are dressed in the same color with varying shades. If the right color is unavailable in the right fabric, choose the fabric in a light color and dye it.

Decoration Decoration includes all the **trim**—buttons, rickrack, lace, and so on—and accessories such as hats, shoes, fans, canes, and jewelry.

Each of these can be used to produce a psychological effect on the observer. As long as decorative items are used sparingly, they serve to emphasize and project details about the character in the play.

Note that essential decorations must be slightly oversized to remain visible. To keep one element from overtaking

Collect fabric swatches for classroom use. Use these small pieces of fabric to engage the students in a discussion of color, hue, and tint. Do some colors work together while others do not? Do the textures of some fabric seem easier to work with than others? Do some of the printed designs work well together? Does it ever work to use a plaid with a stripe?

ACTivity Give students two swatches of fabric and tell them that they must find one additional fabric swatch that will work well in the building of a costume for one of these characters: a Russian tsar, a Spanish dancer, a Native American tribal leader, a torch singer in 1930s Germany, or any others you devise. The possibilities are endless. Have the students discuss the swatch they added and why.

ACTivity Ask students to bring in lots of trim—anything they can think of. Collect these over a period of days, then put them all in a big box and have students pick out two or three pieces without looking. The assignment: Create a small hat for a particular character using these pieces of trim (and any other fabric they care to use).

Quotable

When you don't have the money to build costumes, you start collecting costumes from other productions, other theatre companies, actors' closets, your closet. I had to wear a corduroy blazer to the opening night of Nine, *my biggest show, because all my evening clothes were being used as costumes for another show.*

William Ivey Long, Costume Designer

Here's How

Making costumes that fit the part sometimes means making costumes that are neither tasteful nor pleasing to the eye. Not every actor should look fabulous onstage. Some characters are dowdy, plain, or off-putting in appearance, and it is up to the costume designer to see that they fit the bill. The temptation to add a bit of flair or insert a little artistic "something" has to be avoided. The actor must not look like someone in a costume. The actor must look like a person inhabiting his or her own clothes.

The Question of Comfort

Tell students that costume designers must look to the director for information about any quick changes of costume that will be necessary for the show. Then the costume crew must build the costumes with that in mind. If a quick change is called for, the designer adapts the design to include Velcro™ closures instead of buttons or a zipper. You might also discuss the need for a "dresser" backstage at the crucial quick-change moments. A dresser helps the actors, either backstage or in the dressing room, whenever extra help is needed for a costume change during the show.

others, remember that white or light-colored tights are eye-catching, that glitter steals focus, and that personal jewelry destroys the illusion of the character, not to mention the time and place of the entire play! Be sure that all actors leave their personal jewelry at home. Before they go onstage, give the actors any jewelry that will serve to enhance their characters.

Here's How
To Make the Actor Fit the Part

Sometimes the actor is built differently than the character he or she is to play. Costumes can help create the right illusion. You can use fabric, color, and line to make people appear taller, shorter, heavier, or thinner than they actually are.

Use fabric with long, vertical lines to make a person appear taller and thinner. Also use dark colors to create a slim silhouette. Velvet, which absorbs light, tends to make people appear smaller and thinner as well. Long skirts, high hats, and v-necks add height.

Satin and other glossy fabrics add bulk to a figure, as do glaring colors, loud patterns, and horizontal lines. Placing the waistline of an outfit a bit high can obscure a small waist—and layering fabric adds actual inches.

Of course, these principles are only the most basic elements of design. But they will help you make sure your costumes complement and support the mood, the style, and the message of a play.

The Question of Comfort

Fashion often cares little for the comfort or ease of movement of the wearer. Onstage, however, in order to perform convincingly, actors must be able to move nimbly and perform comfortably onstage. Their costumes should not get in the way. This means that the costume designer should collaborate with the actors, listening to what they have to say about their characters' clothes. The actors should try on the costumes before the designer completes them. If an actor feels awkward in a costume, it will show onstage. No matter the play's time period, the goal is to have the actor look like a person inhabiting his or her own clothes.

For this reason, it is helpful to have costumes ready as early as possible so that actors can rehearse in the armor, hoopskirts, tights, and corsets they will wear during the show. If this is not possible, the costume crew should try to provide rehearsal garments that simulate the costumes. Rehearsal shoes are imperative for both men and women.

Backstage Gossip: Padding Problems

Donald Wolfit's padding for Falstaff was a monstrous piece of old-fashioned engineering. Hot, heavy, and Gothic, it caused the actor to sweat mercilessly. Between matinee and evening performances it would be hung from the flies with a powerful light shining on it, in the hope that the heat would dry it. But the worst drawback of the padding was that it had to be removed entirely if the actor was to relieve himself during the performance. Falstaff, luckily, is offstage for some length of time during the course of the play, and this provided Wolfit with the necessary opportunity. "Brilliant craftsman, Shakespeare. Knew the actor would want to pee and constructed the play accordingly. A master, a master!"

from *Theatrical Anecdotes* by Peter Hay

270 Unit Five Technical Theatre

Keeping Track of It All

Costume designers work at the intersection of the big picture and the tiny details. They need to keep track of each costume piece for each character in every scene of a play. That's not easy under any circumstances. Following are the tools that designers use to stay organized.

Costume Plot A costume designer's most valuable tool is a **costume plot.** It lists every character and costume for each scene. It also offers a way to record the stage of development for each costume. To use a costume plot effectively, make a separate page for each scene of the play. For each scene, list every character who appears in the scene, and describe his or her costume and accessories. It can be helpful to list each accessory separately, in order to track the progress of each character's costume. Some designers make a separate costume list for this purpose.

Costume Plot

Name of Play *The Crucible by Arthur Miller*

The Time *1692* **The Place** *Salem, MASS*

Act *One*

Reverend Parris (45 years old–a righteous man):
- *Black sleeveless gown with tabs and skullcap*
- *Black Pilgrim suit with collar, hat*

Thomas Putnam (40 years old–a wealthy man):
- *Pilgrim suit of fine cloth, white collar and pilgrim hat*

John Proctor (35 years old–a farmer):
- *Leather sleeveless jerkin, rough shirt and homespun Pilgrim suit (wears coat only for Trial scene)*

Abigail Williams (17 years old–niece of Reverend Parris):
- *Typical Pilgrim dress with white collar, cap*

Betty Parris (a young girl–daughter of Reverend Parris):
- *Nightclothes*

Acquisitions List This is a chart headed "Pull/Rent/Borrow/Buy/Build." Some theatre companies can pull items from their own stock or borrow them from other theatres. Sometimes, they build costumes from scratch. Often, however, at least some costumes and accessories must be bought, borrowed, or even rented from costume shops. In order to keep track of what you have, what you need, and where things will come from, you keep a Pull/Rent/Borrow/Buy/Build list, entering each item in the appropriate slot. Some costume designers attach this list to their costume plot. Others keep that list separate so they can lend it to members of the costume crew. However you decide to use it, use it faithfully. It will help you keep the details in your grasp.

From the Field: Heel to Toe

I never like to know what the budget is until I'm through with my design work. I have people who must be covered up with costumes. I need to solve the design problems first and the fiscal problems later. If I have to think about how much money I've got for shoes, that will be in my way while I'm drawing a heel.

Patricia Zipprodt, Costume Designer

Keeping Track of It All

Be sure each actor's name is securely attached to the inside of each piece of clothing. Dressing rooms can be hectic during a performance, and costume pieces can get lost. Having the actor's name inside the costume can help in locating lost items. At the end of each evening's performance be sure all costumes are hung neatly and all accessories are stored in the proper container.

When you're taking your show down, you'll need to return costumes that don't belong to the theatre. So don't just mark an item bought, rented, or borrowed. Instead, use initials that tell you where the item came from. If you can, add a label to each item that tells where it must be returned.

Also, when you return any clean borrowed items, add a thank you card signed by the cast and crew of the show.

ACTivity To help prepare the students to work on their costume design, try this exercise as a warm-up. Read several short scenes from a play. Draw a chart on the board—another way to begin a costume plot. Ask the students to help you fill out the chalkboard plot. Begin by listing the scene numbers, then the characters' names, then the costume pieces for each character, and then any accessories. The students might pull fabric swatches from your fabric box and explain why they would build a certain character's costume in a particular color or fabric.

Be sensitive to students' concerns about weight and body image. In our culture, young people are wrestling with eating disorders. The listing of weight and dress size may not be appropriate for the measurement cards if the cards are accessible to other students. Be careful to limit access to this information.

ACTivity Beginning Students Have students practice their sewing skills. Give them a needle and thread and piece of fabric, preferably fabric in a solid color. Ask them to use a series of common stitches, such as the running stitch, a basting stitch, and a slipstitch. Consult a local fabric shop for books of various stitch techniques. What stitches are used for what purpose and why?

ACTivity Advanced Students Ask the students to design the costumes for a cartoon character, but tell them that the costume must be different than the comic book costume or the movie costume. Suggested characters might be Spiderman, Batman, Catwoman, or Superman. How would they design the costume for one of these characters that expresses the traits of the character, but is not the familiar costume usually associated with the character?

Measurement Cards For costuming purposes, it might not be enough to know that Martha is a size 10. You might need to know the circumference of her head, the length of her inseam, and so on. The sensible thing to do is to take detailed measurements of each actor, and write them on measurement cards. Even if you're not building a costume, measurements are still important. They can help you pull, rent, borrow, or buy costumes that fit.

Costume Spaces To encourage continued organization, assign a hanger or piece of shelf space for each costume piece. Label the space so that anyone in the production can find any piece at any time. This will not only prevent losses, it will allow the costume crew to check costumes periodically for possible repair or cleaning.

Costume Parade When the costumes are almost finished, have each actor move onstage in costume. Ask for comments about the comfort, utility, and movement of the clothes and accessories. Be aware of how the lights play on the costumes. Take notes during the costume parade, and make final alterations so that there are no surprises on opening night.

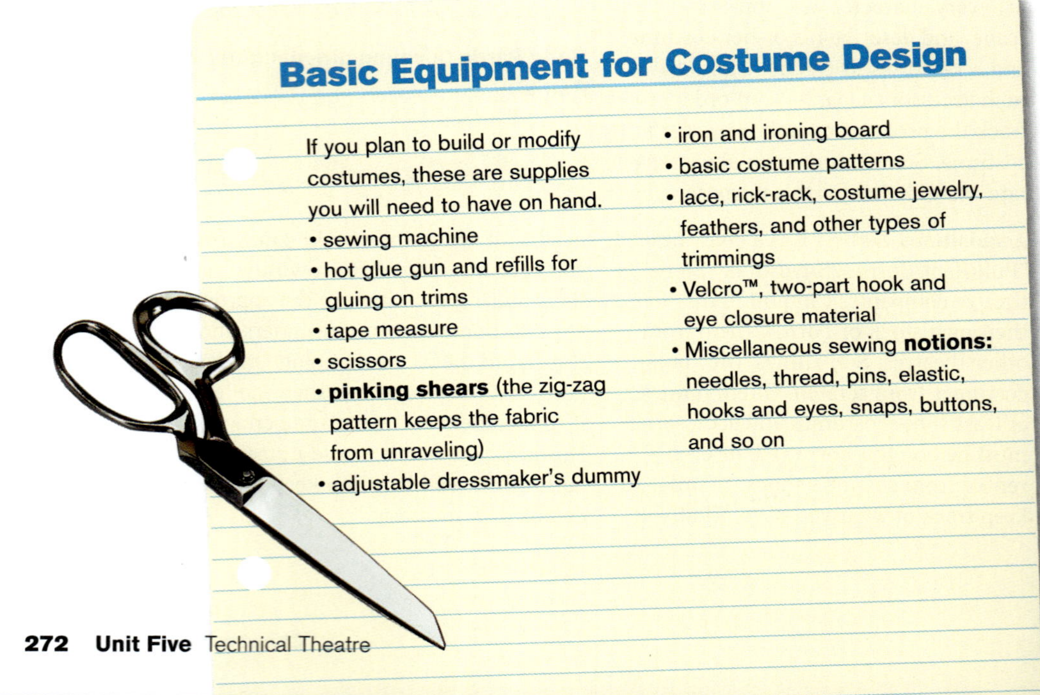

Basic Equipment for Costume Design

If you plan to build or modify costumes, these are supplies you will need to have on hand.

- sewing machine
- hot glue gun and refills for gluing on trims
- tape measure
- scissors
- **pinking shears** (the zig-zag pattern keeps the fabric from unraveling)
- adjustable dressmaker's dummy
- iron and ironing board
- basic costume patterns
- lace, rick-rack, costume jewelry, feathers, and other types of trimmings
- Velcro™, two-part hook and eye closure material
- Miscellaneous sewing **notions:** needles, thread, pins, elastic, hooks and eyes, snaps, buttons, and so on

272 Unit Five Technical Theatre

Quotable

Clothes do not make the woman, and the lack of them doesn't make the actress.

Carroll Baker, Actor

PREPARE

Costume a Character and Prepare a Talk

For this assignment, you will read a play and do research about the time and place it portrays. Your research will allow you to accurately develop a set of wardrobe designs for a particular character in the play.

1. Read a one-act or full-length play that has been approved by your teacher. After you have read the play once, choose a character to costume. Go through the script again and take notes from passages that provide clues to your character.
2. Research the time period of the play.
3. Using your research and notes from the script, make a list of colors, fabric, and decorations that will help define the time, place, and character.
4. Fill in the costume chart on the Activity Sheet for this chapter, which your teacher will provide.
5. Create from three to five drawings of costumes suitable for one character in the play. Draw each costumed figure as large as you can, then complete your sketches with colored pencils, pens, watercolor, or acrylic paint. Be sure your drawings are neat and detailed. For each costume, try to include a swatch of the material you would use.
6. If you feel your completed costume drawings will be too small for your classmates to see easily, reproduce them in color on a transparency for use with an overhead projector. Your teacher can help you with this.
7. Prepare a five- to ten-minute presentation on the costumes you have sketched. This report should begin with a short summary of the play and a description of the character's personality, age, and social status, as well as the mood and period of the play. The body of your talk should refer to the costumes you have created. Support your presentation of the costumes by describing the styles of the period and explaining why you chose the fabric, color, line, and decoration elements you did. Conclude with a summary.
8. Rehearse your talk before class so that you can give it in an interesting, fluid way. Stay within the ten-minute time limit.

Theatre Journal

What are the style elements of your generation? Describe, and if possible, sketch, the shape or basic silhouette of the clothes you and your friends wear. Why do you think these styles are popular?

PREPARE

Costume a Character and Prepare a Talk

Go over each of the eight steps that students will take to complete this project. Have plenty of plays and scenes available for them to look through.

Meet with students individually after they have completed step 4 to be sure that they have gathered all the information necessary to begin their drawings.

Students who are not comfortable with having to draw should be encouraged to think of this step as a way to visually present their understanding of the costuming needs of the play. Remind them that their artistic skills will be evaluated only in so far as they relate to their interpretations of character, mood, time period, and theme.

Some students may find this project more enjoyable if they can work on a computer. Suggest that they transfer their designs into a PowerPoint® presentation. This exercise might also be done in small groups, with students working on the part of the presentation that employs their natural strengths.

Help any students who are having trouble with the time limit. If they are running too long, suggest ways they might cut information. If their presentations are running less than five minutes, suggest areas that need strengthening.

Theatre Journal

Use the following as an additional or substitute prompt:

Pretend you are a bright yellow bird. Write a description of yourself based on the color yellow. How would you describe your mood and character traits?

What if you were an olive green bird? What would change concerning your mood and character traits based on this different color?

Backstage Gossip: A Midsummer's Nightmare

Even the greats can't always manage a dignified exit. Before the war, Vivien Leigh and Robert Helpmann starred in a production of *A Midsummer Night's Dream* in Regent Park. One evening several members of the Royal Family came to see the show. At the end of the performance, Leigh and Helpmann gave a special bow to the royal party and as they did so found to their horror that their elaborate headpieces had locked together and refused to part. Miss Leigh nestled in closer to Helpmann and the two of them were then forced to back offstage, smiling inanely at the royals as they went.

from *Great Theatrical Disasters* by Gyles Brandreth

PRESENT

Show and Discuss Your Costume Designs

Be sure that any students using PowerPoint® or overhead transparencies are well acquainted with their use in presentations. Have all necessary equipment functioning and ready for them.

Remind the students that they must be as good an "audience" member as they are a "performer" or presenter. Class presentation has much in common with performing, and being an active listener in class is much like being in the audience at a show. Active listening requires good manners, quiet concentration, and reflection. Tell students that you will be evaluating how insightful their questions to the speaker are.

Keep a stopwatch on hand to time the students. If they are getting close to the ten-minute limit, give them a warning in order to allow them time to reach the conclusion of their presentation without rushing the final sentences.

PRESENT

Show and Discuss Your Costume Designs

When your name is called, hand your costume designs or Activity Sheet to your teacher and go to the front of the class. Pause and look at the class before you begin to speak. With poise and with a pleasant, audible voice, present your costume designs. If your drawings are large enough, or if you have reproduced them as handouts or on a transparency for use in an overhead projector, point to elements in each design and discuss their significance. If you complete your talk before the ten-minute time limit, ask the audience for questions. Answer any questions as thoroughly as you can.

Sketch and actual costume from a production of Shakespeare's *Twelfth Night.*

From the Field: The Gravity of the Situation

Once an errant chair escaped the rear end of an actor during a production of *She Stoops to Conquer*. The actor's trousers were merely safety pinned in the back of the waistband and the pressure from the fall caused the pin to pop open. When he stood up, his trousers did not. I like to remind everyone that the laws of nature apply on stage as well.

Jamie Bullins, Designer, Stage Manager, and Assistant Professor of Theatre and Performance at Kennesaw State University, Kennesaw, Georgia

274 **Unit Five** Technical Theatre

CRITIQUE

Evaluate a Classmate's Designs and Presentation

Choose a design presentation by one of your classmates and evaluate it on a scale of 1 to 5, with 5 being "outstanding" and 1 being "needs much improvement." Think about the appropriateness of the costumes and the thoroughness of the presentation. Ask yourself these questions as you prepare your critique:

- In what way are the costumes appropriate to the time and place of the play?
- What was memorable about any of the costumes in terms of the theme of the play?
- What mood did the costumes evoke?
- What did the costume communicate about the personality and status of the character?
- How did the presenter use fabric, color, and decoration to support conclusions about the character in the play?
- How well did the speaker understand this character based on the costumes?
- How did the speaker present the important elements of the costumes?

Write a paragraph defending the number grade you gave this presenter.

Career Focus

Costume Designer

Are you
(a) visionary (b) creative
(c) hands-on (d) practical
(e) all of the above?

If your answer is (e), the art of costume design might be for you. Costume designers need to understand or imagine the general style of people in various times, places, social positions, and occupations. They need to harmonize the differing styles in one production. They need to develop skill at drawing or using computer programs to draw silhouettes and costumes. They need to learn enough about sewing to understand which designs are simple and which are complex. They also need to be able to beg, borrow, and shop for the cloth, costumes, and accessories they need—usually on a budget that is too small.

Luckily, you can develop each of these skills before you get a job in the theatre. You can read history or fantasy, study costume books and historical photos and paintings. Learn to sew. Hold a period costume party and provide the clothes.

Then volunteer to help out in a community theatre or school production in the costume or wardrobe department.

Backstage Gossip: Heads Up!

It was the costume designer Irene Sharaff who probably gave the greatest impetus to Yul Brynner's career. When the practically unknown actor was cast for *The King and I* (1951) he was almost bald, but with a black fringe around the back and a few strands on top.

After discussing the costumes he asked what he should do about his hair. "Shave it!" said Miss Sharaff impulsively.

"Oh no! I can't do that," Brynner protested. He was worried about a dip on the top of his head. After the designer reassured him that she could always get him a wig if the operation proved unsuccessful, Yul Brynner shaved his head, rubbed his pate with oil, which became his personal trademark, and for a while at least made baldness sexy in America.

from *Broadway Anecdotes* by Peter Hay

CRITIQUE

Evaluate a Classmate's Designs and Presentation

Give the evaluation rubric to the students as they begin their project so that they will know the criteria on which the evaluation will be based. Discuss each of the questions they should be thinking about as they listen to their fellow classmates' presentations. Remind them that they will be asked to defend their evaluations in a written paragraph.

Career Focus

Engage the students in a discussion of possible jobs related to costume design that would mean working outside the theatre. Possibilities are tailoring, alterations, fashion design, teacher, commercial design, store displays, convention design, photography, and fashion marketing. Ask the students to see how many jobs they can think of that are related to costume design.

Chapter 21 Test

The test for this chapter is available in blackline master form in the Resource Binder, page 88.

For More Information

Books

Braun and Schneider, *Historic Costume in Pictures,* Dover Publications, Inc., 1974.

Covey, Liz, and Rosemary Ingham, *The Costume Designer's Handbook, A Complete Guide for Amateur and Professional Costume Designers,* Heinemann, 1992.

Covey, Liz, and Rosemary Ingham, *The Costume Technician's Handbook, Third Edition,* Heinemann, 2003.

Gorsline, Douglas, *What People Wore: 1,800 Illustrations from Ancient Times to the Early Twentieth Century,* Dover Publications, 1994.

Nunn, Joan, *Fashion in Costume 1200-2000*, New Amsterdam Books, 2000.

Vogue / Butterick Step-by-Step Guide to Sewing Techniques; Butterick Publishing Company, 1999.

Other Media

www.costumes.org

www.costumedesignersguild.com

www.fashion-era.com

Insight Media 800-233-9910

Additional Projects

1. Report on a specific costume period, such as ancient Rome or China, medieval or Renaissance Europe, feudal Japan, or the 17th, 18th, or 19th century in Europe or the United States. From your research, explain the reason for the style, its basic characteristics, and its accessories. Show pictures.
2. Using sheets, demonstrate correct draping of a Greek or Roman costume.
3. Report on the influence that men's fashions have had on women's fashions throughout the ages or on the impact women's fashions have had on men's fashions.
4. Prepare a chart showing the silhouettes of basic costume periods in America.
5. Report on women's shoes or another decorative element from Greek to modern times.
6. Design and create a period costume that you might wear in a favorite play.
7. Read the scene found in Unit Eight from either *Cyrano de Bergerac* by Edmond Rostand or "Baucis and Philemon" by Mary Zimmerman, and design a costume for one of the characters.

276 Unit Five Technical Theatre

Substitute Teacher Activities

Here are a few suggestions for one or more days when you will be out of the classroom:

- Assign the Create Your Own Costumes Worksheet on page 86 of the Resource Binder.
- Assign one or more of the Additional Projects on this page.
- Teach the appropriate sections of Part Three, Costumes, pages 577-579, of the Student Handbook.
- **Students Design and Create a Hat.** Provide a selection of construction paper, scissors, felt tip pens, colored pencils, glue, glitter, beads, ribbon, feathers, fabric swatches, etc. Have the students design a hat that tells the others in the class something about themselves. Are they flamboyant, crafty, organized, a dreamer? Discuss with the students what visual clues might be needed to put these ideas into a three-dimensional object.

Master of the Craft

Julie Taymor

Director, designer, puppet master, and writer, Julie Taymor is involved in every creative aspect of making plays. Her work has been informed by her studies at Oberlin and at Bread and Puppet Theatre, and it has been deeply influenced by her travels in such locales as Sri Lanka, Paris, Indonesia, and Japan. Pulling together all these influences, Taymor has developed her creative vision.

Taymor launched her first major production, *Way of Snow,* which was based on Inuit legend, using both puppets and masks. Later she designed the set, costumes, puppets, and masks for *The Odyssey* at Baltimore's Center Stage. This successful production led to work with the New York Shakespeare Festival, The American Repertory Theatre, and the La Jolla Playhouse, among others.

To date, Taymor has worked on theatrical productions as diverse as Wagner's *The Flying Dutchman,* Shakespeare's *Titus Andronicus,* and Disney's *The Lion King.* In film, she is most famous for directing *Frida,* about the artist Frida Kahlo.

Taymor has been called "one of the most imaginative and provocative directors in theatre arts today." Her work is effective because she knows what is important. In *The Lion King,* for example, she recalls an argument over whether to use real glass or fake plastic beads. Taymor explains, "I knew they had to be real even if the audience couldn't tell the difference. I knew that the people wearing the beads would know, and that the spirit . . . of craftsmen would be in the fabric and materials."

That spirit infuses Taymor's entire body of work, so that in her hands, theatre regains the magic of ritual and the wonder of make-believe.

"Imagination is much better than reality."

—Julie Taymor

Julie Taymor and her replica of the head of Titus Andronicus.

Master of the Craft

More About Julie Taymor

Julie Taymor had this to say about the design of the costumes for The Lion King:

"During this developmental stage, one of my first tasks was to complete the designs of the hundreds of animals that populate the story. Having made the decision not to hide performers within animal suits or behind masks, the challenge was to convey the animals' essence while maintaining the presence of the human. I was particularly inspired by the minimalist way animals are portrayed in African art. The style meshed with my visual esthetic, and reaffirmed that one did not have to represent the whole of an animal's body in literal detail . . . The cut of the fabrics, their decorations, tones, and patterns, would evoke an animal's contours and surfaces without sacrificing the character's human qualities."

History and Costume Design: William Ivey Long

William Ivey Long is a four-time Tony winner for his costume designs for *Nine, Crazy for You, The Producers*, and *Hairspray*. In her article about Long for the Spring/Summer 2003 issue of *William & Mary,* Melissa V. Pinard states that the study of history taught Long "how to conduct historical research, which is essential for creating costumes." Long acknowledged that he would "recommend to anybody what I did—the study of history has so influenced my work."

For More Information

Books

Taymor, Julie with Alexis Green, *The Lion King: Pride Rock on Broadway,* Hyperion, 2003.

Other Media

Behind the Scenes; Julie Taymor: Setting a Scene, Learning Designs and Thirteen/WNET, New York.

Quotable

You can lead actresses to water and drink, but you can't make them wear what they don't want to.

Edith Head, Costume Designer

Theatre Then and Now

The Art of Costuming

Ancient Greece
The costumes in ancient Greek performances were quite elaborate, possibly long tunics and cloaks. The performers also wore masks that expressed a specific emotion.

Noh Drama
Stock characters were all dressed in very colorful, intricate, and elegant costumes in a Noh drama performance. Masks specific to each character were worn by the actors. The masks told the audience which character the actors were portraying.

16th-Century Italy
The stock characters of the *commedia dell'arte* wore costumes and masks that distinguished each character from the other. Dottore was a doctor or lawyer and wore an academic robe. Capitano wore a sword with his cape and an outlandishly embellished headdress. Arlecchino, or Harlequin, wore a suit with a blue, red, and green diamond-shaped design. The audience could tell what character was on stage by looking at the actor's costume.

17th-Century French Theatre
In France during the 17th century, the actors were responsible for providing their own costumes for the stage. However, this requirement was not difficult to accomplish as most costumes for the stage were contemporary clothing. Most actors could, therefore, simply wear their own garments.

Theatre Then and Now

The Art of Costuming

Costumes in the Middle Ages
Spectacle has always been part of the theatrical experience; in the late Middle Ages, it was sometimes the whole thing. Costumes were very elaborate—often intricately embroidered or bejeweled. Leather was used to clothe many a character—from the devil's body suit (equipped with tails and scales) to a young man's breeches—and angels often wore halos of gold. As the Middle Ages progressed in Europe, miracle plays, in which actors were costumed in elaborate Oriental or Byzantine costumes, evolved into morality plays, based on stories from the Bible.

In secular drama, the May Day games and Mumming plays, a kind of pantomime, of rural England drew crowds of folks to watch the antics. Tournaments in which royals and nobles could challenge each other to contests were also held in elaborate and rich costumes. Performers were often colorfully costumed as they sang and danced during the course of these tournaments.

Interludes, short and simple plays performed between longer and more serious presentations, grew ever more elaborate—and more popular. In England, they came to be called masques, and they were often sponsored by the court. Beginning in the early 1600s, English court masques were lavish and spectacular events held once or twice a year at court. Some of the costumes were designed by Inigo Jones, one of the most famous theatrical designers of all time.

Mythic characters wore striking and amazing costumes in English masques, such as the costume Inigo Jones designed to represent a "Fiery Spirit."

Notes

Costumes Today

Today, authentic-looking costumes are the norm, but flights of fancy are common in large-scale productions, especially on Broadway. Productions with simple fairy tale themes, such as *Cats, Beauty and the Beast,* and *The Lion King,* fill theaters with adults who marvel at the effects. Scenery and lighting in these shows are spectacular, but so are the costumes. They include capes that look like wings, patterns that express character traits, and striking masks and headpieces. Some of these incorporate both realistic and fantastic elements by allowing the actor's face to be seen beneath or below the character mask.

Performance art and experimental theatre groups such as Mummenschanz expand the costume repertoire even further by creating costumes made of unusual materials such as brightly colored tubes and other shapes. The group has even utilized rolls of toilet paper to create witty and expressive costuming.

The performers in such dance-based productions as *Rent* and *Stomp,* which are relatively gritty and raw, wear outfits that make extravagant use of color to define their characters.

By embracing fantasy and inventiveness, the costumes of today offer not only a feast for the eyes but for the intellect also.

Mummenschanz exhibits a creative approach to costuming.

Beth Fowler is cleverly costumed as Mrs. Potts in *Beauty and the Beast.*

Beauty and the Beast Trivia

The information that follows gives just a hint of what can be involved in a large-scale production such as *Beauty and the Beast*.

- The musical's Tony-Award-winning costumes were worn and removed 201,000 times during Broadway's first 1,000 performances.
- Over the course of these same 1,000 Broadway performances, securing the 84 wigs and hairpieces that are worn during each show took 3,763 pounds of hairpins.
- The lighting design for *Beauty and the Beast* requires over 1.2 million watts—enough to light a football stadium.
- The fireball that the Enchantress uses, which transforms the prince into a beast, is a patented device that took over a year to develop, enabling her to hold the ball of fire in her hand without being burned.
- Lumiere uses about four pounds of butane fuel a month—that's an ounce of fuel per show per arm. The show uses six pounds of butane per month.
- Each of the 38-member cast wears a wireless microphone.
- When touring, the production uses 27 semi-trailer trucks to move the production from city to city.
- During the first 1,000 performances on Broadway, champagne bottles in the musical number "Be Our Guest" used nearly two tons of explosives; that's 3,720 pounds of solid explosives and 187.5 pounds of liquid butane.

For More Information

Books

Brooke, Iris, *English Costume from the Early Middle Ages Through the Sixteenth Century*, Dover Publications, 2001.

Buhrer, Michel, *Mummenschanz*, Rizzoli, 1986.

Crowfoot, Elizabeth, Frances Pritchard, and Kay Staniland, *Textiles and Clothing: Medieval Finds from Excavations in London, c.1150–c.1450*, Camden House, 2002.

Dryden, Deborah, *Fabric Painting and Dyeing for the Theatre*, Heinemann, 1993.

Norris, Herbert, *Medieval Costume and Fashion*, Dover Publications, 1999.

Thursfield, Sarah, *The Medieval Tailor's Assistant: Making Common Garments 1200–1500*, Quite Specific Media Group Ltd; 2001.

Other Media

For a large selection of theatre supplies visit *www.costumers.com* and *www.thecostumer.com.*

Visit the Mummenschanz group at *www.mummenschanz.com.*

Chapter 22

Makeup

This chapter will introduce students to the techniques used by the makeup artist to create characters for the stage. Students will learn how to apply makeup and will discuss the process.

Objectives

1. to understand the job of the makeup artist
2. to understand the purpose of and techniques of applying makeup
3. to analyze a character for age makeup or character makeup
4. to apply character makeup creatively and safely

National Standards

Chapter 22 meets the following National Standards:

Proficient 3a, 3c, 3d, 4b

Advanced 3g

Project Specs

For this chapter you should have a basic supply of makeup for each student. The ideal would be to provide theatrical makeup, but that is not necessary to begin an exploration of makeup.

Advanced Students

To complete the project, the advanced student should be able to design and execute old-age makeup in addition to the character makeup required by the chapter project specs.

On Your Feet

Ask the students to continue this activity by drawing other faces with distinctive features. What emotions and disposition have the students drawn in these faces?

Chapter 22 Makeup

Women used to speak jokingly about "putting on their face." This is not a joke in the theatre, where skillfully applied makeup can enhance—even greatly alter—the image the actor projects.

Project Specs

Project Description You will apply character makeup and give a five- to ten-minute talk about the process.

Purpose to learn and use the principles of effective stage makeup

Materials hand-drawn makeup plan or the Makeup Activity Sheet provided by your teacher; standard makeup kit; character makeup items

Theatre Terms

acetone
cake makeup
character makeup
collodion
complementary colors
creme foundation
crepe hair
makeup morgue
putty wax
spirit gum
stippling
straight makeup
water-soluble foundation

On Your Feet

Using the chalkboard or large pad of paper, draw a face with a distinctive facial feature such as a raised eyebrow or pursed lips. Ask classmates to identify the personality characteristics they associate with the feature as you have drawn it.

Actress Kathryn Harries performs the role of the sorceress Kundry in Richard Wagner's *Parsifal.*

Theatre Terms

acetone a solvent used to remove spirit gum

cake makeup makeup that is pressed into a round container

character makeup makeup that completely changes an actor's appearance

collodion liquid used to make scars

complementary colors colors that are opposite each other on the color wheel

creme foundation a foundation with an oil base that stays on well

crepe hair artificial hair made of wool

makeup morgue a compilation of pictures of faces to use as a reference point when applying makeup

putty wax medium used to reshape areas of the body, particularly the nose

spirit gum an adhesive used for applying items such as a false beard to the face

stippling adding texture by using small, short strokes in applying makeup

straight makeup makeup that enhances natural features and coloring

water-soluble foundation makeup that can be washed off with water

PREVIEW

Makeup: An Overview

In real life, people wear makeup to cover perceived flaws in their appearance. In the theatre, the purpose of **straight makeup,** that is, makeup that enhances natural features and coloring, is to make actors more visible and distinctive on stage. If it is applied well, makeup can both communicate a character's personality as well as enhance the actor's own features. Stage makeup can reflect the character's age, health, occupation, physical characteristics, and even attitudes. For example, a young character who plays tennis every day would probably have a ruddy or tanned face. An ancient scribe might look shriveled and wise.

Cory Claussen wears straight makeup in this scene from the Des Moines Playhouse production of *Damn Yankees.*

The style of the play and the size of the theatre space must be considered when determining how makeup is applied. If the play is realistic, the makeup should look natural to the audience. If the play is a fantasy or has many symbolic elements, then elaborate, imaginative makeup can be used to obtain special effects. If the actors are performing in a large space with strong lighting, makeup must be bold, even slightly exaggerated. Otherwise, their features may be "washed out" or made pale by the bright lights. In an intimate space, makeup should be subtle. As a rule of thumb, the objective is to create an acceptable effect for the first few rows of the audience while also making sure that the actor's face can be seen in the back rows.

PREVIEW

Makeup: An Overview

First discuss with the students the difference between straight makeup and character makeup and the fact that the amount and type of makeup needed varies for a small, medium, or large stage.

ACTivity Divide the class into partners. Have a digital camera or two available to the students. Set each camera on the black-and-white mode and have students take several close-up shots of their partner's face. Print out the students' images on your computer. Ask the students to study their own photos and try to decide their face shape: round, square, oval, heart-shaped, rectangular, or diamond-shaped. Ask the students to describe what the shape of a face might mean in the design of makeup for the stage.

Visual Cues

Have students compare and contrast the pictures of Kathryn Harries in *Parsifal* and Cory Claussen in *Damn Yankees* and answer the questions that follow.

- What is the difference in their emotional states?
- How does their makeup define those emotions?
- What differences do you see in "character" makeup and "straight" makeup?
- What do you think the "style" is of both of the productions pictured?

Resource Binder

- Makeup Activity Sheet, p. 89
- Fanciful Makeup Worksheet, p. 90
- Critique Sheet: Create Character Makeup, p. 91
- Makeup Test, p. 92
- Character Makeup Form, p. 146

Handbook Connections
page 583

To Have on Hand

- Digital camera for student use
- Computer access
- Makeup kit
- Makeup books and articles
- Washcloths
- Mirrors
- Spotlight and large white paper
- Color wheel
- Gel swatches

Showing a clip from a movie that uses character makeup would be a good way to help develop interest in the topic. There are many movies that use special-effects makeup designers. Try to steer clear of too much gore, but movies such as *Planet of the Apes* and *The Lord of the Rings*™ are good examples of how makeup is used to develop character.

Applying Straight Makeup

Go over with the students the steps in applying straight makeup. You may want to choose a volunteer to work on as you model each step so the students can see how it is done. Another way to start is to have students work in groups of three, one reading the instructions, one applying the makeup, and the third being made up. They should alternate positions as they go through the steps.

ACTivity Divide the students into groups of three with the digital camera still set on the black-and-white mode. Give one of the students a large flashlight; give one of them the camera. The third student in the group will be the model. Have the student with the flashlight shine the light on the model's face to create shadows, while the student with the camera documents those shadows by taking pictures of the model's face. Let the students swap positions until each one has taken a turn at each job. Print out the pictures on your black-and-white printer. Give the students the photos of themselves. Using dark and light shades of makeup, students should make up their faces to match their photos. Remind the students that light tones and colors advance the features, while dark tones or colors make them recede.

Ron Perlman in character makeup as the Beast in the television show *Beauty and the Beast.*

While straight makeup is the norm, there are times when an actor must wear **character makeup,** additional makeup that changes his or her appearance drastically. A young person playing someone who is bald, bearded, or elderly will need character makeup, as will an actor portraying an animal, a gnome, or anyone with unusual features.

Most stage actors are closely involved in designing and applying their own makeup. They have developed a sense of facial bone structure and skin texture. They know faces. You too should try to be aware of faces—and how age, emotion, and other factors affect them. Most important of all, get to know your own face from crown to chin.

Applying Straight Makeup

Following are general instructions for applying straight makeup.

1. **Clean your face.** Remove all street makeup with either soap and water or cold cream and tissues. If you use cold cream, make sure it is completely removed before applying stage makeup. Also use a toning astringent to obtain a clean, dry face.
2. **Apply your foundation.** Use either **creme** or **water-soluble foundation** in a color that is close to your own natural skin tone. Creme, which comes in round plastic containers, blends well, holds up well when the actor sweats, and can be reworked until finally set with powder. Water-soluble foundation, also called **cake makeup,** is applied with a damp sponge, but washes off easily when sweating, and is harder to blend. Most students usually find cremes easier to manage. Whichever you use, just be sure that the makeup you apply has a formula similar to your foundation. Apply creme with your fingers or a dry sponge wedge and cake with a damp sponge. Then blend smoothly and evenly. Cover all visible areas of your face, including the chin, neck, and ears. Fade out at least two inches down the neck to avoid a line at the jaw. Make sure there are no streaks.
3. **Add shadows.** Shadows of a darker color than the foundation are added to help emphasize the features of the face. This will help audience members sitting at a distance see the actor's facial features clearly. You can easily see the areas of the face that need shading:
   - The cheek hollows are shaded to give them dimension.

Quotable

The most exciting kind of acting, to me, is when the actor is almost unrecognizable in the part.

Swoosie Kurtz, Actor

- Shadow below the jaw line to make it stand out from the face and neck.
- Add shadow to the crease above the eye to give the eye socket more dimension.
- Shadow the sides of the nose so it doesn't flatten.

4 Add highlights. Highlights of a lighter shade than the foundation are added next to further define the features of the face. Here too you can see the areas that need highlighting by following the contours of the face:

- Highlight directly under the brow to counteract the effects of overhead lights that tend to create hollows in the socket.
- Add highlights to the cheekbone to balance the shadows you added to the hollow of the cheek.
- Create subtle highlights down the ridge of the nose.
- Add subtle highlights to the chin area.

5 Accent the eyes. We've already shadowed the crease and highlighted the brow bone; now using an eyeliner pencil (which has a thicker form of creme), we will continue to define the eyes. Starting at the outside of the eye, draw a fine line along the roots of the lower lashes with a dark brown pencil or cake liner. Do not use black, as it looks hard and artificial. On the upper lid, start at the inside corner

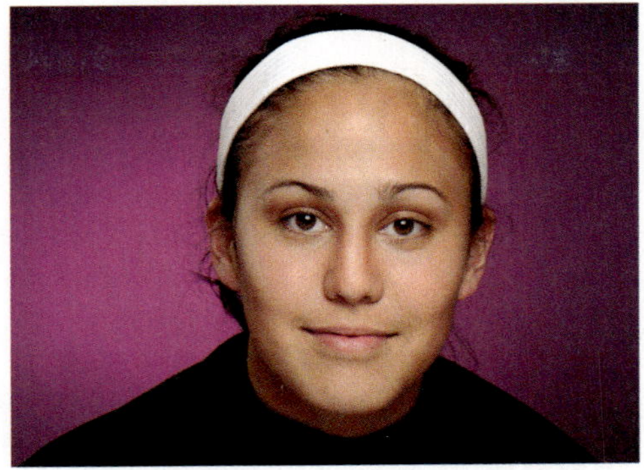

With foundation and cake makeup already applied, shadows are added.

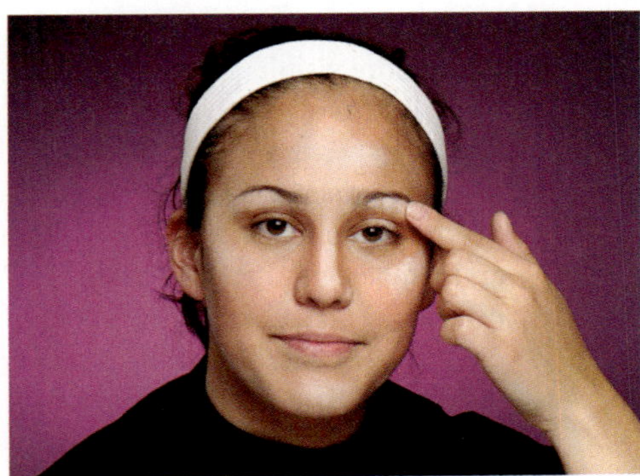

Highlights are now added to further accentuate bone structure.

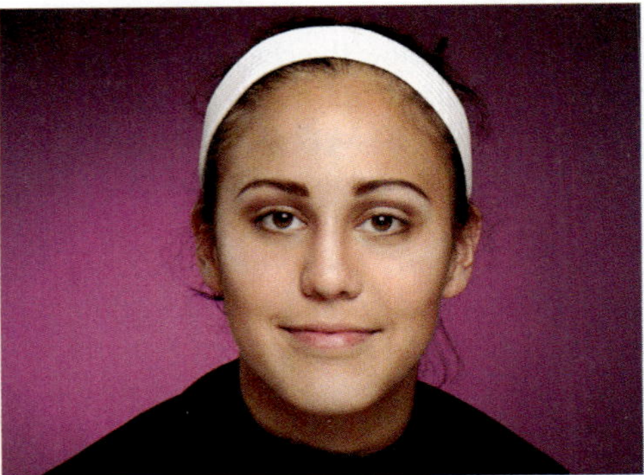

Eyeliner and mascara are added to bring out the eyes.

Notes

Give students information about how the application of makeup differs depending on how close the actors are to the audience. While all actors will probably wear some kind of foundation, rouge, lipstick, and eye shadow to highlight their facial structure, the amounts will vary depending on the size of the stage.

Small Stage
Less makeup is used in general

Lighter colors for the cheeks and lips

Soft, light eye shadow

Medium Stage
More makeup in stronger colors

Highlights on the nose

Shading along the jowls

Large Stage
Same as above, but added highlights just below the brow

False eyelashes are optional

ACTivity Divide the students into small groups and let them practice applying the foundation, shadows, and highlights used for straight makeup. This will be more of a challenge for the boys, so try to pair boys with at least two girls.

ACTivity Have the students research makeup styles from past decades. What was the predominant makeup look for women in the 1920s? What did makeup look like in the 1950s? What was the most prevalent color used for eye shadow in the 1960s? How would the students describe the "punk" look from the 1970s and 80s? What is the style of makeup now?

ACTivity Have students continue applying straight makeup to themselves. They should accent the eyebrows, apply rouge, accent the lips, and then dust the face with powder.

Once the students have completed their makeup applications, ask them to assess their work. Is everyone pleased with the results? If there are any students who felt out of their depth during this process, let them know that practice will improve the results dramatically.

ACTivity Ask students to bring in photos and works of art that they feel contain people with interesting facial structures. Using these pictures as a base, ask students to create a three-dimensional head from clay. The students can either make the head in the shape of a mask so that it can be hung on the wall, or they can create a "bust" type head to sit on a shelf. This activity will help the students become familiar with the human face and head. This is a good tool to help the students in their study of shapes, shadows, and contours.

Very basic sculpting lessons can be found at *www.kinderart.com*, and there are books available such as *Sculpting in Clay with Dale Power* available at *www.schifferbooks.com.*

(by the nose) and follow close to the lashes, extending the line about 1/4 inch beyond the outside corner. The bottom is the most important. On the lower lids, start the line at the outside and fade the line off at the middle of the eye. Do not go all around the edge. Apply one or two coats of brown mascara to all the upper lashes and to the outer portion of the lower lashes.

6 **Accent the eyebrows.** If necessary, darken your eyebrows to make them more visible. Using a medium or dark brown pencil, apply short, feathery lines drawn in the normal direction eyebrow hairs grow. Eyebrows should extend 1/4 to 1/2 of an inch beyond the eye to frame it properly. The heaviest color should be near the center, with the brows tapering at the outer end. Keep the effect soft and natural looking.

7 **Apply rouge.** Use rouge sparingly; a little goes a long way. Using your finger, dot the rouge in a crescent shape just below the cheekbone. Blend to soften all edges. The color should be strongest just below the cheekbone and should grow weaker as it moves away until it blends unnoticed into the base. There should not be a sharp delineation. For a healthy glow, males should carry rouge farther into the temples than females do, and farther down the jaw.

8 **Accent the lips.** Females should use lipstick made for stage use in a shade that matches their rouge. For a clean line, apply lipstick with a personal lipstick brush. To make lips smaller, draw the new shape using red lip-liner pencil. Then apply foundation and powder over the part of the lip you are eliminating. Men can either softly outline their lips with a brown pencil or apply a brownish-red moist rouge that they then gently wipe off, leaving only a suggestion of color.

9 **Apply the finish.** Use a powder puff to apply a thin dusting of translucent powder over the face. Remove excess powder with a powder brush. If necessary, touch up your cheeks and eyelashes.

Quotable

For an actress to be a success, she must have the face of a Venus, the brains of a Minerva, the grace of Terpsichore, the memory of [historian Thomas] Macaulay, the figure of Juno, and the hide of a rhinoceros.

Ethel Barrymore, Actor

Only amateurs appear outside the theatre in stage makeup. As soon as the play is over and curtain calls are complete, remove creme makeup with cold cream and facial tissue followed by soap and water.

Applying Character Makeup

The techniques for applying character makeup are more complex and time-consuming that those for straight make-up. Following are suggestions for the most common character makeup effects.

The Eyes and Brows With the use of shadows and liners, you can make the eyes appear larger, often indicating eagerness, innocence, or exuberance. You can make eyes appear sunken for an evil or threatening look. Eyebrows, as a natural frame to the eye, can do a lot to establish character. Changing the position or size of the eyebrows will create a character. To change the shape, you must first mask out all or part of your own brow. Block out and highlight your natural brows with foundation, or rub them with a cake of very wet soap. When they are dry, apply foundation over them and draw new brows in the desired position and shape. **Crepe hair,** artificial hair made of wool, can be added to make the brows bushier. The sketches at the right indicate a few of the eyebrows you can create.

Common Character Eyebrows

Normal

Sad/Pathetic

Evil

Surprised/Innocent

Mischievous

Backstage Gossip: He Knows the Nose

Actor Hal Holbrook, in his brilliant recreation of Mark Twain, is as meticulous in his makeup as in his acting. No detail is too small or too unimportant to be given careful attention each time the makeup is applied. And for every performance he devotes more than three hours to perfecting those details . . . . Mr. Holbrook says . . . . "His nose was very distinctive . . . the nose alone takes an hour . . . ."

from *Stage Makeup* by Richard Corson

Applying Character Makeup

The Eyes and Brows
With the students, discuss all the character eyebrows on this page. Ask students to try to replicate these looks by manipulating their brow area. Then discuss how much more impact actually creating these eyebrows would have when playing a character with each of these characteristics.

Discuss familiar characters from plays the students have read and assign eyebrows to these characters. Examples might be:

- Puck= Mischievous
- Hamlet = Sad/Pathetic or Normal
- Iago = Evil
- Ophelia = Surprised/Innocent or Sad/Pathetic

ACTivity Have students work in pairs to create a character for one another using basic makeup and character eyebrows. They may also choose to add costume elements to create their character's look. When they are in character, the rest of the class must guess who they are.

ACTivity Divide the class into partners. Each student will take a turn as model and as artist. One student will sit in profile against the wall on which you have taped a large piece of white paper. Shine a bright light at the student so that the student's shadow is cast upon the paper. The other student will now trace the model's shadow on the paper to make a silhouette. Be sure all of the students are at about the same distance from the paper so that all the shadows will be about the same size. Hang these silhouettes on your classroom wall. Ask the students why shadow and light are important in stage makeup. Does the brightness of the light and its distance from the student affect the picture that is cast on the wall? How?

The Nose, Mouth, and Hair
Discuss the various ways that the size of a nose and mouth can be changed and the materials used to help the makeup artist do so. Talk about what clues someone's hairstyle might give about that person. What era would you assume a woman with "big hair" piled high, teased, and sprayed might be representing in a play?

Show Don't Tell Show the film *Roxanne*, starring Steve Martin. Then read the "nose" soliloquy from Edmund Rostand's *Cyrano de Bergerac*. Compare these same two scenes in the film and the play. Finally, discuss the makeup used on Steve Martin in the film to create his character's nose.

ACTivity Brainstorm with the students to make a list of all the types of noses: such as pug nose, crooked nose, witch's nose, Jimmy Durante's nose, etc. Make a "nose" art gallery for your classroom. Have the students cut noses from magazines or have the students draw pictures of different noses. Make captions for the nose gallery from various plays. Let the students find all the lines from Shakespeare that have to do with smell, or noses, such as:

"A rose by any other name would smell as sweet." *Romeo and Juliet*

"I smell sweet savours ...." *Taming of the Shrew*

"...and will as tenderly be led by the nose." *Othello*

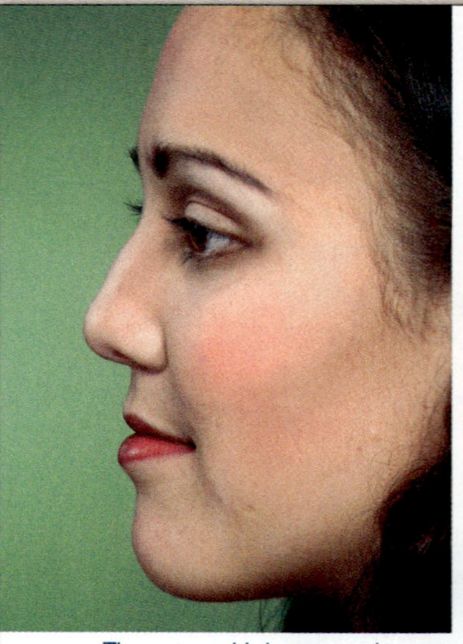
The actor with her natural nose.

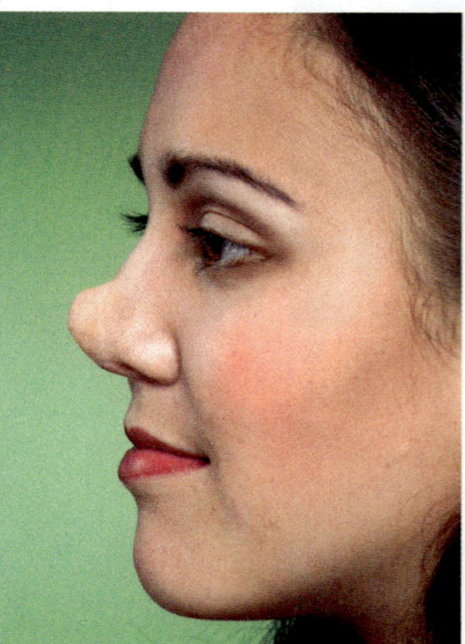
The same actor with an upturned, puckish nose.

The Nose and Mouth
You can vary nose proportions with shadow and highlighting, or you can create a three-dimensional change such as a large, upturned, or misshapen nose with **putty wax** (also called derma wax or nose putty). Prepare the putty by gently kneading it with your fingers until it is soft and pliable. Next apply **spirit gum** adhesive to a clean area of the nose. Embed a few fibers from a cotton ball into the spirit gum to create a "rug" to hold the wax onto your nose. Form the wax into the desired shape using the back of your thumb and place it over the dried spirit gum rug, molding it to the shape of your nose. Smooth out the edges until they blend into the face, and cover the wax with makeup as needed. This may take a bit of practice. Use hair gel to smooth the overall surface. To remove the nose, pull a thread tight and run it along the area under the wax.

You can alter the size of the mouth and change its expression by painting the corners up to suggest happiness or painting them down to indicate sadness, pain, or meanness.

Hair Hair can be slickly combed, messy, or elaborately coiffed as an indication of the character's personality. Women can make their hair look longer by using hairpieces or extensions. Men should get an appropriate haircut three to four weeks before performance and then let their hair grow until after the show. Sprays, gels, and pastes can be used to "mold" the hair into the desired style. To change hair color, use temporary tints found in drugstores. For gray, use a liquid hair whitener. A bald head is achieved with the use of a rubber skullcap. Since wigs are expensive to rent and difficult to fit, avoid them if possible.

Beards and Mustaches Before you apply a beard, observe men who have them. You will notice that facial hair has certain boundaries and that it grows forward under the chin and downward at the sides. It is thinner where the growth starts and becomes thicker farther down on the face. If your character hasn't shaved in a few days, create a stubble effect by **stippling,** or dabbing the face with gray-blue makeup.

Backstage Gossip: Something's Fishy

[Orson] Welles always wore a false nose when he was working on stage, largely because he hated his own and in one performance of *Moby Dick*, while Ahab was delivering one of his big speeches, the nose began to fall apart. "Tell him his nose is falling off," hissed one actor to another. It was too late. The nose had beaten them to it and was already slipping down over Welles's mouth. As the great actor screamed, "Get that white whale, men!" the nose dropped off completely, landed at his feet, and was sent curling into the audience with a deft drop-kick.

from *Theatrical Anecdotes* by Peter Hay

Here's How
To "Grow" Beards and Moustaches

To prepare crepe hair for your beard, unbraid the amount and colors you'll need. To straighten the kinks, dampen the hair, put it between two pieces of muslin or other light cloth, and press it with an iron. Since beards are rarely one solid color, combine the colors needed and then comb the pressed hair.

When applying beards:

1. Be sure the face is shaved and the part to be covered is free of foundation.
2. Define the bearded area by applying spirit gum. If you want to use the beard again, apply 2 layers of liquid latex as a base.
3. Hold a small piece of crepe hair in your hand and cut the ends on an angle. Do not use too thick a piece of hair, but have it longer than the desired finished length.
4. Paint a second coat of adhesive just above the larynx and apply a layer of hair, sticking it out toward the front. Hold until it is dry.
5. In this same manner, cut the hair, apply the adhesive, and work up in layers–like shingles on a roof–until the front of the chin is covered with hair pointing down. Continue until you reach the desired shape.
6. When completed, let spirit gum get completely dry, then gently comb out any loose hairs. Shape it into the desired style, and do a final trim. A light coat of hairspray will help it hold its shape.
7. At the top of each beard, you may need to pencil in hairs to blend the beard's edge so that it looks natural.

To create a mustache, complete steps 1–3 above. Then apply the hair at the outer corner of the lip. Work in several layers toward the center. Follow the lip line. Hold each layer in place until dry. Comb and trim.

1. Cover under the chin, pointing the hair out.

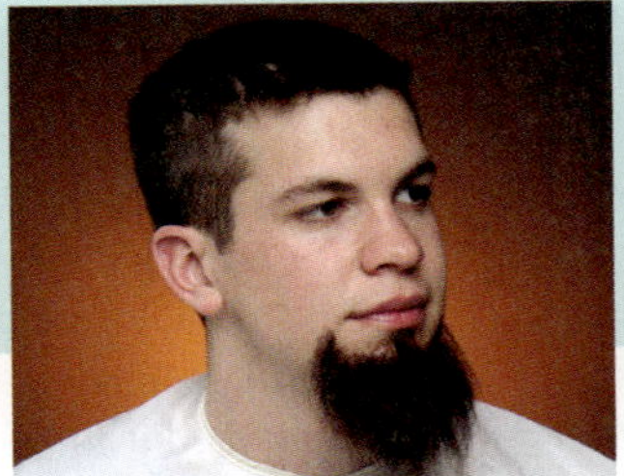

2. Add more crepe hair and cover the chin, pointing the hair down.

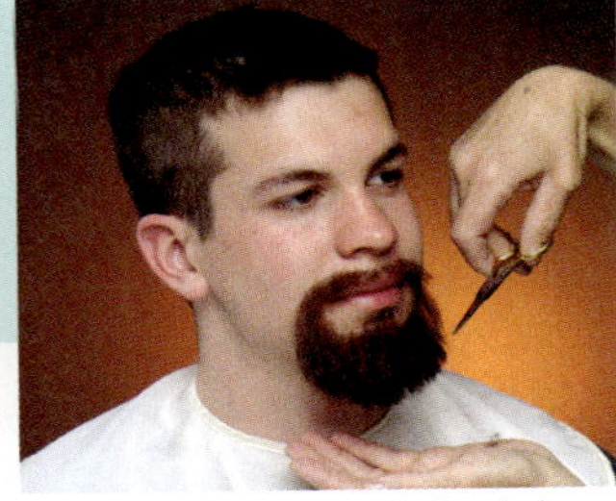

3. Cover the sides, pointing hair down, and trim to shape the beard.

Notes

Here's How

Show, Don't Tell Use one of your male students as a model and show the class how you would go about building a beard. Talk about where you buy crepe hair and let them feel it before you press it. Show them how to blend colors to match your model's hair color, and then proceed to layer and trim the beard.

Have *www.anniescostumes.com* available on the class computer or give the address to the students so that they might see the images of different types of mustaches found on the site. In addition, bring in images of famous men who wore mustaches, such as Charlie Chaplin, Wyatt Earp, Theodore Roosevelt, and Fu Man Chu. Let the students study the distinctive characteristics of each. Then pass out the crepe hair.

ACTivity Pair up students, one male and one female or two males, and give them enough crepe hair to make a mustache. Ask them to research the kind of mustache they would like to create. Have them follow steps 1 through 3 to create their mustache and encourage them to experiment. If time permits, let each of the males in a two-man pair try this activity.

Scars, Missing Teeth, and Stage Blood

Give students a chance to experiment with scars, missing teeth, and stage blood by supplying the necessary ingredients. When students have created a character using one of these elements, ask them to present a short scene involving this character (perhaps joining up with other students to create an ensemble presentation).

Aging a Face

ACTivity Have the students bring in pictures of themselves as well as pictures of the women or men (based on the gender of the student) in their families. Suggestions for a female: your mother at different ages in her life, your grandmother, your mother's sisters, you as a child, you now. Students should then compare and contrast the photos to see how the aging process works on the members of their family. Talk to your mother, father, or other family members about how they have perceived their own aging process. What does age do to skin tone and coloring? Based on your research, what might you look like when you get older?

Scars To make a fresh scar, build up the center of the scar in an irregular shape with putty wax or tissue and liquid latex. If a healed scar is desired, apply three to four coats of nonflexible, or rigid, **collodion,** a clear, thick liquid, directly to the skin, drying between each coat. Collodion will give a drawn, indented look. Collodion can irritate the skin, so be very careful and try a small test patch first. Remove collodion with **acetone,** which can be found in common nail polish remover. Follow the cleaning by applying skin moisturizer.

Missing Teeth To make teeth look like they are missing or broken, use black tooth enamel or black wax directly over the teeth.

Stage Blood Below is the standard recipe for stage blood:

Recipe for Gore

One 16-oz. bottle of corn syrup
One tablespoon red food coloring
1/4 cup liquid laundry detergent
Blue food coloring

- Mix first three ingredients in a jar.
- Add blue food coloring, one drop at a time, to achieve the desired color.
- Shake well before using.
- Keep jar shut tightly between uses.

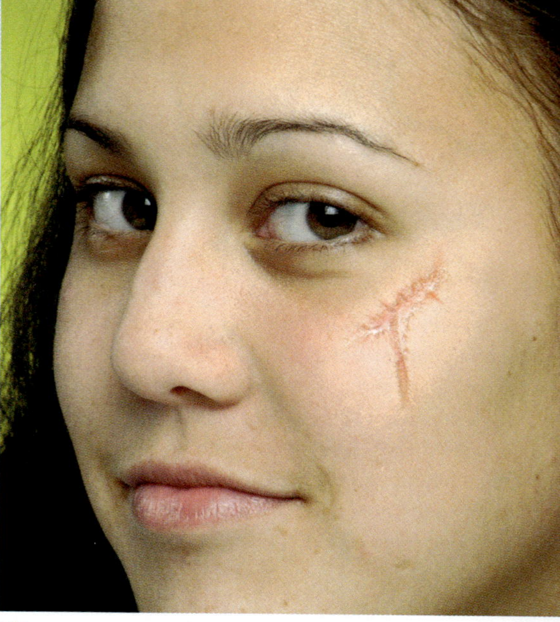

This scar was created using nonflexible collodion.

Aging a Face

As people age, the flesh sags around the bone structure. Wrinkles form, the texture of the skin changes, and the contours of the face shift and sag. All of these features can be reproduced on young actors through sculpting in the contours that begin to form using highlights and shadows.

Remember that age occurs gradually. When applying makeup, you must guard against making yourself look older than your character actually is. If you are playing someone who is forty or so, you will need different makeup than playing someone who is over sixty. To look in your forties, apply darker rouge lower down on the cheeks to indicate the beginning of sagging facial muscles.

Backstage Gossip: Is There a Dentist in the House?

[Actor] Richard Dennis, who was appearing in *Murder by Murder,* had a small pouch of stage blood secreted in his mouth so that when he was punched at the end of Act II, a trickle of blood could dribble down his chin. Unfortunately, the pouch burst at the beginning of Act II and he had to stay on the stage for forty minutes constantly apologizing to the other characters for his relentlessly bleeding gums.

from *Great Theatrical Disasters* by Gyles Brandreth

Shadow softly in the eyebag area. Begin a soft shadow in the crease that runs from your nostrils toward your mouth (the smile line). Use less lipstick if you are a female and brown liner if you are a male.

To appear in your fifties or sixties, increase the darkness of the sculpted shadows under the eyes and smile lines, follow this by adding wrinkles, which should accent the natural lines on your face. Frown and then smile, or make a characteristic expression, and then outline the natural wrinkles that appear with liner. Break up the texture of your skin by stippling the surface slightly by using a sponge and a darker base color.

Eye pouches should be more pronounced the older the character. Indicate facial hollows and sags with brown shading, and subtly highlight them with white.

Emphasize wrinkles in the forehead, around the eyes, and from the nose to the mouth. Gray the hair at the temples, and add a few gray streaks elsewhere for more aging. Apply gray to eyebrows also.

Spotlight on

The Makeup Morgue

A **makeup morgue** is a visual reference tool for creating special makeups. To create one for yourself, page through magazines and cut out any interesting faces you find. Glue each picture to a blank page, and label it with a designation that tells how you might use it, i.e. as an example of age, gender, race, skin texture, eyebrows, mouth, and so forth.

After you have gathered enough images, organize them by category and put them in a binder or accordion file. As it continues to grow, your makeup morgue will become a rich resource for future makeups.

ACTivity Have the students use makeup to practice three different designs for aging mouths, cheekbones, and chins. Have them begin with a 50-year-old person, progress to 60-year-old, and finish with someone who is 70 years old. Have them focus on adding contours to the cheeks, chin, and mouth to show advancing age.

Spotlight on

The Makeup Morgue Bring in samples of makeup morgues for students to look through. Get them started on creating their own morgues.

ACTivity Ask students to choose a favorite character from a play, book, or movie. Have students draw an image of the character as though this character were in a play, using all they know about applying makeup.

Quotable

Father Time is the make-up man responsible for the physical changes that determine the parts the average actor is to play.

Fred Allen, Comic Actor

Create a Very Old Face

Go through each of the steps for creating a very old face with the students. You might want to use a drawing of a face on the chalkboard to illustrate some of the techniques indicated.

ACTivity Give students the opportunity to try to age a partner by following the steps for aging a face on this and the following page. Be sure they use the partner's makeup kit. Be available to assist any students having trouble getting the right effect.

Show, Don't Tell Get a copy of *Mark Twain Tonight*, starring Hal Holbrook. (VHS and DVD available from *www.amazon.com*) Show selected scenes of Mr. Holbrook performing the role of Mark Twain. Mr. Holbrook was considerably younger than the character he played. Engage the students in a conversation about how they would play an old man or woman. How would makeup contribute to the aging process? What would they need to do with their bodies and voices?

Foundation and sculpting shadow is first applied to the face.

Highlights are added and blended.

Create a Very Old Face

1. Apply a pale creme foundation—lighter for a frail character and darker for a healthy character.
2. With the fingertips and a brown liner, add soft shadows to
   - **a** eye sockets
   - **b** indentations below the cheek bones
   - **c** hollows at each temple
   - **d** the sides of the nose
   - **e** the corners of the mouth
   - **f** under the jaw and chin
   - **g** the depressions on both sides of the throat
3. Using off-white liner for highlights above each shadow, apply soft highlights to the bone
   - **a** over each eyebrow
   - **b** in each cheek
   - **c** at the point of the chin
   - **d** along the line of the lower jaw
   - **e** at the throat
4. To further define wrinkles, use brown liner to create them where they naturally form
   - **a** on the forehead
   - **b** between the eyebrows and outer eye corners (worry lines and crow's feet)
   - **c** in the smile lines from the nose to the corners of the mouth
5. With off-white liner on a brush, highlight below all the wrinkles.
6. With the fingertips, blend the edges of the highlight, shadow, and base.
7. Thin the lips using a dark reddish color. Stipple rouge, and apply texture

Backstage Gossip: Makeup Maestro

Once during a matinee at the Haymarket Theatre, [actor Beerbohm] Tree, made up as Falstaff, met Coquelin in the wings. The great French actor was tremendously impressed by the way Tree had made up his features. "Pardon me," he said, "but how do you pad your cheeks?" Tree invited him to touch them. Coquelin did so and with a mild French oath exclaimed: "Why there is nothing!" Tree's effects were gained not by padding and such like devices, but simply by sheer skill as a grease-paint artist.

from *Theatrical Anecdotes* by Peter Hay

Lips are made thinner and hard edges are added around the eyes.

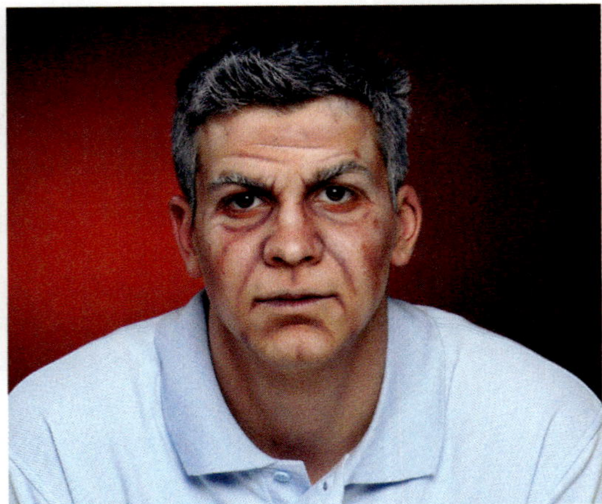

Deep wrinkles are added, hair is whitened, and liver spots can be added.

(i.e. liver spots) if desired. Allow a thin portion of the natural lip to show.

8 Whiten hair and eyebrows. Make eyebrows bushy by brushing them the wrong way. Apply whitener at temples as desired.

9 Powder creme makeup.

Makeup Essentials

Every student of acting should have his or her own makeup kit. This is not only more convenient but hygienic. Many actors outfit a fishing tackle box or toolbox. You should purchase a small makeup kit made for students. Theatrical makeup companies sell them inexpensively. Makeup can get expensive, however, so use only what is necessary, and always replace lids tightly.

On the following page are lists of the essential materials you will need for straight and character makeup.

Theatre Journal

Observe the facial characteristics and hairstyles of the people in a public place, such as a park, mall, or supermarket. Capture a few of these people in your journal by drawing their faces and writing short descriptions of their features.

Makeup Essentials

Continue discussing old-age makeup and then show students your own makeup kit. Talk about the items you consider essential, how to care for each product, where you find the items, and so on.

ACTivity In class, read some selections from T. S. Eliot's *Old Possum's Book of Practical Cats* to the students. Then ask them to design the makeup for several of the cats, such as Gus the Theatre Cat, Grizabella the Glamour Cat or Rum Tum Tugger, based on how they are described in the poems. Encourage students to see a production of Andrew Lloyd Webber's musical *Cats,* which is based on the book, onstage or on DVD or video. Compare the students' designs to the ones used in the musical.

Theatre Journal

Use the following as an additional or substitute prompt:

Observe several older people. Write your observations in your journal. Notice their movement, posture, and vocal patterns. Do older people move with ease or are their movements slower and less sure than a younger person? What words would you use to define the older person's posture? How do the vocal timber, strength, and volume differ from someone younger?

Quotable

The ideal makeup artist has the eye of the caricaturist, the hands of the sculptor, the brush of the portrait painter, and the curiosity of the student.

Greer Garson, Actor

List of Makeup Essentials
Look over the list of makeup essentials on this page with the students. Have them open their makeup kits and check to be sure they have all of the items listed—at least those for straight makeup. Let students know of stores you are aware of in town that sell any of these items at reasonable prices.

ACTivity Take your students to a play that you know incorporates a lot of makeup technique at a community or professional theatre. Tell students to pay particular attention to the actors' makeup. Then, back in the classroom, have them describe the use of makeup in the show. Did the makeup characterize the roles? Did it help the audience understand the occupation, age, lifestyle, or social status of each character? Why or why not? Was most of the makeup straight makeup or was character makeup used also? Were the makeup choices effective for the production?

ACTivity Schedule a "wacky hands" day in your class. Ask the students to design a weird and wacky makeup application only for use on their hands. The design can compliment their old-age makeup project by designing old-age hand-makeup to go with their faces. Or they can be wild and crazy and design the hands for any fantasy creature they desire. Celebrate their creativity with a "finger foods party." Have everyone wear their weird hand-makeup and bring a food item to contribute to the party.

The Essentials for Straight Makeup

1. **Foundation** in creme or cake. Include white, light, and medium shades.
2. **Liners (highlight** and **shading colors)** give the face a three-dimensional effect by providing shadows and highlights. Basic liners are black, brown, maroon, yellow, off-white, and blue.
3. **Lipsticks** in shades of red for women and a brownish shade for men.
4. **Rouge** in red or medium-red for women; reddish-brown for men.
5. **Powder (and puffs)** sets creme so it won't smudge or create a glare under the lights. Choose a shade lighter than the foundation, or use a translucent powder you can apply over any foundation.
6. **Eyebrow pencils** to darken eyebrows and line eyes. Use either medium or dark brown.
7. **Fluff brushes** to apply dry rouge, powder, and eye shadow and to remove excess powder.
8. **Lining brushes** made of sable to line the eyes and to give the appearance of wrinkles and to paint the lips. A common size is 3/16-inch or 1/4-inch.
9. **Mascara** in dark brown.
10. **Cold cream** for removing makeup.
11. **Miscellaneous** sponges, hand mirror, thread, scissors, soap, comb, tissue, brush cleaner, cotton balls, and a pencil sharpener.

The Essentials for Character Makeup

1. **Putty wax** for making false noses, warts, scars, and so forth.
2. **Liquid latex** liquid rubber that can be used for building up facial features such as chins, jowls, noses, eye pouches, and scars and for attaching crepe hair.
3. **Nonflexible collodion** a clear, thick solution used on the skin to make scars.
4. **Crepe hair** for fashioning beards and mustaches. Choose several colors including gray and one that is close to your own color.
5. **Spirit gum** an adhesive for attaching hair, false noses, scars, and so on.
6. **Rubbing alcohol** to remove spirit gum and **acetone** to remove collodion.
7. **Hair whitener** liquid or spray.

Notes

292 Unit Five Technical Theatre

Makeup Hygiene

For the sake of safe hygiene it is strongly recommended that you have your own makeup kit and use only your own makeup. Be sure to have a good supply of:

- sponges
- powder puffs (or cotton balls)
- tissue
- soap or cleanser

Sponges should be thrown away after each use. Take a tissue and clean the surface of all makeup before using it. Although a liquid brush cleaner is available and is certainly effective, you may also clean your brushes in hot, soapy water. Clean them after every use. You may be tempted to borrow someone else's lipstick. This is not recommended, but if you are careful, you can use a cotton swab to remove a small amount of lipstick from another's tube (after wiping the area with a tissue first). Apply a small dab of the lipstick from the swab to your own lip brush.

Also be aware that you should never take makeup directly from containers with your fingers. Instead, squeeze a bit of makeup onto a paper towel or use a small spatula to remove a bit of makeup from jars, pots, sticks, or tubes. Always keep the lids securely closed. Wash your hands well with soap and water before applying your makeup.

Makeup Hygiene

Read over this section with the students to impress upon them the importance of good hygiene in drama class. Discourage sharing of any makeup. Demonstrate for them how to use a spatula for lipstick, rouge, and so on, and show them the correct way to use foundation and powder. Also be sure to alert students that they should do a patch test on the inside of the arm 24 hours before using any new product on the face.

Share the following rules with the students. You might also want to make a copy and post it in the dressing rooms.

Dressing Room Do's and Don'ts

- No food or drink in the dressing room. Water is allowed in a closed container.
- Never borrow and never share makeup.
- Go outside to use hairspray or other aerosol sprays. Do not wear perfume. Some people are allergic to strong odors–aerosol sprays can be very irritating.
- Pay attention to your own personal hygiene. Bathe every day and use a deodorant. Dressing rooms are close quarters, and running from scene to scene can make the room seem even smaller if others haven't showered.

Backstage Gossip: The Bright Blue Tin Man

Why did Jack Haley replace Buddy Ebsen as the Tin Man during the production of the film classic *The Wizard of Oz?* Because the aluminum dust in Ebsen's makeup turned him bright blue and sent him to the hospital with respiratory problems.

Always Adjust Makeup to Lighting

Bring in a large color wheel (or use the one on page 225) and discuss it with students. Tell them that a color wheel is arranged so that primary colors (red, yellow, or blue) are separated by the secondary colors (orange, violet, and green—and for the purposes of lighting, pink). Primary colors cannot be mixed from other elements, but two primaries can be mixed to obtain a secondary color.

Complimentary colors are color opposites. These colors contrast with one another. They also help to make one another more active. In a color wheel, complimentary colors are opposite one another. So, green and red are compliments, blue and orange are compliments, and violet and yellow are compliments.

ACTivity Give students gel swatches and a strong light source (such as a spotlight). Have a volunteer who has been made up in either straight or character makeup position his or her face under the light. Have students experiment with the effect on the face and makeup of different color gels. Do pink lipstick and rouge look better under the red gel? Does rouge need to be heavier under a strong amber gel? What does a green gel do to a person's face? Have students keep notes and report their findings to the class.

ACTivity For a library of ideas to use for nonrealistic makeup, have students cut out pictures of insects, flowers, animals, trees, birds, snakes, spiders, and other interesting plants or animals. They can keep these pictures in their makeup morgue for inspiration when they must devise fantasy makeup.

The illustration above shows the effect of various colored lights on a color wheel.

Always Adjust Makeup to Lighting

Colored lights dim similar colors on stage and completely darken **complementary colors** (those colors opposite each other on the color wheel). Use these techniques to adjust makeup to the existing lighting.

- A red light subdues red makeup and makes green look black. Consequently, if you have red lights on stage, you'll need to apply heavy pink base and a rouge with a blue tint.
- If you have strong amber stage lights, apply rouge heavily and use a pink base, since amber "eats up" red.
- With blue lights, the reds look purple or black, so for a blue moonlight scene use a light foundation and very little rouge.
- Since green light makes the face look ghastly, it is rarely used unless that effect is needed.

Backstage Gossip: Harry's Hoax

One day during the production of the film *Harry Potter and the Sorcerer's Stone,* Daniel Radcliffe, who played Harry Potter, arrived on the set with immense bruises all over his face. He explained that he had been in "a bit of a scuffle." According to Robbie Coltrane, who played Hagrid in the film, the makeup designer "had a minor heart attack . . . before she figured out it was a hoax."

294 Unit Five Technical Theatre

PREPARE

Apply Your Makeup

For your project, you will apply character makeup to yourself to achieve the look of an older or unusual character. You may prefer a character who is more animal than human, such as the creatures in Edward Albee's *Seascape*. Whichever character you choose, be sure to think about this character seriously before you begin experimenting with makeup. You will want to do a bit of research into the time period of the play and read closely any descriptions of the character in the script. Keep notes, and use this information as you create your character. Follow these steps to complete the project.

1. Create a character makeup sheet like the one below or use the Activity Sheet for this chapter, which your teacher will provide. Consider what colors you should use based on your own face, the play's time period and setting, the character you are portraying, the size of the performance space, and the lighting conditions.
2. Secure a makeup kit.
3. Prepare a desk or table at home by spreading papers over it and placing it near a light source. Lay out your makeup, including cold cream, facial tissues, and a large mirror. Wear a smock or old shirt to protect your clothes. Tie your hair back if necessary.
4. Use the step-by-step procedure for applying your makeup found on the previous pages. As you proceed, keep notes as to what you are doing and why. Then practice explaining your choices to the class within the five- to ten-minute framework.

Character Makeup Sheet

Name: ______________________ **Date:** ____________________

Character/Description

Materials	Color	Directions
foundation		
shadows		
highlights		
eyes		
rouge		
lips		
powder		

From the Field: Work from the Outside In

I am the kind of person who tends to work from the outside in. I like to think of the way a person looks, and how I'm going to fit into her walk and mannerisms. Then I start building the character's inner self within that framework.

Frances Sternhagen, Actor

PREPARE

Apply Your Makeup

Give students the Makeup Activity Sheet, page 89, as well as the Character Makeup form on page 146 of the Resource Binder. Before they begin to work on their makeup, go through the directions and your expectations step-by-step. Explain to the students that research and note-keeping are both an important part of this project. Be sure the students have an adequate supply of makeup to accomplish the goals of the design.

Remind the students to take pictures of their makeup designs and to keep them safely stored in their portfolio. A portfolio is not only a tool for college entrance; it is also a life-long souvenir of all the work done and all the new ideas learned in the field of theatre.

PRESENT

Discuss Your Makeup Choices

Keep a stop watch on hand to time the students. If they are getting close to the ten-minute limit, give them a warning in order to allow them time to reach the conclusion of their presentation without rushing the final sentences.

If time allows after students have presented their makeup artistry, ask them to share with the class how they arrived at their artistic choices for this character.

CRITIQUE

Evaluate a Classmate's Makeup and Presentation

Remind students that they must be as good an "audience" member as they are a "performer" or presenter. Class presentation has much in common with performing, and being an active listener in class is much like being in the audience at a show. Active listening requires good manners, quiet concentration, and reflection.

Go over with the students the questions they should be asking themselves as they critique fellow classmates. Remind them that they are not only evaluating how well the makeup was applied, but how appropriate this makeup is to the character.

PRESENT

Discuss Your Makeup Choices

When your name is called, walk throughout the classroom in such a way that all your classmates and your teacher can get a good look at your makeup. Continue to the front of the class. Describe the character you are representing. If you prefer not to come to class in makeup, videotape and edit the process of applying character makeup and show it to the class with live narration. Or you could bring in "before" and "after" photographs showing your makeup process. Be prepared to explain to the class how you achieved your character's look.

Whichever way you choose to present your final character makeup, be sure to use your notes and makeup worksheet or the Activity Sheet to talk about the considerations that went in to the makeup choices you made. Be sure your talk does not exceed ten minutes.

CRITIQUE

Evaluate a Classmate's Makeup and Presentation

Evaluate a classmate's makeup as well as the reasons behind the makeup, on a scale from 1 to 5, with 5 being "outstanding," and 1 being "needs much improvement." Ask yourself these questions:

- How effective is the actor's makeup when viewed fairly closely?
- Is the effect of the actor's makeup visible from a distance?
- In what ways does the makeup represent the character?
- What other choices could have been made to better bring out the character?
- How well did the presenter explain the reasons for applying the makeup in this way?

Write a paragraph that tells why you gave this classmate the rating you did.

Career Focus

Makeup Artist

Makeup artists are employed in professional theatres and for film and video productions, as well as in photo studios that do actors' headshots and commercial photo shoots. Many makeup artists begin as photographers' assistants. Others begin as cosmetologists or hair stylists, and then apply their skills in theatrical venues.

You can develop your own skills as a makeup artist with practice. Check out makeup books and videos and practice the techniques they offer. When you have gained some skill, try to replicate effects you see in still photos. Invite friends to come over in costumes, and apply makeup that matches their attire.

Jot down the steps you use to apply makeup and take photographs for reference. Attach the photos to the notes to create a personal makeup handbook.

Backstage Gossip: Palm Reader

One evening the great actress Sarah Berhardt was finishing her makeup for the role of Cleopatra when fellow actress Mrs. Pat Campbell entered the dressing room.

Sarah was absorbed for the moment and could spare little attention: she was painting her hands, staining the fingertips and palms with the dusky red of henna. Mrs. Campbell watched with some impatience . . . . "What you are doing will never show from the front. Nobody will see it."

"I shall see it," replied Sarah slowly. "I am doing it for myself. If I catch sight of my hand, it will be the hand of Cleopatra. That will help me."

from *Theatrical Anecdotes* by Peter Hay

Additional Projects

1 Demonstrate the application of putty wax to alter facial features such as the nose, ears, chin, or cheeks.

2 Report on special makeup techniques used in the movies and in television.

3 Create an "available materials" makeup. Choose any character you wish from fiction or real life. For makeup, use only the materials you have available at home other than actual makeup. Avoid anything that will stain the face, such as some food dyes. An example of available materials makeup is to create old age using white liquid glue as a base and potting soil as a beard. Or, an owl might be created with wheat paste and raw oatmeal on your face. Use your imagination.

4 Start your makeup morgue by collecting magazine pictures of various faces. Share your morgue with others in your class and discuss the ideas for makeup that you find there.

5 Research and explain how science and technological advances have impacted set, light, sound, makeup, and costume design and implementation for the theatre.

6 Working with a partner, create one of the following on each other:

   a A forty-year-old woman

   b An eighty-year-old man with a beard

   c a young rabbit

7 Choose a specialized character from Unit Eight, such as the old woman in *Driving Miss Daisy* or Sam in *The Janitor,* and describe how you would create the makeup for this person.

Chapter 22 Test

A chapter test is available in blackline master form in the Resource Binder on page 92.

For More Information

Books

Arnink, Donna J., *Creative Theatrical Makeup,* Prentice Hall, 1984.

Corson, Richard, *Stage Makeup, Eighth Edition,* Pearson Allyn & Bacon, 2000.

Power, Dale, *Sculpting in Clay with Dale Power,* Schiffer Publishing, 2000.

Thudium, Laura, *The Actor's Complete Step-By-Step Guide to Today's Techniques and Materials,* Back Stage Books, 1999.

Other Media

www.makeupbooks.com

www.stageandtheatremakeup.com

www.fun-shop.com

www.anytimecostumes.com

Insight Media 800-233-9910

Substitute Teacher Activities

Here are a few suggestions for one or more days when you will be out of the classroom:

- Assign the Makeup Activity Sheet on page 89 of the Resource Binder.
- Assign one or more of the Additional Projects on this page.
- Teach the appropriate sections of Part Five, Makeup, page 583 of the Student Handbook.
- **Design a Mask.** Provide construction paper, scissors, colored pens, glue, glitter, yarn, beads, ribbon, feathers, and so on for the students. The mask students design should reveal some aspect of their own personality. It can be affable, grumpy, proud, silly, and so on. Discuss with the students what visual clues might be needed to put these ideas into a three-dimensional object.

Theatre Then and Now

Kalidasa's Sakuntala

Kalidasa is known as the "Shakespeare of India," and his famous play *Sakuntala*, from the *Mahabharata*, is a story of grand proportions. It is known in the West chiefly through the *Bhagavad Gita*, the magnificent dialogue between Lord Krishna and the hero Arjuna.

The story of *Sakuntala* has all the passion, intrigue, and danger of any classic drama. While hunting one day, King Dushanta arrives at the home of Sakuntala. Struck by her beauty and kindness, Dushanta asks her to marry him. Sakuntala offers a condition that the king must promise to hand over his kingdom to a son born to them, and Dushanta agrees. They marry and are happy, but the king must return to the capital. Sakuntala later gives birth to a son named Sarvadamana.

Six years pass and Dushanta has not sent for his wife or son. Sakuntala journeys to Dushanta's residence, but he has no memory of her. Sakuntala is grief-stricken. Then a heavenly voice commands Dushanta, saying, "He is your son. Accept him." The king then remembers all that has passed and acknowledges his son, who later becomes renowned as Bharata.

Other Cultures, Other Times

Makeup is very important in Japanese Kabuki theatre. The style of makeup most associated with Kabuki is called *kumadori*. The actor applies a base coat of white for most characters. Then heavy, exaggerated lines and shadows are applied that emphasize the emotion and temperament of each character. Each emotion has its own color, for example, light blue indicates calmness, while deep red indicates anger and obstinacy.

For more on Kabuki, visit *www.lightbrigade.demon.co.uk*

Theatre Then and Now

The Actor's Face

The Face of Ancient Asia

Sanskrit drama as performed in India is probably the oldest existing classical theatre form in the world, having originated close to 2000 years ago. It is said to have come from the ancient custom of reciting poetry at social and religious gatherings. The *Natyasastra* by Bharatha Muni is the oldest text on theatre performance.

Acting in ancient India was an art that made great use of both costume and makeup. Actors were rigorously trained, adhering to strict dietary and exercise regimens. The characters they depicted included gods, kings, heroes, jesters, courtiers, and common folks. Everyone involved in the drama—actors, dancers, and musicians alike—were committed to presenting the audience with a luscious feast for the eyes and ears.

Kalidasa is generally agreed to be the greatest of Indian playwrights. He is thought to have lived between about 375 A.D. and 450 A.D. Three of his plays exist today, including *Sakuntala,* the story of a humble girl loved by King Dushanta. The couple must overcome the curse of a sage to find happiness in the final act.

Throughout India and Southeast Asia, the influence of the great Indian epics *Ramayan* and *Mahabharata,* whose stories appear in the form of dance and drama as well as puppet theatre, are still performed. In these dramatic dances, gods such as Shiva and Krishna are often integrated into the stories. The dances are very stylized and exuberant, with each dancer made up and dressed as befits the character.

The ancient theatre of India and Southeast Asia is still alive and well, and its face is as beautiful and colorful as ever.

Arunja, one of the characters in the *Mahabharata,* wears the green makeup typical of the heroes of Sanskrit drama. This performance was given in Kerela, India.

Quotable

Unlike classical masks and those of China and Japan, commedia *masks did not express any particular emotion like joy or sorrow. Instead, they gave a permanent expression to the characters, such as cunning or avarice.*

from *Theatre: A Way of Seeing* by Milly S. Barranger

298 Unit Five Technical Theatre

Actors in straight makeup in Rebecca Gilman's *Spinning into Butter.*

Contemporary Dramatic Faces
Of course, worldwide contemporary drama uses makeup in any number of ways. Makeup must reflect the intention and style of the play. In plays such as *Spinning into Butter* or *Proof,* the actors use straight makeup that reflects their characters' contemporary, day-to day situations.

Other plays, however, must approach the actor's face as a way to tell more of the story. In *A Streetcar Named Desire,* for example, while other characters in the play may wear straight makeup, Blanche often requires heavy applications of lipstick, mascara, and rouge to indicate a woman trying desperately to remain youthful and attractive. And Nobel Prize winner Wole Solinka's blend of Western experimental theatre and Nigerian folk tradition often requires special makeup. The Yoruba pageantry—"masks" and dances—must be depicted in an authentic, yet symbolic way.

Then there are the plays that pull out all the stops. The face becomes a canvas, a playground for the makeup designer, a way for the actor to reflect the theme of the play itself. In *Starlight Express* the actors become trains. In *Cats,* each actor is a very specific breed of cat, and each cat has his or her own personality as reflected in the costume and makeup. And, of course, the faces and bodies of the actors in *The Lion King* are converted not only into lions, but also into jackals, antelopes, and giraffes.

Using just some paint and putty, a bit of crepe hair, a few feathers, and perhaps a new hairdo and some glitter, an actor is transformed. In turn, the actor transforms the world on the stage.

In Wole Solinka's *The Road,* the masked character represents the spiritual level of the play.

Contemporary Dramatic Faces

Starlight Express
Starlight Express opened in March of 1984. In its long run at London's Apollo Victoria Theatre, 5,500 false eyelashes, 2,700 lipsticks, 14,000 cold creams, 12,755 eye shadows, 10,750 makeup pencils, and 4,800 powders have been used.

Blue Man Group
In an article for the *Courier-Journal,* Louisville, Kentucky, March 28, 2003, Thomas Nord interviewed Collin Hurd, a member of Blue Man Group. Nord describes the process of getting into the blue makeup that is the signature of the actors in the group.

Nord wrote:

"It takes two hours for Hurd to transform himself from an ordinary guy into a blue man. When he arrives at the theater, he uses a defoliating soap to scrub off any traces of last night's makeup, then dons a latex skullcap to cover his close-cropped hair. Because the cap covers his ears, Hurd plugs wireless monitors into them to ensure he can hear his musical cues. The cap is affixed with theater glue, which can be tricky stuff . . . . After a warm-up and sound check, the last step is applying the trademark blue makeup, which is, simply enough, gobs of cobalt blue greasepaint applied liberally to the face, head, and neck—even up into the nostrils, for full effect."

For more information on Blue Man Group, see page 53.

For More Information

Books

Brandon, James R., editor, *The Cambridge Guide to Asian Theatre*, Cambridge University Press, 1997.

Kalidasa, W. J. Johnson, editor, *The Recognition of Sakuntala: A Play in Seven Acts*, Oxford World's Classics, 2001.

Kehoe, Vincent J-R, *Special Make-Up Effects*, Focal Press, 1991.

Morawetz, Thomas, *Making Faces, Playing God: Identity and the Art of Transformational Makeup*, University of Texas Press, 2001.

Sartor, David, and John Pivovarnick, *Theatrical FX Makeup*, Heinemann, 2001.

Other Media

Lars Carlsson of Sweden offers a portfolio of very interesting makeup and mask techniques on his Web site: *www.makeup-fx.com.*

Tim Northon also has interesting masks, forms, and makeup on his site: *www.atomictimmy.com/3n.htm.*

Chapter 23

Props

This chapter introduces students to the methods of gathering or making props for a stage production. Students will learn methods of research and how to design, build, find, and borrow props, culminating in the creation of a prop plot.

Objectives

1. To learn the job of the prop master and prop crew
2. To analyze and research a play to determine appropriate props
3. To learn methods of building simple props
4. To develop a prop plot for a play

National Standards

Chapter 23 meets these National Theatre Standards:

Proficient 3a, 3b, 3c, 3d, 4a, 4b, 4c, 5a, 7a

Advanced 3g, 3h, 4d, 4e, 5b, 6e

Project Specs

Advanced Students
In addition to a prop plot for a play, the advanced student should document his or her research and bring examples of the props to include as a part of the presentation.

ESL and Special Needs Students
Students may need help organizing and keeping track of all the new vocabulary and information involved in creating a prop plot. You might want to team these students with those who are more knowledgeable.

On Your Feet

Bring several pairs of eye glasses to class. Have the students define a specific character type that would wear each pair of glasses. What type of character might be expected to wear a monocle? Glasses with bright red frames? Wire-rimmed "granny" glasses? How can character be defined by the props that are selected?

Chapter

23 Props

One of the final pieces of the production puzzle is the addition of properties—or props. The right props can provide the set with crucial details that help to bring the audience into the world of the play.

Project Specs

Project Description For this assignment, you will create a prop plot (a detailed list of props) for a full-length play and describe it in a three- to eight-minute presentation.

Purpose to understand the different kinds of props, how to acquire them, and their function in the play

Materials a prop plot for a play or the Props Activity Sheet your teacher provides

Theatre Terms

- decorative props
- hand props
- prop plot
- props master
- pull
- set dressing
- set props

On Your Feet

Look around the room and imagine that you are making a prop list for a play about this class. As your instructor calls on various people, each should name a prop that would be important to include, such as books, desks, or a chalkboard.

The Balcony, a play by Jean Genet, abounds in characters, costumes, and props.

Theatre Terms

decorative props details on stage, such as paintings, newspapers, or curtains; also called *set dressing*

hand props items used directly by the actors during the show, such as letters and telephones

prop plot a list of props needed for each scene

props master the person in charge of obtaining and organizing all of the props for a play

pull retrieve costumes or props from storage

set dressing anything onstage that adds to the visual representation, including actors

set props items used to create the set, such as furniture, carpets, and lighting fixtures

PREVIEW

Props and What They Do

Imagine the set for a play that takes place in a dining room. On the set there are shelves of china and knickknacks, potted plants, thick brocade drapes, a mirror, paintings, and a huge table set with silverware, dishes, and goblets. There are piles of food on the plates. There are place mats, a tablecloth, and napkins. Which of these items are considered props?

The answer is: all of them. A show's props include anything the actors handle onstage as well as any furniture, draperies, carpets, or paintings on the set. To obtain suitable props, a **props master** may borrow, build, buy, rent, or **pull** them. Pulled props are those you already own—you pull them from storage.

Furniture, carpets, and lighting fixtures—known as **set props**—work along with the other technical elements of the play to establish time period, place, income level of the characters, and so on. Details such as paintings, newspapers, and curtains, which make up the **decorative props** or **set dressing,** can tell an audience a lot about the characters that inhabit this environment. Then there are the **hand props**—items used directly by the actors during the show. These might include a letter, a manuscript, a gun, a telephone, and so on. Hand props can help establish a specific character—think of the elegant heroine gazing demurely out from behind her fan or the poverty-stricken young man who, despite hardship, can't bring himself to part with his father's gold watch.

PREVIEW

Props and What They Do

Discuss the purpose of props in a play. What do props do and why are they useful? Some suggested ideas for the discussion might be: How do props help define a time period? How can a prop tell the audience something about the social and economic status of the characters? In what way can a prop provide focus for a scene? How might a prop help to create a specific mood?

Show clips from films such as *You've Got Mail, Men in Black,* or *Father of the Bride*. Ask the students to discuss some of the props and what they represent for each of these films. Examples might be: shelf after shelf of books for *You've Got Mail,* the futuristic weapons and set pieces used in *Men in Black,* and the tents, tables, plates, glassware, silverware, and so on used in *Father of the Bride.* Discuss the fact that for stage productions props are equally important, though not usually as abundant. For example, a shelf or two painted to look as though it has books in it, with a few actual books scattered about would serve to suggest a bookstore like the one in *You've Got Mail.*

ACTivity Ask students to analyze a scene from one of the films above and list the props that were necessary to the scene. Then ask them to write the scene for the stage, indicating only the props that would enhance the scene's focus.

The following prompts can be used to exercise **critical viewing skills.**

- List three different props in the picture on this page. What is the purpose of each?
- How would you go about obtaining these three props for a production of this play at your school?

Resource Binder

- Props Activity Sheet, p. 93
- Make Your Own Props Worksheet, p. 94
- Critique Sheet: Props for a Play, p. 95
- Props Test, p. 96
- Prop Plot, p. 147
- Pull/Rent/Buy/Borrow/Build List: Properties, p. 148
- Lending Agreement, p. 149

To Have on Hand

- Paper, pencils, scissors
- Books that show historical scenes, various types of furniture, buildings, household items, etc.

Handbook Connections
page 584

Analyzing a Script for Props

Have on hand several scripts and several prop plots from shows you have worked on. Demonstrate ways of locating and determining what props are needed for each script. Show the students how props may be hidden in the dialogue and not just listed on the page. Discuss set props and hand props and how they function in a play

ACTivity Divide the class into small groups. Using a book like *An Illustrated Treasury of Fairy and Folk Tales,* edited by James Riordan or any other folktale source, assign the students a folktale from a culture different from their own. Examples include "The Demon of Stone Mountain" (Vietnam), "The Selkie Wife" (Scotland), "The Golden Goose" (Germany), "Children of the Wind" (Africa), or "Lotus Blossom" (China). Ask the students to research the culture in which the folktale was first told. Topics to research include climate, geography, religion, clothing, foods, ceremonies and festivals, music and dance, etc. Ask the students to use the research to draw the designs of three props to be used in performance of the folktale.

ACTivity Divide the class into groups of five. Select a short play for the students to read. Hold a production meeting, in which students can choose to be the director, costume designer, light designer, sound designer, or props master for this play. The students will then discuss their ideas for staging the play. What is the director's concept? In what time period and in what style will the play take place? What style of costumes, colors for the lights, and what props will be used? The students will need to work together to come to a consensus, based on the director's vision. The students will then write a short description of the play as they each see it on the stage.

The props used in this production of Noel Coward's *Private Lives* reflect the early 1930s.

Analyzing a Script for Props

You wouldn't use a boom box as a radio prop for a play set in 1930. If your play is set in 1970, the magazines on the coffee table, if they are visible to the audience, must be from 1970 (or at least appear to be so). Even if they are not visible, some props masters insist that the authenticity of the prop is mandatory if the actors are to believe in the setting. When it comes to props, even small oversights can take the audience (and the actors) right out of the play. So it's important that the props crew analyzes the script very carefully. If necessary, the props master must do research into the time period to make sure that once the props crew begins to build, borrow, buy, rent, or pull existing props, they have all the information they need to get just the right articles.

> **Be a Good Borrower!**
>
> Remember that props are used in each performance, and they can take a real beating. Check with the director and producer before borrowing anything to use onstage. Don't borrow any prop your school would be unwilling to pay to replace. Above all else, be sure to return items promptly and in good, clean condition.

Some published scripts feature a prop list that offers a breakdown of all the props needed for each scene. But if the play your school is producing doesn't have one, you will need to create your own **prop plot.** This will require that you go through each scene line by line, paying particular attention to the stage directions, and write a list of the props needed. You should code the items in terms of those already available at your school—those items you will pull. Your list should be specific. Rather than simply saying, "clock," describe the ideal clock ("contemporary clock radio with large digital numbers" or "metal alarm clock from the 1950s"). Once you have completed your prop plot, you can begin the gathering process. Note that the props crew must work closely with the set and lighting crews to make sure that furniture, rugs, and draperies don't clash with the walls, flooring, or lighting effects.

Gathering Props

If you don't have a necessary prop in storage, the easiest way to obtain it is to buy it. However, for reasons of budget and/or practicality, this is not always possible.

Large set pieces such as beds can be constructed by the set crew. Your

From the Field: Stripped of His Dignity

When I was in high school I was the prop master for the show *South Pacific.* The prop list given to me said "landing strip." It sounded militaristic to me so I went to the National Guard station, outside of town, and asked them if they had a landing strip. They responded with hilarious laughter. Needless to say, it would have helped to have done a little research first.

Robert Kallos, Technical Director, Atlanta, Georgia

school may already have some smaller furniture, such as tables and chairs, in stock. Assess the school's inventory carefully. Sometimes you can make an old lamp or piece of furniture look new or different with a new shade, a coat of paint, or other decoration.

Remember, it's the illusion that counts. The audience will be sitting out in the house, not onstage. From that distance, an inexpensive, shiny-finished fabric can simulate silk, a papier-mâché vase can become a priceless marble urn, and chunks of foam covered with painted canvas can look exactly like boulders.

Prop Plot

Name of Play What the World Needs Now

Characters Who Handle Props:

Lisa (Sally Klein)

Kent (Damon Warner)

	Scene Description	Properties Needed
ACT I	Living Room 1950s	TV, sofa, 2 chairs, book, coffee table, 2 water glasses, newspaper, an orange
Scene No. 1		TV—wooden floor model small screen Sofa—clean lines, wood trim 2 Chairs—wood, no arms Coffee table—glass top, metal legs with book on top
Scene No. 2		Same as No. 1 / Add orange, 2 water glasses (remove at end of scene)
Scene No. 3		Same as No. 2 / Add newspaper (remove at end of scene)
ACT II	Porch of same house 1950s	Porch swing wooden, old Shrubs
Scene No. 1		

Gathering Props

Discuss the prop plot with students and be sure they know how and when to use it. Tell them it is important that they are very familiar with the prop plot because they will soon be creating one.

As students begin to make their own prop plots, ask them to think about these questions:

- If the prop is a large item, how heavy or cumbersome is it?
- Will it have to be moved during the show?
- How many people will be needed to move the item?
- Do you have enough crew members?
- Can the prop be moved safely, quietly, and quickly?
- Can it be stored in a place that will not present a hazard to the actors or the crew?

ACTivity Advanced Students
Have students read a scene from *The Glass Menagerie* in which Laura looks at her glass animals. Then give them a supply of colorful origami paper and have them read *Practical Origami* by Rick Beech or *Paperart* by Michael G. Lafosse or look on Web sites such as *www.origami.com* to learn how to create origami animals. Have students read the scene using the paper props they have created. This activity should help students understand the importance of using their imaginations and creativity to build props.

ACTivity Beginning Students
Tell students they are producing a play called "My Room." They must list the most important props in the room and tell why they would be necessary.

Notes

Here's How

Another important aspect of being a props person is knowing what to do with your knowledge of props once you have gained it. Keeping a props scrapbook is just as important for the props master as keeping a makeup morgue is for the makeup designer. Props masters should collect images not only of the props they have created, borrowed, or rented, but of objects they might need to fabricate one day.

ACTivity Ask the students to begin to gather pictures of and articles about designs in architecture, nature, fashion, furnishings, weaponry, food products, automobiles, and so on. Have students share one that has meaning for them with the class.

Perishable Props

ACTivity Ask students to brainstorm other ways to create perishable props. Have groups of students try to create one or two of the suggestions to see if they are viable.

ACTivity Have the students experiment with papier mâché by making a small prop. For instance, they can make faux fruit, like an apple or an orange, from a balloon and papier mâché, or they can make a bowl from the bottom of a soda bottle and papier mâché. The recipe for papier mâché and some help in designing several different items can be found at *www.frugalcrafts.com*. How-to books are available at most craft stores.

Here's How
To Search for Props

A true props person is an imaginative scavenger who can see prop potential in things other people throw away. Here are some ideas for locating items on your prop list.

- Scour secondhand stores like the Salvation Army and Goodwill.
- Become a garage sale fanatic.
- Shop at outlets and discount stores.
- Borrow from family and friends.
- Check with other theatre groups in your area, such as other high schools, colleges, and community theatres.
- Skim through books on stagecraft to see what the stage crew could build.
- Send out a list of needed items to classmates and teachers.
- Broadcast your "most wanted" list over the school PA system.
- Get yourself an interview on school or local access radio or television shows.
- Post your list on bulletin boards in school, at supermarkets, and other public locations.
- Research prices at rental stores.
- Ask local shops if you can borrow their window dressing props.

Perishable Props

Plants and food are often found on prop lists. If possible, invest in plastic or silk plants that can be reused for other shows. Real plants tend to wilt under stage lights and need constant watering and tending.

Food can be faked if the actors aren't going to be eating it onstage. For example, the Christmas roast goose on the set's dining table may be built out of papier-mâché—as long as no one has to carve or eat it. But if the play calls for the actors to actually consume the food, then it must be prepared, stored, and disposed of properly so that it doesn't spoil or attract pests. The important thing to remember about stage food is that it only needs to *appear* to be real.

Imagine that your production calls for a character to come in eating French fries. Instead of cooking up a batch of fries for each performance, you might bring in a few pieces of toast cut into the long thin shape of fries. The audience will believe these are French fries if they are told that's what they are. And cut-up dry toast won't get the actor's fingers greasy!

Mashed potatoes are used to simulate ice cream on stage. It doesn't melt, so it can be stored backstage and brought on at the appropriate time.

304 Unit Five Technical Theatre

Quotable

A man who works with his hands is a laborer; a man who works with his hands and his brain is a craftsman; but a man who works with his hands and his brain and his heart is an artist.

Louis Nizer, Lawyer and Author

The fruit looks tasty in this scene from *Reflections*, but it is actually colorful plastic.

Avoid using salty foods as they may cause dry mouth or even choking. In a play that requires a character to drink alcohol, the liquid in the bottle may be tea to simulate whiskey and grape or cranberry juice to be red wine. The props crew should always check with the actors who will be eating the food to see if they are allergic to anything.

During Rehearsal and Production

The props crew's work is not complete when all props have been acquired. They are also responsible for managing the props during rehearsals and the show itself. Hand props, in particular, should be obtained as quickly as possible so that actors can become used to working with them. However, an actor should never be allowed to walk away backstage with these props in hand. They need to be available and accounted for at all times. Most props masters set up a prop table on both sides of the stage. The table is covered with plain paper and all props needed on that side of the stage are placed on the table. Outlining and labeling the items with black marker will help both actors and crew keep track of the items.

The props crew also has a job to do during the run of the show. These are the people that remove and replace props between scenes and acts. They must choreograph their work with that of the stage crew so scene changes can occur quickly and quietly.

During Rehearsal and Production

ACTivity Ask student to make an inventory of the props at your school. Discuss the best way to catalogue and store them. Are there some props that need repair? What might you need to add to your basic stock? Does the budget allow for the increase in the inventory?

Have students be aware of the following questions as they prepare the prop table for a show and check over the props they have gathered.

- Are the props sturdy and safe for the actors to use and the crew to handle?
- What will be done if something breaks during the show?
- Is this a prop that is so important to the show we might need to buy or build a second one just in case?

ACTivity Ask the students to research types of musical instruments from different cultures and time periods. Books such as *The Illustrated Encyclopedia of Musical Instruments* (published by Könemann, Belgium) may be helpful. The students might research drums from Africa, bells from China, tambourines from Turkey, and mandolins from Italy. Ask the music teacher from your school to come to your class to review the research and to bring some interesting historical musical instruments to share with your class. Brainstorm about musical instruments that might be used on stage in the plays of Molière, Chekhov, or Beckett.

Notes

PREPARE

Work on a Prop Plot and Talk

Read the scene with the students and discuss the stage directions. Practice finding props in scenes from a few other plays written in different eras. Demonstrate how you would list each prop in a scene using different colored chalk on the board:

- black for set props
- red for hand props
- blue for decorative props

As the students prepare their prop plots, ask them to verify the time period of the props they are selecting. The Web site *www.artslynx.org/theatre/props2.htm* might prove helpful in answering the following questions:

- Would you have a box of Kleenex on the stage of a play set in 1923?
- Could a bottle of ketchup appear in a play written in 1920?
- If the play takes place in 1935, can an electric carving knife be used?
- Would a ballpoint pen in be acceptable in a play of the 1940s?

ACTivity Have the students make an historical timeline of different props. How has the look of specific items changed throughout the years? Suggestions for the students to research might be phones, kitchen stoves, roller skates, washing machines, and radios.

PREPARE

Work on a Prop Plot and a Talk

Choose a play to use as the basis for a detailed prop plot. Read the complete play. Make a note of each prop you will need, scene by scene. For example, consider a stage direction such as this one:

(The morning sun streams in through the window. A breeze ruffles the curtains. Iris is asleep in the easy chair by the door. Clutched in her hand is a letter. Agnes enters with a can of aerosol room deodorizer. She sprays it all around the room. The noise wakes Iris, who quickly slips the letter into her pocket. Agnes snaps off the lamp on the small table next to Iris without speaking. She then moves to the portrait of their mother on the wall and straightens it ever so slightly.)

In just one stage direction, there are:

- four set props—the curtains, the easy chair, the lamp, and the small table
- two hand props—the letter and the can of aerosol room deodorizer prop
- one decorative prop—the portrait

These would all be listed on your prop plot. Try to be as specific as possible by providing a description of the props you see in your mind's eye. For example, is the lamp a reading lamp, a fancy glass lamp, or a fringed silk-shaded lamp? Decide and then write down that description.

When you have made your way through the play once, read it again and look for anything you may have missed. When you are sure you have recorded every prop, complete your prop plot.

Beginning with the first scene, list each prop. Use three different pens to color code your list. Use a black pen for set props, a red pen for hand props, and a blue pen for decorative props. When you get to scene two, make a new scene heading, and continue listing the props.

Set props need only be listed once as long as they are not removed from the stage at any time. The same is true for decorative props. But hand props should be listed each time they appear in a new scene. So you might have to list the same letter, book, or gun in every scene of the play.

Backstage Gossip: A Stone's Throw

Of all the props that fail to work properly on stage, firearms are the worst. During a presentation of an old American melodrama . . . one character challenges another to shoot him, and is obliged. But one night the pistol failed to fire. "Why don't you shoot?" the first actor ad-libbed, while the second pulled frantically at the trigger. "Shoot, damn it, shoot!" he urged again. No luck. Desperately, the second actor looked for another weapon and found it in a prop boulder, which he tugged from the ground and threw. The papier mâché rock looked as if it weighed half a ton, but it didn't. It struck the first actor on the shoulder, and then floated gracefully to the floor like a balloon as the curtain was quickly and mercifully pulled.

from *All Wrong on the Night* by Maurice Dolbier

Once you have completed your prop list, write a synopsis of the play. Then imagine that you are the props master for a production of this play. Think about what you would say in a meeting about the play's props. What special prop challenges does the play present? What will the props add to the play's mood and tone? Where will you begin your prop search process? Can you make some of the props? What will you need to buy? Prepare a three- to eight-minute talk about these elements. Rehearse your talk a few times, being sure that you do not go over the time limit.

Career Focus

Properties Master

If you have an eye for detail and you've always enjoyed a good treasure hunt, a career as a props master might be a good fit for you. Many who work in props say that the thrill of the hunt is an integral part of the job. Let's say you need a 19th-century grandfather clock . . . and you have to get it for twenty dollars or less. Maybe your show needs an ancient samurai sword . . . one that collapses. Where will you find such things? Can you rent or borrow them? Or will you have to make them? A props master looks at these dilemmas as a challenge.

As in other technical theatre fields, props masters and their crews are responsible for hundreds of small and large tasks before, during, and after every single performance. A good memory is one prerequisite. The ability to take detailed notes is another. A props master also needs good communication skills. After all, he or she must build strong relationships with prop rental houses, other theatres, and the rest of the production crew.

A career as a props master can begin with a theatre degree or with practical experience in community or professional theatre. To see if this work appeals, try working as a props assistant on a play at your school or in your community.

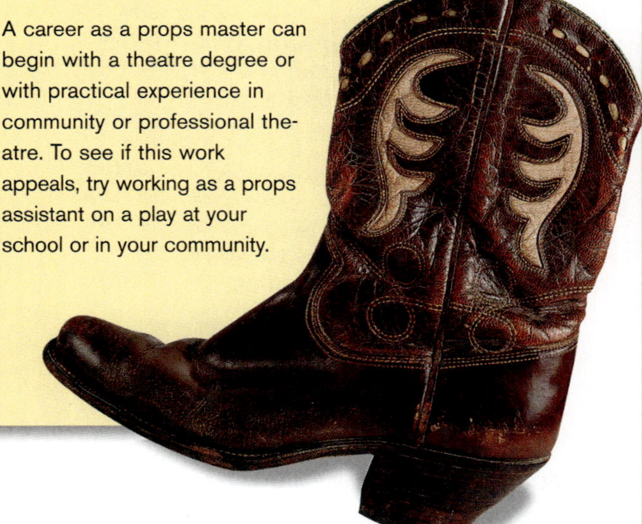

Notes

When students have completed their prop lists and written synopses of the play, go over their work with them using the play for reference. Be sure that the students can answer the important questions about special prop challenges, the play's mood and tone, and the search and creation of props.

Career Focus

Other jobs that a student interested in props might look into are industrial design, theme parks, themed restaurants, and retail widow displays.

PRESENT

Talk About Your Prop Plot

It might make the presentation more interesting if the students bring pictures or (if they are a manageable size) several of the actual props in to show to the class. The pictures could be displayed with an overhead projector or on computer through a PowerPoint® presentation.

Theatre Journal

Use the following as an additional or substitute prompt.

If you could only choose five props to decorate a set meant to be a classroom, what would they be? Write about the five props and why they would be important to the set.

CRITIQUE

Evaluate a Classmate's Prop Plot and Talk

Hand out the Critique Sheet for this project or have students use their own paper. You might also want to see that they have a sample of the Prop Plot handy for reference as they listen to each speaker.

After all the critiques have been turned in, ask pairs or groups of students to get together to compare and evaluate their critiques. Encourage students to be open to the ideas and suggestions of their classmates and, more importantly, to be willing to take an honest and critical look at their own work.

PRESENT

Talk About Your Prop Plot

When your name is called, hand your prop plot or Activity Sheet to your teacher and walk to the playing area.

Introduce the play and give a short synopsis. Then discuss the props you plan to use, how they relate to the play's mood, and how you plan to obtain them. (Which you will make, which you can pull or borrow, and which you will have to rent or buy.) When you have finished, thank your listeners, and return to your seat. Your instructor may wish to pass the prop plot around to your classmates.

Theatre Journal

Think of a recent conversation you had with a friend. If your conversation were a scene in a play, what props would be needed? To answer this, you need to think about where your conversation took place. Write down everything you can remember about the setting of your conversation. Then make a list of what props and set pieces the staging of your conversation would require.

CRITIQUE

Evaluate a Classmate's Prop Plot and Talk

Choose one classmate's presentation to evaluate. You will rate the presentation taking into consideration several aspects of the talk. Use a scale of 1 to 5, with 5 being "outstanding," 4 being "very good," 3 being "good," 2 being "needs some improvement," and 1 being "needs much improvement." Ask yourself the following questions as you critique your classmate's presentation.

- How informative was the synopsis of the play?
- To what degree did the presenter understand the prop needs of this play?
- Was the speaker's prop plot sufficiently thorough or did it need work?
- How realistic were the speaker's plans for making, renting, borrowing, or purchasing the items?
- In what ways might the speaker make or fabricate props that he or she intends to buy or rent?
- How well did the speaker impart the information?

Remember that to do the job well, a props person must be detail-oriented. Although the presentation's time limit is short, evaluate your classmate in terms of how efficiently he or she used the allotted time. Write a paragraph explaining why you gave the rating you did.

Backstage Gossip: The Stalking of Camille

An unexpected arrival from the wings brought a confusion to Lillie Langtry one evening when she was playing Camille. When she was onstage with her lover in the play, she noticed that the white camellia, which she was shortly to give him, was not in its usual place. She managed to sidle towards the wings and whisper "My camellia!" One of the stagehands responded instantly, and, without looking at what she had been given, Mrs. Langtry returned to her lover, saying, "Take this flower, Armand. It is rare, pale, senseless, cold—but sensitive as purity itself. Cherish it, and its beauty will excel the loveliest flower that grows, but wound it with a single touch and you shall never recall its bloom or wipe away the stain," with which she handed him a half-chewed stick of celery.

from *Theatrical Anecdotes* by Peter Hay

Additional Projects

1 Create a short pantomime on a specific theme using a few symbolic props.

2 Bring to class an object that you feel symbolizes your life. Share your feelings and perceptions of this "prop" with your classmates.

3 Create a prop portrait. You can do this by copying a photograph, enlarging it, and painting over it to make it appear completely painted. Build and decorate a frame for the portrait.

4 Experiment to create edible and inexpensive prop foods that look like the real thing. Share your results with your classmates.

5 Read the scene from *The Glass Menagerie* by Tennessee Williams found in Unit Eight. Create a prop list based on this scene. Which of these props might be symbolic or emblematic?

Chapter 23 Test

The test for this chapter is available in blackline master form in the Resource Binder on page 96.

For More Information

Books

Beech, Rich, *Practical Origami*, Hermes House, 2002.

Lafosse, Michael G., *Paperart*, Rockport Publishers, 1998.

McGraw, Sheila, *Papier Mache Today*, Annick Press, 1991.

Riordan, James, *An Illustrated Treasury of Fairy and Folk Tales*, Xs Books, 1987.

Rossol, Monona, *The Artist's Complete Health and Safety Guide, Third Edition,* Allworth Press, 2001.

Sweet, Harvey, *Scenery, Properties, and Lighting: Scenery and Props, Vol. 1,* Pearson Allyn and Bacon, 1994.

Thurston, James, *The Theatre Props Handbook,* Betterway Books, 1990.

Thurston, James, *The What, Where, When of Theatre Props,* Betterway Books, 1992.

Other Media

www.productionresource.com/theater/prop

www.paragonprops.com

www.frugalcrafts.com

Substitute Teacher Activities

- Assign the Make Your Own Props Worksheet, p. 94
- Discuss the information in the Student Handbook concerning Props on page 584.
- Assign one or more of the Additional Projects on this page.
- **Plan a Props Pantomime.** Divide the students into small groups. Decide on pantomime scenarios such as camping, cooking dinner, or getting ready for school. The students will discuss with their group the order in which the actions need to be performed. After the students have worked out their movements, they will choose one prop to use in the performance. This activity helps students understand how much "information" props convey to an audience.

Theatre Then and Now

Symbolic Props Across Time

The Chinese Theatre

In Chinese theatre, the Chinese property man was an important member of the company. He had thorough knowledge and an accurate understanding of all the plays in the company's repertoire. All property was brought in and removed in full view of the audience on the Chinese stage. The stagehands as well as the actors appeared on the stage during a performance.

The Elizabethan Stage

In the Elizabethan theatre, the work of the stagehand was done in part by the characters in the drama. For example, in the banquet scenes, the chairs, table, and food were brought in by the actors who played the servants.

Theatre Then and Now

Symbolic Props Across Time

14th Century Noh Drama

In the Japanese Noh drama of the 14th century, stage props were few—but those that were used were highly symbolic and crucial to the performance. Among these props, the fan was the most important. Because the drama was presented in a formal, aristocratic language that the average viewer could not understand, the actors used fans to accentuate or illustrate almost every gesture throughout the performance.

The fan was manipulated to illustrate anything from the rising sun to a long journey. A character might open a fan to simulate a vast mountain range when mountains were described on the stage. Shortly thereafter, a character might use a closed fan to simulate a boat's oar in water—thereby symbolizing the emotions of someone who feels emotionally adrift.

The scenery in Noh plays consisted entirely of impressionistic props that formed the outlines of buildings, coaches, boats, and just about any other important object in the play. The result was a spare staging with an emphasis on precision movements and the symbolism of important props.

A Noh actor uses a fan to convey meaning.

A Japanese fan

Quotable

Some people weave burlap into the fabric of our lives, and some weave gold thread. Both contribute to make the whole picture beautiful and unique.

Anonymous

A 20th-Century Reinterpretation
Hundreds of years later, in the 1940s and '50s, German playwright and director Bertolt Brecht became intrigued with Japanese theatrical forms. He also worked with the idea of sparse but symbolic props. His plays *The Caucasian Chalk Circle* and *The Good Woman of Setzuan* reflect his great interest in Asian theatre. Like practitioners of Noh and Kabuki, Brecht was not interested in presenting a "realistic" depiction of life.

In his study of Asian theatre, Brecht saw a way to use non-realistic sets and props to keep the audience in an intellectual state of mind. His goal was to keep the audience thinking about the characters' situations and the themes of the play. He accomplished this goal through a variety of means, among them masks and other symbolic items.

One of his favorite Asian-influenced prop tricks was to have the actors sling a board across two chairs to simulate a bridge. Brecht also favored having stage personnel bring on and take off props in full view of the audience. This technique comes from the Kabuki theatre practice of using a *kurogo* (man in black), who shifted props, costumes, and scenery, and even served occasionally as a prompter. Because the *kurogo* was not a character in the play, the audience was able to disregard him.

The chair simulates a speaker's platform in this scene from *The Caucasian Chalk Circle.*

Notes

Rooted Props
"We discovered...the modern trend to reduce the theatrical experience to essentials. Grotowski's "poor theatre" and Samuel Beckett's minimalist theatre are perhaps the most widely publicized examples of this trend today. However, in the American theatre, the trend has its roots in the 1938 Broadway production of Thornton Wilder's *Our Town*. Director Jed Harris took Wilder's straightforward play about recognizable townspeople in Grover's Corner, U.S.A., and placed the actors on a bare stage framed simply by the theatre's back wall. Virtually no scenery was used, costumes were muted, and hand properties were minimal . . . The actors told the story using only those properties, such as chairs and umbrellas, that they could move on and off stage for themselves."

Milly S. Barranger, from *Theatre: A Way of Seeing, Third Edition*

For More Information

Brecht, Bertolt, Hugh Rorrison, James Stern, Tania Stern, and W. H. Auden, translators, *The Caucasian Chalk Circle and Notes*, Methuen Publishing Ltd, 1984.

Holt, Michael, *Stage Design and Properties*, Phaidon Press,1988.

Hutt, Julia, and Helene Alexander, *Ogi: A History of the Japanese Fan*, Dauphin Publishing Ltd, 1992.

Konparu, Kunio, *Noh Theater: Principles and Perspectives*, Weatherhill Publishers, 1984.

Lee, Sang-Kyong, *East Asia and America: Encounters in Drama and Theatre*, Wild Peony Book Publishers, 2000.

Unit **Five** Review

PREVIEW

Examine the following key concepts previewed in Unit Five.

1 Draw a simple diagram of the three common stages.

2 Identify the following stage elements:

fly gallery	teaser	back wall	drop
batten	wings	trap	

3 The illustration at the right is a common set piece. What is it called, and how is it used?

4 Discuss the functions of stage lighting.

5 What are the important safety issues in lighting design?

6 List a few of the duties of the sound crew.

7 What does it mean to pull, rent, borrow, buy, or build?

8 Match the color below to the mood it evokes

danger	purple
restfulness	white
tragedy	green or blue
royalty	red
purity	black

9 What makeup product is used to create the appearance of a scar?

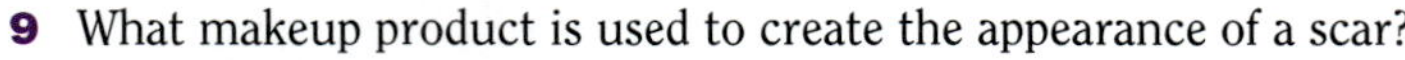

10 Why is a prop plot important?

PREPARE

Assess your response to the preparation process for projects in this unit.

11 In preparing your set design according to the ground plan, how did you keep all the elements in scale?

12 What difficulties did you encounter in working on your lighting plan?

13 What was the most inventive thing you did when preparing your sound effects for a scene?

14 In designing your costume for a character in a play, how did you determine the amout of detail to include?

PREVIEW

1 Students should draw simple sketches of a proscenium, thrust, and arena stage.

2 **fly gallery** narrow platform about halfway up the backstage side wall from which the lines for flying scenery are worked.

batten long pipes from which curtains, lights, or flats are hung.

teaser heavy curtains or canvas-covered wooden frame hung above the proscenium opening to adjust its opening.

wings the offstage area to the left and right of the stage.

back wall the area opposite the proscenium opening.

trap opening in the stage floor.

drop a canvas or muslin curtain that forms part of the scenery.

3 It is a *periaktoi,* or prism set. It is a set piece that can be moved or pivoted. Each of the three sides can be a different scenic element.

4 The functions of stage lighting are to provide visibility, create emphasis and mood, and to provide logical lighting sources.

5 A few possible answers: Wear gloves to protect your hands from heat; be sure your tools are safety clipped or tied to your belt; wear appropriate clothing and close-toed shoes; inspect each instrument for damage and repair as needed; know the wattage and type of each instrument to ensure proper connections.

6 A few duties of the sound crew include putting together a detailed list of sound cues needed for the show and finding the necessary sound effects or music; obtaining the rights to use music; setting up, checking, and maintaining all of the sound equipment; supplying accurate and timely sound effects and music during the performance.

7 **pull** taking the costume from storage.
rent renting a costume from a costume house.
borrow asking for the loan of a costume.
buy purchasing costumes.
build making your own costumes.

8

danger	red
restfulness	green or blue
tragedy	black
royalty	purple
purity	white

9 A scar is made with putty wax or tissue and liquid latex, or with nonflexible collodion applied directly to the skin.

10 A prop plot is important because it is the list of props needed in each scene in the play, identifying the name of the character that uses the prop, and the description of the location in the scene. The list identifies whether the prop is available at your school or must be borrowed, built, bought, or rented.

15 Did you make your presentation in full makeup or did you take photos or videotape the process? Why did you decide to do it this way?

PRESENT

Analyze the experience of presenting your work to the class.

16 Did your audience understand your intentions in creating the set design the way you did? Why or why not?

17 How did your lighting plot reflect the theme of the play?

18 Is there anything you would change about the costume designs that you presented?

19 Were you able to convince your audience that the makeup you created for your character captured his or her spirit?

CRITIQUE

Evaluate how you go about critiquing your work and the work of others.

20 How heavily do you stress originality when evaluating someone's creative efforts? Why?

21 Which do you feel is more important in a costume, that it conveys the time and place of the play or the personality of the character? Explain.

22 Do you think the audience responded better to makeup presented in person, on videotape, or in photographs? Why?

EXTENSIONS

- Gather together scraps of fabric and other items that you feel represent a character in a play of your choice. Discuss how you might use these elements to create a costume for the character.
- Think of ways you might create props for such perishable items as fruit, vegetables, bread, and a chocolate soda.

Resource Binder

Unit Five Test, p. 97

PREPARE

11 Students should indicate that they measured each element and used a standard scale, perhaps 1' = 1/4", in preparing their set design.

12 Answers will vary.

13 Answers will vary, but should illustrate a creative sound element.

14 Answers will vary; the use of detail is a subjective matter.

15 Answers and reasons will vary.

PRESENT

16 Most students should say that they were able to help the audience understand their design.

17 Most students should feel that their lighting plot enhanced the play's theme.

18 Answers will vary but some students may indicate they had ideas that were not fulfilled.

19 Answers will vary.

CRITIQUE

20 Students should indicate that originality is an important part of the creative effort.

21 Most students will answer that the personality of the character is the most important.

22 Most students will say that the audience responded better to makeup presented in person because it is real and more immediate.

EXTENSIONS

- Fabric used by students to represent a character and their ideas for building a costume should be well thought out.
- Creating fruit, vegetables, and so on from papier mâché, clay, plaster, Styrofoam, and even carved wood are viable options.

Unit Six

Theatre and Its Counterparts

Unit Six covers musical theatre and other theatrical forms, including performance art, multimedia, puppet theatre, and Readers Theatre. Chapters on film and television explore how stories and plays may be adapted to the screen. Finally, the elements of criticism are explored. Projects in this unit enable students to plan and write adaptations, present plans and proposals, perform, and review a performance.

Project Preview

Chapter 24 Musical Theatre
Creating and presenting a proposal for a musical

Chapter 25 Other Theatre Forms
Creating and performing a poem for a poetry slam

Chapter 26 Stage to Film
Adapting and directing a scene from a screenplay

Chapter 27 Movies
Planning and presenting an idea for a screenplay

Chapter 28 Television
Writing an outline for a television play

Chapter 29 Critique a Performance
Writing a review

Unit Six

Theatre and Its Counterparts

Quotable

After all, there have only been three forms of musical stage entertainment in the history of Western culture that in their day have been huge money-makers and also perfected art forms. These three are Italian grand opera, the Viennese operetta, and the American musical comedy. We can be proud that one of these belongs to us.

Deems Taylor, Opera Composer and Music Critic

315

Discussion Questions

The following questions are intended to tap into students' **prior knowledge** about the subject matter of the unit.

- Have you ever sung and/or danced on stage? Describe the experience.
- Describe a stage or screen musical you have seen. Did you feel elated or irritated when the characters burst into song?
- Have you seen a puppet performance since you were a young child? What did you think of it?
- Have you ever read a poem aloud? How does the experience of speaking or hearing a poem differ from the experience of reading it silently?
- Have you ever seen a film that was based on a book you had read? What was good or bad about the film version?
- Have you ever daydreamed of yourself as a movie star? What kind of films do you star in?
- What kind of television shows do you most enjoy? Describe one of your favorites.
- Have you ever argued with a friend over what was good or bad about a movie? How did you settle your disagreement (or didn't you)?

Theatre Journal

The person in the photograph is a street performer. Think about the character he is portraying and then write a short monologue for this character.

Visual Cue

British performance artist Wayne Scott imitates a stressed-out businessman on Las Ramblas Boulevard in Barcelona, Spain, in 2002. Use the following prompts to help students use **critical viewing skills** as they look at this photograph.

- How would you describe the way the performer is moving?
- How does the audience seem to be reacting?
- Does this man strike you as a "stressed-out businessman"? Why or why not?

ACTivity Have students take turns moving across the playing area in the character of a businessperson. Discuss the various interpretations.

Chapter 24

Musical Theatre

This chapter gives a brief history of musical theatre, describes the functions of various musical theatre personnel, and asks students to prepare and pitch a proposal for an original musical.

Objectives

1 to understand the elements of musical theatre

2 to analyze a potential musical idea in terms of viability, characters, setting, plot, and audience appeal

3 to create and develop characters and a plot of sufficient interest and importance to carry a musical

National Standards
Chapter 24 meets these National Theatre Standards:
Proficient 1a, 3e, 6b, 6c, 8c
Advanced 1b, 4b, 6f

Project Specs

As they follow the four steps on pages 324–325, students should consider how to make these elements support the one-story concept. That is, characters, setting, and plot elements should be of a consistent style, and the music should be consistent with these.

Suggest that certain stories imply certain treatments. That is, the simple cartoons on which *You're a Good Man, Charlie Brown* is based call for a small cast and simple staging, whereas the sprawling narrative of the novel *Les Misérables* demands a large cast and imposing staging.

Beginning Students
Writing a proposal for a musical may seem overwhelming. Suggest that students concentrate on a broad outline of a familiar story.

On Your Feet

As an alternative, have students write new lyrics for a familiar melody.

Chapter

24 Musical Theatre

When people say the word *Broadway* these days, they are usually referring to musical theatre. In the mid-20th century, **straight plays** (nonmusical comedies and dramas) were a major component of Broadway theatre, but today the big musical productions are the ones that typically bring the crowds.

Project Specs

Project Description For this assignment, you will create and present a five-minute proposal for a new musical.

Purpose to understand the elements of musical theatre

Materials written notes on the proposal or the Musical Theatre Activity Sheet provided by your teacher

Theatre Terms
choreographer
chorus
musical
musical comedy
music director
onstage director
pitch
principals
production numbers
straight plays

On Your Feet

With a classmate, create lyrics for a short song. Alternate lines so that each of you creates some of the lyrics. Then work together to come up with a simple tune that fits the rhythm, emotions, and style of the lyrics you co-wrote.

A scene from the popular musical *Camelot*.

Theatre Terms

choreographer the person responsible for designing a show's dance numbers

chorus a group of singers that provides backup vocals for principal performers

musical a dramatic production accompanied by song and dance

musical comedy a comedic drama featuring song and dance

music director the person who directs the actors, singers, and dancers in a musical

onstage director the director in a musical who directs the non-musical aspects of the play

pitch to try to convince a person or group to accept your proposal of an idea

principals actors in major roles

production numbers elaborate song-and-dance sequences in which most of the cast takes part

straight plays nonmusical plays

PREVIEW

The American Musical

The modern **musical** is a uniquely American art form. While other kinds of musical theatre, such as opera, have existed for centuries, plays set to music began in the 1920s, with the compositions of George Gershwin, Irving Berlin, and others. These musical craftsmen wrote popular songs that became the perfect accompaniment for the light plots of the comedies of the day. They were called **musical comedies,** appropriately enough. The shows typically featured a slight—even silly—story, plenty of tuneful melodies, and a chorus of leggy dancers.

In 1927, musicals took a dramatic turn. Jerome Kern's *Showboat* changed everything. First, it dealt with serious subject matter: racism, spousal abuse, and abandonment. Second, it did something that was revolutionary: It tied the songs into the plot of the play. Suddenly, songs were being used not just as background and distraction, but also as a way of actually *telling* the story. Another innovation occurred in 1943, when *Oklahoma,* the Richard Rogers and Oscar Hammerstein musical, opened to rave reviews. Some consider this the true beginning of the modern musical because every element—music, dialogue, dance, and plot—were seamlessly woven together to create a totally integrated production.

The gals sing and dance in a 1998 Lyceum Theatre production of *Oklahoma.*

Since then, musicals and musical comedies have been a favorite American theatre form. And the musical has gotten richer, more complex, and more dramatic than ever. Such award-winners as *Bye-Bye Birdie,* which

PREVIEW

The American Musical

Students may not be familiar with some of the musicals mentioned in this brief history. Find and display as many images as you can of these and other musical theatre productions showing a variety of set designs from simple to elaborate, costume designs from contemporary to fanciful, and stages from black-box to those with large, elaborate prosceniums.

Encourage students to talk about musicals they have seen on stage and in films. You might make the point that whereas a stage musical might show a scene in a stylized set piece in front of black curtains, a movie version of the same scene would almost certainly open up to a set with real-world exteriors.

Play recorded examples of different kinds of musical numbers from a variety of shows—such as the introspective solo, the love duet, and the company production number—and discuss how these songs contribute to the dramatic development of the plot.

Visual Cue

Lerner and Loewe's *Camelot,* based on T. H. White's novel *The Once and Future King,* ran from December of 1960 to January of 1963. The prompts below should help broaden students' **visual learning skills.**

- Which of these actors do you think is playing King Arthur and which is Guinevere?
- What do you think is happening in this scene?
- Which actor is the main focal point of the scene?

Resource Binder

- Musical Theatre Activity Sheet, p. 98
- From Book to Musical Worksheet, p. 99
- Critique Sheet: Pitch a Proposal for a Musical, p. 100
- Musical Theatre Test, p. 101
- Production Budget Form, p. 131

Handbook Connections
pages 555, 561-562

To Have on Hand

- Recorded clips of musical numbers for students to watch or listen to and discuss.
- Information on your school's dramatic facilities based on Here's How to Choose a Musical for Your School on page 326.
- Copies of George Bernard Shaw's *Pygmalion* and *My Fair Lady* (See For More Information on page 328.)

Share with your students the types of show songs below, identified by conductor, teacher, and author Lehman Engel.

- *Ballad* Characterized by tunefulness and a smooth quality, often speaking of love or introspection
- *Charm song* Characterized by steady rhythmic accompaniment and an optimistic feeling
- *Comedy song* Characterized by clever lyrics, often with punch lines designed to make the audience laugh out loud
- *Musical scene* Usually longer than the others and composed of several elements, characterized by a progression of emotions or a development of understanding

ACTivity Play a few minutes of music from a variety of different numbers in a wide range of popular musicals. Ask students to try to identify which of Engle's four types of show songs is being played.

Visual Cue

Ask students to look closely at this photograph from *Rent* then have them answer the questions below.

- Try to read the body language of three of the people in the photograph. What does it tell you?
- If they were singing a song, would the lyrics speak of hope and happiness or frustrations and despair?

incorporated rock and roll into the plot; *West Side Story,* a dramatic retelling of *Romeo and Juliet* set in New York with powerful songs and dances; *Hair,* all exuberance and counter-culture; the rollicking *Jesus Christ Superstar,* and others, reflected not only the musical interests but the social issues of America.

Today's musicals often feature complex staging with multiple sets, elaborate costumes, and huge casts. It takes a lot of money and a large team of professionals to produce the kind of full-scale musical you might see on Broadway. Many communities just can't afford to produce these kinds of shows and don't have the seating capacity to draw the large-scale traveling productions. Luckily there has also been a recent movement toward smaller-cast, simpler musicals such as the popular *I Love You, You're Perfect, Now Change.* These small-cast musicals are produced on a much lower budget, and consequently can charge a much lower admission price, thus helping the musical gain an even wider audience.

The acclaimed musical *Rent* combines catchy music and lyrics with a powerful statement about urban gentrification and homelessness.

318 Unit Six Theatre and Its Counterparts

Quotable

From the songwriter's point of view, the dirty little secret of musical theatre writing is: If the story doesn't work, nothing else you put onstage will work very well, either. Grab any passing Broadway producer by the lapels and ask him why a specific show flopped, and I guarantee he'll blink and then say, "Book problems."

Nancy Golladay, Broadway and Regional Literary Advisor

The stage musical *Fosse* is constructed around the choreography of the late Bob Fosse.

More and more musicals are full of singing but feature almost no dancing, for example, *Les Misérables* and *The Spitfire Grill*. Others, such as *A Chorus Line* and *Chicago,* feature an abundance of singing and dancing. And at least two major musicals, *Contact* and *Movin' Out,* choreographed by Twyla Tharp, are told entirely in dance. *Contact* features only a prerecorded tape of pop songs, and *Movin' Out* has a live singer at the side of the stage singing the hits of pop star Billy Joel. There are those who may not consider these two pieces musical theatre; however, *Contact* won the Tony Award for Best Musical of 2000.

Another recent group of musicals are actually modern operas—all singing and no spoken dialogue. These include *Joseph and the Amazing Technicolor Dreamcoat, Tommy, Jesus Christ Superstar,* and *Les Misérables.*

If you're going to be auditioning for a musical, it's a good idea to have some vocal training and to be able to execute at least a few basic dance steps.

Musical Personnel

As is the case in the professional theatre, high school musicals are much more complicated to produce than straight dramas. This is because musicals feature orchestral music, multiple elaborate sets, larger casts requiring huge numbers of costumes and, often, special effects. This complexity demands a larger production staff than is typically needed for a play.

Visual Cue

The stage musical *Fosse* celebrated the work of choreographer Bob Fosse by showcasing several of his best-known musical numbers. Challenge students' **visual learning skills** by using the prompts to the right.

- From the costumes and the physical attitudes of the dancers, what can you say about Bob Fosse's choreography?
- How does it compare to that of more traditional shows you have seen?

Musical Personnel

Discuss with students the fact that there are often non-singing and non-dancing roles in musicals, but auditions often ask that you perform one or more songs for a musical. Have students honestly analyze their own strengths in terms of vocal quality, as well as the ability to move gracefully on stage and to learn a certain amount of choreography. Talk to them about any vocal or dance training you may have had.

Additionally, talk about the idea that while most musicals try to hire actors with strong, lyrical singing voices, a number of great musical roles have starred actors with very little singing training (or ability). Rex Harrison and Richard Burton, in *My Fair Lady* and *Camelot,* respectively, did very little actual singing in their Broadway roles. What they did instead was use rhythm, cadence, emotion, and superb acting to make their parts come alive and *seem* like singing.

Talk to students about high school musicals you have directed or been a part of. What made the musical more complicated than the typical drama or comedy?

ACTivity Give students, singers and non-singers alike, the opportunity to use their acting skills to recite one of the following songs:

- "I Wonder What the King Is Doing Tonight" from *Camelot*
- "Why Can't a Woman (Be More Like a Man)" from *My Fair Lady*
- "Just You Wait, Henry Higgins" from *My Fair Lady*
- "Can You Feel the Love Tonight?" from *Lion King*
- "All That Jazz" from *Chicago*

Visual Cue

Based on a play written in 1926, *Chicago* tells the story of chorus girl Roxie Hart. Having killed her unfaithful husband, Roxie is able to use her trial to launch a career in show business—with the help of her lawyer, flim-flam man Billy Flynn.

The show first opened in 1975, with Gwen Verdon as Roxie and Jerry Orbach as Billy. For years it was overshadowed by *A Chorus Line,* but in 1997 it was revived and went on to win six Tony Awards, including "Best Revival of a Musical," "Best Choreography" and "Best Direction of a Musical." The motion picture *Chicago* won the 2003 Academy Award for Best Picture, with Catherine Zeta-Jones winning the Best Supporting Actress award for her performance as Velma. Have students answer the questions below about the photograph from the film.

- What elements of blocking create the visual picture in this scene?
- What elements of posture tell you about the character Ms. Zeta-Jones is portraying?
- What seems to be the attitude of the men in the picture?
- Do you think you would enjoy participating in a musical? If yes, in what capacity? If no, why not?

Performers who can sing, dance, and act are in high demand on Broadway and in films based on Broadway productions. Pictured here is Catherine Zeta-Jones, who sang and danced along with Richard Gere and Renee Zellweger in the movie version of *Chicago.*

Backstage Gossip: Diva Dish

For almost twenty years Ethel Merman had reigned supreme and unchallenged as the queen of musical theatre, when Mary Martin scored a sensation in *South Pacific.* Asked what she thought of the young star's performance, "Oh, she's all right," La Merman replied with a shrug, "if you like talent!"

from *Broadway Anecdotes* by Peter Hay

The Actors The songs performed in musicals are typically used to heighten the emotions of the audience. Musical theatre actors must be able to bring their characters to life through song—in other words, they must have the confidence to "sell it." Of course a trained voice is also essential, but many successful musical theatre actors have interesting as opposed to traditionally beautiful voices.

Good actors who can sing are in great demand in the world of today's professional musical theatre. But most **principals** (actors in major roles) begin their careers as members of the **chorus.** This is the group of singers that provides the backup for the principals. Sometimes chorus members have short solos, but most often they are asked to harmonize and to serve in crowd scenes and production numbers.

The Two Directors Most musicals have two directors—one who directs the actors onstage and another who directs the musicians (both onstage and off). The **onstage director** functions much as a director would in a straight play. He or she blocks the actors (except for dance numbers), coaches the actors in their non-singing scenes, and sees to the overall style and flow of the show. The onstage director is also in charge of casting the show, although most directors collaborate with the music director on this part of the process. The director may be a teacher with a theatre background or a hired theatre professional.

The **music director** works with the actors, singers, and dancers throughout the rehearsal process to ensure that they are on key, up to speed, and creating the best sound possible. He or she guides the performers through the musical part of the rehearsal process and often serves as conductor during performances. The music director's job is very important to the overall effect of the show because so many of a musical's dramatic moments are conveyed through song. He or she must be able to collaborate effectively with the director and choreographer.

The music director is usually responsible for selecting the show's instrumentation. Depending on the performance space, the play, and the budget, the instrumentation might include a single piano, a small band with just a few instruments, or a full-scale orchestra. The music director usually holds special rehearsals with individual principals and periodic rehearsals for just the chorus members. He or she is typically a teacher who works with musicians in the school's band and/or orchestra programs, or is the school's music teacher (however, some schools hire outside music professionals).

ACTivity Ask students to imagine they are musical directors. Give them the following list of subjects for a musical and ask them what kind of instrumentation and musical interpretation they would suggest. Students should be able to justify their artistic choices.

- a story about an Appalachian girl who falls in love with a trapper
- the story of a GI in Viet Nam who helps a boy find the mother he lost
- a tale of two jockeys riding horses destined for the Kentucky Derby
- a story based on Mighty Mouse comic books

Vocabulary Enhancement

In Broadway's more traditional days, shows were often planned so that a large, show-stopping number (such as "Rose's Turn" in *Gypsy*) came just before the finale. These often happened to fall just about 11:00. So even today, a large, important song that comes just before the climax is often referred to as an *eleven o'clock number.*

From the Field: Lip Sync/Choreography

Have the students work in pairs on this one (less intimidating). They will pick out a favorite song, school appropriate, and choreograph a dance to it. The students will perform their song, in costume, for the rest of the class. (The kids loved this one!)

LeAnn Gausman, Theatre Teacher, Parma, Ohio

One of a choreographer's great achievements is to receive an American Choreography Award. Once called the L.A. Dance Awards, these annual honors are given in order to honor and draw attention to the art of choreography for the camera.

Each year the ACA recognizes outstanding achievements in film, television, commercials, and music videos. They also honor individuals and organizations that have made significant contributions to dance as an art and a profession, giving awards for career achievement, educational excellence, and innovation.

Past honorees have included the choreographers Michael Kidd and Bob Fosse, as well as The Gap® for their "visionary" commercials that focus on dance.

ACTivity Advanced Students
Ask students to choreograph a short dance sequence based on a favorite pop song, ballad, rap, classical orchestration, and so on. Emphasize that students should bring their own beliefs and cultural experiences into their work. Have them share their creations with the class, discussing their interpretations afterward.

The Choreographer The person responsible for designing a show's dance numbers is the **choreographer.** Many musicals feature **production numbers,** elaborate song-and-dance sequences in which almost the entire cast takes part. The choreographer must be knowledgeable about music and movement and must have a facility for working with large groups of performers all at once. At the high school level the choreographer will typically be working with individuals at a variety of experience levels and abilities. It takes both talent and patience to create a unified choreographic vision.

Career Focus

Choreographer

Choreographers are among the most multifaceted of all theater professionals. Ask them how they define themselves, and they'll tell you they are dancers, actors, directors, scene designers, mediators, and more.

Like directors, choreographers do their most important work during the rehearsal period. They begin by reading the script. They think about the mood and style of the play and look for important moments in the plot. Then they develop movements to express the emotions in those moments. When they work on musicals, choreographers develop dances and train dancers. But they also direct other movements in other kinds of productions. They design the movements for pratfalls and fight scenes. They make sure entrances and exits flow smoothly. In short, they make sure the movements in every scene are effective.

If you think you might want to become a choreographer, you can begin by studying dance. You don't need to become a great dancer, but you will need to know a lot about movement. When you think you have learned enough to help others, you can volunteer your time and talent on a school or community play or teach dance classes. Through these experiences, you will learn what works and what doesn't work in actual practice.

Once you have gained both education and experience, you can collaborate with directors you admire or you can create dance pieces of your own. You might want to test your abilities in some of the competitions that take place all over the world.

From the Field: Exit Right...No, Left!

Once choreography is set, it's set. One person's wrong movement can affect all the other cast members and the outcome of the show. In a production of *Annie,* one of the little orphan girls turned offstage in the wrong direction. Because she was his cue to enter, she threw off Daddy Warbucks, and because she was on the wrong side of the stage, she bumped into scenery being moved for the next scene. That resulted in Miss Hannigan's having no desk, and the orphan's missing her next entrance cue.

To recoup, we closed the curtain and sent Rooster and Lily out front to adlib the rest of the scene. But the show went on!

Alisha Fran-Potter, Choreographer and Dance Teacher, Glenview, Illinois

Designers Just as in straight plays, the set, lighting, and costume designers must contribute their creative expertise to the overall vision of the production. (See Unit Five for chapters devoted to these theatre personnel.)

The Producer No matter what the production level, a large-scale musical is an expensive proposition. The number of actors, sets, and production staff needed for a musical is very large compared to a straight dramatic work. A high school musical can cost anywhere from $2000 to $15,000. (A professional-level musical may cost up to $10 million.) At the front end, this means that a good producer must be very savvy about recognizing a potential show's marketability. The question is often not so much "Is it good?" as "Will it sell?"—the point being that if it won't sell, it won't matter if it's good. So although a high school production has a built-in audience of friends, classmates, and family members, most producers try to market the show to a larger cross-section of the community in order to ensure sufficient ticket sales to meet the budget.

Often several producers—a teacher and selected students or a group of affiliated teachers—may work together to secure funding for the production and to manage the show's marketing. The musical producer's job is made up of the same general tasks as that of a straight play producer (see Chapter 14).

The Technical Crews The crews for musicals are usually larger than those for smaller-cast straight plays. But they are similar in terms of the types of tasks they fulfill. (For more on technical crews and their functions, see Chapter 14.)

The Business Manager Like any business manager, the business manager for a musical production is in charge of the budget. Musicals, however, can present special challenges because they are often extremely expensive to produce, due to the additional cost of hiring musicians, a conductor, dancers, a choreographer, special technicians, creating lavish costumes and sets, and so on. The business manager may decide that ticket prices have to be higher or that the advertising budget must be doubled—all in the hopes of bringing in money to finance the production.

Backstage Gossip: The Gypsy Robe

It's called the *gypsy robe,* and it's a musical theatre tradition. The member of the chorus with the most Broadway credits receives the gypsy robe on opening night. Members of the show then attach something to the robe that represents some part of the show. Everyone signs it. That cast member will then take the robe to the next Broadway opening and give it to the chorus gypsy of that show who has the most credits.

Of course a show must be financed in order to be produced, must be produced in order to be seen, and must be seen in order to capture an audience. But gaining a production is no guarantee of quality.

Tell students that before they begin their proposals they should determine that being original and doing their best work are their main goals. You might discuss with them the age-old debate between quality and popularity. Ask them if they would rather create a work that they felt good about and that they knew represented their best efforts or a work that was popular and made money? Why?

ACTivity Have students pretend they are producers and play the Marketability Game. Give them a list of musicals, including *The Fantasticks, Cats, Into the Woods, Chicago, Grease,* and *Camelot,* and ask them to rank these shows in order as to the market potential for your high school. Remind them to consider the cost of the production in terms of the musicians you will need for each, the potential audience for each production, the numbers and talents of your student body, any extra crew or cast they may need to hire, and so on.

PREPARE

Create a Proposal for a New Musical

To conceive of a musical show from scratch is a difficult procedure. Students are not asked to write a whole show for their project, merely a proposal. However, it may help them to focus their work if they think of a novel or play they would like to adapt.

Adaptation creates its own special problems: Students must consider carefully which characters are necessary and which might be eliminated. They must focus on the main actions, possibly eliminating subplots or extraneous actions. They also must consider whether scenes can be combined, so that—for example—only four sets are required, rather than eight.

As students work on Step 2, tell them that a main character is frequently given a "want song" that expresses what it is he or she wants. Typically, this would come rather early in the show, and it provides a good way for the audience to get to know the character and to empathize with him or her.

The want doesn't have to be overtly stated; frequently it is phrased in such a way that the audience has to infer the want from what is actually said. Either way, what a character wants should not be a matter of confusion for the audience. Suggest that students use their notes for what the character wants when they come to placing songs in Step 3.

PREPARE

Create a Proposal for a New Musical

These days, the subject of a musical can be just about anything. There are musicals about war, politics, race, immigration, parenting—even taxes! What would *your* musical be about?

You're now going to create a proposal for an original musical that will appeal to your fellow students. Everyone in your class is a potential backer. Your musical can be comic or dramatic. You are not restricted by subject matter. Your musical can tackle any issue you would like. Of course it's always best if the subject has a special meaning for you and will interest an audience. All the proposals will be rated by the entire class, and your teacher will tabulate the votes to see who will get to "produce" his or her show.

Possible Musical Subjects

Begin by writing down some broad ideas for the subject of your musical. Possibilities might include:

- professional sports
- dating
- family relationships
- friendship
- crime and punishment
- working

Four Steps to Creating Your Proposal

1 **Decide on a Subject, Size, and Setting.** Once you have decided on the subject of your musical (something you find interesting or meaningful), you must think about its size. Will it have a small cast or be a large-scale musical? Some musicals feature only two characters; others require a cast of thirty or more. The size of the musical will strongly affect the way you tell your story. Then, decide on a setting. It might be a beach, a party, a museum, or anywhere else your imagination takes you.

2 **Develop the Characters.** Think about the people who will give your musical personality. Remember that, just as in a straight play, the characters in a musical must have objectives (goals or needs). Ask yourself these questions:

- Who is the main character?
- What does he or she want?
- Who or what stands in the way of the character accomplishing the goal?
- Who are the other characters?
- What do they want?

Write a brief sketch of each character. Include his or her age, personality type, physical appearance, and anything else you feel will allow a reader to understand the character's basic qualities. If you envision a large chorus for your musical, you don't have to write sketches for the choral roles. Just include sketches of the characters that will be crucial to the advancement of the play's main plot.

Quotable

I learned about playwriting from the jackets of show albums because I always noticed that the first or second song in any musical was the "want" song—"All I want is a room somewhere." I want. I want.

John Guare, Playwright

3. **Write a Plot Synopsis.** In order to plot your musical, ask yourself the questions below and jot down your ideas.
   - Where does the story begin?
   - What is its theme?
   - What happens first?
   - What happens next?
   - What happens after that point?
   - How does the story end?
   - Does the main character attain his or her goal?
   - Does the main character learn an important lesson?

   Now write a plot synopsis. You do not need to tell every moment in the story—just chart the main course of the action. Include indications of where songs might be placed and what those songs might be about. Try to come up with titles for each song. For example: "Adrian sings 'What Next?' which expresses her shock and excitement at the incredible turn her life has taken."
4. **Write a Theme Statement.** Now review your character sketch and your plot synopsis. What is the dominant idea expressed? Write one sentence that sums up the play's theme.

Once you have completed your character sketches, plot synopsis, and theme statement, give your musical a tentative title. Now think about how you would use all the elements of your musical to gain interest and support for its creation. In other words, think about how you might try to sell, or **pitch,** your idea for the musical to your classmates—your potential backers. What will they find intriguing about your theme, characters, and plot? Jot down a few specifics. You can use your notes in your presentation.

Rehearse Your Proposal

You will not be required to memorize your proposal, but you should be familiar enough with it that you can cover all the necessary information in the time allotted. Use expressive language and convey your ideas in an enthusiastic manner. Your job is to excite your classmates' interest, so make every moment count. You may refer to your notes, but it's important that you don't read them aloud. Time your presentation to make sure it does not exceed the five-minute time limit.

Notes

As students work on Step 3, point out that songs should not be arbitrarily scattered throughout a show. Theoretically, a character starts singing when his or her emotions grow too large to be expressed in mere dialogue. That is why every show song should be considered as the response of a particular character to a particular dramatic situation.

At this point in the proposal process, you might want to let students exchange their plot synopses and discuss what their theme statements should be. Go over the concept of what constitutes theme if you feel the students need help with this.

Advanced Students
Give students a copy of the scripts of both *Pygmalion* and *My Fair Lady*. Have students do a scene-by-scene analysis of what was kept from the original play, what was dropped, and what was adapted when the play was turned into a musical.

Vocabulary Enhancement

Point out that the word *pitch* has multiple meanings in theatre. It can refer to the amount of slant or rake described in Chapter 5. It can also refer to a musical key. Here, of course, it means "to speak for or promote."

Rehearse Your Proposal

Before students begin the rehearsal process, be sure that they are satisfied with the proposal they have written. Meet with students who feel they need help with any aspect of the proposal. If necessary, go over the four steps to creating the proposal, focusing on any that seem especially problematic.

Special Needs Students
If students are still having trouble getting their proposals organized, use a checklist to go over the four steps with them. Check off each step when you are satisfied that this point has been covered. Then help them write the plot synopsis based on the first two steps. Finally, help students see how you can pull the theme out of the plot and come up with the sentence that sums up the theme of their musical.

Here's How

Unless your school has a drama club that also functions as a production agency, students may have little access to information about money or budgets. However, they can analyze available theatre space as well as potential cast, production staff, and audience. One way to choose a show that fits your particular production facilities is by studying the cast breakdowns in catalogues of play script publishers such as Samuel French.

For example, *The Fantasticks* requires a cast of seven, while *I Do, I Do* requires only two. Both can be performed in a limited space with very simple scenic elements and minimal costuming. This kind of analysis can be invaluable to any production company planning to put on a musical.

PRESENT

Pitch Your Idea for a New Musical

Point out that in their presentations, students are simply using the same skills that enhance any public presentation. Encourage them to demonstrate their own enthusiasm for their proposals; a speaker's enthusiasm has a way of infecting an audience—even an audience made up of potential theatrical backers.

Here's How

To Choose a Musical for Your School

You should always try to stage a musical that you find exciting and interesting, but there are a number of things to consider before you make a commitment. Below are a few things you should think about.

- **Money** How much will things cost (consider all the elements)? How much do you have to spend? How many tickets need to be sold to break even?
- **Space** Do you rent a space or use school facilities? Musicals require large spaces for the dance numbers. How much room will the production need both onstage and off?
- **Cast** Are there good singers, dancers, and musicians available who can handle the requirements of the show?
- **Production staff** Are a music director and choreographer available? What about a knowledgeable designer and the large, experienced tech crew you will need?
- **Audience** Will it be large enough to support the cost of the show and the efforts of everyone involved? Will the audience be receptive to the theme, style, and message of the play?

PRESENT

Pitch Your Idea for a New Musical

When your teacher calls your name, gather your notes and head to the front of the room. Take a moment to prepare. Breathe deeply and relax your muscles while maintaining good posture.

Present your proposal as you rehearsed it. Remember to stay positive, enthusiastic, and upbeat. If you lose focus for a moment, use your notes to get back on track. Remember that your class will be voting on which proposal will actually become a new musical.

When you have finished your presentation, thank your audience, give your notes or your Activity Sheet to your teacher, and return to your seat.

Quotable

Before Neil Armstrong walked on the moon. . . . before Wilt Chamberlain completed the first of his seven consecutive years as basketball's top scorer, "Try to Remember" and "Soon It's Gonna Rain" from The Fantasticks *were part of our national culture. . . . And as proof that a sunny, funny musical about love has lasting value, consider that the show's original 44 investors have received a 19,465% return on their $16,500 total investment.*

from *The Fantasticks* Official Web site

CRITIQUE

Evaluate a Classmate's Pitch

The critique for this presentation will be a little different from others you have done in this drama class. This time, you will listen carefully to all the proposals your classmates present, taking notes based on the four points below—plot, characters, theme, and audience appeal. You are not evaluating the presenter's speaking ability; you are evaluating his or her ideas for a new musical. Use the scores you give for each of the four points to determine the overall rating for the proposal.

Plot
1 2 3 4 5

Characters
1 2 3 4 5

Theme
1 2 3 4 5

Audience appeal
1 2 3 4 5

Overall proposal
1 2 3 4 5

Write specific comments describing what you believe was or was not successful in each category. Keep your comments constructive and realistic. Then cast your vote for the musical you would produce and explain why you voted as you did. Base your vote on the descriptions below.

5 = Sold!

4 = I'm interested, but I would need to hear more.

3 = Has potential, but it needs work.

2 = Risky business.

1 = This one has less than a slim chance.

Theatre Journal

What does it take to "sell" a song to an audience? Think about a musical performer whose work you have admired either in a musical play or in a non-theatrical medium. What is it about this person's style that attracts and intrigues you? Write your thoughts and impressions.

CRITIQUE

Evaluate a Classmate's Pitch

Hand out one Critique Sheet per student and assign the presenter that each person will critique. As this critique differs from those done previously, go over the ratings and their meanings carefully. Encourage students to take as many notes as they wish, but explain that their final votes will be based on the total of the rating numbers. Have students circle the four numbers that represent their ratings. Then have students average the four numbers to arrive at their overall proposal number, from 1 (Less than a slim chance) to 5 (Sold!).

Alert students to also think about how creative, clever, and unusual the proposal is, and whether it contains an inventive collaboration of theme and voice; and of course—would they be willing to contribute money to see it onstage?

After all the proposals have been pitched and rated, give students time to compare their own rating numbers and choose the one with the highest score. They should then vote for that proposal by class ballot and turn in their Critique Sheets.

After you have reviewed student critiques, trim off the evaluators' names and hand out the sheets to the subjects of the evaluations.

Theatre Journal

Use the following as an additional or substitute prompt.

We're often impressed by performers who can take center stage and "sell" a show-stopping song, yet that is only a small part of the musical theatre experience. Think about a quieter musical moment that impressed you in some special way.

Backstage Gossip: Birth of a Musical

One day in 1949, Meredith Wilson was reminiscing to a group of friends about his boyhood in Mason City, Iowa. Among his listeners was composer Frank Loesser. Suddenly Loesser jumped to his feet. "What an idea!" he shouted. "Why don't you write a musical about it? Maybe you can start with the fire chief. Let's make him the leader of the town band. Maybe *you* can play the fire chief. And maybe instead of a pit orchestra, you can have a real brass band in the pit. And you're the leader of the band . . . . It would be real Americana!"

When Wilson opened *The Music Man* on Broadway eight years later, it bore little resemblance to this original concept, but Loesser had planted the idea in Wilson's mind.

from *The World of Musical Comedy* by Stanley Green

Chapter 24 Test

The test for this chapter is available in blackline master form in the Resource Binder, page 101.

For More Information

Books

Andrews, Richard, *Writing a Musical,* Hale, Robert Limited, 1997.

Bordman, Gerald Martin, *American Musical Theatre: A Chronicle,* Oxford University Press, 2001.

Davis, Sheila, *The Craft of Lyric Writing*, Writer's Digest Books, 1985.

Engel, Lehman, *The Making of a Musical: Creating Songs for the Stage*, Limelight Editions, 1988.

Frankel, Aaron, *Writing the Broadway Musical,* Da Capo Press, 2000.

Goldstone, Richard H., editor, *George Bernard Shaw's Pygmalion and My Fair Lady,* Signet, 1975.

Jones, Tom, *Making Musicals: An Informal Introduction to the World of Musical Theatre,* Limelight Editions, 1997.

Peterson, Bernard L., Jr., *Musicals in Black and White: An Encyclopedia of Musical Stage Works by, about, or Involving African Americans,* Greenwood Press, 1993.

Other Media

www.stageplays.com

The American Musical Theatre, VHS (2 tapes), Insight Media, 2000.

Broadway! History of the Musical, VHS (5 tapes), Insight Media, 1989.

Dance Class for the Actor, VHS (2 tapes), Insight Media, 2002.

Principles of Choreography, VHS, Insight Media, 1996.

Step by Step: an Amateurs' Guide to Choreography, VHS, Insight Media, 1992.

West End Story: an Anatomy of the Musical Theatre, VHS (2 tapes), Insight Media, 2001.

Additional Projects

1. Write the lyrics for the opening number of a musical about an aspect of your school.
2. Prepare a musical audition piece, and perform it for the class.
3. Collaborate with a classmate to perform a duet from a musical.
4. Rent a videotape of *The Music Man* or *West Side Story* and write a review of the play, the music, and the overall production.
5. Rent a video of the film version of the musical *Chicago.* Discuss the changes that might have been made to transform this stage piece into a movie. How would the film differ from the stage version?
6. Design a promotional plan for the new musical one of your classmate's proposed.
7. Read the scene from *Promenade* by Maria Irene Fornes or *The Dining Room* by A. R. Gurney, Jr. found in Unit Eight, and create an original song that might appear in a musical based on your chosen scene.

Substitute Teacher Activities

Here are suggestions for one or more days when you will be out of the classroom:

- Assign the From Book to Musical Worksheet on page 99 of the Resource Binder.
- Discuss the information found in the Student Handbook concerning the Musical Audition on page 555 and Musical Theatre on pages 561-562.
- Assign one or more of the Additional Projects on this page.
- **Play What's the Rhyme?** with students. Start them off by singing two lines in which the ends rhyme using a familiar tune. Students continue the theme and tune of the song you've started, rhyming each of their own two lines as they go.

Master of the Craft

Andrew Lloyd Webber

Ask most people to name a modern musical, and the chances are good that they will answer with a work crafted by the English composer Sir Andrew Lloyd Webber.

Born into a musical family in 1948, young Andrew began playing the violin at age three. By the age of six he was writing his own songs, and by nine, one of his pieces was published in a magazine for music teachers. An aunt introduced him to the theatre, and he was thrilled by such musicals as *My Fair Lady* and *South Pacific.*

When he was 17, Webber met the lyricist Tim Rice. A short time later, they were hired to co-write a musical for a London prep school. They chose a story from the Bible about Joseph and his coat of many colors. The resulting rock opera was *Joseph and the Amazing Technicolor Dreamcoat.* Although the music was strong, the lyrics catchy, and the story entertaining, *Joseph* didn't get much notice. Webber and Rice's next collaboration was the successful international hit *Jesus Christ Superstar.* This was followed by *Evita* in 1976, a full-scale blockbuster.

In 1981, writing the music entirely on his own, Webber wrote *Cats,* based on T. S. Eliot's *Old Possum's Book of Practical Cats.* The year 1984 brought *Starlight Express,* and two years later came the musical many consider his masterpiece, *The Phantom of the Opera.* Throughout the 1990s Webber's success continued.

The Musicals of Andrew Lloyd Webber

Joseph and the Amazing Technicolor Dreamcoat (1968)
Jesus Christ Superstar (1970)
Jeeves (1975)
Evita (1976)
Variations (1977)
Tell Me on a Sunday (1979)
Cats (1981)
Song and Dance (1982)
Starlight Express (1984)
The Phantom of the Opera (1986)
Aspects of Love (1989)
Sunset Boulevard (1993)
By Jeeves (1996)
Whistle Down the Wind (1998)
The Beautiful Game (2000)
Bombay Dreams (2002)

From an early and profound fascination with music, Andrew Lloyd Webber has become one of the world's most popular composers.

Sir Andrew Lloyd Webber

Quotable

Musicals, whether small, medium, or big, are alive and well as long as someone wants to write one and someone wants to produce one.

Andrew Lloyd Webber, Composer

Master of the Craft

More About Andrew Lloyd Webber

It was Andrew's Aunt Vi who turned him on to the theatre and especially musical theatre. She took him to big musicals like *My Fair Lady* and movies like *Gigi* and *South Pacific.* Soon after, he built a small theatre at home and wrote musicals for it. In 1965 Andrew received a letter:

Dear Andrew, I've been told you're looking for a "with it" writer of lyrics for your songs, and as I've been writing pop songs for a while and particularly enjoy writing the lyrics I wonder if you consider it worth your while meeting me.

Tim Rice

Andrew (age 17) and Tim (age 21) started to collaborate, and their first musical became *The Likes of Us.* The musical was never produced.

Visit an Andrew Lloyd Webber Web site at: *hem.passagen.se/musicals/bio_and.html.*

Theatre Then and Now

Peking Opera

Peking Opera, which was performed in the Beijing dialect, was a blend of highly stylized action, mime, singing, stage combat, acrobatics, dance, and dialogue. The plays were divided into two categories—martial (featuring stunts and acrobatics) and civil (featuring singing). Some were a combination of both.

Traditionally the four main roles were *sheng* (male), *dan* (young female), *jing* (painted face, male), and *chou* (clown, male and female), all of which were played by men. The brightly colored facial makeup symbolized different characters and personalities. Yellow and white meant cunning; red was an indicator of uprightness and loyalty; black meant valor and wisdom; blue and green indicated the manly rebellious character of heroes; and gold and silver represented mystic or supernatural power.

Hoping to attract new and younger audiences, many Peking Opera performances now use both Chinese and Western music that has been electronically amplified. Many have added high-tech lighting and design elements.

Theatre Then and Now

The Common Language of Music

Peking Opera

Peking Opera, China's most famous and popular theatrical form, isn't an opera at all. Westerners began calling it this because of the music and singing that often accompany it. The Peking Opera originated in 1790 when, at the order of the imperial court, four performance companies from Anhui Province came to Peking (Beijing) on a tour. The tour was successful, and the troupes stayed on in Beijing. Over time, the artists absorbed the music and techniques of the local opera companies. The result was a new kind of theatre—formed from the talents of many.

The Peking Opera performances were full of spectacle and included actors in brightly colored face paint. The colors of the faces signified different characters and personalities.

The music of the Peking Opera was typically graceful and pleasing to the ear. The musicians played wind, percussion, and a variety of stringed instruments including *jinghu,* which has two strings and a very high register, and *yueqin,* which has four strings and is played by plucking.

Today, as in the old days, the repertoire of Peking Opera is drawn from tales of previous ages, notable historical events, and legends of emperors, geniuses, and other important people. Having thrived for more than two centuries, Peking Opera is considered the quintessential Chinese art form.

A Peking Opera performer displays his martial arts prowess.

Notes

High-Tech Spectacle and Small-Scale Wonders of Today

Today's musical theatre is bigger, glitzier, and more expensive to produce—and to attend—than ever before. Part of this is due to the audience's increased expectations regarding the level of a show's spectacle. After all, when one is used to seeing incoming helicopters landing onstage (as in Claude-Michel Schönberg and Alain Boublil's *Miss Saigon*) or action played out on a roller rink featuring a 5.5-ton steel suspension bridge and a set built from 6 miles of timber, 2.5 acres of plywood, and 60 tons of steel (as in Andrew Lloyd Webber's *Starlight Express*), it's hard to imagine a musical on a smaller scale being truly exciting.

Yet smaller-scale musicals continue to draw crowds as well. *Pump Boys and Dinettes* is one example of a simple yet lively musical that still holds audience interest, and only recently did the simple, but ever-popular *The Fantasticks* close in New York after 17,162 performances. Today's musicals tackle almost any subject. Adam Guettel and Tina Landau's musical *Floyd Collins* is based on the true story of a Kentucky man who became trapped while exploring a cave in 1925. People continue to be drawn to and moved by musicals of all sizes and subjects. Perhaps that is at least in part because music offers a common language that everyone can understand and enjoy.

The famous helicopter hovers over the actors on the stage of *Miss Saigon*.

Miss Saigon was written by Alain Boublil and Claude-Michel Schönberg, who also wrote *Les Misérables.* Set during the final days of the American evacuation of Saigon in 1975, it tells the story of a young GI and the Viet Namese girl he comes to love. They are parted by ill fate yet bonded by passion and the life of their child.

For More Information

Books

Hay, John M., editor, *Boundaries in China,* Reaktion Books, 1995.

Hsia-Feng, P'An, *The Stagecraft of Peking Opera,* New World Press (China), 1995.

Kondo, Dorinne K., *About Face: Performing Race in Fashion and Theater,* Routledge, 1997.

Mackerras, Colin, *Peking Opera,* Oxford University Press, 1997.

Mackerras, Colin, *Rise of the Peking Opera, 1770-1870: Social Aspects of the Theatre in Manchu China,* Oxford University Press, 1972.

Viagas, Robert, with Donald C. Farber, *The Amazing Story of the Fantasticks: America's Longest-Running Play*, Kensington Publishing Corporation, 1998.

Other Media

To learn more about the long-running musical *The Fantasticks* and to hear a bit of the music, visit *www.thefantasticks.com.*

Backstage Gossip: Whistling the Sets

Sometimes stage design can seem to get out of hand. The lumbering movement of the gigantic set pieces used in *Les Misérables* was found to be distracting to many audience members. And a joke circulated after the opening of *Camelot* that one came out of the theatre "whistling the sets."

Chapter 24 Musical Theatre **331**

Chapter 25

Other Theatre Forms

This chapter covers five theatre forms that have not been dealt with in earlier chapters–performance art, multimedia, puppet theatre, Readers Theatre, and poetry slams.

Objectives

1 to explore theatrical forms outside the realm of traditional theatre

2 to utilize a variety of response strategies appropriate to the media under consideration

3 to write and perform a poem suitable for a poetry slam

National Standards

Chapter 25 meets these National Theatre Standards:

Proficient 1a, 2b, 6a, 6b, 6c, 7b

Advanced 1b, 3i, 4d, 6d, 6e, 7e

Project Specs

Some students may resist the idea of performing poetry. You might assure them that performance poetry doesn't have to rhyme or contain obvious rhythms. One way to think about it might be as a soliloquy expressing the thoughts and feelings of a character—yourself.

ESL Students

Some students might find it easier to write and perform their poems in their original languages. Allow this, but then encourage them to translate their work into English and, perhaps, to perform both versions. (Don't penalize them for running overtime if they do.)

On Your Feet

Show, Don't Tell Demonstrate this activity yourself, using common words like *please, hurry,* and *why*? Show students how vocal inflection can add a meaning to a single word. With students, brainstorm and list a number of words that they can choose from for their three words.

Chapter 25 Other Theatre Forms

Although we typically associate theatre with the production of plays, there are a number of other forms that fall into the basic category of theatre.

Project Specs

Project Description You will create a performance poem and take part in a classroom poetry slam. Your performance must last no longer than three minutes.

Purpose to combine writing and performance skills, and to explore forms outside the realm of traditional theatre

Materials the text of a performance poem or the Poetry Slam Worksheet your teacher will provide

Theatre Terms

Bunraku
multimedia
nonlinear
performance art
poetry slam
Readers Theatre

On Your Feet

Work with three other classmates to represent a common emotion or concept (loneliness, joy, curiosity, fear, political struggle, and so on) using only three words, your voice, gestures, and movement.

Suheir Hammad, Beau Sia, and Georgia Me perform in *Russell Simmons Def Poetry Jam on Broadway* at Longacre Theatre in New York.

Theatre Terms

Bunraku Japanese puppetry in which puppeteers appear onstage while manipulating the puppets

multimedia using more than one medium onstage, including TV, film, dance, etc.

nonlinear not chronological

performance art unstructured dramatic events in which movement, music, improvisation, and games are presented, often making a political statement

poetry slam a competitive poetry reading in which speakers present short, original poems

Readers Theatre a form of drama in which seated actors read aloud from a script

PREVIEW

The "Other" Theatre

Theatre began as ritual performance, and over the centuries the art form has taken many different paths and transformed itself many times over. As you read through this section, notice the similarities as well as the differences among these various forms.

Artist Laurie Anderson creates performance pieces that are visually and musically exciting.

Performance Art

With its roots in music, dance, and storytelling, theatre has given rise to **performance art,** which has in turn become its own popular form. Performance art came from the "happenings" of the 1960s. Often politically charged, happenings were a spontaneous combination of movement, music, improvisation, and sometimes even theatre games. They were, for the most part, unstructured events, usually held in a venue that was not typically associated with theatre or performance—public parks were often the best place to see happenings. Performance artists often experimented with the conventions of traditional theatre. Performance art is often seen in nontraditional performance spaces—parking garages, churches, parks, galleries, and so on.

Performance art tends to be **nonlinear** in its structure—in other words, it does not attempt to tell a chronological story. It typically focuses on neither character nor plot, but instead concerns itself with putting across a statement that is political or in some way controversial. Many politically charged performers use humor to express their ideas. Danny Hoch, Margaret Cho, and John Leguizamo all use comedy in performing works of social, political, and artistic relevance.

Multimedia

The advent of film and video has had a lasting impact on the theatre. Early in the 20th century, innovative stage directors began using film projections

Resource Binder

- Other Theatre Forms Activity Sheet, p. 102
- Re-create a Classic Worksheet, p. 103
- Critique Sheet: Take Part in a Poetry Slam, p. 104
- Other Theatre Forms Test, p. 105

Handbook Connections
pages 562-563, 564-565

To Have on Hand

- Books of poetry
- Videos or DVDs of performance artists, poets, puppet shows, etc.
- Marionettes, puppets, and similar items
- Slide projector, screen, and slides
- Sheet
- Floor lights or spotlights

PREVIEW

The "Other" Theatre

Many students will not have experienced all the other theatrical forms described in this chapter. If you can locate video clips of innovative performance art, puppetry, or poetry slams, and so on, have them on hand.

Performance Art

Show, Don't Tell Wearing dark glasses and a sling, enter the classroom, sit in a chair facing the class, and do nothing. After four minutes, leave the classroom. When you return, explain to students that one of the avowed purposes of performance art is to cause audiences to look at common events in new and fresh ways. Ask students to share their reactions to what just happened. If students mention emotions or motivations or even bits of business, you might discuss whether they were parts of the performance or their own interpretations or expectations.

Finally, go over the text on this page and discuss why what students have seen may be considered performance art. Explain that performance art takes on a multitude of different forms and meanings. In many ways, performance art is where new forms of theatre are invented.

Have students look at the three poetry jam performers and use the prompts below to help them exercise **critical viewing skills.**

- Do you think these three artists are talking about the same thing?
- Name all the parts of the body they are using in the performance.

Multimedia

ACTivity Bring a slide projector and a variety of colorful slides to class. Project a slide on the screen or on a blank wall and call on students, in turn, to improvise a short monologue or scene that relates to the slide.

ESL or Special Needs Students You might want to adapt the activity on page 333 to allow students to stand next to the slide and describe what they see.

Puppet Theatre

Ask students to talk about puppets they have seen in person or on television or in the movies. Most students will probably have experienced a puppet performance at one time or another, but they might resist thinking of puppets as a serious, adult artistic medium. You might show portions of a film on video or DVD, such as *Being John Malkovich,* in which puppets (and the concept of control) play an important part, or even a movie like *Chicken Run,* in which the claymation might be thought of as a form of puppetry.

Show, Don't Tell Try to improvise a shadow puppet performance by using a sheet and floor lamps or spotlights. Demonstrate to students that you can use just about any movable object to create the shadow, including your hands, kitchen utensils, scissors, and so on. Here's where the imagination can really take over.

ACTivity Leave the sheet up and the lights on and ask volunteers to create shadow puppet shows in pairs or groups.

Despite the fact that shadow puppets are seen only as shadows by the audience, they are colorfully decorated and detailed.

as a design element in their plays. And as time went on, using more than one medium to achieve a desired effect became increasingly popular and elaborate. In addition to using film and video, **multimedia** might incorporate live painting, dance, music, puppetry, animation, and computer and laser technology on stage. More and more plays are being written in cyber collaborations—multiple playwrights working via the Internet—and some theatre groups are using the Internet as the very latest in high-tech performance space.

Puppet Theatre

Puppetry is a very old art form—some claim it is nearly as old as humankind itself. The **Bunraku** puppetry of Japan, the water puppets of Vietnam (which shoot up from underwater via long rods), and the shadow puppets of Java (which are viewed through a backlit screen), are but a few of many puppetry forms that are centuries old. (Read more about Bunraku on page 342.)

In ancient times, puppetry was closely linked to feats of magic and conjuring. Throughout history, magicians and other entertainers have used puppets in street performances and later on the stage. The puppets Punch and Judy, who battle with one another throughout their show, are famous icons throughout Europe. Puppetry has enjoyed a popular resurgence in contemporary theatre. It has moved from being primarily a children's theatre form to one that charms and mesmerizes adults as well.

With the emergence of the Bread & Puppet Theatre in the early 1960s, American puppetry became politicized. The shows Bread & Puppet produced were both visually stunning and ideologically compelling. (See Theatre Then and Now on page 343.) Since then, similar puppet theatres have sprung up around the globe. Some of these puppet theatres focus on adaptations of literary works as well as commissioning original works. The puppets they use comprise everything from finger puppets to gigantic, incredibly complex and detailed figures that can simulate intricate human movements and expressions.

Readers Theatre

Readers Theatre is a form in which two or more actors read aloud from a script. The basis of the performance is usually a standard play script, but it can also involve anything from poetry to letters

From the Field: The Making of a Puppeteer

A nun taught us the primary colors, and a little later the public school teacher showed us the wondrous things you could do with clay and chalk and introduced us to tempera paints. What next? There came another teacher who used marionettes as an aid to teaching literature and history. We were transported! Then my twin cousins (not many years older than I) took me on a trip to the opera. We heard *Il Trovatore,* and I still am thrilled with the memory of watching that great, fringed curtain sweep open time after time to reveal caves and castles, while the massive orchestra and chorus and soloists poured their musical hearts out over the plight of Leonora and Manrico. Sixty-five years later I still take pleasure in realizing how those teachers helped form my career as an artist.

Bill Fosser, Puppeteer, Founder of Opera in Focus, Rolling Meadows, Illinois

The Bread & Puppet Theatre—humans in a puppet mode.

to journals to fiction. The actors usually sit on stools and read from scripts set on music stands. Sometimes all the performers dress in similar attire.

Readers Theatre uses a stage convention that allows the actors to deliver their lines out front while reacting as if they were speaking directly to their scene partners. Many larger cities have theatres that produce Readers Theatre exclusively. A. R. Gurney, Jr.'s popular *Love Letters* is a play that is performed in Readers Theatre style. Because this play requires only two actors and no memorization, it is a popular vehicle not only for theatres but also for arts fund-raising events.

Young performers enjoy the relaxed atmosphere of Readers Theatre.

Readers Theatre

In many ways, watching a Readers Theatre performance is like listening to a radio play—the audience gets to use its imagination to create sets, costumes, and actions. Readers Theatre is not new. One of its defining productions was the acclaimed 1951 reading of *Don Juan in Hell* from G. B. Shaw's *Man and Superman* with Charles Boyer, Sir Cedric Hardwicke, Charles Laughton, and Agnes Moorehead.

ACTivity Ask students to pair up or get into groups and pick a scene from a play they would like to read to the class. Each person should have a part. Have them sit at the front of the class. Tell them to read their parts with emotion and honestly. Try to be sure that each group has a mix of talents and abilities.

The following prompts can help students exercise **critical viewing skills** while looking at the photograph at the top of this page.

- What qualifies this performance as puppetry?
- From the masks, costumes, and physical attitudes of the performers, do you think the story being told is a fanciful fairy tale or something else? What?
- What might be some advantages to acting in a mask? What might be some disadvantages?

From the Field: Puppetry Workout

There are no fat puppeteers, I can tell you. The work is too strenuous. Even a large one is at a disadvantage; there's not enough room for him backstage. If a hand puppeteer is too short, he raises himself on high cork soles. Special muscles come into play depending on what one is holding and how. We learn to talk and sing in a bent-over position while manipulating heavy marionettes. The lifting muscles in the arms of rod puppeteers become very strong—I know from personal experience.

Bil Baird, Puppeteer

Poetry Slams

If possible, try to get videos or audiotapes of poetry slam participants in action. Discuss with students the visual and aural impact of these performances. What makes them different from a poetry reading? How do they differ from acting or other kinds of performing? How are they similar?

ACTivity To practice reading poetry before an audience, have students memorize a poem that has real meaning for them. They need not memorize the entire poem, but they should know enough of it by heart to be able to feel some emotion while reciting it. Ask students to present the poem to the class, calling on as much emotional memory and deep meaning as they can.

ESL Students

Encourage these students to recite a poem in their native language, perhaps with another student who can translate as the poem is spoken.

Career Focus

A good stage manager can make the difference between a production running smoothly and things falling apart. If an emergency arises during a performance, the stage manager has to take care of it. The stage manager keeps track of the production schedule and times rehearsals as well as the performance, often taking notes on the performances to share with cast and crew.

It is not unusual for a stage manager to be experienced in just about every area of theatre, including directing, casting, and acting.

ACTivity Ask students to choose just one aspect of the stage manager's role and make a list of all the duties that would entail for a performance of their choosing.

Poetry Slams

A **poetry slam** is a form of competitive performance poetry that was born in Chicago in 1987. Since that time, slams have become enormously popular and there are national and international competitions administered through an organization called Poetry Slam Inc. The Nuyorican Café, founded by Reg E. Gaines, Bob Holman, and others, in New York City is famous for its poetry slams.

At these rousing celebrations of the spoken word, poets are judged on both the writing and the performance aspects of their work by a panel of judges who use a 0–10 rating system.

Career Focus

Stage Manager

One of the hardest working people in any production is the stage manager. This is a job that requires organizational skills, a sharp sense of timing, the ability to work with many different kinds of creative people, a cool head in a crisis, and the confidence to oversee all elements of a production. It is also a job that most people learn by doing. Most stage managers get their start as members of other technical crews or as assistant stage managers.

During rehearsals, the stage manager writes down all the blocking and sometimes writes down and hands out the director's notes to the cast between rehearsals. During the actual performances, the stage manager takes over where the director leaves off. He or she is responsible for seeing that each performance runs smoothly. A small sample of the stage manager's duties include:

- cueing the performers before and during the show
- cueing the technical crews before and during the show
- supervising the stage crew
- making sure performers and crew know their call times for all rehearsals and performances
- relaying notes to the performers or technical team from the director
- scheduling and overseeing meetings and rehearsal times for the technical personnel

In the professional theatre, stage managers are typically members of Actors' Equity Association (AEA), the professional union for actors and stage managers. Qualified stage managers are typically very much in demand.

Notes

Following are the basic rules for a poetry slam:

- Each poem must be an original work by the poet.
- Each poet gets three minutes of performance time. If the poet goes over that period of time, points will be deducted.
- Poets may not use costumes, props, or musical instruments.
- Of the scores from five judges, the highest and lowest are subtracted and the three middle scores are added together to give the poet a total score of anywhere from 0 to 30.
- The judges are selected from among the audience members.

Poetry slams are designed to be audience interactive. In other words, the audience members are free to react to the performances in any way they see fit.

Theatre Journal

What if someone asked you to create a performance piece about your day so far? Would you create performance art, a poem, a dance, or a monologue? Write a short description of the kind of project you would like to work on.

PREPARE

Work on Your Poem

You are going to write an original poem and use it to compete with your classmates in a modified version of a poetry slam.

As you prepare to write your poem, keep in mind that it need not rhyme, and there is no limitation in terms of style. Here's an excerpt from the performance poem "After Cages" by well-known performance poet Cin Salach:

But you are feeling the wind in your hair, finally
After all these years
And the answer is almost too easy:
Send history packing,
But keep the future panting.
Claim this sky for yourself.
Make it sacred.
Declare it off limits to anyone
Who isn't madly in love with you.
Understand that not everyone will be.

Recite the excerpt aloud a few times. Experiment with its rhythm and sound. Choose specific words to emphasize. Think about what the poem is saying but also how it sounds as you speak it. Think about movements that might enhance the poem.

Now you're ready to try your hand at writing your own poem.

From the Field: Variety Show

Prepare a variety show containing acts such as a brief one-act monologues, improvisation selections, lipsyncs, and perhaps a small sketch about the faculty.

Next have other classes sign up to view your show. Each day your variety show can be taken to new classrooms.

LeAnn Gausman, Theatre Teacher, Parma Ohio

Go over the rules for the poetry slam with students. Tell them that they will be expected to write their own poem for the slam, but remind them that three minutes to perform the poem is actually a short time. Ask them to think about a subject for their poem while you time three minutes—calling out "One, two, three" as the minutes pass. This should help them get a feel for the length of time they have to work with.

Encourage students to use props or costumes if this will help them with their performance. Also remind them that they should be responsive to their fellow performers in a positive, encouraging way.

Theatre Journal

Use the following as an additional or substitute prompt.

Do you feel more comfortable performing in front of an audience when you are "yourself" or when you are playing a character? Many people prefer the feeling of security that can come from speaking as someone else. In your journal, explore your feelings as a performer.

PREPARE

Work on Your Poem

Tell students that their performance poems will be more effective if they use their own voices. That is why it's important for students to speak their lines out loud as early as possible. Tell students to ask, "Does it sound like me?" In addition, complete sentences and correct grammar are not necessarily required. Some students may express themselves best in sentence fragments or images. Again ask, "Does it sound like me?" The most effective poems will probably have intense personal meaning to the student.

Chapter 25 Other Theatre Forms **337**

Writing a Performance Poem

Discuss with students the idea that distinctions between types of theatrical performances have blurred over the years. Grand opera has adopted many of the design elements of the musical, which has sometimes resulted in more stylized, less cumbersome settings and quicker, smoother scene changes. Musicals, at the same time, have evolved in the direction of opera, with many musical plays now *through-sung* (with little or no spoken dialogue, as in *Evita* and *Les Misérables*). Some musicals that started out on Broadway, such as Stephen Sondheim's *Sweeney Todd*, are now being performed by opera companies.

The gap is also breaking down between performance art, stand-up comedy, and one-person concerts. HBO, MTV, and other media showcase some of the younger and often radical performers that defy easy categorization.

Suggest that interested students research some of these performance artists and new performance pieces (see Substitute Teacher Activities on page 340).

It would be a good idea to preview your students' poems before they present them to be sure they have not crossed boundaries established by you or your school for language or sexual content.

Writing a Performance Poem

Follow the steps below to write a poem of your own.

1. Relax your mind and body, and let images and words come to you. Spend five minutes writing down the images as they pass through your mind. Don't judge them; just let them in. At the end of five minutes, stop writing. Read through what you've written, and decide which image or line appeals to you most. Use that as a jumping-off point for creating your poem.
2. Make sure what you're writing is something you care about. Your poem might be about anything: a favorite photograph, a deep fear, a lonely feeling, or a great day. Whatever you choose to write about, try to come up with images that paint verbal pictures and/or make strong statements.
3. Once you've written a few lines, begin to speak them out loud. This should lead you to other images and lines.
4. Get your body into it. Performance poets tend to use their bodies expressively, so don't feel as if your feet are nailed to the floor. You can use your voice, body, and expressions to enhance the meaning of your poem.
5. Pay attention to the rhythm of your poem, and think about where you might pause or extend a moment for effect.
6. Rework your poem based on the movement you can add to it. When choosing words, think in terms of how they will help you perform the poem. Think about how the words sound as you say them aloud.

When you feel that you've created a poem that fulfills your intentions, rehearse it a few times to make sure it comes in under the three-minute time limit. You don't have to memorize your poem; you may prefer to read it. However, if you can memorize it, do so. This will add to your freedom of movement and help you better "feel" the language. However, whether you choose to memorize your poem or not, you should be familiar enough with it to be able to move and create a relationship with your audience as you perform.

Notes

PRESENT

Perform Your Poem

When your name is called, take your poem and/or your Activity Sheet with you to the front of the room. Wait as your teacher randomly chooses five judges from among your classmates. The teacher will also choose a timekeeper.

When the judges have been selected, take a moment to center yourself. A few deep breaths will help you. When you are ready, nod to the timekeeper, who will then begin timing your presentation. Introduce the title of your poem. Then begin to perform. Remember that this is a poetry slam—the way you perform your poem will greatly affect your score. Keep your performance fresh and exuberant.

When you have finished, take a brief bow, hand in your poem and/or Activity Sheet to your teacher, and return to your seat. The judges' results regarding your performance will be tabulated at the end of the class.

CRITIQUE

Evaluate a Classmate's Poetry Performance

As a judge for the class poetry slam, listen carefully and then take a moment to create a Poetry Slam Rating Sheet similar to the one below. You will be giving an overall rating from 0 to 10, with 10 being the best possible score. Here are some pointers from the official Poetry Slam Inc. Web site:

- "We use the word poem to include text and performance. Some say you should assign a certain number of points for a poem's literary merit and a certain number of points for the poet's performance. Others feel that you are experiencing the poem only through the performance, and it may be impossible to separate the two. You will give each poem only one score."
- "Trust your gut; and give the better poem the better score."
- "Be fair. We all have our personal prejudices, but try to suspend yours for the duration of the slam. On the other hand, it's okay to have a prejudice that favors the true and the beautiful over the mundane and superficial, the fascinating over the boring and pedestrian."

Poetry Slam Rating Sheet

Judge:

Poet:

Title of Poem:

Score from 0 to 10

Under three minutes?
(If NO, subtract 1 point.)

Final score:

Notes

PRESENT

Perform Your Poem

Tell students that they have the option of making eye contact with audience members during their presentations or of maintaining a private focus. A poem that seems directly addressed to others (especially if it contains the word *you*) will benefit from the performer's making eye contact. Tell them to:

- Look directly at an audience member and establish eye contact.
- Address a few lines directly to that person.
- Find another audience member to establish eye contact with.
- Look directly at that person, and so on.

A poem that is more introspective (that is centered on the word *I*) might be performed with a private focus. Here's how:

- Find a spot on the back wall slightly above the heads of your audience.
- Keep your eyes focused in that general area as you perform.

CRITIQUE

Evaluate a Classmate's Poetry Performance

Hand out the Take Part in a Poetry Slam Critique Sheets or have students copy the Rating Sheet in their books on a piece of paper. In either case, they will be expected to give a final score of 0 to 10 and to work with the rest of the class to establish an overall winner of the slam.

You may wish to point out that few performers will achieve a "perfect" score of 10, while 0 should probably be reserved for performers who fail completely to meet the criteria of a performance poem. (That is, merely performing may be considered worth a few points.)

Have students turn in their Rating Sheets for you to tabulate. After you have reviewed student critiques, trim off the evaluator's name and hand out the sheets to the subjects of the evaluations.

Chapter 25 Test

The test for this chapter is available in blackline master form in the Resource Binder, page 105.

For More Information

Books

Bell, John, *Puppets, Masks, and Performing Objects,* MIT Press, 2001.

Coger, Leslie Irene, and Melvin R. White, *Readers Theatre Handbook: A Dramatic Approach to Literature,* Scott, Foresman and Company, 1982.

Dennison, George, editor, Geoffrey Gardner, editor, Taylor Stoehr, editor, *An Existing Better World: Notes on the Bread and Puppet Theatre,* Autonomedia, 2000.

Eleveld, Mark, editor, *The Spoken Word Revolution: Slam, Hip Hop & the Poetry of a New Generation,* Sourcebooks, 2003.

Tanner, Fran Averett, *Readers Theatre Fundamentals,* Clark Publishing/Perfection Learning, 1993.

Other Media

www.slamnews.com
www.e-poets.net/library/slam/
www.theaterofmemory.com/art/bread/bread.html

By Word of Mouth: Storytelling in America, VHS, Insight Media, 1984.

Jay O'Callahan: A Master Class in Storytelling, VHS, Insight Media, 1983.

Jamaican Storyteller/Performer Thomas Osha Pinnock, VHS, Insight Media, 2000.

Additional Projects

1 Make your own puppet. It can take any form you like: finger puppet, marionette, sock puppet, or a design of your own.

2 Work with a small group of classmates to create a multimedia performance using the spoken word, live and recorded music, and movement.

3 Choose a literary selection or a collage of shorter pieces from newspapers, magazines, or letters from which to create a Readers Theatre performance. Direct the performance piece for the class, and then explain and justify your artistic choices and interpretation.

4 Make a videotape of the performance poem you created for this chapter's project. Use it to further refine your poem and your performance.

5 Research and write a report on a theatre counterpart such as Bunraku, shadow puppets, Punch and Judy, and so on, or other popular poetry forms such as the television program *Def Poetry.* Be prepared to present your report to the class. Include two visual aids.

6 Choose a monologue or scene from those found in Unit Eight and create a performance piece based on that play—change the play in any way you see fit in order to make a statement.

Substitute Teacher Activities

Here are a few suggestions for one or more days when you will be out of the classroom:

- Assign the Re-create a Classic Worksheet on page 103 of the Resource Binder.
- Assign one or more of the Additional Projects on this page.
- Teach the Performance Art section of the Student Handbook on pages 562-563 and the Readers Theatre section on pages 564-565.
- Have students use the Internet to research some of these performance artists: Danny Hoch, Eddie Izzard, Ali G, Don L. Lee, Reg E. Gaines, Bob Holman, Henry Rollins, and Lydia Lunch.
- Have students **Write a Description** of how they would combine at least three media to tell a news story. Students can browse news magazines and papers to find their stories.

Master of the Craft

Marc Smith: The "Slampapi"

"Smith's almost visionary on the need to rescue poetry from its lowly status in the nation's cultural life."

—*Smithsonian* magazine

Not many people can lay claim to single-handedly creating a brand-new art form. But in 1987, poet Marc Smith had a big idea. It was spawned from his feeling that poetry needed a public forum beyond the sometimes academic readings at colleges and bookstores. He wanted a forum for competitive performance poetry. The big idea began to take shape in 1987 when he persuaded the owner of Chicago's Green Mill Tavern to open its doors to the first ever poetry slam. And from that point on, the poetry slam phenomenon has just kept growing. Today more than 150 American cities host their own slams. And now there are even versions of the slam going on in England, Germany, Israel, and Sweden.

The man who made it all happen—the father of the poetry slam, or "Slampapi," as he is called in the performance community—is a terrific poet in his own right. Smith's innate sense of rhythm and his grittily realistic, urban poems tend to break poetic boundaries. His performances, both as a soloist and with his ensemble of performance poets and jazz musicians, blend the eloquence and beauty of poetry with the drama of theatre. His work has gained an international following—and Smith has become one of the most influential performance poets in the world.

In addition to a heavy touring schedule, Smith writes, performs, and continues to host and perform for the Uptown Poetry Slam's avid standing-room-only houses.

Marc Smith, aka the Slampapi

Kiss It

If you need to kiss it,
Kiss it.
If you need to kick it,
Kick it.
If you need to scream it,
Scream it.
But kiss it, kick it, scream it
Now.

–Marc Smith

Master of the Craft

More About Marc Smith

Marc Smith's first book, *Crowdpleaser,* celebrates The Green Mill Tavern and the people who frequent the poetry competitions that take place there. The book is illustrated by Michael Acerra, and it is a fascinating document filled with Smith's poetry and stories. As with Smith's best poetry slam work, *Crowdpleaser* defies labels and presents new ways of sharing the poetic form.

Visit Marc Smith's Web site at: *www.slampapi.com.*

Visit the Poetry Slam Web site at: *www.poetryslam.com.*

Quotable

One thing, though, is for sure: Carl Sandburg jump-upstarted me. Lover, populist, Swede . . . passionate eyeball scrutinizing the world, he could be just as damn everything as everybody else . . . including careless. (That's where he connects to me.) But when there's a lot to get done, who's got enough daylight to worry about how many Ps and Qs are in the soup?

Marc Smith, Poet

Theatre Then and Now

Bunraku

Bunraku may be an ancient form, but elements of its puppetry format are still very much alive today. For example, members of the Thistle Theatre of Seattle, Washington, perform a Bunraku version of "Little Red Riding Hood." The scenes in which the Wolf opens his huge mouth to swallow Grandma and Little Red whole are especially scary—and funny.

Much Asian theatre makes use of theatrical conventions that are unfamiliar to Western culture—or are only recently coming to be appreciated. For example, in Japanese Noh theatre, stagehands dressed in black appear at appropriate times to hand an actor a fan or a sword or to position a stool for the actor to sit on. These stagehands are presumed by the experienced audience to be invisible. Likewise, the puppeteers in Bunraku—although they are fully visible at all times—are presumed to be invisible, which allows the audience to focus on the fluid and delicate movements of the puppets.

Theatre Then and Now

Puppetry for All Time

Bunraku: An Ancient Puppetry Form Many consider Japanese Bunraku the most highly evolved form of puppetry in the world. Offering a unique combination of puppet manipulation, recitation, and music, Bunraku takes many years to master. Its name, loosely translated, means "puppets and storytelling."

Bunraku developed from an ancient Japanese tradition of traveling storytellers. At the same time there were also traveling puppeteers. It is not clear when these two art forms came together, but Bunraku is thought to have come about in 1684. That is when the first known Bunraku theatre opened in Osaka.

Bunraku puppets were about half the size of human beings. They had many moveable parts: Their eyes (and eyebrows) moved, their mouths opened and shut, and their arms and hands moved in very human-looking ways.

The puppeteers in Bunraku were always visible to the audience. They brought the puppets onstage in full view of the audience. Three puppeteers were needed to operate each main character puppet.

The narrator, meanwhile, told the entire story—also in full view of the audience—using a variety of vocal techniques. In addition to telling the story, he or she whispered, chanted, sang, or wept the dialogue for each puppet in the play. A musical accompanist provided music and sound effects to simulate rain, wind, and so on.

Today Bunraku is enjoying a revival. In 1985, The National Bunraku Theatre was granted a permanent home in the place of its origin, Osaka, where it produces four shows a year. Bunraku masters and puppet-makers are aging, however, and there is some question as to whether there will be sufficient interest from the younger generation to continue the Bunraku tradition.

A Bunraku puppetry performance.

342 **Unit Six** Theatre and Its Counterparts

For More Information

Books

Ando, Tsuruo, *Bunraku: The Puppet Theater*, Walker/Weatherhill, 1970.

Baird, Bil, *The Art of the Puppet*, Macmillan, 1965.

Other Media

Visit the Puppeteers of America Web site at: *www.puppeteers.org.*

Bread & Puppet Theatre: Today's Political Puppetry

Peter Schumann founded the Bread & Puppet Theatre in 1962. During the Vietnam War era, Schumann and his collaborators staged outdoor performances on New York City's Lower East Side. These were often in the form of block-long processions of papier-mâché puppets depicting anti-war themes. Bread & Puppet's figures moved hypnotically. They also varied greatly in scale: The smallest puppets fit on one finger. The largest were more than eight feet tall and were designed to be held high above the audience by means of long poles draped with fabric and manipulated by several puppeteers.

The Bread & Puppet Theatre became widely known for its unique brand of puppet-and-mask political theatre, and its work has inspired and influenced a generation of artists. In 1974, the group moved to Vermont and settled on a farm just outside the tiny village of Glover. One of the outbuildings became a museum for the retired puppets, masks, and paintings once used by the company. The museum is open to the public from May through October, and admission is free, in keeping with Bread & Puppet's egalitarian philosophy.

Members of Bread & Puppet Theatre display their creations.

One of the oldest nonprofit, self-supporting theatre companies in the United States, Bread & Puppet Theatre tours its shows all over the world. But during the summer months, visitors can often catch a performance at the farm.

A typical puppet from the Bread & Puppet Theatre collection.

Other Cultures, Other Times

Punch and Judy

Punch and Judy go back hundreds of years in British history, and prior to that, Punch is believed to have been based on a character in Italian *commedia dell' arte.* He may even go back as far as the ancient Romans and Greeks. His persona is aligned with that of mischief-makers and trickster figures found in most cultures.

Punchinello, as he was originally named, was at first a puppet on strings. The slapstick-swinging hand puppet that became known as Mr. Punch developed later. No one knows exactly when he teamed up with Judy, but the duo has been battling it out for decades. Recently there has been some opposition to Punch's violent attacks on all the puppets around him, particularly his better half, but The Punch and Judy College of Professors and the Punch and Judy Fellowship, both located in Great Britain, are sworn to keep Punch and Judy puppetry true to its historical form—whacks, smacks, and all.

For more information on these organizations and their namesakes, visit *www.punchandjudy.com* and *www.punchandjudy.org.*

Notes

Chapter 25 Other Theatre Forms **343**

Chapter 26

Stage to Film

This chapter discusses theater and early films as well as theatre scripts and screenplays, with an emphasis on how screenplays differ from theatre scripts. Students will be introduced to writing for the screen.

Objectives

1. to understand how the elements of theatre and film differ
2. to direct and present an informal reading of an original screenplay
3. to evaluate a screenplay from the point of view of a producer
4. to adapt a scene from a play into a screenplay

National Standards

Chapter 26 meets these National Theatre Standards:

Proficient 4a, 4c, 7b
Advanced 1b, 4e, 4f

Project Specs

The object of a screenplay is to tell a story that an audience can relate to, so encourage students to tell their stories simply but dramatically. Scenes that contain two shots can run for several speeches without a cut, whereas scenes that are made up mostly of closeups need a cut with each change of speaker.

On Your Feet

Show, Don't Tell Let the students know that you will re-enact a moment in history with a speech given to a particular audience. They must then react as the audience did when the words were first spoken. In your best presidential-Bostonian-German accent say, *"Ich bin ein Berliner."* Students should cheer this statement. Discuss the historical reasons for the speech and why it has gone down in history. To hear the entire speech, visit *www.ex.ac.uk/german/abinitio/chap5-10.html.*

Chapter 26 Stage to Film

The inspiration for a film can come from many different sources. Autobiographies, news stories, historical events, and novels are just a few of the possibilities. Live theatre plays are another rich resource for film plots.

Project Specs

Project Description For this assignment, you will turn a scene from a play into a screenplay of no more than ten minutes and then direct it.

Purpose to understand how the elements of theatre and film differ

Materials an outline or the Stage to Film Activity Sheet your teacher provides

Theatre Terms

adapt
screenplay
storyboard
takes

On Your Feet

In a group with three or four classmates, improvise a scene from an important moment in history. Have members of the "audience" try to be the first to guess what historical event you are portraying.

Donald Sutherland, Stockard Channing, and Will Smith appear in the film adaptation of John Guare's *Six Degrees of Separation.*

Theatre Terms

adapt to modify a text from its original form to another

screenplay a text that has been written for performance as a movie or television show; it includes dialogue as well as audio information and camera shots

storyboard a series of rough sketches that depict the chronological sequence of a film

takes shots that are recorded on film

PREVIEW

Theatre and Early Film

In the very early days of film, moviemakers borrowed heavily from the theatre—a dramatic art form that could easily be translated to this new medium. Films made in the early 1900s were essentially nothing more than plays captured on film. The camera took the place of the audience—sitting in a fixed position, taking in all the action in its limited range of view. The camera looked straight ahead, to the left a bit, and to the right a little. And just as on the stage, the actors played to their audience—the camera.

By the 1920s, innovations had been made that revolutionized film. Editing became an art, so that scenes on film could now be shifted, shortened, rearranged, or cut out completely. The camera could move in many directions: up and down and in close enough to allow the audience to see the actor's face alight with joy or stained with tears. New types of lights were being created for the sole purpose of lighting movies. Indeed, a brand-new industry was born to supply filmmakers with all the technical equipment they needed.

Theatre was also changing during this period. The stage and sets were being used in new ways, and innovative approaches to conveying the themes and plot of the play were introduced. But never again would the stage and the screen be so closely aligned as they were in those early days of movies.

The Theatre Script and the Screenplay

The script is the basic tool of both theatre and film. Producers, directors, actors, and technical professionals working on the stage and in the movies rely on the script for its plot, characters, and language—then they apply their own creative inspiration and expertise. The kinds of scripts used in these two mediums are very different.

Although theatrical scripts provide varying amounts of information about characters' attitudes and technical elements such as lighting and scenery, the main emphasis is on what characters say—the dialogue. Technical professionals are often left to their own devices and directors to their own concepts in communicating the details of time, place, movement, and mood of a play.

A film script, or **screenplay,** on the other hand, is much more of a technical document. It includes all the characters' dialogue, but it also provides audio and visual information. Settings, camera shots and angles, and other

PREVIEW

Theatre and Early Film

Because of the comparatively primitive nature of early camera and lighting equipment, the first movies were filmed on sets constructed out-of-doors with no ceilings, so that the filmmakers could take advantage of natural lighting. Some of the best and most consistent natural lighting in the U. S. was on the Pacific coast, which is one reason the film industry moved early in its development to California and the area that would become Hollywood.

The Theatre Script and the Screenplay

Until the advent of the "talkies" in 1927, film dialogue had to be presented in written form projected on the screen. This meant that the dialogue of even the most eloquently written stage play had to be reduced to its bare essentials. But a study of these early silent films may reveal that an amazing amount of storytelling can be done without a word.

There may be a great deal of difference from one script to another regarding stage directions. Shakespeare used almost no stage directions beyond enter and exit. George Bernard Shaw was famous for his extended stage directions, which often make as interesting reading as the dialogue itself.

The play *Six Degrees of Separation* was originally presented on stage with simple, stylized set pieces, highlighted with expressive lighting. As usual, the movie version made use of elaborate, realistic backgrounds. The following prompts can be used to exercise **critical viewing skills.**

- Based on the characters' clothing and location, what can you tell about where and when the story takes place?
- Do you think this story looks like a comedy or a drama? Why?

Resource Binder

- Stage to Film Activity Sheet, p. 106
- Analyze Camera Techniques Worksheet, p. 107
- Critique Sheet: Scene for a Screenplay, p. 108
- Stage to Film Test, p. 109
- Camera Shots, p. 150
- Script Format, p. 151

To Have on Hand

- Examples of screenplays, preferably adaptations from plays
- Videotapes or DVDs of the film versions of the same screenplays
- A sample storyboard

Handbook Connections
pages 556-557

A play does not necessarily need a lot of stage directions; one with few directions gives the director and actors a greater degree of latitude as to how they stage a scene. A shooting script, however, contains much more than dialogue and stage directions. It also includes camera shots and angles, sound effects and special effects, and—in the byplay of intercuts described—an implied outline for film editing.

The Film Script Up Close

Show, Don't Tell To help students visualize such technical terms as MEDIUM SHOT and SPLIT SCREEN, collect and mount a number of pictures that demonstrate these camera techniques. Display them while students work on this chapter. Other terms, such as DISSOLVE and PAN, because they involve movement, can best be understood through film clips.

Technical Terms for the Screenplay

Discuss all the technical terms with the students until you are certain that they understand each one. If possible, create a video montage that includes all of these techniques and discuss them one by one as they appear on the video. Alert students to the fact that some shots are much more difficult to achieve than others.

Following are more technical terms to share with students.

BIRD'S-EYE VIEW a camera shot from a very high angle

WORM'S-EYE VIEW a camera shot from a very low angle

IMPACT ANGLE a quick cut from one subject to another

EYE-LEVEL SHOT a shot from a motionless camera, positioned about the height of a person's eyes

AROUND-THE-WORLD SHOT the camera pans 360° around the scene

ABSTRACT ANGLES the camera is positioned on a tilt

Students may use Camera Shots, page 150 in the Resource Binder, or the list of terms on these pages as they develop their ideas.

effects are all described. A page of a film script usually equals one minute of film time. If a character appears on film for ten seconds, his or her part must take up no more than an inch or so of space on a page. If a scene goes on for five minutes, the writer must describe elements of the action for five pages.

Writers who **adapt,** or modify, theatrical work for film must consider all the audio and visual elements of their scenes. Each element must appear in the script at the time it will appear in the film. Thus, screenplay writers must think in audio, visual, and verbal terms throughout each scene they write. In order to describe camera angles and shots, visual effects, scene descriptions and so forth, screenwriters use special terminology. You will use these terms as you adapt a scene.

The Film Script Up Close

The common film script terms below should be indicated in all caps.

Technical Terms for the Screenplay

INT. interior shot

EXT. exterior shot

CLOSE SHOT a shot that shows only the head and shoulders of a person

CLOSEUP (CU) a shot that shows only a person's head

DISSOLVE a gradual fading out of the picture

DOLLY when the entire camera is moved toward or away from the subject

FREEZE FRAME when the image is momentarily stopped, or "frozen"

INTERCUT camera shots that go back and forth between scenes or people

INSERT a momentary closeup shot of an important person, place, or thing that cuts into another shot

LONG SHOT (LS) a long-distance shot that shows people from head to toe along with considerable background

MATCH CUT shot that cuts from highlighting something in one situation to highlighting the same thing in a different situation

MEDIUM SHOT (MS) a shot of people or a person from the waist up

MONTAGE two or more related scenes blended onscreen at the same time (label "MONTAGE" and "END OF MONTAGE")

O.C. off-camera sounds or dialogue

MOVING SHOT indicates that the camera moves with the characters

PAN a shot that moves slowly from left to right or right to left

P.O.V. point of view, a shot seen from the point of view of the character

SERIES OF SHOTS shots showing different aspects of a scene

SFX special effects, either audio or visual

SPLIT SCREEN one or more subjects shown on screen at the same time, as from two different films

Notes

SUPER superimpose one object over another, such as title over a setting

TWO SHOT a camera shot of two people

V.O. voiceover; a voice is heard, but the speaker is not seen in the shot

ZOOM the camera lens is used to create a rapid closeup

Requirements for Stage vs. Film

Following are different ways of approaching movie and theatre presentations.

Acting Smaller gestures and more nuanced expressions are needed by the film actor because the camera is so close. Theatre calls for broad gestures.

Makeup Age can't be camouflaged on film—even with makeup. Makeup needs to pass the "closeup" test. Makeup can take off or add years onstage.

Voice and Sound Unlike stage actors, film actors don't have to worry about projecting to "the last row of the theatre."

Costumes and **Scenery** must look real on film even in closeups.

Takes When working in film, actors get as many **takes,** or filmed scenes, as is necessary to get it right. Stage actors can't go back and repeat misspoken lines.

Continuity Hair, costumes, sets, and so on, need to match from shot to shot in film (the actor holding a glass in the right hand for one shot, can't be holding it in the left for the next).

Sequence A play is done from beginning to end. With film, scenes are done in any order that makes sense financially—usually organized by setting. All the scenes for one location are done at the same time.

Cast of thousands Film can use hundreds of extras; even with a small cast, film needs many people.

```
                    EDDIE
          Where are they?

Angie stares back defiantly.

                    EDDIE (cont'd)
          I don't have time for this.
               (to Ushers)
          Take her back the theatre. Call Luther
          and tell him we got her.

Two ushers advance on Angie. She plants her heavy boot in one of
their guts. He goes down. Two others grab her from behind and drag
her fighting all the way to the van.
```

Megaplex by Oliver Oertel

Formatting for a screenplay includes a margin of about 1.25 inches for scenes and 1.75 inches for directions and scene headings. Dialogue margins are deeper–about 2.25 inches. Technical directions are set on a line length of 58 characters.

Beginning Students
Encourage students to use mostly long shots, medium shots, and two shots, so that their scenes can run for several lines of dialogue without needing cuts.

Advanced Students
Some students will undoubtedly want to experiment with moving shots or pans, SFX, and so on. Even so, encourage them not to try to cram every kind of effect into their ten-minute scenes but to make judicious choices of the special kinds of shots that will best present their stories.

Vocabulary Enhancement

Transposing a scene from a comparatively limited stage space to—for example—an outdoor scene with unlimited vistas is called *opening up.*

From the Field: Bringing a Play to Television

The biggest challenge [in translating a play into television theatre] is that you only have so much money and that tells you how many days you'll have to shoot the film . . . . We had a 100-page script to shoot in 12 days, which was a Herculean task for the director and actors, and that ripples out to the entire crew. You have to shoot a lot of pages each day, and that means you have to have all the tools available every minute. The actors are always working, 12 hours a day. You're always working under the gun.

Dennis Doty, Producer of the PBS film *Collected Stories*

PREPARE

Work on Your Screenplay

Remind students that if they are adapting a published story or play for a film project, they would need to obtain permission from the copyright holder before making a commercial film of it. However, school projects usually come under the heading of "fair use."

Discuss that a scene from a play that takes place in a limited space with limited characters may often be opened up in a film version to include more backgrounds and more actors (possibly nonspeaking extras). That is, a scene that takes place in a restaurant may be represented on stage by a table and two chairs and only two characters plus a serving person. In a film, that same scene would probably show the entire restaurant with dozens of diners, serving people, cooks, etc., all going about their business. In such a case, it becomes the responsibility of the director, camera operator, and film editor to maintain what focus is necessary on the principals and their dialogue.

Show, Don't Tell Using a scene from a play students are familiar with, demonstrate how one might begin to create a storyboard by drawing a few panels on the chalkboard. Try to show various camera angles. Then explain that a storyboard may look rather like a comic strip, but contains more detailed panels and may or may not suggest dialogue.

In a play, the primary focus is usually on dialogue, while in a film, the primary focus is usually on action. For this reason, it is rarely possible—or desirable—to retain all of a play's dialogue, no matter how well written. Tell students to look for ways to condense and telescope dialogue or—often better—to take advantage of film's unique characteristics to suggest meaning without explicit dialogue.

PREPARE

Work on Your Screenplay

Create an outline or use the Stage to Film Activity Sheet your teacher has given you. Use the sample screenplay, the abbreviations found in Technical Terms for the Screenplay on pages 346–347, and the formatting suggestions discussed previously to help you.

First, choose a scene to adapt. Try to choose a play that you are very familiar with and that you find interesting. Remember that you are adapting only a small portion of this play into a screenplay, so choose a scene with a good deal of impact.

Second, plan your camera shots. Visualize how you will shoot the action. Where will each character be relative to the camera? How will the camera follow each character? How much of the setting will be included? Will you start with a long shot or a closeup? Will one scene dissolve into the next? To help answer these questions, you should create a **storyboard.** A storyboard is a series of drawings showing the sequential shots needed in a scene. A simple drawing of each important camera shot will give you a concrete idea as to the angle and distance of the shot, as well as showing how each shot relates to the next. You can also use a small box with a square cut out at each end to look through in order to "frame" the shot and get an idea of how it would look on camera. Also, ask yourself what can be shown visually in each scene rather than being talked about in the dialogue?

Next, work on the script. Indicate audio and visual elements on the script in the appropriate places, as well as the camera shots needed based on your storyboard. Have fun with the flexibility film offers. Remember that cameras allow quick changes in time and place that are much more difficult in theatre. Then, think about the dialogue. Will you use all the dialogue that appears in the play, leave some out, or condense it?

Then, do an informal reading. When you have a rough draft of your screenplay, ask classmates to help you with a reading. In addition to assigning each role, assign one person the job of reading the audio and visual elements you have incorporated into the screenplay. Time the reading to make sure it does not exceed ten minutes. Make notes indicating any necessary changes.

Last, have a final reading and rehearsal. When you have written a draft with which you are completely satisfied, call for a final reading and a rehearsal.

Backstage Gossip: Unresponsiveness of Film

Critic Walter Kerr says that the difference between theatre and movies is the way a live audience reacts to the actors and how the actors respond to the audience.

"This never happens at a film because the film is already built, finished, sealed, incapable of responding to us [the audience] in any way. The actors can't hear us or feel our presence; nothing WE do in our liveness, counts. We could be dead and the film would purr out its appointed course, flawlessly, indifferently."

PRESENT

Hold a Reading of Your Screenplay

When your name is called, give a copy of your screenplay and the original play script to your teacher. With the actors who will be helping you present the screenplay, walk to the playing area. Be sure chairs are arranged facing the audience with the actors arranged in a line across the playing area.

Stand to the side and announce the title of your screenplay. Then identify the play on which it is based and the scene your actors will read. As in your rehearsals, one of the actors will read any camera, lighting, or sound directions aloud. Take your seat and enjoy the performance.

When the actors have finished reading your screenplay, initiate a short round of applause. The actors should then stand, bow, and return to their seats.

Answer any questions your classmates may have about your screenplay.

Theatre Journal

Realistic scenic elements are more important in film than they are in theatre. To practice thinking in terms of film, highlight or list the set directions from a play you enjoy. Then jot down possible film settings that might communicate the same mood or stand in for the settings indicated in the play.

CRITIQUE

Evaluate Your Classmate's Adaptation

Choose one of the screenplay readings presented in class and evaluate it. Think of yourself as a producer being pitched a plan for a film. Ask yourself the questions below.

- Were you able to visualize the film from the presenter's description?
- Did the technical directions add to the drama or effectiveness of the script?
- How effective were the writer's choice of camera shots and special effects?
- Did the screenplay's plot incorporate enough action to be suitable for filming?

Based on your evaluation of the screenplay, give it a rating between 5 and 1, with 5 being "outstanding " and 1 being "needs much improvement." Write a paragraph explaining the reasons for scoring the screenplay the way you did.

PRESENT

Hold a Reading of Your Screenplay

Remind students that they will have to allow time in their ten minutes for stage directions and visual elements to be read. That is, ten minutes of dialogue may take longer than ten minutes with narration added.

Students should check in advance to be sure that chairs are arranged properly, all actors have their scripts, and so on. Presenters should plan in advance who sits where and practice graceful entrances and exits.

Theatre Journal

Use the following to help students with the prompt.

As you think of real settings in which to place your adapted stage scenes, keep in mind possibilities for long shots that establish the general scene and for moving shots, pans, dollies, and series shots that take advantage of the greater space and the possibilities of multiple angles.

CRITIQUE

Evaluate Your Classmate's Adaptation

Go over with students the points they should consider as they listen to the presentations. You may want to assign individual students to evaluate particular presenters so that everyone is evaluated once.

Encourage students to have a copy of Camera Shots, page 150 in the Teacher's Resource Binder, handy as they evaluate their classmate's adaptation.

Notes

Spotlight on

What the Stage Does That Film and Video Can't

ACTivity Suggest that three or four students form a panel to discuss the opposite proposition: What film and video can do that the stage can't. They might extend their discussion by indicating which they prefer and why.

Spotlight on

What the Stage Does That Film and Video Can't

When talking movies first appeared on the scene, there were many who thought theatre was dead. When television developed, people thought film had seen its last days. Neither of these predictions came true, of course, because each medium has something special to offer. Theatre is unique in the following ways:

Theatre is active. While film and television audiences are largely passive viewers of events, theatre audiences are active participants in the shows they attend. Their responses to the action affect the performances onstage. And in some cases, their active participation is requested or even required for a full performance.

Theatre is multidimensional. When they attend a theatrical production, audiences have to look around. Even proscenium arch theatres have characters that enter and exit from various locations. Sometimes, actors use the house for exits and entrances, and sometimes they even play scenes with or among audience members.

Theatre is a multimedia event. Many stage productions make use of visual arts in the production of a set and costumes. Some make use of video, film, and dance. There can be a lot going on up on the stage, with lots of different places for audience members to cast their eyes.

Every performance is unique. Because theatrical events are live, they are different every time they are performed. Each performance is open to new understanding and therefore, new opportunities for improvisation. You can see or perform in a theatrical performance a hundred times, and each time it will be different in some way.

Quotable

I want to resuscitate an idea of total spectacle, where the theatre will know how to take back from the cinema . . . . all that has always belonged to it.

Antonin Artaud, Actor, Director, and Theorist

350 Unit Six Theatre and Its Counterparts

Additional Projects

1. Videotape the screenplay you created using the actors who worked with you. Be aware of safety issues as you work. Share it with the class.
2. Research the differences between one-camera and three-camera scripts. Write a scene for a screenplay with each of the two formats in mind.
3. Film an improvised skit, and then write a screenplay taking into consideration what worked and what didn't work in your film.
4. Write a screenplay based on a scene that you thought was particularly effective in a play you've seen within the last year.
5. Do a reverse adaptation: Acquire a film script for a film you admire, and then adapt it for the stage.
6. Create and implement a production schedule for a scene from a film script of your choice.
7. Adapt the scene from *Copenhagen* by Michael Frayn or *The Prisoner of Second Avenue* by Neil Simon found in Unit Eight for use as a screenplay.

Chapter 26 Test

The test for this chapter is available in blackline master form in the Resource Binder, page 109.

For More Information

Books

Church, John, and Pamela Gibson, *The Oxford Guide to Film Studies*, Oxford University Press, 1998.

Corrigan, Timothy, *A Short Guide to Writing About Film*, Pearson Education, 2000.

Doyle, Christopher, *Backlit by the Moon*, Idea Books Amsterdam, 1997.

Ferrell, William K., *Literature and Film as Modern Mythology*, Greenwood Publishing Group, Incorporated, 2000.

Sklar, Robert, *A World History of Film,* Abrams, Hardback, 1993.

Other Media

More information on film can be found at *www.movies.yahoo.com.*

Substitute Teacher Activities

Below are a few suggestions for one or more days when you will be out of the classroom:

- Assign the Analyze Camera Techniques Worksheet on page 107 of the Resource Binder.
- Teach the Film section of the Student Handbook, pp. 556-557.
- Assign one or more of the Additional Projects on this page.
- Have students develop a **Play Evaluation Sheet** they can use while reading a play to determine its possible adaptation into a film. They should include such elements as characters, settings, theme, and a brief scene outline, plus a section for notes on why they think the play would make a good film.

Theatre Then and Now

Homer to Home Viewing

The two Homeric epics, *The Iliad* and *The Odyssey,* are so rich in complex characters, thrilling actions, and evocative cultural icons that they have stimulated the imaginations of storytellers and other artists for centuries. Two famous 20th-century novelizations are Nikos Kazantzakis's *The Odyssey: A Modern Sequel* and James Joyce's *Ulysses,* which transposes the story to 1904 Dublin, Ireland. Two musical stage versions are *The Odyssey* and *The Golden Apple,* which places the story in the state of Washington.

Theatre Then and Now

Homer to Home Viewing

Homer's *The Odyssey*

The Odyssey is an epic poem attributed to an author we call Homer. The story is probably 3000 years old, and the written version is about 1000 years old. *The Odyssey* was written to be recited—and perhaps read. Though not written as a play, it has nevertheless inspired many a poet, playwright, and filmmaker to adapt and expand its themes and plot.

The Odyssey tells the story of Ulysses, a hero of the Trojan War, who attempts to return to his home in Ithaca after the war. Unfortunately, he has angered the gods, who present him with a series of obstacles. During his ten-year journey, Ulysses encounters a land with a flower that causes deep sleep; a one-eyed monster called the Cyclops; Circe, the enchantress who turns men into beasts, and many others. All the while, his wife, Penelope, waits patiently for his return.

Homer's epic is exciting and beautifully written, and should certainly be read for its own sake as well as for an understanding of all the poems, paintings, plays, and films that allude to it.

"Every day in rehearsal there are moments that I feel . . . the presence and the weight of this text and its history and its long life, and how we're the part of this telling that has gone on for twenty-seven hundred years."

–Mary Zimmerman

Ulysses and Penelope

Mary Zimmerman's *The Odyssey*

Mary Zimmerman's adaptation of *The Odyssey* tells a tale much like the original poem. While Ulysses battles monsters and escapes the deadly sirens' call, his wife is being heavily pressured by suitors to forget him.

Like the poem, Zimmerman's play uses flashback and interesting details to tell the story. It also takes advantage of

Notes

Hermes and his men march onstage in Mary Zimmerman's 2000 production of **The Odyssey.**

contemporary technology. For example, gigantic video projections help create the setting for the underworld. And the lighting designed by Daniel Ostling represents settings ranging from "rosy-fingered dawn" to stormy seas.

The production draws on traditions in dancing and music, and the lyrical poetry of the original to communicate the breadth of Homer's epic tale.

O Brother, Where Art Thou?

Joel and Ethan Coen also owe much of their film *O Brother, Where Art Thou?* to Homer. They don't try to hide the fact—their references to the ancient epic are fairly easy to spot. But someone who didn't know a thing about Homer would think it was a modern tale.

The movie is a quirky comedy set in 1930s Mississippi. It tells the story of a chain-gang escapee, appropriately named Ulysses, who endures a series of trials as he makes his way home. It comes complete with sirens, a cyclops, and suitors for his estranged wife. In the end, Ulysses is restored to his family.

In the Coen brothers' adaptation, Homer is not only retold in a new medium—it is given a new translation, and a new audience.

John Turturro, Tim Blake Nelson, and George Clooney star in *O Brother, Where Art Thou?*, the contemporary film based on *The Odyssey.*

For More Information

Books

Ferrell, William K., *Literature and Film as Modern Mythology,* Greenwood Publishing Group, Inc., 2000.

Hamilton, Edith, *Mythology: Timeless Tales of Gods and Heroes,* Warner Books, 1999.

Homer, *The Odyssey,* tr. Robert Fitzgerald, Noonday Press, 1998.

Zimmerman, Mary, *The Odyssey: A Play,* Northwestern University Press, 2003.

Other Media

Homer's Odyssey, from Book I through Book XXIV and translated by Samuel Butler, can be read on the Internet by visiting *www.uoregon.edu/~joelja/odyssey.html* or *http://classics.mit.edu/Homer/odyssey.html.*

Visit *http://www.pbs.org/now/transcript/transcript_zimmerman.html* for the transcript of an interview with Mary Zimmerman conducted by Bill Moyers.

Films by the Coen Brothers

If you enjoyed the film *O Brother, Where Art Thou?* you might also enjoy the following films by Joel and Ethan Coen:

Blood Simple (1984) Film noir with plot twists and complex characters about a man who hires a private eye to spy on his wife.

Raising Arizona (1987) A dark comedy in which a childless couple decide to "borrow" a baby from a wealthy couple with quintuplets.

Miller's Crossing (1990) Set during prohibition, this film focuses on two rival gangs fighting for control. An advisor to the head of one of the mob families falls in love with his boss's love interest, which leads to a major battle.

Barton Fink (1991) One of the brothers' most bizarre films, this one involves a screenwriter holed up in a room with nothing to write.

The Hudsucker Proxy (1994) This film is the Coen brothers' first big studio picture. A young man is set up to be a corporate puppet but instead invents the Hula Hoop and becomes a national icon.

Fargo (1996) Chosen as number 84 in the American Film Institute's top 100 films of all time, this is another black comedy with lots of action. It tells the story of a man who plots his wife's kidnapping so that his wealthy father-in-law will pay a ransom.

The Big Lebowski (1998) A strange offering that follows "The Dude" as he tries to get compensation for a ruined rug. The film is officially recommended by the Norwegian Bowling Association.

The Man Who Wasn't There (2001) Reminiscent of *Blood Simple,* this film noir tells of a man who attempts to blackmail his wife's lover to get the cash he needs for an investment. When the lover is found dead, the plot begins to take some twists.

Chapter 27

Movies

This chapter presents the four phases of the filmmaking process: development, preproduction, production, and postproduction. Problems of continuity are explained. Students will learn how to develop an idea for an original screenplay.

Objectives

1. to learn about early and contemporary filmmaking and to understand the filmmaking process
2. to develop an idea for an original screenplay and follow it through all phases of development and production
3. to present the screenplay concept and production considerations to potential producers

National Standards

Chapter 27 meets these National Theatre Standards:
Proficient 4a, 4b
Advanced 1b, 4d, 4e

Project Specs

Writing an original screenplay is, of course, a very large undertaking. Here students are not asked to write a screenplay but simply to describe an idea for a film. The larger part of the project, however, involves considering that idea from the viewpoints of director, producer, and various technical personnel to get an idea of what would be involved in the actual filming.

On Your Feet

Suggest that students work with partners or in small groups to brainstorm and list as many movie-related jobs as they can think of. Then bring the class together to compare lists and to compile a master class list, classifying the jobs as best they can.

Chapter 27 Movies

Film and theatre share many common characteristics. They are both based on story and character, and they both have a lot to tell us about the human condition. Movies, however, approach storytelling in their own, unique way.

Project Specs

Project Description You will develop an idea for an original screenplay, follow it through all phases of development and production, and present your plan in five to ten minutes.

Purpose to understand the filmmaking process and to develop the art of conceptualizing a script and presenting it to others

Materials paper or the Movies Activity Sheet your teacher provides

Theatre Terms

backlot
continuity
development
final cut
postproduction
preproduction
production
rough cut
shooting script
soundstage
trailer
working script

On Your Feet

Think about the many jobs associated with making movies. There are actors and a director, of course. But many more people are needed to make even a small, low-budget movie. As a group, brainstorm and list as many of these as you can.

James Cameron's 1997 film *Titanic*, with Leonardo DeCaprio and Kate Winslet, used spectacular special effects.

Theatre Terms

backlot an outdoor lot where sets are created

continuity the cohesion of visual elements from take to take and from scene to scene

development the creation of a script and the plan by which the film will be produced

final cut the finished film

postproduction the phase of filmmaking when the editor does his or her work

preproduction the phase of filmmaking that must be completed before the film can be shot

production the phase of filmmaking in which the film is shot

rough cut the "first draft" of a film

shooting script a script version in which each shot is tracked by a number and type

soundstage the location in a studio where the production of a film is shot

trailer a film preview ad

working script a script-in-progress

354 **Unit Six** Theatre and Its Counterparts

PREVIEW

If you've ever sat through all the credits at the end of a movie, you have some idea of just how many people are involved in making a typical film. From the producer to the screenwriter to the cameraperson to the caterer, the making of most films requires the skills and talents of hundreds of professionals.

The Four Phases of the Filmmaking Process

Phase One: Development

The first phase of the production process is called **development.** This term refers to the actual creation of a script as well as the plan by which the film will be produced. The producer generally handles much of a film's early development work, which includes

- hiring or approving the director
- hiring or approving screenwriters or the script
- securing the financial resources needed to make the film

Once the director, screenwriter(s), and financial backing have been secured, the director puts together a plan for getting the best writing, acting, and technical

PREVIEW

The Four Phases of the Filmmaking Process

Show a film clip of the credits of an actual movie, preferably a comparatively technical one, such as an Indiana Jones or X-Men movie. Be prepared to pause the film frequently so that students can focus on job titles. (Some credits move far too fast to do this easily.) Some of the jobs (such as scenic carpenter) will be obvious; other jobs (such as best boy) do not immediately convey just what it is these people do. Suggest that volunteers take one job title each, research it, and report back to the class.

Students should understand that who works on what phase of the filmmaking process may be fluid, depending on the individual production circumstances. That is, in small-scale productions the producer and director may be the same person. This person may also be involved in the design and film editing. The same fluidity may hold true when any one of the production team—writer, producer, director, actor, and so on, is especially powerful or has been instrumental in putting together the whole production package. In the making of many movies, however, these jobs are clearly delineated.

Discuss the **development phase** with students including hiring the various personnel and finding backing.

In this scene from *Titanic,* the ship is beginning to sink. The following prompts can be used to exercise **critical viewing skills.**

- What are these people doing?
- How might this same scene be represented on the stage?
- From what you can see in the photo, what are some further prop pieces that might be appropriate in this setting?

Resource Binder

- Movies Activity Sheet, p. 110
- Create a Storyboard Worksheet, p. 111
- Critique Sheet: Concept for a Screenplay, p. 112
- Movies Test, p. 113
- Camera Shots, p. 150
- Script Format, p. 151

Handbook Connections
pages 556-557

To Have on Hand

- A collection of published screenplays
- Videotapes or DVDs of the film versions of the same screenplays
- A list of movie job titles and descriptions for students to compare with their class list of jobs
- Photographs or film footage that shows typical soundstages

Discussions about filmmaking most often concentrate on the production phase—the actual filming of scenes. Yet the development, preproduction, and postproduction phases are equally important and usually take far more time than does the actual filming.

Discuss the **preproduction phase,** including the schedules and budgets that need to be worked out.

ACTivity Have students work with partners or in small groups to chart an imaginary production schedule. Tell them to imagine a production schedule of six weeks (for a relatively simple, straightforward film). Then have them back up and chart the weeks and months they think would be necessary for conceptualizing, scriptwriting, design, construction, casting, wardrobe, and so on—then to move forward and chart the time they think it would take for postproduction work, including editing and marketing. Have students chart the whole process on a blank calendar.

crew for the project. A part of the director's job is creating the production schedule, a detailed plan that maps out all the film's stages of production.

To attract investors, the producer puts together a marketing packet containing the **working script** (a script-in-progress that is subject to change during the development, preproduction, and production phases). The packet also includes a list of the artists who will most likely be working on the film and a preliminary budget. Depending on the presentation, the script, and the artists involved, investors may opt to back the film financially. To do so, they usually must have a strong sense of the film's marketability or its potential for winning an audience. The investors make a percentage of the film's profits, so they naturally want the largest audience possible. Put simply, the investors pay advertising and production costs before the film is made in the hope that they can make money when the film is shown in theatres.

Phase Two: Preproduction

The next phase of the process is called **preproduction.** There are many tasks that must be completed during this phase before the director and the staff can move on to the actual shooting of the film. The production manager has key duties having to do with finalizing the shooting schedule and developing a workable budget.

An artist looks over the storyboard.

Quotable

Russell Carpenter, Director of Photography on the film, *Titanic,* had this to say about the dining room set.

Everything had to be bolted onto [a] steel frame so the set could withstand the pressure of being raised and lowered, with tons of water dumping into it . . . . First we'd film the scenes in which everything looks as elegant as possible, representing all the hope and innocence of the time; then, after some modifications to the set, we'd sink it and watch everything go belly up.

Next, actors must be auditioned for the various roles. Typically, the producer and the director work with a casting director (see the Career Focus on page 175) to find just the right actor for each role.

Once the casting is complete, there may be time in the schedule to have a brief rehearsal period before actual production begins. However, rehearsals are not necessarily a part of every preproduction phase—the film process differs from theatre in this crucial way. Without rehearsal, it's very difficult to put on a play. However, many film actors are used to doing films with little or no rehearsal. The director may work with the writers to create a storyboard—the series of images roughly depicting the chronological sequence of the film. From the storyboard process comes the **shooting script.** In a shooting script, each shot in the film is tracked by a specific number and type of shot. (See Technical Terms for the Screenplay on pages 346–347 of Chapter 26.) The shooting script usually goes through quite a few changes as preproduction and production move along.

Phase Three: Production

When a film moves into **production,** the work most people associate with moviemaking begins. The director works closely with the actors and crew and begins to shoot the film. Shooting may take place at a variety of locations—some films are shot on location in the actual place where the story is set; this might be anywhere from the Iowa countryside to a mountaintop in Nepal. Other films may be shot on a **backlot,** an outdoor lot where sets are created to simulate the location specified in the script. Indoor scenes can be shot on a **soundstage,** where a set has been built, or at an actual indoor location that has been rented for the shoot.

Films are hardly ever shot in the chronological sequence of the script. There are many factors that dictate what the shooting sequence will be. One major factor is location. Filmmakers typically shoot all the scenes that take place in a given location at the same time, rather than in the sequence in

Theatre Journal

Have you ever seen a movie that seemed to speak directly to you? Maybe it was about a family situation, a friendship, or an incident that reminded you of your own life. Maybe it spurred your imagination. Write about how the film affected you, and identify the reasons why you think it made such a strong impression.

Show, Don't Tell Discuss with students the casting process (including the use of agents) and the **production phase** of filmmaking.

Try to find images that show soundstages. Have students see if they can identify any of the cameras, lights, or other technical equipment in the images. Also ask students to try to identify the functions of the various individuals in the photographs.

Theatre Journal

Use the following as an additional or substitute prompt.

You might want to use the journal entry about the film that made a strong impression on you as a model for the screenplay concept you are going to write. Keep a list of the film's strong points and try to use equally strong ideas in your screenplay concept.

ACTivity Advanced Students Have students do research to compare the roles of the set designer, casting director, and costume designer involved in making a film as opposed to creating a theatre production.

Notes

Vocabulary Enhancement

There are two devices filmmakers use to help keep track of the many takes that may be shot. A *slate board* is held in front of the camera to begin each take. On it are written the name of the film, the number of the scene and the take, and whatever other information is thought necessary. That way, a film editor can tell immediately what take is on view.

A *daily sheet* lists every take and serves as a written index to the filmed scenes and where they are on the film reels or videotapes. *Breakdown sheets* are used during film production to help the director and technicians know what scenes will be shot where, when, and in what order.

Visual Cue

". . . when I was ten years old, my family crossing the Great Plains was wiped out by a band of wild Indians." Thus begins the story of *Little Big Man,* a film based on a book by Thomas Berger and directed by Arthur Penn. In the film, Dustin Hoffman plays a role that ranges from being a teenager to being the old man in the picture at the right. Use these prompts to stimulate students' **critical viewing skills.**

- Describe the appearance of the character Jack Crabb.
- How do you think the old man's voice would sound?
- How do you think his aged appearance was achieved?
- Do you think this scene would be shot early or late in the filming schedule? Why?

which they will appear in the film. For example, if several scenes take place at a restaurant over the course of the film, all the restaurant scenes will likely be shot at the same time. This saves setup time and money.

There are also situations in which the actors' makeup must be taken into account. For example in the 1970 film *Little Big Man,* Dustin Hoffman begins as a hundred-year-old man, and most of the film is shown in flashbacks as Hoffman's character remembers his life as a much younger man. At the end of the film, he is an old man again. The scenes of Hoffman in his hundred-year-old-man makeup were all shot at the same time, even though they actually appear at the beginning and at the end of the film. The makeup took several hours to apply, and it was more efficient in terms of both time and money to shoot those scenes all at once.

Dustin Hoffman as the ancient Jack Crabb telling his story in *Little Big Man.*

The director's job is split between coaching the actors in terms of performance and position, and collaborating with the camera crew. Most scenes are usually done in more than one take. To be sure that the shot will be workable later in the process, it may be filmed from a variety of angles, using different film techniques and performance perspectives. In other words, multiple takes allow the film crew to make sure the job is done right.

As the shots are completed, they are sent on to a special lab for processing and printing. The unused takes are not thrown away—they may be needed later during the editing process.

After shooting has been completed each day, the director, production manager, and cinematographer (shot designer) discuss the shooting that will take place on the following day. Each day, the shooting script is likely to change a bit

Quotable

Many years after he first saw Arthur Penn's classic film *Bonnie and Clyde,* critic Roger Ebert had this to say about it:

When I saw it, I had been a film critic for less than six months, and it was the first masterpiece I had seen on the job. I felt an exhilaration beyond describing. I did not suspect how long it would be between such experiences, but at least I learned that they were possible.

358 Unit Six Theatre and Its Counterparts

place to that point. The actors must keep themselves up to speed on the most current version of the script. At the end of a typical day's shoot, the actors study the script for the following day, and the film editor makes a copy of the best takes.

While the production phase is going on, the producer is taking care of the business aspects of the film. The producer usually becomes involved with the day-to-day artistic aspects only if there is a problem involving personnel changes, budget concerns, or scheduling questions. Otherwise the producer is generally taken up with issues of how to market the film. To that end, he or she (or they) will create a **trailer.** A trailer is a special preview advertisement that provides publicity for the film's upcoming release. Timing is important when it comes to advertising the film. The trailer is usually released six months before the film itself begins playing in theatres. Other advertising, such as that in newspapers, magazines, or outdoor signage, precedes the film's release by about a month.

Phase Four: Postproduction
After production of the film is complete, the crucial **postproduction** phase of the filmmaking process begins. At this stage, the editor steps into the spotlight. It is the editor who mixes the sound tape—including the music and sound effects needed—with the film images, matching them up for maximum effect. The editor performs one of

America in Film

The American film industry has reinforced cultural values since cameras began rolling. Silent films often featured the strong, handsome hero saving the beautiful and innocent girl from the grips of danger. During the Great Depression, movie audiences wanted to see idealistic and hopeful images. *Gone with the Wind,* even though it dealt with the devastation of the Civil War, portrayed the beautiful and genteel plantation South with strong characters who could solve their own problems. Shirley Temple made people sing, the Marx Brothers made people laugh, and that classic Depression-era film *The Wizard of Oz* encouraged audiences to forget their troubles and travel down that "yellow brick road" to a better future.

In the 1940s and 50s, Westerns gave life to the American belief in rugged individualism and self-reliance. Films about World War II reinforced the patriotism of the American public, in stark contrast to he darker films of the Vietnam War era.

This is why America loves the movies—to see who they are and what they can become.

Discuss Phase Four, the **postproduction phase,** with the students. This is where the editor's expertise is vitally important. Share with them any film editing experiences you have had or read about.

In recent years, especially with the advent of DVDs, some directors have reissued what are called *director's cuts*. Usually these reedits restore scenes that the director filmed and considered worthy of the film, but that were cut for various reasons from the final cut of the distributed film. Sometimes these DVDs even contain directors' comments on the scenes and how they contribute to the whole.

If you or any of your students have had the opportunity to view a director's cut and the original final cut for distribution, describe some of the restored scenes and comment on their function in the film as a whole.

ACTivity Have students bring in a list of films they know well. Have the class as a whole choose one film to discuss. Direct students as they talk about the film in terms of its setting, locations, director, cinematography, actors, and so on. Ask if there are any scenes they feel should have been cut, and why.

Vocabulary Enhancement

An *indie* is an independent film turned out by an independent filmmaker. (The filmmaker may also be referred to as an indie.) Indies are people who have broken away from the multimillion-dollar Hollywood machine to make smaller films on smaller budgets, often on topics that interest them, rather than topics considered commercial. In recent years independent filmmakers have received more awards and more attention, and there are now festivals devoted to them, such as Robert Redford's Sundance Film Festival.

Notes

Overseeing continuity is a very important job, but in many films a slip or two is made. Most viewers won't catch the continuity errors because the slips are usually very subtle and happen in a flash. For fun, rent a video or DVD and try to catch the continuity errors. One you might want to try is *Jerry McGuire*, which is reputed to have over ten continuity errors, four of them in the first half hour. Watch for this one: Jerry picks up Dorothy for their date, and she has her shoes on. Yet when Laurel comes out to bring Dorothy her forgotten key, she has her shoes in her hand.

ACTivity Tell students they are going to be taking careful note of the continuity in a scene you and a volunteer are about to perform. Tell them that, at the end of the scene, you will call a halt to the day's shooting and it is their job to take continuity notes so that the next scenes filmed will flow seamlessly into the work already done. Be sure to include a number of props and costume elements in your performance. Students' notes should include such things as what the actors onstage are wearing, who is sitting or standing where, the props actors are holding, the position of props actors have set down or picked up, and exact details of an actor's costume, including whether an actor's tie is tied or loose, whether an actor is wearing a hat or carrying it, which earrings an actress is wearing, and so on. After the students have written all their continuity notes, discuss what may have been missed.

the most important functions in the production process. The editor's assistant keeps a careful log with notations about every single shot. Often, the editor makes a **rough cut** first. This is similar to a writer's first draft. And like a writer, the film editor will probably continue to rework the raw material for some time. Others then view the rough cut and make suggestions for adding, rearranging, and cutting scenes. After again rearranging and cutting the film based on this input, the editor presents the **final cut,** or finished film, similar to a writer's final draft. At this stage, it is agreed that the film is as good as it is going to get. The final cut can make the difference between a good film and a great one.

A Little Thing Called Continuity ...

If you see a lot of movies, you may have occasionally noticed a problem having to do with **continuity.** Continuity is the cohesion of visual elements from take to take and from scene to scene. For example, if the top button of an actor's shirt is unbuttoned in one take and it is buttoned in another take there is an error in continuity. Continuity problems are common—and some go unnoticed all the way through to final film. To avoid this embarrassing situation, most film sets designate a particular member of the crew to watch for continuity in every scene.

PREPARE

Develop a Concept for a Screenplay and Work on Its Production

To help you gather your ideas and to understand the art of the screenplay, you might first want to read a classic screenplay, such as one of those listed below. You can find plays in your local library and also on the Internet.

- *Ordinary People*
- *Adaptation*
- *The Hours*
- *The Effect of Gamma Rays on Man-in-the-Moon Marigolds*
- *In the Bedroom*
- *The Grapes of Wrath*

After reading the screenplay, obtain a videotape or DVD of the film. As you watch the movie, pay attention to the plot, characters, theme, and dialogue. Notice how camera angles and lighting affect the mood of the film, how the actors interpret their characters, and how the director goes about presenting the story. Ask yourself whether the film met or exceeded your expectations based on your reading of the screenplay.

Use your understanding of the screenplay and the film as a springboard to help you develop a concept of your own. What story would you like to tell? How would this story translate to film? Remember, it is always best to tell a story that has meaning for you personally—a story that you think is important and

PREPARE

Develop a Concept for a Screenplay and Work on Its Production

If possible, provide screenplays and filmed versions for students to compare. Note that this activity will take several hours at the least. Assign it as homework several days in advance so that students can complete this task by the time they need it.

From the Field: It's the Tale Not the Technology

Periodically, I am asked how I think the "digital revolution" will change the role of the cinematographer. It's true that advances in digital camera and postproduction technologies have made images more accessible and easier to manipulate . . . . Digital technology might make it easier to record moving images, but it is the skill of the people who have mastered the art of cinematography that will create the most powerful images—which will endure. In my experience, the best films have always been those that used great imagery to tell good stories in ways that had the greatest emotional impact on an audience. The technology or tools used to tell the story may have been sophisticated or simple, but it was the storyteller that made the real difference.

John Toll, Cinematographer

360 **Unit Six** Theatre and Its Counterparts

worthwhile. Then, follow the steps below or use the Movies Activity Sheet to create your presentation.

1 **Describe Your Story** Write a short description of the story you would like to film. Give it a title, describe the characters, and give a brief plot description.

2 **Pitch Your Idea** Next, assume you have completed your screenplay. What happens next? How will you get the script made into a film? How will you convince investors that this is an idea worth backing? What kind of audience will it appeal to and why? Why will your idea draw an audience?

3 **Hire the Development Team** List the various personnel who will be needed to bring your script to the screen. Some people, such as the camera crew and other technicians, may be listed by title. Others, such as the director and actors, should be listed by personal name, with reasons given for these particular selections.

4 **Develop the Preproduction Storyboard** Create four to six important scenes that show the sequence of the plot on a storyboard. You needn't be an artist to accomplish this task, just sketch the progress of the scene as it would appear on the screen.

5 **Plan the Production Location and Sequencing** Decide where the film should be shot. Make a list of the various locations, keeping in mind that the budget to produce your first film will probably be very small. As you think about the locations, consider which scenes will need to be shot at the same time (and perhaps out of chronological order), and make a list of these also.

6 **Include Postproduction Considerations** Imagine that most of the film based on your screenplay has been shot. What sound effects will be needed to add to the reality of the film? What kind of music would best set the tone for the movie? Write a short description of the music and special sound effects needed, or make a tape or CD of these sounds, and discuss how they will enhance the film.

Next, gather all your material, and use it to practice convincing your audience that your screenplay and the film produced from it will be a worthwhile undertaking. You might want to use a computerized presentation program such as Power Point™ to help in your presentation. Be straightforward and sincere, and be sure that you do not exceed the ten-minute time limit.

From the Field: An Indie Film Festival

I think the modern student will respond quite favorably to the possibility of making a movie for under $1,000. The challenge to Spielberg and Lucas, et al., is fascinating. Perhaps a film challenge on a local level would be a nice project for a high school . . . . connect local bands, local individual music artists, actors, visual artists, set and costume designers, and writers. A nominal entry fee and then a charge for the screening, followed by the awards, would put a school on the arts map and fulfill a very important arts gap.

John Landers, University of Miami, Coral Gables, Florida

Beginning Students
You may want to have beginning students limit their comparisons to a scene or a few scenes. Familiarize yourself with the materials they will be using so that you can help them choose scenes to compare.

For this project a list of all production personnel is not necessary when naming a development team. It will be enough to list electrician, for example, and to presume all the various jobs and sub-categories that may come under that heading.

Choosing locations can be a complex task. Suggest that students try to list locations that are within easy travel distance of each other (rather than the New York subway, Chicago's Sears Tower, and a Texas oil well). Students should also take into account special conditions that may be required, such as rain, snow, or nighttime. Movie scenes have been shot on busy city streets, for example, but they are logistically very difficult—and very expensive—to achieve.

Play assorted film clips containing background music. Have students listen for the musical style (rock, jazz, classical, etc.), the mood established, and the tempo of the music as compared to the tempo of the action. Have students comment on how such musical backgrounds might enhance or detract from the scene on the screen.

ACTivity Ask volunteers to bring in recordings and to describe the kinds of movie scenes they might be used to enhance.

PRESENT

Share Your Concept

Tell students to double-check all their presentation materials in advance to be sure that they are all there and in the correct order. If students are using PowerPoint® or other electronic presentation methods, they should rehearse in advance to assure a smooth and confident presentation.

CRITIQUE

Evaluate a Classmate's Presentation

Class discussion of the presentations might be simplified by asking: What was the one best aspect of this presentation? What was one aspect of this presentation that needed improvement?

After you have reviewed student critiques, trim off the evaluator's name and hand out the sheets to the subjects of the evaluations and discuss with them any issues you feel are important.

PRESENT

Share Your Concept

When your instructor calls your name, bring all of your material or the Activity Sheet with you to the playing area. You may wish to use a bulletin board or easel to display your storyboards or you may want to use your computer and a monitor to present your work. Talk about each phase of your concept point by point, from 1 through 6.

Invite classmates to ask questions and offer comments as you present your ideas.

When you are finished discussing your concept, exhibiting your storyboards, and perhaps playing the music and sound effects, thank everyone and give your materials to your teacher.

CRITIQUE

Evaluate a Classmate's Presentation

Select one classmate's presentation to evaluate. Ask yourself the following questions as you think about the speaker's proposal:

Was the presentation well organized and clearly presented?

Did the speaker cover all the important points, or was something missing?

Were the speaker's ideas imaginative and interesting as well as feasible?

Did the speaker engage the audience?

Was the speaker articulate in his or her presentation?

Would you invest in this proposed new film? Why or why not?

Use a scale of 1 to 5 to evaluate the presentation, with 1 being "needs much improvement" and 5 being "outstanding." Write a one-sentence evaluation of each of these elements, and then write a paragraph explaining why you rated the presentation in this way on each point.

Notes

Spotlight on

What Film Does That Theatre Can't

Although film and theatre share some common elements, there are stark differences between the two in terms of performance techniques, production elements, and audience experience.

The Intimacy Factor Stage actors are taught to project their voices to fill the auditorium. In a film, an actor can speak softly and make slight gestures. The camera picks up incremental but telling changes in facial expression. To be a good actor in either medium requires hard work, dedication, and emotional honesty.

Playing the Angles Stage directors must block the actors in such a way that they can be seen by the audience at all times. In film, the camera can be angled first one way and then the other to show exactly the movement the director intends. The audience's vision is focused by the camera's lens. As film audience members, we see *only* what the director and cinematographer intend us to see.

A Picture Is Worth a Thousand Words The expression on an actor's face can convey his or her innermost feelings more clearly than a monologue would. In general, a film accomplishes as much with its visual world as a play does with its verbal world. Screenplays typically have much less dialogue than plays, yet a screenplay has more pages than a play because of its formatting and its detailed scenic directions.

Transcending Time and Space Film can jump time and place in a matter of seconds. In the 2001 film *Traffic,* for example, the central action takes place in southern California; Mexico; and Washington, D.C. The filmmaker, Steven Soderbergh, created three highly specific worlds. One of the techniques he used involved subtle changes in light at each separate location; the scenes in Mexico had a sepia tone; the scenes in Washington, D.C., were cool blue. As a result, the viewer was aware on several levels each time there was a change of location.

Spotlight on

What Film Does That Theatre Can't Suggest that students review the Spotlight on: What the Stage Does That Film and Video Can't on page 350 and compare the two. If you had students do the ACTivity that suggested discussing what film and video do that the stage can't, remind them of that discussion and have them compare their own ideas to those given on this page.

Quotable

Playwrights tell stories verbally. Screenwriters tell stories visually. Visual storytelling in films places much less reliance on voice than the verbal process of plays. That's not surprising. And it's not surprising that lots of playwrights can write well for film, while screenwriters are hardly ever able to return the favor. . . . the fact is, most screenwriters don't have the voice for theatre. What they do have is a kind of visual voice that makes them good at what they do.

Richard Toscan, Educator and Writer

Chapter 27 Test

The test for this chapter is available in blackline master form in the Resource Binder, page 113.

For More Information

Books

Ascher, Steven, and Edward Pincus, *The Filmmaker's Handbook: A Comprehensive Guide for the Digital Age,* Dutton/Plume, 1999.

Craddock, Jim, *VideoHound's Golden Movie Retriever 2004: The Complete Guide to Movies on Videocassette and DVD,* Gale Group, 2003.

Erickson, Gunnar, and Mark Halloran, *The Independent Film Producer's Survival Guide: A Business and Legal SourceBook,* Omnibus Press, 2002.

Flinn, Denny Martin, *How Not to Write a Screenplay: 101 Common Mistakes Most Screenwriters Make*, Lone Eagle Publications, 1999.

Katz, Stephen D., *Film Directing Shot by Shot: Visualizing from Concept to Screen,* Butterworth-Heinemann, 1990.

Lagos, Egri, *The Art Of Dramatic Writing,* Simon & Schuster, 1972.

Lumet, Sidney, *Making Movies,* Random House, 1996.

Malkiewicz, Kris, and Jim Fletcher, *Cinematography: A Guide for Film Makers and Film Teachers,* Simon & Schuster, 1992.

Vineyard, Jeremy, *Setting up Your Shots: Great Camera Moves Every Filmmaker Needs to Know,* Michael Wiese Productions, 2000.

Other Media

www.eonline.com
www.imdb.com

Additional Projects

1. Use the storyboards you created while studying this chapter to videotape at least a portion of your screenplay. Try to incorporate several different kinds of camera angles.
2. With two other classmates, develop an idea for a screenplay about the life of a high school student. Brainstorm scenarios and create a detailed outline.
3. Research and report on your favorite film. Tell who wrote it, who produced it, who directed it, and any interesting details about how it came to be made.
4. Choose two classmates as actors to work with you on a scene from a screenplay. Rehearse the actors briefly. Then, using a handheld video camera, have them do several takes of the scene. Play the scene back on the monitor, and see if the three of you agree on which take is the best.
5. Create a poster or graphic that advertises the film based on the screenplay you planned for this project.
6. Using the scene from *A Jamaican Airman Foresees His Death* by Fred D'Aguiar found in Unit Eight, decide how you would recreate this scene on film. Write a detailed description of your concept for the scene.

364 **Unit Six** Theatre and Its Counterparts

Substitute Teacher Activities

Below are a few suggestions for one or more days when you will be out of the classroom.

- Assign the Create a Storyboard Worksheet on page 111 of the Resource Binder.
- Teach the Film section of the Student Handbook, pp. 556-557.
- Assign one or more of the Additional Projects on this page.
- Assign the ACTivity of charting development, preproduction, production, and postproduction phases on page 356.
- Have partners play **Storyboard to Scene.** One person draws a series of four or five scenes for a story and the partner writes the scene. Then they trade off.

Master of the Craft

Spike Lee: On the Scene with a Wake-up Call

When Spike Lee first came to the attention of the film world in 1986, young African-American filmmakers were a rarity. But Lee quickly made a name for himself, not only because of his impressive skills, but also because of his reputation as an independent, outspoken black artist.

Lee's New York University thesis film, *Joe's Bed-Stuy Barbershop: We Cut Heads,* won a Student Academy Award in 1984 (Bed Stuy is short for Bedford Stuyvesant, a neighborhood in Brooklyn, New York). Lee later said: "I thought that now that I had this plaque on top of my television that Columbia, Warner Brothers . . . Spielberg, Lucas, would call me. So I just sat by the phone. Then the phone got turned off. That's when I decided to try to do it more independently."

Lee's stylish and ably directed independent feature debut, *She's Gotta Have It,* used what he later described as "guerrilla filmmaking." He focused on controversial social issues in a unique, unorthodox, and even combative way. Lee's second feature, *School Daze,* released in 1988, secured backing from Columbia Pictures, who offered him a third of what they typically paid filmmakers. Despite lukewarm reviews, *School Daze* earned more than twice what it had cost to make. It satirized issues of class and race differentiation at an all-black college in the form of a musical comedy, establishing Lee as a director who would not compromise his vision.

Lee's 1989 film *Do the Right Thing* scored him an artistic and commercial success. Many films followed, including *Mo' Better Blues* (1990), *Malcolm X* (1992), *He Got Game* (1998), *Bamboozled* (2001), and *25th Hour* (2002). In all his films Lee focuses on the divisions within American society as well as in the black community.

He continues to make films with his production company, 40 Acres and a Mule, in which he asks viewers to wake up and open up their minds.

Spike Lee

Spike Lee appears in his own film *Do the Right Thing.*

Master of the Craft

More About Spike Lee

In a talk delivered in San Francisco in 1996, Spike Lee said, "I was very fortunate because my parents were very creative. My father is Bill Lee, the jazz bassist, and I grew up with him taking me to hear him playing in clubs in the Village. And my mother taught art. We were raised, all my siblings, we were raised in a very creative environment.

I remember going to see Broadway plays, *The King and I,* stuff like that. Now I could see that that exposure was very important, even though I didn't know that was what I wanted to do, even though I didn't want to see those plays, I did not want to see my father play jazz. Now I see that if my parents didn't insist on it, even with me kicking and screaming, I'd have not become a filmmaker."

For More Information

Books

Hardy, James Earl, *Spike Lee,* Chelsea House, 1995.

McDaniel, Melissa, *Spike Lee: On His Own Terms,* Scholastic Library, 1999.

Other Media

Directors: Spike Lee, Robert J. Emery, Winstar, VHS, DVD, 1997.

Theatre Then and Now

Other Cultures, Other Times

The most prolific film capitol in the world isn't Hollywood—it's Bollywood, the nickname of India's Bombay-based film industry. Its products, made in seventeen Indian languages, have enthralled the people of India for a century. So big is the industry that in one recent year an average of two or three films *a day* were churned out. The films range from stirring epics of gods and heroes to modern-day stories of love and sacrifice—and they all contain song and dance!

Although the simplistic good-versus-bad formula has barely changed in a century, some contemporary filmmakers are becoming dissatisfied with what they perceive as Bollywood's inertia and the perpetuation of a lie. For the movies that are supposed to represent the essence of Indian culture suffer from many taboos and scarcely acknowledge the crushing poverty of seventy percent of India's people.

Charlie Chaplin produced, directed, and starred in *The Kid* in 1921, and it made him a full-fledged star. It took over a year to produce—a very long time in those days—and ran a whopping sixty-eight minutes. It's the story of a young baby abandoned by his unwed mother and unofficially adopted by Chaplin's character the Little Tramp. Much of the humor is as funny today as it was when the film was first released.

- What in their costumes tells you this image if from an earlier time?
- Describe the boy's clothing. In what way do they make him sympathetic?

Theatre Then and Now

Chicago to California . . . and on to Toronto

Film in the Early 1900s: Essanay
When it comes to American movies, many people think it all began in Hollywood, California. But in fact, the early days of filmmaking were ruled by Essanay Studios in Chicago, Illinois.

Essanay was founded in 1907 by George K. Spoor and Gilbert "Bronco Billy" Anderson. (The name comes from a combination of the two men's initials, S and A.) The company they built produced hundreds of early silent films, many of them featuring such movie stars as Charlie Chaplin and Gloria Swanson. Anderson himself was a silent film star who became the world's first western movie hero. Bronco Billy cranked out action-packed tales featuring himself as a brave and noble cowboy. Essanay's films were short, which was common in those early days.

But Chicago was well known for something else besides moviemaking: bad weather. Spoor and Anderson realized that it would be more cost effective if they could film outdoors year-round, so they built themselves a new studio in Niles, California. They continued to maintain their Chicago studios, but the big stars—Chaplin, in particular—preferred California.

By 1915, audience tastes were changing. Longer (feature-length) films were becoming popular. After ruling the industry in its early days, Essanay began to decline and went out of business in 1916.

Charlie Chaplin and Jackie Coogan in the silent film *The Kid.*

Backstage Gossip: Money Troubles

Charlie Chaplin was wise to maintain tight control of *The Kid.* When it came time for the production company to pay him for it, they offered only the money that would traditionally cover a two-reel film, even though Chaplin's film was a six-reeler. Chaplin left the state with the reels until they agreed to pay him what he was rightfully due.

Jackie Coogan, who played the little boy in *The Kid*, had a long film career. At the age of eighteen, however, he discovered that his guardians had spent all the money he had earned until that time. This led to a lawsuit and a trial that resulted in what came to be called "The Coogan Law," which protects the earnings of minor children. Coogan later played Uncle Fester on the television series *The Addam's Family.*

Film in the Early 2000s: Toronto Film and Television Office

Established in 1979 in Toronto, Ontario, The Toronto Film and Television Office has built the city a reputation as one of the top locations for making movies and television shows. The original purpose of the company was to coordinate location filming by means of supplying easily attainable film permits. This would bring international business to Canada, which would in turn create jobs for Canadian citizens.

Today, Toronto is an international hotspot for filmmakers. It ranks number three in film and TV production in North America (after Los Angeles and New York), and it is the second largest exporter of TV programming. The streets of Toronto are typically teeming with crews from feature films, made-for-television movies, and television series. Particularly for those projects on a tight budget, the producers are drawn to the lower costs, the experienced Canadian technical crews who are willing to work long hours to get the job done, and the state-of-the-art technical services Toronto offers—from preproduction all the way through postproduction. Combine those factors with a favorable exchange rate on the Canadian dollar—and recently introduced tax credits for shooting in Toronto—and the cost of making a film or TV show in Toronto can be about half that of shooting the same film in the United States.

The popular independent film *My Big Fat Greek Wedding* was filmed in Canada.

The film industry has changed its physical location to fit its goals over the years. As the international film world continues to reinvent itself, the primary locations for shooting are apt to continue to shift as well.

Notes

Filming in The Czech Republic

Because it's historic buildings were not destroyed in WWII, Prague, Czechoslovakia, is a popular location for filmmakers shooting period pieces. In the two quarters called Hradčany and Malá Strana the streets and edifices are much as they were hundreds of years ago.

Cinematography has always been a popular artform in Prague, and the Barrandov studios are the most important film studios in the nation. Although costs are increasing, Prague remains a more economical place to shoot a film than anywhere in the United States. Some of the films shot in Prague in recent years include *Amadeus, Mission Impossible, The Bourne Identity, Shanghai Knights, A Knight's Tale, Bad Company, Kafka,* and *The Shooter.*

Chapter 28

Television

This chapter discusses early TV, daytime TV, controversial TV, public TV, and satellite and cable technologies. Students will explore writing for television and will present a proposal for a television show.

Objectives

1 to explore the unique aspects of television

2 to understand the demands of writing for television

3 to analyze a particular TV show in terms of characters, plot elements, settings, tone, and target audience

4 to write an outline for an episode of an established TV series

National Standards

Chapter 28 meets these National Theatre Standards:

Proficient 6f, 7a, 7d

Advanced 1b, 3g, 6f, 8g

Project Specs

Not all students may have discretionary access to a television set at the times when their chosen program airs, so you may want to provide recordings of episodes of several favorite series and arrange a time and a place for viewing.

Special Needs Students

The episode outline described on page 377 requires paying attention to several elements at once during viewing. Suggest that students concentrate on who the characters are and where the scenes take place. Then they can create an original scene.

On Your Feet

This activity could be a class game. Stick to contemporary shows or the real classics; not everyone watches enough reruns to be familiar with their theme songs or signature lines.

Chapter 28 Television

When we watch TV, we often see the same personalities or characters one or more times a week. Eventually, we come to know and care about the people we see on our household screens.

Project Specs

Project Description You will write an outline for an episode of a well-known television drama or situation comedy, then present your outline in five to ten minutes.

Purpose to explore the unique aspects of television and to understand the demands of writing for this medium

Materials paper or the Television Activity Sheet provided by your teacher

Theatre Terms

demographic
PBS
pilot
reality TV
sitcoms
syndication
target audience

On Your Feet

How influential is television? Does it really have an effect on people's thoughts? Take turns with your classmates humming a theme song or saying a signature line from a popular television show from the past or present. Challenge your classmates to identify the show from the song or line you've provided.

Courtney Cox, Jennifer Aniston, and Matthew Perry in what has become a television classic–*Friends*.

368 Unit Six Theatre and Its Counterparts

Theatre Terms

demographic an advertising term used for a group of people

PBS Public Broadcasting Service, a group of television stations that specialize in educational programming

pilot one episode of a television show that introduces a potential new series

reality TV a form of television programming in which participants who are not actors speak and act as they do in real life while the cameras roll

sitcoms situation comedies

syndication when a television program that has already aired on a network is sold to several stations at once

target audience a group of people that advertisers have determined a television show is most relevant to

PREVIEW

Early Television and Beyond

Television, when it emerged, did not compete with theatre so much as other recorded media. Movies had established themselves as a strong competitor to theatre with their first silent films. Television, in turn, threatened radio and film. TV offered an alternative home for the drama, comedy, and documentary. And its flexibility made it useful for news and other live programming as well.

TV is an intimate medium, so it is perfect for presenting the continuing dramas and situational humor of everyday life. It is also ideal for acts with a more subtle approach to entertainment.

George Burns and Gracie Allen

Aside from news programs, the first things shown on television were entertainment shows such as wrestling and variety shows, full of dancing, singing, sketches, and so on. The most popular and memorable of these were Milton Berle's *Comedy Hour* and *The Ed Sullivan Show.*

Situation comedies, or **sitcoms,** became popular too. Among the most-watched early shows were programs such as *The George Burns and Gracie Allen Show, The Jack Benny Show* (both of which had their roots in radio), and *I Love Lucy.* Each of these programs was supported by corporate sponsors who paid to have their products advertised during the shows.

PREVIEW

Early Television and Beyond

This chapter's preview provides a brief history of television and descriptions of several different kinds of television programs. Students may not be familiar with some of these shows. Encourage discussion of programs that students know about or substitute the names of additional programs that fit into the various categories outlined here. Ask: What is it about the show you're describing that makes it a sitcom (or other genre)?

The picture of George Burns and Gracie Allen on this page is typical of a publicity still of that time. Contrast that image to the production still of *Friends*. Use the following prompts for both images in order to exercise **critical viewing skills** as well as to make comparisons.

- Compare the actors' costumes and hairstyles in both pictures.
- What is Gracie supposed to be doing? What does this imply about her character and about their show?
- What do the characters on *Friends* seem to be doing? What might this imply about their show?

ACTivity To reinforce the meaning of sitcoms, or situation comedies, have students list and describe shows they watch today that fit that category.

Resource Binder

- Television Activity Sheet, p. 114
- Write an Idea for a Television Episode Worksheet, p. 115
- Critique Sheet: Write an Outline for a Television Episode, p. 116
- Television Test, p. 117
- Camera Shots, p. 150
- Script Format, p. 151

Handbook Connections
pages 556-557

To Have on Hand

- One or more episodes of several comedy, drama, crime, etc. series for students to research
- TV monitor and VCR or DVD player

Chapter 28 Television **369**

Daytime TV

Most students probably don't get much chance to watch daytime TV. Try to tape and bring in some typical fare from the major networks. Game shows can still be found, but today there are many offerings along the lines of "Judge Judy" and confrontational programs such as Jerry Springer's show. Ask students to discuss the difference in the programming today compared to what they have learned about early daytime TV.

Television and Controversy

From its early days, television has created controversy of one kind or another, and one of the most disturbing has been the question as to the effect it has on young people. In 1980, Boys Town published a review of thousands of studies conducted over a twenty-five year span concerning television's impact on children. The conclusion of these studies was much as one might expect: TV is a powerful force in the lives of most Americans, and children are no exception. It was determined that exposure to some kinds of programming impacts adversely on children's verbal skills and interest in school. For example, some studies showed that when children watch predominately action or cartoon programs their cognition suffers as well as their ability to control their impulses. However, it was also found that other types of programming can improve children's cognitive skills and school performance. Peggy Charren, director of Action for Children's Television, notes that when "properly used, quality television introduces children to a world beyond their classroom and motivates them to learn."

Vanna White spins the big letters on *Wheel of Fortune.*

Daytime TV

In television's infancy the daytime viewer had little to choose from. Viewers watched fifteen-minute programs, which ranged from talk shows to recitals and continuing dramas. These came to be known as soap operas because in the days of radio soap companies had sponsored similar shows, and the name stuck. Over time, these shows became longer, more dramatic and complex, with convoluted plots and characters of all ages and socioeconomic levels.

Next, producers added game shows and children's programming to the daytime mix. Shows such as *The Price Is Right* became popular, and soon offerings such as *The $64,000 Question, Jeopardy, Wheel of Fortune,* and *Family Feud* became popular nighttime fare as well. Programming in each of these areas expanded until around-the-clock television was no longer a novelty, but the norm.

Television and Controversy

Because it depends on a wide audience base, television tends to avoid taking programming risks. Nevertheless, innovative television writers throughout the years have used comic and dramatic forms in new ways. The 1971 sitcom *All in the Family* brought contemporary social issues to television by presenting in a humorous way the conflicts between a bigoted middle-aged man and his liberal son-in-law. The *Mary Tyler Moore Show* presented positive images of professional women when the idea was still novel. *The Jeffersons, Sanford and Son,* and *Chico and the Man* brought minority issues to the mainstream. Politically inspired shows such as *The Great American Dream Machine* and even *The Smothers Brothers Comedy Hour* were often in trouble with their sponsors over the issues they raised and the stances they took.

More recently, makers of dramas such as *Hill Street Blues* and *West Wing* have developed new standards regarding subject matter and character development. Experimental dramas such as *Twin Peaks* included alternative approaches to plot, character, lighting, and sound. Comedies such as *Seinfeld* and *Friends* brought a contemporary sensibility to the airwaves that sometimes caused critics to assert that they were going a bit too far. The network known as MTV is often credited as

Backstage Gossip: An "Enchanted Sense of Play"

"It is so important to have what I like to call the enchanted sense of play," commented famed TV comedienne Lucille Ball. "Many, many times you should think and react as a child in doing comedy. All the inhibitions and embarrassments disappear. We did some pretty crazy things in *I Love Lucy*, but we believed every minute of them. It's like getting drunk without taking a drink."

From *The TV Guide TV Book*

The Bunkers of *All in the Family* were played by, from left to right, Rob Reiner, Sally Struthers, Carroll O'Connor, and Jean Stapleton.

being the first to expand on conventional ideas of programming. It turned single songs into miniature movies, with the songs as soundtracks. In the process, it drew in thousands of young people to watch its innovative visual style and creative programs.

Producers of cable television shows such as *The Osbournes* and *Sex and the City* have stretched public perceptions of who—and what—are worthy of dramatic treatment, and of what is considered suitable for home viewing.

Despite the controversy surrounding some of these programs, the fact is that over time, we often come to care about the characters we watch each week on the small screen.

Television for the Public Good

Educational programming made its debut in 1953, when station KNXT in Los Angeles set aside an hour of "public service time" on Saturdays. Like commercial

Sarah Jessica Parker, Cynthia Nixon, Kristin Davis, and Kim Cattrall appear in the controversial cable program *Sex and the City*.

Television for the Public Good

ACTivity Bring in *TV Guide* magazines from the last year or so and pass them around. Ask students to look through and find programs they watched and responded favorably to. Keep track as to whether these shows were found on PBS, the major networks, or on cable. Discuss which of these got the most votes and try to determine why.

Backstage Gossip: The Man You Love to Hate

Archie Bunker is one of the most indigenous American types. He is a funny yet tragic figure. James Baldwin says–and I am paraphrasing–"The American white man is trapped by his own cultural history. He doesn't know what to do about it." No character fits this "trapped American" better than Archie Bunker. Archie's dilemma is coping with a world that is changing in front of him. He doesn't know what to do, except lose his temper, mouth his poisons, look elsewhere to fix the blame for his own discomfort. He isn't a totally evil man. He wouldn't burn a cross. He's shrewd. But he won't get to the root of his problems, because the root of his problems is himself, and he doesn't know it. That is the dilemma of Archie Bunker.

Carroll O'Connor, star of *All in the Family*, quoted in *TV Guide*, 1971

Chapter 28 Television **371**

If you can find episodes of *American Playhouse* or *Masterpiece Theatre* to share with the students, do so. Compare selections from each of these popular series. Ask students if they now seem dated in any way or if they are as interesting to them as they were to audiences years ago.

Big Bird and friends continue to instruct and entertain children on the PBS program *Sesame Street.*

television, it owed a debt to theatre. A professor named Frank Baxter agreed to appear during that hour to present a show about Shakespeare. To everyone's surprise—including Baxter's—Shakespeare was a hit! Over the years, Baxter won six Emmy awards and numerous other honors.

Eventually, through government and corporate sponsorship and the dedication of various producers, educational programming expanded into public television. The community of stations that produce public programming came to be known as the Public Broadcasting Service, or **PBS.**

In 1961, public television unveiled its first hit dramatic series—which was also based on Shakespeare. *An Age of Kings* presented Shakespeare's history plays. Until this series aired, public television had been more plainly instructional. But *An Age of Kings* signaled the onset of more vivid and varied programming. It was followed over the years with the kinds of series that public television is known for. They included *Hollywood Television Theatre, American Playhouse,* and Britain's *Masterpiece Theatre.*

These offerings were balanced by college courses, news programs, and children's educational programming. Charming and innovative children's shows such as *Mister Rogers' Neighborhood* and *Sesame Street* set the standard for children's programming in both public and commercial television.

Eventually that spirit of experimentation reached adult educational programming,

Backstage Gossip: Miss Piggy Reprograms TV

TV Guide: If you were in charge of TV programs, what changes would you make?

Miss Piggy: Ah, let *moi* see. First, I would put on no more than six shows that were exactly the same in any one week. It is very confusing when you cannot remember whether it is the two girls in Minneapolis who are sharing the apartment with the boy or the three girls in Cincinnati who are really boys dressed up like girls. Second, when a show became very popular, I would not have the stars go off to other shows and open restaurants. Third, I think there are altogether too many action shows where the best parts are given to automobiles. And finally, when there is something really good on, the other channels should run something you don't care about, like "The History of Socks."

and stations began running cooking shows, home building shows, and episodic historical programs in addition to their traditional offerings. The documentary also gained a strong foothold and hit its stride with fine programs such as *Eyes on the Prize,* a history of the civil rights movement; *The Atomic Café,* which documents how the atomic bomb changed our world; and Ken Burns' *Lewis and Clark: The Journey of the Corps of Discovery.*

Until recently, all of this programming was free of commercial interruption, though corporate sponsors were listed and thanked for their involvement in various programs.

Beyond the Networks

Today, cable and satellite television, offered by subscription, are the place to go for more varied programming. For the most part, both satellite and cable offer the same kind of fare as network television, but cable offerings often seem more varied and innovative and more willing to explore controversial subjects than network TV, and satellite television broadcasts programs from around the world.

More conventional programs have reached into experimentation, as well. Young adult shows like *Lizzie McGuire,* for example, mix cartoons with live actors while allowing for a running commentary on the action, as *The George Burns and Gracie Allen Show* once did. Continuing hour-long dramas like *The Sopranos* and *Six Feet Under* explore little-known subsets of American culture and are able to foster strong viewer emotions—from repulsion to empathy and from laughter to tears.

Reality programming, such as *Road Rules* and *The Real World,* incorporates elements of the sitcom and drama, as real people encounter various challenges followed by (and playing to) the camera lens. **Reality TV** breaks boundaries between entertainment and real life. Many of the programs are criticized for their poor aesthetic quality, but because they have gained audiences, they are having an overwhelming effect on mainstream television.

Kelly Clarkson was voted the winner on the first *American Idol.*

Beyond the Networks

Discuss with students the programs they watch on cable and satellite television. How many hours a week do they spend watching these programs? Tabulate whether experimental, drama, comedy, or reality programs are the most watched.

Suggest that students write an entry in their Theatre Journals about reality programming. They can follow these prompts.

- Describe a reality program you have seen. What is its basic concept or "gimmick"?
- What was the outcome of this particular show? What made you want to watch the next episode?
- What do you think is the main appeal of this show to a general audience (or to a target audience)?
- What is it about programs like *American Idol* that draws viewers? It is the variety-show atmosphere, the possibility of seeing a star being born? Or is it the secret longing to see someone suffer humiliation?

Notes

Here's How

Ask students to take turns reading this chart out loud. Tell them to jot down any points they strongly agree with as well as those whose validity they may question. Have students discuss their impressions of these points and how they might impact their television and film viewing in the future.

Here's How
Television Differs from Film

Whether you're an actor, director, producer, or crew member, you'll find that working in television is different from working in film. Here are some of the ways they differ:

	Television	Film
Performance	• Programming can be presented live. • It lends itself to intimate, confessional styles. • It requires hooks and cliff-hangers to grab audiences. • Audiences are casual and expectations are low. • Many shows have a laugh track; the soundtrack is minimal.	• Film is not presented live. • It lends itself to dramatic, heroic styles. • It can build slowly toward a climactic event. • Audiences buy tickets, therefore expectations are higher. • There is no laugh track; the soundtrack is important.
Structure	• Programs vary in length—most are about 30 minutes; some are three hours. • Programs are interrupted by commercials. • Many programs are weekly or daily serials.	• Programs vary in length from about 1 1/2 to 3 1/2 hours. • Programs usually run uninterrupted. • Though sequels exist, each movie must stand on its own.
Technical Elements	• Close-ups can be extremely effective. • Mid-range shots are also effective. • Panoramic shots are rarely effective. • Characters tend to seem approachable and real.	• Close-ups are less effective. • Mid-range shots are effective. • Panoramic shots can be extremely effective. • Characters and topics sometimes seem larger than life.

Quotable

The theater is the actor's medium. Movies are the director's medium. Television is nobody's medium.

Lee J. Cobb, Actor, quoted in *TV Guide,* 1963

374 Unit Six Theatre and Its Counterparts

If you are a sports enthusiast, particularly a fan of athletic events not covered in the United States, satellite television offers a wide range of programs from all over the globe. If you love soccer, steeple chasing, sumo wrestling, or kick boxing, satellite offers all that and more.

Theatre Journal

Keep a running journal of the television shows you watch during one week. What are your viewing habits? Do you surf or do you park? What programming appeals to you most? During commercial or station breaks, make a few notes about each show you watch. What do you like and dislike about the show? Does your life resemble the life of any character you see on television?

Producing a Pilot Program

Producing a television program is a complex process, requiring the cooperation of people with many different talents. A single program that introduces a potential new series is called a **pilot.** It airs initially as a single program with the expectation that if it is popular, it will become the introduction to a new series. Like any other large and risky project, the making of a pilot program is achieved step by step.

Cable television broadcasts athletic events not carried by networks, such as the semifinals of the French Open, in which Venus Williams participates.

1 **Acquire the Script and Director.** It is the job of the producer to obtain or commission the writing of a pilot script and also to find the right director for the project.

2 **Hire Production Specialists.** This step is often delegated to the art director, who hires the technical crew, a costume designer (who obtains costume elements), a property manager (who obtains props, furniture, and equipment), and a production manager (who coordinates the production specialists). The producer must, however, oversee the day-to-day operations of these elements.

3 **Audition and Hire Talent.** Actors, composers, musicians, and other talented individuals must be auditioned for their suitability for the tasks at hand. Contracts must be negotiated, and everything must be in place before production begins.

Theatre Journal

Use the following to extend the Journal prompt.

Suggest that a team interview all the other students in the classroom about their viewing habits. They can present their findings in a large chart or series of charts that show hours of viewing per week, favorite types of programs, and so on.

Producing a Pilot Program

Have students read the steps carefully to discern the differences, if any, between producing a TV pilot and producing a new play or musical. Have them think critically about how much effect a demographic analysis, leading to a "target audience," is likely to have upon a new television program, as opposed to a new play or musical.

Notes

Career Focus

Being a cameraperson for motion pictures may be a dream job for many high school students, but the assistant cameraperson is also in an enviable position. The assistant is responsible for setting up the camera and seeing that the camera is in focus, which can be quite a challenge on an active set with all kinds of crew walking around. The assistant can learn a lot about camerawork from those around him or her. And an added bonus is the potential for exotic and interesting locations, sometimes quite challenging, such as jungles with wild animals close by, highways with cars zooming by, helicopters flying immediately overhead, and so on.

Show, Don't Tell Many students will probably be old hands at handling video cameras and recorders, but if there are some who have never had hands-on experience with a video camera, give them a chance. Arrange for a video camera in your classroom and allow time for every student (who wants to) to do some filming. Viewing the resulting tape later, you can point out such things as: How fast should a pan move? How close is a closeup? What results can you get from unusual camera angles?

Vocabulary Enhancement

Screenwriters often write *on spec* or on the speculation of payment, without any contract or specific promise of payment.

4 **Hold Rehearsals.** Actors will need off-camera rehearsals. When they are ready to perform, a camera rehearsal is held in which everyone runs through the script together.

5 **Tape the Show.** Some producers present a show live and simply keep the tape as an archive. Most, however, tape a show one scene at a time.

6 **Edit the Tape.** Some producers simply edit out extraneous elements, leaving a show mostly intact. Most, however, edit each segment they tape, and then join them together to create the final product.

Career Focus

Cameraperson

Camera crew members in television and movies straddle the line between technical theatre and art. They must know about lighting, camera shots, and angles, but they must also understand creative composition and visual styles.

You can gain an introduction to all these things through classes in photography, television, and film, but the way to master them is through experience. As in theatre and film, you become a cameraperson by working as a cameraperson. That is, try it out on your own time.

Cameraperson Sidney Lubbitch explains, "The most important thing is to learn the language of the viewfinder." By that, he means that you must learn how the camera frames images and action.

You can start out small. Video cameras are expensive, so you can begin working with still cameras. From them, you can learn about light and speed. You can learn how to focus a lens and experiment with camera angles and composition. After you feel comfortable with the basics, you can begin experimenting with stylistic shots.

If you're still in love with the work, progress to video. You may be able to find used equipment that is inexpensive. Then you can be in charge of filming family occasions, producing your own documentaries, or collaborating with someone who has a story to tell. If you feel confident enough to work with a production team, you might find that a cable access show in your area needs your help.

Make sure you keep a record of your work by holding onto still shots and videotapes; you can review them in order to learn from them. You can also use the successful pieces as samples of your work for a video portfolio.

From the Field: We Shot Anything That Moved

In the 1970s, Jim Arnold was videographer for Evening Magazine, *a television show in San Francisco, California.*

We shot anything that moved; we loved adventure. It was exciting, but occasionally, people got hurt. I talked our host, Steve Fox, into making two parachute jumps out of an airplane, and he twisted an ankle on the second jump. In the worst incident, the host of the Baltimore show was actually killed flying a hang glider for one of their stories. We put cameras on rafts going through river rapids, on the top of mountains, in hot air balloons, everywhere . . . . One story was about the Swiss Air Rescue–the people who use helicopters to rescue injured skiers. At one point, I was hanging from a steel cable, suspended below a helicopter thirteen thousand feet up. It was really exciting footage . . . .

PREPARE

Outline Your Proposed Episode for a TV Show

For this project, you will develop an outline for an episode of a television show with which you are very familiar—a drama or a comedy.

Television writers often write concepts, outlines, and pilots or other scripts "on spec." That is, they work without any up-front payment, in the hopes that a producer will either buy the work or hire them as staff writers. Before you begin your outline, try to obtain a copy of the program's writer's guidelines. These can help you understand what producers are looking for in scripts for their particular show. If this is not possible, use a writer's handbook with guidelines for writing scripts and screenplays. Be sure you consider the following points as you write your outline.

Your Outline Should Reflect:

- **The TV Category** Your proposal will be easier to sell if you can identify it as part of a specific kind of programming, such as a sitcom, an adult cartoon, a family drama, a medical drama, a crime drama, an action series, or a law and justice series.
- **The Correct Tone** Each TV series has its own distinctive tone. *Friends,* for example, is breezy, but *The X-Files* is dark science fiction. Producers are apt to buy scripts in keeping with the usual tone of the show.
- **The Right Plot Elements** Some shows feature a continuing plot thread, while others are self-contained. As an outside writer, you must show an understanding of plot developments that have happened so far without imposing any new plot line.
- **Familiar Character Types** Characters in most television programs have specific roles. Many characters feature one or two defining characteristics, such as bossy, fun-loving, goofy, predatory, spacey, suspicious, innocent, sweet, malicious, and so on.
- **A Target Audience** Most shows are aimed at a specific **demographic,** or group of people (for advertising purposes), such as white males who are 18–35 years old. This would be called your **target audience.** If you know a particular show's demographic, you can include references and topics that appeal to this group.
- **Commercial Breaks** Think about the time slot your particular episode is likely to fill. Then find out where commercials are inserted into programming for that time slot. Structure your script so that suspenseful moments fall just before commercials. This will reel your audience in—and hold them during the commercial break.

Backstage Gossip: Set with Six-Pack

"Hey, Mae! Hey Mae!" is a phrase used by sit-com writers to describe the cliff-hanging end of a segment of a 30-minute show. The theory is that the American couch-potato husband sits in front of the set with his six-pack and, if intrigued, yells to the little woman in the kitchen: "Hey Mae! You gotta see this!"

from *Ned Sherrin's Theatrical Anecdotes* by Ned Sherrin

PREPARE

Outline Your Proposed Episode for a TV Show

Show, Don't Tell Many television series make writer's guidelines available to prospective writers. If possible, obtain at least one to show students what is specified in such guidelines and what is left open to a writer's imagination.

Consideration of the time slot is crucial. Most obviously, there is a great difference between a half-hour program and a full-hour program in terms of how many characters can be featured and how many plot elements or subplots can be introduced. (In a sense, it is like the difference between a one-act and a full-length play.) Less obviously, the programming time slot may hold implications for program content. Although what is permissible in prime time has changed greatly over the years, many audience members still have expectations for language, sexual references, and so on—especially during "family" viewing hours.

Vocabulary Enhancement

Prime time refers to the most-watched hours of a viewing day, generally thought of as between 7:00 to 10:00 p.m. in any time zone.

PRESENT

Share Your Outline for a Proposed TV Episode

Before students present their outlines go over with them one last time the six points that their outline should reflect. Write each on the board and suggest that they give a minute to their introductions, a minute to each of the points, a minute for the conclusion, and a minute for questions from you or the audience.

CRITIQUE

Evaluate a Classmate's Outline

You can choose whether every student will evaluate every other classmate's outline or whether every student will evaluate only one other student, so as to make possible a more thoughtful, more detailed evaluation. If the latter, you will have to assign evaluators so that everyone receives at least one critique from a classmate.

After you have reviewed student critiques, trim off the evaluator's name and hand out the sheets to the subjects of the evaluations.

PRESENT

Share Your Outline for a Proposed TV Episode

When your name is called, step to the front of the room and share your outline with the class. First, give the name of the television program to which your episode pertains. Then read your outline. Be sure to stay within the ten-minute time limit.

When your presentation is complete, hand your outline or your Activity Sheet to your teacher and return to your seat.

CRITIQUE

Evaluate a Classmate's Outline

You will choose one outline and rate it on a scale of 1 to 5, with 1 being "needs much improvement" and 5 being "outstanding." Ask yourself the following questions as you evaluate your classmate's presentation.

- In what ways did the outlined episode seem suitable (or unsuitable) for this particular TV series?
- Did the plot and characters seem to fit in smoothly with the TV program as you have experienced it?
- In what way would the episode outlined in this presentation draw in the target audience of this show?
- Did the presentation seem well researched and well thought out in terms of the time slot, demographics, and style of the show?

Write a short paragraph explaining why you gave this outline the rating you did.

Notes

Spotlight on

Reality TV

Based on how they feel about it, people tend to think of reality TV as either a new innovation or a new low in television. Actually, neither one is true. CBS unveiled the first show in this format more than thirty years ago. It was called *Wanted,* and it focused on alleged criminals in much the same way that *America's Most Wanted* and *Cops* do today. Allen Funt's *Candid Camera* revealed long ago how people act under stressful circumstances–and this same premise is found today in an updated *Candid Camera,* as well as in *The Jamie Kennedy Experiment* and *America's Funniest Home Videos.*

Continuing reality stories have a history, as well. PBS aired the first reality show, called *An American Family,* in 1973. It featured the Louds, a seemingly typical family, who opened up their home to video cameras for a period of seven months. This footage was heavily edited, but the resulting twelve-hour program included the breakup of the Louds' marriage and the coming out of their son Lance. Viewers found it riveting. Thirty years later, a new Loud family program was aired–this time following the death of Lance due to AIDS.

An American Family was the inspiration for MTV's *The Real World,* in which people video their lives together for a period of weeks. The action-oriented *Survivor,* which challenges people to live and compete under difficult conditions, is a variation on this same theme, as is *Get Me Out of Here! I'm a Celebrity!* Similar in nature are the romance-inspired shows *The Bachelor, Blind Date,* and *The Bachelorette.*

Many reality shows lack aesthetic value, but they are popular with networks because they cost very little to produce. They are popular with audiences because they are novel and unpredictable. And they are popular with sponsors because they are popular with audiences. The down side of these types of programs is that they will probably never make any money in **syndication.** That is, the network will never be able to resell these reality programs (as they have such stalwarts as *Star Trek, The Dick Van Dyke Show,* and *M*A*S*H*) for millions of dollars because the reality won't be there and neither will the audience.

Nevertheless, PBS is experimenting with the reality format. In 2002, it aired *Pioneer House,* which challenged people to attempt to live in the manner of the American pioneers. It also featured *1900 House,* a program produced in England, in which the Bowler family moved into a home from the year 1900. These programs have been reasonably successful.

Reality TV is in its infancy, and it is clearly ready to become more of an art form.

Candid Camera actually has its roots in radio! Allen Funt began his career by taping the complaints of his fellow servicemen and airing them for a broadcast audience.

Backstage Gossip: Reality TV's Granddaddy

The granddaddy of the reality TV genre is *Candid Camera*, which has been on television on and off since 1948 (yep, almost since the dawn of the medium itself). The show actually has its roots in radio. When Allen Funt taped and broadcast his fellow servicemen on Armed Forces Radio and took his idea to network radio in 1947, it was called *Candid Microphone.* The television version followed a year later. Funt was still active on the show when he died in 1999.

Beth Rowen in *History of Reality TV* on *infoplease.com*, 2000.

Spotlight on

Reality TV

ACTivity **Beginning Students**
Have students research and compare a reality television show seen in America to a reality program offered in another country. Have students present their findings to the class.

ACTivity **Advanced Students**
Ask these students to choose two countries to analyze in terms of their television production. Comparisons should include production practices and theatrical traditions.

Chapter 28 Test

The test for this chapter is available in blackline master form in the Resource Binder, page 117.

For More Information

Books

Brooks, Tim, and Earle Marsh, *Complete Directory to Prime Time Network and Cable TV Shows: 1946-Present,* Random House, 2003.

Chayefsky, Paddy, *The Television Plays*, Applause, 1995.

DiMaggio, Madeline, *How to Write for Television*, Simon & Schuster, 1993.

Garner, Joe, *Stay Tuned: Television's Unforgettable Moments* [includes an audio CD and DVD disk], Andrews McMeel Publishing, 2002.

Gwinn, Alison, editor, *The 100 Greatest TV Shows of All Time,* Time Inc., 1998

Smith, Evan S., *Writing Television Sitcoms*, Perigee Books, 1999.

Stoppard, Tom, *The Television Plays*, Faber and Faber, 1993.

Whitcomb, Cynthia, and Philip Martin, *How to Write Great Screenplays for Movies and Television,* Writer Incorporated, 2002.

Wiese, Judith Weston, *Directing Actors: Creating Memorable Performances for Film and Television,* Michael Productions, 1995.

Wilen, Joan, and Lydia Wilen, *How to Sell Your Screenplay: A Realistic Guide to Getting a Television or Film Deal,* Square One Publishers, 2001.

Other Media

Here are a few other television-related Web sites:
abc.go.com
www.fox.com
www.mtr.org
www.pbs.org
www.mtv.com
www.nbc.com
www.infoplease.com,/spot/realitytvt.html

Additional Projects

1 Write a satire on or a tribute to an early television program.

2 Produce a live television program featuring a school play or talent show.

3 Experiment! Develop a plan for a mixed-genre program, such as a news/game show or a reality/sitcom.

4 Read a teleplay by a playwright such as Paddy Chayevfsky or Arthur Miller, and write a plan for a sequel.

5 Research the career and life of an early television pioneer such as Lucille Ball, Ernie Kovacks, Ed Sullivan, or Sid Caesar. Share your findings with the class.

6 Research and write about the history of public television, focusing on popular programs such as *Sesame Street* and *Mister Rogers' Neighborhood.* Create a timeline to accompany your report.

7 Choose an existing television series, and write a short script for this program based on one of the scenes found in Unit Eight of this book. You must adapt the scene so that it will appeal to the people who typically watch this TV show.

380 Unit Six Theatre and Its Counterparts

Substitute Teacher Activities

Here are a few suggestions for one or more days when you will be out of the classroom.

- Assign the Write an Idea for a Television Episode Worksheet on page 115 of the Resource Binder.
- Teach the Television section of the Student Handbook, pp. 567-568.
- Assist students as they interview each other on viewing habits.
- Assign one or more of the Additional Projects on this page.
- Play a game of **Television Charades.** Divide the class into two teams. Ask students to write the names of television shows on separate slips of paper. Check to eliminate duplication and then continue with the game. A member of one group picks a title from the other team's TV names and has three minutes to pantomime it for his or her team.

Master of the Craft

Larry Gelbart

"One doesn't have a sense of humor. It has you."
—Larry Gelbart

Writer Larry Gelbart's professional career began at the age of 16. His father, a barber in Los Angeles, had been bragging about him while cutting the hair of early radio and television star Danny Thomas. To his surprise, Thomas gave Larry a job as a staff writer for a popular radio show called *The Maxwell House Coffee Hour.*

With this credit under his belt, Gelbart won writing jobs with other major stars, including comedian Bob Hope. Gelbart has high regard for the demands of radio, especially the show *Duffy's Tavern,* which he says required that he demonstrate his verbal skill and dexterity on a weekly basis.

After serving a one-year tour in the military at eighteen, Gelbart began a civilian career with Bob Hope as a member of Hope's comedy writing team. He toured much of the world with Hope and then made the transition to television. Here he worked with writers Carl Reiner, Mel Brooks, and Neil Simon on shows starring comic greats such as Sid Caesar and Danny Kaye.

Gelbart lived for a time in London, where he wrote the pilot for *M*A*S*H,* a sitcom that satirized the Korean War and lasted for ninety-seven episodes. After *M*A*S*H,* Gelbart worked on the pilot for *Three's Company,* as well as the feature-length television movie *Barbarians at the Gate.*

Over the past sixty years, Larry Gelbart has won Emmy and Peabody Awards for *M*A*S*H;* Tony Awards for the theatrical plays *A Funny Thing Happened on the Way to the Forum* (recently revived on Broadway) and *City of Angels;* and Academy Award nominations for *Tootsie* and *Oh, God.*

Larry Gelbart has been honored for a lifetime of excellence by the Writers Guild of America and its Freelance Writers Committee. But it is not the awards that people remember. It's the warm and incisive humor that has informed all of his work.

Larry Gelbart

Chapter 28 Television 381

Master of the Craft

More About Larry Gelbart

Larry Gelbart has won over a dozen different awards including three Emmys, three Tonys, and the 1981 Laurel Award for outstanding career achievement in television writing from the Writer's Guild of America. He wrote a book about his life as a writer called *Laughing Matters* (Random House, 1998).

Backstage Gossip: Family Togetherness

Larry Gelbart and a collaborator Burt Shevelove were in London in the 60s where they dined with Tony Walton and his wife Julie Andrews. Ms. Andrews skipped dessert and nonchalantly began to breast-feed her baby. The following evening they visited producer Richard Pilbrow, whose wife was also breast-feeding her child. The next day Larry asked Shevelove, "Burt, are we booked in for any good breast-feedings tonight?"

from *Ned Sherrin's Theatrical Anecdotes* by Ned Sherrin

Theatre Then and Now

Theatre and Television: The Odd Couple

The days of the television anthology series, which featured plays written for television—often by some of the country's finest playwrights—and performed live are called television's "Golden Age." Many of these plays have been anthologized. Suggest that students find and read TV plays by Paddy Chayefsky, Horton Foote, Reginald Rose, and Rod Serling (*The Twilight Zone*).

Theatre Then and Now

Theatre and Television: The Odd Couple

Theatre and television have had a love-hate relationship from the start, but, when they share their expertise with each other, both are enriched.

Theatre on the Small Screen
Theatre's early influence on television came in the form of the anthology series—plays written for television and performed live by both rising theatrical stars and hopeful unknowns.

Early television series such as *Philco Television Playhouse, Goodyear Television Playhouse, Kraft Television Theatre,* and *Revlon Theatre* opened a new door for writers, and they responded with timeless TV dramas such as Paddy Chayefsky's *Marty,* Horton Foote's *A Young Lady of Property,* and Reginald Rose's *Twelve Angry Men.* Each of these teleplays dealt with what Chayefsky called "the marvelous world of the ordinary."

During the 1950s, sponsors became increasingly uncomfortable with the controversy some of the early teleplays aroused. These theatrically-based shows were then replaced with an era of shorter action shows and a myriad of sitcoms. Most of these new programs catered to sponsors who preferred to underwrite light entertainment.

New programs featured dashing, unsullied heroes like the eligible young Dr. Kildare or the dedicated detective Ellery Queen. Situation comedies such as *Ozzie and Harriet* presented a sweet, comforting view of family life as television settled into an entertainment routine, with the occasional game show, news show, or mini-drama thrown in. For a time, authentic drama was all but forgotten.

David, Ricky, and their mom, Harriet Nelson, in *Ozzie and Harriet.*

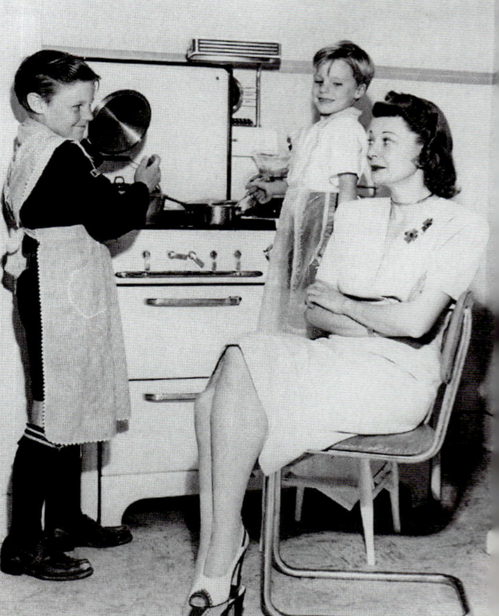

382 **Unit Six** Theatre and Its Counterparts

For More Information

Books

Hoopes, Ned E., and Patricia Neale Gordon, editors, *Great Television Plays, Volume 2*, Dell, 1975.

Kaufman, William I., editor, *Best Television Plays,* Harcourt Brace, 1957.

Mercer, David, *Collected T.V. Plays*, Calder, 1981.

Vidal, Gore, *Best Television Plays*, Ballantine, 1956.

Other Media

Ozzie and Harriet, 4-Pak, Good Times Home Video, DVD, 2002.

The Twilight Zone–Collections 1-4, Rod Serling, et al., Image Entertainment, DVD, 2002.

The X-Files–The Complete Eighth Season, Twentieth Century Fox Home Video, DVD, 2003.

Small Screens Onstage
These days, playwrights creating television drama is not as common as it once was. Theatre's influence on television is perhaps more subtle, while film techniques have become more obvious.

It should not come as a surprise to learn that over the years television has influenced theatre to some degree. Recently, theatrical professionals have begun using television as a dramatic tool.

At their most ordinary, televisions are just set pieces with characters watching them onstage. But TV sets have also been used as a technical element of theatre. They are sometimes featured as alternative narrators or as symbolic characters. American directors have begun to incorporate television technology into their dramatic images. The Wooster Group in New York used television monitors in its staging of *Our Town* by Thornton Wilder. The group feels it plays "a pivotal role in bringing technically sophisticated and evocative uses of sound, film, and video into the realm of contemporary theater."

Tony Hernandez of the Actors Gymnasium's Flying Griffin Circus in Evanston, Illinois.

Television also has fostered audience participation by moving theatrical professionals to offer what television cannot. It has spurred theatrical productions to be daring, in order to woo audiences away from their TV sets, and it has inspired productions based on television, from tributes to *Gilligan's Island* and *The Brady Bunch,* to Green Mamba's satirical take on *Big Brother.*

ACTivity Beginning Students
Have students research and write about ways in which television has impacted theatre, music has reshaped movies, or electronic media has influenced both television and theatre. Choose the best reports and ask these students to present their findings to the class.

ACTivity Advanced Students
Ask students to create a short presentation that integrates several art forms, such as theatre and film or television, the spoken word and music or electronic media, and so on. Have volunteers share their presentations.

Notes

Chapter 29

Critique a Performance

This chapter discusses the principles of theatrical criticism and of critical ethics. Students will learn to focus on important aspects of theatrical production–writing, acting, directing, and design–as they view a performance. Teams will present a review of that performance.

Objectives

1. to understand and explore the elements of criticism
2. to write an objective and fair review of a theatre, film, or television performance
3. to present the review as a member of a team

National Standards

Chapter 29 meets these National Theatre Standards:

Proficient 5a, 6a, 7c, 7d
Advanced 6f, 7e, 7f

Project Specs

Stories about critics and criticism often focus on the clever—often nasty—barbs of critics. Emphasize to students that while responsible criticism does not preclude personal opinion, it does not invite cleverness at others' expense.

Special Needs Students
Suggest that students choose a 30-minute TV program to review rather than a full-length movie or stage play because of its shorter length and easier accessibility.

On Your Feet

Students can also do this activity in pairs or small groups.

Chapter

29 Critique a Performance

"Everybody's a critic." While this statement is often made in jest, it contains a nugget of truth. The fact is, we all have opinions and make judgments about nearly everything, including dramatic performances.

Project Specs

Project Description As part of a group, you will write a review of a performance of your choice in theatre, film, or television. Then the group will give an eight- to ten-minute presentation.

Purpose to understand and explore the elements of criticism

Materials an outline of your presentation or the Critique a Performance Activity Sheet your teacher provides

Theatre Terms

American Theatre Critics Association (ATCA)
dramatic criticism
Goethe's principles
pan
rave review
suspend disbelief

On Your Feet

Name a currently popular film or television show and take about a minute or so to tell the class your opinion of it. Call on one of your classmates to explain what he or she thinks of the same show. Compare the two opinions and discuss any differences.

An interior view of the Avalon Theatre on Catalina Island in California.

384 **Unit Six** Theatre and Its Counterparts

Theatre Terms

American Theatre Critics Association an organization of theatre critics designed to support critics and the theatre and to recognize emerging playwrights

dramatic criticism the act of criticizing a dramatic work

Goethe's principles three questions composed by German philosopher Goethe used to critique a work of art:
1) What was the artist trying to do?
2) How well did the artist accomplish it?
3) Was it worth doing?

pan to review negatively

rave review a positive review

suspend disbelief the ability of viewers to forget they are watching a show and to accept what they see and hear as real life

PREVIEW

You Be the Critic

Dramatic criticism is an area in which nearly everyone takes part now and then. Viewers of plays, movies, and television are quick to evaluate and judge. In so doing, they are stating their opinions about an artistic product. But opinions vary, and often people have conflicting views concerning the same subject. One of your classmates may praise a play and give it a **rave review;** another may **pan** it, that is, give it an extremely negative review.

How, then, are you to know which opinion to respect? You might begin with the question "Why?" "Why did you think the play was good (or weak)?" The viewer who answers with a shrug, or with a statement such as "I don't know—it just was," will probably not be taken seriously. But the viewer who can back up his or her opinion with intelligent reasons and insights deserves your attention.

Of course, the best way to decide the worth of a play, film, or television drama is to see it yourself. But your evaluation will depend to a large extent on what you bring to it as an audience member. If you understand the various aspects of dramatic criticism, you might very well become an intelligent, discerning critic. You will know why a production succeeds or fails.

PREVIEW

You Be the Critic

Some students may not have read enough reviews to be familiar with this literary form. Make available a number of examples for students to use as models. If possible, choose a typical review to reproduce as an overhead transparency or as photocopies for each student. As students study the points of reviewing that follow, invite them to find corresponding parts of the model and to compare them.

Visual Cue

The Avalon Theatre was built in the 1920s. Use the following prompts to help students use **critical viewing skills** as they look at the photograph.

- How does this movie theatre compare to the one in your hometown?
- Do you think sitting in a theatre like this one would enhance your movie-going experience?

Resource Binder

- Critique a Performance Activity Sheet, p. 118
- Critique a CD or Audiotape Worksheet, p. 119
- Critique Sheet: Write a Critique and Discuss a Production, p. 120
- Critique a Performance Test, p. 121

To Have on Hand

- Selection of VCR or DVD recordings of movies and TV shows
- Monitor and VCR or DVD player
- Selection of written reviews from various newspapers and magazines for students to model for style, tone, and coverage

Here's How

ACTivity Have students look critically at one of the model reviews with the Critical Ethics at the right in mind. Ask: Are opinions backed up with valid reasons? Is the review objective and fair? Is the whole production taken into account? Does the review attempt to be constructive and not merely negative? Does the critic exhibit an arrogant cleverness at the expense of the artists involved in the performance?

Vocabulary Enhancement

The phrase *suspend disbelief* refers to an explanation by Samuel Taylor Coleridge in his 1817 *Biographia Literaria,* in which he discusses theories of the creative imagination: "In this idea originated the plan of the 'Lyrical Ballads;' in which it was agreed, that my endeavours should be directed to persons and characters supernatural, or at least romantic; yet so as to transfer from our inward nature a human interest and a semblance of truth sufficient to procure for these shadows of imagination that willing suspension of disbelief for the moment, which constitutes poetic faith."

Here's How
To Practice Critical Ethics

There are ethical considerations to being a good critic. Read each point below before you begin your project.

- Back up your opinions with valid reasons based on appropriate standards. Your critical opinion is only worthwhile if you can soundly substantiate it.
- Be objective and fair. Recognize your own biases and tastes and make allowances for them. Keep an open mind.
- Evaluate the whole production. Although in this exercise you will focus on one aspect of the production, you must be aware of the production as a whole to know whether the aspect you are reviewing is working within its context.
- Be constructive. Indicate good points along with those that need improvement. No matter what your criticism is, be diplomatic.
- Be sincere. Believe in what you say. The opinion must be your own. Although in many cases you will be guided by professional critics, you must learn to develop and stand behind your own beliefs—provided they are grounded in knowledge and understanding.
- Don't be overly negative.
- Don't try to be clever at the expense of the artist. Your job is to evaluate, not to ridicule.
- Don't sweat the small stuff. Always approach a performance with an idea that you'll enjoy it. If you constantly look for something to go wrong, you won't be able to give a fair review. You will dwell on minutiae—fluffed lines or poorly executed light cues—and miss the possible wonders of the production.
- Don't be arrogant. As a critic, you need humility, understanding, and kindness.

Unfortunately, the word *criticism* often has a negative connotation. Many drama critics have a reputation for being derogatory or overly harsh. However, if you begin to pay attention and read drama reviews regularly, you will find that many critics also have many positive things to say. In fact, theatre producers often use quotes from the reviews to advertise a show.

A Critical Foundation

The performance arts should be emotionally and intellectually involving. They should challenge, thrill, or inspire us; make us laugh one moment and cry

Backstage Gossip: "How Bad Was It?"

Below are some famous examples of critics being clever rather than constructive.

George S. Kaufman: "There was scattered laughter in the rear of the theatre, leading to the belief that somebody was telling jokes back there."

Eugene Field: "All through the five acts of the Shakespearean tragedy [*King Lear*] he played the king as though under the premonition that someone was about to play the ace."

John Mason Brown: "Tallulah Bankhead barged down the aisle as Cleopatra and sank. As the serpent of the Nile she proves to be no more damaging than a garter snake."

Robert Benchley: "It is one of those plays in which all the actors unfortunately enunciated very clearly."

the next. But if a production bores us, it has failed. While we watch a play, film, or other dramatic presentation, we should be suspended in an intensified illusion of reality. We see more of life on stage or screen over the course of two or three hours than we could live in the same amount of time in the real world. We don't turn to the dramatic arts to see smaller interpretations of our lives; we come to see larger ones. Yet what we see must appear truthful and believable in the moment. The characters, events, and dialogue must remain consistent and true. The viewers must accept what they see and hear. This is often called the ability to **"suspend disbelief,"** and good critics must be able to do this to give the dramatic work a proper understanding.

When a play receives raves, it often uses them in advertisements.

PREPARE

Work on Your Review of a Dramatic Performance

Divide into groups of four. As a group, choose the play, film, or television show you would like to evaluate. You will all review the entire production, but each of you will also be required to give special attention and consideration to one particular aspect of the show. Decide which of you will be responsible for reviewing the production's

- writing
- acting
- directing
- staging (set, lights, costumes, make-up, technical execution)

Once you have decided who is responsible for each element, use the Critique the Performance Activity Sheet or create an outline to help you focus on your assignment. Then follow these four steps to work on the first part of this project.

PART ONE: Preparing Your Portion of the Review

1 **Appoint a chairperson for your group.** This person will make all the necessary arrangements for obtaining reservations for the play, coordinating the starting times of the film, play, or television show, and deciding where the group should meet in order to see the performance together.

Notes

PREPARE

Work on Your Review of a Dramatic Performance

Working on a collaborative review does lighten the responsibility for each student, allowing that student to concentrate on one aspect of a production. But emphasize that students will also be judged on their collaboration (see Critique on page 392) and that they should take that group effort as seriously as the review itself.

PART ONE: Preparing Your Portion of the Review

Be prepared to help the chairperson of each group make arrangements for viewing a chosen performance. If attending a live performance will be problematic in your area, advise student groups to choose a play or television program available on videotape or DVD. That way you can also arrange for a time and place for viewing.

ACTivity Read an act or a scene or watch a video of a scene from a well-known play with students. Discuss cultural, historical, and symbolic elements of the play based on the viewing. Try to evaluate the validity of the viewpoints of the playwright and/or director of this play.

Goethe's Principles of Criticism

Johann Wolfgang von Goethe (GER tuh) was a poet, dramatist, novelist, and scientist. His genius led him into studies of most areas of human endeavor: law, art, music, biology, physics, politics, history, languages, and philosophy. His great dramatic poem *Faust* is considered one of the masterpieces of world literature. Go over each of the three points of Goethe's Principles with the students. Discuss what each point entails and how you expect it to impact on the group's reviews.

Be prepared to expedite students' choices of shows to evaluate. You might provide a list from which students may select. It might also be wise to review students' choices before they put in a lot of work reviewing a show that might not have the breadth or depth to warrant close critical inspection. (See Goethe's third question, "Was it worth doing?")

ACTivity Often a reviewer will mention past productions of the same play or other films by the same artists so as to make comparisons. Ask students if they are more likely to trust the critical judgment of a reviewer who can make such comparisons or who has seen many productions over the years. Explain why or why not.

2 **Follow audience etiquette at all times.** Get to the theatre early, and stay on your best behavior. (See page 36 for more on Audience Etiquette.) Good behavior should also hold true if you are watching television at the home of one of your friends.

3 **Enjoy the show.** Leave yourself open to the possibility of both tears and laughter. Use your imagination. Suspend disbelief. Take notes throughout the performance about what you see and how you feel. Pay close attention to the particular production aspect to which you have been assigned.

4 **Write your review.** The best time to do this is immediately after the show. Don't wait too long—you want your impressions fresh. First, judge the overall quality of the production—script, performance, direction, and technical elements—according to **Goethe's principles** of criticism. Then write several paragraphs analyzing the production aspect to

Goethe's Principles of Criticism

Critics in many fields tend to agree that the principles of Goethe (1749–1832), a German philosopher, critic, and playwright, provide a sound basis for criticism. Goethe's critical methodology always used three questions:

1 **What was the artist (author, actor, director, designer) trying to do?** Did the author mean to write a tragedy? A fantasy? A farce? What was the author trying to tell us? What world was the director trying to illuminate? Was the actor showing off his or her own personality or attempting to embody a character? What was the aim of the designer?

2 **How well did the artist accomplish it?** Was the artist successful? Does the author's tragedy/fantasy/farce contain the necessary elements of that genre? Were the actor's technique and the director's methods effective?

3 **Was it worth doing?** Here you must form your own opinion as to whether or not the time and effort were worthwhile for both artists and audience. Even if the artist succeeds in achieving his or her aim, the efforts may not be of value to everyone. After considering the entire production, you must decide its worth.

These three questions provide a valuable foundation for criticism because they allow you to judge the work of an artist only after you have considered the purpose, use of technique, and intrinsic value of the individual efforts.

Backstage Gossip: "I Can Take It"

Noel Coward, playwright, songwriter, actor, and author renowned for his wit, once claimed, "I can take any amount of criticism, as long as it is unqualified praise."

388 **Unit Six** Theatre and Its Counterparts

which you were specifically assigned. Back up your opinions with reasons and examples. This written report will be used later when your group creates its full presentation.

The following questions should help you as you evaluate specific elements of a dramatic presentation. Be sure to give concrete, detailed examples in support of your opinions.

Playwriting
Consider these questions when you critique a script. Did the work have:

- the necessary elements of its genre?
- a general appeal wide enough to interest most audience members?
- individuality and freshness of style?
- subtle suggestion (subtext)?
- clear organization, so that events rise to a strong climax?
- clearly drawn, believable characters who are able to arouse audience empathy?
- clear and expressive dialogue that draws the audience into the plot?
- a unified effect that builds interest through variety and contrast?
- A good balance of emotional climax and release?

Acting
Evaluate the following elements when considering the actor's performance:

Theatre Journal
Pay attention to the way your friends speak about films they have seen or television shows they've watched. Are there certain people whose opinions you trust more than others? Write your thoughts on the subject.

- Was each character believable? Was each true to the intent of the production?
- Was the acting spontaneous (did it have the illusion of the first time)?
- How did the actors project visually and verbally? Did they communicate with economy, clarity, control, and conviction?
- Were the quality, interpretation, and projection of the voice suitable for the character? Did the actors use proper tempo and rhythm in their line delivery and cue pickup?
- Were gestures and movement motivated, clear, varied, and appropriate?
- Was there a good balance between emotion and control? Were reactions true? Was the mood sustained? Were the climaxes of scenes achieved?
- Did the actors establish the proper relationships among the characters? Was there teamwork? Ensemble playing?

Notes

Theatre Journal
Use the following as an additional or substitute prompt.

What about the opinions of parents and teachers? Do you think they are as valuable as those of your friends? Write about this issue in your journal.

ACTivity Listen for mentions of plays or movies on television talk shows such as *Late Night with David Letterman*. Are the people who talk about these productions expressing critical opinions, or are they simply promoting their own works?

Go over the playwriting questions with the students using a familiar play as your basis for discussion. Be sure students back up their answers with concrete examples and well-reasoned conclusions.

Also discuss the questions addressed to evaluating the actors. Use as an example a video, play, or television drama all the students have seen.

ACTivity Have students write a short scene that integrates several arts or media (such as incorporating computer images or video) into a play or using television during a musical presentation.

Follow the same discussion process using the questions about directing and design work. Use a familiar television program, DVD or video, or play for this purpose.

PART TWO: Putting It All Together

Help students who are having trouble organizing the various parts of their presentation. Go over the steps involved in putting the presentation together with them, helping them to judge whether their paragraphs are arranged in a logical order and what material can be cut or reworked.

As students rehearse their presentations, have them work out the order in which they are to present. Be sure they practice clear introductions and smooth transitions between sections. Students should also plan where they are to stand or sit while they are not speaking and rehearse graceful entrances and exits. Be available to listen to any students who need a friendly ear during rehearsal.

ACTivity Share with students images of sets and costumes from a variety of nontraditional productions, cinematic as well as theatrical. Ask students to discuss their personal impressions of these designs as well as how they might impact the performance.

Directing
When assessing the work of the director, think about the following issues:

- Were all aspects unified and faithful to the author's purpose?
- Was scene composition handled effectively and smoothly with proper emphasis on balance, variety, and contrast?
- Did rhythm and tempo provide the right mood, with appropriate climax and release in each scene and act?
- Was there a good balance of aesthetic distance and empathy?
- Did each actor suit the part he or she was playing?

Set and Costume Design
Consider these technical aspects of the production when evaluating the staging:

- Did the set design provide appropriate background and mood?
- Were the costumes and makeup in harmony with the character, period, mood, and style of the work?
- Were the lights, sound effects, special effects, etc., handled effectively?

Collaborate with Your Fellow Critics
At this point, you and each of your three fellow critics have created a portion of a review of a dramatic presentation. Now you will put your various responses together into a unified whole.

PART TWO: Putting It All Together

1. **Have a group discussion.** Discuss your impressions of the entire performance, focusing on the plot, theme, staging, acting, directing. What do you all agree on? What are some issues you disagree about? Make note of these.
2. **Read your individual paragraphs.** Read aloud the review you each wrote about your specific aspect of the production. Discuss how your opinions connect and how they vary. Keep notes on these.
3. **Listen for overlap.** For example, if the person reviewing the script brings up a point about the acting, there may be a way to use this area as a transition into the portion of the review dedicated to the actors' performances.
4. **Write and edit your presentation.** Work together to write and edit your presentation. Use the transitions that have come up in your discussions to help present a smooth, seamless flow from one aspect of the production to the next. This will help you to decide the order of the presentation
5. **Rehearse your presentation once.** Be aware that your individual parts of the review don't have to agree with one another. One person may think the acting is wonderful, while another thinks it needs a lot of work.

Notes

390 **Unit Six** Theatre and Its Counterparts

Practice presenting your review together. Make sure the transitions are clear and that each of you knows exactly when to begin reading. Be sure that it can be given in between eight to ten minutes. If it is too long, decide where to cut text. If it is too short, go over your notes and add pertinent information.

6 **Rehearse your presentation again.** Practice your presentation from start to finish without interruption. Whoever begins the presentation will also introduce the group and tell the name of the production and a little bit about it. Each of you will pick up where the previous person leaves off, introduce the element on which you will focus, and read through your presentation.

Career Focus

Theatre Critic

Becoming a critic at a major newspaper, magazine, or radio or television station today typically requires a college education in theatre, dramaturgy, and/or criticism—or considerable direct experience working in the professional worlds of theatre and journalism.

Many smaller or alternative newspapers do not have a full-time critic but instead deal with writers who review on a show-by-show or freelance basis. Some of these freelancers are highly trained and educated professionals; others are basically enlightened audience members with an interest in theatre but little or no direct education or training.

Most professional American critics are members of the **American Theatre Critics Association** (ATCA). The purpose of this organization, according to its bylaws is, "To make possible greater communication among United States theatre critics; to encourage absolute freedom of expression in theatre and in theatre criticism; to increase public awareness of the theatre as an important national resource; and to reaffirm the individual critic's right to disagree with his colleagues on all matters including the above."

The organization also gives awards for outstanding achievement in the theatre at its annual conference. The members vote on the Theatre Hall of Fame awards, give recommendations for the annual Tony Award for Regional Theatre, honor an emerging playwright with the M. Elizabeth Osborn Award, and present the annual American Theatre Critics/Steinberg New Play Awards and Citations at the Humana Festival of New American Plays at the Actors Theatre of Louisville.

Backstage Gossip: Horse Sense

[Actor Henry] Irving was putting on one of his Shakespearean pageants in which it was necessary that he should be mounted. A horse was accordingly obtained...and Irving, who was not much of a horseman, anxiously inquired if it was quiet. "It's as quiet as a lamb," was the reassuring answer; "it's just finished an engagement at His Majesty's Theatre carrying Mr. Beerbohm Tree in *Richard II.*" At this point the horse yawned. "Ah!" said Irving, "he's a bit of a critic too, I see."

from *Theatrical Anecdotes* by Peter Hay

Career Focus

ACTivity Ask students to choose a name from the list below and do some research on this person. Have them present their findings to the class.

Audrey Ashley
Robert Benchley
Chad Jones
Dorothy Parker
Elliott Norton
Gerald Berkowitz
Jonathan Kalb
Richard Christiansen
Susan Pellowe
Walter Kerr

ACTivity **Advanced Students** Have students find a collection of reviews by two different professional critics. Tell them to read several of them and see if they can discern the particular critical principles each critic operates on. Have students analyze, compare, and evaluate the different critiques. If possible, have them find a review by each critic about the same performance. Students can then prepare their own critical analysis of the two reviews and report to the class.

Chapter 29 Critique a Performance **391**

PRESENT

Read Your Group Review of a Dramatic Performance

Remind students to give the name of the performance they will be reviewing and to speak with commitment and assurance. Tell students that while others in your group are speaking they must be attentive to them and their ideas even though they have heard it all in rehearsal (even here the acting technique of the illusion of the first time is applicable).

CRITIQUE

Review the Reviewers

If students are to review only one presentation, you may want to make some assignments so that each group will receive at least one peer review.

When the entire class has finished writing their critiques, you might ask class members to share their thoughts. Ask: What was the best part of group A's presentation? What one area could have used some more work? Which group had the smoothest, most unified presentation?

After you have reviewed student critiques, trim off the evaluator's name and hand out the sheets to the subjects of the evaluations.

PRESENT

Read Your Group Review of a Dramatic Performance

When your names are called, go with your group to the playing area. Don't forget to bring your reviews or the Critique a Performance Activity Sheets with you, as you will be reading from them.

When your turn comes, read your portion of the review with expression, just the way you rehearsed it. Try to leave as few gaps as possible between the sections. Remember that this is a performance. The idea is to try to present the collaborative review as a unified whole.

When your group has finished presenting your review, take a short pause before leaving the playing area. Hand your materials to your teacher on your way back to your seat.

CRITIQUE

Review the Reviewers

Choose one of the group presentations to evaluate. Remember that it is best to begin with the positives. Rate the presentation on a scale of 1 to 5, with 1 being "needs much improvement," and 5 being "outstanding." Ask yourself the following questions as you listen to each group:

- Were the group members able to present their material in a well-organized and well-structured way?
- How well was the group able to articulate ideas and concepts?
- Did the individuals in the group have clear and pleasant vocal projection and expression?
- How were the group members able to convince you that their opinions were well-supported?
- Did members of the group seem poised and comfortable in their presentations?
- How unified was the group's presentation?

Write a paragraph explaining why you gave this group the rating you did.

Notes

Additional Projects

1. Compare the criticisms of two different professional critics concerning the same dramatic production—a play, a film, or a television show. Suggested sources: the *New York Times, The Washington Post, The New Yorker,* and *Time.* Notice the difference between the two points of view—and the similarities. Do both reviews appear to use the criteria presented in this chapter?
2. Write a review of a current film. Read your review to the class and discuss other interpretations.
3. After attending a stage production, survey several audience members about their reactions. Compare the results to your own evaluation. Think about what might account for the discrepancies.
4. Choose a small group to review a current television show. Each of you will write a complete review. Then get together to present and discuss your impressions.
5. Read the scene from *A Star Ain't Nothin' but a Hole in Heaven* by Judi Ann Mason found in Unit Eight, and write a short critique of the dialogue and the general appeal.

"A good drama critic is one who perceives what is happening in the theatre of his time. A great drama critic also perceives what is not happening."

—Kenneth Tynan, British theatre critic

Chapter 29 Test

The test for this chapter is available in blackline master form in the Resource Binder, page 121.

For More Information

Books

Brustein, Robert, *The Theatre of Revolt: An Approach to Modern Drama*, Little, Brown, 1964.

Palmer, Richard H., *The Critics' Canon: Standards of Theatrical Reviewing in America*, Greenwood Press, 1988.

Smith, Samuel Stephenson, *The Craft of the Critic*, Books for Libraries Press, 1969.

Other Media

Visit the American Theatre Critics Association Web site at: *www.americantheatrecritics.org.*

Substitute Teacher Activities

Following are suggestions for one or more days when you will be out of the classroom:

- Assign the Critique a CD or Audiotape Worksheet on page 119 of the Resource Binder.
- Assign one or more of the Additional Projects on this page.
- Being a good critic requires **using descriptive language.** Select five or six interesting objects in the classroom and challenge students to write paragraphs that fully describe them. Ask students to read their descriptions.

Theatre Then and Now

Alexander Pope

Below is a an excerpt from Pope's *An Essay on Criticism.* Read it to the students and ask for their interpretations.

A perfect Judge will read each Work of Wit
With the same Spirit that its Author writ,
Survey the Whole, nor seek slight Faults to find,
Where Nature moves, and Rapture warms the Mind;
Nor lose, for that malignant dull Delight,
The gen'rous Pleasure to be charm'd with Wit.
But in such Lays as neither ebb, nor flow,
Correctly cold, and regularly low,
That shunning Faults, one quiet Tenour keep;
We cannot blame indeed—but we may sleep.
In Wit, as Nature, what affects our Hearts
Is nor th' Exactness of peculiar Parts;
'Tis not a Lip, or Eye, we Beauty call,
But the joint Force and full Result of all.
Thus when we view some well-proportion'd Dome,
The World's just Wonder, and ev'n thine O Rome!
No single Parts unequally surprize;
All comes united to th' admiring Eyes;
No monstrous Height, or Breadth, or Length appear;
The Whole at once is Bold, and Regular.
Whoever thinks a faultless Piece to see,
Thinks what ne'er was, nor is, nor e'er shall be.
In ev'ry Work regard the Writer's End,
Since none can compass more than they Intend;
And if the Means be just, the Conduct true,
Applause, in spite of trivial Faults, is due.
As Men of Breeding, sometimes Men of Wit,
T' avoid great Errors, must the less commit,
Neglect the Rules each Verbal Critick lays,
For not to know some Trifles, is a Praise.
Most Criticks, fond of some subservient Art,
Still make the Whole depend upon a Part,
They talk of Principles, but Notions prize,
And All to one lov'd Folly Sacrifice.

Theatre Then and Now

Strong Views and Famous Feuds

Alexander Pope: Brilliant Early English Critic

Critic, poet, essayist, and playwright Alexander Pope was born in England in 1688, the son of a Roman Catholic merchant. During those days, Catholics suffered from repressive legislation, which denied young Pope access to both a university education and public employment. He would have had very little education had it not been for an aunt who taught him to read. He went on to learn Latin and Greek from a local priest. Sometimes he attended secret Catholic schools, but for the most part, he steadily consumed his father's large library. According to one relative, he "did nothing but write and read." In 1711 he contracted Potts disease, a form of spinal tuberculosis, which resulted in a severe curvature of the spine. As a grown man he was only four feet six inches tall. His deformity made him the object of ridicule, but as time went on, no one could dispute his brilliance. At the age of twenty-three he published a monumental work called *An Essay on Criticism.* In it he penned an ironic line that is still used today: "A little learning is a dangerous thing."

Alexander Pope

Pope was famous not only for his witty satires and his brilliant, quotable essays, but also for his bitter feuds with other writers. When one of his literary works was attacked by his peers, he shot back with a raucously savage poetic send-up entitled *The Dunciad.* In it he ridiculed bad writers, scientists, and critics. A representative line reads: "While pensive poets painful vigils keep, / Sleepless themselves to give their readers sleep."

He was a man of small worldly experience but wide learning. There wasn't much that didn't interest him, including, late in his life, the study of horticulture and landscape gardening. He scored huge successes with excellent translations of Homer's *Iliad* and *Odyssey.* In 1717, with the publication of his collected writings, cantankerous Alexander Pope became one of the leading literary figures of his day. He died in 1744.

Quotable

There are two ways of disliking poetry. One is not to like it, and the other is to read Pope.

Oscar Wilde, Novelist and Playwright

Robert Brustein: Feisty Critic for Our Time

Born in 1927, Robert Brustein has developed many talents throughout his life. He is a respected critic, teacher, director, playwright, and one of America's leading thinkers on the subject of, among other things, the theatre. He does not shy away from thorny issues, as you might be able to tell from a quick scan of the titles of some of his books of theatre criticism and commentary: *The Theatre of Revolt* (1964), *Who Needs Theatre?* (1986), and *Dumbocracy in America* (1994).

Brustein is credited with bringing dramaturgy (see Spotlight on the Dramaturg on page 157) into America by way of academia, which then brought it into the theatre community at large. As a professor at Yale University, he lobbied to move the study of theatre criticism from the English Department to the Drama Department.

He believed that theatre critics must be something more than just enlightened audience members. To that end, his students learned the basics of acting, directing, and the technical side of theatre. In addition to learning the ins and outs of journalism, they studied plays and playwrights. This caused some turmoil within the program and brought about a split that divided future theatre critics/journalists from future theatre professionals/dramaturgs. The American theatre community suddenly had a corps of highly educated dramaturgs. And over time, it found a way to make use of them.

In recent years, Brustein grabbed the spotlight by locking horns with celebrated playwright August Wilson (see Master of the Craft on page 149) in a very public and emotional debate over the politics and racial implications of contemporary theatre funding. The debate, complete with name-calling, developed into a full-scale feud between two great men of the theatre.

Robert Brustein

Quotable

"Does America want a theatre? The question is becoming urgent, even fateful, since a country without a theatre is a country without a soul."

From *The Third Theatre* by Robert Brustein

Robert Brustein

Have students discuss the Brustein quote at the bottom of this page. Prompt them with questions such as the following:

- What kind of theatre is Brustein talking about?
- Why should anyone question whether America *wants* a theatre, since it obviously has one, anyway?
- What do you think Brustein means when he says that "a country without a theatre is a country without a soul"?

Unit Six Review

PREVIEW

Examine the following key concepts previewed in Unit Six.

1. Most musicals have two directors. Who are they and what do they do?
2. Which of the following are important considerations when choosing a musical for your school?
   a. length b. humor c. money
   d. space e. cast f. audience
3. What is Bunraku?
4. Is it important to write poetry about things you care about? Why or why not?
5. Compare the dramatic structure of a movie to that of live theatre.
6. What do the abbreviations INT., EXT., O.C., P.O.V., and V.O. stand for?
7. Explain how film, TV, electronic media, and the theatre may be interdependent.
8. What are the four phases of filmmaking, and what do they entail?
9. What is a demographic, and why is it important to a television writer?

PREPARE

Assess your response to the preparation process for projects in this unit.

10. Did you find it more difficult to write character sketches or the plot synopsis for your musical? Why?
11. As you prepared your performance poem, did the ideas and images flow freely or was it a struggle to find the right words? Give details.
12. Do you think it is easier to write an original screenplay or a screenplay adapted from a play? Explain your answer.
13. Compare the challenges in writing a proposal for a TV episode to those of writing a proposal for a new musical.

Unit Review

PREVIEW

1. The music director works with the actors, prepares the cast for the musical portions of the show, and often conducts the orchestra. The onstage director casts, directs, and collaborates with the staff to assure a smooth-running performance.
2. The important considerations are: c) money d) space e) cast f) audience.
3. Bunraku is an ancient Japanese puppetry form that relies heavily on tradition and unique conventions of puppet manipulation, recitation, and music.
4. Yes, writing about topics you care about allows you to bring more of yourself—your deepest thoughts and feelings—into your writing, which results in more sincerity and often more vivid language.
5. Cameras allow for quick changes in time and place. That means that characters can appear in widely separated and elaborate scenes that flash on the screen within seconds of each other. Neither the stage nor the film is confined to straightforward, chronological storytelling, but a movie can make far greater use of flashbacks, quick-cuts, and so on. The stage remains grounded in the practical need of time for scene changes, costume changes, makeup changes, and so on.
6. INT. = interior shot, a scene that takes place indoors
   EXT. = exterior shot, a scene that takes place outdoors
   O.C. = off camera, voices or sounds heard but not seen
   P.O.V. = point of view, a shot that represents what one of the characters sees
   V.O. = voice-over, a voice heard without the speaker's appearance
7. Film, TV, electronic media, and the theatre may be interdependent in that each medium can borrow from the others. These borrowings may be of story elements, since all media are involved in telling stories; these borrowings may be of reference, in which television screens are shown in movies and theatrical performances are shown on TV; or they may be of technology, in which any of the media may share lighting effects, montages or split-screen or simultaneous scene effects, music and sound effects, and so on.
8. The four phases of filmmaking are:
   1) Development Concepts are fleshed out, scripts written, financial resources secured, and a director contracted.
   2) Preproduction Scripts are finalized, a cast is hired, costumes and sets are built, locations secured, and a production plan is developed.
   3) Production Scenes are photographed (not necessarily in order).
   4) Postproduction The film is edited into rough cut and final cut; music and sound effects are added; continuity is checked; advertising, marketing, and distribution come into play.
9. A demographic is an advertising term used for a group of people. Television shows aimed at a specific demographic will have topics and actors who appeal to the target audience.

PRESENT

Analyze the experience of presenting your work to the class.

14 In creating your presentations, which medium did you find the most interesting—musical theatre, film, television, or other theatre forms? Why?

15 Were you able to remember all the important points you wanted to make in presenting your proposal for a new musical? Explain.

16 What were your impressions of sharing your poetry in a slam format? Would you like to do it again? Why or why not?

17 How did you present your screenplay concept? Would you do it differently next time? Explain.

18 Were you able to use any unusual or inventive ways to make any of your presentations? Discuss them.

CRITIQUE

Evaluate how you go about critiquing your work and the work of others.

19 Did the comments, questions, and other feedback after presenting your outline for a TV episode encourage you to write the episode?

20 What did you learn about your own work while critiquing the work of others?

21 Do you feel that most students are sensitive and fair in their evaluations of classmates' work? Explain.

EXTENSIONS

- Choose any art form that interests you and create a short performance piece based upon it.
- Create a ten-minute video using only inanimate objects as your characters.
- Write and perform a theme song for a new television show about a ten-year-old who finds a tiny universe of aliens dressed in formal attire in her bedroom closet.

PREPARE

Questions **10-13** should be answered honestly and thoughtfully by students. Talk to students about any answers you find unsatisfactory.

PRESENT

Questions **14-18** should contain honest accounts of each student's experiences while presenting the projects in this unit. Discuss with students any problems or disappointments they may have experienced.

CRITIQUE

Questions **19-21** should show some insight into the critiquing process and how it impacts not only the student's work but the work he or she is evaluating.

EXTENSIONS

- Before students begin their performance pieces, make sure all content is suitable for performance in the classroom.
- Suggest to students that before beginning this extension project they read up on videography and filmmaking.
- Give students the option of choosing another subject for the TV show. Have any students who write a theme song share it with you before performing it for the class.

Resource Binder

Unit Six Test, p. 122

Unit Seven

Exploring Theatre History

Note: Although this unit has been placed near the end of the text so that students begin their study of drama with a more action-oriented focus, it is possible that some instructors will prefer to begin the year with theatre history. In this case, simply begin with Unit Seven, which has been written in a manner that allows it to be taught at any time.

The Theatre Then and Now features at the end of each chapter in this text have shown students how elements of historical and contemporary theatre are connected. These connections are a preview to the more focused academic approach in this unit, where students will study the span of theatre history from primitive cultures to today.

Unlike previous units in the text, this unit is divided into three parts with suggested projects at the end of each section.

Part One
The Dawn of Theatre
This section covers the theatre of primitive peoples as well as the early theatre of Egypt, Judea, Greece, Rome, China, India, and Japan.

Part Two
The Middle Ages to 1800
In this section Medieval, Renaissance, Elizabethan, Restoration, and 18th-century theatre is explored.

Part Three
1800 to the Present
Part Three begins with the 19th-century theatre of Europe and America and ends with theatre of the 20th century and beyond.

Unit Seven
Exploring Theatre History

To know the development and historical underpinnings of theatre is to understand the development of the human race. As the theatre grows, civilization grows; when theatre flourishes, human culture flourishes; when theatre is suppressed, people live in darkness. Study the theatre of a particular era and you will learn the religious, social, political, and economic influences of that time. You will learn the people's desires, their ideals, and their needs. Perhaps more importantly, looking into the past helps give you insight into the present. A comparison of past eras not only emphasizes the evolution of drama, but also furthers your understanding of the theatre of today, and it points the way to the theatre of tomorrow.

398 Unit Seven Exploring Theatre History

Quotables

Use the quotes below as journal writing prompts, discussion starters, or for your own enjoyment.

The story of theatre is the story of humankind, because in its essential form theatre belongs to no one race, age, or culture.

Joy H. Reilly and M. Scott Phillips
from *Introducing Theatre*

. . . there may be somebody in any theatre at any time to whom you are opening a new door, a new gateway to beauty.

Gabrielle Réjane, Actor

399

Discussion Questions

The following questions are intended to tap into students' **prior knowledge** and attitudes about the subject matter of the unit.

- What do you already know about some aspect of theatre history? Think about information you have gotten from your travels, movies, books, and studies in other classes.
- Why might it be important to know about the history of the theatre in a drama class?
- Think about the Theatre Then and Now features presented in earlier chapters of this book. Which ones did you find most interesting? Why?
- Based on what you have learned so far about theatre history, score your potential interest level in this unit by using the following guide. Rate your interest on a scale from one to five with five being "very interesting" and one being "boring." What is your theatre history interest level?
- In what way might studying the theatre history of a country help you understand its culture?

Visual Cue

The image above is an 18th-century engraving of *commedia dell'arte* players. *Commedia* is a theatrical form that originated in Italy during the Renaissance. It featured a traveling troupe of actors who played stock characters in improvised comic performances. Use the following questions to discuss the image with your students.

Describe the couple in the center of the stage. What do you think the relationship might be between them?

What might be the intent of the character on the right? What do you think his relationship to the couple is?

Part **One**

The Dawn of Theatre

This section of the unit will introduce students to the beginnings of theatre and its growth and refinement in various cultures.

Objectives

1 to learn about the origins of theatre

2 to gain appreciation for the contributions of the early Greeks to the development of theatre

3 to compare and contrast early theatre in both Western and Eastern cultures

National Standards

Part One meets these National Theatre Standards:

Proficient 2b, 3b, 5a, 8b

Advanced 5b, 6d, 6e, 7g, 8g

Primitive Peoples

Timeless Rituals Tribal ceremonies of the sort that gave rise to theatre are not only still practiced but are still respected for their potency. According to the *Seattle Times,* Native American soldiers prepared for the Iraq War by participating in shamanic rituals designed to protect them from harm. Washington's *Tri-City Herald* reported in May, 2001, that the Yakama tribe billed the Bonneville Power Administration $32,000 for two rain dances that the Yakamas contend broke a local drought.

Part **One** The Dawn of Theatre

Primitive Peoples

Drama, a Greek word, means "to do" or "to act." But drama itself is much older than the Greek civilization. It was born out of the dance ceremonies of primitive people, when instinctive rhythmic movements and the desire to imitate evolved into pantomimes that told of various tribal traditions or rites of passage.

Theatre Terms
pacify
ritual
shaman

There were initiation dances to teach the tribe's customs to boys approaching manhood, war dances to kindle bravery in young warriors, story dances to enact events of a hunt or a great battle, and religious dances to **pacify** or try to satisfy the numerous unseen spirits that these tribes believed controlled the world.

From these religious dances evolved a **ritual.** The chief representative of the gods—the medicine man, **shaman,** witch doctor, or priest—donned a mask believed to have powerful magic and prayed, chanted, and danced in an attempt to drive away evil spirits while the tribe assisted or watched. Out of this religious ritual, performed in a circle in front of the temple, drama began to emerge.

Today, we can still see some of these dramatic forms in the dances of South African and Australian tribes. Remnants of ancient ritual are equally evident in Hawaiian hula and American Indian dances, such as the snake dance, the corn dance, and the sun dance.

Egyptian Theatre

As far as we know, the Egyptians were the first people whose ritualistic rites took a form very similar to our idea of a play, performing them as early as 3000 B.C. The Egyptian people were very concerned with life after death. The rulers of Egypt,

Theatre Terms
hieroglyphics
pharaohs

Theatre Terms

pacify to soothe, satisfy, or make tranquil

ritual the established form or order for a ceremony

shaman a priest or priestess who uses magic to cure the sick or predict the future

hieroglyphics a system of writing using pictures

pharaohs the rulers of ancient Egypt

Book of Job 18th book in the Bible's Old Testament which confronts the problem of good and evil in the world

Old Testament the first portion of the Christian Bible

called **pharaohs,** and other wealthy citizens built huge pyramids and furnished them with great splendor, for they intended to dwell there in the afterworld. This philosophy of life and death is illustrated in their dramas, which were sometimes written in **hieroglyphics** on the walls of tombs.

Plays were often written for important events, such as the coronation of a new pharaoh or an important year in the pharaoh's rule. Some plays revolved around magical healing, and some were religious dramas written on tomb walls and enacted by priests.

The hieroglyphics adorning the hallowed walls of this Egyptian tomb display one of the first forms of theatre.

Hebrew Theatre

Although dance and ritual are mentioned in the **Old Testament,** there is no reference to a definite theatre in Judea. However, two books of the Bible read as dramatic literature. *The Song of Solomon,* which was probably chanted at wedding festivals, contains beautiful poetic dialogue spoken by a bride and groom.

Theatre Terms
Book of Job
Old Testament

The play *J.B.*, by Archibald MacLeish, is based on the Book of Job.

The **Book of Job** has many of the elements of a five-act drama with a prologue and epilogue. There is no record, though, of its having ever been performed in ancient times. Today it is usually classified as dramatic poetry rather than drama. However, there have been several modern versions of the story that have been successfully adapted for the stage.

Resource Binder

Lighting Plot, p. 137
Female Figure Outline, p. 143
Male Figure Outline, p. 144
Costume Plot, p. 145

Visual Cues

The image above left shows Egyptian hieroglyphics.

- What event do you think is being dramatized on this tomb wall?

The image above right is from the award winning play *J.B.* by Archibald MacLeish.

- What do the characters' costumes tell you about the play?
- Describe the set and type of stage in the picture. Could your school mount a similar production? Why or why not?

Hebrew Theatre

Song of Solomon Here is a portion of "The Song of Solomon" (chapter five, King James Version), set up in script form, with three speaking parts: Groom, Bride, and Chorus of Women.

GROOM
I am come into my garden, my sister, my spouse: I have gathered my myrrh with my spice; I have eaten my honeycomb with my honey; I have drunk my wine with my milk: eat, O friends; drink, yea, drink abundantly, O beloved.

BRIDE
I sleep, but my heart waketh: it is the voice of my beloved that knocketh, saying, Open to me, my sister, my love, my dove, my undefiled: for my head is filled with dew, and my locks with the drops of the night. . . . I rose up to open to my beloved; and my hands dropped with myrrh, and my fingers with sweet smelling myrrh, upon the handles of the lock. I opened to my beloved; but my beloved had withdrawn himself, and was gone: my soul failed when he spake: I sought him, but I could not find him; I called him, but he gave me no answer. The watchmen that went about the city found me, they smote me, they wounded me; the keepers of the walls took away my veil from me. I charge you, O daughters of Jerusalem, if ye find my beloved, that ye tell him, that I am sick of love.

CHORUS
What is thy beloved more than another beloved, O thou fairest among women? What is thy beloved more than another beloved, that thou dost so charge us?

The Book of Job Perhaps the most successful stage version of the Job story was Archibald MacLeish's *J.B.,* which ran for 364 performances at the American National Theatre and Academy (ANTA) in New York. A 1959 Pulitzer Prize winner, this dramatic poem places the story in a modern-day circus where Mr. Zuss the balloon vendor is God and Nickles the popcorn man is Satan.

Part One The Dawn of Theatre **401**

Greek Theatre

Plato and Aristotle No less an authority than the Greek philosopher Plato rejected the arts, including drama. In book ten of *The Republic* he argues that there are three levels of reality: the loftiest is that of the ideal, then comes the actual, and finally imitations of the actual. Artists, he said, work at the lowest level: Producing imperfect copies of a reality that already consists of imperfect copies, they are far removed from the truth of things. What's worse, he said, artists undermine morality by depicting bad behavior. Aristotle's *Poetics,* with its theory of catharsis, was written to rebut Plato's polemic.

Greek Theatre

The legacy of the ancient Greek theatre has never been surpassed. Only the Elizabethans came close to achieving such a wealth of plays. The Classic, or Golden Age, of Greece (500–400 B.C.) brought human civilization the greatest tragedies of all time, as well as outstanding creativity in such fields as architecture and government.

Theatre Terms
City Dionysia
deus ex machina
dithyrambs
mantle
periaktois
rhetorical
skene
thespian

A Festival of Theatre

Greek theatre had its beginnings in the religious rites that paid homage to Dionysus, the god of wine and fertility. These public celebrations were held around stone altars at the foot of hilly vineyards. There was much dancing and singing of hymns, called **dithyrambs,** to honor Dionysus, and as these religious celebrations gained popularity, choral groups were organized with vocal contests among them.

Out of these dithyrambic rituals developed tragedy, which literally means "goat song" (*tragos* in Greek). There is disagreement among scholars as to why it was called this. There are several possibilities. Perhaps the chorus wore goatskins, or they draped the altar with one. Another theory is that a goat was sacrificed at the end of the festival as an offering to the gods. It is possible that all of these were true.

Of the four Dionysian festivals, the one held in March, the **City Dionysia,** developed into a festival of tragedies, where a coveted prize was awarded to the best series of plays. The festival, which took place in Athens, was both a national and religious ceremony. Since business was suspended for a week, everyone participated. Crowds came from the surrounding villages, and if someone could not afford the nominal ticket price, the state would pay their entrance fee. Both men and women attended, although theatre production and acting were restricted to males (as was the case worldwide for many centuries).

The annual festival lasted five or six days. The first day included a procession that carried the image of Dionysus to the city limits where people spent their time performing religious rites, drinking wine, singing, and making merry. At night the image was returned to the theatre (*theatron* in Greek, or "seeing place") by candlelight.

The final three days were reserved for the play contests. Each day a different dramatist was featured, offering four plays: a trilogy of tragedies and a satire that provided comic relief after the three heavier plays. At the end of the festival, the winning author and his financial backer (*choregus*) were allowed to wear the coveted ivy garland on their heads.

Theatre Terms

City Dionysia one of several drama festivals held in ancient Greece

deus ex machina literally "the god in the machine." In ancient Greek theatre, a giant crane used to "fly" actors in to the playing area

dithyrambs songs of praise to honor the god Dionysus

mantle a long cloak

periaktois in scenery, three flats that form a triangle and are mounted on a revolving platform

rhetorical having to do with speaking

skene a small building near the stage used by actors for dressing or relaxing

thespian an actor

Dug out of the slope under the south side of the Acropolis in the late 16th century B.C., the Theatre of Dionysus was the center for presenting the works of the great Greek playwrights Euripides, Aeschylus, and Sophocles. It was rebuilt many times, so its original shape is difficult to determine.

Comedies (from *komos,* meaning "a band of revelers") were sometimes performed in the afternoon during the City Dionysia. However, most comedies were performed at the Lenaea Festival (in early February), where prizes were awarded for the best comic writer.

Greek Plays in Performance

Plays were performed outdoors. At first, the theatre consisted of crude benches placed on a sloping hill and looking down on a circle of hard-packed ground where the chorus performed around an altar. Later, the side of the mountain was scooped out into a bowl shape, something like our amphitheatres today, and tiers of stone seats in concentric semicircles were built on the hill. These theatres provided seating for up to 20,000, with a special first row reserved for dignitaries. The acting area, called the orchestra, was the circular space marked out on the ground at the foot of the hill. It varied from 65 feet to 85 feet in diameter.

Visual Cue

The image above shows the ruins of an early Greek theatre.

- What do you think it might have been like to see a play in an ancient amphitheatre such as the one pictured?
- Compare and contrast attending a theatrical performance in ancient Greece to attending a modern event in an outdoor arena such as a football or baseball game.

Part One The Dawn of Theatre **403**

Stages The proscenium creates a frame around the stage, through which we see the narrative unfold as a series of apparently two-dimensional images. In order to create a rounder, more realistic effect, such standard variations as the thrust and "in-the-round" stages evolved. Twentieth century experimentalists went further. A good example is Jerzy Grotowski, the Polish director who started staging work in the 1950s. Hoping to strip away everything but what he regarded as the indispensable performer-spectator relationship, Grotowski created staging arrangements in which the action might literally encircle or even engulf the audience.

The actors changed costumes in the **skene,** a small building first situated at the side of the orchestra and later permanently placed behind it. The skene, from which we derive the word *scene,* had three doors through which actors would enter. To the right and left between the skene and the orchestra was a wide passageway, called the *parodos,* which was used for the chorus to enter and exit. Eventually, a platform called a *proskenion* (from which we get the term *proscenium*) was placed in front of the skene for the actors. On each side, two wings called the *paraskenia* were introduced.

Since the theatre was large and the distance between audience and playing area was great, the drama was **rhetorical,** containing more speech than action. The actors used broad gestures and a declamatory vocal style. To be seen by the audience, the actor made himself taller by wearing thick-soled shoes, called *cothurnus,* and a high headpiece, called an *onkus.* In addition, he wore a wooden, cork, or linen mask that fit over his entire head. These masks not only denoted character, station in life, and emotion, they also projected the actor's voice through a type of inside megaphone.

Actors perform a Greek drama in traditional masks.

The image above shows a modern production of a Greek tragedy.

- What emotion do the masks convey?
- Compare these costumes to the drawing at the top of page 405. How authentic are the modern costumes?

From left to right, the *chiton, himation,* and *chlamys* of the ancient Greek attire.

Costumes of both the actor and the chorus consisted of standard Greek attire: the sleeveless *chiton,* or tunic, belted below the breast; the *himation,* or long **mantle,** draped around the right shoulder; and the *chlamys,* or short cloak. These costumes were very colorful and often featured elaborately embroidered patterns.

Staging was accomplished simply with the use of *pinakes,* or scenery painted on boards and placed against the skene, and *periaktois,* triangular prisms that could be revolved for scenery changes. A few properties were also used. Drums were sounded for thunder, and the *eccyclema,* a small wagon platform, was wheeled on to show a corpse to the audience (all killing had to occur offstage and be reported to the audience by the chorus or a messenger). The ***deus ex machina,*** or "god in the machine," was a unique mechanical crane used for lowering and raising gods. The term is still used today for any plot device, such as the death of a rich uncle, that unexpectedly occurs to assist the main character in the convenient solution of a major problem.

The Great Greek Playwrights

The Greek tragedies were based on ancient myths, which were well known to the audience. Most of the plays encompassed certain elements that Aristotle (384–322 B.C.) later identified in his *Poetics.* (See pages 139–140 for more about Aristotle's *Poetics.*)

The first tragedian to win the City Dionysia playwriting prize was Thespis.

Backstage Gossip: The Drama of Politics

Thespis was beginning to act in tragedies, and the people flocked to see the novelty .... Solon the great lawmaker went to see Thespis act. After the play, Solon went backstage and asked the actor if he was not ashamed to tell so many lies before such a large crowd. When Thespis replied that it was no harm to do so in a play, Solon vehemently struck his staff against the ground: "Ah, but if we commend lies on the stage, some day we will find it in politics."

from *Theatrical Anecdotes* by Peter Hay

The Legacy of Plato and Aristotle

The ideas of both Plato and Aristotle have had enormous influence on the theatre, albeit in opposite directions. On the one hand, the Platonic view of art as false and immoral has been invoked throughout the centuries—sometimes consciously, sometimes not—to close theatres. (The fact that Greek drama originated as part of the orgiastic rites of Dionysus didn't help.) On the other hand, Aristotlean notions about the nature and rules of drama have guided the work of playwrights from Jean Racine (1639-1699) to Eugene O'Neill (1888-1953). Aristotle's authority was so great during and after the Renaissance that it wasn't until the 20th century that his precepts met with serious theoretical opposition.

German playwright-provocateur Bertolt Brecht attacked catharsis, saying it discouraged audiences from thinking critically by appealing to—and exhausting—their emotions.

In a 1966 essay called "Against Interpretation," Susan Sontag argued that Plato and Aristotle together had all but destroyed western art by creating a cultural environment in which art could not be appreciated for itself but had to justify its existence by demonstrating its usefulness. The process has gone so far, she said, that the justifications have finally overwhelmed the art entirely.

Part One The Dawn of Theatre **405**

Aeschylus According to the ancient Greek travel writer, Pausanias, Aeschylus's career in the theatre was ordained by a god. When the future tragedian was a child, the story goes, he was sent out to tend grapes. Falling asleep in the vineyard, he dreamed he saw Dionysus, who told him to write plays. Another, more irreverent legend has it that Aeschylus died when an eagle, attempting to crack a turtle's shell, mistook the playwright's bald head for a rock.

The Oresteia trilogy follows the often horrific fortunes of the descendants of two brothers, Atreus and Thyestes, who fought each other for control of the throne of Mycenae. In *Agamemnon,* the eponymous son of Atreus has no sooner returned from his victory over Troy than he is assassinated by his wife, Clytemnestra, and her lover, Aegisthus (who is Thyestes' son by his own daughter, Pelopia). In *Choephori* (The Libation Bearers) Agamemnon's son, Orestes, avenges his father by killing Clytemnestra and Aegisthus. In the *Eumenides,* Orestes is tried and exonerated for his crime. The essential trajectory of the three plays, then, takes us from crime through punishment to redemption.

Sophocles Sophocles won his first victory in the City Dionysia play competition by beating no less a rival than Aeschylus.

Euripides Sophocles is reputed to have said that while he depicted people as they ought to be, Euripides depicted them as they are. Unfortunately, Euripides' psychological realism did not go over very well with many of his peers. Apparently alienated by his comparative lack of success and the harassment meted out to him by satirists like Aristophanes, Euripides left Athens in 409 B.C., to live at the court of King Archelaus of Macedonia. Following Euripides' death in 405 B.C., his son, Euripides the Younger, returned to Athens with the script of The *Bacchae.* It was performed at the City Dionysia and won first prize.

In his plays that year (534 B.C.), he introduced a leader for the chorus. The leader spoke, and the chorus responded in chants. Thus, the leader became the first Greek actor. Thespis also instigated another first in his drama: the use of masks. It is from his name that the word ***thespian*** comes—another way of saying *actor.*

Three great writers of tragedy developed during the Golden Age. Some of their plays have survived and are still performed today.

Aeschylus (525–456 B.C.) has been called the Father of Tragedy. He is considered by many scholars to be the greatest tragic poet of all time. Aeschylus frequently participated in the City Dionysia, winning first prize thirteen times. He is credited with inventing the trilogy and adding a second actor to the plays. He reduced the chorus from fifty to twelve, but that honored group still handled most of the play, relating the events and setting the mood. Aeschylus loved spectacle, and his plays abounded with it. He had one character, Prometheus

The Colosseum, Rome's ancient arena of death and slaughter, reopened its gates for the first time in 1500 years for this performance of *Oedipus Rex.*

406 **Unit Seven** Exploring Theatre History

Notes

(who steals fire and gives it to humans), fall from a cliff. He dressed the Furies (spirits of revenge who chase down those who do not atone for their sins) in such frightful masks that women and children fainted at the sight of them. Of Aeschylus's ninety plays, only seven survive, of which the Oresteia trilogy may be the most enduring.

Sophocles (496–406 B.C.) is the second great writer of tragedies. He was a handsome, well-educated man of many talents: musician, singer, and athlete. He was also interested in civic affairs, becoming the treasurer of Athens. Sophocles, like Aeschylus, had a brilliant career in theatre. He wrote more than a hundred scripts and won eighteen Dionysia festivals. In his plays, he introduced a third actor and changed the number of chorus members to fifteen. Sophocles was a polished literary craftsman who had keen theatrical sense. His plays feature beautiful language, a well-balanced plot, and excellent character development. Today his work is considered the essence of great Greek drama. The best known of his seven surviving plays are *Electra, Oedipus Rex,* and *Antigone.*

Euripides (480–406 B.C.), although apparently good at boxing and painting, confined himself to a literary life. He would often retire to a cave overlooking the sea, and there he would meditate and write. Euripides was an unorthodox thinker who questioned traditional religious ideas. His plays emphasize psychological motivations and social consciousness, particularly accentuating the plight of women and the problem of the outsider. He was the first to humanize drama with little household details and events that appealed to the emotions. His *Medea* is a potent tragedy that shows the mental anguish of Medea, a woman driven mad by jealousy. In *Alcestis,* Euripides created a play that combined both the serious and the humorous.

Besides these three great tragedians, two writers of comedy gained note.

Aristophanes (circa 448–380 B.C.) is considered the finest comic writer of ancient Greece. His biting, bawdy satires, such as *The Birds, The Frogs,* and *The Clouds* abound with humorous ideas and bold attacks.

Menander (circa 342–291 B.C.) was also a celebrated writer of comedy. Unlike Aristophanes, who wrote about aspects of public life, Menander lampooned domestic or private life. His plays are filled with cunning servants, parasitic relatives, protective fathers, and young lovers. Until the 20th century, only fragments of Menander's plays were known; our knowledge of his work was understood mainly from ancient Roman writers who copied him extensively. But in 1957, the complete work of Menander's *The Curmudgeon,* a farce full of physical and slapstick humor, was discovered.

Aristophanes Aristophanes is credited with writing the world's first anti-war play, *The Acharnians,* in which a farmer concludes his own peace with the Spartans and goes on to have a great time while his more warlike neighbor ends up limping home.

Greek Comedy Scholars distinguish three eras of classical Greek comedy: old, middle, and new. The differences among them are not merely chronological; they have to do with style, subject matter, political realities, and the evolution of the City Dionysia itself from an orgiastic ritual honoring Dionysus to an entertainment for Athens' upper classes.

Old Comedy was the raucous, vulgar, often scathing child of Athenian democracy—formally unrefined and politically outspoken. Middle Comedy arrived in the wake of the catastrophic defeat of Athens at the hands of Sparta (404 B.C.), when demoralized Athenians wanted, as one commentator put it, "to be amused, not lectured." Playwrights—including Aristophanes—abandoned the harsh social criticism so essential to Old Comedy while moving toward greater decorum in language and greater naturalism in style. The era of the New Comedy began when Athenian independence was crushed entirely under Macedonian rule. Whether by choice or compulsion, Menander and his contemporaries steered clear of politics, focusing instead on the comic possibilities of thwarted love and mistaken identity—and thereby providing the pattern for the modern comedy of manners.

Notes

Roman Theatre

Slaves The Romans owed their slaves an enormous cultural debt. After all, it was a Roman slave of Greek origin, Livius Andronicus (284-204 B.C.), who gave Rome access to the masterpieces of classical Greece by translating plays—and the *Odyssey,* as well—into Latin. Livius Andronicus wrote the first original Latin tragedy and comedy. He was in such demand as a performer that, according to the Roman historian Livy, he lost his voice and had to have a young assistant sing his part while he acted it. The elegant comic writer, Terence, was also a slave, as was an accomplished author of mime farces named Publilius Syrus.

Mime Theatre The Roman mime theatre was famously degenerate. Female actors appeared in the nude. Sex scenes were not just graphic but literal, and so were death scenes. When the play called for a character to be executed, a condemned criminal was substituted for the actor playing that role, and dispatched onstage. By contrast, pantomime was a more exalted form in which a single masked performer would silently act out a narrative to the accompaniment of an orchestra and chorus.

Greek drama began to deteriorate as Caesar's armies marched over the land. From the seeds of Greek drama, the victorious Romans established their theatre.

Roman Theatre

As the Romans invaded, they began to take special interest in Greek literature and art. Soon, Rome's crude native drama was replaced by translations and adaptations of Greek plays.

Theatre Terms
claque
closet drama

The Roman aristocracy frowned upon theatre, so audiences consisted mainly of the lower classes. They wanted entertainment. Scoffing at the art-loving and intellectual, they demanded spectacle and vulgarity. Thus, the imitated Greek theatre became decadent and hollow. Tragedies gradually degenerated and comedies slipped into common slapstick.

The Circus Maximus, where charioteers raced around the track.

The Stage and the Playwrights

Because the Roman senate was hostile to theatre, the Roman playhouses were merely portable wooden platforms around which the audience stood. But in 61 B.C., the Roman leader Pompey had a huge outdoor auditorium built. In order to make it legal, he erected a small statue of Venus at the top and called it a temple of worship. The steps of this temple, of course, served as seats for the theatre.

Not to be outdone, the next Roman emperor, Caesar, ordered a playhouse built that was in the shape of two wooden theatres, back to back, each of which could be revolved to face the other. After a play presentation, the seats could be swung around into an amphitheatre for chariot races and gladiatorial contests.

The Romans were the first to use a front curtain. It rolled up and down from a trough in the downstage floor. Roman theatre also instigated the **claque,** a person or persons paid to arouse the audience into clapping and shouting. (For more on Roman theatres, see page 206.)

Theatre Terms

claque a person or group hired to applaud at a performance

closet drama drama more suited for reading than performance

408 Unit Seven Exploring Theatre History

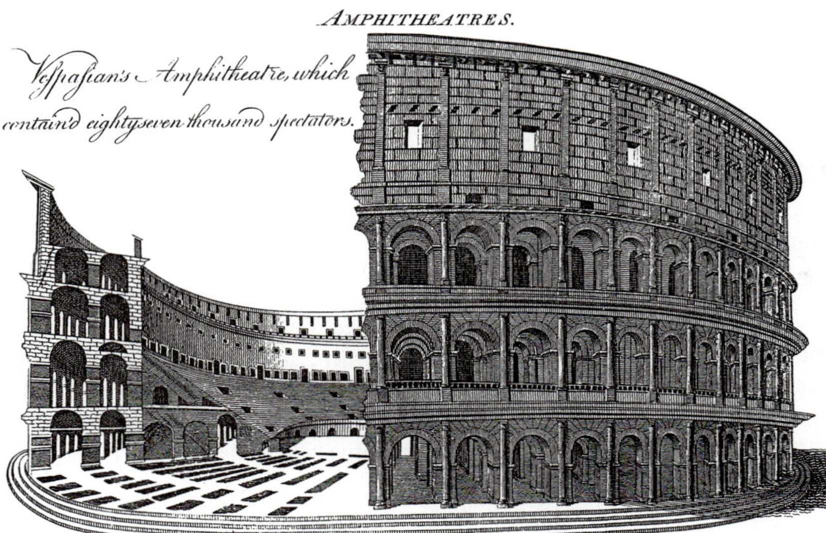

This ancient amphitheatre seated 80,000 spectators.

Seneca (circa 4 B.C.–65 A.D.) was a major Roman dramatist. His plays are so bombastic and full of gory details, however, that they are more effective as **closet drama** (plays to be read rather than performed).

The comic writer **Plautus** (254–184 B.C.) is important mainly because his plays served as a pattern for later writers. His *Menaechmi* influenced Shakespeare's *Comedy of Errors,* and his *Pot of Gold* served as Molière's pattern for *The Miser.*

The Fall of Roman Theatre

Soon Roman theatrical activity gained impetus, with plays and other entertainment being presented for every holiday—and there were many Roman holidays—up to 175 at one point, which would have occupied about six months' time.

The production of plays was eventually overshadowed by sensational spectacles. In the coliseums, gladiatorial contests were interspersed with Christians being fed to lions. Special arenas called *naumachiaes* were filled with water, and slaves on ships fought until all hands were killed.

Finally, theatre entertainment became so base that when Rome fell in 475 A.D., the Christian church banned all theatrical activity. For hundreds of years afterward, theatre lay dormant throughout the continent. The East, however, did not suffer the darkness of Europe. Instead, theatrical forms that had been nurtured from years past, gained momentum throughout India and the Orient.

Plautus Plautus's comedies continue to provide inspiration. His *Pseudolus* provided the basis for the 1962 hit musical, *A Funny Thing Happened on the Way to the Forum.*

Backstage Gossip: When in Rome...

In Greek theatres, refreshments were sold during the performance, as they are at today's sporting events. This was apparently not the custom in Roman theatres. Augustus is said to have been surprised to see a knight drinking during the show, and sent a messenger to tell him: "When the Emperor wants a drink, he goes home." "Ah," said the knight between swigs, "but the Emperor isn't afraid of losing his seat."

Part One The Dawn of Theatre **409**

Chinese Theatre

Masks It is said that a general serving under Emperor Wu of the Han Dynasty (141-87 B.C.) used to wear a fierce mask to intimidate his adversaries. Actors therefore wore masks to portray this general in plays, and the tradition of wearing masks was born.

The Pear Tree Garden The Chinese poet Tu Fu, an almost exact contemporary of Emperor Ming Huang, wrote the following poem in memory of an artist of the Pear Tree Garden:

On Seeing The Pupil of Kung-sun Dance the Sword Dance

Of old times there was a beautiful courtesan Kung-sun,
When she danced the sword dance everyone was moved;
Those who saw her were massed like the hills tense with emotion;
Heaven and earth swayed in sympathy up and down.
For she flashed like the arrow with which the archer Yi shot down the nine suns
And soared as a crowd of spirit kings astride their winged dragons.
She began like a thunderclap with all the anger of rolling echoes,
She finished like the waters of the river and sea shining calm and still on a summery day.
Her red lips, her pearl sleeves are things of the past,
But in the evening of her life there was a pupil to carry on her fragrant traditions.
When the beautiful dancer of Lin-ying, now her successor, danced in Po Ti
She danced wonderfully to the music and her skill triumphed.
When I talked with her we found a common background of memory. . . .
The children of the pear garden have drifted away like smoke,
The remnant of that galaxy of beauty look forward to the bright cold of a winter's day.

From *Selections from Three Hundred Poems of the T'ang Dynasty* [London: John Murray, 1940], translated by Soame Jenyns. Thanks to *Dancezine.*

Chinese Theatre

Theatre Terms
interpretive dance
Peking Opera

The beginning of Chinese drama dates back to 2000 B.C., when **interpretative dance,** that is, dance that tells a story, became more dramatic in form as ancestor worship and military celebrations were staged. These early performances, however, were not presented as entertainment. The Chinese revered their ancestors; dramatic ritual was solely religious with only the emperor, the priests, and the court as participants and audience.

The Blossoming of Chinese Drama Later, the religious rituals developed into definite plays, but it was not until the 8th and 9th centuries A.D. that Chinese drama blossomed, led by Emperor Ming Huang (713–756 A.D.), who founded a school for actors in his garden. The school was so successful that Chinese actors are traditionally called "Children of the Pear Tree Garden." Ming Huang continues as the patron saint of Chinese theatre, and actors traditionally burn incense to his statue before they begin a performance.

The drama of Ming Huang's time was highly formal. It dealt primarily with three themes: ancestor worship, military glory, and faithfulness to a husband. It was written in classical Chinese that only the exceptionally well educated could understand. This classical tradition changed, however, when the Mongols invaded in 1280 A.D. Lacking

A Peking Opera production being performed in present-day Beijing.

Theatre Terms

interpretive dance dance that tells a story

Peking Opera Chinese drama that features chanting, singing, and music

in cultural background, the Mongols demanded action, acrobatic stunts, songs, and dances. It was in this period that such plays as *The Chalk Circle* and *The Lute Song* were written.

The dramas associated with the Mongolian influence became traditional theatre, and throughout the centuries, they were enacted in their original form until the Communists took over China after World War II. After 1949, the Communist government rewrote many of the classical plays using them to preach government policy.

The Peking Opera

Because Chinese drama features chanting, singing, and musical accompaniment, Westerners began calling it **Peking Opera**. Traditional Peking Opera can still be seen today, along with new trends that reveal the influences of the West. Although Chinese drama may seem unusual and exotic to the Western world, its symbolic quality has influenced the writing of many plays, including Thornton Wilder's *Our Town*. (See page 330 for more on the Peking Opera.)

Most of the acting is done by men, who also take women's parts. Acting is regarded as a life study. It uses movements and poses that are highly symbolic. The stylized traditional movements are graceful, and every gesture means something specific. For example, a sleeve passed over the eye denotes weeping; a shaking of the shoulders signifies grief.

Props also have symbolic meaning. White paper falling from a red umbrella means snow; a man with a whip indicates that he is on horseback; an actor carrying a flag indicates an army; a flag with wavy lines symbolizes a river. An onstage prop man, dressed in black, hands properties to the actor. The actors wear dazzling costumes and thick makeup in which color signifies character: red means faithfulness; blue, cruelty; white, evil; and so on. The greatest influence of Chinese drama has been on the theatre of Japan.

Japanese Theatre

Early drama in Japan was probably based on the ritualistic dance of the Shinto religion, but in the 14th century the Japanese **Noh** plays appeared. Similar in form and content to Chinese drama, these pieces were written in a formal, classical language meant only for the aristocrats. They remain remarkably unchanged and are still performed in Japan today. They are short, serious, philosophical studies that combine poetry with dance and music. The dance is completely unlike Western dance, which tends to feature vigorous movements. Instead, Japanese Noh movements

Theatre Terms

Bunraku
flowerway
Kabuki
Kyogen
Noh

Theatre Terms

Bunraku Japanese puppet theatre

flowerway in a Kabuki theatre, a ramp from the back of the audience to the stage

Kabuki a melodramatic, sensational Japanese drama with song and dance, intended for the common man

Kyogen a short comedy presented before or after a Noh drama to offset its serious tone

Noh Japanese dramatic tragedy in classical style performed with poetry, dance, and music

The Chalk Circle tells the story of a young woman named Chang Hai-tang who becomes the second wife of a tax collector, Ma Chun-Shing, and bears him a son. Jealous, and afraid that Hai-tang will take her position and fortune away from her, Ma Chun-Shing's first wife poisons Ma Chun-Shing, blames Hai-tang, and claims the baby as her own. The case is brought to the emperor, who orders that a chalk circle be drawn on the ground and the baby placed at its center. He then tells the two women to grab hold of the child and pull; the one who drags him out of the circle wins. The first wife does as she's told, but Hai-tang refuses for fear of hurting her son. The emperor recognizes Hai-tang's maternal gesture and not only awards her the baby but the opportunity to do as she pleases with the first wife. In 1945, Bertolt Brecht adapted this story into his socialist parable, *The Caucasian Chalk Circle.*

Recent History A notorious figure in the cultural life of communist China was Jiang Qing (1914-1991), the actress who became Mao Ze Dong's second wife in 1939. As a member of the Gang of Four, she helped mastermind the fanatical purges of the Cultural Revolution (1966-1976). She also attempted to remake the Beijing Opera, replacing its traditonal depictions of "emperors, kings, generals, chancellors, literati, and beauties" with paeans to the revolution. She was sentenced to death in 1981, freed in 1991, and reputed to have committed suicide ten days after her release.

Japanese Theatre

Kyogen The word *kyogen* means "wild words" and alludes to a passage in the writings of the Chinese poet, Po Chu-i (772-846): "May the vulgar trade of letters that I have plied in this life, all the folly of wild words and fine phrases, be transformed into a hymn of praise that shall celebrate the Buddha in age on age to come, and cause the Great Wheel of Law to turn."

Actors From the introduction to Arthur Waley's groundbreaking collection, *The No Plays of Japan:* "The training of actors began at seven years old. . . . After twelve the various branches of impersonation are gradually imparted. . . . The danger at twenty-four and twenty-five . . . is that the actor's friends will overpraise him. If he gains applause in his own theatre and happens one day to win in a competition with another troupe, people will begin telling him that he is a master. But such persons are doing him a very ill service; for such temporary success is not the 'true flower.'" Thirty-five is the actor's prime. . . . If at forty-five he still retains his 'flower,' it is certain that it is the 'true flower.'"

A Japanese woodcut by Okumura Masanobu of a Kyogen play being performed before a large audience in the 1700s.

comprise a series of sedate postures in which a specific attitude is expressed.

Noh Drama

Noh stages are always built to specific measurements. They are wooden 18-foot squares, with the audience sitting on three sides. The stage's pointed roof, a carryover from the early days when Noh plays were performed outside, is similar to that of a Shinto shrine and is supported by four pillars. The floor is of highly polished Japanese cypress, specially constructed with large empty jars underneath to provide a unique resonant sound when the actor thumps his feet at a climactic moment.

The characters enter from the greenroom off stage right by means of a narrow upstage corridor. As each character enters, he bows to the audience, announces his name, where he has come from, and what he will do. The chorus, which consists of six to eight men, sits on stage left and provides chanting background music.

Scenery consists of a pine tree tapestry hung on the back wall. Only essential properties are used, and they are often a suggestion rather than an actual representation of the object. For example, a folding fan the actor uses for his various acting poses may at times suggest a dagger, a tray, or a letter, depending on what is needed.

Costumes are ornate silks, worn by all characters whether they are rich or poor. The cut of the costume and the makeup differentiate social class. Major actors wear carved wooden masks that have stereotyped expressions from one of the fifteen standard masks allowed in Noh plays. To offset the often depressing, foreboding quality of the Noh plot, the **Kyogen** was developed to serve as a

The woodcut on this page shows a Japanese Kyogen theatre. To make connections between this and theatres in other countries, have students discuss the following questions:

- Compare this theatre to the inn-yard stage on page 424 and the Globe on page 425. What similarities and differences do you see?
- How attentive is the Kyogen audience? How do audience members meet or not meet the rules for "audience etiquette" on page 36?

comic interlude. Kyogens are farcical comedies performed without music and without masks. Usually five Nohs are presented at one performance, interspersed with three Kyogens. (For more on Noh drama, see page 310.)

Bunraku

In the 17th century another form of Japanese theatre became popular. **Bunraku,** or doll theatre, features four-foot-tall, full-body wooden marionettes, carved in such realistic detail that eyelids, eyebrows, mouth, and fingers can all be moved. Each doll is elaborately costumed. While narrators read the dialogue and a musician plays, three attendants dressed in black and wearing gauze masks (a convention that tells the audience to regard them as invisible) manipulate the dolls. (See page 342 for more on Bunraku.)

Kabuki Theatre

The Japanese drama of the common man is called **Kabuki,** which incorporates song and dance, and is thought to be more melodramatic and sensational than Noh drama. Kabukis have a wide range of subject matter. There are heavy, tension-filled historical tragedies that realistically portray scenes of suicide, murder, and torture; there are domestic love triangles; and there are unspoken dance dramas that often feature grotesque demons.

The Kabuki playhouse uses a wide extended platform, but it dispenses with the roof, pillars, and bridge of the Noh theatre. Actors enter from a **flowerway,** a ramp that extends through the audience from the back of the auditorium up to the stage. The stage floor contains trapdoors where actors may also make spectacular entrances and exits.

Kabuki utilizes colorful, extravagant scenery. Since 1793, most Kabuki theatres have been equipped with a revolving stage, which allows quick and impressive scene shifting. In recent years, theatrical devices such as the ramp, trapdoor, and revolving stage have been borrowed from Japan by the Western world.

Kabuki is noted for its lavish use of elaborate and colorful silk costumes. Although Kabuki actors do not use masks, they apply stylized masklike makeup. The actors wear wigs that denote their character's station, personality, and age; these wigs can weigh as much as twenty-five pounds. (For more about Kabuki, see page 30.)

In both Kabuki and Noh, acting skill is all-important. Actors are traditionally men who are versatile at impersonating women. Today, it is legal for women to act in Kabuki, although few do. For centuries the torch of the acting profession in Japan has been passed along family lines, with children as young as five sometimes appearing onstage as they begin their lifelong profession.

Bunraku The word *bunraku* is derived from the name of a puppeteer, Uemura Bunrakuken, whose eponymous theatre flourished in 19th-century Osaka. The generic term for the form is *ningyo-joruri,* designating the union of puppetry (*ningyo*) with a particular style of chanted storytelling (*joruri*).

Japan's Shakespeare Japan's first professional playwright is also widely acknowledged to have been her greatest. And he achieved this distinction by writing mostly for puppets. Called the Shakespeare of Japan, Chikamatsu Monzaemon (1653-1725) helped found the form that came to be known as Bunraku when he teamed up with another pivotal figure, Takemoto Gidayu, in 1705. His fame is not based entirely on this innovation, however; he is also credited with being the first to write dramas about common people, using the language of the streets. Monzaemon's *The Love Suicides at Sonezaki* deals, for instance, with the star-crossed love of an apprentice clerk and a prostitute. The play was not only popular but notorious, inspiring a spate of love suicides. Monzaemon is said to have written 110 Bunraku and 30 Kabuki plays. Like Shakespeare, he did not shy away from the lurid; his work includes onstage scenes of torture, violent death, and even a Caesarean delivery.

Part One The Dawn of Theatre 413

Hindu Theatre

The *Natysastra* The Hindu equivalent of Aristotle's *Poetics* is the *Natysastra.* Attributed to the legendary Brahman priest and sage, Bharata, its many chapters set out the rules and practices of stagecraft with an encyclopedic comprehensiveness Aristotle does not attempt.

The *Natyaveda* The Natysastra says that theatre was invented by the gods during a time of human degeneracy. People were, as one source puts it, "addicted to sensual pleasures, and jealousy; anger, desire and greed filled their hearts." Led by Indra, a delegation of gods asked Brahma, the creator of the universe, to devise an entertainment that would please and inspire everyone. Brahma took elements from the four Vedas (holy books) and combined them to create a fifth: the *Natyaveda,* or holy book of dance. He gave the new Veda to the gods, but they complained that they were incapable of putting it into practice. Brahma therefore revealed it to the sage Bharata, who, together with his hundred sons, produced the first drama. This premiere of premieres did not go well. The demons in the audience were offended by the story; they took revenge by paralyzing the actors' speech, movement, and memory, which in turn incited the gods to kill many of the demons.

Acting follows the Chinese tradition. It is highly symbolic, presentational, and rhythmic, moving slowly from one studied pose to another. Even the tilt of the finger or the flutter of an eyelash has meaning and can evoke a certain mood in the audience.

Lord Shiva, disguised as a hunter, in the Sanskrit drama *Mahabharata.*

Hindu Theatre

Dramatic form in India is ancient, dating back to 1500 B.C., when dialogue was used in religious hymns. According to Hindu mythology, Brahma invented theatre and commanded the first playhouse be built; but real theatre did not emerge until the 5th century B.C. Plays were composed in **Sanskrit,** the literary language used and understood only by the aristocrats. In fact, most Hindu drama was for the upper classes, being performed in either the gardens or courtyards of the palaces or in specially built palace playhouses.

Theatre Terms
greenroom
Sanskrit

The stage was situated at one end of the room with the audience sitting around. The only scenery was a decorated wall with doors leading to the **greenroom,** a place where the actors changed and relaxed before and after performances. The tradition continues, and today almost every theatre and TV studio has a greenroom.

Theatre patrons had a great love of beauty, and Hindu theatre is very intimate, delicate, and restrained. It is performed strictly for pleasant entertainment, with the plays always ending happily. As far as we know, Hindu theatre was the first to permit women to act onstage. (For more on Sanskrit drama, see page 298.)

Theatre Terms

greenroom a room where actors can relax when they are not on stage

Sanskrit a classical language of India

414 **Unit Seven** Exploring Theatre History

Suggested Projects

1 From current articles, such as those in *National Geographic* magazine, report on the drama of another culture. Show pictures if possible.

2 Draw an idea for a mask that might symbolize a great warrior, an elder leader, a shaman, or a clown.

3 Research and report on some aspect of ancient Egyptian civilization. Use visual aids in your report.

4 Read and report on one of the plays below. Analyze the physical, emotional, and social dimensions of the characters.

Agamemnon, Libation Bearers, The Furies, or *Prometheus Bound* by Aeschylus
Oedipus Rex, Antigone, or *Electra* by Sophocles
Medea or *Alcestis* by Euripides
The Curmudgeon by Menander

5 Read several Japanese haiku, then choose one to read to the class. Discuss how this literary form relates to Japanese acting.

6 Study the puppets of the Far East, including the Japanese doll theatre, Bunraku. Make a puppet in the tradition of the Far East, and share it with the class. (See Haar's *Japanese Theatre,* pages 43–87, for excellent pictures and information on Bunraku.)

7 Report on contemporary theatre trends in China, including recent developments in Peking Opera.

8 Use an Internet site, such as didaskalia.berkeley.edu to learn all you can about ancient Greek theatres. Based on your findings, create a model or drawing of one of them.

9 With two or three classmates, work on a scene from a famous Sanskrit drama, such as *The Fatal Ring* or *Little Clay Cart.* Act out the scene for the class.

Resource Binder

Part One Test, p. 123

For More Information

Books

Beacham, Richard, *Spectacle Entertainments of Early Imperial Rome,* Yale University Press, 1999.

Hadas, Moses (trans.), *Ten Plays by Euripides,* Bantam Doubleday Dell,1981.

Hadas, Moses (trans.), *The Complete Plays of Aristophanes,* Bantam Doubleday Dell, 1976.

Hutton, James (trans.), *Aristotle's Poetics,* W.W. Norton, 1982.

Waley, Arthur (trans.), *The No Plays of Japan,* Grove Press, 1957.

Other Media

The Ancient Greek Theatre, CD-ROM, Insight Media, 1996.

Behind the Mask, VHS, Insight Media, 1990.

A Casebook on Sanskrit Theater, VHS, Insight Media, 1994.

Chinese Opera, VHS, Insight Media, 1992.

Fellini Satyricon (film based on *Petronius*), adapted by Federico Fellini and Bernardino Zapponi, directed by Federico Fellini, VHS and DVD, 1969.

Jowett, Benjamin (trans.), *The Republic of Plato,* The Internet Classics Archive, 1994–2000. *classics.mit.edu/Plato/republic.html*

How Theatre Began, VHS, Insight Media, 1994.

The Mahabharata (stage version of Indian epic), adapted by Peter Brook, Jean-Claude Carriere, and Marie-Helene Estienne, directed by Peter Brook, VHS and DVD, 1992.

Oedipus Rex, VHS, Insight Media, 1986.

The Tradition of Performing Arts in Japan, VHS, Insight Media, 1990.

Part Two

The Middle Ages to 1800

This section of the unit begins with the liturgical plays of the Middle Ages and proceeds through Renaissance, Elizabethan (including Shakespeare), and Restoration drama.

Objectives

1 to learn about Medieval and Renaissance theatre including *commedia dell'arte*

2 to gain appreciation of Elizabethan playwrights, actors, and theatres, especially Shakespeare and the Globe

3 to understand Restoration and 18th-century theatre, especially the comedy of manners

National Standards

Part Two meets these National Theatre Standards:

Proficient 2b, 3b, 5a, 8b

Advanced 5b, 6d, 6e, 7g, 8g

Medieval Theatre

Opposition The early church fathers made no secret of their opposition to the theatre. In a disquisition called *De Spectaculis* (*Of Spectacles*), Tertullian (c. 160-225) wrote, "No, we certainly nowhere find it enjoined with the same clearness as; 'Thou shalt not kill,' 'Thou shalt not worship an idol,' 'Thou shalt not commit adultery' or 'fraud'; we nowhere find it expressly laid down, 'Thou shalt not go to the circus, thou shalt not go to the theatre, thou shalt not look on the contest or spectacle.' But we find relevant to this type of thing that first word of David; 'Happy is the man,' he says, 'who has not gone to the gatherings of the impious, who has not stood in the way of sinners, nor sat in the chair of pestilences."

English translation by T.R. Glover.

Part **Two**

The Middle Ages to 1800

Medieval Theatre

Theatre Terms
cycles
feudalism
guilds
mansions
miracle play
morality play
mystery play
passion play
trope

The Middle Ages in Europe was a period often called the Dark Ages because there was little or no cultural activity. The Middle Ages began with the fall of Rome in 476 A.D. and continued until the 15th century. **Feudalism,** in which peasants worked land and paid rent to landowning lords, was the political system of the time. Poverty and illiteracy among the masses was common. Travel and the exchange of ideas all but vanished. For approximately 400 years there was no theatre, except for sparse folk festivals and a few wandering jugglers and minstrels, who managed to stir the theatrical coals that were routinely extinguished by the church.

Theatre Born of the Church

Strange as it may seem, the church that buried drama in the 5th century resurrected that same art sometime during the 9th century when it introduced the **trope,** short dramatized scenes, into the mass. The trope began in France, but the idea soon spread throughout the European subcontinent. At first, brief Easter and Nativity tableaus (representations of a scene performed by motionless people in costume) were given to help the illiterate congregation understand the service. Pantomimes developed, which soon gave way to dialogue, first in Latin and then in the common language. Priests and choirboys enacted this religious drama. The scenes became so popular that whole stories began to be enacted. Small platforms called **mansions,** or stations, were placed within the cathedral. Separate scenes were performed on these with the crowd moving from one mansion to another until they had seen the whole story.

Theatre Terms

cycles a series of short plays based on religious history, often performed on pageant wagons in Medieval times

feudalism a social system whereby peasants worked the land and paid rent to the landowning nobles

guilds trade unions

mansions small platforms on which short scenes are played

miracle play drama about the life of a saint

morality play drama that teaches moral lessons

mystery play drama based on a biblical story

passion play drama based on episodes of Christ's life

trope short dramatized scenes added to the Catholic mass

Three types of plays were presented in the Middle Ages.

1 **Mystery plays** Bible stories re-enacted

2 **Miracle plays** Enacting the lives of the saints

3 **Morality plays** Stories teaching right from wrong in which characters personified abstract qualities.

An excellent example of a morality play is *Everyman,* which is still performed today. As Everyman journeys to Death, his Friends, Worldly Goods, and so on, all leave him. Only Good Deeds accompanies him to the grave.

In the 10th century, a nun, Hrosvitha, wrote religious comedy that was performed on the cathedral mansions.

An early artist's interpretation of a scene from a miracle play.

Drama in the church became boisterous when comedy was added, and the crowds became so large that in the 13th or 14th century, the mansions were moved outside to the marketplace. The comedy vein persisted: Herod became a devil and the audience laughed at his antics; Noah's wife stubbornly refused to enter the ark and had to be carried inside kicking and screaming; devils with pitchforks prodded the wicked.

Staging the Plays

Elaborate staging devices were contrived, such as Hell's Mouth, which would open and close amid smoke and flames, as well as a rack that exhibited tortured souls, complete with realistic screams. Eventually, the trade **guilds** (unions) sponsored the plays, with each guild presenting an applicable episode. The shipbuilders staged Noah's Ark;

A recent European passion play is presented just as it was in the Middle Ages.

Backstage Gossip: Deadly Dominoes

A play given in Sweden in the late Middle Ages set a dismal record for quick deceases. It was a religious drama called *The Passion of Our Savior,* and an actor named Lengis plunged his lance into the side of the actor on the cross and killed him. The dead man, falling from the cross, struck the actress playing the Virgin Mary, and she was fatally injured. The King of Sweden, John the Second, who was in the audience, swung a scimitar at Lengis and killed him; and the audience, who liked Lengis rather more than they liked their King, rose in their wrath and killed John the Second.

from *All Wrong on the Night* by Maurice Dolbier

"Feast" plays The Middle Ages had its own form of guerrilla theatre. Secret societies produced annual "feasts"—such as the Feast of Fools, the Feast of the Ass, and the Feast of the Boy Bishop—that used vulgarity, nonsense, and a touch of paganism to satirize the Mass and temporarily invert the social order. Possibly older than the mystery plays themselves, these events occurred throughout Europe but enjoyed a special popularity in France, where troupes included Les Enfant sans Souci (The Carefree Children). Though it was argued that the feasts served as an important societal safety valve, they were outlawed by the Council of Basle in 1435.

Hrosvitha (c. 935-1002) According to Adolphus William Ward, Hrosvitha's plays "were devised on the simple principle that the world, the flesh, and the devil should not have all the good plays to themselves." She wrote six of them, occasionally employing rhyme and even elements of farce to illuminate sacred themes. Her plots tend to focus on saints undergoing conversion or enduring martyrdom. Called the "strong voice of Gandesheim," Hrosvitha is thought to have been Europe's first female playwright.

The image at the left shows Martin Norz as Jesus in the Oberammergau passion play, May 2000. Use the following questions to discuss the image with students:

- What episode of Christ's life is pictured?
- Do you think these are professional or amateur actors? Why?
- How might this scene have been different when performed in the 1600s?

Part Two The Middle Ages to 1800 **417**

Oberammergau The present-day Oberammergau Passion Play takes five and a half hours to perform, involves a cast and crew of 2,200 (nearly half the town's population), and takes place in a theatre that seats 4,700.

Anti-Semitism In 1984, Samuel Weintraub of the American Jewish Committee evaluated six American passion plays and found various degrees of anti-Semitism present in all of them. The plays, Weintraub said, tend to demean and stigmatize Jews while excusing the conduct of the Roman curate, Pontius Pilate, and obscuring the Jewish cultural context out of which Jesus arose.

The report calls one play "deliberately and maliciously anti-Semitic," but praises the producers of another for working to rid it of bias. (According to a *Chicago Tribune* story dated July 2, 2000, even the original Bavarian passion play has changed in this respect: "The. . . text used since 1860 has been reworked this year," the article says, "to erase implications that the Jews killed Jesus and that women played only a minor role in Jesus' life.")

the cooks handled Hell's Mouth, since they were used to smoke and flames. Each scene was prepared in great detail and was carefully rehearsed. The productions, which were often quite spectacular, were presented to throngs of people on festival days in an atmosphere of gaiety and fun.

In England, France, and the Netherlands, pageant wagons were often used instead of stationary mansions. These were double-decker wagons. The lower story was curtained off and served as a changing room. The play's action was staged on the upper level and sometimes on the street around the wagon. Audience members would find vantage points and remain there as the wagons were brought to them, episode by episode—something like our parade floats today. In England the plays performed on pageant wagons were called **cycles,** and they were given in the spring on Corpus Christi day. Four of these cycles still exist: those of York, Chester, Wakefield, and Coventry. These old plays are periodically performed today in England during special summer festivals. (For more about medieval staging and pageant wagons, see page 230.)

The **passion play** evolved during the late Middle Ages. It depicted scenes from Christ's life, particularly the last days of his suffering and his resurrection. Of these, the passion play at Oberammergau, Germany, is still performed. More than 300 years ago, residents of that small village prayed that if they were spared the black plague that was laying waste to the continent, they would periodically dramatize a passion play. Their village was spared, and they kept their vow. In 1633 they presented their first play. Since then, the Oberammergau Passion Play has been performed every ten years, at the turn of the decade. Only in 1940, during WWII, were the townspeople unable to give a show. Today thousands throng to see this intriguing play from the past. Similar passion plays, though on a smaller scale, are enacted in the United States in Spearfish, South Dakota; Lake Wales, Florida; and Eureka Springs, Arkansas.

The effects of medieval theatre would be felt in later drama. Because audience members were brought close to the performers, and because the playing area provided increased freedom, the art of acting became as important as the dialogue. Medieval drama also brought in a mixture of the comic and the serious, a combination that would be imitated by both the improvisational players in Italy and the Elizabethan writers in England.

Renaissance Theatre

The Renaissance, which means "rebirth" in French, took place largely in the 15th and 16th centuries, and was an exciting time for theatre. As the ancient classic

Notes

418 **Unit Seven** Exploring Theatre History

A scene from a recent American production of a *commedia dell'arte* play by Molière.

writers were rediscovered, a rebirth of learning occurred throughout Europe, with vigorous activity in all of the arts and sciences. The Renaissance started in Italy, and men such as Petrarch, Leonardo da Vinci, Michelangelo, and Machiavelli contributed to a great flowering of knowledge and ideas.

Italian Theatre of the Renaissance
An important form of theatre that originated in Italy at this time was the ***commedia dell'arte.*** Developed years before from mimes and pantomimes that may have been remnants of ancient Roman comedy, this art was flourishing by 1550. *Commedia dell'arte* was professional improvised comedy performed in the streets for the masses. A company, consisting usually of seven men and three women, would ad lib action, dialogue, song, and dance around a scenario that usually involved love and intrigue. To improvise effectively, actors had to be inventive, clever, and witty, with agile bodies for the many acrobatic stunts, fights, and dances.

Stock characters developed: Harlequin, who wore patches that later evolved into the stylized diamond costume still used today, was the clever, witty servant; Pierrot was lovelorn and moody; Columbine was flirtatious and pretty; Pantalone, who wore baggy trousers (and from whom we derive the word *pantaloons*), was the gullible father. The cast of a *commedia dell'arte,* which included the first women on the stage since Indian drama, wore half masks. The popularity of this art form spread throughout Europe and was particularly well received in France, where it would later influence the writings of Molière. (For more on *commedia dell'arte,* see page 38.)

Theatre Terms
commedia dell'arte
neoclassicism

Theatre Terms

commedia dell'arte improvised comedy with stock characters, which began in Renaissance Italy

neoclassicism a form in which dramatists follow the classic unities and write in verse

Renaissance Theatre

Arte In his book, *The Tricks of the Trade,* Italian Nobel laureate and comic genius Dario Fo reminds us that *arte,* as in *commedia dell'arte,* does not necessarily translate as "art." "In the Middle Ages," he says, "*arte* also meant "guild," and there existed an arte, or guild, of woolworkers, of silkworkers, of masons, and so on . . . . *Commedia dell'Arte,* then, means primarily comedy staged by professional actors."

Zanni One *commedia* character was a comic servant named Giovanni but known by his nickname, Zanni. It is from him that we get the word *zany.*

Lazzi Also from *The Tricks of the Trade:* "The [*commedia*] actors had at their disposal an incredible store of stage business, called *lazzi*—situations, dialogues, gags, rhymes, and rigamaroles which they could call up at a moment's notice to give the impression of on-stage improvisation . . . . The players were past masters at dismantling and re-assembling the different elements, and in this style the most unlikely twists and turns could be extended over the entire script."

Goldoni and Gozzi Though he borrowed heavily from *commedia* storylines and characters, Carlo Goldoni (1707-1793) disdained the form's cartoonishness and brought a transformation to the Italian stage by writing more naturalistic, dimensional, character-based comedy in the manner of Molière. Goldoni's primary opponent was Count Garlo Gozzi (1720-1806), who championed traditional Tuscan culture. Gozzi's fantasies, *King Turandot* and *A Fable of the Love of Three Oranges* (the latter written—in *commedia* style—to lampoon Goldoni and Pietro Chiari [1700-1788]), have inspired operas by the likes of Puccini and Prokofiev.

Part Two The Middle Ages to 1800 **419**

Spanish Theatre Called *Monstruo de la Naturaleza*—"Prodigy of Nature"—by Miguel de Cervantes (1547-1616), Lope de Vega (1562-1635) was as prodigal as he was prolific. He quarrelled, loved, soldiered, and reproduced with remarkable gusto even as he was writing more plays than any single individual is known to have written either before or since. Nor did he slow down when he joined the priesthood in 1614. Where the plays of Calderon de la Barca (1600-1681) tend to be abstract and contemplative in tone, Lope's are given to action and often draw on contemporary events. In his based-on-fact drama, *Fuenteovejuna,* for instance, the lord of the eponymous village rapes a young woman and is murdered by angry villagers; when King Ferdinand's judge arrives to investigate, he finds that, even under torture, the villagers will say only that Fuenteovejuna killed him. Ultimately, their courage earns them the pardon and protection of the king.

French Theatre The two titans of French neoclassicism were Pierre Corneille (1606-1684) and Jean Racine (1639-1699). The paths of their careers were remarkably similar. Each was born into a bourgeouis setting and received a solid, religiously based, classically oriented education (although Corneille's was Jesuit and Racine's Jansenist). Each came early under the wing of an important patron (Corneille's was Cardinal Richelieu; Racine's, Molière) from whom each soon became alienated. Each had a blockbuster, epoque-making hit (Corneille's: *Le Cid,* Racine's: *Andromaque*) followed by a series of successes in the tragic mode, characterized by stylistic rigor and emotional power. And each finally turned his back on the theatre (Racine, because of attacks against his greatest play, *Phedre;* Corneille, at least partly because of Racine).

Spanish Theatre of the Renaissance
While Italy was developing its *commedia* and opera, Spain became interested in drama. From about 1550 to 1680, Spanish theatre flourished. It was influenced by both *commedia dell'arte* and Italian court staging. Three major playwrights evolved at this time: Miguel de Cervantes (1547–1616), who is better known today for the novel *Don Quixote* than for his 30 plays; Lope de Vega (1562–1635), who wrote a phenomenal 2000 plays, many of them full of beautiful poetry, vigorous action, and dashing romance; and Calderon (1600–1681), who created 200 plays, which were distinguished by their spiritual emphasis and elevated poetry.

These dramatists were all successful in establishing an original art form, free from the classical rules that fettered so many Italian and French writers. Spanish dramatists, ignoring the unities of time and place, wrote beautiful flowing dialogue and centered their action around adventure, romance, and chivalry.

French Renaissance Theatre
Because of France's many wars, and because one theatre group had exclusive rights to the public playhouse, the Renaissance came late to French theatre, reaching its height during the 17th century. At that time the increased theatre activity gave rise to **neoclassicism,** a form in which dramatists were supposed to observe the classic unities and write in a restricted verse form. This French drama developed into entertainment mainly for royalty. Playhouses were ornate, with carvings

This open-air production of *Entremeses* by Miguel de Cervantes was performed in Guanajuato, Mexico.

Visual Cue

Use the following questions to discuss the open-air production pictured above:

- What other theatres have you either studied or attended that could be considered open-air?
- As an audience member, would you find such a performance more or less theatrically satisfying than a play seen in a regular theatre?
- What production problems would need to be solved in order to perform in an outdoor setting?

420 **Unit Seven** Exploring Theatre History

washed in gold, velvet-covered seats, and lavish drapes, following the Italian tradition of luxurious surroundings for the nobles.

Molière (1622–1673) represents the high point of French Renaissance drama. He wrote such witty satire that his plays continue to entertain audiences around the world. Molière's real name was Jean-Baptiste Poquelin, but when he chose the theatre as his life's work, he also chose another name so that his parents would not be disgraced by having an actor in the family.

Molière toured for twelve years as an actor in a *commedia dell'arte* company. As he began to write comedies, he drew from the *commedia's* farcical style. His many plays, performed both for the public and for the court of Louis XIV, are masterpieces of satire, a perfect blend of the humorous and the caustic. In *The Doctor in Spite of Himself,* Molière lampoons the field of medicine; in *Tartuffe* he satirizes hypocrisy; in *The Imaginary Invalid* he spoofs hypochondria. Throughout his writing career, Molière continued to act. In his last years he was ill from tuberculosis, and, ironically, he died onstage just after completing a performance of *The Imaginary Invalid.* (For more about Molière, see page 132.)

Although the theatrical activity in Italy and Spain (and later, in France) advanced Renaissance drama, it was not in these countries where drama realized its greatest potential. Instead, we look to England for a unique form that reached staggering heights.

Elizabethan Theatre

Elizabeth and the Playwrights

There was great vitality, zest, and intellectual curiosity throughout England during Queen Elizabeth I's reign (1558–1603). Her country swelled with national pride over its voyages of discovery, its defeat of the Spanish armada, its expanding trade markets, and its increased literary vistas—the result of the introduction of printed books in 1475.

Theatre Terms
discovery space
groundlings
masques
soliloquies
tiring house
Wooden O's

When Elizabeth became queen of England, the theatre gained a friend, for even though the Lord Mayor and other civil authorities were hostile to drama (because of the fear that the crowds would spread disease and start fights), Elizabeth loved the theatre. She commanded many court performances, protected groups of players through court sponsorship, and looked upon London's feverish dramatic activity with approval.

The Elizabethan period was an age of literary enlightenment. There were many brilliant playwrights, and most of them wrote with great freedom, disregarding the classic unities of time and

Theatre Terms

discovery space in an Elizabethan theatre, a space at the back of the stage used for small interior settings

groundlings audience members who stood in the pit around the Elizabethan stage

masques extravagant court entertainments that included dance, music, and poetry

soliloquies types of monologues that reveal the character's inner thoughts

tiring house in an Elizabethan theatre, a backstage area where actors changed clothes

Wooden O's Elizabethan theatres which were usually round or octagonal

Interestingly, in attempting to describe the difference between Corneille and Racine, one observer felt compelled to paraphrase Sophocles's remark about the difference between himself and Euripides: Corneille depicted people as they ought to be while Racine depicted them as they are.

Corneille's *Le Cid* made such a strong impression on Parisian society that "Beautiful as *Le Cid*" became a catchphrase.

Molière produced Racine's first two tragedies. Racine repaid him by seducing one of his leading ladies and coaxing her to jump to a rival company. Molière reputedly never spoke to Racine again.

Elizabethan Theatre

The Role of Age A sidelight: The greatest figures of the Italian, Spanish, and French Renaissances lived to be very old men. Goldoni, Gozzi, Chiari, and Calderon reached their 80s; Lope de Vega and Corneille lived into their 70s; Cervantes saw his 69th birthday; and Racine died relatively young at 60. The tendency for writers of the English Renaissance is exactly opposite. Of the eleven leading writers listed in this section, only three made it out of their 50s, with Thomas Heywood the grand old man at 67. Shakespeare and John Lyly both died at 52; Greene, Kyd, Peele, Webster, Beaumont, and Fletcher were all spent by their 30s or early 40s. And of course, Marlowe famously lost his life at 29. One wonders if there is a correlation between the greater vigor of the English Renaissance and the shorter life spans of its participants. Did the expectation of death paradoxically enliven their work? Did the long lives of the Italian, Spanish, and French lions discourage competition and therefore innovation?

Part Two The Middle Ages to 1800 **421**

Christopher Marlowe was the adventurer par excellence. It is thought that he spied for the English crown during his college years, keeping tabs on its Catholic adversaries in France, and that after taking his M.A. he went to the Low Countries (the present day Netherlands and Belgium) to fight alongside Protestant rebels. Back in London, he was an outspoken, ostentatiously dressed dandy before the term was coined. His incautious, irreverent mouth made him the target of charges of heresy, for which he might have been prosecuted if he had not been killed first in a fight over a bar tab. (Some think the fight was intentionally provoked in order to get Marlowe out of the way.)

Marlowe's roommate, Thomas Kyd, was arrested for heresy and tortured into informing against Marlowe. He died a year later.

Ben Jonson's valediction "To the Memory of Shakespeare" compares the Bard favorably not only to his contemporaries but to the greatest writers of the Classical period. It contains these lines: "Soul of the age!/The applause! delight! the wonder of our stage! . . . /He was not of an age, but for all time!" Jonson himself is the only person buried vertically under the floor at Westminster Abbey. His headstone reads, "O rare Ben Johnson" (sic). Legend has it that this epitaph was an afterthought, requested and paid for by an admirer who happened to be present when masons were closing the grave.

Like so many other theatre artists of the Renaissance, Ben Jonson (1572-1637) did time in jail. In 1597, he was imprisoned for co-writing—with Thomas Nashe—a seditious satire called *The Isle of Dogs*.

The following year he killed an actor named Gabriel Spencer in a duel and was convicted of murder. He escaped hanging, but forfeited his possessions and was literally branded (on the thumb) as a felon.

place, and the rule—left over from the ancient Greeks—that violence should not be seen on stage. Moreover, they mixed poetry with prose and interspersed comedy with tragedy. Competent though they were, Thomas Kyd, John Lyly, Robert Greene, George Peele, John Webster, Thomas Dekker, Thomas Heywood, and Beaumont and Fletcher were overshadowed by the three giants of Elizabethan theatre: Christopher Marlowe, Ben Jonson, and William Shakespeare.

Christopher Marlowe (1564–1593)
Next to Shakespeare, Marlowe is considered the greatest dramatist of tragedy in England, even though he lived only to the age of twenty-nine. Marlowe's blank verse is often termed "Marlowe's Mighty Line." In his short life, he wrote seven plays. *Tamburlaine, Edward II, The Jew of Malta,* and *Dr. Faustus* became his best known.

Ben Jonson (1572–1637)
Like Marlowe, Jonson scorned Shakespeare at first because Shakespeare knew "small Latin and less Greek." Jonson was a classic writer, always correct, always abiding by the Aristotelian unities. Much of his work is biting, humorous satire. *Everyman in His Humour, Volpone,* and *The Alchemist* are but a few of his plays. When James I inherited the throne, Jonson entertained the court with **masques,** great extravaganzas of song, dance, and recitation. It is said that on one Jonson production alone, James spent the equivalent of $500,000 on lavish costumes and sets designed by Inigo Jones, who had studied perspective scenery in Italy.

William Shakespeare (1564–1616)
Considered the greatest of all English dramatists, it is strange and unfortunate that we know so little about Shakespeare's life. Born in Stratford-upon-Avon, where his father was a glover and, for a time, a respected town official, Shakespeare attended grammar school, his only formal education. At eighteen, he married Ann Hathaway, eight years his senior. Although the exact reason is not known, he left his wife and three children and went to London, where he began working in the theatre world as an actor, manager, and writer. By 1596, he was well established and in royal favor, for Queen Elizabeth granted him a coat of arms.

In the thirty-eight plays attributed to him, Shakespeare created histories, comedies, tragedies, and fantasies. His plays combined skillful plot and character development with majestic use of language. Among his masterful creations are the melancholy Hamlet, Prince of Denmark; the fat, braggart Falstaff; the impish Puck; the boyish Rosalind; the impetuous Hotspur; the youthfully passionate Juliet; and the jealous Othello.

Notes

422 **Unit Seven** Exploring Theatre History

Shakespeare's luminous **soliloquies** (speeches where actors talk alone to reveal their thoughts aloud) encompass great breadth of emotion and intellect and are beloved throughout the world. But his less grand phrases are a part of our world as well. We quote Shakespeare without even knowing it. Phrases such as "grim necessity," "as luck would have it," "Greek to me," "the short and long of it," "a rose by any other name," "haven't slept a wink," "all the world's a stage," "the unkindest cut of all" and "eating out of house and home," are straight out of Shakespeare's playful, compelling, and inventive language.

The Theatres

The first public playhouse to be erected during this time was The Theatre, constructed by James Burbage in 1576, accommodating about 1,500 people.

Shakespeare is as popular today as he was over 400 years ago, as can be seen in this lively and imaginative scene from a recent production of his *Twelfth Night*.

William Shakespeare There are those who argue that Shakespeare's plays are too great to have been written by Shakespeare. They claim that the historical Shakespeare—whom they prefer to call the Stratford Man (for his hometown of Stratford-upon-Avon), or Will Shakespeare (for the way he signed documents)—was too unschooled, untraveled, and plebian to have given the world the profundity of *Hamlet,* the sophistication of *As You Like It,* the humanity of *King Lear,* or the sweetness of *A Midsummer Night's Dream.* (Apparently it escapes them that Marlowe was the son of a shoemaker and Jonson was raised by a bricklayer.) They have therefore written fat books purporting to prove that Shakespeare was a front for someone else who could not afford to be associated directly with the seamy world of the theatre. Candidates include Francis Bacon, Edward de Vere, King James I, and Queen Elizabeth. Christopher Marlowe has been put forward, also, on the theory that he faked his death in order to confound his enemies, and then continued his career in secret.

For an entertaining and sensible refutation of the "anti-Stratfordian" argument, see William M. Murphy's 1964 lecture, "Thirty-Six Plays in Search of an Author."

Shakespeare's children were a daughter named Susanna and a pair of twins, Hamnet and Judith. On August 11, 1596, 11-year-old Hamnet died of unknown causes.

Visual Cue

Ask students to study the image from the *Twelfth Night* production above. Discuss the concept of Shakespeare in modern dress with your students.

- The photo caption says that Shakespeare plays are as popular today as they were 400 years ago. Do you agree with this statement? Why or why not?
- What is your opinion about Shakespeare in modern dress? Does it help with comprehension or does it detract from the majesty of the plays?
- What would you think of a modern language Shakespeare along with the modern dress? In other words, changing the language to contemporary English?

Lord Pembroke's Men performed some of Shakespeare's earliest plays, including the lurid *Titus Andronicus.* By the 1590s Shakespeare was a principal member of the Lord Chamberlain's Men, the company that built the Globe Theatre. When James I succeeded Queen Elizabeth to the throne in 1603, he became their patron and the company was renamed the King's Men.

The Theatres The Globe Theatre's motto was *"Totus mundus agit histrionem,"* or "an entire world of players." The converse, of course, is, "All the world's a stage."

From the Web site of the Rose Theatre Trust: "Built in 1587 by Philip Henslowe, the Rose was the first theatre on London's [Thames] Bankside. In 1989 its remains were discovered and partially excavated amidst a blaze of international press coverage. Despite their huge archaeological and cultural significance, they were promptly covered up again for conservation reasons. Nearly ten years later, the theatre site was reopened to the public as part of an historical exhibition. Meanwhile, thanks primarily to the efforts of the late American actor Sam Wanamaker, the Globe has been rebuilt as faithfully as possible and reopened as a performance venue."

It was placed outside of London to escape the city's jurisdiction. Other theatres, including The Rose, The Fortune, The Swan, Blackfriars, and The Globe, were soon built. Although we do not know the exact nature of Elizabethan theatre structure, we know that the playhouses were modeled upon the inn yards where earlier plays had been presented. Called **Wooden O's,** the theatres were usually round or octagonal with two or three tiers of thatched roof galleries surrounding an open court on three sides. One end served as a multiple acting area with a large platform (equipped with trapdoors), which was elevated by four to six feet and extended into the open court. Each theatre also had a **discovery space** located between two doors at the back of the stage and used for small interior settings, such as Juliet's burial vault. The two doors at the back of the stage led to the **tiring house,** or backstage area, where the actors would go to change costumes.

On the second level of the stage facade, there was another acting space (an "inner above"), as well as balcony windows and a terrace. A third level could also provide a playing area but was used mainly for the musicians as they accompanied songs and dances and played musical interludes. A fourth level was a structure called the hut, which housed stage machinery for the special effects.

Stage in an inn yard, around 1565. Portable platforms upon which plays were performed were set up in the inn yards. This image is based upon a sketch from the 16th century by Pieter Breughel the Younger.

Plays were held in the afternoon (with the daylight serving as lighting system), and to announce performances, a flag—white for comedy, black for tragedy—was raised at the top of the theatre. All classes of people attended, for the theatre was to Elizabethans not only their drama, but also their movies, novels, radio, television, and newspapers rolled into one. The **groundlings**—usually tradespeople, soldiers, apprentices, and servants—paid a penny and stood in the pit around the acting platform. Lords and ladies paid more and had seats in the gallery. A few rich, young gallants might

Notes

424 **Unit Seven** Exploring Theatre History

even occupy a portion of the stage. The whole atmosphere was joyful and at times boisterous. Peddlers sold oranges and nuts that were noisily eaten—and sometimes thrown—by the audience.

There was no scenery. The spectators used their imaginations as they listened to the playwright's descriptions and the characters' dialogue. Some properties were used, and so were certain sound effects. In fact, the burning of The Globe Theatre in 1613 was the result of the thatch roof catching a spark from the cannon shots that announced the king's entrance in Shakespeare's *Henry VIII.* By June of 1614 it was rebuilt and in use again.

Since costumes were usually handsome styles of the day donated by patrons, there was little attempt made toward historical accuracy. Julius Caesar, along with Dr. Faustus, wore Renaissance clothes on the Elizabethan stage.

The modern Globe, an open-air theatre reconstructed through the efforts of many, including American actor Sam Wanamaker. The original Globe was destroyed in 1644.

Backstage Gossip: Cockney Catastrophe

When a "super" [extra] graduates to a "bit part," the margin for error is sizably increased. In an early nineteenth-century provincial production of *Richard III,* an amateur actor entered toward the end of the first act and told the astonished king, "My Lord, I 'ave cut off the Dook of Buckingham's 'ead." "Oh, you 'ave, 'ave you?" King Richard retorted. "Well, you've gone and spoiled the 'ole bloomin' play, that's wot you've done!"

from *All Wrong on the Night* by Maurice Dolbier

Part Two The Middle Ages to 1800 **425**

Edward Alleyn became very wealthy as an entertainment entrepreneur. One of his businesses was the Bear Garden, a venue for bearbaiting.

Will Kempe was the great theatrical clown of his day, famous for jigging the entire way from London to Norwich—a distance of about 100 miles as the crow flies. Some scholars think that part of Hamlet's famous speech to the Players ("...and let those that play your clowns speak no more than is set down for them, for there be of them that will themselves laugh, to set on some quantity of barren spectators to laugh too, though in the mean time some necessary question of the play be then to be considered. That's villainous and shows a most pitiful ambition in the fool that uses it.") was Shakespeare's not-so-subtle gibe at Kempe.

The Jacobean Age The reign of James I was called the Jacobean Age. In the theatre it was characterized by cynicism, melancholy, and a preoccupation with evil. *Hamlet,* Webster's *The Duchess of Malfi,* and Jonson's *Volpone* embody the Jacobean mood.

Only a few stylized costumes, those for fairies, witches, lawyers, and churchmen, were used.

The Players
Actors were all men, with the women's parts being taken by boys whose voices had not yet changed to masculine lowness or by men with higher-than-usual voices. Acting was a strenuous life, for often roles required singing, dancing, fighting, and fencing. Three great actors emerged during this period:

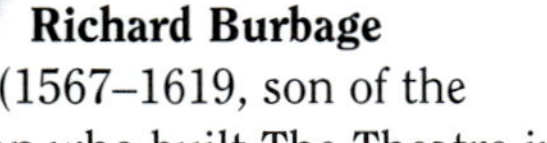

Richard Burbage

Richard Burbage (1567–1619, son of the man who built The Theatre in 1576) Born, like Shakespeare, in Stratford-upon-Avon, Burbage played many of Shakespeare's tragic figures, including Hamlet, Othello, Richard III, and King Lear. He and his brother Cuthbert built The Globe Theatre in London.

Edward Alleyn

Edward Alleyn (1566–1626) Alleyn played the title roles in *Tamburlaine* and *Dr. Faustus* as well as Barabas in *The Jew of Malta,* all written by Christopher Marlowe. In 1600, Alleyn and his partner Philip Henslowe constructed The Fortune Theatre north of London to compete with the Globe.

William Kemp or Will Kempe
(circa 1560–about 1603)
Kemp's greatest success came from the role of Nick Bottom in *A Midsummer Night's Dream.* Shakespeare created this character with the supposed intention of ridiculing the scene-stealing actor, but Kemp made the character his own, even down to Bottom's donkey ears. In early manuscripts Shakespeare inadvertently identifies Bottom as "Kempe."

James I (1603–1625) reigned after the death of Elizabeth I. The political unrest that had been brewing throughout his reign continued after Charles I was crowned in 1625. Eventually, civil war broke out, and Oliver Cromwell, the Puritan leader, gained control. Charles was beheaded, and the rest of the Stuart line fled to France. The Puritans, always against the theatre, closed what they considered "dens of iniquity" in 1642. Public theatre died in England until Charles II regained control of England in 1660. During Cromwell's time, however, plays were performed surreptitiously, as the historical record of arrests of actors and audience members shows.

Backstage Gossip: Will vs. Richard

This story comes from an actor in Shakespeare's company, who noted the following in his diary under March 13, 1601:

Upon a time when Burbage played Richard III, there was a citizen grew so far in liking with him that before she went from the play she appointed him to come that night unto her, by the name of "Richard the Third." Shakespeare, overhearing their conclusion, went before, was entertained, and at his game ere Burbage came. Then, message being brought that Richard the Third was at the door, Shakespeare caused return to be made, that William the Conqueror was before Richard the Third.

from *Theatrical Anecdotes* by Peter Hay

Restoration and 18th-Century Theatre

The Restoration came about with the reestablishing of the monarchy in England in 1660 under Charles II. When Charles returned from France and was restored to the English throne, he started a new era of drama that was fashioned after the theatre he had seen in Paris.

Since the Elizabethan playhouses had been torn down by the Puritans, new indoor theatres were built with a deep apron on which to act and with a proscenium arch, behind which a series of flats were painted in perspective and were set parallel to the curtain. These flats were spaced upstage of each other to give the

Theatre Terms
bombastic
legitimate theatre
the Restoration

Theatre design in the 18th century featured box seats, a pit, a wide apron in front of the curtain, and a gallery for the audience. The scene depicted here is the wrestling match in Shakespeare's *As You Like It* at the Drury Lane Theatre, London, 1841.

Part Two The Middle Ages to 1800 **427**

Theatre Terms

bombastic pompous and high-flown language

legitimate theatre a term originally based on England's Licensing Act of 1737 in which plays could only be performed in two specific playhouses.

the Restoration an era that began with the restoration of the British monarchy in 1660 under Charles II

The Restoration

Aphra Behn A sometime English spy with the code name "Astrea," Aphra Behn (1640-1689) became one of the most prolific playwrights of the Restoration and the first European woman to earn her living by writing. Though she also wrote fiction and poetry, she was well known for racy comedies with titles like *The Forced Marriage, The Amorous Prince, The Feigned Courtesans,* and *The Lucky Chance.*

"All women together ought to let flowers fall upon the tomb of Aphra Behn . . . ," Virginia Woolf wrote, "for it was she who earned them the right to speak their minds. It is she—shady and amorous as she was—who makes it not quite fantastic for me to say to you tonight: Earn five hundred a year by your wits."

Sarah Kemble Siddons was especially famous for her portrayal of Lady Macbeth, and she chose the role for her farewell performance in 1812. It is said that the audience at that performance was so taken with Siddons in the sleepwalking scene that they would not let the play proceed beyond it.

illusion of distance. Candles and oil lamps provided lighting in these indoor theatres, and women were allowed to perform.

The audience was the sophisticated aristocracy. Broadly generalized, this crowd was witty, insincere, and apt to indulge in foolish pleasures. The plays staged at this time were comedies of manners that satirized the artificiality of the day, and so they, too, were witty and concerned with foolish pleasures.

Plays of the Restoration include John Dryden's *All for Love,* George Etherage's *Love in a Tub,* William Wycherly's *The Country Wife,* George Farquhar's *The Beaux' Stratagem,* and William Congreve's *The Way of the World.*

The Restoration ended in 1737, when Parliament passed the Licensing Act, which limited London's public playhouses to two: Covent Garden and Drury Lane. All others were illegal. Thus, evolved the term **legitimate theatre,** which today has changed meaning and refers to all live play performances (as opposed to film).

The Comedy of Manners

Later in the century and roughly corresponding to the period of the American Revolution, two other English dramatists carried on the comedy of manners tradition with a brilliance and inoffensiveness that must have pleased the licensing board. Oliver Goldsmith (1728–1774) unveiled his witty, upbeat *She Stoops to Conquer,* and Richard Brinsley Sheridan (1751–1816) fashioned the best English comedies since those of Shakespeare.

During this period, some great actors made their names on the English stage. David Garrick (1717–1779), both actor and director, is credited with establishing a less **bombastic** style of acting, that is, one that didn't appear pompous or overdone. He did many Shakespearean revivals, often rewriting, deleting, or adding scenes. The tragic actress Sarah Kemble Siddons (1755–1831) and her brother John Phillip Kemble (1757–1823) were also famous stage personalities. Later, Edmund Kean (1787–1833) achieved great acclaim, particularly for his role as Shylock in Shakespeare's *The Merchant of Venice.*

Backstage Gossip: The Worst Audience Award

Restoration audiences have a fair claim to being considered the worst that any actors in the world have had to play to—the theatre being looked on as a place to eat, drink, brawl, pick up prostitutes or merchants' wives and, from time to time, damn the play and the players loudly. On several occasions, fights that broke out in the audience were carried to the stage itself and ended in fatal sword thrusts.

from *All Wrong on the Night* by Maurice Dolbier

428 Unit Seven Exploring Theatre History

Suggested Projects

1 Read one of the following plays, and discuss the elements in it that depict life and philosophy in the Middle Ages:

The Second Shepherd's Play
Master Pierre Patelin
Everyman
Gammer Gurton's Needle

2 Do Internet research to find out more about the Oberammergau Passion Play today. Write a report on the production preparation, playing procedures, and so on.

3 Read Simonson's description of medieval staging in his book *The Stage Is Set* and use the information to stage a scene from *Everyman.*

4 Write a plot outline for a morality play. List the sequence of events and describe each character.

5 Research *commedia dell'arte* characters and draw costumes for each. Select a few fabric samples for each costume also.

6 Pretend that you are an Italian manager of a *commedia dell'arte* troupe, and write an original scenario from which your actors will improvise.

7 Rehearse and present a scene or soliloquy from a Shakespeare play. Read the complete play from which the scene is taken so you will better understand your character's motivation.

8 Compare Elizabethan theatres with those of Renaissance Spain. (See *The Living Stage* by Macgowan and Melnitz.)

9 Read and act out scenes from one of Molière's comedies, such as *The Doctor in Spite of Himself, The Would-Be Gentleman, The Miser, The Affected Young Ladies, The Imaginary Invalid,* or *Tartuffe.*

10 Learn more about The Globe and take a virtual tour by visiting www.shakespeare.palomar.edu/theatre.htm#Globe. Discuss your impressions with your classmates.

Resource Binder

Part Two Test, p. 124

For More Information

Books

Cawley, A.C. (ed.), *Everyman and Medieval Miracle Plays,* Everyman Paperback Classics, 1993.

Gordon, Mel; *Lazzi: The Comic Routines of the Commedia dell-Arte,* PAJ Publications, 1987.

Ogburn, Charlton; *The Mysterious William Shakespeare: The Myth & the Reality,* EPM Publications, 1992.

Smith, Dawn (trans.), *Eight Interludes [by] Miguel de Cervantes,* Everyman Paperback Classics, Orion Publishing Group and Charles E. Tuttle Co., 1996.

Spencer, Jane (ed.), *Aphra Behn: The Rover and Other Plays,* Oxford University Press, 2000.

Wilbur, Richard (trans.), *Tartuffe, by Molière,* Harcourt Brace & Co., 1968.

Other Media

Approaching Literature: Aphra Behn's the Rover, VHS, Insight Media, 1997.

Binda, Hilary (ed.), *The Complete Works of Christopher Marlowe: An Electronic Edition, 2000. www.perseus.tufts.edu*

Commedia dell'Arte, VHS, Insight Media, 1997.

Everyman, VHS, Insight Media, 1991.

French Literature: Molière, VHS, Insight Media, 1985.

The N-Town Passion Play, VHS, Insight Media, 1990.

The Restoration Theatre: From Tennis Court to Playhouse, VHS, Insight Media, 1990.

The Way of the World, VHS, Insight Media, 1977.

Part **Three**

1800 to the Present

The third part of Unit Seven addresses 19th-century theatre on the continent and in America and concludes with an overview of theatre in the 20th and 21st centuries.

Objectives

1 to learn about theatre in the 19th century

2 to understand realism and romanticism and the playwrights who dominated these movements

3 to introduce 20th-century theatrical movements and dramatists

National Standards

Part Three meets these National Theatre Standards:

Proficient 2b, 3b, 5a, 7a, 8b, 8c

Advanced 5b, 6d, 6e, 8g

Continental Theatre in the 19th Century

August Strindberg According to one account, August Strindberg's ferocious talent was set loose by a dose of opium he thought would kill him. Despondent, young Strindberg (1849-1912) attempted suicide but fell into a deep sleep instead. When he awoke he found he'd released a torrent of repressed memories and began to write. Even in his naturalist period, the sense of a torrent is vivid. *Miss Julie,* his drama about the sexual power struggle between a young countess and her father's servant, is fraught with a barely socialized energy. Later works like *A Dream Play* bypass the social aspect and attempt to access the unconscious source of that energy directly.

Henrik Ibsen kept Strindberg's portrait above his desk. It is reported that he once said, "I cannot write a line without that madman standing and staring down at me with those mad eyes."

Part Three 1800 to the Present

Continental Theatre in the 19th Century

Theatre Terms
realism
romanticism

Romance and Realism

The dramatic style that firmly established itself in the early 19th century was **romanticism,** an emotional escape into adventure, beauty, and sentimental idealism. Started by Goethe (1749–1832) and Schiller (1759–1805) in Germany, the movement blossomed in France with the works of Victor Hugo (1802–1885) and Alexander Dumas (1802–1870), who adapted for the stage his well-loved adventure stories, such as *The Three Musketeers.*

In the mid-19th century, however, drama radically changed direction. **Realism,** which depicts a selected view of real life, emerged. The dominant figure in this theatre movement was Henrik Ibsen (1828–1906), a Norwegian who is often called the father of realism. His work was well written and constructed, and it had keen insight into characterization. Although his plays seem mild to today's audiences, his themes completely revolutionized the theatre of his day, shocking the spectators and bringing on a storm of criticism about the way his plays dealt with social problems. In *A Doll's House,* Nora leaves her husband and children; this single action presented to the world a new position of women in society. Ibsen's other plays, among them *Hedda Gabler, The Master Builder, An Enemy of the People,* and *Ghosts,* have equally provocative themes that realistically revealed the problems of Ibsen's time and place. His work influenced other dramatists, such as August Strindberg of Sweden, who wrote expressionistic drama that became the forerunner of today's avant-garde theatre. (For more about Henrik Ibsen, see page 98.) Anton Chekhov's *The Cherry Orchard* and Maxim Gorki's *Lower Depths* continued the movement away from romanticism. Konstantin Stanislavski (1863–1938), the great Russian director, also contributed to the movement with his experimental Moscow Art Theatre, where he trained actors in a technique of realistic acting. (For more on Stanislavski, see page 18.)

Theatre Terms

realism a type of literature that depicts life objectively and accurately

romanticism a literary movement of the late 18th and early 19th centuries that emphasized imagination and emotions

In England, George Bernard Shaw (1856–1950) introduced Ibsen to the larger theatre world by producing *Ghosts.* Shaw then continued his own realistic bent by writing comic satire in which he attacked all cherished beliefs, leaving little untouched by his caustic yet delightful wit. Considered the finest English playwright since Shakespeare, Shaw was also very prolific. *Androcles and the Lion, Pygmalion, Major Barbara, The Devil's Disciple, Arms and the Man, The Doctor's Dilemma,* and *Candida* are but a few of his successes. Shaw hoped that his comic writings would reform the world. That they failed to do so, he felt, was no fault of his own.

Although realism grew to great heights, many authors around the world continued to write noteworthy romantic, symbolic, or mystical plays. In England, Oscar Wilde (1854–1900) produced witty farces. *The Importance of Being Earnest* is in the best 18th-century comedy of manners style. Sir William Gilbert (1836–1911) and Sir Arthur Sullivan (1842–1900) wrote hugely popular operettas such as *The Mikado, HMS Pinafore,* and many others. In France, Edmond Rostand (1868–1918)

Ian McKellen performs with a young actor in Ibsen's *An Enemy of the People,* at the Royal National Theatre.

Konstantin Stanislavski In 1907 Stanislavski tried breaking away from realism, staging an expressionist version of Leonid Andreyev's *The Life of Man.* The show was a popular success, but Stanislavski believed it failed to challenge his actors. As James Roose-Evans reports in his book, *Experimental Theatre: From Stanislavsky to Today,* the experience marked a turning point. "From that moment on," Roose-Evans writes, "[Stanislavski's] work and his attention were devoted almost completely to the study and teaching of inner creativeness" as opposed to scenic show.

Anti-Stanislavski In Russian and early Soviet theatre, Vsevolod Meyerhold (1874-1940) was the anti-Stanislavski. A former actor with impeccable realist credentials (he originated the role of Treplev in Chekhov's *The Seagull*) Meyerhold became a proponent of the "Theater Theatrical" which exalted spectacle. His 1920 production of *The Storming of the Winter Palace* involved 8,000 performers and a cannon blast from a warship.

Bernard Shaw A thoroughgoing pedant, albeit an entertaining one, Bernard Shaw never lost a chance to educate the public. He was famous for publishing his plays with introductory essays that might exceed the play in length.

Ubu Roi In 1896 Alfred Jarry staged the premiere of *Ubu Roi,* a grotesque, gleefully coarse travesty of *Macbeth* in which a pear-shaped king of Poland tries to take over the world. It caused an uproar and supplied a prototype for post-World War II absurdism. It was originally written as a school prank, to burlesque a mathematics teacher.

Quotable

The nineteenth century was a time of change in Europe. Of all centuries, it was the century of revolution—political revolution and industrial revolution . . . . The outcome of all these upheavals was a slow march towards political and social democracy . . . . The theatre was greatly affected by the peculiar nature of the 19th century. There was revolution in playwriting . . . . The story of the theatre throughout the full 19th century is a story of definite and important progress. Playwrights moved from classicism to romanticism to realism.

from *The Theatre and Its Continuing Social Function* by William Melnitz

Part Three 1800 to the Present **431**

American Theatre in the 19th Century

Royal Tyler Aside from writing plays, fiction, and poetry, Royal Tyler (1757-1826) was Chief Justice of the Vermont Supreme Court. *The Contrast* is a satire on city and country manners. It includes a scene in which Jonathon, a country Yankee, goes to the theatre and watches an entire performance of *The School for Scandal* without realizing it's a play. He thinks all the houses in New York must have curtains that rise, to "let us look right into the next neighbor's house." One reason for President Washington's enthusiasm over the play (aside from Tyler's stature as a jurist) might have been the fact that the hero of the piece, Colonel Manly, appears to have been modeled after him.

Edwin Booth, of course, was the older brother of presidential assassin John Wilkes Booth (1838-1865). Before he made his treasonous appearance in President Lincoln's box at Ford's Theatre on April 14, 1865, John Wilkes had appeared there onstage in thirteen productions. Lincoln himself had seen him perform at the Ford, in a play called *The Marble Heart.*

The Barrymores Mrs. Drew's daughter, Georgiana (1856-1893), was a popular comedienne who married Maurice Barrymore (1847-1905), a popular leading man. Their three children, Lionel, Ethel, and John, were among the preeminent stage and film actors of their generation. Drew Barrymore of *Charlie's Angels* fame is Georgiana and Maurice's great-granddaughter. The story is told that "when Maurice Barrymore was being laid to rest, the straps supporting the lowered coffin became twisted and the coffin had to be raised again for an adjustment to be made. 'How like Father,' Lionel Barrymore whispered as the coffin reappeared, 'a curtain call!'"

wrote *Cyrano de Bergerac* in 1897; and in Russia in 1836, Nikolai Gogol (1809–1852) wrote *The Inspector General.*

Among the famous continental actors of the 19th century were France's Sarah Bernhardt and Coquelin; Italy's Eleanora Duse; and England's Sir Henry Irving and his leading lady, Ellen Terry, who together were largely responsible for returning the acting profession once again to respectability.

American Theatre in the 19th Century

Early American Theatre
The theatre of the American colonies had been sparse, as most people regarded the entire art form as sinful. In fact, in the New York colony the governor's council passed an act in 1709 forbidding "playacting and prizefighting." Theatre fared better in the Virginia colony, where students at the College of William and Mary performed a play in 1702, and where the first playhouse in America was built in Williamsburg in 1716.

Theatre Terms
minstrel shows
vaudeville

The first American play worthy of consideration was written by Royal Tyler in 1787. Called *The Contrast,* it was a pleasing comedy dealing with American problems. Apparently, the play was most successful, for when it was published, President George Washington's name was first on the subscription list. In fact, Washington was a theatre lover and periodically attended plays where he saw Shakespearean and other classic revivals.

American Theatre Comes into Its Own
It was not until the 19th century, however, that theatre blossomed in America. By then, most of the moralist opposition had disappeared. Numerous showboats entertained up and down the Mississippi. Playhouses were built in major American cities. These buildings followed the new trend of smaller auditoriums, narrow aprons, box settings (instead of wings and backdrops), and after 1880, incandescent lighting.

Powerful managers formed stock companies where groups of actors received excellent training in repertory theatre. This was the age of the actor, and many outstanding stars found fame. Edwin Booth (1833–1893) was considered to be America's greatest actor; appearing as Hamlet, he played one hundred nights, a record broken by few other Hamlets. Joseph Jefferson (1829–1905) made a name for himself with his many performances as Rip Van Winkle; the brilliant Richard Mansfield (1857–1907) starred in many productions; Maude Adams delighted audiences in such plays as *Peter Pan;* and Mrs. John Drew, whose daughter married a Barrymore and started that famous acting family, found success in Sheridan's *The Rivals.*

Theatre Terms

minstrel shows shows performed in black face makeup featuring African American songs and jokes

vaudeville variety shows featuring singers, acrobats, comedians, animal acts, and other types of entertainment

absurdism a belief that life is meaningless and that searching for order only brings conflict

epic theatre drama that asks the audience to think seriously about a political or social issue and in which theatricality overrides realism

impressionistic in painting, the use of color and line to suggest mood and setting rather than realistic representations

regional theatres theatres in major American cities other than New York

432 **Unit Seven** Exploring Theatre History

Many of these beloved actors toured America with their shows playing frequent one-night stands. During this time, touring shows did great business. For more than fifty years, road companies traversed the country until the competition of radio and movies and the increased railroad rates brought about a decline in business. With the disappearance of road shows and repertory companies, the long-run performances on Broadway began, and New York City became the theatrical center of the United States. There, the theatre again burgeoned into big business.

Three major types of native theatrical activity developed in 19th-century America. The **minstrel shows,** performed in black face and featuring African-American songs and jokes, were exceptionally popular throughout America and England. **Vaudeville** was even more popular. It was a variety show featuring everything: trained seals, singers, acrobats, jugglers, dancers, comedians, and animal acts. Shows were relatively inoffensive so the whole family could enjoy the entertainment. Vaudeville was an important part of the American entertainment scene for many years until movie and radio competition made it obsolete. Now it is almost a lost art, except for a few nightclub variety shows. **Melodrama** that dripped with sentimentality also thrived during this time, as audiences throughout the country wept at the plight of poverty-stricken heroines in the clutches of evil villains.

Theatre in the 20th Century and Beyond

At the beginning of the 20th century, new stagecraft methods revolutionized the theatre. Through the creativity of such innovative designers as Switzerland's Adolphe Appia and England's Gordon Craig, the theatre was introduced to **impressionistic** settings that used color and line to evoke the mood of a place rather than realistic painting. Also implemented were revolving stages, projected scenery, and a variety of amazing lighting effects.

Theatre Terms
absurdism
epic theatre
impressionistic
regional theatres

Theatre on the Continent
Continental playwrights made numerous contributions. In Germany, Bertolt Brecht (1898–1956) developed his **epic theatre,** where he hoped to encourage audience members to think critically and to promote social reform through political action. To do so, Brecht purposely broke the realistic illusion and stressed theatricality. He deliberately inserted narration and songs between episodic scenes; he made stage light units visible to the audience; he used placards, projections, and any other effect to get the spectator to think and

New Vaudeville In the late 1960s and 1970s, vaudeville-style performance made a comeback in the form of what came to be known as New Vaudeville. Peaking in the mid-80s, when a New Vaudeville version of Shakespeare's *The Comedy of Errors* played Chicago's Goodman Theatre and traveled to the Olympic Arts Festival in Los Angeles, the playful, slapstick, tongue-in-cheek style attracted seriously skilled artists like Bill Irwin, the Flying Karamazov Brothers, Avner the Eccentric, and juggler Michael Moschen.

Theatre in the 20th Century and Beyond

Audience Response "The dramatic theatre's spectator says: Yes, I have felt that way too—Just like me—It's only natural—It'll never change—The sufferings of this man appal me, because they are inescapable—That's great art; it all seems the most obvious thing in the world—I weep when they weep, I laugh when they laugh."

"The epic theatre's spectator says: I'd never have thought it—That's not the way—That's extraordinary, hardly believable—It's got to stop—The sufferings of this man appal me, because they are unnecessary—That's great art: nothing obvious in it—I laugh when they weep; I weep when they laugh."

Bertolt Brecht, in an essay called "Theatre for Pleasure or Theatre for Instruction" (translated by John Willett), describing the difference in audience response between Aristotlean theatre and his own.

Quotable

It is not enough to demand insight and informative images of reality from the theater. Our theater must stimulate a desire for understanding, a delight in changing reality. Our audience must experience not only the ways to free Prometheus, but be schooled in the very desire to free him. Theater must teach all the pleasures and joys of discovery, all the feelings of triumph associated with liberation.

from "Essays on the Art of Theater," by Bertolt Brecht

Theatre of Cruelty In 1938 the mad French theatrician Antonin Artaud published a series of essays under the title *Le Théâtre et son Double* (*The Theater and its Double* that became the manifesto of the Theatre of Cruelty, a post-linguistic, theatre of communal ritual and spectacle calculated to free people from the empty tyranny of things and restore the "magic relation to reality and danger." "If there is still one hellish, truly accursed thing in our time," Artaud declared, "it is our artistic dallying with forms, instead of being like victims burnt at the stake, signaling through the flames." Artaud spent nine years in an asylum for the insane; when he emerged in 1946, two years before his death, the greatest names in the French theatre honored him at the Theatre Sarah Bernhardt in Paris.

ask questions that would encourage societal changes. His most popular plays include *Mother Courage, The Caucasian Chalk Circle, The Good Woman of Setzuan,* and *The Three Penny Opera.* (For more on Bertolt Brecht, see pages 111 and 311.)

In France, Jean Giraudoux (1882–1944) wrote the popular *Tiger at the Gates, Ondine,* and *The Madwoman of Chaillot.* Jean Anouilh (1910–1987) wrote a modern version of *Antigone* and a play about Joan of Arc called *The Lark.* In each, he showed an uncompromising protagonist maintaining integrity by choosing death.

In Spain, Federico García Lorca (1898–1936) achieved acclaim with themes of love and honor in *Blood Wedding* and *The House of Bernarda Alba.* In Italy, Luigi Pirandello (1867–1936) wrote about appearance versus reality in *Six Characters in Search of an Author.*

Ireland's John M. Synge (1871–1909) wrote in poetic prose about the Irish people and the conflict between a desire for freedom and an oppressive way of life in his play *The Playboy of the Western World* and in *In the Shadow of the Glenn.* Sean O'Casey (1880–1964) dealt with the effects of the Irish rebellion on ordinary people in *The Shadow of a Gunman, Juno and the Paycock,* and *The Plough and the Stars.*

Popular English dramatists in the first half of the century include: T. S. Eliot (1888–1965), who wrote poetic drama in *The Cocktail Party and Murder in the Cathedral;* Christopher Fry (1907–), who created intellectual comic verse plays with *The Lady's Not for Burning* and *Venus Observed;* and J. B. Priestly (1894–1984), who wrote mysteries such as *An Inspector Calls.* James M. Barrie (1860–1937) wrote *Peter Pan,* and Noel Coward (1899–1973) developed witty, sophisticated comedies including *Blithe Spirit* and *Private Lives.*

Post-War Drama and the Absurdists Opening up a new post-World War II era of English drama, John Osborne's *Look Back in Anger* became a rallying cry for a group of playwrights who became known collectively as the "angry young men." In the 1950s and '60s innovative playwrights such as Peter Shaffer (*Black Comedy, Five Finger Exercises, Equus,* and *Amadeus*) and Tom Stoppard (*Rosencrantz and Guildenstern Are Dead, Travesties, Hapgood,* and *Arcadia*) came to prominence. Many of the playwrights of this period have become even more prolific in recent years. Tom Stoppard, in particular, has created a phenomenal series of plays covering everything from love to astrophysics to mathematics to world history.

One school of playwrights are often combined together, not because of nationality, but because they are

Notes

Italian playwrights Dario Fo and Franca Rame

exponents of the avant-garde theatre called **absurdism.** In their plays, the absurdists argue that all life is meaningless. Characters speak and act at random with no societal (or theatrical) rules. Proponents of the Theatre of the Absurd include Samuel Beckett (1906–1989), whose plays *Endgame, Happy Days,* and *Waiting for Godot* concern the sense of loneliness and alienation that results when people face the task of establishing real communication with one another. Eugene Ionesco (1912-1994) in *Rhinoceros, The Chairs,* and *The Bald Soprano,* rejected traditional plot lines and consistent characters and instead wrote comic plays about the meaninglessness of a life ruled by chance. Other examples are Jean Genet's *The Balcony,* Harold Pinter's *The Dumb Waiter,* Dario Fo and Franca Rame's *Accidental Death of an Anarchist* and *We Won't Pay! We Won't Pay!,* and Edward Albee's *The Sandbox.*

The American Scene

The United States began developing its own unique theatre, largely through the efforts of Professor George Pierce Baker and his playwriting course at Harvard. This remarkable teacher nurtured many of the century's most notable American dramatists, including Phillip Barry, Robert Sherwood, Sidney Howard, S. H. Behrman, and Eugene O'Neill. These playwrights were aided by Baker and two major theatre companies willing to stage their work, the Washington Square Players and the Provincetown Players.

Eugene O'Neill

Of these new writers, Eugene O'Neill (1888–1953) became the leading

The Bald Soprano A classic scene in Ionesco's "anti-play" *The Bald Soprano* has a man and a woman sitting in the drawing room of a home to which they have been invited for dinner. "Excuse me," says the man, "but haven't we met before?" It seems possible, but how? They discover they both come from Manchester. "How curious!" they say. Not only that but they both left Manchester about five weeks ago in the same car of the same train. "That is curious! How very bizarre! And what a coincidence!" Could that be where they met? Perhaps, but they don't recall it. Now it also happens that they live on the same floor in the same building on the same street. And not only that but they sleep in the same bed in the same room. "How curious it is, how curious it is, how curious it is, and what a coincidence!" Perhaps it is there that they met, suggests the man. "How curious it is and what a coincidence!" the woman replies. "It is indeed possible that we have met there, and perhaps even last night. But I do not recall it, dear sir!" Well," says the man, "I have a little girl, my little daughter, she lives with me, dear lady. She is two years old, she's blonde, she has a white eye and a red eye, she is very pretty, her name is Alice, dear lady." Amazingly, the woman has a daughter with precisely the same attributes. They cannot avoid concluding that they are husband and wife, and fall into each other's arms.

Voodoo *Macbeth* During the Great Depression, President Roosevelt instituted the Works Progress Administration to provide jobs for the unemployed. The WPA had a cultural wing that hired 40,000 artists representing all disciplines, including the theatre. In 1936, under the direction of a 20-year-old Orson Welles, the Negro Unit of the Federal Theater Project mounted an all-black "Voodoo" *Macbeth* set in 19th-century Haiti. The show sold out in Harlem, then transfered downtown before touring to Bridgeport, Hartford, Dallas, Indianapolis, Chicago, Detroit, Cleveland, and Syracuse.

Backstage Gossip: Not My Cup of Tea

Memories of the opening run of *Waiting for Godot* still haunt Peter Bull, who played Pozzo. Not everyone who went to see Beckett's masterpiece enjoyed it. Cries of "Rubbish," "It's a disgrace," and "Take it off," were commonplace. One night when Vladimir said to his companion, "I am happy," and Estragon replied. "I am happy too," a man in the stalls called out, "Well, I'm bloody well not." Attempts to silence the protester simply provoked him further: "And nor are you. You've been hoaxed like me."

from G*reat Theatrical Disasters* by Gyles Brandreth

Part Three 1800 to the Present **435**

Tennessee Williams had his first literary success at the age of 16, when he won third prize and $5 for an essay titled, "Can a Good Wife Be a Good Sport?" He would later win two Pulitzers, for *A Streetcar Named Desire* and *Cat on a Hot Tin Roof.*

American dramatist in the first part of the 20th century. His plays were both realistic and expressionistic, often dealing with difficult psychological truths. After mastering the one-act form, O'Neill turned to writing longer scripts. *The Emperor Jones, The Hairy Ape, Strange Interlude, A Long Day's Journey into Night, Mourning Becomes Electra,* and many other plays made him—and the American theatre scene—famous throughout the world.

Other U.S. playwrights who came to prominence were George S. Kaufman and his comedies *You Can't Take It with You* and *The Man Who Came to Dinner;* Lillian Hellman with *The Little Foxes* and *The Children's Hour;* Robert Sherwood with *Idiot's Delight* and *Abe Lincoln in Illinois;* Maxwell Anderson, who penned the poetic dramas *Winterset* and *Elizabeth the Queen;* and Clifford Odets with *Waiting for Lefty* and *Golden Boy.*

Special attention should be given to the following four American dramatists:

Thornton Wilder (1897–1975)
Wilder contributed to dramatic literature one of the world's best-loved and most frequently produced plays—*Our Town.* This play depicts American small-town life in the early 1900s and shows the eternal patterns of human existence. In *The Skin of Our Teeth* Wilder exhibits zany humor and great passion in portraying humanity's ability to overcome disaster.

Tennessee Williams

Tennessee Williams (1911–1983)
Southern characters that were often neurotic and nearly always desperate were his specialty, but Williams's unique form of poetic realism got inside the hearts and minds of these characters, telling universal truths. This has continued to make an indelible impression on audiences. His best-known works include *The Glass Menagerie, A Streetcar Named Desire,* and *Cat On a Hot Tin Roof.*

Arthur Miller (1915–)
Miller writes of the dilemma of American families and the tragedy of common citizens in such plays as the classic *Death of a Salesman* and the WWII morality play *All My Sons.* In *The Crucible* Miller used the historical setting of the Salem Witch Trials to criticize the methods of Senator Joe McCarthy and the House Un-American Activities Committee. (To read more about Arthur Miller, see page 99.)

Neil Simon (1927–)
Simon remains one of the world's most popular and prolific writers of comedy. He combines wisecracks and barbed wit with family realism and serious themes.

Quotable

Arthur Miller describes the moment during the first production of *Death of a Salesman* when actor Lee J. Cobb truly transformed himself into the character of Willy Loman.

The theatre vanished. The stage vanished. The chill of an age-old recognition shuddered my spine; a voice was sounding in the dimly lit air up front, a created spirit, an incarnation…a new human being was being formed before all our eyes… In an empty and dusty theatre, he cast the shadow of a being that was not himself but the distillation of all he had ever observed….

Some of his best-known works are *The Odd Couple, Lost in Yonkers, Brighton Beach Memoirs,* and *Biloxi Blues.* (For more information on Neil Simon, see page 133.)

Other Playwrights

Other notable living American playwrights include Sam Shepard (*Buried Child, Fool for Love*), David Mamet (*American Buffalo, Glengarry Glen Ross*), Marsha Norman (*'Night, Mother*), Beth Henley (*Crimes of the Heart*), Lanford Wilson (*Tally's Folly, The Fifth of July*), Tony Kushner (*Angels in America*), Christopher Durang (*Sister Mary Ignatius Explains It All for You*), Arthur Kopit (*Wings, Y2K*), A. R. Gurney, Jr. (*The Dining Room*), Wendy Wasserstein (*An American Daughter*), Rebecca Gilman (*Spinning into Butter*), Kia Corthron (*Breath, Boom*), and Julie Jenson (*Two-Headed*).

African-American theatre has been enriched by the work of Lorraine Hansberry (1930–1965), who wrote *A Raisin in the Sun,* and by August Wilson (1945–), who is in the process of writing a history of black America with a cycle of plays set in different decades of the 20th century. His works include *Ma Rainey's Black Bottom, Fences,* and *The Piano Lesson.* (To read more about August Wilson, see page 149.) Charles Fuller (1939–) won success with *A Soldier's Play.* He is writing a series of plays about African Americans since the freeing of the slaves. Suzan-Lori Parks, with her vibrant language and overtly political themes, won the 2002 Pulitzer Prize for her play *Topdog/Underdog.*

Lorraine Hansberry

Beyond Broadway

Today, the theatre is alive with activity. Broadway is still considered the hub of professional theatre in the United States, but rising costs have kept producers away from many newer, more risky ventures. Most Broadway shows are comedies or musicals with mass appeal to ensure their status as commercial hits. Consequently, new plays have had to find homes elsewhere. Off-Broadway theatre (New York theatres seating fewer than 299 people) welcomes new names and plays because shows can be produced less expensively—and therefore at less risk to investors. Not being tied so tightly to the box office allows for the staging of experimental productions. Some of these shows become hits and occasionally move to Broadway.

Notes

Viola Spolin Not all of contemporary American theatre is playwright-centered. Organizations like The Second City build shows through improvisational ensemble work. The Second City approach grew out of games Viola Spolin invented during the 1930s, while working with immigrant teenagers at a settlement house. Having noticed that the structure of a game gives people permission to put aside their inhibitions, she created a bunch of them for her shy young clients to play. Her son, Paul Sills, subsequently worked with her to adapt the games for theatrical use. The same principle applies in either case: The game establishes a free zone for creative interaction.

Part Three 1800 to the Present **437**

Regional Theatre As an indication of the vigor of American theatre, consider that the League of Chicago Theaters reports a membership of about 130 professional companies, big and small.

John Belluso "Being in a wheelchair shapes my existence every moment that I'm awake. Many people ask me, "Do you ever want to not write about it?" I think the answer is no. I feel that because this is my experience, because this is something that shapes my life moment to moment, then it sort of seems nonsensical to me to not write about it. It seems that this is an identity worth taking pride in and therefore exploring it as such. I think that is sort of the through line through my plays. They often are plays about the body and about the body politic, and how society creates this notion of what it is to be disabled, through culture, through assigning stereotypes, through actual oppression."

from an interview published in the *Providence Phoenix*.

Laura Esping and Judson Pearce Morgan in *Comedy of Errors* at the Guthrie Theatre in Minneapolis.

Professional productions also thrive outside of New York City. In the 1960s, **regional theatres** were established in many major cities across the United States. The first began under the direction of Tyrone Guthrie in 1963 in Minneapolis, Minnesota. The Guthrie Theatre remains among the top regional theatres in the country. Later, other companies opened in San Francisco, Chicago, Louisville, Seattle, Dallas, Los Angeles, and Denver, to mention a few.

These resident companies encourage new talent and playwrights, including those who represent various ethnic groups and social minorities. For example, David Henry Hwang writes about the Chinese and Chinese-American culture, as do Frank Chin and James Yoshimura. José Rivera, Migdalia Cruz, Maria Irene Fornes, and Edwin Sanchez concern themselves with Hispanic issues and culture. John Belluso and others focus on disability issues. Still other playwrights concentrate on plays for children.

Nonprofessional community theatre is strong almost everywhere. Community theatres usually perform New York successes several years after the original run. Most also produce musicals and sometimes classical plays. They attempt to involve townspeople, and their enthusiasm and imagination help them to overcome the barriers of insufficient funding and/or facilities.

In recent years, voices have sporadically cried that the theatre is becoming decadent, a wasteland filled with plays of questionable merit. Theatre, of course, depends to a great extent upon the tastes of the audience. If an audience demands good theatre—that which not only entertains but stimulates worthwhile thinking and feeling—and insists that its wishes be satisfied, then the theatre must respond accordingly. You who are today's dedicated student of drama will be tomorrow's talented practitioner and/or audience member. Your desires and expectations will help to shape the future of theatre.

Quotable

Fortunately for the theatre, it does not have to keep pushing to the edge of human experience. It must be remembered that the most popular forms of theatre are light comedy, farce, murder mystery, and musical comedy—the musical without a message. These are some of the ways audiences enjoy themselves... There is no exclusive form of theater. It is not now, and never has been, the preserve of some intellectual minority.

from *All the World's a Stage* by Ronald Harwood

438 Unit Seven Exploring Theatre History

Suggested Projects

1 Read and report on one of the following plays, briefly giving its plot and telling how it realistically shows life at the time it was written.

A Doll's House or *An Enemy of the People* by Henrik Ibsen
The Cherry Orchard or *The Seagull* by Anton Chekhov
Arms and the Man or *Pygmalion* by George Bernard Shaw

2 Read and report on one of the following plays, highlighting its contribution to the dramatic world.

The Importance of Being Earnest by Oscar Wilde
Cyrano de Bergerac by Edmond Rostand
The Inspector General by Nikolai Gogol
Six Characters in Search of an Author by Luigi Pirandello

3 Write and present a biographical sketch on a great American actor or actress of the 19th century.

4 Create and stage a class vaudeville show.

5 Hold a panel discussion on "Television and Its Contribution to the Theatre World."

6 Read a play by a 20th-century author. Cast the play and present a fully rehearsed scene to the class.

7 With a group of classmates, attend a community or university theatre production. Arrange to visit backstage. Find out about the theatre's use of advanced technology in set, light, costume, and sound design. Take notes and discuss these implementations in class.

8 Report on how the Elizabethan stages have influenced the style of our modern thrust stages. You might find help at www.bartleby.com/216/1017.html.

9 Report on the style and success of famous actors in the 20th century. The book *Famous Actors and Actresses on the American Stage* by William C. Young might prove helpful.

10 Select a current playwright from a culture other than your own and, after research, give an oral report on the contribution of that person's dramatic work to modern theatre.

Resource Binder

Part Three Test, p. 125

For More Information

Books

Artaud, Antonin (translated by Mary Caroline Richards), *The Theater and Its Double,* Grove Weidenfeld, 1958.

Bartow, Arthur, *The Director's Voice: Twenty-One Interviews,* Theatre Communications Group, 1988.

Brook, Peter; *The Empty Space,* Macmillan Publishing Co., 1968.

Callow, Simon, *Being an Actor,* Grove Press, 1988.

Fo, Dario (translated by Joe Farrell), *Tricks of the Trade,* Routledge, 1991.

Innes, Christopher, *Avant Garde Theatre 1892-1992,* Routledge, 1993.

Savran, David, *In Their Own Words: Contemporary American Playwrights,* Theatre Communications Group, 1988.

Spolin, Viola, *Improvisation for the Theatre,* Northwestern University Press, 1985.

Sweet, Jeffrey (ed.), *Something Wonderful Right Away: An Oral History of The Second City and the Compass Players,* Avon Books, 1978.

Tynan, Kenneth, *The Sound of Two Hands Clapping,* Da Capo Press, 1976.

Other Media

Bertolt Brecht, VHS, Insight Media, 1996.

Chekhov and the Moscow Art Theatre, VHS, Insight Media, 1982.

The Cherry Orchard, VHS, Insight Media, 1968.

Dario Fo and Franca Rame: A Nobel for Two, VHS, Insight Media, 1998.

The Federal Theatre, Project 8891, and the Mercury Theatre, VHS, Insight Media, 1999.

George Bernard Shaw and His Times, VHS, Insight Media, 1984.

Ubu Roi, VHS, Insight Media, 1977.

Vaudeville Videos, VHS, Insight Media, 1999.

West End Story: An Anatomy of the Musical Theatre, VHS, Insight Media, 2001.

Unit **Eight**

Monologues and Scenes

440 **Unit Eight** Monologues and Scenes

441

Monologues

Monologues for a Woman

Monologues for a Man

*Indicates annotated monologue

442 **Unit Eight** Monologues and Scenes

Romeo and Juliet

by William Shakespeare

Attending a dance, Juliet meets Romeo, and they fall in love. Later, Romeo hides in her garden. When she walks onto her balcony and romantically speaks aloud to herself about Romeo, he discloses his presence. Embarrassed, Juliet addresses him.

JULIET. Thou know'st the mask of night is on my face,
Else would a maiden blush bepaint my cheek
For that which thou hast heard me speak tonight.
Fain would I dwell on form, fain, fain deny
What I have spoke; but farewell compliment!
Dost thou love me? I know thou wilt say "Ay,"
And I will take thy word; yet, if thou swear'st,
Thou mayst prove false: at lovers' perjuries
They say, Jove laughs. O gentle Romeo,
If thou dost love, pronounce it faithfully;
Or if thou think'st I am too quickly won,
I'll frown and be perverse and say thee nay,
So thou wilt woo; but else, not for the world.
In truth, fair Montague, I am too fond,
And therefore thou mayst think my 'haviour light;
But trust me, gentleman, I'll prove more true
Than those that have more cunning to be strange.
I should have been more strange, I must confess,
But that thou overheard'st, ere I was ware,
My true love's passion; therefore pardon me,
And not impute this yielding to light love,
Which the dark night hath so discovered.

Charlotte Randle as Juliet in the National Theatre production of *Romeo and Juliet*

Monologues **443**

Saint Joan by George Bernard Shaw

Joan of Arc has been sentenced to life in prison, instead of burning at the stake, for leading soldiers into battle based on voices she has heard from Heaven. When she realizes that she is to be continually confined, she recants her confession and boldly addresses her inquisitors.

JOAN. Yes: they told me you were fools *[the word gives great offence]*, and that I was not to listen to your fine words nor trust to your charity. You promised me my life; but you lied *[indignant exclamations]*. You think that life is nothing but not being stone dead. It is not the bread and water I fear: I can live on bread; when have I asked for more? It is no hardship to drink water if the water be clean. Bread has no sorrow for me, and water no affliction. But to shut me from the light of the sky and the sight of the fields and flowers; to chain my feet so that I can never again ride with the soldiers nor climb the hills; to make me breathe foul damp darkness, and keep from me everything that brings me back to the love of God when your wickedness and foolishness tempt me to hate Him: all this is worse than the furnace in the Bible that was heated seven times. I could do without my warhorse; I could drag about in a skirt; I could let the banners and the trumpets and the knights and soldiers pass me and leave me behind as they leave the other women, if only I could still hear the wind in the trees, the larks in the sunshine, the young lambs crying through the healthy frost, and the blessed, blessed church bells that send my angel voices floating to me on the wind. But without these things I cannot live; and by your wanting to take them away from me, or from any human creature, I know that your counsel is of the devil, and that mine is of God.

The Prisoner of Second Avenue by Neil Simon

When Edna's husband Mel is laid off, she takes a job to tide them over. Although the playwright deals with a serious subject, he adds a good deal of humor to the situation. Here, Edna has rushed home during her lunch break.

EDNA. Mel?. . . Mel, I'm home. *(She closes door and crosses to living room, turns off radio, then into kitchen.)* You must be starved. I'll have your lunch in a second . . . *(Takes things out of package.)* . . . I couldn't get out of the office until a quarter to one and then I had to wait fifteen minutes for a bus . . . God, the traffic on Third Avenue during lunch hour . . . I got cheese soufflé in Schrafft's, is that alright? I just don't

444 **Unit Eight** Monologues and Scenes

have time to fix anything today, Mr. Cooperman wants me back before two o'clock, we're suddenly swamped with work this week. . . He asked if I would come in on Saturdays from now until Christmas but I told him I didn't think I could . . . *(She is crossing into kitchen and getting out pots.)* . . . I mean we could use the extra money but I don't think I want to spend Saturdays in that office too. We see each other little enough as it is . . . Come in and talk to me while I'm cooking, Mel, I've only got about thirty-five minutes today . . . *(Edna has put the casserole on the stove and is now crossing into kitchen, setting up two places with dishes and silverware.)* My feet are absolutely killing me. I don't know why they gave me a desk because I haven't had a chance to sit at it in a month . . . Hi, love. I bought you *Sports Illustrated* . . . Mr. Cooperman told me there's a terrific story in there about the Knicks, he thought you might be interested in it . . . *(Mel tosses the magazine aside with some contempt . . .)* You just can't move up Third Avenue because there's one of those protest parades up Fifth Avenue, or down Fifth Avenue, whichever way they protest . . . Fifteen thousand women screaming "Save the Environment" and they're all wearing leopard coats . . . God, the hypocrisy . . . Come on, sit down, I've got some tomato juice first. . . *(She pours tomato juice into two glasses. Mel listlessly moves to table and sits.)* Isn't that terrible about the Commissioner of Police? . . . I mean kidnapping the New York Commissioner of Police? . . . Isn't that insane? I mean if the cops can't find him, they can't find anybody . . . *(She sits, picks up her glass of juice and sips.)* . . .

"Trudy" from The Search for Signs of Intelligent Life in the Universe

by Jane Wagner

In this one-woman show written for Lily Tomlin, the playwright investigates the lives of many characters, including Trudy, a bag woman with a mind of her own.

TRUDY. Here we are, standing on the corner of "Walk, Don't Walk." You look away from me, tryin' not to catch my eye, but you didn't turn fast enough, *did* you?

You don't like my *ras*py voice, do you?
I got this raspy voice
'cause I have to yell all the time
'cause nobody around here ever
LISTENS to me.

You don't like that I scratch so much;
yes, and excuse me,
I scratch so much
'cause my neurons are
on *fire*.

Monologues 445

And I admit my smile is not at its
Pepsodent best
'cause I think my
caps must've somehow got
osteo*porosis.*

And if my eyes seem to be twirling
around like fruit flies—
the better to see you with, my dears!

Look at me,
you mammalian-brained LUNKHEADS!
I'm not just talking to myself.
I'm talking to you, too.
And to you
and you
and you
and you and you and you!

I know what you're thinkin'; you're
thinkin' I'm crazy.
You think I give a hoot? You people
look at my shopping bags,
call me crazy 'cause I save this junk.
What should we call the
ones who
buy it?

It's my belief we all, at one time
or another, secretly ask ourselves
the question,
"Am *I* crazy?"
In my case, the answer came back:
A resounding
YES!

You're thinkin': How does a person
know if they're crazy or not?
Well, sometimes you don't know.
Sometimes you can go through
life suspecting you *are*
but never really knowing for sure.
Sometimes you know for sure
'cause you got so many people tellin'
you you're crazy
that it's your word against
everyone else's.

Another sign is when you see life so
clear sometimes
you black out.
This is your typical visionary variety
who has flashes of insight
but can't get anyone to listen to 'em
'cause their insights make 'em sound
so *crazy*!

In my case,
the symptoms are subtle
but unmistakable to the trained eye.
For instance, here I am,
standing at the corner of
"Walk, Don't Walk,"
waiting for these aliens from outer
space to show up.
I call that crazy, don't you?
If I were sane,
I should be waiting for the light like
everybody else.

They're late
as usual.

You'd think,
as much as they know about time travel,
they could be on time *once* in a while.

446 Unit Eight Monologues and Scenes

I could kick myself.
I told 'em I'd meet 'em on the corner of
"Walk, Don't Walk"
'round lunchtime.
Do they even know what
"lunch" means?
I doubt it.

And "'round." Why did I say "'round?"
Why wasn't I more specific? This is so
typical of what I do.

Now they're probably stuck somewhere
in time, wondering what I meant by
"'round lunchtime." And when they get
here, they'll be dying to know what
"lunchtime" means. And when they
find out it means going to Howard
Johnson's for fried clams, I wonder,
will they be just a bit let down?

I dread having to explain
tartar sauce.

This problem of time just points out
how far apart we really are.
See, our ideas about time and space are
different from theirs.
When we think of time, we tend to
think of clock radios, coffee breaks,
afternoon naps, leisure time,
halftime activities, parole time,
doing time, Minute Rice, instant tea,
mid-life crises, that time of the month,
cocktail hour.
And if I should suddenly
mention *space*—aha! I bet most of
you thought of your closets.
But when they think of time and space,
they really think
of
Time and Space.

They asked me once my thoughts on
infinity and I told 'em
with all I had to think about,
infinity was not on my list
of things to think about.
It could be time on an ego trip,
for all I know. After all, when you're
pressed for time,
infinity may as well
not be there.
They said, to them, infinity is
time-released time.

Frankly, infinity doesn't affect
me personally one way or the other.

You think too long about infinity,
you could go stark raving mad.
But I don't ever want to sound
negative about going crazy.
I don't want to overromanticize
it either, but frankly,
goin' crazy was the *best* thing ever
happened to me.
I don't say it's for everybody;
some people couldn't cope. . . .

Monologues **447**

Clear Glass Marbles by Jane Martin

A young woman is standing next to an end table with a lamp on it, holding a crystal bowl filled with ninety clear glass marbles.

LAURIE. (1) The day my mother found out she was dying she asked me to go out and buy her these clear glass marbles. Dad and I hadn't even known she was ill which was nothing new. (2) Whenever you asked my mother if she was ill she would throw things at you, sesame buns, the editorial page, a handful of hair ribbons. "Do not," she would say, "suggest things to suggestible people." (3) Anyway, I brought her the marbles and she counted ninety of them out and put them in this old cut-glass bowl which had been the sum total of great Aunt Helena's estate. Apparently, the doctor had given her three months and she set great store by doctors. She said she always believed them because they were the nearest thing to the Old Testament we had. "I wouldn't give you two bits for these young smiley guys," she'd say, "I go for a good, stern-furrowed physician." (4) She wouldn't even have her teeth cleaned by a dentist under fifty. So she counted out ninety clear glass marbles and set them in the bowl on her bedside table. Then she went out and spent twelve hundred dollars on nightgowns. She said, "In my family you are only dying when you take to your bed, and that, my darlings, is where I am going." And she did. Oh we hashed it around. Dad said she couldn't possibly be dying but the doctors convinced him. I told her it seemed a little medieval to lie in state up there but she said she didn't want to be distracted from what she loved, us, and what she wanted to mull. . . (5) And she said there was nothing outside except drugstores and supermarkets and drycleaners and that given her situation they were beneath her dignity. I asked her what she intended to do up there and she said study French, visit with us, generally mull and maybe call a few pals. Study French. (6) She said she had made a pledge to herself years ago that she would die bilingual. Dad and I cried a lot, but she didn't. He was fun to cry with. From then on the doctors had to come see *her* because, as she put it, she *came in* with a house call and she was *going out* with a house call. (7) And all day, every day, she would hold one of these marbles in her hand. Why? She said it made the day longer. (8) Mother had her own bedroom. That was the way it always was, for as long as I can remember. She called my father "The Thrasher." Dad could really get into a nightmare. Apparently early on in the marriage he had flipped over and broken her nose and that was it. Separate beds. Her room was very spare really. Wooden floors, an old steel-and-brass bed, oak dresser, bedside table, and don't ask me why, a hat rack. No

(1) In this first sentence, what are the two most important ideas that the actor must emphasize?

(2) What does this tell you about the family?

(3) Besides her mother's words, what attitude of her mother's must Laurie mimic?

(4) In your mind, picture the wrinkled brow of the old physician.

(5) What does *mull* mean in this context?

(6) How do you think the actor should say "Study French"?

(7) What does this indicate about the mother's birth?

(8) Why does the mother want the day to be longer?

448 **Unit Eight** Monologues and Scenes

pictures on the walls. She never understood how people could look at the same darn thing day after day. She said it was bound to "deflate the imagination." We'd sit with her after dinner and talk about "issues." She told us she was too far gone for gossip or what we ate for lunch. Then we'd all turn in and in a little while, just before I'd drift off I'd hear this. . .* *(She rolls one of the marbles across the stage floor.)* Happened every night. After the third or fourth day I saw one on the floor and started to pick it up but she said "leave it." She said it very sharply. (9) I asked, "How come?" She said she was "learning to let go of them." *(From now on the actress frequently rolls marbles across the stage, indicated hereafter by an asterisk, ending up at last with only one.)* Oh, she passed the time. There were things she wanted. She made out a list of children's books from her own childhood and we got as many of them as we could find from the library. She said they were still the only good books she'd ever read.* (10)

She wrote notes to, I don't know, maybe sixty or seventy people, and they told us later on that they were sort of little formal goodbyes, each of them recalling some incident or shared something, not very significant, but the odd thing was that in each one she included a recipe. A recipe in every one of them.

We got out the big cookie tin full of snapshots that somehow never became a scrapbook. She liked that. She showed my father how to do the medical insurance and how she handled the accounts. We went through her jewelry.* She wrote down the names of the roofers and plumbers and air-conditioning people. She called it "wrapping it up." "Well, this is good," she'd say, "I'm wrapping it up."*

She had the television moved up in her room and she called me aside to say that it was entirely possible that she might reach a stage where she really wouldn't know what she was watching but that I must promise her that I'd keep it on P.B.S. (11)

Later on, when it started getting hard,* she told Dad and me that she would like to spend more time alone. "I'm afraid," she said, "that I'm going to have to do this more or less by myself." She said that she was glad, and she hoped we would be, that this was arranged so that you got less attached to the people you loved at the end. The next period isn't worth going into, it was just. . . hard. *(She picks up the bowl of marbles.)* Do you know that from the very beginning down to the very last she never admitted to any pain. Never. She called it "the chills." The last thing she asked for was a picture we had in the front entrance hall of a Labrador retriever she and Dad had

(9) Try to mimic the sharpness in the mother's voice.

(10) What do the marbles symbolize? Why did she want only clear ones?

(11) Use clues in the monologue (Study French, watching P.B.S., etc.) to describe the mother's personality or tastes.

Monologues **449**

(12) Why were there a lot of marbles left to roll on the floor at this point in the monologue?

(13) How should these last three lines be spoken: in sadness, regret, hope, or courage? Are there other alternatives?

owned when they were first married. He was, she said, a perfectly dreadful dog. "When you are young," she said, "you believe in the perfectibility of dogs."

I was in bed two weeks ago Wednesday toward dawn, then this. . . *(She pours the rest of the marbles on the floor. When they have stopped rolling, she speaks.)* (12) Dad and I ran in there. The bedside table was turned over and she was gone. Dead. When the emergency medical people got there they found this. . . *(She opens her hand to disclose one more marble.)* The rest spilled when the table fell, but this one was still in her hand.

(13)

I keep it.

I keep it in my hand all day.

It makes the day longer.

Real Women Have Curves

by Josefina López

Ana is a top-notch student who wants to attend college, but her mother insists that she help in her sister Stela's struggling dress factory. Ana sees that the factory employees work very hard for their pay and that dresses that cost little to make are sold in stores for hundreds and hundreds of dollars. Ana awakens her mother, sister, and coworkers to the idea that they shouldn't be misled by the body image promoted by these stores. In the end, Ana too learns a lesson.

ANA. I always took their work for granted, to be simple and unimportant. I was not proud to be working there at the beginning. I was only glad to know that because I was educated, I wasn't going to end up like them. I was going to be better than them. And I wanted to show them how much smarter and liberated I was. I was going to teach them about the women's liberation movement, about sexual liberation and all the things a so-called educated American woman knows. But in their subtle ways they taught me about resistance. About a battle no one was fighting for them except themselves. About the loneliness of being women in a country that looks down on us for being mothers and submissive wives. With their work that seems simple and unimportant, they are fighting. . . Perhaps the greatest thing I learned from them is that women are powerful, especially when working together. . . As for me, well, I settled for a secondhand typewriter and I wrote an essay on my experience and I was awarded a fellowship. So I went to New York and was a starving writer for some time before I went to New York University. When I came back, the plans for making the boutique were no longer a dream, but a reality. *(Ana picks up a beautiful designer jacket and puts it on.)*

450 **Unit Eight** Monologues and Scenes

Because I now wear original designs from Estela Garcia's boutique, "Real Women Have Curves."

(The lights come on and all the women enter the door wearing new evening gowns and accessories designed by Estela. The women parade down the theatre aisles voguing in a fashion-show style. They take their bows, continue voguing, and slowly exit. Lights slowly fade out.)

Hamlet by William Shakespeare

Polonius, who is the Danish court's Lord Chamberlain, bids good-bye to his son Laertes, who is returning to a French university. Polonius gives some fatherly advice.

POLONIUS. Yet here, Laertes? Aboard, aboard, for shame!
The wind sits in the shoulder of your sail,
And you are stayed for. There—my blessing with thee,
And these few precepts in thy memory
Look thou character. Give thy thoughts no tongue,
Nor any unproportioned thought his act.
Be thou familiar, but by no means vulgar.
Those friends thou hast, and their adoption tried,
Grapple them unto thy soul with hoops of steel;
But do not dull thy palm with entertainment
Of each new-hatched, unfledged courage. Beware
Of entrance to a quarrel, but being in,
Bear't that th' opposed may beware of thee.
Give every man thy ear, but few thy voice;
Take each man's censure, but reserve thy judgment.
Costly thy habit as thy purse can buy,
But not expressed in fancy; rich not gaudy,
For the apparel oft proclaims the man,
And they in France of the best rank and station
Are of a most select and generous chief in that.
Neither a borrower nor a lender be,
For loan oft loses both itself and friend,
And borrowing dulls th' edge of husbandry.
This above all, to thine own self be true,
And it must follow as the night the day
Thou canst not then be false to any man.
Farewell. My blessing season this in thee!

Cyrano de Bergerac
by Edmond Rostand

Although charming and witty, Cyrano de Bergerac, a 17th-century poet, has an exceptionally large nose that brings him excessive ridicule. Tiring of mundane comments about his nose, he imaginatively describes various remarks that could be made about it by a clever person.

Monologues **451**

CYRANO. I'm afraid your speech was a little short, young man. You could have said . . . oh, all sorts of things, varying your tone to fit your words. Let me give you a few examples.

In an aggressive tone. "If I had a nose like that, I'd have it amputated!"

Friendly. "The end of it must get wet when you drink from a cup. Why don't you use a tankard?"

Descriptive. "It's a rock, a peak, a cape! No, more than a cape: a peninsula!"

Curious. "What do you use that long container for? Do you keep your pens and scissors in it?"

Gracious. "What a kind man you are! You love birds so much that you've given them a perch to roost on."

Truculent. "When you light your pipe and the smoke comes out your nose, the neighbors must think a chimney has caught fire!"

Solicitous. "Be careful when you walk; with all that weight on your head, you could easily lose your balance and fall."

Thoughtful. "You ought to put an awning over it, to keep its color from fading in the sun."

Pedantic. "Sir, only the animal that Aristophanes calls the hippocampelephantocamelos could have had so much flesh and bone below its forehead."

Flippant. "That tusk must be convenient to hang your hat on."

Grandiloquent. "No wind but the mighty Arctic blast, majestic nose, could ever give you a cold from one end to the other!"

Dramatic. "When it bleeds, it must be like the Red Sea!"

Admiring. "What a sign for a perfume shop!"

Lyrical. "Is that a conch, and are you Triton risen from the sea?"

Naïve. "Is that monument open to the public?"

Respectful. "One look at your face, sir, is enough to tell me that you are indeed a man of substance."

Rustic. "That don't look like no nose to me. It's either a big cucumber or a little watermelon."

Military. "The enemy is charging! Aim your cannon!"

Practical. "A nose like that has one advantage: it keeps your feet dry in the rain". . . .

There, now you have an inkling of what you might have said to me if you were witty and a man of letters.

452 **Unit Eight** Monologues and Scenes

Death of a Salesman by Arthur Miller

Biff has returned home for a short time. With his brother, Happy, as a sounding board, Biff confesses that he has wasted his life and still does not know what to do. He is torn between the demands of his father and his own self-desires. [If Happy's speech is omitted, the speech becomes a monologue.]

BIFF. Well, I spent six or seven years after high school trying to work myself up. Shipping clerk, salesman, business of one kind or another. And it's a measly manner of existence. To get on that subway on the hot mornings in summer. To devote your whole life to keeping stock, or making phone calls, or selling or buying. To suffer fifty weeks of the year for the sake of a two-week vacation, when all you really desire is to be outdoors, with your shirt off. And always to have to get ahead of the next fella. And still—that's how you build a future.

[HAPPY. Well, you really enjoy it on a farm? Are you content out there?]

BIFF. Hap, I've had twenty or thirty different kinds of jobs since I left home before the war, and it always turns out the same. I just realized it lately. In Nebraska when I herded cattle, and the Dakotas, and Arizona, and now in Texas. It's why I came home now, I guess, because I realized it. This farm I work on, it's spring there now, see? And they've got about fifteen new colts. There's nothing more inspiring or—beautiful than the sight of a mare and a new colt. Add it's cool there now, see? Texas is cool now, and it's spring. And whenever spring comes to where I am, I suddenly get the feeling, my God, I'm not gettin' anywhere! What the hell am I doing, playing around with horses, twenty-eight dollars a week! I'm thirty-four years old, I ought to be makin' my future. That's when I come running home. And now, I get here, and I don't know what to do with myself. *(After a pause)* I've always made a point of not wasting my life, and every time I come back here I know that all I've done is to waste my life.

The Drummer by Athol Fugard

A pile of rubbish is seen on the pavement, waiting to be cleared away. This consists of an over-filled trash can and a battered old chair with torn upholstery on which is piled cardboard boxes and plastic bags full of junk. Distant and intermittent city noises are heard.

At RISE: A BUM *enters. He walks over to the pile of rubbish and starts to work his way through it . . . looking for something useful in terms of that day's survival. He has obviously just woken up and yawns from time to time. After a few seconds he clears the chair, sits down, makes himself comfortable, and*

Monologues **453**

continues his search. One of the boxes produces a drumstick. He examines it and then abandons it. A little later he finds a second drumstick. He examines it. Remembers! He scratches around in the pile of rubbish at his feet and retrieves the first. Two drumsticks! His find intrigues him. Another dip into the rubbish but it produces nothing further of interest. Two drumsticks! He settles back in his chair and surveys the world.

An ambulance siren approaches and recedes stage right. He observes indifferently. A fire engine approaches and recedes stage left. He observes. While this is going on, he taps idly on the lid of the trash can with one of the drumsticks. He becomes aware of this little action. Two drumsticks and a trash can! It takes him a few seconds to realize the potential. He straightens up in his chair and with a measure of caution, attempts a little tattoo on the lid of the can. The result is not very impressive. He makes a second attempt, with the same result. Problem. Solution! He gets up and empties the trashcan of its contents, replaces the lid, and makes a third attempt. The combination of a serious intention and the now resonant bin produces a decided effect. He develops it and in doing so starts to enjoy himself. His excitement gets him onto his feet. He has one last flash of inspiration. He removes the lid from the can, up-ends it, and with great bravura drums out a final tattoo . . . virtually an accompaniment to the now very loud and urgent city noises all around him. Embellishing his appearance with some item from the rubbish . . . a cape? . . . and holding his drumsticks ready, he chooses a direction and sets off to take on the city. He has discovered it is full of drums . . . and he has got drumsticks.

The Beginning

The Janitor by August Wilson

Sam, a janitor, enters an empty ballroom. He is pushing a broom near the lectern. He stops and reads the sign hanging across the ballroom.

SAM. NATIONAL . . . CONFERENCE . . . ON . . . YOUTH. *(He nods his approval and continues sweeping. He gets an idea, stops, and approaches the lectern. He clears his throat and begins to speak. His speech is delivered with the literacy of a janitor. He chooses his ideas carefully. He is a man who has approached life honestly, with both eyes open.)* I want to thank you all for inviting me here to speak about youth. See . . . I's fifty-six years old and I knows something about youth. The first thing I knows . . . is that youth is sweet before flight . . . its odor is rife with speculation, and its resilience—that means bounce back—is remarkable. But it's that sweetness that we victims

454 **Unit Eight** Monologues and Scenes

of. All of us. Its sweetness . . . and its flight. One of them fellows in that Shakespeare stuff said, "I'm not what I am." See. He wasn't like Popeye. This fellow had a different understanding. "I am not what I am." Well, neither are you. You are just what you have been . . . whatever you are now. But what you are now ain't what you gonna become . . . even though it is with you now . . . it's inside you now this instant. Time . . . see, this is how you get to this . . . Time ain't changed. It's just moved. Or maybe it ain't moved . . . maybe it just changed. It don't matter. We are all victims of the sweetness of youth and the time of its flight.

See . . . just like you I forgot who I am. I forgot what happened first. But I know the river I step into now . . . is not the same river I stepped into twenty years ago. See, I know that much. But I have forgotten the name of the river . . . I have forgotten the name of the gods . . . and like everybody else I have tried to fool them with my dancing . . . and guess at their faces. It's the same with everybody. We don't have to mention no names. Ain't nobody innocent. We are all victims of ourselves. We have all had our hand in the soup . . . and made the music play just so.

See now . . . this is what I call wrestling with Jacob's angel. You lay down at night and that angel come to wrestle with you. When you wrestling with that angel, you bargaining for your future. See. And what you need to bargain with is that sweetness of youth. So . . . to the youth of the United States I says . . . don't spend that sweetness too fast! 'Cause you gonna need it. See. I's fifty-six years old and I done found that out. But it's all the same. It all comes back on you . . . just like sowing and reaping. Down and out ain't nothing but being caught up in the balance of what you put down. If you down and out and things ain't going right for you . . . you can bet you done put down a payment on your troubles. Now you got to pay up on the balance. That's as true as I'm standing here. Sometimes you can't see it like that. The last note on Gabriel's horn always gets lost when you get to realizing you done heard the first. So, it's just like—

[MR. COLLINS *(entering).* Come on, Sam . . . let's quit wasting time and get this floor swept. There's going to be a big important meeting here this afternoon.]

SAM. Yessuh, Mr. Collins. Yessuh. *(He goes back to sweeping, as the lights go down to black.)*

Monologues **455**

① Where is Copenhagen?

② Check an encyclopedia to see what role German scientists played in the development of the atomic bomb.

③ What would "quantum ethics" suggest? Check a dictionary. Why was the study of energy so intense during this period in history?

④ Why do you think Heisenberg feels there is a place for the SS man in heaven? Keep reading to find out.

⑤ Who were the Allied troops? It might help you to research the history of World War II.

⑥ What does this sentence suggest about the situation then in Germany?

Copenhagen by Michael Frayn ①

In 1941, the German physicist Werner Heisenberg made a visit to Copenhagen to see his Danish mentor, Niels Bohr. The two had worked together in the 1920s to revolutionize atomic physics. WWII was raging and they were on opposite sides of the conflict. No one really knows what they said to one another, but the play imagines them meeting after their deaths to discuss that mysterious meeting in 1941. Near the end of the play, Heisenberg speaks of the destruction of Germany. ②

HEISENBERG. Then we should need a strange new quantum ethics. There'd be a place in heaven for me. ③ And another one for the SS man I met on my way home from Haigerloch. ④ That was the end of my war. The Allied troops were closing in; there was nothing more we could do. ⑤ Elisabeth and the children had taken refuge in a village in Bavaria, so I went to see them before I was captured. I had to go by bicycle—there were no trains or road transport by that time—and I had to travel by night and sleep under a hedge by day, because all through the daylight hours the skies were full of Allied planes, scouring the roads for anything that moved. ⑥ A man on a bicycle would have been the biggest target left in Germany. Three days and three nights I traveled. Out of Württemberg, down through the Swabian Jura and the first foothills of the Alps. Across my ruined homeland. Was this what I'd chosen for it? This endless rubble? This perpetual smoke in the sky? These hungry faces? Was this my doing? And all ⑦ the desperate people on the roads. The most desperate of all were the SS. Bands of fanatics with nothing left to lose, roaming around shooting deserters out of hand, hanging them from roadside trees. The second night, and suddenly there it is—the terrible familiar black tunic emerging from the twilight in front of me. On his lips as I stop—the one terrible familiar word. 'Deserter,' he says. He sounds as exhausted as I am. ⑧ I give him the travel order I've written for myself. But there's hardly enough light in the sky to read by, and he's too weary to bother. He begins to open his holster instead. He's going to shoot me because it's simply less labour. And suddenly I'm thinking very quickly and clearly—it's like skiing, or that night on Heligoland, or the one in Faelled Park. What comes into my mind this time is the pack of American cigarettes I've got in my pocket. And already it's in my hand—I'm holding it out to him. The most desperate solution to a problem yet. I wait while he stands there looking at it, trying to make it out, trying to think, his left hand holding my useless piece of paper, his right on the fastening of the holster. There are two simple words in large print on the pack: Lucky

456 **Unit Eight** Monologues and Scenes

Strike. He closes the holster, and takes the cigarettes instead . . . It had worked, it had worked! (9) Like all the other solutions to all the other problems. For twenty cigarettes he let me live. (10) And on I went. Three days and three nights. Past the weeping children, the lost and hungry children, drafted to fight, then abandoned by their commanders. Past the starving slave-labourers walking home to France, to Poland, to Estonia. (11) Through Gammertingen and Biberach and Memmingen. Mindelheim, Kaufbeuren, and Schöngau. Across my beloved homeland. My ruined and dishonoured and beloved homeland. (12)

(7) How would Heisenberg say these six sentences?

(8) Why is Heisenberg exhausted?

(9) Why do the American cigarettes yield such power, and why does Heisenberg offer them?

(10) Explain the irony of this situation.

(11) Who were these people? Why were they on the road?

(12) From this monologue what have you learned about Heisenberg? Try to read the complete play.

Monologues **457**

Scenes

Scenes for One Man and One Woman

Scenes for Two or More Men

Scenes for Two or More Women

*Indicates annotated scene

458 **Unit Eight** Monologues and Scenes

Scenes for Mixed Groups

The Imaginary Invalid

by Molière, adapted by Fran Tanner

In this 17th-century French satire, the young girl Louison is teasing her father, Argan, by refusing at first to disclose that her older sister, Angelique, is seeing a gentleman. When forced to speak, she enjoys embellishing her story.

(Louison, a girl of twelve or thirteen, enters.)

LOUISON. Did you call me, papa?

ARGAN. Yes, little one. Come here. *(She advances part way.)*

ARGAN. *(Beckoning slyly.)* A little closer.

Manuel Denis in *The Imaginary Invalid* at the Theatre du Châtelet, 1990.

(Louison comes closer.)

ARGAN. Now then. Look at me.

LOUISON. *(With seeming innocence.)* Yes, papa?

ARGAN. Don't you have something to tell me?

LOUISON. *(Sweetly.)* Well, I can tell you a story. Would you like to hear the Donkey's Skin or the fable of the Raven and the Fox?

ARGAN. *(Angrily.)* That's not what I had in mind.

LOUISON. My apologies, papa.

ARGAN. Don't you obey your father?

LOUISON. Of course, papa.

ARGAN. And didn't I ask you to report all that you see?

LOUISON. Yes, papa.

ARGAN. Have you told me everything?

LOUISON. *(With some doubt.)* Yes, papa.

ARGAN. Haven't you seen something today?

LOUISON. No, papa.

ARGAN. No?

LOUISON. *(Quite doubtful.)* No . . .

ARGAN. Aha. Then I shall have to renew your memory.

(Picks up his cane and starts toward LOUISON.)

LOUISON. *(Frightened.)* Oh, papa.

ARGAN. Is it not true that you saw a man with your sister Angelique?

LOUISON. *(Crying.)* Oh, dear.

ARGAN. *(Raising his cane to hit her.)* I shall teach you to lie.

LOUISON. Oh, forgive me, papa. Angelique made me promise not to tell. But I'll tell you now.

ARGAN. Very well. You shall tell me, but only after I have punished you for telling a lie.

LOUISON. Don't whip me, dear papa. Please don't whip me.

ARGAN. I shall! *(Raises his cane and strikes once.)*

LOUISON. *(LOUISON backs against the couch, crying loudly, pretending to be hurt.)* Oh, I'm hurt. Papa, stop. I'm hurt. Oh, I'm dying, I'm dead. *(She falls on couch, pretending to be dead, but keeping one eye open to see what her father will do.)*

ARGAN. What's this? Louison, my little one. Louison, what have I done to you? Oh, dear. My poor Louison. Oh, my poor child.

460 **Unit Eight** Monologues and Scenes

LOUISON. *(No longer able to hide her laughter, sits up suddenly.)* Come, come, papa. It's all right. I'm not quite dead.

ARGAN. *(Surprised, but relieved.)* Oh, you imp, you. What a rascal I have. Well, I'll overlook it this once, but you must tell me everything.

LOUISON. Yes, papa. But don't tell Angelique I told.

ARGAN. Of course not.

LOUISON. *(Looks to be sure no one is listening.)* Well, while I was in Angelique's sitting room, a handsome man came, looking for her.

ARGAN. *(Eagerly.)* Yes?

LOUISON. When I asked what he wanted, he said he was her new music teacher.

ARGAN. Aha. So that is their little plan. Continue.

LOUISON. Then Angelique came and when she saw him she said *(over dramatically.)* "Oh, go away, for my sake, leave."

ARGAN. *(Disappointed.)* Oh.

LOUISON. But he didn't leave. He stayed and talked to her.

ARGAN. *(Eagerly.)* What did he say?

LOUISON. He told her . . . *(Teasing her father.)* many things.

ARGAN. Yes?

LOUISON. That he loved her passionately, and that she was the most glorious creature in the world.

ARGAN. And then?

LOUISON. And then he fell on his knees before her—

ARGAN. *(Excitedly.)* Yes, yes.

LOUISON. *(Dramatically.)* And kissed her hand— *(Giggles.)*

ARGAN. *(Eagerly.)* And then?

LOUISON. And then—*(Pause full of suspense, followed by a matter of fact.)* Mama came and he ran away.

ARGAN. *(Disappointed)* That's all? Nothing more?

LOUISON. No, papa. There was nothing more. *(She giggles and runs out. Argan groans and sinks into a chair.)*

The School for Scandal

by Richard Brinsley Sheridan

Sir Peter is scolding his young wife for her extravagance. She humorously confronts him with her determination to do as she pleases, in this 18th-century comedy of manners.

SIR PETER. Lady Teazle, Lady Teazle, I'll not bear it!

LADY TEAZLE. Sir Peter, Sir Peter, you may bear it or not, as you please;

Scenes **461**

but I ought to have my own way in everything, and what's more, I will, too. What! Though I was educated in the country, I know very well that women of fashion in London are accountable to nobody after they are married.

SIR PETER. Very well, ma'am, very well; so a husband is to have no influence, no authority?

LADY TEAZLE. Authority! No, to be sure, if you wanted authority over me, you should have adopted me, and not married me. I am sure you were old enough.

SIR PETER. Old enough! Ay, there it is. Well, well, Lady Teazle, though my life may be made unhappy by your temper, I'll not be ruined by your extravagance.

LADY TEAZLE. My extravagance! I'm sure I'm not more extravagant than a woman of fashion ought to be.

SIR PETER. No, no, madam, you shall throw away no more sums on such unmeaning luxury. 'Slife! To spend as much to furnish your dressing-room with flowers in winter as would suffice to turn the Pantheon into a greenhouse and give a *fête champêtre* at Christmas.

LADY TEAZLE. And am I to blame, Sir Peter, because flowers are dear in cold weather? You should find fault with the climate, and not with me. For my part, I'm sure, I wish it was spring all year round, and that roses grew under our feet.

SIR PETER. Oons! Madam, if you had been born to this, I shouldn't wonder at your talking thus; but you forget what your situation was when I married you.

LADY TEAZLE. No, no, I don't; 'twas a very disagreeable one, or I should never have married you.

SIR PETER. Yes, yes, madam; you were then in somewhat a humbler style, the daughter of a plain country squire. Recollect, Lady Teazle, when I saw you first sitting at your tambor, in a pretty figured linen gown, with a bunch of keys at your side; your hair combed smooth over a roll, and your apartment hung round with fruits in worsted, of your own working.

LADY TEAZLE. Oh, yes! I remember it well, and a curious life I led—my daily occupation to inspect the dairy, superintend the poultry, make extracts from the family receipt book, and comb my aunt Deborah's lap-dog.

SIR PETER. Yes, yes, ma'am, 'twas so indeed.

LADY TEAZLE. And then, you know, my evening amusements! To draw patterns for ruffles, which I had not materials to make up; to play Pope Joan with the curate; to read a sermon to my aunt; or to be stuck down to an old

462 Unit Eight Monologues and Scenes

spinet to strum my father to sleep after a fox-chase.

SIR PETER. I am glad you have so good a memory. Yes, madam, these were the recreations I took you from; but now you must have your coach—*viz-à-viz*—and three powdered footmen before your chair; and in the summer, a pair of white cats to draw you to Kensington Gardens. No recollection, I suppose, when you were content to ride double, behind the butler, on a docked coach-horse?

LADY TEAZLE. No; I swear I never did that. I deny the butler and the coach-horse.

SIR PETER. This, madam, was your situation; and what have I done for you? I have made you a woman of fashion, of fortune, of rank; in short, I have made you my wife.

LADY TEAZLE. Well, then, and there is but one thing more you can make me to add to the obligation, and that is—

SIR PETER. My widow, I suppose?

LADY TEAZLE. Hem! Hem!

SIR PETER. I thank you, madam; but don't flatter yourself for though your ill conduct may disturb my peace, it shall never break my heart, I promise you; however, I am equally obliged to you for the hint.

LADY TEAZLE. Then why will you endeavor to make yourself so disagreeable to me, and thwart me in every little elegant expense?

SIR PETER. 'Slife, madam, I say, had you any of these little elegant expenses when you married me?

LADY TEAZLE. Lud, Sir Peter! Would you have me be out of the fashion?

SIR PETER. The fashion, indeed. What had you to do with the fashion before you married me?

LADY TEAZLE. For my part, I should think you would like to have your wife thought a woman of taste.

SIR PETER. Ay, there again: taste! Zounds! Madam, you had no taste when you married me!

LADY TEAZLE. That's very true indeed, Sir Peter; and after having married you, I should never pretend to taste again, I allow. But now, Sir Peter, if we have finished our daily jangle, I presume I may go to my engagement at Lady Sneerwell's.

SIR PETER. Ah, there's another precious circumstance; a charming set of acquaintances you have made there!

LADY TEAZLE. Nay, Sir Peter, they are all people of rank and fortune, and remarkably tenacious of reputation.

Scenes **463**

SIR PETER. Yes, egad, they are tenacious of reputation with a vengeance; for they don't choose anybody should have a character but themselves! Such a crew! Ah! Many a wretch has rid on a hurdle who has done less mischief than these utterers of forged tales, coiners of scandal, and clippers of reputation.

LADY TEAZLE. What! Would you restrain the freedom of speech?

SIR PETER. Ah! They have made you just as bad as any one of the society.

LADY TEAZLE. Why, I believe I do bear a part with a tolerable grace. But I vow I bear no malice against the people I abuse. When I say an ill-natured thing, 'tis out of pure good humor; and I take it for granted they deal exactly in the same manner with me. But, Sir Peter, you know you promised to come to Lady Sneerwell's too.

SIR PETER. Well, well, I'll call in just to look after my own character.

LADY TEAZLE. Then indeed you must make haste after me, or you'll be too late. So, good-bye to ye. *(Exit)*

SIR PETER. So, I have gained much by my intended expostulation; yet, with what a charming air she contradicts everything I say, and how pleasingly she shows her contempt for my authority! Well, though I can't make her love me, there is great satisfaction in quarreling with her; and I think she never appears to such advantage as when she is doing everything in her power to plague me. *(Exit)*

A Marriage Proposal

by Anton Chekhov,
adapted by Fran Tanner

In this Russian comedy, Ivan Vassiliyitch Lomov's proposal of marriage to his neighbor's daughter, Natalia, is thwarted as they quarrel about ownership of the meadows separating their land.

NATALIA. Oh, hello. Father said there was someone here to see me with an important question. How are you Ivan Vassiliyitch? (1)

LOMOV. I am fine my dear Natalia Stepanovna.

NATALIA. You must excuse me for wearing my apron and looking like this, but I've been working. Do sit down. Goodness, you haven't visited us for ages. You should come more frequently. *(They sit.)* May I offer you something to eat? (2)

LOMOV. No, thank you. I've just had lunch.

NATALIA. Well, do smoke if you wish. There are some matches. It's hard to believe that the weather is so wonderful today, when yesterday it rained so much

(1) Russian names may seem difficult to pronounce. Repeat the names of both characters until you are comfortable with them.

(2) What are Natalia's feelings here? Is she matter-of-fact? Embarrassed? Flustered? Uneasy?

464 **Unit Eight** Monologues and Scenes

we couldn't work outside. How many bricks have you made? Wouldn't you know it. I had the workmen mow all of the hay, and now I'm worried for fear it will rot. I suppose I should have waited longer. (3) *(Notices his suit.)* Oh, but what have we here. Why, you are all dressed up. Are you going to a party? You certainly look nice. What is the occasion?

LOMOV. *(Excitedly)* It's—well—my dear Natalia Stepanovna—I have something to ask you—something that will be a surprise, I know, but you must not be angry—for—I—well—*(Aside.)* (4) How cold it is in here!

NATALIA. What are you talking about? *(Pause.)* Well?

LOMOV. Briefly—we have been friends for a long time—since childhood. My aunt and uncle, who gave me their estate—as you know—greatly admired your parents. Indeed your family and my family have been on good terms with each other for generations. In fact, as you know, my property is adjacent to yours. My meadows touch your woods.

NATALIA. Excuse me, Ivan Vassiliyitch, but those meadows. Did you call them yours?

LOMOV. Yes, they are mine.

NATALIA. Well, I'm sorry to differ with you, but the meadows belong to us, not to you. (5)

LOMOV. Not mine? Now my dear—

NATALIA. Why, I've never heard the like of this. What makes you think they belong to you?

LOMOV. Because I'm speaking of the meadows that run between your woods and my brick ground.

NATALIA. Precisely. They belong to us.

LOMOV. No, they belong to me. You are quite mistaken. As far back as I can remember they have belonged to my family.

NATALIA. Not so.

LOMOV. But it is on record, my dear. True, at one time the ownership was disputed, but now it is common knowledge that the meadows are mine, without argument. In fact, my aunt's grandmother permitted your great grandfather's servants to use the land rent-free while they made bricks for my grandmother. They used the meadows for over forty years, with my family's permission. However, when— (6)

NATALIA. But you are mistaken. My great grandfather's land touched the swamp, so the meadows of course are ours. There is nothing more to say. I can't understand your reasoning.

LOMOV. I'll be glad to show you the records, Natalia Stepanovna. (7)

(3) Should Natalia be pausing before each sentence or running all of her sentences together in this speech? Which would seem more in character to you?

(4) What is the question going to be? Notice the play's title.

(5) Natalia should stress "us." From here on, the polite, courteous courtship behavior begins to shift.

(6) Lomov must let the audience sense that he is trying to control his temper as he gives Natalia this explanation.

(7) Would Lomov say these words sweetly, sarcastically, calmly, or angrily?

Scenes **465**

(8) Natalia's sarcasm here reflects back to her earlier comment about Lomov's nice suit.

(9) What gesture might Lomov use as he says these words?

(10) Both characters have become gradually more intense. As you build to the end, use quick cue pickups, topping one another's line. Both voices and bodies should communicate anger.

NATALIA. That is not necessary. Either you are joking or you are trying to make me angry. Whichever the case, you ought to be ashamed of yourself. It is most unpleasant to hear all of a sudden that the property we have owned for almost 300 years is not ours. I will be the first to admit that the meadows are not worth much. They cover less than five acres and would probably sell for only a few hundred rubles, but the principle of the thing is what interests me. I cannot stand peacefully by while you take my land.

LOMOV. Please, let me finish speaking. Your great grandfather's peasants, as I have already stated, made bricks for my aunt's grandmother. She wanted to be nice to them, so she—

NATALIA. Grandmother! Grandfather! Aunt! I don't know a thing about your ancestors but I do know the meadows are mine. And that's that!

LOMOV. No, the meadows belong to me!

NATALIA. You can talk until you're blue in the face, and put on full evening dress for all I care, (8) but the meadows are, and always will be, mine—mine—mine. I have no intention of taking your land, but neither will I relinquish that which rightfully belongs to my family!

LOMOV. Well, the meadows mean nothing to me. I don't need them. Please, let us stop this. I present the meadows to you as a gift. (9)

NATALIA. How can you give them to me when they belong to me? Ridiculous. Here we have always considered you to be our good friend. Why only last year we loaned you our threshing machine when we needed it ourselves—and now you are stealing our property. How dare you give me my own land. I call that a very dirty trick. In fact, to give you a piece of my mind, I'd say—

LOMOV. You are calling me a thief? My dear lady, I'll have you know that I have never taken anyone's land and I will not be accused of doing so now. The meadows belong to me! (10)

NATALIA. Liar. They are mine!

LOMOV. Mine!

NATALIA. So. We'll see who they belong to. This afternoon I'll order my reapers into my meadows.

LOMOV. You'll what?

NATALIA. My reapers will go into my meadows—today.

LOMOV. Then I'll have the pleasure of kicking them out.

NATALIA. How dare you.

LOMOV. The meadows belong to me. Can't you understand. They are mine!

466 **Unit Eight** Monologues and Scenes

NATALIA. It's not necessary to shout. If you want to rant and rave, please leave. In my house you must conduct yourself like a gentleman. (11)

LOMOV. Oh. If my head wasn't throbbing and my heart beating wildly, I would handle you the way you should be handled. *(Loudly.)* The meadows are mine!

NATALIA. Mine!

LOMOV. Mine! (12)

A Doll's House

by Henrik Ibsen,
translated by Michael Meyer

In this Norwegian play written in 1879, the question of women's rights is addressed. Nora is a wife who is treated as a child by Torvald Helmer, her husband. In this scene, Nora realizes what she must do to achieve her own identity.

NORA. *(Looks at her watch.)* It isn't that late. Sit down here, Torvald. You and I have a lot to talk about. *(She sits down on one side of the table.)*

HELMER. Nora, what does this mean? You look quite drawn—

NORA. Sit down. It's going to take a long time. I've a lot to say to you.

HELMER. *(Sits down on the other side of the table.)* You alarm me, Nora. I don't understand you.

NORA. No, that's just it. You don't understand me. And I've never understood you—until this evening. No, don't interrupt me. Just listen to what I have to say. You and I have got to face facts, Torvald.

HELMER. What do you mean by that?

NORA. *(After a short silence.)* Doesn't anything strike you about the way we're sitting here?

HELMER. What?

NORA. We've been married for eight years. Does it occur to you that this is the first time that we two, you and I, man and wife, have ever had a serious talk together?

HELMER. Serious? What do you mean, serious?

NORA. In eight whole years—no, longer—ever since we first met—we have never exchanged a serious word on a serious subject.

HELMER. Did you expect me to drag you into all my worries—worries you couldn't possibly have helped me with?

NORA. I'm not talking about worries. I'm simply saying that we have never sat down seriously to try to get to the bottom of anything.

HELMER. But, my dear Nora, what on earth has that got to do with you?

(11) A lower volume and pitch might be more effective at this point. The audience should feel that Natalia could explode again at any moment.

(12) As the last "Mine!" is spoken, how should each character move?

Scenes 467

NORA. That's just the point. You have never understood me. A great wrong has been done to me, Torvald. First by Papa, and then by you.

HELMER. What? But we two have loved you more than anyone in the world!

NORA. *(Shakes her head.)* You have never loved me. You just thought it was fun to be in love with me.

HELMER. Nora, what kind of a way is this to talk?

NORA. It's the truth, Torvald. When I lived with Papa, he used to tell me what he thought about everything, so that I never had any opinions but his. And if I did have any of my own, I kept them quiet, because he wouldn't have liked them. He called me his little doll, and he played with me just the way I played with my dolls. Then I came here to live in your house—

HELMER. What kind of a way is that to describe our marriage?

NORA. *(Undisturbed.)* I mean, then I passed from Papa's hands into yours. You arranged everything the way you wanted it, so that I simply took over your taste in everything—or pretended I did—I don't really know—I think it was a little of both—first one and then the other. Now I look back on it, it's as if I've been living here like a pauper, from hand to mouth. I performed tricks for you, and you gave me food and drink. But that was how you wanted it. You and Papa have done me a great wrong. It's your fault that I have done nothing with my life.

HELMER. Nora, how can you be so unreasonable and ungrateful? Haven't you been happy here?

NORA. No; never. I used to think I was; but I haven't ever been happy.

HELMER. Not—not happy?

NORA. No. I've just had fun. You've always been very kind to me. But our home has never been anything but a playroom. I've been your doll-wife, just as I used to be Papa's doll-child. And the children have been my dolls. I used to think it was fun when you came in and played with me, just as they think it's fun when I go in and play games with them. That's all our marriage has been, Torvald.

HELMER. There may be a little truth in what you say, though you exaggerate and romanticize. But from now on it'll be different. Playtime is over. Now the time has come for education.

NORA. Whose education? Mine or the children's?

HELMER. Both yours and the children's, my dearest Nora.

468 **Unit Eight** Monologues and Scenes

NORA. Oh, Torvald, you're not the man to educate me into being the right wife for you.

HELMER. How can you say that?

NORA. And what about me? Am I fit to educate the children?

HELMER. Nora!

NORA. Didn't you say yourself a few minutes ago that you dare not leave them in my charge?

HELMER. In a moment of excitement. Surely you don't think I meant it seriously?

NORA. Yes. You were perfectly right. I'm not fitted to educate them. There's something else I must do first. I must educate myself. And you can't help me with that. It's something I must do by myself. That's why I'm leaving you.

HELMER. *(Jumps up.)* What did you say?

NORA. I must stand on my own feet if I am to find out the truth about myself and about life. So I can't go on living here with you any longer.

HELMER. Nora, Nora!

NORA. I'm leaving you now, at once. Christine will put me up for tonight—

HELMER. You're out of your mind! You can't do this! I forbid you!

NORA. It's no use your trying to forbid me any more. I shall take with me nothing but what is mine. I don't want anything from you, now or ever.

HELMER. What kind of madness is this?

NORA. Tomorrow I shall go home—I mean, to where I was born. It'll be easiest for me to find some kind of a job there.

HELMER. But you're blind! You've no experience of the world—

NORA. I must try to get some, Torvald.

HELMER. But to leave your home, your husband, your children! Have you thought what people will say?

NORA. I can't help that. I only know that I must do this.

HELMER. But this is monstrous! Can you neglect your most sacred duties?

NORA. What do you call my most sacred duties?

HELMER. Do I have to tell you? Your duties towards your husband, and your children.

NORA. I have another duty which is equally sacred.

HELMER. You have not. What on earth could that be?

NORA. My duty towards myself.

Blood Wedding

by Federico García Lorca

This opening scene, set in Spain in the early 1900s, suggests the lyrical gloom that envelopes the bridegroom's family and his upcoming wedding to a woman who loves another.

BRIDEGROOM. *(entering)* Mother.

MOTHER. What?

BRIDEGROOM. I'm going.

MOTHER. Where?

BRIDEGROOM. To the vineyard. *(He starts to go.)*

MOTHER. Wait.

BRIDEGROOM. You want something?

MOTHER. Your breakfast, son.

BRIDEGROOM. Forget it. I'll eat grapes. Give me the knife.

MOTHER. What for?

BRIDEGROOM. *(laughing)* To cut the grapes with.

MOTHER. *(muttering as she looks for the knife)* Knives, knives. Cursed be all knives, and the scoundrel who invented them.

BRIDEGROOM. Let's talk about something else.

MOTHER. And guns and pistols and the smallest little knife—and even hoes and pitchforks.

BRIDEGROOM. All right.

MOTHER. Everything that can slice a man's body. A handsome man, full of young life, who goes out to the vineyards or to his own olive groves—his own because he's inherited them . . .

BRIDEGROOM. *(lowering his head)* Be quiet.

MOTHER. . . . and then that man doesn't come back. Or if he does come back it's only for someone to cover him over with a palm leaf or a plate of rock salt so he won't bloat. I don't know how you dare carry a knife on your body—or how I let this serpent *(She takes a knife from a kitchen chest.)* stay in the chest.

BRIDEGROOM. Have you had your say?

MOTHER. If I live to be a hundred I'd talk of nothing else. First your father; to me he smelled like a carnation and I had him for barely three years. Then your brother. Oh, is it right—how can it be—that a small thing like a knife or a pistol can finish off a man—a bull of a man? No, I'll never be quiet. The months pass and the hopelessness of it stings in my eyes and even to the roots of my hair.

470 **Unit Eight** Monologues and Scenes

BRIDEGROOM. *(forcefully)* Let's quit this talk!

MOTHER. No. No. Let's not quit this talk. Can anyone bring me your father back? Or your brother? Then there's the jail. What do they mean, jail? They eat there, smoke there, play music there! My dead men choking with weeds, silent, turning to dust. Two men like two beautiful flowers. The killers in jail, carefree, looking at the mountains.

BRIDEGROOM. Do you want me to go kill them?

MOTHER. No . . . If I talk about it it's because . . . Oh, how can I help talking about it, seeing you go out that door? It's . . . I don't like you to carry a knife. It's just that . . . that I wish you wouldn't go out to the fields.

BRIDEGROOM. *(laughing)* Oh, come now!

MOTHER. I'd like it if you were a woman. Then you wouldn't be going out to the arroyo now and we'd both of us embroider flounces and little woolly dogs.

BRIDEGROOM. *(He puts his arm around his mother and laughs.)* Mother, what if I should take you with me to the vineyards?

MOTHER. What would an old lady do in the vineyards? Were you going to put me down under the young vines?

BRIDEGROOM. *(lifting her in his arms)* Old lady, old lady—you little old, little old lady!

MOTHER. Your father, he used to take me. That's the way with men of good stock; good blood. Your grandfather left a son on every corner. That's what I like. Men, men; wheat, wheat.

BRIDEGROOM. And I, Mother?

MOTHER. You, what?

BRIDEGROOM. Do I need to tell you again?

MOTHER. *(seriously)* Oh!

BRIDEGROOM. Do you think it's bad?

MOTHER. No.

BRIDEGROOM. Well, then?

MOTHER. I don't really know. Like this, suddenly, it always surprises me. I know the girl is good. Isn't she? Well behaved. Hard working. Kneads her bread, sews her skirts, but even so when I say her name I feel as though someone had hit me on the forehead with a rock.

BRIDEGROOM. Foolishness.

MOTHER. More than foolishness. I'll be left alone. Now only you are left me—I hate to see you go.

BRIDEGROOM. But you'll come with us.

Scenes **471**

MOTHER. No. I can't leave your father and brother here alone. I have to go to them every morning and if I go away it's possible one of the Felix family, one of the killers, might die—and they'd bury him next to ours. And that'll never happen! Oh, no! That'll never happen! Because I'd dig them out with my nails and, all by myself, crush them against the wall.

BRIDEGROOM. *(sternly)* There you go again.

MOTHER. Forgive me. *(pause)* How long have you known her?

BRIDEGROOM. Three years. I've been able to buy the vineyard.

MOTHER. Three years. She used to have another sweetheart, didn't she?

BRIDEGROOM. I don't know. I don't think so. Girls have to look at what they'll marry.

MOTHER. Yes. I looked at nobody. I looked at your father, and when they killed him I looked at the wall in front of me. One woman with one man, and that's all.

BRIDEGROOM. You know my girl's good.

MOTHER. I don't doubt it. All the same, I'm sorry not to have known what her mother was like.

BRIDEGROOM. What difference does it make now?

MOTHER. *(looking at him)* Son.

BRIDEGROOM. What is it?

MOTHER. That's true! You're right! When do you want me to ask for her?

BRIDEGROOM. Does Sunday seem all right to you?

MOTHER. *(seriously)* I'll take her the bronze earrings, they're very old—and you buy her. . .

BRIDEGROOM. You know more about that. . .

MOTHER. . . . you buy her some open-work stockings—and for you, two suits—three! I have no one but you now!

BRIDEGROOM. I'm going. Tomorrow I'll go see her.

MOTHER. Yes, yes—and see if you can make me happy with six grand-children—or as many as you want, since your father didn't live to give them to me.

BRIDEGROOM. The first-born for you!

MOTHER. Yes, but have some girls. I want to embroider and make lace, and be at peace.

472 **Unit Eight** Monologues and Scenes

Driving Miss Daisy

by Alfred Uhry

Miss Daisy's son has hired Hoke to drive the elderly Miss Daisy wherever she needs to go. Miss Daisy is a proud, opinionated white woman, and the idea does not sit right with her. In Hoke, an equally determined black man, she has met her match.

DAISY. Good morning.

HOKE. Right cool in the night, wadn't it?

DAISY. I wouldn't know. I was asleep.

HOKE. Yassum. What yo plans today?

DAISY. That's my business.

HOKE. You right about dat. Idella say we runnin' outa coffee and Dutch Cleanser.

DAISY. We?

HOKE. She say we low on silver polish too.

DAISY. Thank you. I will go to the Piggly Wiggly on the trolley this afternoon.

HOKE. Now, Miz Daisy, how come you doan' let me carry you?

DAISY. No thank you.

HOKE. Ain't that what Mist' Werthan hire me for?

DAISY. That's his problem.

HOKE. All right den. I find something to do. I tend yo zinnias.

DAISY. Leave my flower bed alone.

HOKE. Yassum. You got a nice place back beyond the garage ain' doin' nothin' but sittin' there. I could put you in some butterbeans and some tomatoes and even some Irish potatoes could we get some ones with good eyes.

DAISY. If I want a vegetable garden, I'll plant it for myself.

HOKE. Well, I go out and set in the kitchen, then, like I been doin' all week.

DAISY. Don't talk to Idella. She has work to do.

HOKE. Nome. I jes sit there till five o'clock.

DAISY. That's your affair.

HOKE. Seem a shame, do. That fine Oldsmobile sittin' out there in the garage. Ain't move a inch from when Mist' Werthan rode it over here from Mitchell Motors. Only got nineteen miles on it. Seem like that insurance company give you a whole new car for nothin'.

DAISY. That's your opinion.

HOKE. Yassum. And my other opinion is a fine rich Jewish lady like you doan b'long draggin' up the steps of no

Scenes **473**

bus, luggin' no grocery store bags. I come along and carry them fo' you.

DAISY. I don't need you. I don't want you. And I don't like you saying I'm rich.

HOKE. I won' say it, then.

DAISY. Is that what you and Idella talk about in the kitchen? Oh, I hate this! I hate being discussed behind my back in my own house! I was born on Forsyth Street and, believe you me, I knew the value of a penny. My brother Manny brought home a white cat one day and Papa said we couldn't keep it because we couldn't afford to feed it. My sisters saved up money so I could go to school and be a teacher. We didn't have anything!

HOKE. Yassum, but look like you doin' all right now.

DAISY. And I've ridden the trolley with groceries plenty of times!

HOKE. Yassum, but I feel bad takin' Mist' Werthan's money for doin' nothin'. You understand?
(She cuts him off in the speech.)

DAISY. How much does he pay you?

HOKE. That between me and him, Miz Daisy.

DAISY. Anything over seven dollars a week is robbery. Highway robbery!

HOKE. Specially when I doan do nothin' but set on a stool in the kitchen all day long. Tell you what, while you goin on the trolley to the Piggly Wiggly, I hose down yo' front steps. *(Daisy is putting on her hat.)*

DAISY. All right.

HOKE. All right I hose yo' steps?

DAISY. All right the Piggly Wiggly. And then home. Nowhere else.

HOKE. Yassum.

DAISY. Wait. You don't know how to run the Oldsmobile!

HOKE. Miz Daisy, a gear shift like a third arm to me. Anyway, thissun automatic. Any fool can run it.

DAISY. Any fool but me, apparently.

HOKE. Ain' no need to be so hard on yoseff now. You cain' drive but you probably do alota things I cain' do. It all work out.

DAISY. *(Calling offstage.)* I'm gone to the market, Idella.

HOKE. *(Also calling.)* And I right behind her! *(Hoke puts on his cap and helps Daisy into the car. He sits at the wheel and backs the car down the driveway. Daisy, in the rear, is in full bristle.)* I love a new car smell. Doan' you? *(Daisy slides over to the other side of the seat.)*

474 **Unit Eight** Monologues and Scenes

DAISY. I'm nobody's fool, Hoke.

HOKE. Nome.

DAISY. I can see the speedometer as well as you can.

HOKE. I see dat.

DAISY. My husband taught me how to run a car.

HOKE. Yassum.

DAISY. I still remember everything he said. So don't you even think for a second that you can—Wait! You're speeding! I see it!

HOKE. We ain' goin' but nineteen miles an hour.

DAISY. I like to go under the speed limit.

HOKE. Speed limit thirty five here.

DAISY. The slower you go, the more you save on gas. My husband told me that.

HOKE. We barely movin'. Might as well walk to the Piggly Wiggly.

DAISY. Is this your car?

HOKE. Nome.

DAISY. Do you pay for the gas?

HOKE. Nome.

DAISY. All right then. My fine son may think I'm losing my abilities, but I am still in control of what goes on in my car. Where are you going?

HOKE. To the grocery store.

DAISY. Then why didn't you turn on Highland Avenue?

HOKE. Piggly Wiggly ain' on Highland Avenue. It on Euclid, down there near—

DAISY. I know where it is and I want to go to it the way I always go. On Highland Avenue.

HOKE. That three blocks out of the way, Miz Daisy.

DAISY. Go back! Go back this minute!

HOKE. We in the wrong lane!
I cain' jes—

DAISY. Go back I said! If you don't, I'll get out of this car and walk!

HOKE. We movin'! You cain' open the do'!

DAISY. This is wrong! Where are you taking me?

HOKE. The sto'.

DAISY. This is wrong. You have to go back to Highland Avenue!

HOKE. Mmmm Hmmmm.

DAISY. I've been driving to the Piggly Wiggly since the day they put it up and

Scenes 475

opened it for business. This isn't the way! Go back! Go back this minute!

HOKE. Yonder the Piggly Wiggly.

DAISY. Get ready to turn now.

HOKE. Yassum.

DAISY. Look out! There's a little boy behind that shopping cart!

HOKE. I see dat.

DAISY. Pull in next to the blue car.

HOKE. We closer to the do' right here.

DAISY. Next to the blue car! I don't park in the sun! It fades the upholstery.

HOKE. Yassum. *(He pulls in, and gets out as Daisy springs out of the back seat.)*

DAISY. Wait a minute. Give me the car keys.

HOKE. Yassum.

DAISY. Stay right here by the car. And you don't have to tell everybody my business.

HOKE. Nome. Don' forget the Dutch Cleanser now. *(She fixes him with a look meant to kill and exits. Hoke waits by the car for a minute, then hurries to the phone booth at the corner.)* Hello? Miz McClatchey? Hoke Coleburn here. Can I speak to him? *(Pause.)* Mornin sir, Mist' Werthan. Guess where I'm at? I'm at dishere phone booth on Euclid Avenue right next to the Piggly Wiggly. I jes drove yo' Mama to the market. *(Pause.)* She flap a little on the way. But she all right. She in the store. Uh oh. Miz Daisy look out the store window and doan' see me, she liable to throw a fit right there by the checkout. *(Pause.)* Yassuh, only took six days. Same time it take the Lawd to make the worl'. *(Lights out on him.)*

Weebjob

by Diane Glancy

Thou hast fenced me with bones . . .

—Job 10:11

Gerald Long Chalk, or Weebjob (wēb jōb), age 48, is the main character. His name is a play on the Biblical Job because he is beset with problems. Weebjob is a holy man, a Mescalero Apache, and he always seems to be at a crossroads in his life. He lets rich land lie fallow. He paints signs and hangs them on his fence. Signs that say: "He hangs the earth on nothing, Job 26:7," etc.)

Weebjob's friend, Pick Up, age 43, is in love with Weebjob's daughter. He is also a Mescalero Apache.

Suzanne Long Chalk, or Sweet Potato, Weebjob's daughter, is 21. She has a mind of her own. She is unhappy with

476 **Unit Eight** Monologues and Scenes

her life because she doesn't know where she belongs.

The setting is the Salazar Canyon in Lincoln County, New Mexico.

Scene 2

The stage is dark except for a spotlight in the corner which falls on Sweet Potato and Pick Up in the truck.

SWEET POTATO. Why are we stopping? I need to get back to feed Weebjob.

PICK UP. Let him wait.

SWEET POTATO. I'll hear him bellering in the valley if we don't get back soon . . . He'll be painting another sign for the fence by the road . . . *(Pick Up touches her face.)*

PICK UP. Where were you for a week?

SWEET POTATO. You already asked me, and I told you I was on the road. *(Folds her arms.)* Why did you bring me back to him? You know I didn't want to come.

PICK UP. You can't run away, Sweet Potato.

SWEET POTATO. My name is Suzanne Long Chalk.

PICK UP. I'll call you what I please. I can't have you hitch-hiking on the road for anyone to pick up. You shouldn't be out on the road alone. It's not good. What would you do in Gallup?

SWEET POTATO. Get a job. I can cook, wait tables. I worked there last summer, if you remember.

PICK UP. Yes, it's the first time I came to see you . . . I don't want you to go back there.

SWEET POTATO. You sound like my father.

PICK UP. It's not as your father that I'm speaking. Work at the Civil War in Old Lincoln if you must have a job. Let the men gawk at you. Wait tables. *(He pauses and looks at her.)* I care for you, Suzanne. You know that. *(Pause.)* More than as a father. I didn't come to Socorro to see James.

SWEET POTATO. I told you I didn't want to speak of these things.

PICK UP. I didn't for many years. But now I can't wait any longer. You're more than Weebjob's daughter to me.

SWEET POTATO. Maybe we could be like cousins.

PICK UP. I want you as a close friend.

SWEET POTATO. We are close friends, Pick Up, my father's friend.

PICK UP. Yes, I'm his friend.

SWEET POTATO. You wouldn't be if he heard you speak to me like that.

Scenes 477

PICK UP. I know. *(He touches her face again.)*

SWEET POTATO. I remember you, Pick Up, when you used to have a brown Volkswagen, and looked like a prune driving it down the road.

PICK UP. I remember you, Sweet Potato, in a round purple coat, like a plum on narrow legs, with skinny braids sticking out from beneath your cap.

SWEET POTATO. I remember the night you got drunk in the Civil War Bar in Old Lincoln and came to our house and quoted poetry to the weed-clumps.

PICK UP. I remember when the faintest bit of snow blew into the valley and you ran into my truck on William's bicycle and sprang the tire.

SWEET POTATO. I remember—*(Pick Up puts his hands over her mouth.)*

PICK UP. I remember when you fell into the stream. I should have let you drown. *(He kisses her.)*

SWEET POTATO. Would you call him father?

PICK UP. *(He rolls his head back.)* I would rather have a buffalo for a father-in-law.

SWEET POTATO. *(She takes up for Weebjob.)* He's a better man than any I've known.

PICK UP. I know.

SWEET POTATO. Wise and good-hearted. Quick tempered. A little harsh with words and his head too much in the Bible, but a good man.

PICK UP. I don't know what to do, Suzanne. I want you, and I wonder why. I'm almost as old as your father. How could I think of you as a wife? How could you think of me—

SWEET POTATO. Don't talk about it.

PICK UP. Marry me, Suzanne.

SWEET POTATO. I can hear Weebjob roaring about it now.

PICK UP. He will be all right. Think about me, Sweet Potato. *(He kisses her again.)* Marry me.

SWEET POTATO. Maybe it's what you deserve.

FOB

by David Henry Hwang

In this play, Steve has entered the back room of a Chinese restaurant in Torrance, California, and asked Grace, who sits at a table, if they have a certain dish. She tells him they are not yet open, and he proceeds to tell her that he is the legendary Chinese hero Gwan Gung.

478 Unit Eight Monologues and Scenes

STEVE. Tell me, how do people think of Gwan Gung in America? Do they shout my name while rushing into battle, or is it too sacred to be used in such ostentatious display?

GRACE. Uh—no.

STEVE. No—what? I didn't ask a "no" question.

GRACE. What I mean is, neither. They don't do either of those.

STEVE. Not good. The name of Gwan Gung has been restricted for the use of leaders only?

GRACE. Uh—no. I think you better sit down.

STEVE. This is very scandalous. How are the people to take my strength? Gwan Gung might as well not exist, for all they know.

GRACE. You got it.

STEVE. I got what? You seem to be having trouble making your answers fit my questions.

GRACE. No, I think you're having trouble making your questions fit my answers.

STEVE. What is this nonsense? Speak clearly, or don't speak at all.

GRACE. Speak clearly?

STEVE. Yes. Like a warrior.

GRACE. Well, you see, Gwan Gung, no one gives a wipe about you 'round here. You're dead.

(Pause.)

STEVE. You . . . you make me laugh.

GRACE. You died way back . . . hell, no one even noticed when you died—that's how bad off your PR was. You died and no one even missed a burp.

STEVE. You lie! The name of Gwan Gung must be feared around the world—you jeopardize your health with such remarks. *(Pause.)* You—you have heard of me, I see. How can you say—?

GRACE. Oh, I just study it a lot—Chinese-American history, I mean.

STEVE. Ah. In the schools, in the universities, where new leaders are born, they study my ways.

GRACE. Well, fifteen of us do.

STEVE. Fifteen. Fifteen of the brightest, of the most promising?

GRACE. One wants to be a dental technician.

STEVE. A man studies Gwan Gung in order to clean teeth?

GRACE. There's also a middle-aged woman that's kinda bored with her kids.

Scenes **479**

STEVE. I refuse—I don't believe you—your stories. You're just angry at me for treating you like a servant. You're trying to sap my faith. The people—the people outside—they know me—they know the deeds of Gwan Gung.

GRACE. Check it out yourself.

STEVE. Very well. You will learn—learn not to test the spirit of Gwan Gung.

(Steve exits. Grace picks up the box. She studies it.)

GRACE. Fa Mu Lan sits and waits. She learns to be still while the emperors, the dynasties, the foreign lands flow past, unaware of her slender form, thinking it a tree in the woods, a statue to a goddess long abandoned by her people. But Fa Mu Lan, the Woman Warrior, is not ashamed. She knows that the one who can exist without movement while the ages pass is the one to whom no victory can be denied. It is training, to wait. And Fa Mu Lan, the Woman Warrior, must train, for she is no goddess, but girl—girl who takes her father's place in battle. No goddess, but woman—warrior-woman *(She breaks through the wrapping, reaches in, and pulls out another box, beautifully wrapped and ribboned.)*—and ghost. *(She puts the new box on the shelf, goes to the phone, dials.)* Hi, Dale? Hi, this is Grace . . . Pretty good. How 'bout you? . . . Good, good. Hey, listen, I'm sorry to ask you at the last minute and everything, but are you doing anything tonight? . . . Are you sure? . . . Oh, good. Would you like to go out with me and some of my friends? . . . Just out to dinner, then maybe we were thinking of going to a movie or something . . . Oh, good . . . Are you sure? . . . Yeah, okay. Um, we're all going to meet at the restaurant . . . No, *our* restaurant . . . right—as soon as possible. Okay, good . . . I'm really glad that you're coming. Sorry it's such short notice. Okay. Bye, now . . . Huh? Frank? Oh, okay. *(Pause.)* Hi, Frank . . . Pretty good . . . Yeah? . . . No, I don't think so . . . Yeah . . . No, I'm sorry, I'd still rather not . . . I don't want to, okay? Do I have to be any clearer than that? . . . You are not! . . . You don't even know when they come—you'd have to lie on those tracks for hours . . . Forget it, okay? . . . Look, I'll get you a schedule so you can time it properly . . . It's not a favor, damn it. Now goodbye! *(She hangs up.)* Jesus!

(Steve enters.)

STEVE. Buncha weak boys, what do they know? One man—ChinaMan—wearing a leisure suit—green! I ask him, "You know Gwan Gung?" He says, "Hong Kong?" I say, "No, no. Gwan Gung." He says, "Yeah. They got sixty thousand people living on four acres. Went there last year." I say, "No, no.

480 **Unit Eight** Monologues and Scenes

Gwan Gung." He says, "Ooooh! Gwan Gung?" I say, "Yes, yes, Gwan Gung." He says, "I never been there before."

GRACE. See? Even if you didn't die—who cares?

STEVE. Another kid—blue jeans and a T-shirt—I ask him, does he know Gwan Gung? He says, he doesn't need it, he knows Jesus Christ. What city is this now?

GRACE. Los Angeles.

STEVE. This isn't the only place where a new ChinaMan can land, is it?

GRACE. I guess a lot go to San Francisco.

STEVE. Good. This place got a bunch of weirdos around here.

GRACE. Yeah.

STEVE. They could never be followers of Gwan Gung. All who follow me must be loyal and righteous.

GRACE. Maybe you should try some other state.

STEVE. Huh? What you say?

GRACE. Never mind. You'll get used to it—like the rest of us.

(Pause. Steve begins laughing.)

STEVE. You are a very clever woman.

GRACE. Just average.

STEVE. No. You do a good job to make it seem like Gwan Gung has no followers here. At the university, what do you study?

GRACE. Journalism.

STEVE. Journalism—you are a writer, then?

GRACE. Of a sort.

STEVE. Very good. You are close to Gwan Gung's heart.

GRACE. As close as I'm gonna get.

STEVE. I would like to go out tonight with you.

GRACE. I knew it. Look, I've heard a lot of lines before, and yours is very creative, but . . .

STEVE. I will take you out.

GRACE. You will, huh?

STEVE. I do so because I find you worthy to be favored.

GRACE. You're starting to sound like any other guy now.

Spinning into Butter

by Rebecca Gilman

We see a dean's office at Belmont College, a small liberal arts college in Belmont, Vermont. It is a large office, with built-in bookshelves full of books

Scenes **481**

and nice white trim and a large warm rug on the floor. The desk is cluttered with papers and more books, and there are several very comfortable-looking chairs. There may even be a fireplace. Large windows provide a lot of light.

Sitting at the desk is Sarah Daniels, who is the college's Dean of Students. She is earnest in her desire to do right by her students.

There is a knock at the door.

SARAH. Come in.

(Patrick Chibas enters. He is self-assured, dressed in running shorts and a T-shirt.)

PATRICK. Dean Daniels? I think I was next. I got a note in my box that said you wanted to see me?

SARAH. *(Smiles.)* I left notes for a lot of students. *(Patrick stares at her.)* I need you to tell me your name.

PATRICK. Oh. Sorry. Patrick Chibas.

SARAH. Patrick. Great. Have a seat. *(Patrick takes a seat and looks around while she fishes out a file from a pile on her desk. While she looks)* Welcome back. How's moving going?

PATRICK. Fine.

SARAH. *(Finds his file but doesn't open it yet.)* What dorm are you in this year?

PATRICK. Grange Hall.

SARAH. Was that your first choice?

PATRICK. Last.

SARAH. I guess sophomores always get the short straw, don't they?

PATRICK. Yeah.

SARAH. Did you go home for the summer?

PATRICK. For the first part, and then I went to Florida.

SARAH. Did you have an internship?

PATRICK. No. I just bummed around. I waited tables at the Fish Shack.

SARAH. Just relaxed, huh?

PATRICK. Yeah. *(Small beat.)* Am I in trouble?

SARAH. No! No. I'm sorry, Patrick. I actually wanted to talk to you about a scholarship. *(Opens his file.)*

PATRICK. Oh yeah?

SARAH. Yeah. You declared an environmental sciences major last spring.

PATRICK. Yeah.

SARAH. Well, we have a scholarship that's designated for. . . well, it's designated for an outstanding minority student in environmental sciences, and I just. . . Well. . . I wondered if you might be interested.

482 Unit Eight Monologues and Scenes

PATRICK. Sure.

SARAH. Good. There's just one thing, then. I need to ask you, Patrick, on your Belmont application, you... Under the voluntary disclosure of your racial/ethnic background you marked "Other."

PATRICK. Yeah.

SARAH. Okay. I guess I need to know, so I can make a recommendation to the board, just what "other" is. If you don't mind.

PATRICK. I don't mind. I'm Nuyorican.

SARAH. Nuyorican?

PATRICK. Yeah.

SARAH. Huh. Would it be fair for me to say, then, that you're, um, Hispanic?

PATRICK. I prefer Nuyorican.

SARAH. Of course. I just... Well, to simplify things, when I make my recommendation to the board, do you think I could just mention that you're Hispanic?

PATRICK. What's wrong with Nuyorican?

SARAH. Nothing, of course.

PATRICK. Then why don't you just say that?

SARAH. I will. *(Beat.)* And then, I think, I'll probably be asked to explain, and I wondered, could I just explain by saying that you're Hispanic?

PATRICK. Why would you be asked to explain?

SARAH. Because the members of our scholarship advisory board are... well... to be honest, Patrick, they're not culturally sensitive. *(Patrick stares at her.)* If you know what I mean.

PATRICK. I guess I don't.

SARAH. I think they tend to see the world in very... limited terms, as black or white or re... *(She stops herself.)*... racially divided along solid, clearly delineated lines.

PATRICK. So you're saying they're old?

SARAH. Yes. They're old. And they're just... They're not going to know what Nuyorican is.

PATRICK. *(Sighs.)* Look, you understand why I don't want to be called Hispanic, don't you?

SARAH. As I understand it, and correct me, please, if I'm wrong, it's because it really only applies to imperialists of European descent who colonized Puerto Rico.

PATRICK. Yeah. I mean, if you understand, then...

SARAH. Why am I suggesting it?

Scenes **483**

Good question. *(Beat.)* And you're right. I shouldn't compromise your feelings for the sake of expediency. I'm sorry.

PATRICK. That's okay.

SARAH. *(Thinking.)* What about Latino?

PATRICK. *(Irritated.)* No.

SARAH. How 'bout just plain Puerto Rican?

PATRICK. No.

(Beat.)

SARAH. It's a twelve-thousand-dollar scholarship, Patrick.

PATRICK. It is?

SARAH. I want you to get it. It just seems like a shame to me to leave money sitting around in a bank when it could be doing you some good. You're a remarkably talented student and I think you should be rewarded in a meaningful way.

(Long pause.)

PATRICK. You can put Puerto Rican.

SARAH. *(Smiles.)* Thank you. *(She makes a note.)* I'll let you know as soon as I hear.

PATRICK. *(Taking his cue, standing.)* Okay. Sure. Thanks, Dean Daniels.

SARAH. You're welcome. Will you send in whoever's next?

PATRICK. Sure.

The Importance of Being Earnest

by Oscar Wilde

In this 19th-century English comedy, Algernon is quizzing Jack about the latter's proposal of marriage to Gwendolen. The two men spar with clever remarks, for which author Oscar Wilde is famous. (1)

ALGERNON. Didn't it go off all right, old boy? (2) You don't mean to say Gwendolen refused you? I know it is a way she has. She is always refusing people. I think it is most ill-natured of her.

JACK. Oh, Gwendolen is as right as a trivet. (3) As far as she is concerned, we are engaged. Her mother is perfectly unbearable. Never met such a gorgon . . . I don't really know what a gorgon is like, but I am quite sure that Lady Bracknell is one. (4) In any case, she is a monster, without being a myth, which is rather unfair . . . I beg your pardon, Algy, I suppose I shouldn't talk about your own aunt in that way before you.

ALGERNON. My dear boy, I love hearing my relations abused. It is the only thing that makes me put up with them at all. Relations are simply a tedious pack of people who haven't got the

(1) This play pokes fun at the social mores of its time. The cleverness of the dialogue should be maintained with lightness and enthusiasm.

(2) In what part of this speech do you realize to what Algernon is referring?

(3) This is a 19th-century English expression. What does *trivet* suggest about Gwendolen's personality?

(4) In mythology what was a "gorgon"? Realize the humor in this line so you can say it to get chuckles from the audience.

484 Unit Eight Monologues and Scenes

remotest knowledge of how to live, nor the smallest instinct about when to die. (5)

JACK. Oh, that is nonsense!

ALGERNON. It isn't.

JACK. Well, I won't argue about the matter. You always want to argue about things.

ALGERNON. That is exactly what things were originally made for.

JACK. Upon my word, if I thought that, I'd shoot myself. *(A pause.)* You don't think there is any chance of Gwendolen becoming like her mother in about a hundred and fifty years, do you Algy?

ALGERNON. All women become like their mothers. That is their tragedy. No man does. That's his. (6)

JACK. Is that clever?

ALGERNON. It is perfectly phrased! And quite as true as any observation in civilized life should be.

JACK. I am sick to death of cleverness. Everybody is clever nowadays. You can't go anywhere without meeting clever people. The thing has become an absolute public nuisance. I wish to goodness we had a few fools left.

ALGERNON. We have.

JACK. I should extremely like to meet them. What do they talk about?

ALGERNON. The fools? Oh, about the clever people, of course.

JACK. What fools!

ALGERNON. By the way, did you tell Gwendolen the truth about your being Ernest in town, and Jack in the country? (7)

JACK. *(In a very patronizing manner.)* My dear fellow, the truth isn't quite the sort of thing one tells to a nice sweet refined girl. What extraordinary ideas you have about the way to behave to a woman!

ALGERNON. The only way to behave to a woman is to make love to her, if she is pretty, and to someone else if she is plain.

JACK. Oh, that is nonsense.

ALGERNON. What about your brother? What about the profligate Ernest?

JACK. Oh, before the end of the week I shall have got rid of him. I'll say he died in Paris of apoplexy. Lots of people die of apoplexy, quite suddenly, don't they? (8)

ALGERNON. Yes, but it's hereditary, my dear fellow. It's a sort of thing that runs in families. You had much better say a severe chill.

JACK. You are sure a severe chill isn't hereditary, or anything of that kind?

(5) Emphasize the contrast of "how to live" and "when to die" to obtain the humor here.

(6) Again, emphasize the contrasting ideas. Wilde uses contrasts throughout this scene to create humor.

(7) This is a very important line on which the whole plot of the play rests.

(8) Apoplexy is a condition in which the blood supply to the brain is obstructed, causing paralysis or brain damage, now called a stroke.

(9) This is forecasting of a later scene when the two women do meet.

(10) Make the following exchange of dialogue quick and adroit.

ALGERNON. Of course it isn't.

JACK. Very well, then. My poor brother Ernest is carried off suddenly in Paris, by a severe chill. That gets rid of him.

ALGERNON. But I thought you said that . . . Miss Cardew was a little too much interested in your poor brother Ernest? Won't she feel his loss a good deal?

JACK. Oh, that is all right. Cecily is not a silly romantic girl, I am glad to say. She has got a capital appetite, goes for long walks, and pays no attention at all to her lessons.

ALGERNON. I would rather like to see Cecily.

JACK. I will take very good care you never do. She is excessively pretty, and she is only just eighteen.

ALGERNON. Have you told Gwendolen yet that you have an excessively pretty ward who is only just eighteen?

JACK. Oh! One doesn't blurt these things out to people. Cecily and Gwendolen are perfectly certain to be extremely great friends. I'll bet you anything you like that half an hour after they have met, they will be calling each other sister.

ALGERNON. Women only do that when they have called each other a lot of other things first. (9) Now, my dear boy, if we want to get a good table at Willis's, we really must go and dress. Do you know it is nearly seven?

JACK. *(Irritably.)* Oh! It always is nearly seven.

ALGERNON. Well, I'm hungry.

JACK. I never knew you when you weren't . . .

ALGERNON. What shall we do after dinner? Go to the theatre? (10)

JACK. Oh, no! I loathe listening.

ALGERNON. Well, let us go to the Club.

JACK. Oh, no! I hate talking.

ALGERNON. Well, we might trot round to the Empire at ten?

JACK. Oh, no! I can't bear looking at things. It is so silly.

ALGERNON. Well, what shall we do?

JACK. Nothing!

ALGERNON. It is awfully hard work doing nothing. However, I don't mind hard work where there is no definite object of any kind.

486 **Unit Eight** Monologues and Scenes

The Inspector General

by Nikolai Gogol, adapted by Fran Tanner

Arriving penniless in a Russian village, Khlestakov is treated shabbily. But when he poses as a government official, the villagers grant his every wish. In this early scene in the play, Khlestakov orders supper from a servant who has been told to refuse this beggar.

SERVANT. The manager sent me to see what you want.

KHLESTAKOV. Ah, good to see you, old man. How are things going?

SERVANT. All right, thank you.

KHLESTAKOV. Is business booming here at the hotel?

SERVANT. Yes, sir. Thank you, sir.

KHLESTAKOV. Lots of guests?

SERVANT. Adequate, sir.

KHLESTAKOV. Well fine! You know, it's almost past dinner time and I haven't eaten yet. Do a good turn and bring me a tray immediately, or I shall be late for my appointment.

SERVANT. Sorry, sir, but the manager will charge no more dinners to you. In fact, today he almost sent a complaint about you to the police.

KHLESTAKOV. A complaint? That's ridiculous. After all, I've got to eat or I shall starve. The truth of the matter is, I'm quite famished!

SERVANT. Be that as it may. He said he wasn't going to give you anything else until you had cleared up your bill.

KHLESTAKOV. Well, can't you talk to him? Put in a good word for me!

SERVANT. But what can I say?

KHLESTAKOV. Talk to him seriously and tell him I've got to have something to eat. The money—well—tell him just because his kind can go all day without food, doesn't mean that other people can. Preposterous idea!

SERVANT. Yes, sir, I'll tell him. *(Exit Servant.)*

KHLESTAKOV. How disgusting if he refuses to send up dinner. I've never been so hungry. I wonder if I could pawn my clothes? My trousers? No, I'd rather not eat than go home without my Petersburg suit. Too bad that Yokhim wouldn't let me rent a carriage. It would have been great to drive up in style to a landlord's house with my carriage lanterns on and Osip behind in uniform. How impressed they would be. "Who is it? Who has come?" Then my footman would announce *(He imitates footman.)* "Ivan Alexandrovich Khlestakov of Petersburg. Will you receive him?" Those country dunces, though, wouldn't even know what that

Scenes **487**

meant. If any farmer visits them, he stumbles right into the living room like a bear. Hmmm. I'd go up to a pretty young girl and say "Mademoiselle, I am so happy—" Huh! *(He spits.)* I'm so hungry I feel nauseated.

(Enter the Servant.)

KHLESTAKOV. Yes, what do you want?

SERVANT. I'm bringing dinner.

KHLESTAKOV. *(Claps his hands and jumps into his chair.)* Ah, dinner. At last, dinner.

SERVANT. The manager says this is the last dinner he will send you.

KHLESTAKOV. Oh, the manager. Who cares about the manager. What's there to eat?

SERVANT. Soup and roast beef.

KHLESTAKOV. You mean that is all?

SERVANT. That's all, sir.

KHLESTAKOV. Nonsense. I won't hear of it. That's not enough.

SERVANT. On the contrary, sir, the manager says it's far too much!

KHLESTAKOV. But what about the gravy?

SERVANT. There isn't any.

KHLESTAKOV. Why not? When I passed the kitchen I saw them making a lot, and earlier in the dining room, I saw two short-looking men eating salmon and other good things.

SERVANT. Well, there is some and then there isn't.

KHLESTAKOV. What do you mean?

SERVANT. I mean, there isn't any, sir.

KHLESTAKOV. No salmon? No gravy? No chops?

SERVANT. No, sir. Well, yes, sir. But only for those who pay, sir.

KHLESTAKOV. Oh, you knucklehead. Why should I go hungry while they eat. Aren't I as good as they?

SERVANT. No, sir. Well, yes, sir, but the difference is, they have money.

KHLESTAKOV. Oh, it's a waste of time to argue with you. *(Tastes soup.)* What awful soup. Why, it's only hot water you've poured into the bowl. There's no taste at all, only a dreadful smell. I'll not eat it! You must bring me some other.

SERVANT. Sorry, sir. The manager said if you didn't like this, you could go without.

KHLESTAKOV. *(Holding his bowl and plate.)* Well, then leave it. Only, don't talk like that to me. I'll not have it. *(Tastes soup again.)* Heavens, what

488 **Unit Eight** Monologues and Scenes

soup. *(Continues to eat it.)* I'm probably the first to ever eat soup like this. Why, there's even a feather floating on top. *(Spoons a piece of chicken in the soup.)* Ah, even the fowl is foul. Pass me the roast beef. Here, Osip, there's some soup left for you. *(Cuts meat.)* You call this roast beef? It most certainly is not!

SERVANT. Then what is it?

KHLESTAKOV. Only the devil knows, but it is not beef. It tastes more like leather. Cheaters! What they won't give a person. Why, my jaw aches from chewing just one bite. *(Picks teeth with finger.)* It's even worse than tree bark. I can't get it out. Such food is enough to ruin one's teeth. *(Wipes mouth with napkin.)* Isn't there anything else?

SERVANT. No, sir.

KHLESTAKOV. What cheaters they are. Not even dessert. It's terrible the way they always take advantage of travelers!

You Can't Take It With You

by Moss Hart and George S. Kaufman

In this American comedy, the Sycamore family is considered eccentric because of their unusual philosophy. Grandpa Sycamore explains to the stalwart Mr. Kirby that people should not work at jobs they dislike.

KIRBY. *(Outraged.)* I beg your pardon, Mr. Vanderhof. I am a very happy man.

GRANDPA. Are you?

KIRBY. Certainly I am.

GRANDPA. *(Sits.)* I don't think so. What do you think you get your indigestion from? Happiness? No, sir. You get it because most of your time is spent in doing things you don't want to do.

KIRBY. I don't do anything I don't want to do.

GRANDPA. Yes, you do. You said last night that at the end of a week in Wall Street you're pretty near crazy. Why do you keep on doing it?

KIRBY. Why do I keep on—why, that's my business. A man can't give up his business.

GRANDPA. Why not? You've got all the money you need. You can't take it with you.

KIRBY. That's a very easy thing to say, Mr. Vanderhof. But I have spent my entire life building up my business.

GRANDPA. And what's it got you? Same kind of mail every morning, same kind of deals, same kind of meetings, same dinners at night, same indigestion. Where does the fun come in? Don't you think there ought to be something more, Mr. Kirby? You must

Scenes 489

have wanted more than that when you started out. We haven't got too much time, you know—any of us.

KIRBY. What do you expect me to do? Live the way you do? Do nothing?

GRANDPA. Well, I have a lot of fun. Time enough for everything—read, talk, visit the zoo now and then, practice my darts, even have time to notice when spring comes around. Don't see anybody I don't want to, don't have six hours of things I have to do every day before I get one hour to do what I like in—and I haven't taken bicarbonate of soda in thirty-five years. What's the matter with that?

KIRBY. The matter with that? Suppose we all did it? A fine world we'd have, everybody going to zoos. Don't be ridiculous, Mr. Vanderhof. Who would do the work?

GRANDPA. There's always people that like to work—you can't stop them. Inventions, and they fly the ocean. There're always people to go down to Wall Street, too—because they like it. But from what I've seen of you I don't think you're one of them. I think you're missing something.

KIRBY. I am not aware of missing anything.

GRANDPA. I wasn't either, till I quit. I used to get down to that office nine o'clock sharp no matter how I felt. Lay awake nights for fear I wouldn't get that contract. Used to worry about the world, too. Got all worked up about whether Cleveland or Blaine was going to be elected President—seemed awful important at the time, but who cares now? What I'm trying to say, Mr. Kirby, is that I've had thirty-five years that nobody can take away from me, no matter what they do to the world. See?

KIRBY. *(Crossing to table.)* Yes, I do see. And it's a very dangerous philosophy, Mr. Vanderhof. It's—it's un-American.

"Dead Parrot" from *The Complete Monty Python's Flying Circus*

by Graham Chapman, John Cleese, Terry Gilliam, Eric Idle, Terry Jones, and Michael Palin

Mr. Praline walks into the pet shop carrying a dead parrot in a cage. He walks to counter where shopkeeper tries to hide below cash register.

PRALINE. Hello, I wish to register a complaint. . . Hello? Miss?

SHOPKEEPER. What do you mean, miss?

PRALINE. Oh, I'm sorry, I have a cold. I wish to make a complaint.

490 Unit Eight Monologues and Scenes

SHOPKEEPER. Sorry, we're closing for lunch.

PRALINE. Never mind that my lad, I wish to complain about this parrot what I purchased not half an hour ago from this very boutique.

SHOPKEEPER. Oh yes, the Norwegian Blue. What's wrong with it?

PRALINE. I'll tell you what's wrong with it. It's dead, that's what's wrong with it.

SHOPKEEPER. No, no it's resting, look!

PRALINE. Look my lad, I know a dead parrot when I see one and I'm looking at one right now.

SHOPKEEPER. No, no sir, it's not dead. It's resting.

PRALINE. Resting?

SHOPKEEPER. Yeah, remarkable bird the Norwegian Blue, beautiful plumage, innit?

PRALINE. The plumage don't enter into it—it's stone dead.

SHOPKEEPER. No, no—it's just resting.

PRALINE. All right then, if it's resting I'll wake it up. *(Shouts into cage.)* Hello Polly! I've got a nice cuttlefish for you when you wake up, Polly Parrot!

SHOPKEEPER. *(Jogging cage.)* There it moved.

PRALINE. No he didn't. That was you pushing the cage.

SHOPKEEPER. I did not.

PRALINE. Yes, you did. *(Takes parrot out of cage, shouts.)* Hello Polly, Polly *(Bangs it against counter.)* Polly Parrot, wake up. Polly. *(Throws it in the air and lets it fall to the floor.)* Now that's what I call a dead parrot.

SHOPKEEPER. No, no it's stunned.

PRALINE. Look my lad, I've had just about enough of this. That parrot is definitely deceased. And when I bought it not half an hour ago, you assured me that its lack of movement was due to it being tired and shagged out after a long squawk.

SHOPKEEPER. It's probably pining for the fiords.

PRALINE. Pining for the fiords, what kind of talk is that? Look, why did it fall flat on its back the moment I got it home?

SHOPKEEPER. The Norwegian Blue prefers kipping on its back. Beautiful bird, lovely plumage.

PRALINE. Look, I took the liberty of examining that parrot, and I discovered that the only reason that it had been

Scenes **491**

sitting on its perch in the first place was that it had been nailed there.

SHOPKEEPER. Well of course it was nailed there. Otherwise it would muscle up to those bars and voom.

PRALINE. Look matey *(Picks up parrot.),* this parrot wouldn't voom if I put four thousand volts through it. It's bleeding demised.

SHOPKEEPER. It's not, it's pining.

PRALINE. It's not pining, it's passed on. This parrot is no more. It has ceased to be. It's expired and gone to meet its maker. This is a late parrot. It's a stiff. Bereft of life, it rests in peace. If you hadn't nailed it to the perch, it would be pushing up the daisies. It's rung down the curtain and joined the choir invisible. This is an ex-parrot.

SHOPKEEPER. Well, I'd better replace it then.

PRALINE. *(To camera.)* If you want to get anything done in this country you've got to complain till you're blue in the mouth.

SHOPKEEPER. Sorry guv, we're right out of parrots.

PRALINE. I see. I see. I get the picture.

SHOPKEEPER. I've got a slug.

PRALINE. Does it talk?

SHOPKEEPER. Not really, no.

PRALINE. Well, it's scarcely a replacement, then is it?

SHOPKEEPER. Listen, I'll tell you what, *(Handing over a card.)* tell you what, if you go to my brother's pet shop in Bolton he'll replace your parrot for you.

PRALINE. Bolton eh?

SHOPKEEPER. Yeah.

PRALINE. All right.

(He leaves, holding the parrot.)

(CAPTION: 'A SIMILAR PET SHOP in BOLTON, LANCS'

(Close-up of sign on door reading: 'Similar Pet Shops Ltd.' Pull back from sign to see same pet shop. Shopkeeper now has moustache. Praline walks into shop. He looks around with interest, noticing the empty parrot cage still on the floor.)

PRALINE. Er, excuse me. This is Bolton, is it?

SHOPKEEPER. No, no it's, er, Ipswich.

PRALINE. *(To camera.)* That's Inter-City Rail for you. *(Leaves.)*

(Man in porter's outfit standing at complaints desk for railways. Praline approaches.)

PRALINE. I wish to make a complaint.

492 Unit Eight Monologues and Scenes

PORTER. I don't have to do this, you know.

PRALINE. I beg your pardon?

PORTER. I'm a qualified brain surgeon. I only do this because I like being my own boss.

PRALINE. Er, excuse me, this is irrelevant, isn't it?

PORTER. Oh yeah, it's not easy to pad these out to thirty minutes.

PRALINE. Well I wish to make a complaint. I got on the Bolton train and found myself deposited here in Ipswich.

PORTER. No, this is Bolton.

PRALINE. *(To camera.)* The pet shop owner's brother was lying.

PORTER. Well you can't blame British Rail for that.

PRALINE. If this is Bolton, I shall return to the pet shop.

(CAPTION: 'A LITTLE LATER LTD')

(Praline walks into the shop again.)

PRALINE. I understand that this is Bolton.

SHOPKEEPER. Yes.

PRALINE. Well, you told me it was Ipswich.

SHOPKEEPER. It was a pun.

PRALINE. A pun?

SHOPKEEPER. No, no, not a pun, no. What's the other thing which reads the same backwards as forwards?

PRALINE. A palindrome?

SHOPKEEPER. Yes, yes.

PRALINE. It's not a palindrome. The palindrome of Bolton would be Notlob. It don't work.

SHOPKEEPER. Look, what do you want?

PRALINE. No I'm sorry, I'm not prepared to pursue my line of enquiry any further as I think this is getting too silly.

A Jamaican Airman Foresees His Death

by Fred D'Aguiar

Three young Jamaican men are eager to join Britain's Royal Air Force during World War II to fight for a mother country they have yet to see. In the following scene, Alvin Williams, the main character, has his enlistment interview with a civilian, an Air Force man, an Army man and Kojo, in place of the absent Navy representative.

CIVILIAN. You wish to volunteer?

ALVIN. Yes sir!

ARMY. Patriotic.

Scenes 493

AIR-FORCE. Very like a patriot.

ARMY. And honourable.

AIR-FORCE. That too.

ARMY. Patriotic and honourable.

AIR-FORCE. Honourable and patriotic.

ARMY. Same difference.

AIR-FORCE. One must first have honour; with honour one is in a position to be a patriot. Therefore, honourable and patriotic.

CIVILIAN. There will be neither honour nor patriotism or vice versa unless we can recruit men.

ARMY. A man with your muscles would do well in a regiment.

AIR-FORCE. A man of your intelligence would do well in a squadron.

ARMY. I don't see how you could possibly have assessed the man's intelligence when he hasn't said two words.

AIR-FORCE. By the same token, I fail to see how you can talk about his muscles when he is fully clothed.

ARMY. I made a quick assessment as he entered the room and took six steps to his seat. I could tell from the briskness in his opening and closing the door, by the lightness of his step and from his firm handshake, that he is at least a boxer.

AIR-FORCE. All right, let's test your hypothesis. Now, Mr. Williams, if you will kindly enter the room again.

(Alvin goes out of the room, knocks as before, enters, closes the door behind him and waits.)

ARMY. See! I am vindicated. There's the briskness of an athlete.

AIR-FORCE. Nonsense. It doesn't take much to open and close a door.

CIVILIAN. Gentlemen . . .

ARMY. These are military matters. We are assessing Mr. Williams as we see fit. Will you walk over to this desk as before.

AIR-FORCE. Light-footed?! I counted seven steps.

ARMY. The last one was a pigeon-step.

AIR-FORCE. I don't care if it belonged to a caterpillar. You are wrong.

ARMY. Don't jump the gun, he has yet to shake our hands.

(Alvin offers a limp hand.)

ARMY. You are not the man who walked in that door a moment ago.

KOJO. More like an Englishman's, that handshake.

AIR-FORCE. We are all Englishmen, Englishmen abroad, but Englishmen all the same.

494 **Unit Eight** Monologues and Scenes

CIVILIAN. Wrong. We are Jamaicans under British rule.

ARMY. Separate Jamaica from Britain and what are you left with? A poor, small island without a voice or guardian.

CIVILIAN. Hardly.

ARMY. Everything we have, and I mean everything, is given to us by Great Britain. A constitution that is British. Think what that means. . .

KOJO. But at what price?

ARMY. You don't get anything in this world for nothing.

AIR-FORCE. Great Britain does not owe Jamaica a living!

KOJO. Great Britain does not own the lives of our young men.

ARMY. It's the least we can do.

KOJO. Ditch the Brits.

ARMY. We must obey the rule of law.

KOJO. Who in this room had a hand in making that law?

AIR-FORCE. The law doesn't apply any less because we're further from Westminster.

ARMY. Here here.

AIR-FORCE. A principle's a principle.

KOJO. But it has to mean something to the people to whom it applies.

CIVILIAN. Where is all this going?

KOJO. We're Jamaicans.

CIVILIAN. So?

KOJO. And the wonderful constitution you defend is now being contested, right?

AIR-FORCE. The Fascists want to put theirs in its place.

ARMY. We are not here to question the Government. We are here to carry out its orders.

KOJO. Sometimes the Government is wrong.

AIR-FORCE and ARMY. Anarchist!

KOJO. As Jamaicans we can act as conciliators; as a British Dominion we are forced to take sides.

ARMY. As a British Dominion? We are a British Dominion!

AIR-FORCE. We have the monarchy!

KOJO. We have plenty monkeys of we own.

AIR-FORCE. This conversation is stupid.

KOJO. Stupid/he, stupid/she, stupid-all-a-we!

ALVIN. It seems to me, sir, unless we have this kind of conversation things will never change.

ARMY and AIR-FORCE. You too!

Scenes **495**

ALVIN. Don't get me wrong. I am here to enlist. But I am only here because you and you and you told me again and again that was the honourable and patriotic thing to do for the mother country. I haven't been able to see Jamaica and what it is to be Jamaican without seeing an Englishman and the Union Jack. When I do, I'm condemned for being a follower of Marcus Garvey. He's the only one who has held up an alternative. He's shown me it's possible to be something other than British.

ARMY. What do you think of the Army, Mr. Williams?

ALVIN. It's a good force, sir, but my special interest is in the Air Force.

AIR-FORCE. Bravo! But you know, young man, everyone wants to fly.

ALVIN. I've always wanted to fly.

KOJO. Don't be so concrete.

AIR-FORCE. You've got to do better than that.

ALVIN. It's my dream, sir.

KOJO. *(Mocking.)* It's my dream, sir.

AIR-FORCE. What can you contribute to the Air Force?

ALVIN. My youth, my strength, and my intelligence.

KOJO. *(Mocking.)* My youth, my strength, and my intelligence.

AIR-FORCE. I mean what can you contribute to the Air Force? You, Mr. Williams.

ALVIN. When I was a boy, my uncle made me a kite, nearly as tall as me. But when I raised it I was too small to control it. A grown-up had to hold my arms to stop it dragging me away. One day I decided to fly the kite on my own. I was sure if I got the right grip and a sure foothold I could steer it—have fingertip control, like I did with smaller kites. I raised it all right. There was a good breeze and the principle is the same whatever the kite-size. I thought I was on top of it—on top if it and on top of the world. I began to jump up and down. I even called out for everyone to come and see me, Alvin, behind that kite they all thought I'd have to give away. Just then a strong breeze hit the kite. Something pulled me so hard I had to look up. All I saw way up in the sky was this tadpole waving. I thought that small thing can't tug with so much force, it must be the hand of God. I thought, if I could hold on long enough, I'd be hauled up to heaven. And heaven to me was all the things I ever wanted but could never have: shoes, long trousers, black pudding, pepper-pot and souse every day, a new slate for school. Things I dreamed about. Things I knew I would have

496 **Unit Eight** Monologues and Scenes

when I got to heaven. We used to make long lists. We talked to God, but he never replied. When he did answer some people in church we could never understand what they were saying. I tried running along with the pull, but my legs weren't fast enough. I heard the shouts of let go, let go, but I couldn't let go of heaven. I held on for dear life. When I came round they told me I was dragged into a fence. It took me a long time to believe the preacher preaching on Sundays and even longer to get round to praying. But I never doubted for a moment that I had to fly. Not to God. But because in my head that kite is still up there, waiting for me to pilot it to the ground.

AIR-FORCE. Welcome to the Air Force, Mr. Williams.

(They take turns to shake his hand.)

ARMY. I knew you had a firm grip, must've been nerves, eh? Box?

ALVIN. No, sir.

KOJO. You want to fly? We all want to fly.
God's up there in the sky, not down here.
He's up there 'cause he's a bird;
if he's in man's image he'd be down here
getting his hands dirty with the rest of us.
We want to be birds so badly,
we cage them. We teach them our language,
parrot-fashion, in the hope they'll divulge
how it is you grow hollow bones and feathers,
instead of hairs and skin. We consume their
flesh and bones hoping we can digest their wisdom.
But all we get is the stench of our own earthboundness.
We call our women after them 'cause we believe
they were told the secret, but were sworn to silence,
or deliberately withhold it from us for spite.
We spend our lives making paper airplanes,
kites, balloons, airships, real planes, you name it,
even our wishes when we see a star shoot.
We send them all up there to find out
where the birds hide their bird-making formula.
We cry when we're born 'cause the first thing
we notice is that we've got no wings.
So we bawl. We spent the rest of our lives
trying to get back to that comforting, watery,
blub-blub, blub-blub, brilliant dark, in the hope

Scenes **497**

that a second journey will somehow,
anyhow,
sprout wings.
Remember and deliver us, O lord,
O John Crow,
O sparrow, O Pterodactyl; deliver us
this day
from our daily dread of being land-
locked,
sea-locked, from our gravity strait-
jacket.
Deliver us to birddom, till birddom
come,
thy quill be done, on earth as it is
in heaven,
a-bird.

(1) Why does Emilia say this? What has happened in the previous scene?

(2) In Shakespeare's time *incontinent* meant "at once."

(3) Why does Othello want Emilia gone?

(4) In this scene notice that Desdemona obeys her husband in all that he asks.

(5) Desdemona breaks into her speech of love for Othello to direct Emilia in helping her undress. Shakespeare is adding little domestic details.

(6) Desdemona seems to have a premonition of death. Find additional clues to her uneasiness.

Othello

by William Shakespeare

Othello believes that his wife, Desdemona, has been unfaithful. Jealous with rage, he sends her to her room with the intent of killing her. Desdemona is blameless and cannot understand Othello's anger. As she prepares for bed, she discusses the situation with Emilia, her maid.

EMILIA. How goes it now? He looks gentler than he did. (1)

DESDEMONA. He says he will return
incontinent; (2)
And hath commanded me to go to bed,
And bade me to dismiss you. (3)

EMILIA. Dismiss me?

DESDEMONA. It was his bidding;
therefore, good Emilia,
Give me my nightly wearing, and adieu.
We must not now displease him. (4)

EMILIA. I would you had never seen him!

DESDEMONA. So would not I: my
love doth so approve him,
That even his stubbornness, his checks,
his frowns—
Prithee, unpin me—have grace and
favor in them. (5)

EMILIA. I have laid those sheets you bade me on the bed.

DESDEMONA. All's one.
Good faith, how foolish are our minds!
If I do die before thee, prithee, shroud
me
In one of those same sheets. (6)

EMILIA. Come, come, you talk.

DESDEMONA. My mother had a maid
call'd Barbara:
She was in love, and he she lov'd prov'd
mad
And did forsake her.
She had a song of "willow";
An old thing 't was but it express'd her
fortune,
And she died singing it. That song
tonight
Will not go from my mind; I have much
to do

498 **Unit Eight** Monologues and Scenes

But to go hang my head all at one side
And sing it like poor Barbara.
Prithee, dispatch. (7)

EMILIA. Shall I go fetch your nightgown?

DESDEMONA. No, unpin me here.
This Lodovico is a proper man. (8)

EMILIA. A very handsome man.

DESDEMONA. He speaks well.

EMILIA. I know a lady in Venice would have walked barefoot to Palestine for a touch of his nether lip. (9)

DESDEMONA. *(Singing.)*
"The poor soul sat sighing by a sycamore tree,
Sing all a green willow; (10)
Her hand on her bosom, her head on her knee
Sing willow, willow, willow.
The fresh streams ran by her, and murmur'd her moans;
Sing willow, willow, willow;
Her salt tears fell from her, and soften'd the stones;
Sing willow, willow, willow."
Lay by these—
(Singing.) (11)
"Willow"—
Prithee, hie thee; he'll come anon — *(Singing.)*
"Sing all a green willow must be my garland.
Let nobody blame him, his scorn I approve—"
Nay, that's not next—
Hark! Who is 't that knocks?

EMILIA. It's the wind.

DESDEMONA. *(Singing.)*
"I call'd my love false love; but what said he then?
Sing willow, willow, willow.
If I court moe women, you'll couch with moe men—"
So, get thee gone; good-night.
Mine eyes do itch;
Doth that bode weeping?

EMILIA. 'T is neither here nor there.

DESDEMONA. I have heard it said so.
O, these men, these men!
Dost thou in conscience think—tell me, Emilia—
That there be women do abuse their husbands
In such gross kind?

EMILIA. There be some such, no question.

DESDEMONA. Wouldst thou do such a deed for all the world?

EMILIA. Why, would not you?

DESDEMONA. No, by this heavenly light! (12)

EMILIA. Nor I neither by this heavenly light; I might do't as well i' th' dark. (13)

(7) What does *dispatch* mean?

(8) Lodovico had just been entertained in Othello's home.

(9) The *nether* lip is the lower lip.

(10) Find the melody of this plaintive piece in a book of Shakespearian songs.

(11) As Desdemona sings this song, Emilia should be doing appropriate business, such as brushing her mistress's hair or hanging up her dress.

(12) Here we realize that Desdemona is innocent of any unfaithfulness.

(13) Emilia is joking. Emphasize the contrast between *light* and *dark*.

Scenes **499**

(14) A cheap ring made in separate halves.

(15) In the following speech, Emilia suggests that women can (and should) get revenge on husbands who go astray.

(16) What does Desdemona think about Emilia's philosophy? Does Desdemona believe that a husband's ill conduct is an excuse for a wife's behaving badly?

DESDEMONA. Wouldst thou do such a deed for all the world?

EMILIA. The world's a huge thing; it is a great price
For a small vice.

DESDEMONA. In troth, I think thou wouldst not.

EMILIA. In troth, I think I should; and undo't when I had done.
Marry, I would not do such a thing for a joint-ring, (14) nor for measures of lawn, nor for gowns, petticoats, nor caps, nor any petty exhibition; but, for all the whole world—'ud's pity, who would not make her husband a cuckold to make him a monarch? I should venture purgatory for it.

DESDEMONA. Beshrew me, if I would do such a wrong
For the whole world.

EMILIA. Why, the wrong is but a wrong i' th' world; and having the world for your labour, 't is a wrong in your own world, and you might quickly make it right.

DESDEMONA. I do not think there is any such woman.

EMILIA. Yes, a dozen; and as many to th' vantage as would store the world they play'd for.
But I do think it is their husbands' faults (15)
If wives do fall. Say that they slack their duties
And pour our treasures into foreign laps,
'Or else break out in peevish jealousies.
Throwing restraint upon us; or say they strike us.
Or scant our former having in despite;
Why, we have galls, and though we have some grace,
Yet have we some revenge. Let husbands know
Their wives have sense like them; they see and smell
And have their palates both for sweet and sour
As husbands have. What is it that they do
When they change us for others? Is it sport?
I think it is. And doth affection breed it?
I think it doth. Is 't frailty that thus errs?
It is so too. And have not we affections,
Desires for sport, and frailty, as men have?
Then let them use us well; else let them know,
That ills we do, their ills instruct us so.

DESDEMONA. Good-night, good-night. Heaven me such uses send,
Not to pick bad from bad, but by bad amend. (16)

500 Unit Eight Monologues and Scenes

The Glass Menagerie

by Tennessee Williams

In an attempt to help her daughter, Laura, gain skills for the job market, Amanda scrapes up the money to send Laura to typing school. But in her shyness, Laura quits the school without telling her mother. In the following scene, Amanda confronts her daughter about her deceit.

LAURA. Mother, I was just . . .

AMANDA. I know. You were just practicing your typing, I suppose. *(Behind chair R.)*

LAURA. Yes.

AMANDA. Deception, deception, deception!

LAURA. *(Shakily.)* How was the D.A.R. meeting, Mother?

AMANDA. *(Crosses to Laura.)* D.A.R. meeting!

LAURA. Didn't you go to the D.A.R. meeting, Mother?

AMANDA. *(Faintly, almost inaudibly.)* No, I didn't go to any D.A.R. meeting. *(Then more forcibly.)* I didn't have the strength—I didn't have the courage. I just wanted to find a hole in the ground and crawl in it and stay there the rest of my entire life. *(Tears type charts, throws them on floor.)*

LAURA. *(Faintly.)* Why did you do that, Mother?

AMANDA. *(Sits on R. end of day-bed.)* Why? Why? How old are you, Laura?

LAURA. Mother, you know my age.

AMANDA. I was under the impression that you were an adult, but evidently I was very much mistaken. *(She stares at Laura.)*

LAURA. Please don't stare at me, Mother! *(Amanda closes her eyes and lowers her head. Pause.)*

AMANDA. What are we going to do? What is going to become of us? What is the future? *(Pause.)*

LAURA. Has something happened, Mother? Mother, has something happened?

AMANDA. I'll be all right in a minute. I'm just bewildered—by life . . .

LAURA. Mother, I wish that you would tell me what's happened!

AMANDA. I went to the D.A.R. this afternoon, as you know; I was to be inducted as an officer. I stopped off at Rubicam's Business College to tell them about your cold and to ask how you were progressing down there.

LAURA. Oh . . .

AMANDA. Yes, oh-oh-oh. I went straight to your typing instructor and introduced myself as your mother. She didn't even know who you were. "Wingfield," she said? "We don't have any such scholar enrolled in this school." I assured her she did. I said my daughter Laura's been coming to classes since early January. "Well, I don't know," she said, "unless you mean that terribly shy little girl who dropped out of school after a few days' attendance?" No, I said, I don't mean that one. I mean my daughter, Laura, who's been coming here every single day for the past six weeks! "Excuse me," she said. And she took down the attendance book and there was your name, unmistakable, printed, and all the dates you'd been absent. I still told her she was wrong. I still said, "No there must have been some mistake! There must have been some mix-up in the records!" "No," she said, "I remember her perfectly now. She was so shy and her hands trembled so that her fingers couldn't touch the right keys! When we gave a speed-test—she just broke down completely—was sick at the stomach and had to be carried to the washroom! After that she never came back. We telephoned the house every single day and never got any answer." *(Rises from day-bed, crosses R.C.)* That was while I was working all day long down at that department store, I suppose, demonstrating those—*(With hands indicates brassiere.)* Oh! I felt so weak I couldn't stand up! *(Sits in armchair.)* I had to sit down while they got me a glass of water! *(Laura crosses up to phonograph.)* Fifty dollars' tuition. I don't care about the money so much, but all my hopes for any kind of future for you—gone up the spout, just gone up the spout like that. *(Laura winds phonograph up.)* Oh, don't do that, Laura!—Don't play that victrola!

LAURA. Oh! *(Stops phonograph, crosses to typing table, sits.)*

AMANDA. What have you been doing every day when you've gone out of the house pretending that you were going to business college?

LAURA. I've just been going out walking.

AMANDA. That's not true!

LAURA. Yes, it is, Mother, I just went walking.

AMANDA. Walking? Walking? In winter? Deliberately courting pneumonia in that light coat? Where did you walk to, Laura?

LAURA. All sorts of places—mostly in the park.

AMANDA. Even after you'd started catching that cold?

LAURA. It was the lesser of two evils, Mother. I couldn't go back. I threw up on the floor!

502 **Unit Eight** Monologues and Scenes

AMANDA. From half-past seven till after five every day you mean to tell me you walked around in the park, because you wanted to make me think that you were still going to Rubicam's Business College?

LAURA. Oh, Mother, it wasn't as bad as it sounds. I went inside places to get warmed up.

AMANDA. Inside where?

LAURA. I went in the art museum and at the birdhouses at the Zoo. I visited the penguins every day! Sometimes I did without lunch and went to the movies. Lately I've been spending most of my afternoons in the Jewel-box, that big glass house where they raise the tropical flowers.

AMANDA. You did all that to deceive me, just for deception! Why? Why? Why? Why?

LAURA. Mother, when you're disappointed, you get that awful suffering look on your face, like the picture of Jesus' mother in the Museum!

(Rises.)

AMANDA. Hush!

LAURA. *(Crosses R. to menagerie.)* I couldn't face it. I couldn't.

AMANDA. *(Rising from day-bed.)* So what are we going to do now, honey, the rest of our lives? Just sit down in this house and watch the parades go by? Amuse ourselves with the glass menagerie? Eternally play those worn-out records your father left us as a painful reminder of him? *(Slams phonograph lid.)* We can't have a business career. No, we can't do that—that just gives us indigestion. *(Around R. day-bed.)* What is there left for us now but dependency all our lives? I tell you, Laura, I know so well what happens to unmarried women who aren't prepared to occupy a position in life. *(Crosses L, sits on day-bed.)* I've seen such pitiful cases in the South—barely tolerated spinsters living on some brother's wife or a sister's husband—tucked away in some mousetrap of a room—encouraged by one in-law to go on and visit the next in-law—little birdlike women—without any nest—eating the crust of humility all their lives! Is that the future that we've mapped out for ourselves? I swear I don't see any other alternative. And I don't think that's a very pleasant alternative. Of course—some girls do marry. My goodness, Laura, haven't you ever liked some boy?

LAURA. Yes, Mother, I liked one once.

AMANDA. You did?

LAURA. I came across his picture a while ago.

AMANDA. He gave you his picture, too? *(Rises from day-bed, crosses to chair R.)*

Scenes **503**

LAURA. No, it's in the yearbook.

AMANDA. *(Sits in armchair.)* Oh—a high-school boy.

LAURA. Yes. His name was Jim.

The Effect of Gamma Rays on Man-in-the-Moon Marigolds

by Paul Zindel

Act I

Scene 1

(As the house lights fade, a music theme fades in. A light picks up Tillie sitting on the floor R. of the sofa, she is holding a small white rabbit).

TILLIE'S VOICE. *(Recorded.)* He told me to look at my hand for a part of it came from a star that exploded too long ago to imagine. This part of me was formed from a tongue of fire that screamed through the heavens until there was our sun. And this part of me—this tiny part of me—was on the sun when it itself exploded and whirled in a great storm until the planets came to be. *(The lights in the room begin to fade up slowly.)* And this small part of me was then a whisper of the earth. When there was life perhaps this part of me got lost in a fern that was crushed and covered until it was coal. And then it was a diamond millions of years later—it must have been a diamond as beautiful as the star from which it had first come. *(The tape begins to fade and Tillie continues the speech.)* Or perhaps this part of me got lost in a terrible beast, or became part of a huge bird that flew above the primeval swamps. And he said this thing was so small—this part of me was so small it couldn't be seen—but it was there from the beginning of the world. And he called this bit of me an atom. And when he wrote the word, I fell in love with it. Atom. Atom. What a beautiful word. *(Pause. Telephone rings. The lights in the room fade up.)*

BEATRICE. *(Off upstairs.)* Will somebody get that please? *(Phone continues to ring.)* Aaaaa! *(She enters, crosses downstairs.)* No help! Never any help! *(She answers the phone.)* Hello? Yes it is. Who's this? *(Pause.)* I hope there hasn't been any trouble at school? Oh, she's always been like that. She hardly says a word around here either. I always say some people were born to speak and others just to listen. *(Pause.)* You know I've been meaning to call you to thank *you* for that lovely rabbit you gave Matilda. She and I just adore it and it's gotten so big. *(Pause.)* Well, it certainly was thoughtful. Mr. Goodman, I don't mean to change the subject but aren't you that delightful young man Tillie said hello to a couple of months back at the A & P? You were by the lobster tank and I was by the frozen foods? That

504 **Unit Eight** Monologues and Scenes

delightful and handsome young man? *(Pause.)* Why, I would very much indeed use the expression handsome. Yes, and . . . *(Pause.)* Well, I encourage her at every opportunity at home. Did she say I didn't? Both my daughters have their own desks and I put 75 watt bulbs right near them. *(She crosses to the D. end of the counter, turns her back to the audience and puts instant coffee into a cup.)* Yes. . . yes. . . *(She turns front.)* I think those tests are very much overrated, anyway, Mr. Goodman. Well believe me she's nothing like that around this house. *(She crosses to the L. of the table, pulls the chair out, and sits. Pause.)* Now I don't want you to think I don't appreciate what you're trying to do, Mr. Goodman, but I'm afraid it's simply useless. I'd say as long as she's doing well in your class that's all you should be concerned about. I'm sure with all those modern techniques you must have, you can bring her out—that is the phrase, isn't it?—just as well as anyone. *(Pause.)* I've tried just everything, but she isn't a pretty girl—I mean, let's be frank about it—she's going to have her problems. But with all your charm and patience I'm sure she'll respond and improve to your satisfaction. Are you married, Mr. Goodman? Oh, that's too bad. I don't know what's the matter with women today letting a handsome young man like you get away. *(Long pause.)* Well, some days she just doesn't feel like going to school. You just said how bright she is, and I'm really afraid to put too much of a strain on her after what happened to her sister. You know, too much strain is the worst thing in this modern world, Mr. Goodman, and I can't afford to have another convulsive on my hands, now can I? *(She rises, and crosses to the bottom of the stairs.)* I can't tell you how happy I am that you called. Why, believe it or not you're the first teacher that's ever taken the trouble to call me as a preventative measure. And I truly appreciate that, Mr. Goodman. Oh, the others call you when the damage has been done, but I doubt that Ruth would have had that breakdown, if those teachers down there had taken the trouble to call me. . . Well, she never acted strange at home. But don't you worry about Matilda. There will be some place for her in this world. And, like I said, some were born to speak and others just to listen. . . and do call again, Mr. Goodman, it's been a true pleasure speaking with you. Goodbye. *(She hangs up the phone, and crosses D. C. Tillie puts the rabbit in its cage.)* Matilda, that wasn't very nice of you to tell them I was forcibly detaining you from school. Why the way that Mr. Goodman spoke he must think I'm running a concentration camp. Do you have any idea how embarrassing it is to be accused of running a concentration camp for your own children? Well, it isn't embarrassing at all. *(She crosses*

Scenes 505

U. of the kitchen table, to the counter, pours water into the cup with instant coffee, turns the hotplate off, and turns to Tillie.) That school of yours is forty years behind the times anyway, and believe me you learn more around here than that ugly Mr. Goodman can teach you! You know, I really feel sorry for him. Of course, he's not as bad as Miss Hanley. The idea of having her teach girl's gym is staggering. And you have to place me in the embarrassing position of giving them a reason to call me at eight-thirty in the morning, no less.

TILLIE. *(Rising.)* I didn't say anything. . .

BEATRICE. What do you tell them when they want to know why you stay home once in a while?

TILLIE. I tell them I'm sick.

BEATRICE. *(Crosses U. C., gets the pillow from the window ledge, crosses to U. of the L. sofa unit, puts the pillow on the sofa, and pushes the sofa next to the other section. She sits and drinks her coffee. Tillie picks up her school book from the sofa.)* Oh, you're sick all right, the exact nature of the illness is not fully realized, but you're sick all right. Any daughter that would turn her mother in as the administrator of a concentration camp has got to be suffering from something very peculiar.

TILLIE. *(Pause, as she crosses U. of the sofa, to the kitchen table.)* Can I go in today, mother? *(She picks up a second book, and crosses to the L. of Beatrice.)*

BEATRICE. You'll go in, all right. . .

TILLIE. Mr. Goodman said he was going to do an experiment. . .

BEATRICE. Why, he looks like the kind that would do his experimenting after sundown. . .

TILLIE. On radioactivity. . .

BEATRICE. On radioactivity? That's all that high school needs!

TILLIE. He's going to bring in the cloud chamber. . .

BEATRICE. Why, what an outstanding event. If you would've warned me I would've gotten dressed to kill and gone with you today. I just love seeing cloud chambers being brought in. . .

TILLIE. You can actually see. . .

BEATRICE. You're giving me a headache.

TILLIE. *(Pause as she crosses to U. of the end table.)* Please?

BEATRICE. No, my dear, the fortress of knowledge is not going to be blessed by your presence today. I have a good number of exciting duties for you to take care of, not the least of which is rabbit droppings.

506 Unit Eight Monologues and Scenes

TILLIE. Oh, mother, please . . . I'll do it after school.

BEATRICE. If we wait one minute longer this house is going to ferment. I found rabbit droppings in my bedroom even this time and if you don't start moving you're going to smell hasenpfeffer.

TILLIE. *(Crosses to the small table U. of Nanny's door, puts her books on the table, picks up the rabbit cage, crosses to the R. of the sofa, holding the cage between herself and Beatrice.)* I could do it after Mr. Goodman's class. I'll say I'm ill and ask for a sick pass.

BEATRICE. Do you want me to chloroform that thing right this minute?

TILLIE. No!

BEATRICE. Then shut up.

A Shayna Maidel

by Barbara Lebow

Set in New York City in 1946, this play portrays a family separated by the Holocaust. Although born in Poland, Rose, now in her twenties, came with her father to the United States when she was four. Her mother and sister could not follow and were put in concentration camps. In this scene, her sister Lusia, now grown, has just arrived in New York. Her old world ways are a sharp contrast to Rose's "Americanization." Lusia's intent is to find and be united with her husband Duvid. The two sisters discuss their early memories.

(Rose is heard softly humming a popular song. The morning light slowly comes up on her. She is wearing a robe and slippers, but looks dressed up. She is setting the table, trying to be quiet so as not to wake Lusia, although Lusia is not in sight and her bed is made. Rose enjoys arranging the small feast. The doorbell rings, startling her. She goes to the front door.)

ROSE. Lusia! *(Rose follows Lusia as she puts down her handbag. Lusia is wearing the same clothes as when she arrived.)* I thought you were still sleeping. I've been tiptoeing around. What were you doing? Where could you go?

LUSIA. To place I come to first. Where you come to get me.

ROSE. Whatever for? Did you forget something? I'm surprised they're even open today. You went all by yourself?

LUSIA. *(Struggling with language.)* I go read list. In books they got. And new names every day. People they find yet from the camps. Some coming yet from out woods where they been hiding.

ROSE. I know. I know, Lusia. But surely by now—

Scenes 507

LUSIA. New names every day. And so I make mine list. You see? And sometimes maybe I find a person some place alive, some family, some friend. And this how I find Duvid, or he finding me, too.

ROSE. But that would take a miracle.

LUSIA. Is no miracle. Duvid is a . . . a mensch. Is only knowing Duvid is alive.

ROSE. *(Covering her discomfort.)* I see. Come, you'll tell me more. We'll eat. *(Rose proudly leads Lusia to the laden dinette table. Lusia shrinks back, overwhelmed.)*

LUSIA. Too much food! So much. No, too much, I think.

ROSE. You must eat, Lusia. You've got to eat enough. And there's plenty, really, *(Piling food on Lusia's plate.)* I know you're the big sister, but you've got to let me take care of you, for now. Then, when everything's normal again, you'll be the big sister. *(Rose pours a glass of milk. Lusia sips at it, picks at the food. As they continue talking, they remain contrasted in manner. Lusia is still, Rose animated, using her hands a lot.)*

LUSIA. Funny, big sister, baby sister. I have baby sister one time, long time. . .

ROSE. Ago.

LUSIA. Long time ago. So beautiful I think, and I take for walk in. . .

ROSE. Carriage?

LUSIA. Carriage, yes, I take for walk and show to friends mine baby shvester. Make me feel good. Happy. Then gone. And many years no sister but picture from America and letter from Papa and lady who takes care of.

ROSE. Mrs. Greenspan. Tanta Perla.

LUSIA. Yes. And then no more letter. No more sister. *(Voice.)* And carriage stays empty for too much years . . . And baby shvester woman now who want take care me.

ROSE. I don't remember at all. I wish I did.

LUSIA. You don't remember even Mama? *(Rose shakes her head.)* Nothing?

ROSE. I was only four when we left. It's so strange that you have memories of me, that I was part of your life. That I was born in another world. I don't remember any of it. Just a feeling, maybe. Sometimes there's a particular smell when something's cooking or a song comes on the radio and all of a sudden I feel different, like I'm in another place.

LUSIA. How you feel then?

ROSE. Warm. Safe. Sad.

LUSIA. Mama, that is. The feeling from Mama. *(Rose and Lusia look at one another silently across the table, each mirror to the other for a moment.)*

508 Unit Eight Monologues and Scenes

ROSE. Eat some more, Lusia. You're not eating enough. *(Pause while Lusia picks at food.)* Lusia, have you wondered about it, thought why you got sick and not me?

LUSIA. Mama says was plan from God. But she keeps hold our passage, our tickets, till could not read no more. Till thin like old leaf. Till long time after no good, no one . . . they no loz no one . . . no one . . . *(She is frustrated, trying to find the English word.)*

ROSE. Allowed.

LUSIA. Allowed leave Poland no more.

ROSE. And I was playing stickball and going to the movies and eating Mello-Rolls!

LUSIA. What means this?

ROSE. Oh, it doesn't matter. *(She pushes away from the table, gets up.)* He should have gotten you out!

LUSIA. Mama told how whole America changes mind, wants no new Jewish, no new people no more. All fast like this *(Snaps her fingers.)* something happens no one got money. From streets with gold to nothing. And everyone, not just mine father.

ROSE. That was the Depression. It kept you away, but it didn't make any difference in my life. I remember having bad dreams when I was little, but I don't know what about. Everything else stayed the same; the food, the stories on the radio and Tanta Perla, like a bird chirping around me trying to give comfort after the bad dreams. But she never could.

LUSIA. De varemsteh bet iz de mamas. Farshtaist?

ROSE. Yeah, but how could I tell? Mama wasn't real to me. They'd never say her name, or yours. They called you "Them," talking in whispers or in certain looks so I could just pick up little bits of what was going on. And when I was older and could have understood, I knew it was forbidden, Papa wouldn't talk. Not about you, not about Mama. He would just say he was working it out or, later, that Roosevelt would take care of everyone over there. I tried to make myself a family out of the photographs and letters, but they were in Yiddish and I only learned to read English. Tanta Perla used to read them to me and translate. Papa never would. Then, when there were no more letters, I began to forget completely. By the time the war came, it was as if there had been no one there at all. . . until Papa found you. I still don't know exactly how to feel. I mean, I've had it pretty easy and you—

LUSIA. Mine father don't know I'm here yet?

Scenes **509**

ROSE. He'll be in shul all day. We can call him tonight or even go out there.

LUSIA. No. Tuesday I suppose to come on boat.

ROSE. Papa was going to come with me to meet you. He'll be mad if we don't let him know you're here.

LUSIA. This I remember good about Papa. He gets so mad. He makes a big voice, everybody is . . . *(She shakes.)*

ROSE. Nervous.

LUSIA. Nervous.

ROSE. In that way, he hasn't changed.

LUSIA. I remember him. Papa was a man very . . . pretty?

ROSE. Handsome? Papa?

LUSIA. Handsome. And I know from pictures, too. But everything must be certain way or he is so mad. And very . . . *(She gestures.)*

ROSE. Strict.

LUSIA. Strict. But very proud when we all dress up. You, too. And Mama. Family all go out together. I see his face and I'm thinking how happy he is, how proud. He don't say nothing, but I can see. You know this face?

ROSE. I've never seen that look. *(Pause.)* We'll have to call him tomorrow.

Jar the Floor

by Cheryl L. West

Vennie and her friend Raisa have come to visit Vennie's mother MayDee and her grandmother MaDear, although the mother and daughter have long been at odds. Vennie and Maydee can't seem to avoid arguing.

MAYDEE. I find it so astounding that you never fail to make sure everything careens out of control every time you come home.

VENNIE. So this is all my fault?

MAYDEE. Who said anything about fault? Let's just table this. I want MaDear to have a good day. We have plenty of time to discuss this later. How long are you two planning to stay?

VENNIE. You started it.

MAYDEE. Started what? What did I start this time? All I asked you was how long you plan to stay. How is that an invitation for conflict?

VENNIE. Mother please! It's what you start every time I come home . . .

MAYDEE. I have not started one thing today . . . all I asked . . .

VENNIE. You and your little ice pick . . . soon's you see me, you go to town. Pick, pick, pick. My clothes ain't right, pick, my hair ain't right, pick,

510 **Unit Eight** Monologues and Scenes

pick, my grammar ain't right. . .triple pick. . . sum it up, I ain't right. . .

MAYDEE. Whine . . . whine . . . whine . . . grow up, Vennie.

VENNIE. I would if you'd let me.

MAYDEE. That's not true.

VENNIE. *(Sarcastically, but delivered calmly with a smile.)* Oh, let's get real. Y'all have performed for the company so let's take it on down to Front Street. See Raisa, I'm something to be bought for, organized and then laid out so others can marvel at how wonderful MayDee Lakeland is . . . how she overcame every obstacle to get her three degrees in one hand and raise me single-handedly in the other. . . and what's that commercial. . . never let 'em see you sweat. Well that's MayDee Lakeland . . . you'll never see her sweat, queen of control . . . that's what we all love about her . . . *(Feigned innocence, as if the thought just occurred to her.)* Um, do we have an itinerary this weekend, Mother? I was telling Raisa that you always made sure I participated in every activity: karate, dance, art, gymnastics. So did the secretary remember to outline Vennie's activities, you know in those fifteen minute increments. . . what Mother-dear is going to do with daughter-dear this weekend. *(MayDee quietly disposes of the itinerary.)* Oh come on now, you didn't leave our time together to chance. 'Cause then maybe you would have to enjoy me. And that would be too much like right, wouldn't it Mother? S'pecially given that you don't even like me.

MAYDEE. *(Pausing, embarrassed to have this conversation in front of Raisa, MayDee laughs.)* You're just like your grandmother, such a wicked sense of humor. I love you, Vennie. All I ever wanted was to protect you. Don't you know how much I love you, whatever you do?

VENNIE. What I know is being your daughter hurts . . . bad, or should I say badly. . .

MAYDEE. You can't mean that. *(Exits with hair stuff.)*

Macbeth

by William Shakespeare

After helping her husband kill King Duncan, Lady Macbeth is obsessed with her terrible deed. In this sleepwalking scene, her gentlewoman asks the doctor to observe and diagnose the problem.

GENTLEWOMAN. Lo you, here she comes! This is her very guise, and upon my life, fast asleep. Observe her. Stand close.

DOCTOR. How came she by that light?

Scenes 511

GENTLEWOMAN. Why, it stood by her. She has light by her continually, 'tis her command.

DOCTOR. You see, her eyes are open.

GENTLEWOMAN. Aye, but their sense is shut.

DOCTOR. What is it she does now? Look how she rubs her hands.

GENTLEWOMAN. It is an accustomed action with her to seem thus washing her hands. I have known her continue in this a quarter of an hour.

LADY MACBETH. Yet, here's a spot.

DOCTOR. Hark! She speaks. I will set down what comes from her, to satisfy my remembrance the more strongly.

LADY MACBETH. Out, damned spot! Out I say! One, two—why, then 'tis time to do 't. Hell is murky. Fie, my lord, fie! A soldier, and afeard? What need we fear who knows it, when none can call our power to account? Yet who would have thought the old man to have had so much blood in him?

DOCTOR. Do you mark that?

LADY MACBETH. The Thane of Fife had a wife. Where is she now? What, will these hands ne'er be clean? No more o' that, my lord, no more o' that. You mar all with this starting.

DOCTOR. Go to, go to. You have known what you should not.

GENTLEWOMAN. She has spoke what she should not, I am sure of that. Heaven knows what she has known.

LADY MACBETH. Here's the smell of the blood still. All the perfumes of Arabia will not sweeten this little hand. Oh, oh, oh!

DOCTOR. What a sigh is there! The heart is sorely charged.

GENTLEWOMAN. I would not have such a heart in my bosom for the dignity of the whole body.

DOCTOR. Well, well, well—

GENTLEWOMAN. Pray God it be, sir.

DOCTOR. This disease is beyond my practice. Yet I have known those which have walked in their sleep who have died holily in their beds.

LADY MACBETH. Wash your hands, put on your nightgown, look not so pale. I tell you yet again, Banquo's buried, he cannot come out on's grave.

DOCTOR. Even so?

LADY MACBETH. To bed, to bed, there's knocking at the gate. Come, come, come, come, give me your hand. What's done cannot be undone. To bed, to bed, to bed. *(Exit.)*

512 Unit Eight Monologues and Scenes

Blithe Spirit

by Noel Coward

After holding a seance for research on his book, Charles finds that the spirit of his dead wife, Elvira, has appeared. Since only Charles (and the audience) can see her, his present wife, Ruth, thinks he is crazy. In trying to convince Ruth that the spirit of Elvira is indeed present, the following humorous scene ensues.

(Elvira enters by the windows, carrying a bunch of grey roses. She crosses to the writing-table up stage R., and throws the zinnias into the wastepaper basket and puts her roses into the vase. The roses are as grey as the rest of her.)

ELVIRA. You've absolutely ruined that border by the sundial. It looks like a mixed salad.

CHARLES. Oh, my God!

RUTH. What's the matter now?

CHARLES. She's here again!

RUTH. What do you mean? Who's here again?

CHARLES. Elvira.

RUTH. Pull yourself together and don't be absurd.

ELVIRA. It's all those nasturtiums; they're so vulgar.

CHARLES. I like nasturtiums.

RUTH. You like what?

ELVIRA. *(Putting her grey roses into the vase.)* They're all right in moderation, but in a mass like that they look beastly.

RUTH. *(Crosses over to R. of Charles, C.)* What did you mean about nasturtiums?

CHARLES. *(Takes Ruth's hands and comes round to the L. of her.)* Never mind about that now. I tell you she's here again.

ELVIRA. *(Comes to above the sofa.)* You have been having a nice scene, haven't you? I could hear you right down the garden.

CHARLES. Please mind your own business.

RUTH. If you behaving like a lunatic isn't my business, nothing is.

ELVIRA. I expect it was about me, wasn't it? I know I ought to feel sorry, but I'm not. I'm delighted.

CHARLES. Ruth—darling—please. . .

RUTH. I've done everything I can to help. I've controlled myself admirably. And I should like to say here and now that I don't believe a word about your damned hallucination. You're up to something, Charles—there's been a certain furtiveness in your manner for weeks. Why don't you be honest and tell me what it is?

Scenes 513

CHARLES. You're wrong—you're dead wrong! I haven't been in the least furtive—I—

RUTH. You're trying to upset me. *(She moves away from Charles.)* For some obscure reason you're trying to goad me into doing something that I might regret. *(She bursts into tears.)* I won't stand for it any more. You're making me utterly miserable! *(She crosses to the sofa and falls into the R. end of it.)*

CHARLES. *(Crosses to Ruth.)* Ruth—please—

RUTH. Don't come near me!

ELVIRA. Let her have a nice cry. It'll do her good. *(She saunters round to down stage L.)*

CHARLES. You're utterly heartless!

RUTH. Heartless!

CHARLES. *(Wildly.)* I was not talking to you! I was talking to Elvira.

RUTH. Go on talking to her then, talk to her until you're blue in the face, but don't talk to me.

CHARLES. *(Crosses to Elvira.)* Help me, Elvira—

ELVIRA. How?

CHARLES. Make her see you or something.

ELVIRA. I'm afraid I couldn't manage that. It's technically the most difficult business—frightfully complicated, you know—it takes years of study—

CHARLES. You are here, aren't you? You're not an illusion?

ELVIRA. I may be an illusion, but I'm most definitely here.

CHARLES. How did you get here?

ELVIRA. I told you last night—I don't exactly know—

CHARLES. Well, you must make me a promise that in future you only come and talk to me when I'm alone.

ELVIRA. *(Pouting.)* How unkind you are, making me feel so unwanted. I've never been treated so rudely.

CHARLES. I don't mean to be rude, but you must see—

ELVIRA. It's all your own fault for having married a woman who is incapable of seeing beyond the nose on her face. If she had a grain of real sympathy or affection for you she'd believe what you tell her.

CHARLES. How could you expect anybody to believe this?

ELVIRA. You'd be surprised how gullible people are; we often laugh about it on the Other Side.

514 Unit Eight Monologues and Scenes

(Ruth, who has stopped crying and been staring at Charles in horror, suddenly rises.)

RUTH. *(Gently.)* Charles!

CHARLES. *(Surprised at her tone.)* Yes, dear—*(Charles crosses to her, R.)*

RUTH. I'm awfully sorry I was cross.

CHARLES. But, my dear—

RUTH. I understand everything now. I do really.

CHARLES. You do?

RUTH. *(Patting his arm reassuringly.)* Of course I do.

ELVIRA. Look out—she's up to something.

CHARLES. Will you please be quiet?

RUTH. Of course, darling. We'll all be quiet, won't we? We'll be as quiet as little mice.

CHARLES. Ruth dear, listen—

RUTH. I want you to come upstairs with me and go to bed.

ELVIRA. The way that woman harps on bed is nothing short of erotic.

CHARLES. I'll deal with you later.

RUTH. Very well, darling—come along.

CHARLES. What are you up to?

RUTH. I'm not up to anything. I just want you to go quietly to bed and wait there until Doctor Bradman comes.

CHARLES. No, Ruth, you're wrong—

RUTH. *(Firmly.)* Come, dear—

ELVIRA. She'll have you in a strait-jacket before you know where you are.

CHARLES. *(Comes to Elvira—frantically.)* Help me—you must help me—

ELVIRA. *(Enjoying herself.)* My dear, I would with pleasure, but I can't think how.

CHARLES. I can. *(Back to Ruth.)* Listen, Ruth—

RUTH. Yes, dear?

CHARLES. If I promise to go to bed, will you let me stay here for five minutes longer?

RUTH. I really think it would be better—

CHARLES. Bear with me, however mad it may seem, bear with me for just five minutes longer.

RUTH. *(Leaving go of him.)* Very well. What is it?

CHARLES. Sit down.

RUTH. *(Sitting down.)* All right. There!

Scenes **515**

CHARLES. Now listen, listen carefully—

ELVIRA. Have a cigarette; it will soothe your nerves.

CHARLES. I don't want a cigarette.

RUTH. *(Indulgently.)* Then you shan't have one, darling.

CHARLES. Ruth, I want to explain to you clearly and without emotion that beyond any shadow of doubt, the ghost or shade or whatever you like to call it of my first wife Elvira is in this room now.

RUTH. Yes, dear.

CHARLES. I know you don't believe it and are trying valiantly to humor me, but I intend to prove it to you.

RUTH. Why not lie down and have a nice rest and you can prove anything you want to later on?

CHARLES. She may not be here later on.

ELVIRA. Don't worry—she will!

CHARLES. Oh God!

RUTH. Hush, dear.

CHARLES. *(To Elvira.)* Promise you'll do what I ask?

ELVIRA. That all depends what it is.

CHARLES. *(Between them both, facing upstage.)* Ruth—you see that bowl of flowers on the piano?

RUTH. Yes, dear, I did it myself this morning.

ELVIRA. Very untidily, if I may say so.

CHARLES. You may not.

RUTH. Very well—I never will again. I promise.

CHARLES. Elvira will now carry that bowl of flowers to the mantelpiece and back again. You will, Elvira, won't you? Just to please me.

ELVIRA. I don't really see why I should. You've been quite insufferable to me ever since I materialized.

CHARLES. Please!

ELVIRA. *(Goes over to the piano.)* All right, I will just this once. Not that I approve of all these Maskelyne and Devant carryings-on.

CHARLES. *(Crosses to the mantelpiece.)* Now, Ruth—watch carefully!

RUTH. *(Patiently.)* Very well, dear.

CHARLES. Go on, Elvira—take it to the mantelpiece and back again.

(Elvira takes a bowl of pansies off the piano and brings it slowly down stage, below the armchair to the fire; then suddenly pushes towards Ruth's face, who jumps up and faces Charles, who is at the mantel piece.)

516 **Unit Eight** Monologues and Scenes

RUTH. *(Furiously.)* How dare you, Charles! You ought to be ashamed of yourself.

CHARLES. What on earth for?

RUTH. *(Hysterically.)* It's a trick. I know perfectly well it's a trick. You've been working up to this. It's all part of some horrible plan. . .

CHARLES. It isn't—I swear it isn't. Elvira—do something else, for God's sake!

ELVIRA. Certainly—anything to oblige.

RUTH. *(Becoming really frightened.)* You want to get rid of me—you're trying to drive me out of my mind—

CHARLES. Don't be so silly.

RUTH. You're cruel and sadistic and I'll never forgive you.

(Elvira picks up the chair from down stage L., holds it in midair as if to hit Ruth, Ruth flinches, then Elvira puts it back, and stands above the windows. Ruth makes a dive for the door, moving between the armchair and sofa. Charles follows and catches her.)

I'm not going to put up with this any more.

CHARLES. *(Holding her.)* You must believe it—you must—

RUTH. Let me go immediately.

CHARLES. That was Elvira—I swear it was.

RUTH. *(Struggling.)* Let me go.

CHARLES. Ruth—please—

(Ruth breaks away to the windows. Elvira shuts them in her face and crosses quickly to the mantelpiece. Ruth turns at the windows to face Charles.)

RUTH. *(Looking at Charles with eyes of horror.)* Charles—this is madness—sheer madness—it's some sort of auto-suggestion, isn't it?—Some form of hypnotism, swear to me it's only that—*(She rushes to Charles, C.)* Swear to me it's only that.

ELVIRA. *(Taking an expensive vase from the mantelpiece and crashing it into the grate.)* Hypnotism my foot!

The Dining Room

by A.R. Gurney, Jr.

This scene is of a family celebrating a holiday at their homestead. They are confronted by the fact that their elderly mother is living in the past.

NANCY. I've got the plates, Mrs. Driscoll. You've got your hands full with that turkey. *(She sets the plates and carving utensils at the head of the table and calls toward the hall.)* (1) We're ready, everybody! Come on in! *(The singing continues as the family*

(1) What holiday is this family celebrating? Where has the family gathered?

Scenes **517**

(2) Why is Stuart escorting his mother to the dining room and not her other sons?

(3) Why is the Old Lady confused? How old do you think she is? How can you physically show old age without using cliché movements?

(4) What words give clues about how the Old Lady was raised and the economic condition of her family?

(5) How does the Old Lady sound? Is she teasing, or does she really not know her children?

(6) Who are Beth and Nancy? Are they children or daughters-in-law? Which one do you think is married to Stuart?

begins to come into the dining room to celebrate Thanksgiving dinner. The oldest son, Stuart, has his mother on his arm. She is a very vague, very old Old Lady.) (2)

STUART. . . . Now, Mother, I want you to sit next to me, and Fred, you sit on Mother's left, and Ben, you sit opposite her where she can see you, and Nancy and Beth hold up that end of the table, and there we are. *(Genial chatter as everyone sits down. The two sons push in their mother's chair. After a moment the Old Lady stands up again, looks around distractedly.)* (3) What's the matter, Mother?

OLD LADY. I'm not quite sure where I am.

STUART. *(Expansively; arm around her; seating her again.)* You're here, Mother. In your own dining room. This is your table, and here are your chairs, and here is the china you got on your trip to England, and here's the silver-handled carving knife which Father used to use. (4)

OLD LADY. Oh yes. . . *(Genial laughter, ad-libbing: "She's a tired. . . It's been a long day..." The Old Lady gets up again.)* But who are these people? I'm not quite sure who these people are. *(She begins to wander around the room.)* (5)

STUART. *(Following her around.)* It's me, Mother: Stuart. Your son. And here's Fred, and Ben, and Nancy, and Beth. We're all here, Mother. (6)

NANCY. *(Going into the kitchen.)* I'll get the turkey. That might help her focus.

STUART. Yes. *(To Old Lady.)* Mrs. Driscoll is here, Mother. Right in the kitchen, where she's always been. And your grandchildren. All your grandchildren were here. Don't you remember? They ate first, at the children's table, and now they're out in back playing touch football. You watched them, Mother. *(He indicates the French doors.)*

OLD LADY. Oh yes. . . *(She sits down again at the other end of the table. Nancy comes out from the kitchen carrying a large platter. Appropriate Oh's and Ah's from Group.)*

STUART. And look, Mother. Here's Nancy with the turkey. . . Put it right over there, Nancy. . . See, Mother? Isn't it a beautiful bird? And I'm going to carve it just the way Father did, and give you a small piece of the breast and a dab of dressing, just as always, Mother. *(He sharpens the carving knife officiously.)* (7)

OLD LADY. *(Still staring out into the garden.)* Just as always. . .

STUART. *(As he sharpens.)* And Fred will have the drumstick—am I right, Fred?—And Beth gets the wishbone, and Ben ends up with the Pope's nose, am I right, Ben? *(Genial in-group laughter.)*

518 Unit Eight Monologues and Scenes

NANCY. Save some for Mrs. Driscoll.

STUART. I always do, Nancy. Mrs. Driscoll likes the second joint.

OLD LADY. This is all very nice, but I think I'd like to go home.

STUART. *(Patiently, as he carves.)* You are home, Mother. You've lived here fifty-two years.

BEN. Fifty-four.

BETH. Forever.

STUART. Ben, pass this plate down to Mother . . .

OLD LADY. *(Getting up.)* Thank you very much, but I really do think it's time to go.

NANCY. Uh-oh.

STUART. *(Going to her.)* Mother . . .

BETH. Oh dear.

OLD LADY. Will someone drive me home, please? I live at eighteen Summer Street with my mother and sisters.

BETH. What will we do?

STUART. *(Going to Old Lady.)* It's not there now, Mother. Don't you remember? We drove down. There's a big building there now.

OLD LADY. *(Holding out her hand.)* Thank you very much for asking me . . . Thank you for having me to your house. *(She begins to go around the table, thanking people.)*

FRED. Mother! I'm Fred! Your son!

OLD LADY. Isn't that nice? Thank you. I've had a perfectly lovely time. . . Thank you. . . Thank you so much. *(She shakes hands with Nancy.)* It's been absolutely lovely. . . Thank you, thank you. (8)

STUART. Quickly. Let's sing to her.

BETH. Sing?

STUART. She likes singing. We (9) used to sing to her whenever she'd get upset. . . Fred, Ben. Quickly. Over here.

OLD LADY. *(Wandering distractedly around.)* Now I can't find my gloves. Where would my gloves be? I can't go out without my gloves.

BEN. What song? I can't remember any of the songs.

STUART. Sure you can. Come on. Hmmmmmmmmm. *(He sounds a note. The others try to find their parts.)*

BEN & FRED. Hmmmmm.

OLD LADY. I need my gloves, I need my hat. . .

STUART. *(Singing.)* "As the blackbird in the spring. . .

OTHERS. *(Joining in.)* 'Neath the willow tree. . .

(7) What does his sharpening the knife "officiously" tell you about Stuart's personality? How do you physically show being officious while carving the turkey?

(8) How would the Old Lady speak and gesture while saying these words?

(9) To try to distract their mother, the children are eager to start singing. A sense of urgency (and a faster pace) must be accomplished.

(10) Look up the music to "Aura Lee." It was once a popular song, and it is easy to sing and fun to harmonize. You can find the song in a book that features songs from the past.

(11) Notice how the words *carriage* and *tea* (a special meal) place the Old Lady in the past. When would that be?

(12) Both Fred and Ben must communicate their willingness to help their older brother appease their mother. What do you think will happen when they show her that her old house is no longer there?

Sat and piped, I hear him sing,
Sing of Aura Lee . . ." (10)
(They sing in pleasant, amateurish, corny harmony. The Old Lady stops fussing, turns her head, and listens. The other women remain at the table.)

MEN. *(Singing.)* "Aura Lee, Aura Lee,
Maid of Golden Hair . . .
Sunshine came along with thee, and swallows in the air."

OLD LADY. I love music. Every person in our family could play a different instrument. *(She sits in a chair along the wall, Down Right.)*

STUART. *(To his brothers.)* She's coming around. Quickly. Second verse.

MEN. *(Singing with more confidence now; more daring harmony.)*
"In thy blush the rose was born,
Music, when you spake,
Through thine azure eye the morn
Sparkling seemed to break.
Aura Lee, Aura Lee, Maid of Golden
Hair,
Sunshine came along with thee, and
swallows in the air."
(They hold a long note at the end. The Old Lady claps. Everyone claps.)

OLD LADY. That was absolutely lovely.

STUART. Thank you, Mother.

OLD LADY. But now I've simply got to go home. Would you call my carriage, please? And someone find my hat and gloves. It's very late, and my mother gets very nervous if I'm not home in time for tea. *(She heads for the hall.)* (11)

STUART. *(To no one in particular.)* Look, Fred, Ben, we'll drive her down, and show her everything. The new office complex where her house was. The entrance to the Thruway. The new Howard Johnson's motel. Everything! And she'll see that nothing's there at all.

FRED. I'll bring the car around.

STUART. I'll get her coat.

BEN. I'm coming, too. (12)

STUART. We'll just have to go through the motions.

A Raisin in the Sun

by Lorraine Hansberry

Walter and his wife Ruth and sister Beneatha all live with Walter and Beneatha's mother in a cramped apartment in a black neighborhood in a large city. Because some money has come into the family, their mother has put a down payment on a house in a white section of town. Mr. Lindner comes to talk to them about "problems" he foresees in their move.

LINDNER. How do you do.

520 Unit Eight Monologues and Scenes

WALTER. *(Amiably, as he sits himself easily on a chair, leaning with interest forward on his knees and looking expectantly into the newcomer's face.)* What can we do for you, Mr. Lindner!

LINDNER. *(Some minor shuffling of the hat and briefcase on his knees.)* Well—I am a representative of the Clybourne Park Improvement Association—

WALTER. *(Pointing.)* Why don't you sit your things on the floor?

LINDNER. Oh—yes. Thank you. *(He slides the briefcase and hat under the chair.)* And as I was saying—I am from the Clybourne Park Improvement Association and we have had it brought to our attention at the last meeting that you people—or at least your mother—has bought a piece of residential property at—*(He digs for the slip of paper again.)*—four o six Clybourne Street.

WALTER. That's right. Care for something to drink? Ruth, get Mr. Lindner a beer.

LINDNER. *(Upset for some reason.)* Oh—no, really. I mean thank you very much, but no thank you.

RUTH. *(Innocently.)* Some coffee?

LINDNER. Thank you, nothing at all.

(Beneatha is watching the man carefully.)

LINDNER. Well, I don't know how much you folks know about our organization. *(He is a gentle man; thoughtful and somewhat labored in his manner.)* It is one of these community organizations set up to look after—oh, you know, things like block upkeep and special projects and we also have what we call our New Neighbors Orientation Committee. . .

BENEATHA. *(Drily.)* Yes—and what do they do?

LINDNER. *(Turning a little to her and then returning the main force to Walter.)* Well—it's what you might call a sort of welcoming committee, I guess. I mean they, we, I'm the chairman of the committee—go around and see the new people who move into the neighborhood and sort of give them the lowdown on the way we do things out in Clybourne Park.

BENEATHA. *(With appreciation of the two meanings, which escape Ruth and Walter.)* Un-huh.

LINDNER. And we also have the category of what the association calls—*(He looks elsewhere.)*—uh—special community problems. . .

BENEATHA. Yes—and what are some of those?

WALTER. Girl, let the man talk.

Scenes **521**

LINDNER. *(With understated relief.)* Thank you. I would sort of like to explain this thing in my own way. I mean I want to explain to you in a certain way.

WALTER. Go ahead.

LINDNER. Yes. Well. I'm going to try to get right to the point. I'm sure we'll all appreciate that in the long run.

BENEATHA. Yes.

WALTER. Be still now!

LINDNER. Well—

RUTH. *(Still innocently.)* Would you like another chair—you don't look comfortable.

LINDNER. *(More frustrated than annoyed.)* No, thank you very much. Please. Well—to get right to the point I—*(A great breath, and he is off at last.)* I am sure you people must be aware of some of the incidents which have happened in various parts of the city when colored people have moved into certain areas—*(Beneatha exhales heavily and starts tossing a piece of fruit up and down in the air.)* Well—because we have what I think is going to be a unique type of organization in American community life—not only do we deplore that kind of thing—but we are trying to do something about it. *(Beneatha stops tossing and turns with a new and quizzical interest to the man.)* We feel—*(Gaining confidence in his mission because of the interest in the faces of the people he is talking to.)*—we feel that most of the trouble in this world, when you come right down to it—*(He hits his knee for emphasis.)*—most of the trouble exists because people just don't sit down and talk to each other.

RUTH. *(Nodding as she might in church, pleased with the remark.)* You can say that again, mister.

LINDNER. *(More encouraged by such affirmation.)* That we don't try hard enough in this world to understand the other fellow's problem. The other guy's point of view.

RUTH. Now that's right.

(Beneatha and Walter merely watch and listen with genuine interest.)

LINDNER. Yes—that's the way we feel out in Clybourne Park. And that's why I was elected to come here this afternoon and talk to you people. Friendly like, you know, the way people should talk to each other and see if we couldn't find some way to work this thing out. As I say, the whole business is a matter of *caring* about the other fellow. Anybody can see that you are a nice family of folks, hardworking and honest I'm sure. *(Beneatha frowns slightly, quizzically, her head tilted regarding him.)* Today everybody knows what it means to be

522 **Unit Eight** Monologues and Scenes

on the outside of *something*. And of course, there is always somebody who is out to take advantage of people who don't always understand.

WALTER. What do you mean?

LINDNER. Well—you see our community is made up of people who've worked hard as the dickens for years to build up that little community. They're not rich and fancy people; just hard-working, honest people who don't really have much but those little homes and a dream of the kind of community they want to raise their children in. Now, I don't say we are perfect and there is a lot wrong in some of the things they want. But you've got to admit that a man, right or wrong, has the right to want to have the neighborhood he lives in a certain kind of way. And at the moment the overwhelming majority of our people out there feel that people get along better, take more of a common interest in the life of the community, when they share a common background. I want you to believe me when I tell you that race prejudice simply doesn't enter into it. It is a matter of the people of Clybourne Park believing, rightly or wrongly, as I say, that for the happiness of all concerned that our Negro families are happier when they live in their *own* communities.

BENEATHA. *(With a grand and bitter gesture.)* This, friends, is the Welcoming Committee!

WALTER. *(Dumbfounded, looking at Lindner.)* Is this what you came marching all the way over here to tell us?

LINDNER. Well, now we've been having a fine conversation. I hope you'll hear me all the way through.

WALTER. *(Tightly.)* Go ahead, man.

LINDNER. You see—in the face of all things I have said, we are prepared to make your family a very generous offer. . .

BENEATHA. Thirty pieces and not a coin less!

WALTER. Yeah?

LINDNER. *(Putting on his glasses and drawing a form out of the briefcase.)* Our association is prepared, through the collective effort of our people, to buy the house from you at a financial gain to your family.

RUTH. Lord have mercy, ain't this the living gall!

WALTER. All right, you through?

LINDNER. Well, I want to give you the exact terms of the financial arrangement—

WALTER. We don't want to hear no exact terms of no arrangements. I want to know if you got any more to tell us 'bout getting together?

LINDNER. *(Taking off his glasses.)* Well—I don't suppose that you feel. . .

Scenes **523**

WALTER. Never mind how I feel—you got any more to say 'bout how people ought to sit down and talk to each other?. . . Get out of my house, man.

(He turns his back and walks to the door.)

LINDNER. *(Looking around at the hostile faces and reaching and assembling his hat and briefcase.)* Well—I don't understand why you people are reacting this way. What do you think you are going to gain by moving into a neighborhood where you just aren't wanted and where some elements—well—people can get awful worked up when they feel that their whole way of life and everything they've ever worked for is threatened.

WALTER. Get out.

LINDNER. *(At the door, holding a small card.)* Well—I'm sorry it went like this.

WALTER. Get out.

LINDNER. *(Almost sadly regarding Walter.)* You just can't force people to change their hearts, son.

(He turns and puts his card on a table and exits. Walter pushes the door to with stinging hatred, and stands looking at it. Ruth just sits and Beneatha just stands. They say nothing. Mama and Travis enter.)

MAMA. Well—this all the packing got done since I left out of here this morning. I testify before God that my children got all the energy of the dead. What time the moving men due?

BENEATHA. Four o'clock. You had a caller, Mama.

(She is smiling, teasingly.)

MAMA. Sure enough—who?

BENEATHA. *(Her arms folded saucily.)* The Welcoming Committee.

(Walter and Ruth giggle.)

MAMA. *(Innocently.)* Who?

BENEATHA. The Welcoming Committee. They said they're sure going to be glad to see you when you get there.

WALTER. *(Devilishly.)* Yeah, they said they can't hardly wait to see your face.

(Laughter.)

MAMA. *(Sensing their facetiousness.)* What's the matter with you all?

WALTER. Ain't nothing the matter with us. We just telling you 'bout the gentleman who came to see you this afternoon. From the Clybourne Park Improvement Association.

MAMA. What he want?

RUTH. *(In the same mood as Beneatha and Walter.)* To welcome you, honey.

524 **Unit Eight** Monologues and Scenes

WALTER. He said they can't hardly wait. He said the one thing they don't have, that they just dying to have out there is a fine family of colored people! *(To Ruth and Beneatha.)* Ain't that right!

RUTH and BENEATHA. *(Mockingly.)* Yeah! He left his card in case—

(They indicate the card, and Mama picks it up and throws it on the floor—understanding and looking off as she draws her chair up to the table on which she has put her plant and some sticks and some cord.)

MAMA. Father, give us strength. *(Knowingly—and without fun.)* Did he threaten us?

BENEATHA. Oh—Mama—they don't do it like that any more. He talked Brotherhood. He said everybody ought learn how to sit down and hate each other with good Christian fellowship.

(She and Walter shake hands to ridicule the remark.)

MAMA. *(Sadly.)* Lord, protect us . . .

The Actor's Nightmare

by Christopher Durang

To his utter dismay, George finds himself onstage with a role in a play he does not know. In this scene, the famous actress Sarah Siddons is playing the female lead in a play very much like one by Noel Coward. She is in a glamorous evening gown, and she is holding a cocktail glass. After a moment, George arrives onstage, fairly pushed on. He is dressed as Hamlet—black leotard and large gold medallion around his neck. As soon as he enters, several flash photos are taken, which disorient him greatly. When he can, he looks out and sees the audience and is very taken aback. We hear music.)

SARAH. Extraordinary how potent cheap music is.

GEORGE. What?

SARAH. Extraordinary how potent cheap music is.

GEORGE. Yes, that's true. Am I supposed to be Hamlet?

SARAH. *(alarmed; then going on).* Whose yacht do you think that is?

GEORGE. Where?

SARAH. The Duke of Westminster, I expect. It always is.

GEORGE. Ah, well, perhaps. To be or not to be. I don't know any more of it. *(She looks irritated at him; then she coughs three times. He remembers and unzips her dress; she slaps him.)*

SARAH. Elyot, please. We are on our honeymoons.

GEORGE. Are we?

Scenes **525**

SARAH. Yes. *(Irritated, being over-explicit)* Me with Victor, and you with Sibyl.

GEORGE. Ah.

SARAH. Tell me about Sibyl.

GEORGE. I've never met her.

SARAH. Ah, Elyot, you're so amusing. You're married to Sibyl. Tell me about her.

GEORGE. Nothing much to tell really. She's sort of nondescript, I'd say.

SARAH. I bet you were going to say that she's just like Lady Bundle, and that she has several chins, and one blue eye and one brown eye, and a third eye in the center of her forehead. Weren't you?

GEORGE. Yes. I think so.

SARAH. Victor's like that too. *(Long pause)* I bet you were just about to tell me that you travelled around the world.

GEORGE. Yes I was. I travelled around the world.

SARAH. How was it?

GEORGE. The world?

SARAH. Yes.

GEORGE. Oh, very nice.

SARAH. I always feared the Taj Mahal would look like a biscuit box. Did it?

GEORGE. Not really.

SARAH. *(She's going to give him the cue again.)* I always feared the Taj Mahal would look like a biscuit box. Did it?

GEORGE. I guess it did.

SARAH. *(Again)*. I always feared the Taj Mahal would look like a biscuit box. Did it?

GEORGE. Hard to say. What brand biscuit box?

SARAH. I always feared the Taj Mahal would look like a biscuit box. Did it? *(Pause)* Did it? Did it?

GEORGE. I wonder whose yacht that is out there.

SARAH. Did it? Did it? Did it? Did it? *(Enter Meg. She's put on an apron and maid's hat and carries a duster, but is otherwise still in her stage manager's garb.)*

MEG. My, this balcony looks dusty. I think I'll just clean it up a little. *(Dusts and goes to George and whispers in his ear; exits)*

GEORGE. Not only did the Taj Mahal look like a biscuit box, but women should be struck regularly like gongs. *(Applause)*

SARAH. Extraordinary how potent cheap music is.

GEORGE. Yes. Quite extraordinary.

526 Unit Eight Monologues and Scenes

SARAH. How was China?

GEORGE. China?

SARAH. You travelled around the world. How was China?

GEORGE. I liked it, but I felt homesick.

SARAH. *(Again this is happening; gives him cue again.)* How was China?

GEORGE. Lots of rice. The women bind their feet.

SARAH. How was China?

GEORGE. I hated it. I missed you.

SARAH. How was China?

GEORGE. I hated it. I missed... Sibyl.

SARAH. How was China?

GEORGE. I... miss the maid. Oh, maid!

SARAH. How was China?

GEORGE. Just wait a moment please. Oh, maid! *(Enter Meg)* Ah, there you are. I think you missed a spot here. *(She crosses, dusts, and whispers in his ear; exits.)*

SARAH. How was China?

GEORGE. (*With authority.*) Very large, China.

SARAH. And Japan?

GEORGE. *(Doesn't know, but makes a guess.)* Very... small, Japan.

SARAH. And Ireland?

GEORGE. Very... green.

SARAH. And Iceland?

GEORGE. Very white.

SARAH. And Italy?

GEORGE. Very... Neapolitan.

SARAH. And Copenhagen?

GEORGE. Very... cosmopolitan.

SARAH. And Florida?

GEORGE. Very... condominium.

SARAH. And Perth Amboy?

GEORGE. Very... mobile home, I don't know.

SARAH. And Sibyl?

GEORGE. What?

SARAH. Do you love Sibyl?

GEORGE. Who's Sibyl?

SARAH. Your new wife, who you married after you and I got our divorce.

GEORGE. Oh, were we married? Oh yes, I forgot that part.

SARAH. Elyot, you're so amusing. You make me laugh all the time. *(Laughs)* So, do you love Sibyl?

GEORGE. Probably. I married her. *(Pause. She coughs three times, he unzips her dress, she slaps him.)*

Scenes **527**

SARAH. Oh, Elyot, darling, I'm sorry. We were mad to have left each other. Kiss me. *(They kiss. Enter Dame Ellen Terry as Sibyl, in an evening gown.)*

ELLEN. Oh, how ghastly.

SARAH. Oh dear. And this must be Sibyl.

ELLEN. Oh how ghastly. What shall we do?

SARAH. We must all speak in very low voices and attempt to be civilized.

ELLEN. Is this Amanda? Oh, Elyot, I think she's simply obnoxious.

SARAH. How very rude.

ELLEN. Oh, Elyot, how can you treat me like this?

GEORGE. Hello, Sibyl.

ELLEN. Well, since you ask, I'm very upset. I was inside writing a letter to your mother and wanted to know how to spell apothecary.

SARAH. A-P-O-T-H-E-C-A-R-Y.

ELLEN. *(Icy.)* Thank you. *(Writes it down; Sarah looks over her shoulder.)*

SARAH. Don't scribble, Sibyl.

ELLEN. Did my eyes deceive me, or were you kissing my husband a moment ago?

SARAH. We must all speak in very low voices and attempt to be civilized.

ELLEN. I was speaking in a low voice.

SARAH. Yes, but I could still hear you.

ELLEN. Oh. Sorry. *(Speaks too low to be heard)*

SARAH. *(Speaks inaudibly also.)*

ELLEN. *(Speaks inaudibly.)*

SARAH. *(Speaks inaudibly.)*

ELLEN. *(Speaks inaudibly.)*

SARAH. I can't hear a bloody word she's saying. The woman's a nincompoop. Say something, Elyot.

GEORGE. I couldn't hear her either.

ELLEN. Elyot, you have to choose between us immediately—do you love this creature, or do you love me?

GEORGE. I wonder where the maid is.

ELLEN & SARAH. *(Together, furious.)* Forget about the maid, Elyot! *(They look embarrassed.)* You could never have a lasting relationship with a maid. Choose between the two of us.

GEORGE. I choose... oh God, I don't know my lines. I don't know how I got here. I wish I *weren't* here. I wish I had joined the monastery like I almost did right after high school. I almost joined, but then I didn't.

528 Unit Eight Monologues and Scenes

A Waitress in Yellowstone or Always Tell the Truth

by David Mamet

Following is the beginning of the play. A narrator takes the stage. He is dressed as a park ranger.

RANGER. Winnie was a waitress. She worked for tips. Here is a tip: a bad situation generally grows worse.

Things which can get no worse improve. There are exceptions: here is not one. Winnie caught a guy lifting a tip off of her table. Told him "who do you think you are?" and she read him out to the onlooking crowd, what sort of a you-fill-in-the-blank that he *was*. . . which he was.

It turns out this man was a congressman. In an election year. He had to keep a shining image in the public eye, which is exactly where he kept it.

Would have been better off to be what he wished to seem, but barring that he took the secondary course, lived like a thief and made the Public Pay.

Winnie and her son Doug. Had planned a trip to Yellowstone. To celebrate his Tenth Birthday. He'd, as you might imagine, looked forward to that trip all year. And it was the object of much of their talk and much of their joint happiness.

At the restaurant.

WAITRESS. Hey, Winnie, quit dreaming, table number three wants the check!

(Old Couple)

OLD MAN. Could I have the check, please.

WINNIE. Here you are.

OLD MAN. Thank you. See you tomorrow, Winnie. . .

WINNIE. No you won't, sir. Tomorrow my boy and I leave for our vacation. I'll see you in two weeks.

OLD MAN. Where are you going?

WINNIE. Yellowstone Park.

OLD MAN. That's right, you told me. Here's a little extra, you have a fine trip.

(The Old Couple starts up to leave.)

WINNIE. That's *very* generous of you, sir. . . thank you. . . *(Before she can gather the money, etc., she is called to another table.)*

CONGRESSMAN. Miss!

WINNIE *(to Old Man)*. Thank you very much.

CONGRESSMAN. Miss!

WINNIE. I'm coming. *(to Congressman)* Yes, sir?

CONGRESSMAN *(of check)*. What is the meaning of this?

Scenes 529

WINNIE *(checking bill).* Ninety-five cents, for a substitution. You had beans instead of the creamed spinach.

CONGRESSMAN. You never told me that.

WINNIE. Yes, sir, I did.

CONGRESSMAN. You certainly did *not.* You did *not* tell me that.

WINNIE. Yes, sir, I am certain, you said "I'll have the Special." Look: It's not important. If you take the check to the boss, I'm sure that he'll. . .

CONGRESSMAN. Well, that's not the point, is it? The point is that you never *told* me. . .

WINNIE. Well, if that's true, I'm sorry, sir.

CONGRESSMAN. No: *say* you never told me. . .

WINNIE. Excuse me. . .

CONGRESSMAN. You owe me an apology.

WINNIE. I think that I apologized, excuse me. . . *(She walks away. To another waitress.)* Some people have too much salt in their diet. . . *(to Congressman)* WAIT A SECOND WAIT A SECOND WAIT A SECOND: *WAIT* A SECOND THERE!

(She walks back to his table, which he has gotten up from. He is standing near the table vacated by the Old Couple. To Congressman.)

You wanna put something back? *(Pause)* You wanna put something back, or you want me to call the police.

CONGRESSMAN. I don't know what you're talking about.

WINNIE. I'm talking about you just lifted my tip off of that table. Now: you put it back or I call the cops.

CONGRESSMAN. You're saying. . . *(Pause)* You're saying I did whhh. . . ? Get out of my way. *(Tries to push past her)*

WINNIE. In a pig's *eye* I will. Somebody call the cops! Somebody call the cops, this guy took my tip off the. . . *(To Congressman)* You aren't going anywhere!

BOSS. What's the trouble?

WINNIE. This guy took my tip off the table.

CONGRESSMAN. Lady, you're in a world of trouble here.

WINNIE. Well, we're just going to see. . .

COP. What seems to be the trouble?

WINNIE. This guy lifted my tip off the table.

CONGRESSMAN. Not only is it not

530 **Unit Eight** Monologues and Scenes

true, but I want to tell you you've just caused yourself a lot of pain. What's your name, Officer? I'm John Larue, I am the congressman for this district, and this deranged and sick individual has just slandered me. Pick her *tip* off the table? You know WHO I *AM*???

(The Congressman sings about the exalted position he enjoys. He finishes singing.)

CONGRESSMAN. Now: I'll give you one last chance to retract what you said and take back your vicious lie, or you're going to wish you never were born.

WINNIE. Well, to wish you never were born you have to be born. Which gives you the option, and I think I'll stick with the truth. You should be ashamed of yourself. Good-bye.

(The Cop takes the Congressman away.)

WINNIE. What kind of a world is it? That guy should be setting an example . . .

(Winnie and the assembled customers sing "What Kind of a World Is It?" peppering the song with examples from their own lives. The second verse is: "On the Other Hand," where Winnie sings about some of the good things which may be had simply in life, in her case, the trip with her son to Yellowstone Park.

As the clock strikes twelve she sings "My Day Is Done, and I'm Going on Vacation," and leaves the restaurant. She walks home.)

WINNIE. Look at the stars, what a beautiful night it is. Always various. *(She walks into her house.)* Look at my son, isn't he gorgeous. And now we have all this vacation time to be alone together. All the rest is basically illusion.

RANGER. And so she fell asleep, and she and her son dreamed the same dream. In which they were in Yellowstone Park, high upon a ridge, upon a summit, looking down, and they saw mountain sheep, and they saw deer, and when the rain came unexpectedly they made a shelter from a fallen tree. And as in the wild of sleep and as in the wild of the forest their cares fell away. And when Winnie awoke, she saw her son, already dressed, sitting at the breakfast table, and he had made her a cup of tea.

(N.B. They are both dressed in full camp regalia.)

WINNIE. Good morning. What are you doing up so early?

DOUG. Oh, I couldn't sleep.

WINNIE. Why? You worried about school, shouldn't you be off to school?

DOUG. Well, I thought I wouldn't go to school today.

Scenes **531**

WINNIE. Wouldn't go to school? Why, of course, you have to go to school today, why wouldn't you?

DOUG. 'CAUSE WE'RE GOING TO YELLOWSTONE PARK!!!!!

(They jump up and down and sing a song about how they must make sure they've taken the right things. They sing about the contents of a rucksack, and emergency gear, which they inspect on each other's person. This gear includes: waxed matches in a waterproof container [several containers secreted in various parts of the clothing and generally high up to keep them dry should one fall into waist-high water], a compass, a spare compass, a topographic map of the area to be camped in. A candle for helping to light fires, needle and thread, steel wool which, though it is not generally known, is, in its superfine variety, great tinder and can just be wrung out when wet, extra clothing, rain gear, pencil and paper, fishing line and hook, bandages, whistle, etc. They finish the song, and, having checked each other out, decide that they are ready to proceed to the bus, which they have ten minutes to catch. In deciding which coat to wear, they turn on the radio to catch a weather report.)

DOUG. I can't believe we're really going.

WINNIE. Have I ever lied to you?

DOUG. No!

WINNIE. Well, then, there you are.

RADIO ANNOUNCER *(voice over).* In other news, Congressman John Larue, up for reelection, yesterday was accosted for the misdemeanor of Attempting to Defraud of Services or, to put it simply, a waitress at a restaurant he frequents accused the Congressman of lifting her tip off her table.

WINNIE. . . .come on, let's get out of here. . .

CONGRESSMAN *(voice over).* You know, it's easy to accuse, and I think by far the simplest thing would be to let this sick accusation pass, and go my way, but there comes a time. . .

WINNIE. Turn that creep off, let's go to the *country*. . .

DOUG *(turns off radio).* What'd he do?

WINNIE. The creep. Lifted a tip off of a waitress's table. Can you believe that?

DOUG *(opening door).* What a life.

WINNIE. On to the Wilds!

(In the door are two burly plainclothes policemen.)

POLICEMAN. Winnie Magee?

WINNIE. I. . . uh, what is it?

532 Unit Eight Monologues and Scenes

POLICEMAN. Are you Ms. Winnie Magee?

WINNIE. I can't talk to you now, we have to catch a bus.

POLICEMAN. ARE YOU WIN. . . ?

WINNIE. Yes, but I can't talk. . .

POLICEMAN *(simultaneously with "talk").* You're under arrest. Would you come with us, please?

WINNIE. I. . .

DOUG. Wait, you can't, what's this all. . . ?

POLICEMAN. Slander, Malicious Mischief, Defamation of Character, would you please. . . ?

WINNIE. Who, what. . . ?

DOUG. What are you doing to my mother?

SECOND POLICEMAN. She insulted a congressman, kid.

WINNIE. But we. . . we just have ten minutes to catch the bus. . .

(They are in a court of law.)

And we're going to Yellowstone P. . . what is this, what's going on here. . . ?

JUDGE. You are accused of wantonly, maliciously, and with malice aforethought having verbally assaulted, insulted, and impugned the character of one John Larue, Congressman for the Seventh District of. . .

WINNIE. HOLD ON A SECOND. I insulted wh. . . ?

JUDGE. You have no voice in this court, would you please, who is your counsel?

WINNIE. Say that again?

BAILIFF. Who's your lawyer?

WINNIE. I don't have a lawyer, why should. . . What's going on here? *(Pause)* Come on, I have to catch a bus. *(Pause)*

JUDGE. You are accused by the congressman here *(Congressman stands.)* of, in simple terms, of lying about him in such a way as to damage his reputation.

WINNIE. Ah.

JUDGE. When you said that he stole your tip.

WINNIE. He *did* steal my tip.

JUDGE. The court will now appoint you a lawyer.

WINNIE. I don't need a lawyer, I don't *want* one. Let's settle this here and now, 'cause I'm on my vacation time, alright? You tell me how you want to do this, and let's get this done.

JUDGE. You wish to act as your own lawyer?

WINNIE. That's. . . okay. *(Pause)* Okay.

JUDGE. You're making a mistake.

WINNIE. I've made them before. Nothing to be scared of. Now, what is the thing?

DOUG. Mom, what's going on. . . ?

(Winnie and Doug hold a whispered consultation while the Bailiff and the Judge sing about the charge and the procedure in this case. They are joined by the Lawyer for the Congressman and the Congressman, who sing about her heinous behavior and the grave damage that has been done. They stop. Pause.)

WINNIE. Now what?

JUDGE. You may present your case.

A Star Ain't Nothin' but a Hole in Heaven

by Judi Ann Mason

The Lorraine Hansberry award, of which this play is a recipient, is established for the best plays on the black experience in America. The following scene is set in Louisiana, 1969. Pokie, a high school senior who lives with her senile, dying aunt Mamie and her aged, blind uncle Lemuel, struggles to overcome tradition and her family's disapproval to go north to get a good college education.

MAMIE. Lemuel, Lemuel. That man is a great man, Pokie. Good man.

POKIE. I know.

MAMIE. Sometimes you don't understand him. He is hard to understand sometimes.

POKIE. He treats me like I'm a little baby.

MAMIE. He tryin' to protect you.

POKIE. From what?

MAMIE. What he had to go through.

POKIE. Things ain't like that no more. There's a lotta things I have to do and he won't let me. I think he don't want me to graduate.

MAMIE. Aw, Pokie . . .

POKIE. Every time I ask him for something I need, he tells me that I don't need it.

MAMIE. You got to try real hard to make him see.

POKIE. I told him I needed a white dress—

MAMIE. He's always been like that. Like the time I told him I needed some new shoes for my sister's wedding.

534 **Unit Eight** Monologues and Scenes

POKIE. I wouldn't ask him for the dress if I didn't have to have it. . .

MAMIE. All the time before that, all the money had to be spent on things for his pappy.

POKIE. Do you think he'll let me buy it?

MAMIE. "Lemuel, the shoes don't cost but $2. And I'll take good care of them. You won't have to buy me no more. . ."

POKIE. I saw a dress that cost only $12 up at the Woolworth.

MAMIE. He told me that we didn't have the money. But I knew we had the money cause I had worked five days straight down to Miss Blema's store that week and I gived him all the money. . .

POKIE. Aint Mamie, will you listen to me?

MAMIE. So I tells him I had the money and he gets mad at me. "You ain't grateful for all I done for you. Who else gon marry a woman like you? You be thankful for me marrying you . . ."

POKIE. Will you listen to me?

MAMIE. I told him that he didn't have to marry me. If he had to wipe my brow with it, he didn't have to marry me.

POKIE. I got problems, too! But nobody around here never listens to me talk. . .

MAMIE. It was just like talkin' to myself. "You told me you didn't make no mind about children. You told me I was just as much a woman cause I couldn't make babies. Lotsa women can't make babies. I ain't the only one, Lemuel."

POKIE. *(Unable to control her moment of disgust.)* For once can't you hear me? Come back and talk to me!

MAMIE. "I love you, Lemuel. I love Jesus, too. Jesus is the Savior! Save me, Lord! Take this curse from my womb!"

POKIE. Come back and talk Aint Mamie!

MAMIE. Too old now. Life done creeped up on me. It done snatched my breath from my lungs. I'm still a woman.

POKIE. Listen to me! *(Mamie bursts into a fit of tears. Pokie goes to her and starts to shake her.)* Listen! You come back here and listen!

MAMIE. Turn me loose! Jesus gonna remember me! Turn Jesus loose! Take the cross from his back! He's the Son of God! Turn the Lord aloose!

LEMUEL. *(At door.)* Mamie, what's the matter? *(Seeing Pokie.)* Pokie, let her be! You trying to kill her? What you doing? Stop hollin' at her! Turn her loose!

Scenes **535**

POKIE. *(She releases Mamie and stands back staring at Lemuel.)* You saw that?

LEMUEL. It's alright Mamie. All right.

POKIE. How did you see what I was doing to her?

LEMUEL. She was hollin'.

POKIE. No, you saw it. Joretta was right. You can see.

LEMUEL. Girl, stop that barking and help me get her to bed.

POKIE. Do it yourself.

LEMUEL. What you say?

POKIE. Do it yourself. You saw well enough a minute ago. . .

LEMUEL. Go get the alum so you can rub her down.

POKIE. I ain't gonna do it!

LEMUEL. Is this the thank-you we get after all we done for you? You musta forgot we didn't have to take you in. . .

POKIE. I'm leaving, Uncle Lemuel.

LEMUEL. Pokie, shut up that noise.

POKIE. Me and Joretta going up north to college.

LEMUEL. Help me get Mamie to bed.

POKIE. I ain't coming back here. You done all this to keep me here, but I'm going to college. And I'm gonna be an artist!

LEMUEL. Then what we suppose to do?

POKIE. You can move to town.

LEMUEL. This is my land.

POKIE. You can sell it and buy somewhere in town.

LEMUEL. Who gon take care of Mamie? She's your ainnie and you talking about leaving her. A decent girl would stay as close to her kin as she could—

POKIE. I ain't willing to sacrifice my life.

LEMUEL. You know we can't take care of ourselves. We subject to die in this house.

POKIE. I can't stay here. I won't.

LEMUEL. If you think I'll let you leave—

POKIE. How you gon stop me? You can't see, remember? All I got to do is walk out of here.

LEMUEL. You shut up! *(He comes toward her.)*

POKIE. I'm leaving. I don't owe nobody nothing but me.

(Lemuel tries to grab her. Pokie dashes out of the way. Lemuel stumbles on the

536 **Unit Eight** Monologues and Scenes

chair. Pokie rushes to the door and exits.)

LEMUEL. Pokie! Come back here! Pokie!

(Pokie runs toward the tree, lays her head against it and cries. Lemuel looks after the door.)

MAMIE. Lemuel, we need to get Pokie a white dress to graduate in. A nice white dress, with ruffles and a big collar. Lemuel, Pokie needs a white dress . . .

(lights dim)

"Baucis and Philemon" from Metamorphoses

by Mary Zimmerman

Following is the entire segment of "Baucis and Philemon" *from Mary Zimmerman's play,* Metamorphoses, *which is based on the writings of Ovid. Be aware that much of the play takes place in a pool of water.*

(Music. Transition. The raft and candelabra are struck.)

NARRATOR ONE. It happened that one night, Zeus, the lord of the heavens, and Hermes, his son, came down to earth to see what people were really like. They disguised themselves as two old beggars, stinking and poor, ragged and filthy. They knocked on a thousand doors.

(Zeus knocks on the surface of the deck. Both adopt supplicating poses.)

ZEUS. Hello, do you have any spare—?

OFFSTAGE VOICE. Get out of here! Get the hell out of here! I work hard for my money!

NARRATOR ONE. And a thousand doors were slammed on them.

(They knock on the deck, and a woman opens the door.)

HERMES. Hello, we're tired, we live on the street, and we hoped that you might—

WOMAN AT THE DOOR. I'm sorry, I'm . . . um . . . soooo sorry. Sorry. *(She slams the door shut.)*

NARRATOR ONE. At last they came to a little hut on the outskirts of town.

HERMES. Why bother knocking here? We've knocked on houses of all kinds, the homes of people with plenty to spare. Whoever lives here obviously has nothing.

ZEUS. Let's give it a try all the same. We've come all this way.

(He knocks.)

HERMES. This is hopeless. Let's just go ho—

BAUCIS. *(Entering.)* Poor strangers! Philemon, there are guests at our door!

ZEUS. Hello. We are strangers to these parts. We've lost our way and—

Scenes **537**

PHILEMON. *(Entering.)* Baucis, why are you standing there! We must bring our guests inside.

ZEUS. Do you know us?

PHILEMON. Of course.

HERMES. You do?

PHILEMON. Yes—

HERMES. Then who are we?

PHILEMON. Why, you are children of God. Come in, come in.

(At this point, the narrative divides among several members of the company. They enter and exit variously, carrying illuminated candles in wooden bowls, which stand in for all the items they will mention. They hand these bowls to Baucis and Philemon, or place them in the water themselves. The scene is active: The entire surface of the water becomes the "table" being set with illuminated candles.)

NARRATOR TWO. The two immortals, satisfied that their disguises had not been seen through, entered the house, lowering their heads to fit through the door.

BAUCIS. No, don't sit on the floor! Sit on chairs, as quality people do.

NARRATOR THREE. Philemon ran to get another chair.

NARRATOR FOUR. And Baucis fetched two pieces of cloth to pad them so the strangers might rest easy.

NARRATOR FIVE. She stirred the coals in the hearth and fanned the fire to cook them a meal.

NARRATOR ONE. Philemon set out the embroidered cloth that they saved for feast days.

NARRATOR TWO. Baucis saw that one of the legs of the chair was short and she propped it up with a shard of a pot.

NARRATOR THREE. Philemon set out a plate of olives, green ones and black, and a saucer of cherry plums.

NARRATOR FOUR. Then there was cabbage and some roasted eggs . . .

NARRATOR FIVE. For dessert there were nuts, figs, dates, and plums.

NARRATOR ONE. And a basket of ripe apples.

NARRATOR TWO. Remember how apples smell?

(A pause. Everyone inhales and remembers. Then they continue.)

NARRATOR ONE. At last, with a show of modest pride, they brought out a bit of honeycomb for sweetness.

NARRATOR TWO. Philemon poured wine from a bottle, but as he filled the glasses of the guests, he saw that the bottle remained full.

538 **Unit Eight** Monologues and Scenes

ALL NARRATORS. And then they knew.

(Narrators exit.)

BAUCIS. Oh, mercy! Mercy!

(She runs with her husband to kneel in front of the gods.)

PHILEMON. You are divine and we've served you such a simple meal. Baucis, go and kill the goose!

ZEUS. Let it live. We are gods and we thank you. You've done enough, more than your nasty neighbors thought to do.

(The original narrator of the scene enters with three other members of the company, all carrying bowls of candles. As she speaks, they come forward, kneel in the water, and set the bowls floating. There is music under the next line of Narrator One.)

NARRATOR ONE. Suddenly, everything was changing. The poor little house, their simple cottage, was becoming grander and grander, a glittering marble-columned temple. The straw and reeds of the thatched roof metamorphosed into gold, and gates with elaborate carvings sprang up, as ground gave way to marble paving stones.

HERMES. Old man, old woman, ask of us what you will. We shall grant whatever request you make of us.

(Baucis and Philemon whisper to each other.)

BAUCIS. Having spent all our lives together, we ask that you allow us to die at the same moment.

PHILEMON. I'd hate to see my wife's grave, or have her weep at mine.

NARRATOR TWO. The gods granted their wish. Arrived at a very old age together, the two stood at what had been their modest doorway and now was a grandiose facade.

ZEUS. And Baucis noticed her husband was beginning to put forth leaves, and he saw that she, too, was producing leaves and bark. They were turning into trees. They stood there, held each other, and called, before the bark closed over their mouths:

PHILEMON AND BAUCIS. Farewell.

NARRATOR ONE. Walking down the street at night, when you're all alone, you can still hear, stirring in the intermingled branches of the trees above, the ardent prayer of Baucis and Philemon. They whisper:

ALL. Let me die the moment my love dies.

NARRATOR ONE. They whisper:

ALL. Let me not outlive my own capacity to love.

NARRATOR ONE. They whisper:

ALL. Let me die still loving, and so, never die.

Scenes **539**

Promenade

by Maria Irene Fornes

In this excerpt from her offbeat, bright-spirited play, Maria Irene Fornes's every word is a new surprise. With characters named 106, 105, Miss U and Mr. R, you are instantly aware that this play is a bit out of the ordinary. And don't expect linear plot lines and obvious themes. Do expect intelligence and philosophical insight wrapped in zaniness.

Scene 2

The Banquet. There are ladies and gentlemen in evening clothes around the table. The servant sweeps. The waiter serves the guests. 105 and 106 enter. They put on top hats and tails. They sit at the table and eat.

MR. R. Speech . . . speech . . .

MR. S. Let's play croquet . . .

MR. R. Speeches and music . . .

MR. T. Let's call Mr. Lipschitz . . .

MR. S. No speeches . . . No speeches . . .

MR. R. Let's have a song . . .

(105 and 106 clear their throats.)

MISS O. Mr. T, was that you I saw on the corner of Fifth and Tenth?

MR. T. Perhaps.

MISS O. With Mrs. Schumann and her newly clipped poodle?

MR. T. Oh, no, it wasn't I. Friday night I was out of town.

MISS O. Ah! And how did you know it was Friday night I saw you on the corner of Fifth?

(They all laugh.)

MR. T. Well, I must confess. The lady loves me.

(They all laugh.)

MISS U. She shows good taste.

MR. R. Then, introduce us. She'll surely fall for me.

(The ladies giggle.)

(Mr. R writes in a notebook.) Mrs. Schumann . . . lady of taste . . . Bring dog biscuit. *(To Mr. T.)* What is her address?

MR. T. Tch-Tch.

MISS I. Oh, Mr. R, what perspicacity.

MISS O. Are you sure that's what you mean?

(Miss I looks a little embarrassed.)

MR. S. Let's have a song.

(105 and 106 stand and get ready to sing.)

MISS O. And who are these? Dear me.

(105 and 106 realize they have been indiscreet. They sit back at the table

540 **Unit Eight** Monologues and Scenes

and pretend not to hear the others.)

MISS I. They must be friends of Mr. S.

MISS U. My dear. You go right to the point . . .

MISS I. Mr. S. does frequent rather unearthly places, doesn't he?

MR. T. What do you mean?

MISS I. I mean the lower depths.

MR. T. Oh, yes.

MR. S. If I am sometimes in the company of this and that, my dear, it's only because I like to study life . . . I am what you might call a student of life . . . This . . . and that.

MISS U. Oh, how incredibly personal you are, Mr. S. Have I not always said you have the artist in you?

MR. S. I am neither more than I seem to be, nor more than I am, and no less, also.

SERVANT. *(Mimicking in a low voice.)* And no less . . . also.

MR. R. Miss I . . .

MISS I. Yes?

MR. R. Last Saturday I waited for a certain lady who never arrived.

MISS I. You did?

MR. R. Yes.

MISS I. Oh, she couldn't come. She spent all afternoon walking up and down a certain street where a gentleman *(Referring to Mr. T.)* who shall remain nameless lives. She was hoping to have an accidental meeting. . . a sort of unexpected encounter with him. But he never left his house . . . nor did he enter it.

(Miss O and Miss U giggle. The servant is bored by the ladies' and gentlemen's repartee. Through the following speeches she pantomimes their gestures.)

MR. T. He didn't, Madam . . . he didn't. He saw the lady from his window and she did indeed walk up and down his street. But he couldn't receive her . . . his heart was torn. You see, he received a letter from the one he loves *(Referring to Miss U)* telling him his love was unrequited. He spent all afternoon sitting by his window plucking petals from flowers, and the answer always was . . . she loves me not.

MISS O. And who is this he speaks of?

MISS U. She is not free to love. Her heart belongs to he *(Referring to Mr. S.)* whose glance drives her to a frenzy, and whose mere presence brings color to her cheeks.

MR. S. The man who puts you in such a state has eyes only for O. Oh, Miss O.

Scenes **541**

MISS I. Oh! What tension! A name has been mentioned.

MISS U. And what have you to say to that, O?

MISS O. I regret I cannot speak since Mr. S has mentioned me by name. But do you wonder why O shuns you when you are so indiscreet? *(Taking a step toward R.)* And besides, she loves R.
(R takes a step toward I.)
(I takes a step toward T.)
(T takes a step toward U.)
(U takes a step toward S.)
(S takes a step toward O.)
(O takes a step toward R.)
MISS U. You were there when
I was not.
I was there when you were not.
Don't love me, sweetheart,
Or I might stop loving you.
Unrequited love,
Unrequited love.

MISS O. Passionate lips are sweet.
But oh, how much sweeter
Are lips that refuse.
Don't love me, sweetheart,
Or I might stop loving you.

MISS I. Inviting lips,
Alluring lips
Which shape the word no
No no no no no no.
Don't love me, sweetheart,
Or I might stop loving you.

MR. R. You know nothing of life,
You know nothing of love
Till you have tasted
Of unrequited love.
Don't love me, sweetheart,
Or I might stop loving you.

ALL. Unrequited love,
Unrequited love.
There is no love
Like unrequited love.

MISS I. Oh! We sang that well.

MR. R. He who scrubs the pot finds it most shiny.

MR. S. *(To Mr. R.)* And he who soils it, turns up his nose. Mr. R, you were flat.

MISS I. Touché!

MISS U. What a marvelous mind.

MR. S. Just frank.

SERVANT. *(Mimicking.)* Just frank.

(They all look at the servant, shocked.)

MISS I. Mr. S, it's up to you to think of a rejoinder.

MR. S. Dear me, I'm speechless. Wait! Listen to my answer. *(He improvises the following:)*

My frankness, my dear,
My wit, my veneer,
Are something you should revere.

LADIES. A rhyme! A rhyme!

MR. S. Instead, you just think
it queer.

542 Unit Eight Monologues and Scenes

Your unprosperous status
Produces a dubious,
Fallacious, and tedious
Outlook on life.
(The servant makes a face at him.)
You do not know what we're about
We do not know what you're about
Or care to know.
(The servant lowers her head.)
It's sad your career
Depends on our whim.
On with your work, my dear,
Or you'll get thin.
You see, even if you're here,
And we're also here,
You are not near.
Isn't that clear?

MISS U. Oh, Mr. S, how well you rhyme.

MR. S. Not difficult, dear. Just keep the ending of the word in mind. . . it will come.

MISS U. *Incendo, incendis, incendit, incendimos, incenditis, incendunt.*

MR. S. No, dear, the ending, not the beginning.

How I Learned to Drive

by Paula Vogel

Throughout this play, the main character, Li'l Bit, a 40-something-year-old woman, goes back in time to her early years with her family and her uncle Peck. Three separate Greek Choruses (whose members, the author instructs, "should be able to sing three-part harmony") comment on the action and move it forward. The year is 1969 and the family is having dinner.

MALE GREEK CHORUS. *(As Grandfather.)* What kind of things do you want to read?

LI'L BIT. There's a whole semester course, for example, on Shakespeare—

(Greek Chorus, as Grandfather, laughs until he weeps.)

MALE GREEK CHORUS. *(As Grandfather.)* Shakespeare. That's a good one. Shakespeare is really going to help you in life.

PECK. I think it's wonderful. And on scholarship!

MALE GREEK CHORUS. *(As Grandfather.)* How is Shakespeare going to help her lie on her back in the dark?

(Li'l Bit is on her feet.)

LI'L BIT. You're getting old, Big Papa. You are going to die—very very soon. Maybe even tonight. And when you get to heaven, God's going to be a beautiful black woman in a long white robe. She's gonna look at your chart and say: Uh-oh. Dog-ugly mean with blood relatives. Oh. Uh-oh. Voted for George

Scenes 543

Wallace. Well, one last chance: If you can name the play, all will be forgiven. And then she'll quote: "The quality of mercy is not strained." Your answer? Oh, too bad—*Merchant of Venice:* Act IV, Scene iii. And then she'll send you to fry in hell with all the other crackers. Excuse me, please. *(To the audience.)* And as I left the house, I would always hear Big Papa say:

MALE GREEK CHORUS. *(As Grandfather.)* Lucy, your daughter's got a mouth on her. Well, no sense in wasting good gumbo. Pass me her plate, Mama.

LI'L BIT. And Aunt Mary would come up to Uncle Peck:

FEMALE GREEK CHORUS. *(As Aunt Mary.)* Peck, go after her, will you? You're the only one she'll listen to when she gets like this.

PECK. She just needs to cool off.

FEMALE GREEK CHORUS. *(As Aunt Mary.)* Please, honey—Grandma's been on her feet cooking all day.

PECK. All right.

LI'L BIT. And as he left the room, Aunt Mary would say:

FEMALE GREEK CHORUS. *(As Aunt Mary.)* Peck's so good with them when they get to be this age.

(Li'l Bit has stormed to another part of the stage, her back turned, weeping with a teenage fury. Peck, cautiously, as if stalking a deer, comes to her. She turns away even more. He waits a bit.)

PECK. I don't suppose you're talking to family. *(No response.)* Does it help that I'm an in-law?

LI'L BIT. Don't you dare make fun of this.

PECK. I'm not. There's nothing funny about this. *(Beat.)* Although I'll bet when Big Papa is about to meet his maker, he'll remember *The Merchant of Venice.*

LI'L BIT. I've got to get away from here.

PECK. You're going away. Soon. Here, take this.

(Peck hands her his folded handkerchief. Li'l Bit uses it, noisily. Hands it back. Without her seeing, he reverently puts it back.)

LI'L BIT. I hate this family.

Icarus

by Edwin Sánchez

A brother and sister, Primitivo and Altagracia, are living in a remote beachside cabin. Each day Primitivo swims farther and farther out to sea and back again. His sister his helping him train to become a celebrity. Soon

544 **Unit Eight** Monologues and Scenes

the two are joined by Mr. Ellis, his dog Betty, Miss the Gloria, and Beau. Beau challenges Primitivo to a race. Following is a conversation among the members of the small community.

PRIMITIVO. I was kind of afraid of you before but not anymore. You're going to become exhausted out there. Your lungs will collapse, and they'll fill with water, and the only person who can save you will be me, but I'll be too busy touching the sun. *(Pointing to the ocean.)* She's all yours. I'm sure you'll want to practice. I should warn you, she's a little choppy and watch out for her undertow, she doesn't let go easily.

(Primitivo and Altagracia exit. Beau goes to the Gloria. Lights up on the Gloria. She is wearing a facial masque and has a strapped-on ice pack around her eyes.)

the GLORIA. Halt, who goes there?

BEAU. It's just me, Miss the Gloria.

the GLORIA. Ah, my fan. But you shouldn't see me like this. I'm a work in progress. Turn away.

BEAU. You look fine.

the GLORIA. Turn away! Have you?

BEAU. Yes. *(He hasn't.)*

the GLORIA. I'll have to take your word as a gentleman that indeed you have.

(Beau turns around.)

the GLORIA. You're here much too early. The Gloria is best seen under man-made illumination. Nonetheless, I'm so glad you're here. I have so much to tell you.

BEAU. Has it ever occurred to you that every time I see you we only talk about you?

the GLORIA. You say that as if it were a bad thing.

BEAU. Do you ever wonder what I look like?

the GLORIA. You're going to give me frown lines. I won't like you anymore if I get frown lines.

BEAU. Do you ever ask yourself, "Why you?" "Why are you so beautiful?"

the GLORIA. Massage my feet, please.

(Beau does.)

the GLORIA. Because I can handle the stress. Not everyone could, you know. The weight, the burden, the responsibility that comes from being everybody's fantasy.

BEAU. I have my mask off. Do you wanna see me?

the GLORIA. Of course not. I already have my image of you. Whatever you do, whatever it takes, maintain the illusion. It's hard work, it's a full-time job, but it's worth it.

Scenes **545**

BEAU. And what will you do when your beauty is gone?

(Panic-stricken, the Gloria stops him.)

the GLORIA. I haven't faded, have I? This is the only currency I have.

BEAU. No, you're still perfect.

the GLORIA. You frightened me. I mean, who would ever want me without my face?

BEAU. Goodbye now.

the GLORIA. Bye-bye.

(Beau exits. Mr Ellis sits on the beach, a pair of baby shoes by his side. He is too tired to dig.)

MR ELLIS. I'm not staring, I'm not staring, I'm not staring, I'm not staring, am I staring? I'm not staring, I'm not staring, I'm not staring, I'm not staring, I'm. . . not. . . I don't like to remember. I don't.

(Beau stops. He sits by Mr Ellis and takes his shovel and begins to dig for him. Mr Ellis grabs his wrists and stops him.)

MR ELLIS. You weren't invited to help. If you have something you don't want to remember, go find your own beach.

(Altagracia brings Primitivo downstairs to the beach.)

PRIMITIVO. We should be sending out press releases.

ALTAGRACIA. I'm on it.

PRIMITIVO. And we'll need V I P seating.

ALTAGRACIA. Uh-huh.

PRIMITIVO. And maybe baton twirlers.

MR ELLIS. What do you think his losing will do to her?

BEAU. Are you so sure I'm gonna win?

MR ELLIS. You're not gonna win. You're just gonna beat him.

ALTAGRACIA. I need to talk to you. We need to discuss the terms of the race.

PRIMITIVO. The rules.

ALTAGRACIA. Yeah, the rules.

BEAU. We get in the water and swim. One of us wins—

PRIMITIVO. Me.

BEAU. —and one of us loses.

PRIMITIVO. You.

ALTAGRACIA. Primi, let management manage, okay? That's why I'm getting the big bucks. Why don't you practice your victory speech?

PRIMITIVO. Okay, but don't give away the foreign distribution rights.

546 Unit Eight Monologues and Scenes

Remember, I'm right here.

(Altagracia sits on a step.)

ALTAGRACIA. Step into my office.

(Beau sits next to Altagracia, who finds herself too close to him so she moves up a step.)

BEAU. Well, it's almost race time. Primitivo seems really excited.

ALTAGRACIA. Yeah.

BEAU. How's that?

ALTAGRACIA. I said, "Yeah."

BEAU. Are you talking to me or to your feet?

ALTAGRACIA. Why are you doing this?

BEAU. I thought this is what you wanted.

ALTAGRACIA. I wanted Primitivo to swim.

BEAU. He's not swimming?

ALTAGRACIA. Farther and better than ever. No complaining, either.

BEAU. Then what's the problem? You still believe he can touch the sun, right?

ALTAGRACIA. Sure I do.

BEAU. Then you should be grateful I'm staying. I'll give him a chance to prove it.

ALTAGRACIA. You're right.

BEAU. If anybody can, he can. You just lost your faith for a second, that's all.

ALTAGRACIA. Yeah.

BEAU. I guess I should go practice.

(Altagracia grabs his arm.)

ALTAGRACIA. Are you really gonna go through with this?

(Beau nods his head and strips down to his bathing trunks as he goes into the water. Primitivo does his sun touch, stretched arm with splayed fingers as he watches Beau swimming. Altagracia sits next to Mr Ellis, who opens his suitcase and retrieves a brooch from it. He holds it up.)

ALTAGRACIA. Pretty.

MR ELLIS. Cheap. My wife's one piece of Christmas jewelry. She'd wear it exactly from December first to January seventh. I didn't even know I had it.

(Mr Ellis drops the brooch in the hole and buries it.)

ALTAGRACIA. You know, in the summer, some little kid with a sand shovel is gonna find it.

MR ELLIS. It might be her. Reincarnated.

ALTAGRACIA. Oh, please.

MR ELLIS. She'll have a feeling of déjà vu.

ALTAGRACIA. I can barely survive going through this once. Let alone over and over again.

MR ELLIS. Next time it would be different.

ALTAGRACIA. I'd want it in writing, notarized, and blessed by the Pope.

(She picks up Betty and holds her close.)

MR ELLIS. I don't want you to get hurt, little girl. Dreams can protect you so no one can hurt you.

(He slowly opens his suitcase slightly.)

MR ELLIS. I can help you. 'Cause dreams are my business. Reach in, I'll let you have one on account. Go on. A dream to stand between you and reality.

(Altagracia is unsure. Mr Ellis points to Beau in the water.)

MR ELLIS. The beautiful boy is pretty good out there, isn't he?

ALTAGRACIA. I hadn't noticed.

MR ELLIS. One dream. Any dream at all. 'Cause you mean so much to me.

(Altagracia is about to reach in when Mr Ellis suddenly snaps the suitcase shut, barely missing her hand. She hits him and storms upstairs.)

ALTAGRACIA. I hate you! *(She exits.)*

MR ELLIS. Better I should squash your dreams than someone who doesn't love you.

(the Gloria enters her porch, wearing sunglasses, and sees Primitivo laying in the sun. Mr Ellis, upon seeing her, runs under the porch.)

the GLORIA. You were quite the athlete out there.

PRIMITIVO. Miss the Gloria.

the GLORIA. I've never seen anyone swim quite the way you do, with so much passion. Such a handsome boy. Am I making you blush?

PRIMITIVO. Uh, no.

the GLORIA. Yes, I am. That's so sweet. Hardly anybody blushes anymore. Come on up for that drink I promised you; I have tons of good news. I got invited to the party of the year!

PRIMITIVO. That's great.

the GLORIA. Very last minute, you understand, but what do I care. And I can bring a guest. I'd love to show up with someone as handsome as you on my arm. How about it? It's tomorrow night.

PRIMITIVO. I'm. . . booked for another party.

the GLORIA. Well, that's a shame.

548 **Unit Eight** Monologues and Scenes

I would have made it a very special evening for you. Maybe I will afterwards.

PRIMITIVO. Yeah, maybe.

the GLORIA. And there's more. I got a part!

PRIMITIVO. You got another feature?

the GLORIA. Yes! Well, actually I'm just doing it as a favor for a friend, it's sort of a, uh subcameo. I'm in the background, but really the entire scene hinges around me. I'm the center of attention. I've decided I'm going to do it all with my eyes. *(She removes her sunglasses.)*

PRIMITIVO. Congratulations.

the GLORIA. In lesser hands this would just be a glorified extra, in my hands it's a lock on a best supporting actress nod.

PRIMITIVO. I'm sure you'll be wonderful.

the GLORIA. And beautiful.

PRIMITIVO. Very, very beautiful.

the GLORIA. Come on up and give me a little good luck kiss. Don't be so shy.

PRIMITIVO. I can't.

the GLORIA. *(Not hearing him. Looking out at the ocean.)* Who's that walking this way?

PRIMITIVO. Nobody.

the GLORIA. He's beautiful.

PRIMITIVO. Yeah.

the GLORIA. Don't be jealous. You're both very, very attractive.

PRIMITIVO. Yeah, we're equals.

the GLORIA. I'll see you after the party then?

PRIMITIVO. It's a date.

(the Gloria disappears into her bedroom.)

Scenes **549**

Student Handbook

Part One Acting

Acting Styles

There are two main approaches to acting.

Method Acting Actors who have worked or prefer to work by "becoming" the character are influenced by the tradition of Method acting, originated by Konstantin Stanislavski (1863–1938) and currently taught by schools such as the Actors Studio in New York and Los Angeles. This approach asks actors to fully immerse themselves in the general world of the play and the specific world of their characters. Method work is also called *internal* or *subjective* work because actors build the character from within, tapping into the parts of themselves that relate to the character.

Technical Acting Actors who work technically tend to approach a role from a much more objective viewpoint. The technical actor uses powerful vocal and physical work to bring a character to life. The interpretation of the character is often more intellectual or stylized than emotional. Technical work is sometimes called *external* or *objective* work, because the actor builds the character through pacing, projection, vocalization, movement, and emotion. These are intellectualized from the script, but not necessarily "felt" by the actor. Technical acting is an important part of contemporary theatre because it emphasizes the disciplined training of the voice and body.

Are you a method or a technical actor? Your style will be determined partly by type and temperament and partly by the teachers, directors, training methods, and acting companies with which you work. You will also be influenced by the styles of plays in which you are cast. Both approaches will be useful to you as an actor in certain roles and productions.

To prepare for work in either style of acting, the actor must still employ a combination of research and imagination. Actors research the *given circumstances* of the play, and imagination fills in the gaps. Given circumstances include:

- What the playwright says about the character.
- What other characters say about the character.
- What the character says about him or herself.
- What the character does.

This research should be attuned to both the obvious and direct statements, such as one character saying, "You're so selfish," or the more subtle, "What do you expect from her?" The first example is direct text and the second is *subtext,* or what may lie beneath the surface meaning of the dialogue.

550 Student Handbook

Acting Types

In the theatre, and particularly in movies and television, appearance and stage presence have much to do with an actor's ability to be cast and to work. A role can be, and often is, a combination of the following types:

Antagonist The character who opposes the objectives of the protagonist, or main character.

Bit Part A smaller role, such as GUARD #1 or a chorus member.

Character Part Usually a parental, comic, threatening, or eccentric figure. This person often has odd characteristics or personality quirks that serve as a *foil,* or contrast, to the protagonist. Character parts provide comic relief, dramatic tension, and/or color to a play. They are often challenging "stretch" roles for younger actors.

Foil A character that serves as either an antagonist or as a significant character to whom the protagonist may be compared.

Ingenue [AHN•juh•nu] A young female love interest, sometimes the protagonist, and in older plays, an example of idealized womanhood.

Juvenile A young male love interest, sometimes a protagonist or hero. In older plays he is often an example of perfect manhood.

Principal A main or leading role, usually the protagonist, antagonist, or love interest in a play.

Protagonist The main character with whom the audience sympathizes. Usually the character that changes the most during the course of the play.

Supporting Role A smaller role, often a sidekick or secondary love interest.

Straight Part A role that can fulfill some of the same functions as a character part but without the eccentricity. A straight part will not be played as broadly as a character part but may still provide comic relief, dramatic tension, and/or color. Straight roles demand less of a stretch for young actors.

Characterization

There are five basic areas to explore when preparing for a role. They are based on the journalistic questions *Who? What? When? Where?* and *Why?* Try to find the answers by analyzing the script. If the answers are not in the script, create the answers from your imagination.

Who is your character? To understand the world of the play and, therefore, the world of a character, an actor must explore the character's personality. This understanding is formed by a variety of influences: genetics, environment, and social influences, among others. Here are some questions to ask and answer about a character:

- Where were you born?
- Does this location affect your behavior? The way you speak?
- How important are social institutions such as school, government, and church in your world?
- What are your prejudices, if any?
- What is your attitude toward the opposite sex?
- In what way do you have professional power? Personal power? How well do you use what power you have?
- How would you describe your home life? What was your family life like when

Part One Acting **551**

you were growing up? How has it affected your present life?

- How do you want to appear to other characters in the play?

What is going on in the script? First, read the entire play. Then read it again, focusing on your character. Take notes on the following questions:

- What does the playwright say about your character?
- What do other characters say about your character?
- What does your character say about him/herself?
- What does your character do? (Remember that actions speak louder than words.) Does your character say one thing and do another?
- What does your character want and need as written in the script?
- What changes does your character go through over the course of the play?
- What is the playwright trying to communicate? What is the play about?

When? What's going on before, during, and after you are onstage? For every scene you are involved in, you need to be able to answer the following questions:

- Where have I just come from?
- What am I thinking about as I walk into the room?
- How much of my history do I bring into the room with me?
- As I walk into this room, what are my immediate expectations and goals?
- What are my long-range expectations and goals?
- What do I need to accomplish before I leave this room?
- As I leave, where am I going? How do I feel about what just happened? What will I do next?

Where? How do surroundings affect your behavior? If there is more than one setting, ask these questions about each location. People behave differently in different places.

- Where am I and what time is it?
- What kind of room or area is it?
- How does the space I am in impact my behavior?

Why do you do what you do? Every play has a main idea or "spine." In addition to independent character study, you will analyze the play with your director. Once you have a clear concept of the main idea, ask yourself these questions, first for the play as a whole, and then for each scene in which you appear.

- What do I want?
- What am I willing to do to get what I want?
- What is in my way?

Scoring a Role

The term *scoring* has various definitions depending on your instructor. For some teachers, the scoring of a role relates to the character analysis detailed above. For others, scoring is the literal marking in the script of notes and reminders about line delivery and blocking. Each actor develops his or her own personal shorthand for marking a script. The following elements are usually noted:

- Pauses
- Pitch
- Emphasis

552 Student Handbook

- Speed or Tempo
- Movement
- Character Revelation or Discovery
- Stage Business

Another important aspect to scoring is to break scenes into sections and give them names using concrete noun titles for specific actions. Examples of names for scenes might include:

- The Courtship
- The Denial
- The Rejection
- The Request
- The Secret
- The Illusion
- The Trick

Next, define how your character will fit into the scene using the infinitive verb form. What does your character want at this moment, and how will he or she go about getting it? Examples of infinitives to use within scenes are:

- To Romance
- To Seduce
- To Deny
- To Conquer
- To Conceal
- To Beg
- To Criticize
- To Excuse
- To Supplicate
- To Hide

Auditions

There are two main types of auditions:

- **The audition for a specific role or play.** If possible, read the full play before the audition. This will give you a clear advantage when you approach the role for which you are reading. The director may request a specific type of audition piece, such as one of the types of monologues listed on page 554, or he or she may simply ask you to read from the play itself (see **Cold Reading** on page 555). The more you know about the play, the easier it will be for you to make meaning from even the smallest section or scene.
- **The prepared professional audition.** Most audition situations allow you to prepare beforehand. You are expected to keep the audition material short, usually one to two minutes, and you are often called upon to provide two contrasting monologues–one comic or character and the other dramatic or period–all within the allotted time period. Directors know what they are looking for and are used to assessing actors quickly. An experienced director will immediately spot the qualities needed for the role–which means that the professionalism of your approach in that very short amount of time may make the difference between being cast or forever waiting in the wings.

At most auditions, you will be asked to fill out a form with information about yourself. Take the time to fill in the information clearly and completely; you don't want anything to stand in the way of your success. You will then be given a number or a time, or told to wait until your name is called.

When you are called, make a strong cross to center stage or the center of the audition room and smile. When it is clear that the auditors are ready, state your name clearly. Some auditors will expect you to state the name of your audition piece and its source; however, many auditors only need to hear your name (and talent agency if you have representation) and then will expect you to proceed. At the end of your audition, pause in case the director wishes to ask you any questions, give direction, or invite you to do more. Then say, "Thank you," and leave.

The Audition Resume The resume gives the director a thumbnail sketch of who you

Part One Acting **553**

are and what sort of work you have done. Your resume reflects how much you care about your acting career, so be sure it looks clean and professional.

The resume begins with your name, contact information, and any personal information you wish to share. This is followed by a listing of your educational background, then your professional credits, and finally any special abilities that might help you in your work. There are a variety of formats, many of which are detailed in library books, textbooks, and even such handbooks as *Resumes for Dummies.* Here are some basic rules:

- Don't leave anything out you want the director to know.
- Don't exaggerate or fabricate experiences.
- Don't list anything more than ten years old.

Audition Selections Every actor should have between four and ten monologues memorized at all times, including contemporary and classical pieces. Try to find selections that are not overused, but avoid monologues that do not originate from published plays. Talk to teachers, directors, and other actors about which monologues might be right for you. Following are the general categories:

- **Dramatic Monologue** Preferably a recent work featuring a character close to your age and range of experience.
- **Comic Monologue** Again, try to choose something from contemporary literature that relates to your own experience and your "type." Comedy and drama will both work if you enjoy and feel comfortable with the piece.
- **Shakespearean Monologue** Choose something that you enjoy and understand. Analyze the scene carefully so that the language makes sense, and don't allow yourself to be trapped in the iambic pentameter (poetry) of the piece. Read for content and meaning. Many thoughts and sentences expand beyond one line and bridge several poetic phrases. Read the entire play, and be sure the character is within your range.
- **Classical Monologue** Choose a selection from classical literature, ranging from ancient Greek to Restoration comedy to Ibsen and Chekov. Having this material in your repertory will show that you are well versed in theatre styles and history.

Callbacks During the audition process, the director will begin to sort out combinations of people who will make the production the best and most cohesive possible. These actors will be called back to read again, usually for specific roles in the play.

Educational institutions and community theatres will post callbacks. If you are not called back by an educational institution, it is acceptable to wait until the casting process is over and then approach the director for feedback. Be sure to check both the callback sheet *and* the final cast list. Even though you are not called back, you may still be cast.

In a professional situation, most callbacks and casting are done via phone calls or E-mail. Be sure to check your messages. Producers rarely make any contact if you are not cast, and it is considered unprofessional to ask the producer for feedback on your audition. Just keep trying.

554 Student Handbook

The best way to handle a callback audition is to treat the event as if it were a rehearsal. Behave as though you already had the part. Watch for clues about how the director sees the character. If the audition or callback involves a group of people and you are able to stay in the room, listen carefully to what the director is asking from each actor.

Cold Reading Some auditions are *cold,* or unprepared, readings. Many callbacks operate in this manner. You will usually have only a few moments to prepare, sometimes with a partner or two. Use whatever time you have to become as familiar as possible with the material. The best preparation for such an audition is to read plays out loud as often as possible—alone, in class, or with friends.

Musical Audition For musical theatre, you will be required to prepare either sixteen bars of music, or a song of a specific type, such as "Broadway belt," "standard musical comedy," ballad, or even contemporary rock. Avoid using operatic-type material unless the audition specifically calls for it. Bring the music for your audition piece(s) with you and be sure it:

- Is in the key that best fits your voice.
- Has a clearly marked introduction.
- Shows what *tempo* (speed) you want.
- Indicates where you wish to start and stop.

Be prepared to sing more than sixteen bars if you are asked and have at least one additional song ready in case the director or musical director wants an "on the spot" callback. Most musical theatre actors keep a notebook of ten to twenty contrasting songs that are well-rehearsed and memorized.

Preparation

- **Memorize your audition pieces.** Nothing will kill an actor's chance of being cast more quickly than "going up" or "blanking" (forgetting your lines). The director will immediately wonder whether or not you have the discipline to memorize an entire script.
- **Rehearse your material.** Have your material in a notebook. Work with a teacher, director, or your peers to make sure your audition plays as strongly as possible.
- **Read the directions.** Auditions are almost always announced with a simple set of expectations. One of the easiest ways to impress a director is to prove that you can follow directions. If the audition calls for one sixty-second monologue, give exactly that and no more. Find out something about the play or company for which you are auditioning. Don't audition with a David Ives comic monologue for a production of *Macbeth.* If the company does only contemporary dramas, audition with pieces that show your ability to tackle David Mamet or Tom Stoppard. Make sure you know your audition time and location and never, ever arrive late.
- **Dress professionally and appropriately.** You will be dressing for both the character and the audition. You do not need to audition in costume, but what you wear should be compatible with the character you are portraying. How you dress also reflects how much respect you have for the director and the audition process. If you show up in sloppy, wrinkled clothes, the assumption may be made that your life is in similar shape.

Part One Acting **555**

Difficult Acting Scenes

"I have to cry?"
"I have to kiss him?"

If you are a method actor, you solve these problems with substitution–imagine who you'd really like to kiss, or find something from your life to cry about. If you're a technical actor, you address these situations by showing that you know how to kiss or how to cry because you've practiced the technique and it's something actors are called upon to do.

Crying In order to cry on stage, you can practice the principle of substitution by thinking of something sad in your life that will bring up strong enough emotions to generate tears. A more technical approach is to use eye drops just prior to a scene–as long as it's possible to establish that the crying began offstage. Entering with "tears" in your eyes will appear realistic. Technically, crying shows in the voice and body as much as in the eyes. People who are crying often have to catch their breath and fight to keep their voice from wavering or their shoulders from shaking.

Kissing First, check with your director to see if a real kiss is necessary or if an illusion will do. Once this is decided, there are techniques to make a stage kiss simple and believable. The taller partner, usually the man, should stand in front of the woman with his back slightly to the audience. He can then lean in and either actually kiss or place his cheek against her cheek. His head will keep the audience from actually seeing whether a real kiss takes place. The kiss should last at least three to five seconds, depending on the amount of passion that is to be shown. Getting into and out of the kiss is as important as the event itself. The buildup and response show the level of emotion and nature of the relationship.

Film

Acting Much of what you learn about theatrical acting technique has to be relearned for film and television. Many of the skills are the same, and a good actor can be accomplished at both, but the small screen (television) and the big screen (movies) can look at the actor so closely that every acting moment must become smaller and more subtle. Actors who excel in a large theatre can easily be "too big" for the screen. In order to learn to act for television and film, every actor should study with teachers who understand the style. There are classes in all the major regional and national theatre centers. Check the credentials of whomever you study under. Make sure that former students really do get work.

The best piece of advice for an actor who wants to work in television and film is to start doing so on any level. Be an extra, work on the production team, get a job as a driver–just stay close to where films are being made.

The Business of Film

Most actors rely on their agents, managers, and/or entertainment lawyers to serve as buffers and negotiators for their work in motion pictures. While the major studios provide the biggest budgets and the best and most lucrative work for actors, independent films are the wave of the late 20th and early 21st centuries. Many independent films are made "on spec." The actors work at the SAG (Screen Actors Guild) minimum wage and donate the remainder of their normal salary to the

556 Student Handbook

production budget in the hopes that once the film makes the round of independent film festivals, it will be picked up for distribution. If this happens, everyone involved in the film stands to make a great deal of money. The success of an independent film can also make a sudden star out of a relatively unknown actor or generate "heat" for the screenwriter or director. Independent films account for much of the new talent in the industry.

Improvisation

Improvisation is the spontaneous exploration of the journalistic *W's*–the same ones that appear in the section under Characterization on page 551–552. The three principal *W*'s that govern an improv are *Who? Where?* and *What?*

Who? An improvisation can be character-centered. The *who* can provide the most important imaginative content. *Who* might be an old lady, a skunk, a preacher, and so forth.

Where? An improvisation can be location-centered. The *where* can be the basis for much of the comedy or drama of the scene. *Where* could be in a zoo, in an elevator, by the shore of a farm pond, or at a funeral parlor.

What? An improvisation can be situation-centered. The *what* can be an event that provides the imaginative content that drives the direction of the improv. *What* might be a wedding, a robbery, a funeral, or a game show.

An improv based on these examples could end up being the "wedding of an old lady and a skunk in an elevator."

Improvisations will be too short or die out quickly unless there is conflict involved. If there is a situation where one of the characters wants something and the other will not let him or her have it (motivation and obstacle), then these characters are in conflict and the conversation can become quite heated and animated. The basis of energy in improvisation is conflict, either provided in the setup or created by the characters themselves.

Do's and Don'ts of Improvisation

- **Do accept every offer.** Whatever someone else says is an offer to move forward. If an improv partner says, "You wrecked the car," your response might be, "You wanted a new one anyway, and now you have the insurance money to get it."
- **Do accept what is said as fact.** Again, when a partner says, "You wrecked the car," you did! There are a million explanations, or "yes, . . . ands" available to you, such as, "Yeah it's wrecked, but it's not my fault. Your mother was talking on her cell phone, and she rear-ended me!"
- **Do stay in the world you create.** If you establish the roles of a parent and teenager, stay in that world. "You were out awfully late last night," says the parent, to which you might respond, "Oh, I was with Brian, and his parents were downstairs. Didn't they call you?"
- **Do keep focused on your motivation.** (Work to achieve your objective in the improv.)
- **Do listen, observe, and respond as the character you've created.**
- **Don't dead-end an improv with the word "No."**
- **Don't reject offers.** When your partner says, "You wrecked the car," the response, "No, I didn't," leaves little room to maneuver.

Part One Acting **557**

- **Don't reject what is said as fact.** Again, when a partner says, "You wrecked the car," the response, "Huh-uh, you did it. You were driving," creates an almost insurmountable obstacle for your partner.
- **Don't stray from the world you create.** If you are a parent and teenager arguing, remember your world. If your response to "You were out awfully late last night," is "You said I could stay out as late as I wanted, and you didn't come home on time either," we lose the sense of the balance of power in the relationships.
- **Don't spend time explaining.** Theatre is action. Use action statements whenever possible.

Motivation

Finding and using motivation is an extension of character development. It is the most important key to how a character responds to a situation in both improvisations and in written dramatic text. Why does your character act the way he or she does? What does your character truly want? How can you figure these things out and apply them to your acting scenes?

Finding motivation comes from analysis of the script, or in the case of improvised scenes, from creating wants and needs for a character. When you break a script into acting units, even the smallest unit will involve the motivation of your character. When you are perfectly clear as to what your character wants, that clarity drives your actions, inflection, and even movement.

Motivation also creates *subtext,* that which is not said or is hidden between the lines. A good playwright will generally not state a character's motivation directly but will cloak it, just as people do in actual conversation. For example, at the crises of Arthur Miller's *The Crucible,* there is a moment when the characters are virtually screaming out between and beneath the lines. John Proctor wants to prove his abiding love for Elizabeth and to seek her forgiveness by being honest, but Elizabeth wants John to lie just this one time in order to save his life. They are completely trapped by the situation and cannot say what they truly wish to have happen when the other onstage characters are listening. The audience knows the motivation that drives each one, empathizes with both, and is drawn into the tragedy of the moment.

Whether you are preparing for an audition, doing scene work, or rehearsing for a play, be sure you know and play your character's motivation. If you are having trouble, discuss it with your director or teacher. Once you have found your motivation, it will be easier to memorize lines and develop stage business, because you will know the reasons behind your words, thoughts, and actions.

Movement

Physical work is extremely important in theatre. Actors spend a great deal of time warming up and looking for ways to fine-tune working with their bodies. In addition to basic stage crosses and knowledge of stage directions, there are several important terms to remember:

- **Counter** This is the term for a move that allows another actor to take the stage or make a clear and forceful movement. Because that actor is moving, the stage picture might become unbalanced, and another actor may

558 Student Handbook

need to counter the move by stepping back or out of the way.

- **Dress** This term refers to the idea of an actor as a set piece or decoration. The director "dresses" the set with actors as he moves them about. For this reason, the director will sometimes tell an actor to "dress right" or "dress left" (move stage right or stage left) to balance the position of another actor.
- **Gesture** "What do I do with my hands?" Beginning actors tend to work with their minds first. They understand a character intellectually but cannot make physical the traits of the character. Observe people and other good actors, then imitate what they are doing. The skill of observation is very important when seeking to find the right stance or gesture.
- **Leading Center** Each character has an essential "center" to her or his physical being. An overbearing Henry VIII might feel his center in his belly and lead from that center. An intellectual Thomas More from *A Man for All Seasons* might lead with his forehead. Snoopy in *You're a Good Man, Charlie Brown* might lead with his fast-moving feet or lapping and yapping mouth. Whatever your character's center, leading with that in your mind will help your character take on a look and movement that is individual and unique.
- **Master Gesture** Technical actors may plan and method actors discover a master gesture for their characters. This gesture is a distinctive movement that helps separate the character from the actor playing the character. The gesture might be a walk, a twitch, a stance, or the pulling of a strand of hair–some significant act that reflects the inner life and nature of the character. The master gesture also separates one character from another as the audience watches each come to life in the same play. The more stylized the play, the larger the master gesture. In an intense realistic drama, the gesture might be as simple as tapping a pencil nervously. In a broad comedy, the gesture might be a funny walk or an exaggerated expression.
- **Stage Picture** The director looks at each moment on stage and sees a picture made up of characters and set pieces. Each actor not only creates an individual role, but also becomes part of this picture.

Creating Believable Action

- **Use all of your senses and your sense memory.** Where are you in the play? When were you in a similar situation in real life? How did you move? What did you do?
- **Register the environment in your brain.** Let it sink in. This may take a split second or several seconds, depending on the situation, but don't react like you already know how you're supposed to act. The reaction must be in real time. Acting is active rather than reactive. The audience needs to sense you making a discovery rather than simply following what's said in the script or reacting to the other actors on stage.
- **Respond physically to the stimulus.** If your scene takes place in a pizzeria, think about what it smells like and how it makes you feel. Whatever the environment, you should have a physical reaction that the audience can perceive.
- **Respond orally.** How you move and speak will be different depending on

Part One Acting **559**

whether you are hungry, angry, lonely, hot, cold, or tired. Your posture, your physical and verbal reactions, including tone of voice, will be affected by the environment, just as it is in real life. Physical and vocal response to the environment creates belief and represents an opportunity to use your sense of observation in order to be a stronger actor.

Fighting, Slapping, and Physical Force The principal rule in stage combat is that the victim does all the work. If you are flung to the floor, you are actually flinging yourself. The aggressor in any physical stage work or stage combat starts the blow or attack and then "pulls the punch" in a manner imperceptible to the audience. The reaction of the audience is based on the reaction from the actor receiving the blow or attack.

When an abusive husband character grabs his wife by the arm and flings her down, he simply takes hold of her arm and she makes a rapid movement back and forth, then falls to the ground. If the actor then reaches down to slap her, she may hold up a hand which receives a "slap" from the husband, but at the same time snaps her head to one side to create the illusion that he has slapped her face. The audience will watch and believe the victim.

In another example, when the monster in a production of *Frankenstein* picks the doctor up by the throat, the actor playing the doctor simply grabs the arm of the monster with both hands and does a pull up while moving his head back and forth and gasping for air. Virtually no work is done by the monster, but the audience perceives him as having great strength.

Swordplay and Stage Combat Rule one is "Be safe." Stage combat is very technical and requires much discipline and practice from both the method and technical actor. Any combat involving props should be choreographed. The director, more experienced actors, or a stage combat or martial arts professional should work with the actors to plot out every beat and every stroke of any swordplay, fistfight, violent chase sequence, or other form of elaborate fight. There is no room for improvisation in stage combat. Both combatants must have a clear idea of where the fight is going.

Training Many actors attend physical theatre schools such as those mentioned in the following section on mime and pantomime. They also study aerobics, dance, Pilates, and/or yoga. All actors should take some basic dance courses including beginning ballet, tap, and modern dance. This training is good for coordination, and most actors at some time or another are required to do some dancing in connection with a role.

Mime and Pantomime

These terms are often used interchangeably and both imply essentially the same thing–the art of telling a story through body movement and facial gestures alone.

Mime is an art form that involves creating moments of drama and theatricality through movement without vocalization. It is more formal than pantomime. Mimes do not speak, though they may sometimes vocalize. They usually wear simple clown white makeup, often with a touch of personalization such as a tear, a smile, or a frown. Classical mimes usually have

560 Student Handbook

extensive physical training and can create tricks and complete environments with their bodies. Some classical mime movements or illusions include creating a wall, ascending and descending stairs, climbing a rope, blowing up a balloon, as well as entire scenes and stories.

Pantomime, strictly speaking, is simply creating a situation or movement that represents something, such as going fishing or sweeping the floor, usually without props and often without sound. Pantomime is very useful in many theatre situations. In much of what is known as "transformational" theatre, the actors create much of the set and the props with their bodies or they use representational objects such as a hanger, piece of fabric, or small box, that can become anything because of the way the actor works with it. For example, a stick can become a fishing pole, a bat, a fly swatter, a cane, an antenna, or anything else the actor imagines.

Some plays have a combination of pantomimed and realistic props. There might be a real bowl for cooking, but the egg that goes into the bowl is pantomimed. Each play will have its own set of rules for the use of realistic versus pantomime props and situations. A simple example of this is the standard children's theatre production of *Peter Pan* in which the main character may actually "fly" using wire rigging or simply pantomime flying. Again, depending on the rules for the given production, all flying may be pantomimed, but all sword fights might use "real" prop swords.

Training Mimes are well grounded in physical theatre. Mime training is related to clown and new vaudeville training, which is taught in specialized schools. Three of the principal schools of physical theatre training are Le Coq in Paris, started by Jacques Le Coq; Decroux in Paris, founded by Etienne Decroux; and in America, the Dell'Arte school in Blue Lake, California, founded by Carlo Mazzone-Clementi.

Musical Theatre

Musical theatre in its present form—a play driven by songs and music—is one of the most uniquely American theatrical institutions. From early works such as *Babes in Toyland,* to Rodgers and Hammerstein's epic *The Sound of Music,* and from classically derived *West Side Story* through Bob Fosse's *A Chorus Line* to *The Lion King, Rent,* and *Hairspray,* the world of theatre is enriched by plays with memorable music.

An actor in musical theatre needs to be a "triple threat"—one part actor, one part singer, and one part dancer. Many theatre programs offer specialty degrees in each area, but an actor who intends to be successful in musical theatre should have a working knowledge of all three.

Acting Everything in the previous sections on acting applies to musical theatre. However, the actor must be prepared to convey a role with a minimal amount of dialogue, some of which is sung rather than spoken.

Choreography Every musical has a choreographer. The choreographer's vision is sometimes of equal importance to that of the director. Occasionally, they will be the same person. *Chicago* is as much a product of the genius of choreographer Bob Fosse as it is of all the stage directors (and even film directors) who have since interpreted the show. Choreography is the art of creating and directing not only the specific

Part One Acting **561**

dance combinations of any given piece, but also of bringing to life the "look" of the entire production. Some musicals are jazz-based, some modern, and some, like *The King and I,* owe much to the beauty of the waltz and ballroom dancing. In order to learn dance numbers, the actor needs a dance vocabulary. This is achieved through taking basic dance classes and fearlessly trying everything suggested by the choreographer.

Music Voice lessons are important for most actors who seek a professional career but are absolutely necessary for actors who wish to participate in musical theatre. Most colleges will offer voice as part of their curriculum, but there are also excellent private vocal coaches and voice teachers. In addition, you should learn to play a musical instrument, one that requires you to read music. Piano helps you learn the structure and theory of music. Guitar is excellent because it gives you an instrument with which to accompany yourself when you sing. If you don't read music, be prepared to keep a small tape recorder with you at all times so that you can record your parts, both harmonies and solos, and practice them outside of regular rehearsal time.

Networking

Young actors need to be supportive of one another. The good and bad relationships you develop in your career will come back to help or hinder your progress. Theatre is a business of relationships and connections. Many theatre companies are started by frustrated actors who are not getting cast and branch out to become self-producers. The innovative and experimental work created at these theatres often becomes a part of the mainstay theatre scene. Your relationship to such actors becomes important when one of them suddenly becomes the director or playwright of a hit show.

Your teachers, directors, and their peers are also important connections. The acting profession is actually quite a small industry, and cultivating friendships and professional relationships with those who have gone before can pay the dual dividends of increased knowledge of your craft for the present and unique opportunities in the future.

Besides the opportunities you might receive from your theatre connections, you will eventually have the opportunity to give back to others. This is perhaps even more important in a collaborative profession than in the business world. Join professional organizations. Work for free on occasion. Make outreach a part of your theatrical life—outreach to youth, to the aged, to those challenged or less fortunate. Volunteer to share what you've learned and the talent you've cultivated. All that you give, you will receive back, and all that you receive is a gift from those who have gone before in this very small and occasionally brutal business.

Performance Art

Another form of acting is performance art. Performance art is almost always interdisciplinary. Multimedia and mixed media compliment and enhance the theatrical aspects of the presentation, which is often called an *installation.*

During the late 1950s and into the 1960s, performance art was developed as a defiant alternative to more traditional theatrical events. Music was often improvised, slide projection was commonplace, and the performer would express him or herself in an abstract or absurd manner. Some of the

562 Student Handbook

best known early performance artists were John Cage and Yoko Ono. John Cage still has a tremendous influence in the field of classical music, and one of his performance art pieces is still ongoing. This piece adds a brick per year to play a specific pedal note on a German organ. This musical piece will take over 1000 years to complete. Other examples of performance art installations could include:

- Creating a living room in which the artist simply goes about daily life in front of the viewing public.
- Reading from classical plays or literature while dance is going on in response to the reading.
- Musicians improvising while a theatrical artist responds with poetry.

Performance art is all about concept. There is usually no director–the artist fulfills that function. As a result, performance art sometimes has a random or unplanned feel. Although it may appear spontaneous and simple, creating an interesting, multidisciplined environment is easily as difficult as creating an evening of good theatre. The art in both cases is dependent upon content, thought, audience response, timeliness, relevance, and creativity. Being involved in performance art gives the theatre actor a wonderful opportunity to be exposed to new and exciting artists and art forms.

Physical Warm-ups

There is not a sport in the world that doesn't require the athlete to warm up. While theatre is not a sport, it is a very physical process. Most educational and training theatre ensembles will have a group warm-up. Sometimes this is led by the director, at other times by one of the company members. Professional actors are expected to warm up on their own rather than taking up paid rehearsal time.

Because the tools of the acting trade are voice, body, and imagination, all three should be exercised during a warm up. You can develop your own warm-up routines, but you should also be open to learning them from other actors and even other disciplines. Remember to warm up the voice along with the body. Vocal warm-ups can include tongue twisters, over-enunciation, experimenting with your lines from the play, and singing vocalizations. Physical warm-ups should include the entire body, starting slowly and increasing in intensity. Your mental warm-up should include at least a little improvisation, even if it's only by talking with yourself or your character in the mirror. Meditation and guided imagery are other types of mental warm-ups that help clear the mind in preparation for its use onstage.

Radio

Before television, there was radio. The Golden Age of Radio featured nearly as many comedies, news shows, adventure programs, serials, soap operas, and musical revues as there are on television today. Some of the great stars and stories of early television began their careers on the radio, including Jack Benny, Burns and Allen, and *The Lone Ranger.* With the advent of television as the principal media in the American household, radio has become predominantly a vehicle for music, sports, news, and talk or opinion shows. Radio is generally not as lucrative as television for the actor. Jobs include disc jockey, sportscaster, news or weather forecaster, talk radio personality, and voice-over actors for advertising commercials.

Part One Acting **563**

Each of these requires extensive use of the voice. Actors with very unique and distinct voices tend to find work on radio most easily. A quick wit and improvisational ability also contribute to success in this field.

In recent years there has been a resurgence of interest in radio, and many stations are now broadcasting "made-for-radio" comedy, mystery, adventure, and variety shows. One of the most successful of these is *A Prairie Home Companion,* featuring the wit, wisdom, and storytelling of Garrison Keillor.

Most universities with a television and film department provide courses in radio work, and many of these universities allow students to get hands-on experience by working with the university's local FM or AM radio station.

Readers Theatre

Readers Theatre is just that—an opportunity to read a play without memorization. This allows a play to reach an audience in a shorter time period, allows actors to gain valuable experience getting to know plays, and allows audiences to engage their imaginations and discover new material.

Readers Theatre is used for educational purposes, for new play development, and for pure entertainment. In this medium, the level of blocking or movement is up to the director and/or cast members. Much of Readers Theatre is done with actors seated on stools with their scripts on music stands. Words rather than actions are the stars of the show. Performance in this genre is therefore dependent upon a clear commitment by the actor to the vocal work involved in creating a character or characters. (It is possible to reduce a ten-character play to a reading by four or five actors through the doubling of parts.)

Readers Theatre usually, but not always, has a director who also serves as a producer, assigning roles, guiding rehearsals, and planning the evening's reading. Either the director or a stage manager reads any stage directions in the script. Following are ways to stage these performances:

Platform Readings are done with a clear distinction between audience and actors. The actors sit in front of the audience on a bare stage.

Monodrama is the reading of a play or selections from a play by a single actor. Clarity of character and the ability to quickly shift from one voice to the next are essential to maintaining interest during this sort of presentation. Monodrama is also defined as "memorized work that is written for or by a single actor, such as a one-man or one-woman show." Historical figures are often the subjects of monodramas. A prime example is Hal Holbrook's *Evening with Mark Twain.*

Choral Readings involve more than one person reading at the same time. Choral reading is often done to great effect at large events. Actors on one side of the room might read a poem by an American poet such as Walt Whitman, while those on the other side might read excerpts from the daily news in a "call and response" manner. In choral reading, the actors must be keenly sensitive to one another and to the rhythms of the work being read. Choral reading is hard but can be very effective. Many people are familiar with choral reading through their own religious institutions.

564 Student Handbook

There is a profound unity of purpose achieved through choral reading, which is why it is so prevalent in religion and also why the chorus was such an important part of early Greek theatre.

Group Readings One of the most entertaining ways to learn about theatre is to start a play-reading group. The group meets and chooses plays, then reads them, taking turns or choosing roles, sections, or otherwise dividing the material. Group readings are done mostly for the entertainment, education, and artistic development of the group doing the reading.

Chamber Theatre Chamber theatre takes its name from chamber music. Usually smaller than fully-staged theatre, Chamber Theatre often involves some staging. Actors may still carry scripts, but they do the work "on their feet."

Rehearsals

Rehearsals can be both the most exciting and most challenging part of the theatrical process. As an actor, the time you are not on stage may move very slowly. Be sure to use your time wisely. Study your lines and make sure you are ready for your entrances.

There are several types of rehearsals, each with a specific purpose.

Blocking Rehearsals are used to work out stage movement. Actors carry their scripts, carefully writing down stage directions. Nothing frustrates a director, assistant director, or stage manager more than having to go through blocking a second or third time for an actor who was either inattentive or who didn't write down what he or she was to do the first time the direction was given. A pencil and eraser are the best tools for this job, since the second time through, things may change. The director may see a better way to play or stage a scene, and in the case of a new play, the playwright may change a line or even an entire scene.

Working and Polishing Rehearsals follow blocking rehearsals and can be the most fun for both actor and director. When the rehearsal period is long enough, this is the time for exploration and discovery. The play is analyzed, subjected to experimentation, developed, dissected, and put back together.

Technical Rehearsals are not about the actor. During a technical rehearsal, the actor takes a backseat to the sound, lights, stage management, cues, and other elements that will allow the production to shine in its full theatricality. Actor discipline is extremely important during tech rehearsals. The actor must be prepared to start and stop, wait, wait, and probably wait some more—and yet be able to start again with full emotion and clear purpose the moment the rehearsal continues. Some technical rehearsals go "cue by cue," meaning that large chunks of dialogue during which there are no sound or light cues may be skipped. Again, the actor must be ready for this and give a clear and precise performance of the cues so that the technicians can recognize their cues and be prepared to do their part to support the production.

Dress Rehearsals are often difficult for actors. Added to performances that seemed "set" are the sudden distractions of unfamiliar clothing and makeup. This can be especially difficult for a *period* (not contemporary) play that requires elaborate

Part One Acting **565**

costumes and/or complex makeup. Concentration becomes the most important skill an actor can use during this time—that and a positive attitude. "Make it an acting problem," is one of the favorite responses of a costumer, stage manager, or director to actor complaints about wigs that don't feel right or clothes that seem too big or appear unflattering. Actors need to remind themselves that costumes and makeup are similar to personal props. There are often discoveries to be made about characters based on the vision the costume designer and director had when wardrobes were planned. If the fabric of a costume is especially reflective or shiny, that character may also shine and reflect. If a costume flows, then the actor wearing it should give it every opportunity to do so. If costumes include accessories such as kerchiefs, lace, monocle, glasses, pocket watch, or pockets, characters should find ways to use them.

Making these discoveries when first wearing the costume is part of what makes the dress rehearsal feel so different. An experienced director knows that during a dress rehearsal some of the old work will be left behind as characters catch up with their costumes.

Final Rehearsal All elements of the production should be in place during the final rehearsal. Even though every actor will continue to make some new discoveries during the run of a show, the expectation of the production team is that at the final rehearsal they can see how the production will appear to the audience. This rehearsal is their final opportunity to give notes and to tweak the show before the public adds the most important dimension of response.

Previews In professional theatres with long runs, the final rehearsal is often followed by a series of preview rehearsals, which are actually performances of the show in front of an audience. These are especially important for new plays and are always done for shows that plan to move to a major theatre on Broadway, or even onto one of the many strong regional theatre stages. Previews give the production team time to make changes based on how the audience reacts to the material. Comedy can be clarified, timing cleaned up, and dramatic moments crafted for the maximum possible effect.

Press Night is the last preview or first performance depending on the theatre involved. Press night is when the critics are invited in to review the play. Major commercial theatre projects often live and die by the success of their previews and press nights.

Script

Actors create their own working script in a variety of manners. Many actors photocopy the script onto pages that can be put in a notebook. Some actors, like directors, prefer to have the script copied on only one side of each sheet, so the back becomes available for notes. These can be notes on staging and blocking, character notes, or notes received from the director during the course of the show. The actor traditionally highlights his or her lines so that they are easy to find during working rehearsals and for purposes of memorization. The notebook also provides a good place to keep rehearsal schedules and other handouts the actor receives from the stage manager, assistant director, director, producer, and other members of the production team.

566 Student Handbook

Storytelling

Storytellers practice their craft by performing at various venues on the professional storytelling circuit. They may also belong to professional organizations and/or take part in national competitions. In addition, storytellers are in high demand in the world of theatre for youth.

A good storyteller uses the same tools as an actor—voice, body, and imagination. A storyteller combines a strong narrative voice that sets the scene and strong character voices that propel the story through dialogue. The storyteller is really multiple actors in one, creating each character and building the story through the combination of character and dramatic action. Storytellers who create their own stories must work much like playwrights, creating a story structure that includes conflict, rising action, crisis, and climax.

Storytellers usually tell more than one story during a session, and these should have some variety so that the entire session shows a dramatic build and a rhythmic ebb and flow. The strongest stories are usually saved for last.

Television

Next to the movie industry, television provides the most lucrative possibilities for the young actor. Since more "product" is created for television, there are more opportunities for acting jobs.

Most television programs are designed to appeal to the broadest possible audience. For this reason, some actors feel they compromise their "art" when they work in television. Such actors must weigh the relative values of great art with a full refrigerator. Some television shows, made-for-TV movies, and even series are works by important artists and exhibit great artistry.

On the other hand, there is no doubt that some programming is sensationalistic and driven solely by ratings—the industry's determination of what people are watching most frequently. Television reflects the mass culture of our country, while theatre generally reflects the cultural life of artists and their vision. This is not meant to be judgmental. People enjoy comedy, sports, news, and sentimental stories, and the industry is able to provide such fare. The comparison is similar to discussing the relative values of a newspaper and a novel. Fewer people will read the novel, but it may have a longer lasting effect on the aesthetic (artistic) history and strength of a culture.

Most television programming can be grouped into the following categories:

Children's Programming Since the 1950s with its *Captain Kangaroo* and Saturday morning cartoons, television has produced fare for children. In the early years, most programming was commercially driven by sponsors of breakfast cereals and toys. Since then, however, the advent of public television has opened the door for shows with educational as well as entertainment value. Programs such as *Sesame Street* and *Mister Rogers' Neighborhood* play an important role in the national education process.

Dramatic Series Television dramas range from action adventure, such as *ER*, to police and courtroom series, such as *Law and Order.* Drama series and sitcoms (situation comedies) usually include a stock

Part One Acting **567**

(regular) cast of characters and many featured roles around whom each week's drama revolves. Dramatic series tend to choose topical themes and reflect the world as it is. For this reason, most series last anywhere from two to six seasons before the taste of the public and the nature of current events bring new work forward.

Educational and Informational Television Public television and channels such as the History Channel and the Discovery Channel have done much to make historical and factual events entertaining and available to the general public.

Reality TV Reality TV has always been a part of television programming. Early shows such as *The Dating Game, This Is Your Life,* and *Candid Camera* all dealt with reality-based incidents. Currently, however, reality-type programs dominate TV fare. The onslaught of such offerings is due in part to recent strikes by the actors' and writers' unions. Without scripts or actors, producers and networks looked for other ways to fill the holes in their schedules. The result was the development of reality programming such as *Survivor, Fear Factor,* and *The Bachelor.* Networks were delighted to discover that such shows drew large audiences (and thus, sponsors) and, for the most part, avoided the need for expensive professional talent. In fact, the acting industry has suffered because of the popularity of such shows. The artistic value of reality television is an easy target, but the fact that such shows remain popular is a strong statement about the current cultural climate in America.

Science Fiction From the movie houses of the 1930s, serialized adventures of *Flash Gordon* and *Superman* quickly made their way to the small screen. These were followed by such shows as *The Twilight Zone, Alfred Hitchcock Presents,* and *Star Trek.* Recent science fiction series have included further editions of *Star Trek* and newer, edgier shows such as *The X-Files* and *Blade.*

Situation Comedies (sitcoms) From *I Love Lucy, The Beverly Hillbillies,* and *All in the Family* to *Seinfeld, Friends,* and *The Simpsons,* the sitcom is one of the mainstays of television. In historical derivation, the sitcom most resembles commedia dell'arte–comedy based on larger-than-life stock characters in situations that reflect our lives and allow us to laugh at our own mistakes and weaknesses.

Soap Operas Soap operas are the melodramas of today's media. Viewers thrive on the sensationalistic surrealism of characters suffering even more than people do in real life. *Days of Our Lives, The Guiding Light,* and others have evolved and kept their audiences for decades by airing hyper-dramatic situations and the difficulties of both rich and poor.

Sporting Events Some of the highest ratings go to the industry that also consumes the most entertainment dollars–professional sporting events. The NFL, NBA, and collegiate athletics take up a good portion of airtime on commercial channels. These events also provide jobs for those who wish to work in the industry either on camera or behind the scenes.

568 Student Handbook

Voice

Caring for and cultivating the voice take up much of the training time of the professional actor. Without clear diction and a strong instrument, an actor cannot hope to have a successful career in this very competitive business. Some actors and actresses are born with a particularly powerful or unique voice, but others may still aspire to success through diligent work and training.

Actors must develop vocal control of the following elements:

Accents Accents may seem easy, but they are very hard to do correctly. In some comedies, actors will "fake" an accent, having fun with the sound of "pretend" British, French, or German. This is fine for burlesque or broader comedy, but it is not acceptable when trying to create a real character. Some plays, and certainly many movie and television production companies, hire phonetic or diction experts as accent coaches. Actors without such resources can purchase tapes and guides for different dialects and accents. Nothing shouts "amateur" more than a bad accent, and nothing can enrich a play more than a well-researched one. Some actors and actresses have a talent or an "ear" for accents; for others, diction and accents are just another part of the hard work that is the discipline of the professional actor.

Emphasis and Subordination Some words are more important than others, as are some phrases. Your director might ask you to "point" a portion of your speech so that a crucial piece of information is not missed. On the other hand, some speeches or parts of lines are less important and can be "thrown away." This can be done to move quickly through material or even for comic intent.

Where the emphasis in a line is placed, will also have a definite impact on what the line means. Sometimes the playwright will underline or boldface a word or phrase to help make it clear where he or she is going with the line. Note how the emphasis of different words changes the meaning in the following sentences.

I'll take the money to town.
I'll **take** the money to town.
I'll take the **money** to town.
I'll take the money to **town**.

Final Consonants Some beginning actors drop the ends of individual words, not truly finishing consonants. "Give me the hat back, won't you, Fred?" might become "Gimme eh ha ba, on u, Fre?"

Practice speaking your lines, making sure that every consonant is crisp and clear. This may feel unnatural at first, but the more it becomes second nature to you, the easier it will be to command an audience with the clarity of your voice and line delivery.

Pause and Rate Attention to pauses and speaking rates can make vocal acting stronger and more natural sounding.

Pauses are an important part of speaking. On the positive side, a pause creates emphasis. The audience will literally hold its collective breath waiting to hear what you say next. On the negative side, too long a pause can indicate that you've forgotten your next line! Although long pauses occur naturally during real conversation, in the theatre, it often appears like

Part One Acting **569**

a missed cue or a late entrance. If an actor leaves too many long pauses in between sentences or before starting his or her line, the scene will begin to drag.

Rate of delivery is also important. The actor needs to speak clearly and concisely at a pace that allows the audience to follow what's said but not become bored. Picking up cues does not always mean speaking faster–it can mean to speak sooner, one line after the other.

The opposite problem to dragging is rushing. Some actors learn their lines so well that they rattle them off without giving them full meaning. In more declamatory styles, including certain passages of Shakespeare, the actor can actually slow down and play with the poetry of the language. Most of the time, however, it is important to speak naturally but at a reasonable rate of speed.

Swallowing Words Beginning actors who lack experience with breath control, may swallow words–often at the end of sentences. An actor might have a line such as "I'm off and I won't be back until sunrise." If the actor swallows the end of the line it might sound like "I'm off and I won't be b--k t-l s--rse." Although difficult to show on paper, it is easy to spot when an actor rushes the end of a line, dropping pitch and volume while increasing rate.

570 Student Handbook

Part Two Directing and Producing

The Director

Even though the director controls the production and develops its artistic vision, he or she is first and foremost the principal collaborator. A good director establishes unity of purpose through a spirit of cooperation and respect. Below are aspects of the director's work.

Choosing the Play There are several factors that guide the choice of a play. Some of these are artistic and some are practical.

- **Artistic Preference** The director may choose a play based on his or her passion for the specific play or playwright. The director may feel a period piece must be presented because only contemporary plays were done during the previous season. The director may want to explore the unique worlds of David Mamet or Maria Irene Fornes. The director might be committed to new works and may even hold a contest for new plays or select a new play from one of the many play development workshops across the country. Or, the director may simply choose a play because he or she has always wanted to direct it.
- **Box Office** The box office is a big and not always artistic factor in choosing a play. Even in educational theatre, filling the house can make a difference in the ongoing success of the program. Sometimes a theatre can support experimental or edgy work that brings in a smaller audience as long as they are willing to do one or two "box-office hits." Musicals and plays such as *West Side Story, The Odd Couple, Into the Woods, Oliver, A Christmas Carol, My Fair Lady, Camelot,* and many others are almost sure to fill the house.
- **Performance Space** The three main types of performance space are:

1. **Proscenium** The proscenium is the classic theatre framed by the *proscenium arch*—the well-defined sides and top that border the front of the stage. Most proscenium stages have a main front curtain and then a playing area with *wings* (areas on the sides of the stage for the exit and entrance of actors and scenery). The proscenium stage establishes the "fourth wall" through which the audience watches the production.
2. **Thrust** A thrust stage is any configuration in which the stage is built out so that the audience surrounds it on three sides.
3. **Arena** Arena staging is theatre-in-the-round with the audience on all sides of the actors. This is the most intimate of theatre settings, but it presents obvious challenges to actors, the design team, and the director.

After analyzing a script, the producer and the director may decide that they want to present the play in the intimate space of an arena or thrust stage. On the other hand, when doing a production with a large cast and complex sets, they may opt for a full proscenium theatre.

Even when there is only one choice of space, it can sometimes be reconfigured. High schools with full proscenium stages

Part Two Directing and Producing **571**

may seat the audience on the stage in order to present theatre-in-the-round or three-quarter-round.

The choice of space may also be a financial one. If producing a big budget Broadway musical, the theatre must have enough seats to guarantee the income necessary to meet expenses.

The director may also choose a play based on the strengths of available talent. If he or she has a very strong African-American actor who is ready for a large role, the director may chose to showcase that actor by doing *Othello.* If the director has a large number of very talented singers who are strong physical actors, he or she may decide on a show such as *Sweeny Todd* or *Candide.* If the company has its own rock band, the director might consider *Rent* or *Grease* with the band onstage during the performance.

The size of the cast is also a criterion. High school producers may need to use thirty to fifty people and so may have to choose a large musical or Shakespearean production. Most schools have more female actors than male, so a director might look for plays such as *Steel Magnolias* that feature strong female casts.

Developing the Artistic Vision As the director reads and analyzes a script, he or she begins to develop an aesthetic vision. Sometimes this is a concept, such as setting *Romeo and Juliet* during the Civil War. Sometimes the vision is more technical, such as doing *The Glass Menagerie* in the round with as few set pieces and props as possible.

Along with the artistic vision, the director must also consider functional aspects of the script, such as:

- What acting areas are required?
- How many different locations are needed?
- How many entrances and exits occur?
- What levels might be used for various settings?
- What special effects or technical needs are required?

The director shares his or her initial vision and set of requirements with the production team members and then listens to input from them. Their ideas will help to shape, fulfill, and even add to the director's vision. In subsequent design meetings, the designers for costumes, sets, makeup, and lights will bring in sketches, plots, models, and renderings and share them with the rest of the team.

Planning the Blocking and Stage Composition As a director works with the actors, he or she moves them around the stage forming stage "pictures," or arrangements. Stage pictures show the relative power and importance of the characters. Audience focus will always go to the actor in the strongest position. Center stage and downstage right are the most dominant positions. Movement and stage pictures are dictated by issues of appropriateness, feasibility, genre, and intent.

- **Appropriateness** Moving actors around merely for the sake of movement will read as unnatural and unrealistic. In fact, moving people around as a means of holding the audience's interest does

572 Student Handbook

just the opposite. The movement becomes diluted and unimportant. All movement should relate to the content of the scene and be appropriate to the motivation of and relationships among the characters.

- **Feasibility** Actors must not be asked to do something that makes them uncomfortable or puts them in danger. An elderly actor can not suddenly spring across the room. An unskilled actor should not be asked to participate in stage combat or swordplay.
- **Genre** A director responds to genre and style when blocking movement patterns. Classical theatre may require adherence to a different set of rules than modern drama. Melodrama is often very stylized, comedy very broad, and drama very reserved. Sometimes the best movement is no movement at all.
- **Intent** What is the director trying to say with the movement and stage pictures he or she creates? How do these elements reflect relationships among characters as well as the mood and theme of the play?

The blocking developed by the director should be flexible. Actors bring to a production varying amounts of experience as well as their own character research and motivation. Often, after the initial blocking session, the actor may feel that his or her character would move in a manner other than the director has indicated. All such ideas should be explored. Although the final decision remains with the director, actors often provide new and interesting ways to block scenes based on their characters' motivations and impulses.

The Producer

In professional terms, a producer has both the best and worst of all possible jobs. The producer has the greatest possibility of realizing profit and recognition for artistic success as well as the greatest financial risk. Producers are often idea people who provide the backing and backbone for a production. Some are very hands-on, helping to decide which directors, designers, or actors to hire as well as choosing the play. A producer in high school theatre is often the drama teacher and occasionally a fine arts administrator or even the bookkeeper. The producer in a community or not-for-profit theatre setting is often the board of directors. In community theatre, if the production is profitable there will be money to fund the next production and perhaps increase production values as the theatre becomes more successful.

The producer is the money person in professional theatre, gathering the funding to get the show on its feet. Since theatre receives all money on the "back end" (revenue comes only after the production money has been spent), the producer is also the risk-taker. If the show should flop, the producer is the one left holding the bag. Everyone else gets paid for the work done. If the show makes a profit, so does the producer. The following people report to the producer:

The Business Manager The business manager in a high school production may be the school's treasurer or financial officer. In a small theatre, the producer often handles the business manager's duties, which include:

Part Two Directing and Producing **573**

- Working with the producer and director to create a budget.
- Maintaining, updating, and reporting on the budget.
- Collecting and banking receipts.
- Making sure the play does not go over budget.
- Getting approval from the director or producer to go over budget.
- Authorizing and tracking expenses.
- Paying bills.
- Handling the payroll of contract labor and employees.
- Overseeing the box office.

The House Manager The house manager is responsible for the seating and comfort of the audience. He or she sees that the auditorium is a comfortable temperature, that the doors are open early for audience seating at each performance, and that programs are available for distribution. The house manager also supervises the ushers by helping them become familiar with the seating arrangements. Ushers hand out programs and escort audience members to their seats.

Publicity, Ticket, and Program Personnel Members of these crews design and procure printed materials such as posters, ads, and tickets; create advertising campaigns; sell paid advertising for programs; arrange for cast photos; write and place announcements about the show on the radio or in newspapers; distribute flyers; arrange for reviewers; sell tickets; and so forth.

The Production Team

One of the most critical jobs of the producer and director is to bring together an effective production team. In schools, this team may consist of both students and professionals. Students who have a considerable amount of technical experience can often be stage managers and, when given training and the benefit of experience, can even serve as costume or set designers.

Some or all of the following personnel may be part of the production team. Their roles will be discussed further in Parts Three through Eight of this handbook.

- **Choreographer** Plans and teaches all dance and stylized movement for a production.
- **Costume Designer** Designs, supervises, and/or builds the costumes.
- **Fight Choreographer** Plans fight and swordplay scenes and teaches fight techniques.
- **Music Director** If the production has live music, a musical director contacts, hires, trains, and conducts the musicians and works with the singers and sound designer.
- **Set Designer** Designs and supervises set construction and painting.
- **Sound Designer** Designs the soundscape for the show, including sound effects and incidental music.
- **Stage Manager** The stage manager is the unsung hero in theatre. In a good production, the director and stage manager seek to be invisible, allowing the actors and ultimately the play to take center stage. The director technically finishes his or her job on opening night. From that point on, the stage manager is responsible for everything that happens, both on and off the stage. A partial list of the stage manager's duties includes:

574 Student Handbook

- Attending all production meetings.
- Preparing the prompt book.
- Posting the auditions, callbacks, and casting notices.
- Assisting in the selection of crew members.
- Preparing the cast and crew contact sheets.
- Setting up, posting, and updating the rehearsal schedule.
- Marking the ground plan on the stage or rehearsal area floor.
- Keeping track of time during breaks.
- Coordinating all tech and dress rehearsals.
- Calling light, sound, and music cues during the show.

A stage manager usually highlights cues in the prompt book since they are his or her "lines" for running the show. A stage manager also usually writes in a "warn" or "ready" cue so that when calling the show, the lighting and sound operators can be alerted before the cue actually runs. For example, the stage manager would call "Ready lights cue 1," "Ready sound cue 2," "Go cue 1," "Go cue 2," and so on. Sound cues and light cues are often written in different colors so that they are easy to spot.

A positive attitude from all members of the production team will create a positive attitude from the cast and crews serving under them.

The Prompt Book

The prompt book is the place where the director breaks the script down into units, names the units, indicates cues, and pre-plans the blocking. As blocking is given and/or changed and cues are added, the assistant director or stage manager keeps the book up to date. The prompt book should be easy to work with and functional for the duration of the rehearsal and production process. Usually, each page of the script is duplicated on three-hole-punched notebook paper. (The script should already have been paid for so there is no danger of copyright infringement.) In addition, some directors put a copy of the ground plan between each page of the script so that they can visualize the playing area and mark blocking and stage pictures.

The prompt book becomes the most comprehensive record of an individual production. When they are first produced, many plays contain few or no stage directions. In such cases, the prompt book notations become part of the manuscript when the play is published. Many directors and theatres keep copies of their prompt books in case they decide to repeat a production.

The Script

When choosing a script, it is important to consider what type of play you wish to live with as a producer or director. Producers generally choose plays based on box office receipts and profitability. Directors more often choose what appeals to them artistically. The best producer/director teams find a convergence of these two visions. When preparing to choose a script, the team must look at both genre and style.

The Comedy Genre Comedy can be broken down into several categories. *Low comedy* is physical and exaggerated and includes burlesque and farce. *Middle comedy* relies more on situations and mental aerobics than on the physical. Romantic comedy and parody fall into this group.

Part Two Directing and Producing **575**

High comedy is intellectual in form, often mocking the upper classes. This group includes satire and comedy of manners.

The Dramatic Genre Drama includes the most classical form of Greek tragedy, but also refers to many other types of plays dealing with serious or realistic subjects, but not necessarily with the unhappy ending of tragedy. Drama can deal with social issues, family situations, or historical events. Categories include classic and Shakespearean tragedy, melodrama, psychological and social drama, and fantasy.

Experimental Style *Avant garde* or experimental theatre are catchall expressions that encompass whatever is current, new, and exciting in off-Broadway, off-off-Broadway, or street theatre. Once a style is accepted, it is no longer experimental.

Historical Style The style of a script can be defined in historical terms. Major historical styles include: *commedia dell'arte,* Elizabethan, Restoration, romanticism, realism, expressionism, theatre of the absurd, theatre of involvement, and transformational theatre.

Presentational Style When the "fourth wall" is broken, and an actor speaks directly to the audience, the style is called *presentational.*

Representational Style
Representational plays are those in which the actors seem unaware of an audience, The audience watches as though through a "fourth wall."

Post Production

This term has two different meanings. One is theatrical and the other is for film and video work.

In Theatre The show is over. Now what? You *strike*—which means all the company members help take apart and put away sets, props, costumes, etc., and return the theatre to a state of readiness for the next production. The stage manager runs the strike and is usually responsible for putting together a strike duty sheet that everyone follows. In professional companies, each group of workers has its own strike duties. Actors clean up their areas and return their props and costumes. Set crews take apart and store the set; costume crews clean and store the costumes; props crews return or put away props. In most nonprofessional theatres, strike involves everyone who participated in the production.

In Television and Film Post production has a completely different meaning in film and television. In these areas, post production is everything that happens to a film after the footage has been shot and the actors' work is over. Post production includes the following tasks:

- Edit and review the *dailies* and *rushes* (film from each day of shooting).
- Edit the video/film.
- Add sound effects and music.
- Add special effects.
- Create a rough cut for the director's approval.
- Add credits.
- Make and screen the final cut of the film.
- Distribute and promote the film.

576 Student Handbook

Part Three Costumes

Costume Crew

The size of the costume crew for a particular show varies based on the production values of the theatre and the scale of the play being produced. The crew works with the costume designer prior to production week and under the stage manager from that point on. Crew members assist with:

- Organizing available costumes.
- Measuring actors.
- Finding, buying, renting, and borrowing costumes.
- *Building* (making) costumes: sewing, painting, gluing, etc.
- Creating and updating the costume plot and acquisitions list.
- Fitting and altering costumes.
- Serving as "dressers" for actors or actresses who have fast changes.
- Washing, repairing, ironing, and maintaining costumes.
- Keeping the dressing rooms clean.
- Returning any borrowed items after the show closes.

The costume crew *call* (the time to be at the theatre) is usually fifteen minutes to one-half hour before the actor call. Some members of the crew may be able to leave once everyone is dressed, but other crew members will stay for the entire show in order to be available for any emergency sewing or repair. The crew also does a check at the end of each performance to determine laundry and repair needs.

Costume Design

Before working on a costume plan, the costume designer will analyze the play to answer the following questions:

- When does the play take place (period)?
- How many characters are there?
- Who are the characters?
- How are their clothes described?
- Are they rich? poor?
- Over what period of time does the play take place?
- Do characters need to change clothes?
- Are there any special needs, i.e. accommodating a body mic or including pockets, bows, or other things mentioned in the script?

At the first production meeting, the costume designer will listen to the producer and director's vision for the show. Next, the designer will create costume *renderings,* sketches of characters in costume that enable the team to visualize the designer's concept. *Swatches* (small pieces of fabric selected for the costume) often accompany renderings. With the director's approval, the designer begins to supervise the gathering and building of the costumes.

Costume Considerations The creativity of costuming should follow some practical considerations in addition to the artistic concept for the play.

- **Action** What will the actor be doing in this costume: dancing, fighting, loving, falling, running?

Part Three Costumes **577**

- **Changeability** How easy is the costume to put on and take off, especially if the actor has fast changes, wears multiple costumes for different scenes, or plays multiple characters?
- **Comfort** Will the actor be able to work during the entire performance without worrying about the costume?
- **Durability** How well will the costume hold up? (Consider the fabric as well as the assembly.)
- **Historical Accuracy** Does the costume look as though it is truly from the play's historical period?
- **Coordinated Effect** How will all the costumes look with each other?

Costume Efficiency

- Look for ways to layer costumes. Does each change have to be full, or can a change be effected by adding or removing pieces of clothing?
- Plan for an actor's fast changes by having a member of the costume crew waiting in the wings to help.
- Use Velcro™ instead of buttons and snaps.
- Use reversible clothing. This is a quick way to create more than one look for the same actor.

Costume Plot

The costume designer will track all characters through the entire play, noting what each one will wear in any given scene as well as any changes the character might need to make. This costume plot allows the designer to make a clear list of all needed costumes. He or she then determines which are already available in the school or company's costume shop, which need to be borrowed, rented, or purchased, and which may be altered or built.

Decoration

Fabrics and trims can help create a period look. Gold braid, lace, velvet capes, "jeweled" clasps, leather or faux leather fabric, burlap, felt, and other specialty fabrics can transform a simple garment into anything from a peasant girl's dress to a Roman soldier's tunic and cape. Trims can be sewn on or applied with a hot glue gun. Some decorations are painted on with fabric paint or markers. Stenciling or sponging the material can create other effects.

"Distressing"

Often a costume needs to appear well worn, or *distressed.* This can be done by using sandpaper or a wire brush on the elbows, knees, collars, cuffs, and hems of the garment. Stretching clothing until it is baggy and out of shape also adds to the effect. Fabric can also be distressed by simply putting it on the ground and walking on it!

Dyeing

At one time or another, every costume department will find it necessary to dye fabric. Dyes such as Rit™ and Tintex™ are available in fabric stores, as well as grocery and discount department stores. For the deepest shades, you may have to use a unified aniline dye or a disperse dye available from theatrical supply houses. Costumes that need to be the same color should be dyed at the same time. Different batches seem to take to the dye in different ways. Wash all dyed material in cold water or have it dry-cleaned.

578 Student Handbook

Measurements

The important measurements for women and men differ. You should create a standard measurement chart for both genders. Make and date charts for each actor and keep them on file. An actor who does a show two months later may not need a new chart. A year later, however, the actor might have different measurements. Although hair and eye color are not true "measurements," they are often helpful to the costumer in terms of matching costume color to a particular actor and should be added to the chart. Whenever possible, measurements should be taken by persons of the same sex as the actor–especially in school settings.

Patterns

When building costumes, it is often useful to begin with a commercial pattern. These are available in various sizes at any fabric store. Although some "period" patterns are available, you may have to adjust a contemporary pattern to achieve the look you need. Wedding dresses and formal wear often lend themselves to adaptation. Features such as sleeves, vest lengths, hemlines, and necklines can be modified to achieve the necessary silhouette.

Sewing

Sewing is simply a matter of creating a *seam*–which is a line of stitches that joins two or more pieces of fabric. It is necessary to leave some fabric free between the edge of the fabric and the seam–this is called the *seam allowance*–which is traditionally 5/8" wide. Whether stitching by hand or using a machine, use pins to hold the fabric in place while stitching along the seam allowance. To be an effective machine sewer, you have to learn to sew a straight line and keep a steady, medium speed to avoid fabric bunching up. Finish your seams by trimming the seam allowance with pinking shears to create a zigzag cut. This will keep the edges from fraying.

Wardrobe Room

Sometimes called a *costume room* or *costume shop,* the wardrobe room, depending on size, may be used for both the building and storage of costumes. A wardrobe room that is used for building costumes should have the following tools and supplies available:

- **Measuring Tools** Flexible measuring tape, sewing gauge for hems, measurement charts.
- **Marking Tools** Tracing paper and tracing wheel for moving markings from pattern to fabric; chalk for marking fabric during fittings.
- **Cutting Tools** Scissors and pinking shears.
- **Seam Ripper** For taking stitches out.
- **Long Cutting Table**
- **Fitting Equipment** Dress form or dressmaker's dummy.
- **Full-length Mirror**
- **Sewing Machine**
- **Steam Iron, Ironing Board, and Portable Steamer**
- **Storage Bins** For fabrics, scraps, accessories, patterns, and sewing notions.
- **Movable Clothes Rack**
- **Hot Glue Gun and Glue Sticks**
- **Notions** Needles, fasteners, thimbles, pins, snaps, hooks and eyes, Velcro™, buttons, etc.

Part Three Costumes **579**

Part
Four Lighting

Color Effects

Besides its use for illumination, lighting provides design opportunities through the effect of color–including the gel color of the lights and the effects these have on objects being lighted. In addition, certain colors have an emotional effect on the audience. These colors have traditionally been associated with the following qualities:

- Yellow = joyful, youthful, cowardly
- Orange = exhilarating, lively, wealthy
- Red = bloody, passionate, angry, strong, warlike
- Pink = romantic, fantastic
- White = innocent, truthful, virginal, peaceful, pure
- Blue = calm, spiritual, formal, cold, depressing
- Purple = mystical, royal, mournful
- Soft Green = soothing, waterlike, tranquil
- Green = young, natural, springlike, jealous
- Gray = neutral, serious, cloudy, negative
- Brown = poor, earth-bound, peasantlike
- Black = tragic, deathly, somber, eerie

When beginning to plan a lighting design, it is important to know what happens when one color is placed over another. See page 294 of this text for an illustration of the effect of colored lights on a color wheel. While the lighting designer can work ahead of time with the set and costume designers to plan for effect, final adjustments cannot be made until tech rehearsals when the actors can be seen in costume and makeup under lights.

Light Crew

The light crew usually consists of the lighting designer, several technicians, one or more followspot operators (if necessary), and a dimmer board operator. The light crew:

- Maintains the lighting instruments.
- Hangs the instruments according to the plot.
- Gels and focuses the lighting instruments.
- Makes adjustments during technical rehearsals.
- Strikes (takes down) and stores the lights when the production closes.

Hanging and Focusing The light crew works under the supervision of the lighting designer to hang the lights according to the light plot. Lights are hung on the proper battens, which usually have different names. The battens are sometimes called *rails* and are numbered or labeled according to their position.

- **Balcony Rail** is a beam or batten at balcony level.
- **House Rail** #1 might be over the house, but closer to the stage than the balcony rail.
- **First Electric** is a rail or batten with plugs, usually found just behind the proscenium.
- **Second Electric** is the next upstage batten.
- **Third Electric** is further upstage.

Most electrical rails can be lowered for the initial hanging of the lights. Preliminary focus may be done at this time. Because it is difficult to focus lights exactly until they are in place, ladders are still used to focus the lights when the electrics are raised back

580 Student Handbook

up above the stage. Once all the lights are hung and focused and the lighting designer approves the look, the gels are inserted.

The lighting crew then works with the director, stage manager, and lighting designer to do a *dry tech* of the production. The dry tech is simply an opportunity to run through the show from one light cue to the next to make sure that all the cues are in order and that the lighting looks as good as possible without actors or costumes to illuminate. This is a troubleshooting rehearsal during which the lighting designer and director may choose to add or subtract cues.

Most theatres built or renovated after 1993 have computerized light boards. These make the world of lighting much easier. Each light that is plugged in is patched through the computer into a dimmer. Dimmers can then be combined and levels set to create specific looks for each cue. Once programmed, the intensity and duration of each cue can be changed with just the touch of a few buttons.

Older theatres may work from manual dimmers and a manual patch board. A manual patch board has a number for each lighting plug that corresponds to another numbered plug in the light booth which is then plugged into a specific dimmer. These dimmer controls can then be combined on submasters (several of the dimmers put together) and brought up and down (raised and lowered in intensity).

Really old theatres may simply have a way to bring the lights up and down. The potential level of sophistication in your lighting plot will be directly proportional to the quality of the lighting system your school or theatre can provide.

Running the Show A running crew will usually consist of a lightboard operator, one or two followspot operators, a backstage lighting operator or, if necessary, a specials operator. *Specials* are windows, sunlight, lamps, special effects moments, or emphasis lighting.

Followspots are used more frequently in musicals than in any other form of theatre. Usually one followspot is enough to accentuate a singer during a solo. A second followspot is sometimes used to bathe the singer in light or to light two singers during a duet. Most followspots have color wheels so that they can illuminate the singers in a variety of colors that enhance costume, mood, and setting.

Homemade Lights

A drama department on a limited budget can make adequate spotlights for mounting on a teaser batten. Purchase 150-watt PAR-38 spots and screw them into clamp-on swivel sockets that can be mounted on a batten. (To be safe, use wire as well as clamps to attach the spots to the batten.) By using swivel sockets, you can adjust the lamps to any angle. Reflector spots are available in several colors, or you can use a clear lamp and attach spring tension holders that house special glass color filters. For greater color diversity, buy clear lamps and make frames for holding gelatin or plastic. Cut each frame from a large tin can or from sheet aluminum available at the lumberyard or at a metal shop. Fold the frame double, place the gelatin between the frames, and close them with brads at the top. Then wire the frame to the socket with a coat hanger or other heavy-duty wire, allowing space for ventilation between the lamp and the gel. Without such ventilation, the heat will burn or melt the gelatin.

Part Four Lighting **581**

Portable Lighting Systems Many rock bands use small portable lighting systems consisting of PARs mounted on a folding light stand. Most theatrical lighting companies make the stands, or "trees," for such lights and also sell small dimmer packs. These packs can either be plugged directly into a wall outlet or the lights themselves can be plugged in and then controlled from the dimmer board with microphone-type cable. A lighting system such as this usually consists of four lights per tree and most school "gymnatoriums" and multipurpose rooms can support two such trees. These lights can be gelled to provide color.

Lighting Design

The lighting designer must prepare for a production in the same way every other member of the production design team does–by first analyzing the script. The lighting designer looks for answers to the following questions:

- What scenes happen at night? during the day?
- What sources of light are mentioned (lamps, windows, etc.)?
- What sort of day is it? rainy? sunny? foggy? stormy?
- What season is it?
- What is the theme of the play?
- How does the mood change throughout the play?
- What areas must be well-lighted?

After hearing from the director and the other designers, the lighting designer will have new elements to consider:

- What "specials" are needed? (As you know, specials are specific lights used for monologues or to accentuate a certain speech or action. In *Macbeth,* the lighting of the dagger that hangs in midair is an example of a special.)
- What color choices have been made by the director, costumer, and/or set designer, and how may lights accentuate or contrast with those choices?

The Lighting Plan With input from the script, the director, and the other designers, the lighting designer develops a basic lighting plan. The plan shows which instruments will light specific parts of the stage. Each area should be covered by a minimum of two instruments, one from each side. Usually these are a contrast of warm and cool colors to provide depth. A third light can provide a front wash or fill in a color designed to give emotional power to the scene.

As a rule of thumb, lighting designers break the proscenium stage into six areas that must be lighted: upstage left, center, and right and downstage left, center, and right. Lighting instruments are then assigned to these areas. Additional instruments may be added to provide sidelighting, backlighting, color, and additional wash. After these playing areas have been covered, the lighting designer adds instruments to cover the specials. The complete lighting plan is shown visually in a diagram called the *light plot*, which is illustrated on page 240 of this text.

The Hanging Plot This is the compilation of the lighting plot with the instrument list. It provides an organized method of showing which instrument has to go to which position and be placed into which specific circuit or dimmer. The hanging plot is used by the light crew to hang, focus, and gel the lights for the production.

582 Student Handbook

Part Five Makeup

The Makeup Crew

This crew will vary in size depending on the production. For a simple, realistic play, the crew could consist of one or two crew members whose duties will include:

- Ordering, buying, or otherwise supplying all nonpersonal makeup and special effects items (such as crepe hair, nose putty, and spirit gum).
- Setting up the makeup room in advance of makeup call.
- Making sure that all actors have their makeup charts and/or sketches.
- Assisting actors with makeup.
- Cleaning up the makeup area.
- Performing emergency re-application of makeup during the production.
- Striking and restocking makeup at the end of the production.

Makeup Design

The bigger the budget of the theatre, the more likely it is that there will be a makeup designer. Makeup is an intensely personal thing, however, and should be learned by the actor, who is usually expected to be able to do simple "street" makeup. Actors are also expected to provide their own basic makeup kit.

Like other members of the production team, makeup designers begin with an analysis of the script, looking for the theme of the play as well as the following:

- How many characters are there?
- When does the play take place?
- What style of makeup was prevalent during this time period?
- How old are the characters?
- What special features or attributes are mentioned in the script? (i.e., age, scars, coloration, significant features)

Character Makeup Sketches At the first production meeting, the makeup designer will listen to the director's overall production vision and will then begin to work on a plot for each character based on the expectations of the director and the requirements of the script. The designer may decide to sketch out how some characters should look. This is especially important if there are clowns, elves, or other fantastical characters.

Unusual Makeup Designs In fantasy productions such as *The Wiz, Cats,* or *The Lion King* and in many children's theatre productions, it is essential to create a sketch and a plan for animal or creature makeup. These designs can be suggestive or realistic. Suggestive makeup might include feathers, mop heads, fake teeth, and so on. Realistic makeup can be created using crepe hair, latex, and a life mask of the actor's face.

Life Masks A life mask can be made from plaster bandage strips one-inch wide and six- to eight-inches long. Apply petroleum jelly to the actor's face, then put the bandages on one at a time. Leave breathing holes and cover the eyes with waxed paper. When two to three layers have covered the face, use a blow dryer for fifteen to twenty minutes to set the mask. Remove the mask and allow it to dry.

Part Five Makeup **583**

Part Six Props

Prop is an abbreviation of the word *property.* A prop is the "property" of the actor. As such, directors will often say that every actor is responsible for making sure his or her props are available when going on stage. However, props are ultimately the responsibility of a props master, or if the theatre is small, the set designer with help from the stage manager. Props are most closely related to set design, as they are part of the visual aspect of the play.

Consumable Props such as food items must be handled carefully. Remember to consider what actors have to do or say after eating or drinking a certain prop. If their mouths are filled with something dry, there must be water available on stage as well. Make sure whatever you prepare is fresh and kept covered and sanitary. Avoid using something for a prop that will tempt cast or crew members to help themselves. Instead, try to find items that are not particularly desirable but still achieve the effect and look you need.

Making or Finding Props Although it is always preferable to use the real thing, most theatre budgets don't allow the purchase of antiques or even replicas of certain items. The props master's job is to create, borrow, purchase, or otherwise dress the set and provide the actors with working and then final props. Many things can be made quite easily from wood, carved Styrofoam covered with plaster, or papier-mâché. The set crew and set designer can help with particularly difficult or large props to make sure they are in the same style as the set.

The Props Crew Again, depending on the scope of the show and the number of students/actors/volunteers involved, the props crew can be just the props master (who may also be the stage manager), or a complete crew. In small productions, props may be handled by the stage crew under the direction of the stage manager. Along with making or procuring props, the props crew is responsible for:

- Setting up the props table.
- Checking the prop list before and after every scene, act, and performance.
- Re-supplying and making consumable props for each show.
- Assisting the actors with finding props and returning them to the table.
- Striking the props at the end of the production and returning those that were borrowed.

The Prop Table is one of the most important backstage locations. Set up and designed by the props master and/or stage manager, the table will often have a location outlined and labeled for each prop. Actors are responsible for picking up their props from the table before making an entrance and returning them to the table if they exit the stage with a prop.

584 Student Handbook

Part Seven Sets

The Crew

The stage crew works directly for the stage manager and may be responsible for:

- Building and painting scenery.
- Making and painting props.
- Organizing props with the props crew.
- Erecting and bracing scenery.
- Shifting, flying, or rolling scenery in and out during the production.
- Placing props and setting the stage between acts and scenes.
- Operating special effects such as smoke machines, flash pots, trapdoors, revolving stages, etc.
- Re-setting all scenery at the end of the performance.
- Sweeping the stage and backstage areas.

The stage crew customarily dresses in all black so that they will not be noticed when they change scenery in minimal lights or blackouts. The stage crew, like the stage manager, forms the backbone of successful theatre production.

Design

Pre-planning Before the process of design begins, there are several things the set designer must consider. These have to do more with the facility than with artistic considerations. Necessary information includes:

- **Aprons, Fly Loft, and Wings** Where is the storage area for what you build? Is there room to take scenery off and on the stage? Is there tracking? Is there fly space? Is it a full fly? Can you fly your scenery in and out? Is the system manual or automatic? Will the fly system make any noise when it operates?
- **Equipment** What does the theatre have in terms of construction equipment and supplies for building? How many pre-existing flats, drops, and scrims are there? What are the heights and widths of the flats? Is there a permanent cyclorama, or cyc, curtain?
- **The Shop** How big is the shop? When is it available? When can you work? What other shows are being built? What tools are there and are they all fully operational?
- **The Stage** Is there a revolving stage floor? Are there trapdoors? Are there pre-constructed permanent steps, ramps, thrusts, pits, or rakes that you must work around?

The answers to these questions help the designer prepare a plan and budget for the set. If existing equipment can be used, money will be saved, and perhaps spent instead on an interesting design choice that will further the artistry of the production.

Script Analysis The set designer will analyze the play for several specifics before beginning to map out a design. These include:

- What is the director's artistic vision for the play?
- What locations does the play call for?
- When does the play take place?

Part Seven Sets **585**

- What objects or areas are required by the play?
- What entrances and exits are suggested by the script? Are they necessary?
- What is the theme of the play?

Design Principles Keeping all these things in mind and based on the pre-design planning, the designer will develop a preliminary design concept based on the following principles of design:

- **Balance** There must be some balance from one side of the stage to the other. A large double door stage right might be balanced by a large chest of drawers or a stairway stage left. If everything is on one side of the stage, it "tips the boat." Most sets, however, exercise some asymmetrical or informal balance rather than perfect symmetry. (The exception is extreme stylization.)
- **Central Axis** There will be a focal point to the design, usually slightly off center. This can be the highest or lowest point on stage, the bulkiest or sparsest point of the set. This focal point will be balanced by the director's choice of how to populate the stage and space the actors. Actors effectively become part of the stage picture.
- **Line** Lines in columns, costume, draperies, and positioning or height of flats have a psychological and emotional effect on the audience. General principles of line include:

  Crooked lines = chaos, pain, conflict

  Curves and angles = intensity, danger, excitement

  Curved lines = wealth, expanse, comfort

  Diagonal lines = force, strife, conflict, or discord

  Horizontal lines = stability, calmness, peace

  Long vertical lines = dignity, hope, spirituality
- **Mass** Bulk and weight have a profound effect. Both can bring the play closer to audience members, making them feel closed in.
- **Proportion** The set will appear realistic if all elements are scaled to a six-foot-tall person. Nonrealistic sets can have people overshadowed by high peaks, tall buildings, or, when the person is more important than the background, placed in abstract settings such as pipe grids.
- **Shape** This is the outline provided by the set. The background can appear circular, triangular, pointed, or linear in order to create a sense of realism, impressionism, or expressionism as fits the genre of the play.

Final Design When the design concept is complete, the designer will create *renderings* (drawings) and a three-dimensional model of the set. Once this is accepted by the director, the designer puts together the working drawings so that the construction and stage crews can begin to build the sets. The stage manager often has input into the practicality of these working drawings and renderings.

Set Construction

Sets consist not only of backdrops and flats, but also things such as ramps, platforms, boxes, and stairs. Although muslin or canvas flats are more traditional, many contemporary theatres have shifted to lightweight lauan or plywood construction. However the set is created, it must be

586 Student Handbook

safe and stable as well as being functional and visually interesting.

Erecting Flats Sets are often built in pieces and then assembled on the set. They can be moved into place by stagehands who either lift one edge up and then tilt it into place or who "walk" the flat up by having one crew member place a foot against the bottom while another lifts the top and slowly walks it into place. Flats can also be flown into place by lifting them up on a flyline, swinging them to where they need to be, and lowering them into position. This method is called *floating* and is the most time-consuming but easiest on the stagehands.

Joining and Bracing Flats Once in place, flats can be joined by either lashing them together using cleat hooks and rope, or hinging them. Using loose pin hinges will allow for easy removal, especially if the set is designed for touring or repeat usage. When the flats are all in place, *dutchman* (muslin strips dipped in sizing) is applied to cover the seams. If flats are perfectly matched, a strip of masking tape can be substituted. In the case of plywood or lauan flats, a small amount of wood putty, caulking, or sheetrock mud between the flats can cover the seams.

Flats are kept upright with stage braces. Commercial, adjustable stage braces can be used that are anchored to the floor with screws. If there are restrictions against nails or screws, you can build a plywood floor plate with a rubber adhesive bottom and then attach the stage brace to that. Such a plate should be weighted with stage weights in order to make it sturdy and slip-proof. You can also use a simple triangular wooden bracing, called a *jack*. This brace consists of three pieces of wood that form a triangle: one going up the back of the flat, one extending out at a right angle from the bottom of the flat, and a third on an angle connecting the first two. The jack should also be weighted with sandbags, or stage weights, or screwed into the floor with a foot iron.

Changing the Set Sets can be constructed in ways to make set changes go smoothly. Here are three useful methods:

- **Revolves** You must have a stage with a large, built-in revolve or build a round platform that will serve as a revolve. The revolve allows you to build up to three "looks" that can be revealed as the set is turned mechanically or by hand. Revolves give a very distinct and dramatic look, especially if the change occurs as an actor walks "into a scene."
- **Wagons** Platforms on wheels, from 4' x 8' to 8' x 16', can be preset in the wings, depending on available wing space. Called *wagons,* they can be furnished or "dressed" backstage during a prior scene. The same wagon can be used for multiple locations depending on what furniture, props, or flats are set on it and what scenic units may be flown in to join the wagon once it is in place. Many high-tech theatres have hydraulic wagons that can roll sets in from all sides as well as the back of the stage.
- **Jackknifing** This involves either two wagons on either side of the stage or simply braced scenery on sliders that are easy to move. One scene is simply pivoted out from right or left as the other scene is pivoted into place. When the scenery is in place, it is flush with

Part Seven Sets **587**

the proscenium. When it is out of the way, it rests flat against the stage right or stage left side of backstage. The full set is pivoted so the previous set cannot be seen. This is best done in a blackout or when the main curtain is down as it is not as smooth a transition as a revolve and requires several stage crew members.

Set Painting

Base Coat All flats need a primer and a base coat of color. With some careful planning, you can change the color of the base coat to match the details of the set. For example, blue paint might be used where windows will be created, a brick-red color could be used for the fireplace, and beige for the rest of walls.

Kinds of Paint There are several types of paint that make scenic painting easy, including:

1 **Casein paints** These are used for professional scenery and will hold up outdoors or in dampness.
2 **Latex paint** This covers well, cleans up easily, and is cheap and readily available. Painting with latex on muslin may reduce the life of the flat as the paint tends to crack as the cloth absorbs it.
3 **Vinyl and acrylic-base scenic paints** These have pure colors and strong durability.

Texturing A painted set can look far more interesting if you use one of the following methods of texturing to add depth and dimension:

- **Dry brushing** Use a dry brush lightly coated with paint. Move it quickly back and forth. Change colors and do the same in a different direction.
- **Feather dusting** This quick-texturing technique involves dipping an inexpensive feather duster into paint, brushing off the excess, and pressing the duster against the flat. Turn the duster gently and you will get a different pattern each time it moves. This effect can look like leaves or brush.
- **Rag rolling** A rag or rolled-up piece of frayed burlap dipped in paint can be rolled over the base coat in order to make it look like plaster.
- **Spattering** Use two or more colors, one lighter and the other a shade darker than the base. Fill the brush with paint and remove the excess. Stand a short distance from the flat and strike the brush handle with a hand, a board, or other surface so that the paint spatters onto the flat. Spattering may take some practice.
- **Stippling** This is done using a sponge or crumpled rag pressed against the base coat. Stippling should create a random pattern—do not make it look uniform.

Production Design

Each production has its own look or style. The production design is a composite of the visions of the producer, the director, and all the principal designers. The best production designs are based on these four qualities:

1 **Informative** Lets us know something about the piece, such as time and place.

588 Student Handbook

2. **Expressive** Shows us something about the theme and mood of the play.
3. **Appropriate** Fits the world of the play, based on elements taken from the play.
4. **Usable** The set must have levels and be flexible and dramatically dynamic.

The production design can also be concept-driven, for example, setting *Romeo and Juliet* during the Civil War with the Montagues as a rich Southern family and the Capulets as a poorer family from the North. This concept begins to rule all aspects of the production. During meetings, the production team may make variations on the original design, perhaps deciding to do costumes in traditional antebellum period style but setting all the action in the middle of a battlefield, representing the war that separates the two families. The production design is an element that emphasizes theatre as a collaborative art form. The set in this case still remains informative, expressive, appropriate, and usable.

Technical Considerations for Three Types of Theatre Spaces

	Scenery	Lights	Sound	Makeup
Proscenium	Has the most options—sets can be flown in, rolled in from sides, turned, and set while mid-drop is down. This is most flexible for large sets and period shows.	Front lights (side possible). Easy to accomplish. The audience is never "in the light." Flexible	Audience is at a distance, so sound must be clear. Floor or hanging mics often used. Need monitors. Most difficult to create sound in this space.	Most difficult because of space between actor and audience. All effects must read from a distance, but not seem unrealistic close up.
Thrust	Backdrops are possible, but most set pieces must be low because sightlines become a problem. Actors may be blocked by sets.	Light is from front. Side light is more difficult. Must be careful not to shine light on audience. Can do effects on back wall.	Actors are easier to amplify, closer to audience. Orchestra can be a problem; no pit. Floor mics helpful. Monitors helpful.	Less makeup needed, as audience is closer (except for special makeup).
Arena	Most difficult, but very freeing. No drops. Unit sets work best; must be small because of sightlines. Everything must be brought on in full view of audience.	Most difficult to light, but light is important to delineate areas. Lights from above and sides. Must be careful not to shine light in eyes of audience.	In a smaller theatre, less amplification is needed. Speakers can "surround" the audience for effect, or sound can come from above.	Little makeup needed, as audience is so close (with the exception of special makeup).

Part Seven Sets **589**

Part Eight Sound

Sound Crew

The head of the sound crew usually runs the cues called by the stage manager. There may be more than one crew member if the sound is coming from multiple sources. The microphone mixer or board operator hooks up the wireless mics, sets the floor mics, and makes sure that they all have batteries and are turned on and off at the appropriate moments.

Guidelines

1. Be sure that the sound operator is in the house where the balance can actually be heard. Placing a sound operator in a booth with glass doors and expecting him or her to adjust sound based on what is heard through a headset is a recipe for disaster.
2. Replace the batteries in all cordless microphones every night. Make sure the actors know how to turn their microphones off and on and that they keep them on during the show so that all control is done by the soundboard operator.
3. Never leave a wireless microphone turned up after an actor leaves the stage.
4. Make sure there are monitors for musical productions. Singers may be off key if they cannot hear each other or the orchestra accompaniment.
5. Balance live music with the amplified voices. Orchestras in contemporary musicals are often slightly amplified so that the sound can be balanced and equalized between voices and instruments.
6. Don't touch the equalizers. These should not be used to increase amplification. The professionals who installed the equipment or who are hired to set up the sound design for a show will adjust the equalizers, which should then be left at those levels unless there is a serious problem with either feedback or highs and lows.
7. Every performance will be unique. The sound operator must be aware of where laugh lines are and how the audience might react. The operator should also watch carefully because actors may unexpectedly change positions and deliver their lines at different places on stage relative to fixed hanging or floor microphones. The sound operator's job is to follow the action with the microphone levels.
8. Make sure a sound check is done every night. Each actor should do a few lines and all microphones should be tested.
9. Sound operators must play the mics like musical instruments. They should know when a performer is going to enter, speak, and leave. The sound

590 Student Handbook

operator should not be afraid to speak with actors about correcting anything that affects sound quality.

10 When touring, or even in an auditorium where additional sound is used, be sure to tape cords and cables down with gaffer's tape.

Sound Design

Like all other designers, the sound designer does an analysis of the play for meaning as well as needed sound effects and then begins to develop a *soundscape* for the production. The sound designer will attend the initial production meeting and amend the original concept to fit the overall production design. At the next production meeting, the sound designer should have examples of music choices and important sound effects as well as a chart of microphone placement and wireless microphone usage.

Soundscape A soundscape is the "color palette" of the sound designer. It contains his or her interpretation of the overall feel of the production design. For example, in a recent production of *Frankenstein,* the powerful soundscape consisted of a combination of odd and organic laboratory sounds and industrial 1980s music between scenes. The soundscape for *The Robber Bridegroom* might consist of bluegrass music with a few electronically altered versions of the same pieces threaded throughout the show.

Sound Recording and Construction

The sound crew gathers the sounds to be used in the play and puts them together in a logical and simple playback method. Occasional sounds like the crashing or breaking of glass can be constructed, but most of these sounds are available either on recordings or on many sound effects sources on the Internet. Today's digital technology makes it easy to compile sounds and use digital editing to create either a DAT or a CD that will have all the cues lined up one after the other so that sound operation is done by push-button control. Digital editing is so precise that the simplest changes can be made in tempo, pitch, and volume and a new CD burned or DAT made quickly from one rehearsal to the next. If your school or theatre does not have such technology, you can usually find a student or professional who has the necessary equipment and will be willing to help create a sound score for your production.

Part Eight Sound **591**

Part
Nine The Business of Theatre

Agents, Lawyers, and Managers

Agents Finding an agent is the "catch 22" of the acting industry. Often you can't be seen until you have an agent, and you can't get an agent until you've worked and been "seen." In the early days of your career, an agent can help you become "marketable." You still have to the do the essential work of proving yourself in auditions, but the agent can get you through the door for movies, television, and stage acting. And an agent will certainly help you in negotiations once success starts to come your way. Agents also represent writers and directors in both the film and television industries. Agents receive a percentage (generally ten percent) of every contract they negotiate for you.

Lawyers Entertainment lawyers serve a more specific function than agents do. They negotiate contracts and help protect the actor/director. Entertainment lawyers usually work for a fee rather than a percentage. Many very successful artists have both a lawyer and an agent. Don't worry about finding a good entertainment lawyer—when you are successful, they will find you.

Managers Some actors also find it helpful to have a manager. Managers are concerned with all aspects of an actor's career, often serving as counselor, friend, image consultant, and career guide. Like an agent, managers receive a percentage of what the actor earns.

Auditions

In larger cities, audition calls are listed in trade and industry magazines and newspapers. New York and Los Angeles have trade magazines such as *Backstage* and *Onstage,* as well as Web sites that list auditions. In other areas you may need to do some investigating to discover how and where auditions are held. Read the local newspapers and study the theatre scene where you are living. Attend shows and introduce yourself. If you see a theatre company that you like, ask them if and when they hold open auditions and always check listings and bulletin boards at local Actors' Equity Association offices.

Some auditions are open and others are exclusive. Exclusive auditions require you to have an agent set up the appointment. If you don't have an agent, the best thing to do is to attend every possible open audition that seems to fit your age and type. Don't waste the time of directors and producers by showing up for auditions where you clearly won't be cast. You may also hear about auditions for talent "showcases" or volunteer/ internship programs. Study all of these carefully. Doing some work for free in hopes that it may lead to money and publicity later is a gamble that sometimes pays big dividends. Too much free work can devalue you as an actor, but it is also a way to network and meet other people in the business.

592 Student Handbook

"Foot-in-the-Door" Jobs

Below is a list of jobs that are not ones you left home to pursue. However, they all may help you make the connections you need to move up the industry ladder.

- *Box Office Worker* Sells tickets.
- *Drama Specialist* If you have some training, particularly college or university training, you might find work at a youth program or camp that needs a drama specialist. You may be expected to teach theatre, direct, or even act with young people ranging from the very privileged and experienced to at-risk students.
- *Dresser* Like a costume assistant, a dresser simply works backstage and helps a principal actor with quick costume changes.
- *Extra* Extras get paid next to nothing, but they do get screen time and once in a while are picked out for speaking roles or extra on-camera opportunities in a movie.
- *Food Service Provider* This can range from working in a concession stand to working a catering job for a company that provides meals for production personnel.
- *Grip* This term comes from simply "gripping" equipment–moving things on location, holding microphones, pulling cables, and otherwise assisting on a movie set.
- *Intern* An intern is sometimes paid a minimal amount but often works for free in order to learn some aspect of the trade. This is a good stepping stone; just don't get stuck.
- *Production Assistant* This is a catchall title that can include jobs as diverse as appointment book manager, errand runner, props collector, script-reader, or even tutor.
- *Receptionist* This person answers phones and greets visitors for directors, producers, or production companies.
- *Stagehand* Although these jobs are usually held for trained technical people, it is sometimes possible to get hired as a stagehand for a particular production. Technical theatre people probably have the easiest time finding work in the industry.
- *Stand-in* Most television and movie stars do not stand and wait while the camera angles are set and lights arranged. They have a stand-in of the approximate height, build, and hair color who "stands in" the position until it's time to do the scene. Although this can be very boring work, it puts your face in front of directors, camera people, and the actors on a regular basis.

Headshots, Portfolios, Demo Reels, and Resumes

Headshots When you go to an audition, you will be expected to bring a *headshot,* a photo of your head and shoulders. Most actors have at least one current headshot–as recent as two years for a young person and within five years for an adult. Some actors have several photos. They choose whichever one is most appropriate to the audition or job interview at hand.

Headshots will cost $100 and up, depending on the photographer. They should be done by a professional photographer who is experienced in this field. Your senior picture is *not* a headshot. Ask a fellow actor or a talent agent to recommend someone.

Part Nine The Business of Theatre **593**

Once you've had your sitting, the photographer will give you contact sheets from which you will pick your favorite shot. Get help in choosing the image that will best serve you. If possible, ask a director and/or casting director who looks at headshots on a daily basis to help you. They can give you feedback on how your photo compares to other actors' and how well it reflects your appearance. Glamour shots that give a false impression can work against you. You then need prints made of your headshot. You can order 300 to 500 copies of your picture for under $100. Don't scrimp here. You need plenty of photos so that you are not afraid to leave a trail of them at auditions and with directors and theatre companies. Make this investment before you start trying to sell yourself as a performer.

A Portfolio A portfolio can be a very useful tool. Most directors, educators, and designers use a portfolio to show examples of their work when a "live" audition isn't appropriate. The portfolio consists of sketches, photographs, programs, drawings, and other documentation of your work. It is an excellent interview tool for actors looking for work with a company, though rarely is such evidence called for in an audition.

Demo Reels The *demo reel* is a film portfolio featuring clips from television or motion picture work you have done. As with headshots, ask other people in the industry to recommend professionals who can help you put together your demo reel.

Resumes You must have a resume. (See pages 553–554 of this handbook.) In fact, you might want to have multiples–each designed to showcase the aspect of your work most likely to get you a specific job. For example, if you are auditioning for film, list your film and/or video credits first. If you are auditioning for a Shakespearean play, be sure to place prior Shakespeare credits early in the resume.

Location

Some actors are comfortable in New York, others in Los Angeles, and many at regional theatre centers in between such as Chicago, Minneapolis, Seattle, San Francisco, and so on. You need to find a place where you can make connections and have the least amount of fear. Of course, New York and Los Angeles are the biggest markets, but they are also the most competitive. In both regional and major urban markets there are many smaller theatre companies willing to work with new actors. You don't have to wait for the "big audition" to begin developing your craft.

Networking and Connecting

Networking is one of the greatest keys to success. You must do your best to know who is doing what sort of work in the business and try to find ways to get close to people who are having success. Sometimes this means working at a related job, such as becoming a paramedic for film or television sets or helping to organize extras for a casting director. Apprenticeships and opportunities to further others in the business can only help you later on.

Connecting is similar to networking but has more to do with consciously seeking out those who might help you. You need to be courteous and not pushy, but it never hurts to try making a connection with someone who might be able to help you. Often people who are successful in the business

594 Student Handbook

are very willing to serve as mentors to others. This may be the way they got their start, and successful people are often willing to share their expertise. Just remember when you become successful to help others along the way.

Organizations and Unions

Larger cities offer alumni groups from universities or colleges you might join. These groups provide a valuable service, allowing you to meet others who may work in the industry and who may have experiences to share. Join any such organizations that you can. It is also an excellent idea to join professional organizations such as TCG (Theatre Communications Group), ASSITEJ/USA (The United States Center for the Association of Theater for Children and Young People), or AATE (The American Alliance for Theatre and Education). You may also soon qualify for the various unions including AEA (Actors' Equity Association), SAG (Screen Actors' Guild), AFTRA (American Federation of Television and Radio Actors), IATSE (International Alliance of Theatrical Stage Employees), WGA (Writers Guild of America), or DGA (Dramatists Guild of America).

Joining a union will take money and time and is not always the best decision. Many companies have a certain number of union vs. nonunion jobs and young actors can price themselves out of the market by becoming union members too soon. On the other hand, the union provides a safety net in terms of pay scale and health insurance as well as connecting the young actor to others in the business. Certain large film or television roles may require actors to join SAG or AFTRA, which may, by the time of this printing, be merged into one union. Consulting with friends or officers in the various unions is a great way to find out what you should do in your location with your particular skills.

Self-Esteem

While you are waiting for your career to take off, be sure you are also living your life to the fullest–doing things for other people as well as for yourself. You should always have a "fall-back" trade in case you become frustrated with your progress in the theatre. Don't base your self-esteem on what others think of your work or how often you get a role.

Stamina and Commitment

Theatre is a rough business. You must be fully committed to a career in theatre and aware that for most people success doesn't come overnight. Actors who are "discovered" are much less frequent occurrences than careers launched through determination and commitment. Try your best to not take things personally, to move past rejection, and to find things that satisfy your soul as you're making the journey. Also, remember that the journey itself is part of the career, even if it means living through many rejections and setbacks.

Finances and Taxes

Finances are difficult for a young actor. The best advice is to find a job that is flexible enough to allow you to audition and perform, but still lucrative enough to support you when theatre and acting jobs are not coming in. Remember that to make money, you must spend money–on headshots, resumes, training, makeup, travel

Part Nine The Business of Theatre **595**

to auditions, and so on. Waiting tables is the obvious parallel profession to acting, but there are other jobs that will allow you time to audition and work, including temp agency work, especially in the larger markets.

Some of your theatre earnings will likely be "contract" income rather than "employee" income. Remember that when you are hired on contract, you are responsible to the government for both income tax and the full amount of your Social Security tax. This is a tax that is matched by your employer when you are "employed" rather than "contracted." It is always easier to be an employee at tax time, but writers, designers, and directors are often contracted and must, therefore, take care of their own Social Security deductions. For this reason, you must keep very careful records of all your income and expenses. The costs each time you travel, do your hair for a specific role, spend money going to an audition, or take a director to lunch are deductible business expenses. If you have a reasonable amount of self-employment, it will probably be worthwhile for you to itemize your deductions rather than use the short tax form. A good accountant who is knowledgeable about the industry will be able to advise you on which form will be most advantageous for you and whether or not you need to pay quarterly tax estimates. Of course he or she will charge a fee, but remember that even this expense is tax-deductible.

596 Student Handbook

Glossary

accent the sound and patterns of speech from a specific region

acetone (ASS•ih•tohn) a solvent similar to nail polish remover used to remove spirit gum

act the main sections of a play

active listening using what you hear to build meaning

adapt to change a text from one form to another

adrenaline a hormone that produces the feel of sudden increased energy

amphitheater a round structure arranged around an open space with tiered seating

amplifier a device that provides the power supply to sound equipment

antagonist a main character who opposes the protagonist

apron the stage floor between the front edge of the stage and front curtain

archetype (AR•kih•typ) a character who represents a certain type or idea

arena stage staging in the center of a room with the audience sitting on all sides of the playing area; also called *theatre-in-the-round*

articulation clearly pronouncing words

artistic selectivity selecting the minimal amount of information needed to portray a character while still communicating necessary ideas and emotions

aside words spoken by a character to the audience rather than to the other characters who supposedly do not hear the speech

audible able to be heard

audience participation when the audience takes part in the action of the play

auditions tryouts for a part in a play

auditorium the part of a theatre where the audience sits

auditors the people conducting auditions

avant garde (ah•vahn•GARD) experimental new work; unorthodox

backdrop or drop a painted curtain without fullness, hung from a batten

backlot at a motion picture studio, an outdoor lot where sets are created to simulate a location

backstage the area behind the scenery not visible to the audience

barn door an accessory for Fresnel lighting instruments that houses moveable flaps to control the light beam

base foundation color used for stage makeup

batten a horizontal pipe suspended over the stage, from which scenery, lights, or curtains are hung; also called a *rail*

bit part a role with very few lines

blackout when all stage lights go off simultaneously

blocking the director's planned movement for the characters

body language using expressions and body movement to communicate rather than words

body mic a small microphone that can be hidden in the performer's clothing or hair

book the written script for a musical

border lights long, narrow, metal enclosures that house a row of lamps and reflectors; also called *strip lights*

Glossary

box office 1. where tickets are purchased for theatrical events 2. the amount taken in for ticket sales

box set a set representing the walls of a room, sometimes with a ceiling

build 1. to make a costume from scratch 2. the increase of vocal intensity toward a climactic point

Bunraku (bun•RAH•koo) traditional Japanese puppetry

burlesque (bur•LESK) physical comedy that uses exaggeration that is directed at a person, custom, artifact, or event

business detailed bits of action such as knitting, setting the table, etc., as distinguished from broad stage movement; also called *stage business*

business manager the person in charge of finance, publicity, ticket sales, programs, and other business relating to a theatrical production

call posted announcement of rehearsals, etc., placed on the call-board near stage entrance

callback a second audition at which only those actors under serious consideration for roles are called in

cameo a one-scene part

casting the process of selecting actors for various roles

catharsis (kuh•THAR•sis) emotional purging or an uplifting release that the audience feels during a play, particularly at the end of a tragedy

CD-R (compact disk, recordable) a compact disk used for recording and playing back sound

character a role that an actor portrays in a play

character makeup makeup that changes an actor's appearance drastically

character role a role in which character traits and appearance differ from that of the actor

cheating out playing a bit toward the audience while conversing with others on stage

choreographer the person responsible for designing a show's dance numbers

chorus 1. In Greek drama, a group of actors who speak in unison and comment on the action of the play 2. the singers in a musical other than the principal performers

climax the high point of the play at which the protagonist makes an irrevocable decision; also called the *turning point*

closed audition an audition open only to union members or those represented by an agent

close-up a camera shot that shows only an actor(s) head

clown white white makeup often used by mimes

cold reading when an actor auditions for a role without having read the script

collodion (kuh•LOH•dee•un) a clear, thick liquid used on the skin to make scars

comedy a play that ends happily and arouses laughter through humorous treatment of an aspect of life

comedy of manners comedy that originated in the later 1600s which makes fun of upper-class pretentiousness and the attitudes of the wealthy

commedia dell'arte (kuh•MAY•dee•uh del•AR•tay) improvised comedy featuring stock characters that began in Renaissance Italy

conflict the dramatic opposition of the protagonist with society, with his or her peers, or with him or herself

console the lighting control panel; also called a *dimmer board panel*

continuity in film or television, the matching of visual elements from take to take and from scene to scene

costume designer person in charge of designing or otherwise obtaining costumes for a show

costume parade when actors walk onstage in full costume for the purpose of determining comfort, utility, movement, and proper lighting

costume plot a list of every character and his or her costume for each scene

costume shop the place where costumes are built and stored

counter-cross moving in the opposite direction—and out of the way—of another actor who is moving across the stage

counterweight system a system that uses lines, cables, and weights to raise and lower the battens, that hold scenery, drops, and lights

crash box a heavy box filled with glass or broken shards, used for sound effects

creme foundation a makeup foundation with an oil base

crepe hair artificial hair made of wool used for making beards and mustaches

crinolines full, stiff underskirts

crisis an event that occurs just when it seems things could either resolve or worsen; the crisis leads to the climax

cross an actor's move from one side of the stage to another

cross light when two spotlights are placed on opposite sides of the stage at a 45 degree angle to minimize shadows on an actor's face

cue **1.** the last words or action of one actor that immediately precede another actor's speech **2.** signal for light changes, curtain, etc.

curtain set a set that uses the cyclorama at the back of the stage to act as a wall or drapery

cut **1.** delete **2.** a command to stop action and dialogue

cyc or cyclorama **(sy•kluh•RAH•mah)** a curtain or wall at the back and sides of the stage

DAT (digital audiotape) a small tape used for recording and playing back sound

dead zone an area of the stage without adequate lighting

decorative props details on stage such as paintings, newspapers, or window curtains; also called *set dressing*

demographic an advertising term meaning a group of people

denouement **(day•noo•MAH)** the outcome of the main problem in a drama

deus ex machina **(DAY•us eks MAH•kih•nah)** literally, "god in the machine"; a mechanical crane used to lower and raise gods in ancient Greek theatre

development the creation of a script and the plan by which the film will be produced

dialogue conversation among characters

diaphragm **(DY•uh•fram)** the muscle below the rib cage

diction the style, dialect, rhythm, and words of the characters

Glossary

digital audio software computer software that allows the user to mix sounds

dimmer board a lighting control panel

dimmers controls that change the level of lighting intensity

director the person who interprets a play, casts, blocks, and helps actors develop their characters

discovery space in Elizabethan theatres, the space located between two doors at the back of the stage used for small interior settings

dissolve in film and TV, when one shot is faded out and another is faded in

double cast selecting two actors for each role; the casts then split the performances

downstage the area of the stage closest to the audience

dramatic criticism the act of reviewing a dramatic work

dramaturg a person who performs a variety of tasks to assist with the production of a play, including reading and evaluating scripts, researching historical and societal issues, and sharing pertinent information with the director and cast

dress rehersals the final rehearsals before opening night run without stopping; actors are in full makeup and costume and all production elements are in place

dress the stage keep the stage picture balanced

drop a canvas or muslin curtain that forms part of the scenery

dry tech a rehearsal run without actors in order to check technical cues

dual role the actor's two realities onstage—the actor-as-character and the actor-as-actor

dutchman thin strips of muslin used to cover the gap between flats

elevation sketch a drawing that shows how the stage will look from the perspective of the audience

ellipsoidal (ih•lip•SOY•dul) reflector spotlight a spotlight with an ellipsoidal reflector, usually hung from the auditorium ceiling to light downstage acting areas; also called a *Leko*

emoting expressing emotions

empathy emotional feedback between performer and audience

ensemble a group of actors working together to create an artistic whole rather than stressing individual players

epic a long narrative poem that tells the story of a legendary hero

epic theatre a drama in which the audience is encouraged to think critically about political and social issues; theatricality overrides realism

equalizer a device on the sound board that balances high, medium, and low frequencies to achieve a desired blend of sounds

etiquette appropriate conduct

exposition information that gives you an idea about what has happened before the play began and what is happening as the play begins

external traits characteristics that make up physical appearance, such as posture, gestures, mannerisms, voice, and clothing

farce a physical comedy that exaggerates situations until they are hardly believable

final cut the finished film

flats pieces of canvas stretched over wooden frames that are painted and linked together to create scenery such as walls and doorways

floodlights lights that illuminate broad areas of the stage

floor plan a diagram that shows the walls, doors, windows, furniture, and other important architectural details on the stage drawn to scale

fly space the area above the stage where scenery, drops, and lights are hung when not in use

foil a character whose personal attributes contrast sharply with the main character or protagonist

followspots spotlights that produce strong beams of light that follow an actor onstage

foundation makeup the color of one's skin

fourth wall the imaginary wall through which the audience views the play

Fresnel (**fruh•NEL**) a spotlight with a step-lens that throws an efficient and soft beam, usually hung from the teaser batten to light upstage areas

full back/full front facing completely away from or completely toward the audience

gelatins (gels) transparent color sheets inserted into a frame in front of a spotlight or floodlight

genre a type or classification of literature

gestures movements of separate parts of the body such as waving an arm or shrugging a shoulder

gobo a template of thin metal inserted into an ellipsoidal reflector spotlight to create a light pattern on stage

Goethe's (GUR•tuz) principles three criteria posed by German philosopher Goethe used to critique a work of art: 1. What was the artist trying to do? 2. How well did the artist accomplish it? 3. Was it worth doing?

going up forgetting one's lines during a rehearsal or performance

grand drape the front curtain on a proscenium stage, usually made of a heavy, luxurious fabric

greasepaint heavy, oil-based theatrical makeup

greenroom a room where actors relax before and after performances

grid or gridiron the framework high over the stage that supports the curtain and scenery riggings

groundlings (in Elizabethan times) tradespeople and lower class citizens who stood in the pit around the stage to watch a performance

ground plan a diagram drawn to scale that shows the walls, doors, windows, furniture, and other important architectural details of the stage

hand props items handled and/or carried on stage by actors during the show, such as letters, books, guns, dishes, and so forth

hanging plot the plan created by the lighting designer that shows where the crew should hang the lighting instruments

high comedy comedy such as satire and comedy of manners that makes fun of political situations, cultural habits, and accepted social standards

holding for laughs waiting for audience laughter to diminish before continuing dialogue

hot spot a place area where too much light hits a small area of the stage

Glossary

house another name for auditorium, the place where the audience sits

house lights auditorium lights used before and after the play and during intermission

house manager the person who oversees the box office, supervises the ushers, and attends to conditions in the auditorium

illusion of the first time the actor's ability to perform in a show over and over while making it appear that the dialogue and situations are happening for the first time

impressionistic relying on colors and lines to create mood and setting rather than on realistic representations

improvisation an impromptu scene where the actors make up the dialogue and action

inciting incident the first event that suggests the situation of the drama will change; the event to which all other actions in the play can be traced

inflection variety of vocal pitch

ingenue (AHN•juh•nu) a young female lead character, often the love interest in the play

installation a presentation of performance art

instrument the term used to refer to a stage light

internal traits the characteristics that make up personality, such as family circumstances, environment, occupation, level of education, interests, and so on

interplay interaction between characters

Kabuki (kuh•BOO•kee) stylized Japanese drama which originated in the 1600s

kill eliminate; for example, "kill the noise" means to be quiet

Kyogen (ky•O•gen) a short Japanese comedy performed without music and masks

lamp the bulb for a lighting instrument

larynx (LAR•inks) the part of the throat that contains the vocal cords

lavalier (lah•vuh•LEER) mic See *body mic*

left the left side of the stage from the actor's perspective when facing the audience; also called *stage left*

legitimate theatre originally evolved from England's Licensing Act of 1737, in which plays could only be performed in two specific playhouses, today the term refers to all live play performances (as opposed to film)

Leko (LEE•ko) another name for an ellipisoidal reflector spotlight

lighting designer the person responsible for creating a lighting plan for a theatrical production

light plot a plan showing the position of lighting instruments

low comedy comedy that is physical and sometimes vulgar; it includes outlandish behavior and oddly harmless violence

makeup cosmetics, false hair, and other products that an actor uses to change his or her appearance

makeup designer the person responsible for creating makeup designs for a production

makeup morgue a collection of portrait pictures or photos used as a reference when creating a character's makeup

mansions small platforms or stations where scenes of plays were performed; and viewers moved from place to place to view the entire story

masques extravagant entertainments held at court that included dance, song, and recitation

master gesture a distinctive gesture used to establish a character's personality

melodrama an overly dramatic play that focuses more on cliff-hanging action and intense emotions than on character development or real problems

Method acting an acting approach that calls on the actor to use personal experience and sense memory to develop a character

middlebrow comedy comedy based on plot and sentimental situations; often used in romantic and situation comedies

mime an actor who communicates through movements of the body and face, but does not speak; a more formal and disciplined version of pantomime

minidisk a small disk for use in digital recording

minimal set a set made of two- or three-fold flats that create walls or hide furniture; also called the *profile set*

miracle play a drama depicting the lives of the saints

mixer See *sound board*

modified authenticity the idea that a costume does not have to replicate a historical design exactly, but rather give the impression of that design

monologue a long speech by one character

morality play a drama that teaches right from wrong

motivation a specific reason for saying or doing something; to show a character's desires through voice and movement

multimedia using more than one medium onstage, including TV, film, dance, etc.

muscular memory when you know the role so well that your actions become effortless and appear completely natural

musical a dramatic production accompanied by song and dance

music director the person who directs the actors, singers, and often the orchestra in a musical

musical comedy a comedic drama featuring song and dance

mystery play a drama based on a Bible story

neoclassicism with regard to drama, a form of writing in which playwrights were to observe classical influences and adapt them to their work

Noh traditional Japanese theatre in which the story is communicated through poetry, dance, and music

nose putty a pliable substance used in a character makeup to build a false nose, chin, or forehead

objectives goals

observation recognizing a fact or event

obstacle anything that gets in the way of an objective

off book having a part memorized so that a script is no longer needed

offstage any part of the stage that the audience cannot see

onstage any part of the stage that is visible to the audience

open stance when an actor faces the audience; full front

Glossary

outcome result

pan 1. to review negatively 2. to move a film or TV camera from left to right or vice versa

pancake makeup makeup that is pressed into a hard round cake and applied with a wet sponge

pantomime telling a story or presenting an idea through bodily movement and expression rather than words

parody imitate in a humorous way

passion play a drama depicting scenes from Christ's life, especially the days of his suffering and resurrection

PBS Public Broadcasting Service, a group of television stations that specialize in educational and arts programming; partly funded by government money and private donations

Peking Opera Chinese drama that features chanting, singing, and musical accompaniment

performance art unstructured dramatic events in which movement, music, improvisation, and games are presented, often with the purpose of making a political statement

periaktoi **(pair•ee•AK•toy)** the Greek word for a triangle of flats that can be revolved for scenery changes; also called a *prism set*

permanent set a set that remains in place throughout the production

pilot the first episode of a television show that introduces a potential new series

pinking shears a kind of scissors that cuts a zigzag edge, used to prevent fabrics from unraveling

pitch 1. the relative highness or lowness of a voice 2. to present a plan or idea in hopes of convincing others to invest in or accept it

pliable 1. adaptable to varying conditions 2. flexible

plot the story of a play from beginning to end

poetry slam a competitive poetry reading in which poets present short, original poems that are judged by the audience

postproduction the phase of filmmaking when the film editor does most of his or her work including mixing the sound tape with film images and arranging and cutting scenes to make the final cut

preproduction the phase of filmmaking that must be completed before the film can be shot

presentational a style of play in which the actor may speak directly to the audience

principals actors in major roles

prism set See *periaktoi*

producer a person who secures financial backing for a play or film, chooses the director, and oversees the day-to-day business of the production

production the phase of filmmaking in which the movie is shot

production numbers elaborate song-and-dance sequences in which most of the cast takes part

profile facing sideways to the audience so that they only see one side of your body

project to increase voice or actions so they will carry to the audience

prompt book a book (usually a three-ring binder) that contains the script annotated with the director's ideas about details such as movement as well as technical cues for lights, sound, etc.

props or properties set furnishings including furniture, pictures, ornaments, drapes, and so on. See *hand props* and *set props*

props master the person in charge of obtaining and organizing all of the props for a play

props plot a list of props needed for each scene

prop table a backstage location where hand props are kept

proscenium stage a stage with a permanent framed opening through which the audience sees the play

protagonist the main character with whom audience empathy lies

public domain a work that belongs to the public; royalty-free

pull to retrieve costumes or props from storage

quarter turn a 90-degree turn

quick study one who can memorize a part rapidly

rail **1.** the top or bottom board of a flat **2.** another term for *batten*

raked stage a slanted stage, where upstage is slightly higher than downstage

rate the speed at which one speaks

rave review a very positive review

Readers Theatre a form of drama in which actors are seated and read aloud from scripts

realism a type of literature that depicts life objectively and accurately

realistic play a play that imitates real life

reality TV a form of television programming in which non-professional participants speak and act as they would in real life

recall to remember a fact or event so as to re-create it

regional accent the sound of speech from a particular region

rehearsal a session where the play is practiced in preparation for performance

rendering a colored drawing of a set or costume

repertory a group of plays presented in rotation over a period of time by the same company of actors

representational a theatrical style, in which the actors are "unaware" that the audience is watching

resolution the end of a plot when the conflict is resolved

resonance a rich, warm vocal tone

Restoration comedy See *comedy of manners*

rhetorical involving speech (rather than action)

right the stage area to the actor's right as he or she faces the audience; also called *stage right*

role a part in a play

romanticism a literary, artistic, and philosophical movement of the late 18th and early 19th centuries that emphasized the imagination and emotions

rough cut the "first draft" of a film that has been roughly edited

roundels colored glass disks used in border lights

royalties the fees paid to the rights holder of a play, other literature, or music in order to use or perform it

rule of three the belief that pratfalls, accidents, and misunderstandings designed to make the audience laugh are only funny three times in a row

run through a rehearsal without interruption

Glossary

rushes or dailies in film, the unedited footage shot each day

satire comedy that ridicules the foolish behavior of certain people

scenario an outline of a play

scene a part or division of an act of a play

scenery the background pieces such as flats and drops that create the play's setting

scene shop the place where scenery and props are constructed

scoring a role **1.** marking the script with notes on blocking and delivery **2.** analyzing the script as an aid to character development

screenplay a script for a film

scrim a loose-weave curtain on a batten used for "visions," "flashbacks," and so on, opaque when lighted from the front, transparent when the set behind it is lighted

script a printed copy of the play

sense memory tapping into memories in order to recapture an experience

set the scenery used onstage

set designer the person in charge of creating a plan for the set(s) of a production

set dressing anything on stage that adds to the visual representation, including actors

set piece a three-dimensional scenery piece that stands by itself, such as a rock or tree

set props items used to dress the set, such as furniture, carpets, and lighting fixtures

shooting script a version of the script for a film in which each shot is tracked by number and type of shot

sightlines imaginary lines indicating visibility of stage areas from different areas of the house

sitcoms situation comedies

skene (SKEE•nee) in ancient theatres, a building behind the stage used by the actors

social drama a play that focuses on serious, real-life problems of ordinary people

soliloquies speeches in which one actor speaks aloud, revealing his or her inner thoughts

sound board a device that controls sound sources and allows them to be manipulated and balanced; also called a *mixer*

sound designer the person responsible for planning the sound for a show

soundscape the sound designer's artistic vision for a production's sound

soundstage the location in a studio where a film is shot

spectacle everything the audience sees, including scenery, costuming, dance, pantomime, and swordplay

spiking marking the rehearsal area with masking tape to show the positions of furniture, doors, etc.

spill light leakage from stage lights

spirit gum an adhesive used for applying items such as a false beard or nose putty

spotlight a generic term for several types of lighting instruments

stage business See *business*

staged reading the reading of a drama in which actors use manuscripts and rough blocking

stage fright feeling nervous before a performance

stage left/stage right See *left, right*

stage manager the person who directs the backstage crews and runs the show once it goes into performance

stakes the consequences that result from an outcome

stealing the scene taking audience attention away from the proper focal point

step on to cut off or interrupt another character by speaking over his or her lines

stiles the vertical boards that make up the sides of a flat

stippling adding color and texture to a surface by dabbing it lightly with a paint-filled sponge or rag

stock character a character with a set of recognizable traits such as, the young lover, the irate father, the clever servant, and so on—often seen in *commedia dell'arte* productions

storyboard a series of rough drawings depicting the chronological sequence of a film, TV show, or ad

straight makeup makeup that enhances natural features and coloring

strike **1.** to remove something from the set; **2.** to take down set and props after the show's final performance

strip lights See *border lights*

subtext information that is implied in the dialogue but not stated

supporting roles roles that support a leading role

suspend disbelief the ability of a viewer to accept what he or she sees and hears as real

swatch a small sample of fabric

symbol an object that is used to represent an abstract concept or principle

syndication when a television program that has already aired on a network is sold to other stations

tableau a visual effect in which actors create a picture by standing in a frozen position

tag line the final line of a play or scene

tape **1.** a cassette or videotape **2.** to record on tape

target audience the group of people to whom advertisers believe a television show or film is most relevant

teaser the overhead curtain that masks the first batten of lights and adjusts the height of the proscenium opening

teaser batten a batten that is hung behind a teaser curtain

technical acting an acting approach that calls on the actor to use learned techniques for movement, speech, and character development rather than emotions and sense memory

theatre-in-the-round See *arena stage*

theatre of the absurd a type of drama based on the idea that life is meaningless and that searching for order only brings about confusion and conflict

theme the underlying message or meaning of a play or other piece of literature

thespian an actor

three-quarter turn a 270-degree turn

thrust stage a stage that juts into the audience area, with the audience usually sitting around its three sides

timing to move and say one's lines at the most effective moment

Glossary

tiring house in an Elizabethan theatre, the backstage area where actors would go to change costumes

tormentors side curtains or flats that adjust the proscenium width

tragedy a drama in which a protagonist struggles against some force, usually making an ennobling sacrifice before going down in defeat (usually death)

tragic flaw a weakness of character that ultimately causes the protagonist's destruction

trailer a preview that provides publicity for a film's release

transmitter a device that sends a signal from the microphone to the receiver

trapdoor an opening in the stage floor that allows actors to enter and exit

travesty a humorous imitation

trilogy three related works of literature

trim decorative items such as buttons, lace, ribbon, jewelry, etc.

tryouts auditions for parts in a play

turning point See *climax*

typecasting casting someone over and over again in the same type of role

understudy an actor who learns a role in case a lead actor cannot perform

unit set a set made of several pieces that can be rearranged to produce more than one scene

unity a balance in the variety and kinds of movement in a play

upstage the stage area farthest away from audience, toward the backstage wall

upstaging drawing the audience's attention to yourself when it should be focused on another character

vaudeville (VAWD•vil) a variety show featuring many acts, including trained animals, singers, acrobats, dancers, and comedians

villian a despicable character, especially in a melodrama

visualize to picture in one's mind

vocalizing singing without words

voice-over the voice of an unseen narrator

volume the relative loudness of a voice

wagon stage platforms on which scenery is placed and rolled onto the stage

walk-on a part in which the actor walks on and off stage without having any lines to say

warn to notify that a cue is approaching.

wings offstage to right and left of the acting area

Wooden O's round or octagonal theatres such as Shakespeare's Globe with two or three tiers of thatched roof galleries on three sides of an open court

working script a script-in-progress that will change as a film is made

work lights white lights used solely for rehearsal

Acknowledgments

Text Credits (continued)

Excerpt from *Clear Glass Marbles* by Jane Martin. Copyright ©1981 by Alexander Speer, Trustee. Reprinted by permission of Alexander Speer, Actors Theatre of Louisville. Caution: Professionals and amateurs are hereby warned that *Clear Glass Marbles* is subject to royalty. It is fully protected under the copyright laws of the United States of America, the British Commonwealth, including Canada, and all other countries of the Copyright Union. All rights, including professional, amateur, motion pictures, recitation, lecturing, public reading, radio broadcasting, television, and the rights of translation into foreign languages are strictly reserved. In its present form, the play is dedicated to the reading public only. No part of this work may be reproduced, stored in a retrieval system or transmitted in any form, by any means, now known or yet to be invented, including mechanical, electronic, photocopying, recording, videotaping or otherwise, without the prior written permission of the Trustee. Particular emphasis is laid on the question of amateur or professional readings, permission and terms for which must be secured in writing from Alexander Speer, Trustee, 316 West Main Street, Louisville, KY 40202-4218.

Excerpt from *Copenhagen* by Michael Frayn. Copyright ©1998 by Michael Frayn. Reprinted by permission of Methuen Publishing Limited, London.

Excerpt from *Cyrano de Bergerac* by Edmond Rostand, translated by Lowell Bair. Copyright ©1972 by Lowell Bair. Used by permission of Dutton Signet, a division of Penguin Group (USA).

Excerpt entitled "Dead Parrot" from *Monty Python's Flying Circus: All the Words, Volume One* by Graham Chapman, John Cleese, Terry Gilliam, Eric Idle, Terry Jones and Michael Palin. Reprinted by permission of Python (Monty) Pictures Limited.

Excerpt from *Death of a Salesman* by Arthur Miller. Copyright 1949, renewed ©1977 by Arthur Miller. Used by permission of Viking Penguin, a division of Penguin Group (USA).

Excerpt from *The Dining Room* by A.R. Gurney. Copyright ©1981 by A.R. Gurney as an unpublished dramatic composition. Copyright ©1982 by A.R. Gurney, Jr. Reprinted by permission of Dramatists Play Service, Inc. Cauion: The reprinting of *The Dining Room* included in this volume is reprinted by permission of the author and Dramatists Play Service, Inc. The stock and amateur performance rights in this play are controlled exclusively by Dramatists Play Service, Inc., 440 Park Avenue South, New York, NY 10016. No professional or non-professional production of the play may be given without obtaining in advance, the written permission of the Dramatists Play Service, Inc., and paying the requisite fee. Inquiries regarding all other rights should be addressed to Gilbert Parker, William Morris Agency, Inc. 1325 Avenue of the Americas, New York, NY 10019.

Excerpt from *A Doll's House* by Henrik Ibsen, translated by Michael Mayer. Copyright ©1966 by Michael Mayer, renewed ©1994 by Michael Mayer. Reprinted by permission of Harold Ober Associates Incorporated. Caution: This play is fully protected, in whole, in part or in any form under the copyright laws of the United States of America, the British Empire, including the Dominion of Canada, and all other countries of the Copyright Union, and is subject to royalty. All rights including motion picture, radio, television, recitation, public reading, are strictly reserved.

Excerpt from *Driving Miss Daisy* by Alfred Uhry. Copyright ©1987 by Alfred Uhry as an unpublished dramatic composition. Reprinted by permission of Dramatists Play Service, Inc. Caution: The excerpt from *Driving Miss Daisy* included in this volume is reprinted by permission of the author and Dramatists Play Service, Inc. The stock and amateur performance rights in this play are controlled exclusively by Dramatists Play Service, Inc. 440 Park Avenue South, New York, NY 10016. No professional or non-professional performance of the play may be given without obtaining in advance, the written permission of the Dramatists Play Service, Inc., and paying the requisite fee. Inquiries regarding all other rights should be addressed to Flora Roberts, Incorporated, 393 West 49th Street, #5G, New York, NY 10019.

The Drummer by Athol Fugard. Copyright ©1989 by Athol Fugard. Reprinted by permission of Samuel French Inc. Caution: Professionals and amateurs are hereby warned that *The Drummer*, being fully protected under the copyright laws of the United States of America, the British Commonwealth countries, including Canada, and the other countries of the Copyright Union, is subject to a royalty. All rights, including professional, amateur, motion picture, recitation, public reading, radio, television and cable broadcasting, and the rights of translation into foreign languages, are strictly reserved. Any inquiry regarding the availability of performance rights, or purchase of individual copies of the authorized acting edition, must be directed to Samuel French Inc., 45 West 25 Street, New York, NY 10010 with other locations in Hollywood and Toronto, Canada.

Excerpt from *The Effects of Gamma Rays on Man-in-the-Moon Marigolds* by Paul Zindel. Copyright ©1970 by Paul Zindel. Reprinted by permission of Curtis Brown.

Excerpt from *FOB* by Henry David Hwang. Copyright ©1990 by David Henry Hwang. All rights reserved. All inquiries regarding rights should be addressed to the author's agent, William Craver, Writers & Artists Agency, 70 West 36th Street, #501, New York, NY 10018. Reprinted by permission of the author.

Acknowledgments

Excerpt from *The Glass Menagerie* by Tennessee Williams. Copyright 1945 by Tennessee Williams and Edwin D. Williams. Reprinted by permission of New Directions Publishing Corp. Caution: Professionals and amateurs are hereby warned that *The Glass Menagerie,* being fully protected under the copyright laws of the United States of America, the British Empire, including the Dominion of Canada, and all other countries of the Copyright Union, is subject to royalty. All rights, including professional, amateur, motion picture, recitation, lecturing, public reading, radio and television broadcasting, and the rights of translation into foreign languages, are strictly reserved. Particular emphasis is laid on the question of readings, permission for which must be obtained in writing from author's agent. For British Commonwealth Rights (excluding Canada), refer to Tom Erhardt, Casarotto Ltd., National House, 60-66 Wardour Street, London WIV 2HP, England.

Excerpt from *How I Learned to Drive* by Paula Vogel. Copyright ©1998 by Paula Vogel. Reprinted from *The Mammary Plays* by Paula Vogel. Reprinted by permission of Theatre Communications Group.

Excerpt from *Icarus* by Edwin Sanchez. Copyright ©1999 by Edwin Sanchez. Reprinted by permission of the Joyce Ketty Agency.

Excerpt from *A Jamaican Airman Forsees His Death* by Fred D'Aguiar. Copyright ©1995 by Fred D'Aguiar. Reproduced with permission of Curtis Brown Ltd., London.

Excerpt from *The Janitor* by August Wilson. Copyright ©1985 by August Wilson. Reprinted by permission of the author.

Excerpt from *Jar the Floor* by Cheryl L. West. Copyright ©2002 by Cheryl L. West. Reprinted by permission of the Joyce Ketty Agency.

Excerpt from *Metamorphoses: A Play* Based on David R. Slavitt's translation of The Metamorphoses of Ovid by Mary Zimmerman. Copyright ©2002 by Mary Zimmerman. Reprinted by permission of Northwestern University Press. All rights reserved. Caution: Professionals and amateurs are hereby warned that this material, being fully protected under the Copyright Laws of the United States of America and all other countries of the copyright union, is subject to royalty. All rights including but not limited to, professional, amateur, recording, motion picture, recitation, lecturing, public reading, radio and television broadcasting and the rights of translation into foreign language are strictly reserved. All inquiries regarding performance rights for this play should be addressed to the author's agent, Bruce Ostler, at Bret Adams Ltd., 448 West Forty-fourth Street, New York, NY 10036.

Excerpt from *The Prisoner of Second Avenue* by Neil Simon. Copyright ©1972 by Neil Simon. Reprinted by permission of Gary N. DaSilva, Attorney at Law. Caution: Professionals and amateurs are hereby warned that *The Prisoner of Second Avenue* is fully protected under the Berne Convention and the Universal Copyright Convention and is subject to royalty. All rights, including without limitation professional, amateur, motion picture, television, radio, recitation, lecturing, public reading and foreign translation rights, computer media rights and the right of reproduction, and electronic storage and retrieval in whole or in part and in any form are strictly reserved and none of these rights can be exercised or used without written permission from the copyright owner. Inquiries for stock and amateur performances should be addressed to Samuel French, Inc., 45 West 25th Street, New York, NY 10010. All other inquiries should be addressed to Gary N. DaSilva, 111 N. Sepulveda, Suite 250, Manhattan Beach, CA 90266-6850.

Excerpt from *Promenade* by Maria Irene Fornes. Copyright ©1987 by Maria Irene Fornes. Reprinted by permission of Helen Merrill Ltd. On behalf of the author.

Excerpt from *A Raisin in the Sun* by Lorraine Hansberry. Copyright ©1958 by Robert Nemiroff as an unpublished work. Copyright ©1959, 1966, 1984 by Robert Nemiroff. Reprinted by permission of Random House, Inc.

Excerpt from the stage play *Real Women Have Curves* by Josefina Lopez. Copyright ©1996 by Josefina Lopez. Reprinted by permission of the author. All rights reserved.

Excerpt from *Saint Joan* by George Bernard Shaw. Reprinted by permission of The Society of Authors, on behalf of the Bernard Shaw Estate.

Excerpt from *The Search for Signs of Intelligent Life in the Universe* by Jane Wagner. Copyright ©1986 by Jane Wagner Inc. Reprinted by permission of HarperCollins.

Excerpt from *A Shayna Maidel* by Barbara Lebow. Copyright ©1984 by Barbara Lebow as an unpublished dramatic composition. Copyright ©1988 by Barbara Lebow. Reprinted by permission of Dramatists Play Service, Inc. Caution: The reprinting of *A Shayna Maidel* included in this volume is reprinted by permission of the author and Dramatists Play Service, Inc. The stock and amateur performance rights in this play are controlled exclusively by Dramatists Play Service, Inc. 440 Park Avenue South, New York, NY 10016. No professional or non-professional production of the play may be given without obtaining in advance, the written permission of the Dramatists Play Service, Inc., and paying the requisite fee. Inquiries regarding all other rights should be addressed to Mary Hardin, Hardin-Curtis Associates, 850 Seventh Avenue, Suite 405, New York, NY 10019.

Excerpt from *Spinning Into Butter: A Play* by Rebecca Gilman. Copyright ©2000 by Rebecca Gilman. Reprinted by permission of Faber and Faber, Inc., an affiliate of Farrar, Straus and Giroux, LLC.

Excerpt from *A Star Ain't Nothin' but a Hole in Heaven* by Judi Ann Mason. Copyright ©1977 by Judi Ann Mason. Reprinted by permission of the author.

Excerpt from *A Waitress in Yellowstone* by David Mamet. Copyright ©1984 by David Mamet. Reprinted by permission of Grove/Atlantic, Inc.

Excerpt from *Weebjob* from *War Cries, Plays by Diane Glancy* by Diane Glancy. Copyright (c)1997 by Diane Glancy. Originally published by Holy Cow Press, Duluth, MN. Reprinted by permission of the author.

Excerpt from *You Can't Take It With You* by Moss Hart and George S. Kaufman. Copyright 1937 by Moss Hart and George S. Kaufman. Copyright renewed ©1964 by Anne Kaufman Schneider and Catherine Carlisle Hart. Reprinted by permission of Dramatists Play Service, Inc. Caution: The reprinting of *You Can't Take It With You* included in this volume is reprinted by permission of the author and Dramatists Play Service, Inc. The amateur performance rights in this play are controlled exclusively by Dramatists Play Service, Inc. 440 Park Avenue South, New York, NY 10016. No professional or non-professional production of the play may be given without obtaining in advance, the written permission of the Dramatists Play Service, Inc., and paying the requisite fee. Inquiries regarding all other rights should be addressed to Anne Kaufman Schneider 26 E. 63rd Street., New York, NY 10011.

Image Credits

Cover photos: top, left to right: Richard Feldman/Theatre Pix; © David Cooper/Photostage; Reuters NewMedia Inc./ CORBIS; bottom: Richard Feldman/Theatre Pix

3: © Robbie Jack/CORBIS; 4–5: © David Turnley/CORBIS; 12–13: © Donald Cooper/Photostage; 13: Photofest; 17: Photofest; 18: © Bettmann/CORBIS; 19: © Bettmann/CORBIS; 20–21: © Reuters NewMedia Inc./CORBIS; 27: © Steve Prezant/CORBIS; 28: © Franz-Marc Frei/CORBIS; 29: Corel; 30 top: © Charles & Josette Lenars/CORBIS; 30 bottom: © Michael S. Yamashita/CORBIS; 31: © Michael S. Yamashita/ CORBIS; 32–33: Michael Brosilow; 38 left: © Leonard de Selva/CORBIS; 38 right: Michael Brosilow; 39: Michael Brosilow; 43: © Robbie Jack/CORBIS; 44–45: © Robbie Jack/CORBIS; 48: Corel; 49: Burdette Parks, Roundlake Studios; 52: Corel; 53 top: © Neal Preston/CORBIS; 53 bottom: MICHAEL HALSBAND/Landov; 54–55: Chris Bennion/Theatre Pix; 62–63: © The Newark Museum / Art Resource, NY; 63: Des Moines Community Playhouse; 64–65: © Robbie Jack/CORBIS; 66: Corel; 67: © Robbie Jack/ CORBIS; 71: © Roger Ressmeyer/CORBIS; 73: © HOWARD JACQUELINE/CORBIS SYGMA; 74: Connie Verkade; 75: © 2002 David Polenberg; 76–77: Michael Brosilow; 79: © Robbie Jack/CORBIS; 80: Donald Cooper, Photostage; 84: Lisa Ebright; 85 top: Jeffery St. Mary Sunrise Foundation, photograph by Jeffery St. Mary; 85 bottom: Lisa Ebright; 87: Burdette Parks, Roundlake Studios; 89: © Robbie Jack/ CORBIS; 90–91: © Robbie Jack/CORBIS; 93: Michael Brosilow; 95: Michael Brosilow; 97: Library of Congress; 98: © FOGEL FRANCOIS/CORBIS SYGMA; 99: CBS/Landov; 100–101: Kevin Berne; 102 top: Western Michigan University; 104: Utah Shakespearean Festival; 106: College of Southern Idaho; 107: © Robbie Jack/CORBIS; 110: ArtToday; 111 top: © Bettmann/CORBIS; 111 bottom: © Robbie Jack/CORBIS; 112–113: Corel; 114: Joan Marcus/Bloomberg News/Landov; 115: Burdette Parks, Roundlake Studios; 119: City of Westminster Archive Centre, London, UK/Bridgeman Art Library; 121 top: THE KOBAL COLLECTION / CASTLE ROCK ENTERTAINMENT; 121 bottom: THE KOBAL COLLECTION / RENAISSANCE FILMS/BBC/CURZON FILMS; 122–123: © CORBIS; 123: © Bettmann/CORBIS; 124–125: Corel; 125: Des Moines Community Playhouse; 126: © Robbie Jack/CORBIS; 127: THE KOBAL COLLECTION / ODYSSEY; 131: AP Photo/E Pablo Kosmicki; 132: © Leonard de Selva/CORBIS; 133 left: © Robbie Jack/CORBIS; 133 right: AP Photo/File; 135: Corel; 137: RAFAEL PEREZ/Reuters /Landov ; 138–139: AP Photo/Alan Solomon; 140: Richard Feldman; 147: A. Vincent Scarano; 149: AP Photo/Tina Fineberg; 150 top: ArtToday; 150 bottom: © Robbie Jack/CORBIS; 151: AP Photo/Kenneth Lambert; 152–153: © Micheline Pelletier/CORBIS SYGMA; 163 left: THE KOBAL COLLECTION / MARAT SADE/UNITED ARTISTS; 163 right: © Colita/CORBIS; 164: © Lindsay Hebberd/CORBIS; 165 top: © Jacques M. Chenet/CORBIS; 165 bottom: AP Photo/Ted S. Warren; 167: © Robbie Jack/CORBIS; 179: Western Michigan University; 180: The Harvard Theatre Collection, The Houghton Library; 181: Richard Feldman; 182–183: The Flying Karamazov Brothers; 186 top: Corel; 187: Burdette Parks, Roundlake Studios; 194: © Francis G. Mayer/CORBIS; 195: Richard Feldman; 196 top: Corel; 196–197: Western Michigan University; 199: Digital Vision; 201: Neo Futurists; 205: Burdette Parks, Roundlake Studios; 206: © Roger Wood/CORBIS; 207: Michael Rubottom; 210–211: Donald Cooper/Photostage; 212–213: Clive Barda/ArenaPAL; 213: Wayne Kischer; 221: Corel; 224 bottom: Richard Feldman; 226: Richard Feldman; 229: G.W. Mercier; 230: North Wind Archives; 231: Tallahassee Little Theatre, Susan Stripling photography; 232–233: Richard Feldman; 234 top to bottom: Strand; Strand; Guy Currier,

Acknowledgments

Altman Lighting;Lighting Innovation; Strand; Oasis Stage Werks; 235 top to bottom: University of Indianapolis; PLC Collection; PLC Collection; PLC Collection; DHA Lighting Limited; PLC Collection; 236: Corel; 237: Western Michigan University; 238: Goodman Theatre, Eric Y. Exit; 242: Wallace Photography; 245: Corel; 250: © Historical Picture Archive/CORBIS; 251 right: Beinecke Rare Book and Manuscript Library, Yale University; 251 left: Richard Feldman; 253: © Robbie Jack/CORBIS; 254–255: Liquid Library; 256: Michael Brosilow; 257: Art Today; 261: THE KOBAL COLLECTION / COLUMBIA; 263 left: THE KOBAL COLLECTION; 263 right: Michael Brosilow; 265: © Robbie Jack/CORBIS; 269: © RAAB SHANNA/CORBIS SYGMA; 274 top: Nan Zabriskie; 274 bottom: ©1996 Liz Lauren; 277: © MAIMAN RICK/CORBIS SYGMA; 278: The Devonshire Collection, Chatsworth. Reproduced by permission of the Duke of Devonshire and the Chatsworth Settlement Trustees.; 279 top: Mummenschanz; 279 bottom: © CORBIS SYGMA; 280–281: © Robbie Jack/CORBIS; 281: Des Moines Community Playhouse; 282: CBS-TV / THE KOBAL COLLECTION; 298: Cynthia Clampitt; 299 top: Western Michigan University; 299 bottom: Goodman Theatre; 300–301: Corel; 302: Corel; 305: Corel; 310 left: Photos.com; 310 right: ArenaPAL; 311: Henrietta Butler/ArenaPAL; 315: AP Photo/Denis Doyle; 316: © Kelly-Mooney Photography/CORBIS; 317: Michael Le Poer Trench/ArenaPAL; 318: Carol Rosegg/ArenaPAL; 319: Colin Willoughby/ArenaPAL; 320: THE KOBAL COLLECTION / MIRAMAX / JAMES, DAVID; 329: AP Photo/Stephen Chernin; 330: © Liu Liqun/CORBIS; 331: Michael Le Poer Trench/ArenaPAL; 332: AP Photo/Robert Spencer; 333: © DICKINSON TIM/CORBIS SYGMA; 334: © Michael S. Yamashita/CORBIS; 334: AP Photo/Anat Givon; 335 left: Robert Strickland; 335 right: Corel; 341: AP Photo/Harry Cabluck; 342: © Michael S. Yamashita/CORBIS; 343: Bread and Puppet Theatre Headquarters; 344: THE KOBAL COLLECTION / MGM/MAIDEN/NEW REGENCY / ARONOWITZ, MYLES; 352: © Bettmann/CORBIS; 353 top: T. Charles Erickson; 353 bottom: THE KOBAL COLLECTION / TOUCHSTONE/UNIVERSAL; 355: THE KOBAL COLLECTION / 20TH CENTURY FOX/PARAMOUNT / WALLACE, MERIE W.; 356: THE KOBAL COLLECTION / 20TH CENTURY FOX / NITKE, BARBARA; 358: THE KOBAL COLLECTION / CINEMA CENTER; 365 left: THE KOBAL COLLECTION / UNIVERSAL; 365 right: © Reuters NewMedia Inc./CORBIS; 366: © Bettmann/CORBIS; 367: THE KOBAL COLLECTION / IFC FILMS / GIRAUD, SOPHIE; 368–369: THE KOBAL COLLECTION / WARNER BROS TV/BRIGHT/KAUFFMAN/ CRANE PRO; 369: © Bettmann/CORBIS; 370: THE KOBAL COLLECTION; 371 top: THE KOBAL COLLECTION / CBS-TV; 371 bottom: THE KOBAL COLLECTION / DARREN STAR PRODUCTIONS / BLANKENHORN, CRAIG; 372: THE KOBAL COLLECTION / CTW/JIM HENSON PROD; 373: © Reuters NewMedia Inc./CORBIS; 375: © Reuters NewMedia Inc./CORBIS; 381: AP Photo/Bob Galbraith; 382: THE KOBAL COLLECTION / ABC-TV; 383: © William Burlingham/The Actors Gymnasium; 385: © David Butow/CORBIS SABA; 387: The Advertising Archive Ltd.; 394: © Bettmann/CORBIS; 395: Richard Feldman; 399: © Bettmann/CORBIS; 400–401: Corel; 401: Kati Wilson, Loyola Marymount University Costume Design student and costume designer for JB; 403: Art Today; 404: © Robbie Jack/CORBIS; 405 middle: Art Today. 406: © AFP/CORBIS; 408: Art Today; 409: © Bettmann/CORBIS; 410: © Marc Garanger/CORBIS; 412: Cynthia Clampitt; 413: © Burstein Collection/CORBIS; 416–417: AP Photo/Diether Endlicher; 419: Michael Brosilow; 420: © Lindsay Hebberd/CORBIS; 423: Burdette Parks, Roundlake Studios; 424: Utah Shakespearean Festival; 425: Andrea Pistolesi/Getty Images; 426: Art Today; 431: © Robbie Jack/CORBIS; 435: AP Photo/Luca Bruno; 436, 437: © Bettmann/CORBIS; 438: Michal Daniel; 441: Nigel Norrington/ArenaPAL; 442–443: Pete Jones/ArenaPAL; 459: © ELBAZ SOPHIE/CORBIS SYGMA

Mike Aspengren Illustrations: 56, 58, 65 top, 103, 145, 184, 185, 186 bottom, 188, 189, 190, 204, 214, 215, 217, 218, 219, 222, 223, 224 top, 225, 240, 241, 262, 285, 294, 405 left and right,

William Burlingham Photographs: back cover, 6, 7, 22, 23, 24, 25, 35, 37, 46, 57, 61, 69, 94, 143, 154, 156, 160–161, 169, 172, 193, 228, 258, 259, 266, 267, 268, 283, 284, 286, 287, 289, 290, 291, 292, 293, 304–305, 309

The editors wish to thank the playwrights, publishers, and agents who have allowed their copyrighted materials to be used in this book. Every effort has been made to contact all copyright holders. If we have omitted anyone, please let us know and we will include a suitable acknowledgment in subsequent editions.

Index

Index

Index

Index

Index

Index

Index

National Standards for Theatre Education

Grades 9 through 12

In grades 9–12, students view and construct dramatic works as metaphorical visions of life that embrace connotative meanings, juxtaposition, ambiguity, and varied interpretations. By creating, performing, analyzing, and critiquing dramatic performances, they develop a deeper understanding of personal issues and a broader worldview that includes global issues. Since theatre in all its forms reflects and affects life, students should learn about representative dramatic texts and performances and the place of that work and those events in history. Classroom work becomes more formalized with the advanced students participating in theatre, film, television, and electronic media productions.

1. Content Standard Script writing through improvising, writing, and refining scripts based on personal experience and heritage, imagination, literature, and history

Achievement Standard, Proficient: Students

a. construct imaginative scripts and collaborate with actors to refine scripts so that story and meaning are conveyed to an audience

Achievement Standard, Advanced: Students

b. write theatre, film, television, or electronic media scripts in a variety of traditional and new forms that include original characters with unique dialogue that motivates action

2. Content Standard Acting by developing, communicating, and sustaining characters in improvisations and informal or formal productions

Achievement Standard, Proficient: Students

a. analyze the physical, emotional, and social dimensions of characters found in dramatic texts from various genres and media

b. compare and demonstrate various classical and contemporary acting techniques and methods

c. in an ensemble, create and sustain characters that communicate with audiences

Achievement Standard, Advanced: Students

d. demonstrate artistic discipline to achieve an ensemble in rehearsal and performance

e. create consistent characters from classical, contemporary, realistic, and nonrealistic dramatic texts in informal and formal theatre, film, television, or electronic media productions

3. Content Standard Designing and producing by conceptualizing and realizing artistic interpretations for informal or formal productions

Achievement Standard, Proficient: Students

a. explain the basic physical and chemical properties of the technical aspects of theatre (such as light, color, electricity, paint, and makeup)

b. analyze a variety of dramatic texts from cultural and historical perspectives to determine production requirements

c. develop designs that use visual and aural elements to convey environments that clearly support the text

d. apply technical knowledge and skills to collaboratively and safely create functional scenery, properties, lighting, sound, costumes, and makeup

e. design coherent stage management, promotional, and business plans

Achievement Standard, Advanced: Students

f. explain how scientific and technological advances have impacted set, light, sound, and costume design and implementation for theatre, film, television, and electronic media productions

g. collaborate with directors to develop unified production concepts that convey the metaphorical nature of the drama for informal and formal theatre, film, television, or electronic media productions

h. safely construct and efficiently operate technical aspects of theatre, film, television, or electronic media productions

i. create and reliably implement: production schedules, stage management plans, promotional ideas, and business and front of house procedures for informal and formal theatre, film, television, or electronic media productions

4. Content Standard Directing by interpreting dramatic texts and organizing and conducting rehearsals for informal or formal productions

Achievement Standard, Proficient: Students

a. develop multiple interpretations and visual and aural production choices for scripts and production ideas and choose those that are most interesting

b. justify selections of text, interpretation, and visual and aural artistic choices

c. effectively communicate directorial choices to a small ensemble for improvised or scripted scenes.

Achievement Standard, Advanced: Students

d. explain and compare the roles and interrelated responsibilities of the various personnel involved in theatre, film, television, and electronic media productions

e. collaborate with designers and actors to develop aesthetically unified production concepts for informal and formal theatre, film, television, or electronic media productions

f. conduct auditions, cast actors, direct scenes, and conduct production meetings to achieve production goals

5. Content Standard Researching by evaluating and synthesizing cultural and historical information to support artistic choices

Achievement Standard, Proficient: Students

a. identify and research cultural, historical, and symbolic clues in dramatic texts and evaluate the validity and practicality of the information to assit in making artistic choices for informal and formal productions

Achievement Standard, Advanced: Students

b. research and describe appropriate historical production designs, techniques, and performances from various cultures to assist in making artistic choices for informal and formal theatre, film, television, or electronic media productions

6. Content Standard Comparing and integrating art forms by analyzing traditional theatre, dance, music, visual arts, and new art forms

Achievement Standard, Proficient: Students

a. describe and compare the basic nature, materials, elements, and means of communicating in theatre, dramatic media, musical theatre, dance, music, and the visual arts

b. determine how the nondramatic art forms are modified to enhance the expression of ideas and emotions in theatre

c. illustrate the integration of several arts media in informal presentations

Achievement Standard, Advanced: Students

d. compare the interpretive and expressive natures of several art forms in a specific culture or historical period

e. compare the unique interpretive and expressive natures and aesthetic qualities of traditional arts from various cultures and historical periods with contemporary new art forms (such as performance art)

f. integrate several arts and/or media in theatre, film, television, or electronic media productions

7. Content Standard Analyzing, critiquing, and constructing meanings from informal and formal theatre, film, television, and electronic media productions

Achievement Standard, Proficient: Students

a. construct social meanings from informal and formal productions and from dramatic performances from a variety of cultures and historical periods, and relate these to current personal, national, and international issues

b. articulate and justify personal aesthetic criteria for critiquing dramatic texts and events that compare perceived artistic intent with the final aesthetic achievement

c. analyze and critique the whole and the parts of dramatic performances, taking into account the context, and constructively suggest alternative artistic choices

d. constructively evaluate their own and others' collaborative efforts and artistic choices in informal and formal productions

Achievement Standard, Advanced: Students

e. construct personal meanings from nontraditional dramatic performances

f. analyze, compare, and evaluate differing critiques of the same dramatic texts and performances

g. critique several dramatic works in terms of other aesthetic philosophies (such as the underlying ethos of Greek drama, French classicism with its unities of time and place, Shakespeare and romantic forms, India classical drama, Japanese kabuki, and others)

h. analyze and evaluate critical comments about personal dramatic work explaining which points are most appropriate to inform further development of the work

8. Content Standard Understanding context by analyzing the role of theatre, film, television, and electronic media in the past and the present

Achievement Standard, Proficient: Students

a. compare how similar themes are treated in drama from various cultures and historical periods, illustrate with informal performances, and discuss how theatre can reveal universal concepts

b. identify and compare the lives, works, and influence of representative theatre artists in various cultures and historical periods

c. identify cultural and historical sources of American theatre and musical theatre

d. analyze the effect of their own cultural experiences on their dramatic work

Achievement Standard, Advanced: Students

e. analyze the social and aesthetic impact of underrepresented theatre and film artists

f. analyze the relationships among cultural values, freedom of artistic expression, ethics, and artistic choices in various cultures and historical periods

g. analyze the development of dramatic forms, production practices, and theatrical traditions across cultures and historical periods and explain influences on contemporary theatre, film, television, and electronic media productions

Correlation to National Standards

Standard	Proficient	Advanced	Chapter Number or Part*
1a	✓		1, 11, 12, 13, 24, 25, 27
1b		✓	12, 13, 17, 24, 25, 26, 28
2a	✓		1, 2, 3, 6, 7, 8, 9, 10, 11, 12, 13, 15, 16, 17
2b	✓		10, 11, 25, TH1, TH2, TH3
2c	✓		1, 4, 5, 8, 9, 10, 12, 16
2d		✓	2, 4, 5, 7, 8, 9, 10, 11, 12. 15, 16
2e		✓	8, 10, 11, 15
3a	✓		18, 19, 20, 21, 22, 23
3b	✓		18, 19, 20, 21, 23, TH2, TH3
3c	✓		6, 18, 19, 20, 21, 22, 23, 26
3d	✓		19, 20, 22, 23
3e	✓		14, 24
3f		✓	18, 19, 20, 21
3g		✓	20, 21, 22, 23, 28
3h		✓	23, 25
3i		✓	25
4a	✓		14, 23, 26, 27
4b	✓		6, 14, 22, 23, 27
4c	✓		4, 23
4d		✓	23, 25, 27
4e		✓	14, 23, 26, 27
4f		✓	14, 26
5a	✓		9, 23, TH1, TH2, TH3
5b		✓	9, 10, 23, TH1, TH2, TH3
6a	✓		3, 25, 29
6b	✓		2, 24, 25
6c	✓		4, 24, 25
6d		✓	3, 25, TH1, TH2, TH3
6e		✓	23, 25, TH1, TH2, TH3
6f		✓	24, 28, 29
7a	✓		10, 14, 17, 23, 28, TH3
7b	✓		3, 10, 12, 14, 15, 17, 25, 26
7c	✓		2, 4, 5, 6, 7, 8, 9, 11, 12, 13, 14, 15, 16, 17, 29
7d	✓		2, 5, 6, 7, 8, 9, 11, 12, 17, 28, 29
7e		✓	12, 14, 16, 25, 29
7f		✓	4, 11, 16, 17, 29
7g		✓	9, 10, 11, TH1, TH2
7h		✓	9, 11, 12, 14, 17
8a	✓		5, 7, 8, 9, 12, 13, 14, 16
8b	✓		7, 13, 14, 15, 17, TH1, Th2, TH3
8c	✓		8, 14, 17, 24, TH3
8d	✓		12
8e		✓	7, 13, 14, 15, 16
8f		✓	15, 16, 17
8g		✓	5, 7, 8, 12, 13, 14, 15, 16, 17, 28, TH1, TH2, TH3

*TH1, TH2, and TH3 refer to the parts in Unit Seven (Theatre History).

Bibliography

ACTING

Aaron, Stephan. *Stage Fright – Its Role in Acting.* Chicago: University of Chicago Press, 1988.

Adler, Stella. *The Art of Acting.* New York: Applause, 2000.

Albright, Hardie. *Acting: The Creative Process.* 3rd ed. Belmont, CA: Wadsworth, 1980.

Barton, Robert. *Acting On Stage and Off.* New York: Harper, Row, and Winston, 1989.

_________. *Style for Actors.* Mountain View, CA: Mayfield, 1992.

Benedetti, Robert. *The Actor at Work.* 5th ed. Englewood Cliffs, NJ: Prentice Hall, 1990.

Bernard, Ian. *Film and Television Acting.* Stoneham, MA: Focal Press, 1993.

Boleslavsky, Richard. *Acting: The First Six Lessons.* Routledge, 2003.

Bowskill, Derek. *Acting: An Introduction.* Englewood Cliffs, NJ: Prentice Hall, 1977.

Chekhov, Michael. *To The Actor.* New York: Barnes and Noble, 1985.

_________. *On the Technique of Acting.* New York: Harper-Collins, 1991.

Callow, Simon. *Being an Actor.* New York: Grove Press, 1986.

Cohen, Robert. *Acting Power.* Mountain View, CA: Mayfield, 1988.

Cole, Toby, editor. *Acting: A Handbook of the Stanislavski Method.* New York: Crown Publishing Group, 1955.

Cole, Toby and Helen Chinoy. *Actors on Acting.* Rev. ed. New York: Crown Publishing Group, 1980.

Crawford, Jerry and Joan Snyder. *Acting in Person and in Style.* 4th ed. Dubuque, IA: William Brown, 1991.

Delgado, Ramon. *Acting With Both Sides of Your Brain.* New York: Holt, Rinehart and Winston, 1986.

Desberg, Peter. *Controlling Stage Fright.* Oakland, CA: New Harbinger, 1989.

Duer, Edwin. *The Length and Depth of Acting.* New York: Holt, Rinehart and Winston, 1962.

Felner, Mira. *Free to Act: An Integrated Approach to Acting.* New York: Holt, Rinehart, and Winston, 1990.

Franklin, Miriam, and James Dixon. *Rehearsal.* 6th ed. Englewood Cliffs, NJ: Prentice Hall, 1983.

Funke, Lewis, and John Booth. *Actors Talk About Acting: Fourteen Interviews with Stars of the Theatre.* New York: Random House. 1961.

Grote, David. *Script Analysis.* Belmont, CA: Wadsworth, 1984.

Hagan, Uta. *A Challenge for the Actor.* New York: Macmillan, 1991.

Hagan, Uta, and Haskel Frankel. *Respect for Acting.* New York: Macmillan, 1973.

Harrop, John, and Sabin Epstein. *Acting With Style.* 2nd ed. Englewood Cliffs, NJ: Prentice Hall, 1990.

Kahan, Stanley. *Introduction to Acting.* 4th ed. New York: Allyn and Bacon, 1997.

Kuritz, Paul. *Playing: An Introduction to Acting.* Englewood Cliffs, NJ: Prentice Hall, 1982.

Lewis, Robert. *Advice to the Players.* New York: Harper and Row, 1980.

McGaw, Charles. *Acting Is Believing.* 9th ed. Wadsworth Publishing, 2003.

Morris, Eric. *Being and Doing: A Workbook for Actors.* Los Angeles: Ermor Enterprises, 1990.

Moore, Sonia. T*he Stanislavski System.* 2nd ed. New York: Viking Penguin, 1984.

_________. *Training an Actor.* Rev. ed. New York: Viking Penguin, 1979.

Spolin, Viola. *Improvisation for the Theatre: A Handbook of Teaching and Directing Techniques.* 3rd ed. Evanston, IL: Northwestern University Press, 1999.

_________. *Theatre Game File.* Evanston, IL: Northwestern University Press, 1989.

Stanislavski, Konstantin. *An Actor Prepares.* New York: Theatre Arts Books, 2002.

_________. *Building a Character.* New York: Theatre Arts Books, 2002.

Tanner, Fran. *Creative Communication.* 5th ed. Topeka, KS: Clark Publishing, Inc., 1995.

Thomas, James. *Script Analysis for Actors, Directors and Designers.* Stoneham, MA: Focal Press, 1992.

Whelan, Jeremy. *The ABC'S of Acting.* Portland, OR: Grey Heron Books. 1990

ACTING IN SHAKESPEARE

Barton, John. *Playing Shakespeare.* Portsmouth, NH: Heinemann, 1988.

Brine, Adrian, and Michael York. *A Shakespearean Actor Prepares.* Lyme, N.H.:Smith and Krause, 2000.

Brubaker, Edward S. Shakespeare Aloud: *A Guide to His Verse on Stage.* Lancaster, PA: Brubaker, 1977.

Chute, Marchette. *Shakespeare of London.* New York: Viking Penguin, 1991. Background and feel of Elizabethan times.

Gielgud, John, and John Miller. *Acting Shakespeare.* New York: Scribner's, 1993.

Halio, Jay L. *Understanding Shakespeare's Plays in Performance.* Los Angeles: Martin, 1990.

Hodges, Walter. *Shakespeare and the Players.* New York: Coward McCann, 1963. Elizabethan actors and acting.

Joseph, Bertram. *Acting Shakespeare.* New York: Theatre Arts Books, 1969.

Loney, Glenn, ed. *Staging Shakespeare.* New York: Garland, 1990.

Maher, Mary Z. *Modern Hamlets and Their Soliloquies.* Iowa City, IA: University of Iowa Press, 1992.

Silverbush, Rhona. *Speak the Speech!: Shakespeare's Monologues.* NY: Faber and Faber, 2002.

AUDITIONS

Black, David. *Actor's Audition.* New York: Random House, 1990.

Callen, K. *How to Sell Yourself as an Actor.* Studio City, CA: Sweden Press, 1992.

Ellis, Roger. *Audition Handbook for Student Actors.* Chicago: Nelson-Hall, 1985.

Finchley, Joan. *Audition.* Englewood Cliffs, NJ: Prentice Hall, 1984.

Harmon, Renee. *How to Audition for Movies and T.V.* New York: Walker, 1992.

Hunt, Gordon. *How to Audition.* 2nd ed. New York: Harper and Row, 1992.

Markus, Tom. *The Professional Actor: From Audition to Performance.* New York: Drama Book Specialists, 1980.

Merlin, Joanna. *Auditioning: An Actor-Friendly Guide.* NY: Vintage Books, 2001.

Oliver. Donald. *How to Audition for the Musical Theatre.* Rev. ed. New York: Drama Book Specialists, 1988.

Richardson, Randall. *The Audition Sourcebook: Do's, Don'ts, and an Online Guide to 2100+ Monologues and Musical Excerpts.* Portsmouth, NY: Heinemann, 2002.

Shurtleff, Michael. Audition: *Everything an Actor Needs to Get the Part.* New York: Bantam, 1980.

Silver, Fred. *Auditioning for the Musical Theatre.* New York: New Market, 1985.

CAREERS

Alterman, Glenn. *Promoting Your Acting Career.* NY: Allworth Press, 1998.

Babcock, Dennis, and Preston Boyd. *Careers in the Theatre.* Minneapolis, MN: Lerner, 1975.

Blum, Richard. *Working Actors.* Stoneham, MA: Focal Press, 1989

Cohen, Robert. *Acting Professionally: Raw Facts About Careers.* 3rd ed. Mountain View, CA: Mayfield, 1982.

Engel, Lehman. *Getting Started In the Theatre.* New York: Collier Books, 1973.

Fridell, Squire. *Acting in Television Commercials for Fun and Profit.* New York:

Crown, 1980.

Greenberg, Jan. *Theatre Careers.* New York: Holt, Rinehart and Winston, 1983.

Hines, Terence, and Suzanne Vaughn. *An Actor Succeeds: Management.* New York: Samuel French, 1989.

Logan, Tom. *How to Act and Eat at the Same Time.* 2nd ed. Washington, D.C.: Communication Press, 1988.

Moore, Dick. O*pportunities in Acting Careers.* Skokie, IL: NTC, 1985.

Padol, Brian, and Alan Simon. *The Young Performer's Guide: How to Break into Show Business.* Crozet, VA: Better Way, 1990.

COSTUMES

Baker, Georgia, and Helen Pullen. *A Handbook of Costume Drawing.* Stoneham, MA: Focal Press, 1992.

Baker, Patsy. *Wigs and Makeup for the Theatre.* Stoneham, MA: Focal Press. 1992.

Barton, Lucy. *Historic Costume for the Stage.* Rev. ed. Boston, MA: Walter Baker, 1961.

Bicât, Tina. *Making Stage Costumes: A Practical Guide.* Marlborough, England: Crowood, 2001.

Cassin-Scott, Jack. *The Illustrated Encyclopedia of Costumes and Fashion from 1066 to the Present.* NY: Sterling, 1995.

Cunningham, Rebecca. *The Magic Garment.* White Plains, NY: Longman, 1989.

Cumming, Valerie, and Aileen Ribeiro. *The Visual History of Costume.* New York: Drama Book Specialists, 1990.

Davenport, Millie. *Book of Costumes.* New York: Crown, 1964.

Emery, Joy. *Stage Costume Techniques.* Englewood Cliffs, NJ: Prentice Hall, 1981.

Holkeboer, Katharine. *Costume Construction.* Englewood Cliffs, NJ: Prentice Hall. 1989.

Hunnisett, Jean. *Period Costume for Stage and Screen.* New York: Drama Book Specialists, 1991.

Ingham, Rosemary, and Elizabeth Covey. *The Costumer's Handbook.* Englewood Cliffs, NJ: Prentice Hall, 1980.

Jackson, Sheila. *Costuming for the Stage.* New York: Dutton, 1988.

Litherland, Janet, and Sue McAnally, *Broadway Costumes on a Budget: Big-Time Ideas for Amateur Producers.* Colorado Springs, CO: Meriwether, 1996.

Musgrove, Jan, *Make-up, Hair, and Costume for Film and Television.* Boston, MA: Focal Press, 2003.

Prisk, Berneice. *Stage Costume Handbook.* Westport, CT: Greenwood, 1979.

Wilcox, Ruth Turner. *Five Centuries of American Costume.* New York: Charles Scribner's Sons, 1963.

________. *The Mode in Costume.* 4th ed. New York: Charles Scribner's Sons, 1983.

DIRECTING

Ball, William. *A Sense of Direction.* New York: Drama Book Specialists, 1984.

Benedetti, Robert. *The Director at Work.* Englewood Cliffs, NJ: Prentice Hall, 1985.

Bogart, Anne. *A Director Prepares: Seven Essays on Art in Theatre.* London: Routledge, 2001.

Catron, Louis E. *The Director's Vision: Play Direction from Analysis to Production.* New York: McGraw-Hill, 1989

Clurman, Harold. *On Directing.* New York: Macmillan, 1974.

Cohen, Robert, and John Harrop. *Creative Play Direction.* 2nd ed. Englewood Cliffs, NJ: Prentice Hall, 1984.

Cole, Toby. *Directors on Directing.* Indianapolis, IN: Bobbs-Merrill, 1963.

Converse, Terry John. *Directing for the Stage: A Workshop Guide of Creative Exercises and Project.* Colorado Springs, CO: Meriwether, 1995.

Dean, Alexander, and Lawrence Carra. *Fundamentals of Play Directing.* 5th ed. New York: Holt, Rinehart and Winston, 1989.

Hodge, Francis. *Play Directing.* 3rd ed. Englewood Cliffs, NJ: Prentice Hall, 1988.

Kirk, John, and Ralph Bellas. *The Art of Directing.* Belmont, CA: Wadsworth, 1990.

Sievers, W. David. *Directing for the Theatre.* 3rd ed. Dubuque, IA: William Brown, 1974.

Vaughn, Stuart. *Directing Plays.* White Plains, NY: Longman, 1993.

IMPROVISATION & THEATRE GAMES COLLECTIONS

Barker, Clive. *Theatre Games.* Portsmouth, NH: Heinemann, 1988.

Frost, Anthony, and Ralph Yarrow. *Improvisation in Drama.* Los Angeles: Martin, 1990.

Hodgson, John, and Ernest Richards. *Improvisation.* New York: Grove Press, 1987.

Owens, Fred. *Theatre Games.* San Francisco, CA: Diamond Heights Publishers, 1979.

Polsky, Milton. *Let's Improvise.* Lanham, MD: University Press of America, 1989.

Spolin, Viola. *Improvisation for the Theatre.* 3rd ed. Evanston, IL: Northwestern University Press, 1999.

________. *Theatre Games for Rehearsal.* Evanston, IL: Northwestern University Press, 1985.

LEISURE READING & THEATRE HUMOR

Allen, John. *Great Moments in the Theatre.* London: Phoenix House, 1958.

Brandreth, Gyles. *Great Theatrical Disasters.* St. Martin's Press, 1982.

Brook, Peter. *The Empty Space.* New York: Atheneum, 1968.

Cottrel, John. *Laurence Olivier.* Englewood Cliffs, NJ: Prentice Hall, 1975.

DeMille, Agnes. *And Promenade Home.* New York: Little, Brown, 1958.

Dolbier, Maurice. *All Wrong on the Night.* New York: Walker, 1966. Vignettes of humorous theatrical errors.

Funke, Lewis and John Booth. *Actors Talk About Acting.* New York: Random House, 1961. Very good for the serious drama student.

Gielgud, John. *Stage Directions.* New York: Random House,1963.

Gillmore, Margalo. *Four Flights Up.* New York: Houghton Mifflin, 1964. Most entertaining.

Grotowski, Jerzy. *Towards a Poor Theatre.* New York: Simon and Schuster 1968.

Guthrie, Tyrone. *Life in the Theatre.* New York: McGraw-Hill, 1959.

Hart, Moss. *Act One.* New York: Random House, 1959. Excellent.

Hay, Peter. *Broadway Anecdotes.* New York: Oxford University Press, 1989.

________. *Theatrical Anecdotes.* New York: Oxford University Press, 1987.

Hayes, Helen. *My Life in Three Acts.* New York: Touchstone, 1991

Holbrook, Hal. *Mark Twain Tonight.* New York: McKay, 1959.

Houseman, John. *Final Dress.* New York: Touchstone, 1984.

Lewes, George. *On Actors and the Art of Acting.* New York: Grover Press, 1957.

Martin, Mary. *My Heart Belongs.* New York: William Morrow, 1976.

Mosel, Tad, and Gertrude Macy. *Leading Lady: Katharine Cornell.* Boston, MA: Little, Brown, 1978.

Redgrave, Michael. *The Actor's Ways and Means.* London: Heinemann Ltd., 1953.

Shaw, George Bernard. *Shaw on Theatre.* New York: Hill and Wang, 1958

Stanislavski, Constantin. *My Life in Art.* New York: Theatre Arts Books, 1948.

MAKEUP

Baygan, Lee. *Makeup for Theatre, Film and Television.* New York: Drama Book Specialists, 1982.

Buckman, Herman. *Stage Makeup.* Rev. ed. Cincinnati, OH: Watson-Guptill, 1989.

Corson, Richard. *Fashions in Hair.* New York: Hillary House, 1980.

________. *Stage Makeup.* 8th ed. Englewood Cliffs, NJ: Prentice Hall, 1990.

Swinfield, Rosemarie. *Stage Makeup Step-by-Step.* Cincinnati, Ohio: Betterway Books, 1994.

________. *Period Makeup Step-by-Step.* Cincinnati, Ohio: Betterway Books, 1994.

MONOLOGUE COLLECTIONS

Alterman, Glenn. *Two Minutes and Under: Original Character Monologues for Actors.* Newbury, VT: Smith and Kraus, 1993.

Edwards, Gus. *Monologues on Black Life.* Portsmouth, NH: Heinemann, 1997.

Ellis, Roger. *Competition Monologues.* Lanham, MD: University Press of America, 1989.

Emerson and Grumbach. *Monologues for Men.* New York: Drama Book Specialists, Vol. 1, 1976; Vol. 2, 1981

________. *Monologues for Women.* New York: Drama Book Specialists, Vol. 1, 1976; Vol. 2, 1981.

________. *Monologues for Young Actors.* New York: Drama Book Specialists, 1991.

________. *Actors' Guide to Monologues.* New York: Drama Book Specialists, Vol. 1, 1972; Vol. 2, 1981.

Harrington, Laura. *One Hundred Monologues.* New York: Dutton, 1989

Karshner, Roger. *Monologues They Haven't Heard.* Toluca Lake, CA: Dramaline, 1983.

________. *Monologues For Teenagers.* Rancho Mirage, CA: Dramaline, 1994.

London, Todd, editor. *Contemporary American Monologues for Women.* New York: Theatre Communications Group, 1998,

________. *Contemporary American Monologues for Men.* New York: Theatre Communications Group, 1998,

Marshall, Michael. *The Book of Comic and Dramatic Monologues.* New York: Hamish Hamilton, 1982.

Pomerance, Susan. *For Women: Monologues They Haven't Heard.* Toluca Lake, CA: Dramaline, 1985.

Rudnicki, Stefan. *Classical Monologues, One: Shakespeare.* New York: Drama Book Specialists, 1979; *Two: Shakespeare and Friends,* 1979; *Three: The Age of Style,* 1985; *Four: Warhorses,* 1985.

________. *The Actor's Book of Monologues for Women.* New York: Viking Penguin, 1991.

________. *The Actor's Book of Unusual Monologues.* New York: Viking Penguin, 1990.

Slaight, Craig, and Jack Sharrar. *Great Monologues for Young Actors* (Vol I and II). Lyme, NH: Smith and Kraus, 1999.

Smith, Marisa, and Kristin Graham. *Monologues from Literature.* New York: Fawcett, 1990.

Uno, Roberta. *Monologues for Actors of Color.* New York: Routledge, 2000.

MOVEMENT & MIME

Baker, Hendrik. *Stage Movement and Theatrecraft.* New York: Theatre Arts, 1981.

Davies, Gil. *Staging a Pantomime.* London: A&C Black, 1995.

Hobbs, William. *Stage Combat: The Action to the Word.* New York: St. Martin's, 1981.

King, Nancy. *A Movement Approach to Acting.* Englewood Cliffs, NJ: Prentice Hall, 1981.

Kipnis, Claude. *The Mime Book.* Colorado Springs, CO: Meriwether, 1988.

Martinez, J. D. *Combat Mime: A Non-Violent Approach to Stage Violence.* Chicago: Nelson Hall, 1982.

Oxenford, Lyn. *Playing Period Plays.* Chicago: Coach House Press, 1984.

Rubin, Lucille. *Movement for the Actor.* New York: Drama Book Specialists, 1980.

Russell, Douglas. *Period Style for the Theatre.* 2nd ed. Rockleigh, NJ: Longwood, 1987.

Sabatine, Jean, and David Hodge. *The Actor's Image: Movement Training.* Englewood Cliffs, NJ: Prentice Hall, 1983.

Stolzenberg, Mark. *Be a Mime.* New York: Sterling, 1991.

White, Edwin, and Marguerite Battye. *Acting and Stage Movement.* New York: Meriwether, 1985.

OTHER THEATRE FORMS

Alpert, Hollis. Broadway, *125 Years of Musical Theatre.* New York: Arcade Publishing, 1991.

Ando, Tsuruo, *Bunraku: The Puppet Theater,* Walker/Weatherhill, 1970.

Baker, Hendrik. *Stage Movement and Theatrecraft.* New York: Theatre Arts, 1981.

Baird, Bil *The Art of the Puppet,* New York: Macmillan, 1965.

Beddow, Margery. *Bob Fosse's Broadway.* Portsmouth, NH: Heinemann, 1996.

Bell, John. *Strings, Hands, Shadows: A Modern Puppet History.* Detroit: Detroit Institute of Arts, 2000.

Bering, Rüdiger. *Musicals.* Hauppauge, New York: Barron's, 1998.

Bloom, Ken. *American Song: The Complete Musical Theatre Companion.* New York: Schirmer Books, 1996.

Brown, Gene. *Show Time, a Chronology of Broadway and the Theatre from Its Beginnings to the Present.* New York: Macmillan, 1997.

Citron, Stephen. *The Musical From Inside Out: A Guidebook.* Chicago: Elephant Paperbacks, 1997.

Coger, Leslie Irene, and Melvin R. White. *Readers Theatre Handbook: A Dramatic Approach to Literature,* Glenview, IL: Scott, Foresman and Company, 1982

Conrad, Christine. Jerome Robbins, *That Broadway Man/That Ballet Man.* London: Booth Clibborn Editions, 2000.

David Currell, David. *Puppets and Puppet Theatre.* Marlborough, England: Crowood Press, 1999.

Davis, Lee. Bolton and Wodehouse and Kern, *The Men Who Made Musical Comedy.* New York: Heinemann, 1993.

DeVenney, David P. *The Broadway Song Companion, An Annotated Guide to Musical Theatre Literature by Voice Type and Song Title.* Lanham, MD: Scarecrow Press, Inc., 1998.

Eleveld, Mark, editor. *The Spoken Word Revolution: Slam, Hip Hop & the Poetry of a New Generation,* Sourcebooks, 2003.

Filichia, Peter. *Let's Put on a Musical, How to Choose the Right Show for Your School.* New York: Avon Books, 1993.

Flower, Cedric, and Alan Jon Fortney. *Puppets: Methods and Materials.* Schenectady, NY: Davis, 1983.

Gänzl, Kurt. *Musicals, the Complete Illustrated Story of the World's Most Popular Live Entertainment.* London: Carlton Books, 1995.

Hobbs, William. *Stage Combat: The Action to the Word.* New York: St. Martin's, 1981.

Kennedy, Michael Patrick, and John Muir. *Musicals, A Guide to Over 180 Major Musicals.* Glasgow, GA: Harper Collins, 1997.

King, Nancy. *A Movement Approach to Acting.* Englewood Cliffs, NJ: Prentice Hall, 1981.

Mandelbaum, Ken. *A Chorus Line and the Musicals of Michael Bennett.* New York: St. Martin's Press, 1989.

Miletich, Leo N. *Broadway's Prize-Winning Musicals, An Annotated Guide for Libraries and Audio Collectors.* New York: Harrington Park Press, 1993.

Novak, Elaine A., and Deborah. *Staging Musical Theatre, A Complete Guide for Directors, Choreographers and Producers.* Cincinnati: Better Way Books, 1996.

PLAY ANTHOLOGIES – THREE-ACT

Allison, Alexander, Arthur Carr, and Arthur Eastman. *Masterpieces of Drama.* Macmillan, New York, 1979.

Auburn, Mark, and Katharine Buckman. *Drama Through Performance.* Houghton Mifflin, Boston, 1977.

Barnet, Sylvan, Morton Berman, and William Burto. *Types of Drama: Plays and Essays.* 8th ed. Pearson Longman, 2000.

Barranger, M. S., and Daniel Dodson. *Generations.* Harcourt, Brace, Jovanovich, New York, 1971. Seven plays showing a generation conflict.

Bonazza, Blaze, and Emil Roy. *Studies in Drama.* Harper and Row, New York, 1968.

Brockett, Oscar. *Plays for the Theatre: An Anthology of World Drama.* 8th ed. Wadsworth Publishing, 2003.

Cerf, Bennett, and Van Cartmell. *Plays of Our Time.* Random House, New York, 1967.

Gassner, John. *Best American Plays.* Crown Publishers. New York. Six in the series from 1918 to 1967.

__________. *Treasury of the Theatre.* Simon and Schuster. New York. Series 1935, 1940, 1951, 1963, 1967, 1970.

__________. *Twenty-Five Best Plays of the Modern American Theatre.* Crown, New York, from 1929 to 1952.

Goldman, Mark, and Isadore Traschen. *The Drama: Traditional and Modern.* Allyn and Bacon, Boston, 1968.

Goodman, Randolph. *From Script to Stage: Eight Modern Plays.* Rinehart Press, San Francisco, 1971. Plays and discussions on their staging.

__________. *Drama on Stage.* Holt, Rinehart and Winston, New York, 1978.

Hatlin, Theodore. *Drama Principles and Plays.* Prentice-Hall, Englewood Cliffs, New Jersey, 1975.

Hay, David, and James Howell. *Contact With Drama.* Science Research Associates, Chicago, 1974.

Johnson, Stanley, Judah Bierman, and James Hart. *The Play and the Reader.* Prentice-Hall, Englewood Cliffs. New Jersey, 1971.

Perfection Learning Corporation. *Page to Stage: Plays from Classic Literature,* 2002.

__________. *Drama for Reading and Performance, Collection One,* 2002.

__________. *Drama for Reading and Performance, Collection Two,* 2002.

Perrine, Laurence. *Dimensions of Drama.* Harcourt, Brace, Jovanovich, New York, 1973. Comments and study questions.

Pickering, Jerry. *A Treasury of Drama: Classical Through Modern.* West, St. Paul, Minnesota, 1975.

PLAY ANTHOLOGIES – ONE-ACT

Barrows, Marjorie Wescott. *Drama I.* Macmillan, New York, 1962.

Bruchac, Joseph. *Pushing Up the Sky: Seven Native American Plays for Children.* New York: Dial Books, 2000.

Cerf, Bennett, and Van Cartmell. *Thirty Famous One-Act Plays.* Modern Library, Random House, New York, 1949.

__________. *Twenty-Four Favorite One-Act Plays.* Doubleday, New York, 1958.

Coleman, Wim. *Nine Muses: Modern Plays from Classic Myths.* Perfection Learning Corporation, 2001.

France, Rachel. *A Century of Plays by American Women.* Rosen, New York, 1979.

Gassner, John, and Frederick Little. *Reading and Staging the Play.* Holt, Rinehart and Winston, New York, 1967. Excellent Plays with notes on production, setting, and interpretation.

__________, and Mollie Gassner. *Fifteen International One-Act Plays.* Washington Square Press, New York, 1969.

Griffith, Frances. *One-Act Plays for Our Time.* Popular Library, New York, 1973.

Kozelka, Paul. *Fifteen American One-Act Plays.* Washington Square Press, New York, 1971. Paperback. Excellent plays.

Richards, Stanley. *Best Short Plays.* Chilton, New York. Series from 1969 to present.

__________. *Best Short Plays of the World Theatre.* Crown, New York. Three series from 1958 to 1973.

Scanlan, Michael. *Inside/Out.* Bakers Plays, Boston, 1984. Features issues important to teens.

Sweetkind, Morris. *Ten Great One-Act Plays.* Bantam, New York, 1970.

Weiss, Jerry. *Ten Short Plays.* Dell, New York, 1963.

Zachar, Irwin. *Plays as Experience: One-Act Plays for the Secondary Schools.* Odyssey Press, New York, 1962.

PLAY INDEXES

Conner, John M., and Billie Conner. *Index to Plays in Collections.* 5th ed.

Logasa, Hanna. *Index to One-Act Plays.* F. W. Faxon Company. 1966.

Keller, Dean. *Index to Plays in Periodicals.*

Ottemiller, John H., ed. *Index to Plays in Collections.*

Yaakov, Juliette, ed. *Play Index.* H. W. Wilson.

SCENE COLLECTIONS

Beard, Joycelyn. *Great Contemporary Stage Scenes for Women.* Newbury, VT: Smith and Kraus, 1991.

Bert, Norman. *For Actors: Great Monologues and Dialogues.* Colorado Springs, CO: Meriwether, 1990.

Brown, John R. *Shakescenes: Shakespeare for Two.* Woodland Hills, CA: Applause Theatre Books, 1991.

Cassady, Marshall. *The Book of Cuttings for Acting and Directing.* Skokie, IL: NTC, 1991.

__________. *The Book of Scenes for Acting Practice.* Skokie, IL: NTC, 1991.

Cohen, Lorraine. *Scenes for Young Actors.* New York: Avon Books, 1982.

Elkind, Samuel. *Scenes for Acting and Directing.* Studio City, CA: Players Press, 1991.

Franklin, Miriam. *Rehearsal.* 6th ed. Englewood Cliffs, NJ: Prentice Hall, 1983.

Holt, Robin. *Scenes from Shakespeare.* Jefferson, NC: McFarland, 1988.

Karshner, Roger. *Scenes for Teenagers.* Woodstock, IL: Dramatic Publishers, 1986.

Karton, Joshua. *Film Scenes for Actors.* New York: Bantam, Vol. 1, 1983; Vol. 2, 1987.

Lane, Ruth. *Scenebook for Student Actors.* Barbousville, WV: Dickinson, 1973.

Maag, Edith. *Scenes from the Classics.* Woodstock, IL: Dramatic Publishers. 1987.

Olfson, Lewy. *50 Great Scenes for Student Actors.* New York: Bantam, 1984.

Pomerance, Susan. *Modern Scenes for Women.* Toluca, CA: Dramaline, 1989.

Schulman, Michael, and Eva Mekler. *The Actor's Scenebook.* New York: Bantam, 1984.

__________. *Contemporary Scenes for Student Actors.* New York: Viking Penguin, 1980.

Steffensen, James. *Great Scenes from the World Theatre.* New York: Avon Books, 1976.

Stiver, Harry, and Stanley Kahan. *Play and Scene Preparation.* Needham Heights, MA: Allyn & Bacon,1984.

SCENERY, LIGHTING, & PRODUCTION

Arnold, Richard. *Scene Technology.* Englewood Cliffs, NJ: Prentice Hall, 1990.

Boger, Louise. *The Complete Guide to Furniture Styles.* New York: Scribner, 1982.

Buerki, F. A. *Stagecraft for Non-Professionals.* 3rd ed. Madison, WI: University of Wisconsin Press, 1972.

Burris-Meyer, Harold, and Edward Cole. *Scenery for the Theatre.* Boston, MA: Little, Brown, 1972.

Gassner, John, and Frederick Little. *Reading and Staging the Play.* New York: Holt, Rinehart and Winston, 1967.

Gillette, Arnold. *Stage Scenery: Its Construction and Rigging.* 4th ed. New York: Harper and Row, 1989.

Gillette, J. M. *Designing With Light.* 2nd ed. Mountain View, CA: Mayfield, 1989.

________. *Theatrical Design and Production.* Mountain View, CA: Mayfield, 1992.

Govier, Jacquie. *Create Your Own Stage Props.* Englewood Cliffs, NJ: Prentice-Hall, 1984.

Hays, David. *Stage Lighting for Directors and Actors.* New York: Limelight, 1989.

Kelly, Thomas. *A Backstage Guide to Stage Management.* New York: Watson-Guptil, 1991.

Langley, Stephen. *Theatre Management in America.* 2nd ed. New York: Drama Book Specialists, 1990.

Laughlin, Haller, and Randy Wheeler. *Producing the Musical.* Westport, CT: Greenwood Press, 1984.

Palmer, Richard. *The Lighting Art.* Englewood Cliffs, NJ: Prentice Hall, 1985.

Parker, Oren, and Craig Wolf. *Scene Design and Stage Lighting.* 6th ed. New York: Holt, Rinehart and Winston, 1990.

Simonson, Lee. *The Stage is Set.* 3rd ed. Westport, CT: Greenwood, 1975.

Sporre, Dennis, and Robert Burroughs. *Scene Design in the Theatre.* Englewood Cliffs, NJ: Prentice Hall, 1990.

STORYTELLING

Baker, Augusta, and Ellin Greene. *Storytelling: Art and Technique.* 2nd ed. New York: Bowker, 1987.

Biggs, Nancy, and Joseph Wayne. *Children's Literature Through Story Telling and Drama.* 2nd ed. Dubuque, IA: William Brown, 1979.

Breneman, Lucille and Bren. *Once Upon a Time: A Storytelling Handbook.* Chicago: Nelson-Hall, 1983.

Bryant, Sara. *How to Tell Stories to Children.* New York: Gordon Press, 1980.

Chambers, Dewey. *The Oral Tradition: Storytelling Creative Drama.* 2nd ed. Dubuque, IA: William Brown, 1977.

Pellowski, Anne. *The World of Storytelling.* Rev. ed. New York: Bowker, 1990.

Sawyer, Ruth. *The Way of the Storyteller.* Rev. ed. New York: Viking Press, 1977.

Shedd, Charlie, and Martha. *Tell Me a Story.* New York: Doubleday, 1984.

Siks, Geraldine Brain. *Drama with Children.* New York: Harper-Collins, 1977.

Wilson, Jane. *The Story Experience.* Metuchen, NJ: Scarecrow, 1979.

Ziskind, Sylvia. *Telling Stories to Children.* Glenwood Springs, CO: Wilson, 1976.

THEATRE APPRECIATION & CRITICISM

Barranger, M. S. *Theatre: A Way of Seeing.* 3rd ed. Belmont, CA: Wadsworth 1991.

Blurn, Daniel, and John Willis. *A Pictorial History of American Theatre.* Rev. ed. Long Island City, N.Y.: Crown Publishers, 1986.

Brockett, Oscar G. *The Essential Theatre.* 5th ed. New York: Holt, Rinehart and Winston, 1992.

________. *The Theatre: An Introduction.* 4th ed. New York: Holt Rinehart and Winston, 1992.

Brustein, Robert. *Siege of the Arts: Collected Writings, 1994-2001.* Chicago, IL: Ivan R. Dee, 2001.

Carlson, Marvin, and Yvonne Shafer. *The Play's the Thing.* White Plains, NY: Longman, 1990.

Cohen, Robert. *Theatre.* 2nd ed. Mountain View, CA: Mayfield Publishing, 1988.

Corrigan, Robert. *The Making of Theatre.* Glenview, IL: Scott, Foresman, 1981.

________. *The World of the Theatre.* 2nd ed. Glenview, IL: Scott, Foresman, 1990.

Forrest, Tim. *The Bulfinch Anatomy of Antique Furniture.* Boston: Little, Brown and Company, 1996.

Hatlen, Theodore. *Orientation to the Theatre.* 4th ed. New York: Appleton-Century-Crofts, 1987.

Haymon, Ronald. *How to Read a Play.* New York: Grove Press, 1987.

Kernodle, George. *Invitation to the Theatre.* 3rd ed. New York: Harcourt, Brace and World, 1985.

Pickering, Jerry. *Theatre, A Contemporary Introduction.* 3rd ed. St. Paul, MN: West Publishing, 1981.

Porter, Tom, and Sue Goldman. *Designer Primer,* New York: Charles Scribner's Sons, 1988.

Staub, August, and others. *Varieties of Theatrical Art.* 2nd ed. Raleigh, NC: Contemporary Publishing of Raleigh, 1984.

Wilson, Edwin. *The Living Theatre.* New York: McGraw-Hill, 1982.

________. *The Theatre Experience.* 3rd ed. New York: McGraw-Hill, 1985.

THEATRE HISTORY

Allen, John. *Great Moments in the Theatre.* Phoenix House (38 William IV Street, Charing Cross, London, W.C. 2), 1958. Interesting true stories about important happenings in the theatre; good for reading aloud or to use as lecture sidelights.

Berthold, Margot. *History of World Theatre.* Frederick Ungar, 1972.

Blum, Daniel. *A Pictorial History of the American Theatre, 1860–1985.* 6th ed. Crown, 1985.

Bordman, Gerald. *American Musical Comedy.* Replica Books, 2001.

Brockett, Oscar G. *History of the Theatre.* 9th ed. Allyn and Bacon, 2002.

Butler, James H. *Theatre and Drama of Greece and Rome.* Chandler, 1972.

Cheney, Sheldon. *Theatre: 3000 Years of Drama, Acting, and Stagecraft.* McKay, 1972.

Cheney, William Smith. *Chief Patterns of World Drama.* Dover, 1955. Two-volume paperback. Includes outstanding plays and describes the period from which they evolved.

Duer, Edwin. *The Length and Depth of Acting.* Holt, Rinehart and Winston, 1962. A history of acting.

Ernst, Earle. *The Kabuki Theatre.* University Press of Hawaii, 1974.

Freedley, George, and John Reeves. *A History of the Theatre.* Rev. ed. Crown, 1988. Encyclopedic.

Haar, Frances. *Japanese Theatre in Highlight.* 2nd ed. Charles Tuttle, 1971. Excellent pictures.

Hamilton, Edith. *The Greek Way.* Norton, 1952. (Abridged in National Geographic, March 1944.)

________. *The Roman Way.* Norton, 1932.

Hughes, Glenn. *A History of the American Theatre.* Samuel French, 1951.

Kitto, H. D. K. *Greek Tragedy.* Anchor Books, 1954.

Kuritz, Paul. *The Making of the Theatre History.* Prentice Hall, Englewood Cliffs, N. J., 1988.

Macgowan, Kenneth. *Golden Age of Theatre.* Rev. ed. Prentice-Hall, 1978.

________. and William Melnitz. *The Living Stage: A History of World Theatre.* Prentice-Hall, 1955. Very good.

________. and Herman Rosse. *Masks and Demons.* Harcourt Brace, 1923. Readings on primitive theatre.

Meserve, Walter and Mollie. *A Chronological Outline of World Theatre.* Feedback Theatre Books and Prospero Press, NY, 1992.

VOICE & ORAL INTERPRETATION, DIALECT, DICTION, & PRONUNCIATION

Berry, Cecily. *Voice and the Actor.* New York: Macmillan, 1991.

Blunt, Jerry. *Stage Dialects.* New York: Harper-Collins, 1968.

________. *More Stage Dialects.* Dramatic Publishing, 1996.

Bowen, Elbert, and others. *Communicative Reading.* 4th ed. New York: Macmillan, 1990.

Coger, Leslie, and Melvin White. *Readers Theatre.* 3rd ed. Glenview, IL: Scott, Foresman, 1982.

Crannel, Kenneth. *Voice and Articulation.* Belmont, CA: Wadsworth, 1991.

Eisenson, Jon. *Voice and Diction: A Program for Improvement.* New York: Macmillan, 1985.

Hobbs, Bob. *Teach Yourself Transatlantic.* Mountain View, CA: Mayfield, 1986.

King, Robert and Eleanor DiMichael. *Voice and Diction Handbook.* ____: Warland, 1991.

Lee, Charlotte, and Timothy Guro. *Oral Interpretation.* 8th ed. New York: Houghton Mifflin, 1992.

Lessac, Arthur. *The Use and Training of the Human Voice.* New York: Drama Book Specialists, 1967.

Linklatter, Kristan. *Freeing the Natural Voice.* New York: Drama Book Specialists, 1976.

Machlin, Evangeline. *Speech for the Stage.* New York: Theatre Arts Books, 1980

Rizzo, Raymond. *The Voice as an Instrument.* 2nd ed. New York: Odyssey Press, 1979.

Tanner, Fran. *Readers Theatre Fundamentals.* 2nd ed. Topeka, KS: Clark Publishing, 1993.

Turner, Clifford. *Voice and Speech in the Theatre.* 3rd ed. New Rochelle, NY: Sportshelf, 1982.

Yordon, Judy. *Roles in Interpretation.* 2nd ed. Dubuque, IA: William Brown, 1989.

PLAY PUBLISHERS

Anchorage Press, Inc., P.O. Box 8067, New Orleans, LA 70182.

Baker's Plays, 100 Chauncy St., Boston, MA 02111.

Dramatic Publishing Co., 311 Washington St., P.O. Box 129, Woodstock, IL 60098.

Dramatists Play Service, 440 Park Ave. S., NY, NY 10016.

Encore Performance Publishing, P.O. Box 692, Orem, UT 84057.

Samuel French, Inc., 45 West 25th Street–Dept. W, New York, NY 10010 Phone (212) 206-8990 Fax (212) 206-1429

New Plays, Inc., P.O. Box 5074, Charlottesville, VA 22905.

Perfection Learning Corp, 10520 New York Ave, Des Moines, Iowa 50322

Pioneer Drama Service, Inc., P.O. Box 22555, Denver, CO 80222.

Players Press, Inc., P.O. Box 1132, Studio City, CA 91614.

Plays, the Drama Magazine for Young People, 120 Boylston Street, Boston, MA 02116.

Smith and Krause: Books for Actors, P.O. Box 10, Newbury, VT 05051.

www.stageplays.com

SUGGESTED PLAYS FOR SCHOOL PRODUCTIONS

The following listings include these abbreviations:

Baker: Baker's Plays

DPC: Dramatic Publishing Company

DPS: Dramatists Play Service

French: Samuel French

Three-Act Plays
Classics

Arms and the Man. George Bernard Shaw. Comic satire. 5m 3w. French. 1885 costumes. Raina, the romantic daughter of an Hungarian major, assists an enemy soldier who hides in her home. After the war, the soldier returns to add amusing complications to Raina's planned life.

The Doctor in Spite of Himself. Molière. Comic satire. 8m 5w. French. 17th century French costumes. To spite her lazy husband, Martine tells some strangers that he is a wonderful doctor, but will never admit it until he has been beaten. After a beating Sganarelle not only agrees to being a doctor, but "cures" a very sick maiden by arranging for her to elope with her lover.

The Imaginary Invalid. Molière. Comic satire. 8m 4w. DPC. 17th century French costumes. Argan thinks himself ill and wishing to have a doctor with him at all times, decides to have his daughter marry a doctor. She refuses because she is in love with another. Comic disguises on the part of her lover and servant cure her father, and he agrees to her desired marriage.

The Importance of Being Earnest. Oscar Wilde. Farce. 4m 4w. French. Victorian costumes. When Jack courts Gwendolen, he faces numerous problems because he doesn't have the name of Ernest. Merry complications evolve. Excellent farce.

The Inspector General. Gogol. Farce. 19m 9w (many can be doubles). Baker. 19th century costumes. The crooked politicians of a small Russian town mistake a young braggart for an important government official. Only after they have wined and dined him and have nothing left, do they discover the real government inspector.

Lady Precious Stream. Hsiung. Romantic drama. 16m 8w. Extras. French. When Lady Precious Stream, the daughter of a nobleman, marries a humble gardener, her family disowns her. After years of hardship and adventure, her husband becomes king of the western regions and they again live the noble life. Done in traditional Chinese style.

The Miser. Molière. Comic satire. 11m 5w. French. 17th century French costumes. A greedy father refuses to allow his children to marry as they wish, until he loses his money chest. Delightful situations occur before he regains his money and the children get their wishes.

The Rivals. Richard Brinsley Sheridan. Comedy. 8m 4w. French. 18th century costumes. Lydia is attracted to a young man, Beverley, because she believes he is a romantic peasant. Her aunt disapproves because she wants Lydia to marry the wealthy Jack Absolute. Humorous complications result when Beverley turns out to be Jack in disguise, and Lydia refuses to marry him because of his money.

School for Scandal. Richard Brinsley Sheridan. Comedy. 12m 4w. Baker. 18th century costumes. Intrigues of an artificial society are humorously brought to life as we learn the real character of two brothers who are trying to impress their wealthy uncle.

She Stoops to Conquer. Oliver Goldsmith. Comedy. 15m 4w. French. 18th century costumes. A merry intrigue as the Hardcastles attempt to marry off their two children.

Shakespeare, William
As You Like It
Taming of the Shrew
Midsummer Night's Dream
Twelfth Night
Comedy of Errors
(acting editions and streamlined versions are available through French and Baker)

Comedies & Farces

Ah Wilderness! Eugene O'Neill. 9m 6w. French. 1910 costumes. A small-town family becomes involved with the antics of its teenage son as he asserts his independence. Length needs cutting.

Charley's Aunt. Brandon Thomas. 6m 4w. French. 1892 costumes. Farcical fun begins when an Oxford university student disguises himself as a friend's aunt, so that his friends may entertain their lady loves, properly chaperoned. When the real aunt appears, the frolic becomes even more involved.

Cheaper By The Dozen. Christopher Setgel from the book by Ernestine and Frank Gilbreth. 9m 7w. DPC. Father, an efficiency expert, runs his family of 12 children with efficient factory methods that lead to many humorous events. Good family comedy.

The Curious Savage. John Patrick. 5m 6w. DPS. Mrs. Savage has been left a fortune by her late husband. Because she will not give it to her greedy stepchildren, they commit her to a sanitarium. She meets delightful people there and decides to help them with her money.

The Happiest Millionaire. Kyle Crichton. 9m 6w. DPS. 1916 costumes. A millionaire father's zest for life creates many humorous events as he lunges from one interest into another, including "testing" his daughter's boyfriend.

Ladies of the Jury. Fred Ballard. Comedy-drama. 12m 10w. French. Jury members in a murder trial gradually reverse their decisions through the subtle suggestions of a keenly intelligent lady juror.

Life With Father. Howard Lindsay and Russel Crouse. 8m 8w. DPS. 1880 costumes. Amusing family life as Vinnie enlists her children and relatives to help in getting Father baptized against his wishes.

The Loud Red Patrick. John Boruff. 4m 5w. French. 1912 costumes. An Irish widower who has always taught his four daughters the importance of intellectual freedom finds his democratic family council going against him when his oldest daughter decides to substitute marriage for college.

The Madwoman of Chaillot. Jean Giraudoux. 17m 8w. DPS. A "madwoman" decides to free the world of financiers and other materialists whose worship of money breeds unhappiness. She traps them in a unique way and thus saves Paris.

The Matchmaker. Thornton Wilder. 9m 7w. French. 1880 costumes. A rich merchant hires a lady to arrange for him a marriage with a young girl. The farcical events end with his marrying the lady he hired. Light and fun.

Nuts in May. Kristen Sergel from the book by Cornelia Otis Skinner. 6m 10w. DPC. It is the opening of Miss Skinner's new Broadway play, but instead of a quiet day of rest, she is besieged by well wishing family and friends who are more nervous than she. The fun continues when Cornelia's teenage son reveals that he has accidently asked two dates to the opening.

Our Hearts Were Young and Gay. Jean Kerr, adapted from Cornelia Otis Skinner's novel. 9m 8w. DPC. 1920 costumes. The merry adventures of two girls as they sail for Europe and "discover" Paris. Length needs cutting.

Romanoff and Juliet. Peter Ustinov. 9m 4w. DPS. When the son of a Russian ambassador and the daughter of an American ambassador fall in love, humorous trouble ensues.

Scapino. Frank Dunlop, Jim Dale, and Molière. 10m 4w. DPC. The comic romps of Scapino lead to hilarious situations.

The Solid Gold Cadillac. Teichmann and Kaufman. 13m 5w. DPS. When a little old lady with her ten shares of stock attends a stockholders' meeting of a big company, her questions so worry the directors that they hire her to keep her quiet. But she is not easily subjugated. Needs some editing.

The Star-Spangled Girl. Neil Simon. 2m lw. French. Two earnest young men, struggling to put out a "protest" magazine, spin into romance when an All-American girl moves next door. Witty lines and humorous situations.

You Can't Take It With You. Moss Hart and George Kaufman. 9m 7w. DPS. A delightful family, each pursuing different hobbies, lives a pleasing, unorthodox life that almost breaks up the daughter's romance when her boyfriend's family arrives unexpectedly and is shocked by the activities. Excellent.

Was He Anyone? N. F. Simpson. 3m 4w. DPC. A comic "absurdist" satire on organized charity and bureaucracy as various organizations decide how best to help a man drowning in the Mediterranean.

Dramas

The Barretts of Wimpole Street. Rudolph Besier. 12m 5w. Romantic drama. DPS. 1850 costumes. The romance of Elizabeth Barrett and Robert Browning, against the background of Elizabeth's tyrannical father whom she finally resists. Difficult but worthwhile

The Crucible. Arthur Miller. 10m 10w. DPS. An exciting historical drama about the Puritan purge of witchcraft in old Salem. A classic.

The Diary of Anne Frank. Goodrich and Hackett. 5m 5w. DPS. The story of a Jewish family who goes into hiding in World War II and the shining spirit of the young teenage Anne.

The Dining Room. A. R. Gurney. 3m 3w. DPS. Cast portrays a wide array of characters. The action embodies humorous as well as touching scenes that show the vanishing lifestyle of the upper middle class where the now neglected dining room was once a vital center of family life.

The Diviners. James Leonard. 6m 5w. French. A compelling story of the 1930s when a disenchanted preacher makes friends with a disturbed young man who is afraid of water in any form.

I Remember Mama. John VanDruten, adapted from Katharine Forbes' *Mama's Bank Account.* 9w 13w, DPS. Costumes 1900–1910. (Special version for high schools is available.) Life of a Scandinavian immigrant family who meets its problems with humor and pathos, as the children grow up, graduate, and launch careers. Excellent characterizations.

Inherit the Wind. Jerome Lawrence and Robert Lee. 21m 6w. (Many parts can be doubled.) DPS. 1920 costumes. A poignant, meaningful drama of the Scope's trial concerning the legality of teaching Darwin's Theory of Evolution in the schools. Excellent dialogue.

The Night Thoreau Spent in Jail. Lawrence and Lee. 11m 5w. French. Thoreau as a young man struggling with the principles he stands for and learning from Emerson; all placed in montage for a single night's experience.

Our Town. Thornton Wilder. 17m 7w. French. 1901 costumes. A beautiful play of American life in a small village at the turn of the century. The Gibbs and Webbs watch their children grow up, marry, and then meet death. A deeply moving play in all its simplicity.

The Rainmaker. Richard Nash. Romantic drama. 6m lw. French. A man who says he can bring rain comes to a drought area and sells his plan to a family. Through him they learn the value of a dream and their plain sister, who is doomed an old maid, learns to believe she is pretty and becomes so. Terrific pace.

Twelve Angry Men. Reginald Ross. 13m. (Also women's version: *Twelve Angry Women,* or mixed cast version: *Twelve Angry Jurors.*) DPC. Jurors in a murder case attempt to reach a verdict, and in so doing, learn much about themselves.

Fantasies

Berkeley Square. John Balderston. Drama 7m 8w. French. Some 18th century costumes. A modern American goes to England when he inherits an old English ancestral house in London. There he finds he can step into his ancestor's life in the 18th century.

Captain Applejack. Walter Hackett. Mystery fantasy. 7m 4w. French. Pirate adventures develop when Applejohn learns that his late night visitors are trying to find a pirate's treasure hidden in the house. Applejohn's dream on stage as a pirate later becomes an actuality.

Gramercy Ghost. John Holm. Mystery fantasy. 6m 6w. DPS. A young woman inherits the ghost of a Revolutionary soldier and finds that she is the only one who can see and hear him. Entanglements result until the ghost's secret is discovered and his conditions met.

Green Valley. Frank Waltron. Comic fantasy. 11m 7w. Baker. Elden Berry, the last of a long line of Berrys who pioneered California's Green Valley, is losing his land to an unscrupulous promoter who wants the area because vegetables grow to giant size. The spirits of Elden's ancestors return to help him keep the land. Uniquely refreshing story. Good production notes on making special properties.

Mrs. McThing. Mary Ellen Chase. Comic fantasy. 8m 9w. DPS. When a rich woman deprives her son of playing with a witch's daughter, strange things happen that teach her life's values.

Noah. Andre Obey. Drama fantasy. 5m 4w and 3 as animals. French. Stylized Biblical costumes. The story of Noah and his family as they prepare for and meet the flood.

Mysteries

Angel Street (or *Gaslight*). Patrick Hamilton. 4m 3w. French. 1880 costumes. A murderer almost succeeds in making his wife believe she is insane, when an amiable man from Scotland Yard begins investigating. Exciting action emerges as the detective proves the husband's guilt.

The Bat. Rinehart and Hopwood. 7m 3w. French. Houseguests attempt to solve the mysterious happenings in the home of a deceased bank president whose bank was recently robbed. Excellent mystery, but with exacting light cues.

Double Door. Elizabeth McFadden. 7m 5w. French. 1910 costumes. Victoria dominates her sister's and brother's lives with tyrannical firmness. Disapproving her brother's bride, Victoria makes plans for murder. Suspense develops.

A Murder Has Been Arranged. Emlyn Williams. 3m 6w. French. On the night he is to inherit a large fortune, a man is murdered after he has been tricked into writing his own suicide note. Tension mounts as the others learn what has happened and prepare to obtain a confession from the murderer.

A Perfect Alibi. A. A. Milne. 8m 3w. French. In full view of the audience, an English gentleman is murdered by two houseguests. The police declare the death was suicide, but the dead man's nephew and ward prove differently.

Ten Little Indians. Agatha Christie. 8m 3w. French. Ten strangers who are guests at an island house are each accused of a different murder, and then one by one they too are murdered, according to the rhyme "Ten Little Indians." Suspense mounts as each of the remaining tries to determine who the murderer is.

One-Act Plays
Comedies & Farces

Antic Spring. Robert Nail. 3m 3w. French. High school students go on a pantomimed picnic.

Apollo of Bellac. Jean Giraudoux. 9m 3w. French. A girl learns the secret of getting along in the world – telling every man he is handsome. She does, with amazing results.

The Boor. Anton Chekhov. 2m 1w. French. In his attempts to collect a bill from his debtor's widow, a man gets the widow instead.

Box and Cox. John Morton. 2m 1w. French. The same room is rented to two different men; one by day and one by night. The men are at first unaware of the situation, so humorous events evolve.

Dear Departed. Stanley Houghton. 3m 3w. French. A family is quarreling over their dead father's possessions when he walks in, very much alive.

Family Album. Noel Coward. Comedy with music. 5m 4w. French. Gathered together after their father's funeral, a family feigns sorrow until the oldest admits their father was no good. Memories of childhood and many revelations unfold. Some parts charmingly set to music, but may be used without.

Flattering Word. George Kelly. 2m 3w. French. When he is told that he looks like a great actor, a minister who is against the theatre accepts an invitation to attend a play.

The Florist Shop. Winifred Hawkridge. 3m 2w. Baker. A salesgirl in a florist shop arranges a wedding between a spinster and a bachelor by sending flowers to the lady from an "unknown" admirer.

The Ghost Story. Booth Tarkington. 5m 5w. French. A young man, unhappy with the crowd around his girl, decides to tell a ghost story and scare them away so that he can have the girl to himself. A humorous ending ensues.

Goodbye to the Lazy K. Robert Finch. 5m 1w. Chilton Company (East Washington Square, Philadelphia, Pennsylvania 19106). (Non-royalty play; script appears in Zachar's *Plays as Experience.*) The cowboy hero decides to leave his girl and go to the city where he hopes to become rich. Parting is difficult and his friends make matters worse. Song and dance mixed with the comedy.

The Happy Journey. Thornton Wilder. Comedy-drama. 3m 3w. French. Ma and Pa and two children journey to see a married daughter. A simple story, but dramatically and touchingly told. No scenery.

In the Suds. Barnard and Rose Hewitt. 1m 2w. Baker. A henpecked husband gains revenge upon his shrewish wife when she falls into a tub of suds and can't get out.

I'm a Fool. Christopher Sergel from Sherwood Anderson's story. 4m 4w. DPC. To impress an attractive girl, a boy who works at a race track pretends he is a wealthy heir. The girl promises to write him, but unhappily her letters will go to the person he is impersonating.

Ladies Alone. Ryerson and Clements. 3w. French. Three roommates vow to spend a night home together until the telephone rings and each accepts a date.

The Lost Princess. Dan Totheroh. Comedy in Chinese tradition. Sequel to *The Stolen Prince.* 8m 4w, extras. (Or all women or men.) French. The twin sister of the stolen prince is rescued and reared by a notorious outlaw. The girl reforms him and saves his life when she is recognized as the lost princess.

The Lost Silk Hat. Lord Dunsany. 5m. French. When a young man leaves his hat at his girl's house, he sends different people to retrieve it, with an amusing result.

The Man Who Married a Dumb Wife. Anatole France. 7m 3w. French. A French gentleman marries a woman who cannot speak. When he has his doctor cure his wife, he discovers that life was better when she was silent.

The Marriage Proposal. Anton Chekhov. 2m 1w. French. A man comes to propose but ends up in a violent quarrel over land and a dog.

Master Pierre Patelin. Merritt Stone, tran. 4m 1w. French. A lawyer participates in some underhanded business that prove hilarious.

The Neighbors. Zona Gale. Comedy-drama. 2m 6w. Baker. When a spinster receives word that she is being sent a homeless nephew, the neighbors pitch in to help. A touching story.

Opening Night. Roland Fernand from the story by Cornelia Otis-Skinner. 1m 10w. DPC. The day that she is to open in a Broadway play, Miss Skinner's family wants her to rest, but she is besieged by well wishers and nervous family who are so worried about her that they fail to she has left for the theatre.

Overtones. Alice Gerstenberg. 4w. French. While two women carry on a polite conversation, their inner selves reveal their true thoughts and feelings.

The Princess Marries the Page. Edna St. Vincent Millay. 6m 1w. Baker. A princess falls in love with a neighboring king who is disguised as a page.

The Romancers. Edmond Rostand. 5m 1w. French. Two young people flirt over a garden wall while their fathers pretend disapproval, knowing that if they approve, their children will not marry. A fake abduction brings about the marriage. Delightful and self-contained although it is Act I of a 3-act play.

The Still Alarm. George Kaufman. 5m. French. There is a fire in a hotel, but the men are exceedingly unconcerned about it; and there the fun lies.

Spreading the News. Lady Gregory. 7m 3w. French. When one man forgets his pitchfork at a country fair in Ireland, another runs after him. Nosy townspeople add up misinformation and an exaggerated story of a murder is circulated.

The Stolen Prince. Dan Totheroh. Comedy in Chinese tradition. 9m 3w. (Or all men or women.) French. A prince is stolen in infancy and raised by a poor couple. Brought before the Emperor for punishment, the young prince's true identity is discovered. See The Lost Princess as a sequel.

A Sunny Morning. Quinteros. 2m 2w. French. Two people, who were formerly sweethearts, meet again when they are old.

Sure Thing. David Ives. 1m 1w. DPS. Humorous satire of the dating game in which a young man tries and tries again to engage a young woman in conversation. A bell rings each time he goes astray, and he picks up the conversation once more.

The Trysting Place. Booth Tarkington. 4m 3w. French. Humorous complications arise when several pairs of lovers try to meet in a hotel.

The Ugly Duckling. A. A. Milne. 4m 3w. French. A prince and princess are betrothed by their families, sight unseen. Each family in turn arranges a "stand-in" until the wedding, because of their "plain" children. But the real prince and princess meet and fall in love.

Dramas–Serious Plays, Mysteries, Melodramas

The Clod. Lewis Beach. 4m 1w. French. During the Civil War a farm woman is insulted beyond her endurance by two Southern soldiers who are searching for a Northern soldier.

Cathleen ni Houlihan. William Butler Yeats. 3m 3w. French. 1798 Irish peasant costumes. A young man who is about to be married leaves his fiancee and home to fight for his native Ireland. Excellent symbolic drama.

The Game of Chess. Kenneth Goodman. 4m. French. A pre-revolutionary governor of a Russian province is interrupted at chess by an assassin. Through cunning trickery, the governor saves himself.

Ile. Eugene O'Neill. 5m 1w. DPS. A captain of a whale ship obstinately remains at sea while his wife goes insane.

Jacob Comes Home. William Kozlenko. 2m 3w. Baker. A Jewish family in the 1930s await the return of their father who is to be released by the Nazis. Suspense builds to the horrifying climax. Well written.

The Last of the Loweries. Paul Green. 1m 3w. French. An outlaw son returns to the mountains to see his mother, but he is killed.

The Long Christmas Dinner. Thornton Wilder. Comedy-drama. 5m 7w. French. Spans a family's history of Christmas dinners by showing the changing times and American life in general. A moving story.

The Lottery. Brainerd Duffield from a story by Shirley Jackson. 8m 5w. DPC. From a seemingly happy situation of families gathering for a lottery, we gradually suspect the horrible nature of the lottery.

A Minuet. Louis Parker. Poetic-drama. 2m 1w. French. During the French Revolution, a nobleman who has been separated from his wife meets her as both await the guillotine. A show of moral courage that is handled well.

Moonshine. Arthur Hopkins. 2m. French. A revenue officer who discovers a group of dangerous moonshiners is able to trick them into letting him go. Full of suspense.

Night at the Inn. Lord Dunsany. 8m. French. The thieves who have stolen the ruby eye from an Eastern idol are visited by the idol. A thriller.

The Old Lady Shows Her Medals. James M. Barrie. 2m 5w. French. A childless old woman invents a war hero son who surprisingly materializes. Play can be adapted for modern times.

Pawns. Percival Wilde. 6m. Baker. Ignorant but sensitive peasants learn from a crude, Army sergeant that they are to be "mobilized" and sent to kill their next-door neighbors who are "enemies" because of a boundary line. Powerful.

Riders to the Sea. John M. Synge. 1m 3w. French. The sea triumphs as the wife of a fisherman buries her last son, drowned at sea.

The Ring of General Macias. Josefina Niggle. 3m 2w. Music Corporation of America (598 Madison Avenue, New York, New York 10022). During the Mexican Revolution of 1912, the wife of a Federal general is held captive by two Revolutionary soldiers. She succeeds in "saving" her husband's honor by arranging for his death. Exciting melodrama.

The Sandbar. Edward Albee. 3m 2w. DPS. Comedy and Drama mix in play about old age.

Submerged. Cottman and Shaw. 6m. Baker. When a submarine crew is trapped on the ocean floor, one of them must be shot through the torpedo tube so rescue workers will find the crew. How the choice of man is made and what happens is exciting.

The Sun Is a Dead Man's Weapon. Robert Carroll. 2m 2w. French. When their tyrannical father dies, two sisters and a brother think they can pick up life where they left it. The older sister learns something about their past, however, that alters their future.

The Valiant. Hollworthy Hall and Robert Middlezuss. 5m 1w. French. A girl visits a man in prison, hoping he is her long lost brother.

Trifles. Susan Glaspell. 3m 3w. Baker. While the police are searching for clues that will convict a woman of murdering her husband, two friends discover items that would convict her. By keeping still about their discovery, their friend is released. Powerful story.

Two Crooks and a Lady. Eugene Pillot. 3m 3w. French. Two thieves are about to steal an old woman's jewels, but she is cleverly able to get them fighting between themselves.

Where the Cross Is Made. Eugene O'Neill. 6m 1w. DPS. An old man dies and his son is driven insane through a search for a nonexistent treasure.

The Will. James M. Barrie. 6m 1w. French. 1915 and modern costumes. The life of a husband and wife is revealed through the years as they have their will drawn up, first as poor newlyweds; later in middle life; and finally, by the old, wealthy husband who has no one to leave his money to because his wife is dead.

Fantasies

The Actor's Nightmare. Christopher Durang. Fantasy-Comedy. 2m 3w. Grove/Atlantic, Inc. (841 Broadway, New York, N.Y. 10003). To his dismay, George finds himself onstage with no idea what part he is playing. Hilarious antics ensue.

Aria da Capo. Edna St. Vincent Millay. Fantasy-drama. 4m 1w. Baker. Pierrot and Columbine in a play written in protest about war and selfishness.

The Devil and Daniel Webster. Stephen Vincent Benèt. Fantasy-drama. 6m 1w. DPS. Daniel Webster pleads a case against the Devil for a man who has sold his soul to the Devil.

Dust of the Road. Kenneth Goodman. Fantasy-drama. 3m 1w. French. A man, who is about to steal from his friend's son, meets Judas who is walking the earth on Christmas Eve.

Early Frost. Douglas Parkhirst. Fantasy-mystery. 4w. French. When a young girl comes to live with her two old aunts and begins to rummage around the attic, the horrible secret of her "strange" aunt is revealed.

Jest of Hahalaba. Lord Dunsany. 4m. Fantasy-drama. French. An old gentleman, through the powers of an alchemist who conjures spirits, is allowed to see into the forthcoming year. What he sees is a terrible shock—notice of his own death the very next day.

Maker of Dreams. Oliphant Down. Fantasy-comedy. 2m 1w. French. Pierrot, searching for his ideal woman, is assisted by the Maker of Dreams.

Three Pills in a Bottle. Rachel Field. Fantasy-drama. 5m 3w. French. The souls of three people come to play with a sick child, who gives them each a magic pill to cure their particular pains.

This Way to Heaven. Douglas Parkhirst. Fantasy-comedy. 2m 3w. French. A mysterious man appears in Gram's kitchen and makes several, bungling attempts to take Gram with him to heaven, where he wants her to cook for his section so he can earn his wings. Finally he decides to leave Gram, but there is a surprise ending.

The Wonder Hat. Hecht and Goodman. Fantasy-comedy. 3m 2w. French. Harlequin buys a hat that makes him invisible, and Columbine buys a slipper that makes her attractive to men. Humorous situations and a surprising end.

SOURCES & ADDRESSES

DECLAMATION MATERIAL

Orations, monologues, readings, pageants, blackouts, stunts, skits, sketches, etc.

Contemporary Drama Service
885 Elkton Drive
Colorado Springs, Colorado 80933

Hansen Drama Shop
718 E. 3900 S.
Salt Lake City, Utah 84107

PLAYS

To keep informed on new plays, have your name put on the mailing list for current catalogues published by these companies.

Baker's Plays (Baker)
PO Box 699222
Quincy, MA 02269-9222

Brooklyn Publishers
1841 Cord St.
Odessa, TX 79762
1-888-473-8521

Clark Publications
(I. E. Clark)
P. O. Box 246
Schulenburg, Texas 78956

Dramatic Publishing Company (DPS)
3ll Washington St.
Woodstock, Illinois 60098-3308

Dramatists Play Service, Inc. (DPS)
440 Park Avenue South
New York, New York 10016

Samuel French, Inc. (French)
45 West 25th St.
New York, New York 10010

The Drama Book Specialist
821 Broadway
New York, New York 10003
(handles books on every theatre aspect)

Drama Book Shop
250 W. 40th St.
New York, New York 10018
(handles most theatre books)

Perfection Learning Corporation
1000 North Second Avenue
P.O. Box 500
Logan, Iowa 51546
1 800 831 4190

Richard Stoddard
Out Of Print Theatre Books
90 E 10th Street
New York, New York 10013
(212) 982-9440,

Theatre Books, Inc.
1576 Broadway-Room 312
New York, New York 10036
(212) 757-2834.

MUSICALS

Also try other companies listed in this section.

Music Theatre International
421 West 54th St.
New York, New York 10019

Rodgers and Hammerstein Library
229 West 28th St. 11th floor
New York, New York 10001

Tams-Witmark Music Library
560 Lexington Ave.
New York, New York 10022

MELODRAMAS

Also try other companies listed in this section.

Pioneer Drama Service
P. O. Box 4267
Englewood, Colorado 80155-4267

THEATRE SUPPLY HOUSES

These are just a few of the larger supply houses. For a comprehensive list of suppliers, see

The Directory of TCI
P. O. Box 470
Mt. Morris, Illinois 61054

COSTUMES

Broadway Costumes
1100 West Cermak Road
Second Floor
Chicago, Illinois 60608

Dodger Costume Rental, Inc.
601 West 26th Street
Suite 312
New York, New York 10001

Lost Eras
1511 West Howard Street
Chicago, Illinois 60626
773-764-7400

Milliners Supply Company
911 Elm Street
Dallas, Texas 75202

Morris Costumes
3108 Monroe Road
Charlotte, North Carolina 28205

Rubies Costume
1 Rubie Plaza
Richmond Hill, New York 11418

The tdf Costume Collection
601 West 26th St, 17th Floor,
New York, New York 10001
(costumes for non-profit theatre groups)

The Theatre Company
687 North Benson Avenue
Upland, California 91786

Theatre House, Inc
400 West 3rd Street
P.O. Box 2090
Covington, Kentucky 41112

COSTUME SPECIALTIES

Backstage (wigs, accessories, hats)
41 West Broadway
Eugene, Oregon 97401

Costume Armour
P. O. Box 85
Cornwell, New York 12518

Weapons of Choice
4075 Browns Valley Rd.
Napa, California 94558-4144

Costume Shop Supplier
Richard The Thread
8320 Melrose Ave. #201
Los Angeles, California 90069

Rainments Serving the Costumer
P. O. Box 6176
Fullerton, California 92634
(historical patterns, corset kits, etc.)

FABRIC

(For costumes, drapes, and scenery)

Amazon Drygoods
2218 E 11th St.
Davenport, Iowa 52803-3760

Associated Fabrics
104 E. 25th Street
New York, New York 10010

Dazian's Inc.,
27 W. 20th Street
Suite 903
New York, New York 10019

Rose Brand Textile Fabrics
75 9th Ave. 4th Fl.
New York, New York 10001
1-800-225-1624

GELATINS & LIGHTING PLASTICS

Rosco Laboratories
52 Harbor View Avenue
Stamford, Connecticut 06902

Lee Filters
1015 Chestnut Street
Burbank, California 91506

LIGHTING

Grand Stage Lighting Company
630 West Lake
Chicago, Illinois 60606

The Great American Market
826 N. Cole Avenue
Hollywood, California 90038

Hub Electric Company
6207 Commercial Road
Crystal Lake, Illinois 60014

Kliegl Lighting Company
5 Aerial Way
Syosset, New York 11791

Premier Lighting & Production Co.
12023 Victory Blvd.
North Hollywood, California 91606-3318

Stagecraft Industries
P. O. Box 4442
Portland, Oregon 97208

Strand–Century Lighting
18111 S. Santa Fe Ave.
Rancho Dominguez, California 90221

MAKEUP HOUSES

(Send for catalogues)

Joe Blasco Cosmetics
1708 Hilklhurst Ave
Los Angeles, California 90027

Bob Kelly Cosmetics
151 West 46th Street
New York, New York 10036

Mehron, Inc.
45 East Rte. #303
Valley Cottage, New York 10989

Ben Nye
11571 Santa Monica Boulevard
Los Angeles, California 90025

Stein Cosmetic Company
430 Broome Street
New York, New York 10013

PUBLICITY

(posters, news stories on plays)

Package Publicity Service
27 W. 24th Street
New York, New York 10010

RECORDINGS & CASSETTES DIALECTS–

Cassettes are available with Blunt's Stage Dialects, Machlin's Dialects for the Stage, and Stern's Dialect Records

Various accent and dialect cassettes are available from:

Dialect/Accent Specialists
P. O. Box 44
Lyndonville, Vermont 05851
Readings & Discussions (on cassettes)

Center for Cassette Studies
919 Third Avenue
New York, New York 10022
(extensive index)

Listening Library
P.O. Box L
Old Greenwich, Connecticut 06870

SOUND EFFECTS

Dramatists Play Service
440 Park Avenue South
New York, New York 10016

Films for the Humanities
P. O. Box 2053
Princeton, New Jersey 08543
(BBC collection)

Valentino, Inc.
P. O. Box 534
Elmsford, New York 10523

SCENE PAINT

Gothic Color Company
P. O. Box 189
Glen Cove, New York 11542

Playhouse Colors
771 9th Avenue
New York, New York 10019

STAGE HARDWARE

J. R. Clancy, Inc.
7041 Interstate Island Road
Syracuse, New York 13209

Mutual Hardware
5-45 49th Avenue
Long Island City, New York 11101

THEATRICAL SUPPLIES

These houses handle lights, makeup, stage hardware, fabrics, paints, costumes, tools, draperies, etc.

Alcone Company (Paramount Theatrical Supplies)
5-49 49th Avenue
Long Island City, New York 11101
(excellent catalogue)

Globe Theatrical Supply
813 Pearl St
Sioux City, Iowa 51101

Norcostco
825 Phode Island Ave. South
Minneapolis, Minnesota 55422

Olesen Company
1535 Ivar Avenue
Hollywood, California 90028
(informative catalogue)

Theatre and Fabric House
P. O. Box 2090
Covington, Kentucky 41012

Tobins Lake Studio
7030 Old US 23
Brighton, Michigan 48116

TICKETS PRINTED

Sets Tickets
P. O. Box 84
Sierra Madre, California 91025

Ticket Craft
1390 Jerusalem Avenue
Merrick, New York 11566

Weldon, William, and Lick
P. 0. Box 168
Fort Smith, Arkansas 72902

SPECIAL EFFECTS

(projections, lighting, fog, etc..)

The Great American Market
4975 Pico Blvd.
Los Angeles, California 90019

Jauchen and Meeh, Inc.
43 Bridge Street
Brooklyn, New York 11201

VIDEOS & FILMS

Many state universities offer rental videos and films on drama. For a list of teaching videos and films, see:

R. R. Bowker's Educational Film Locater. A consortium of university film centers. Excellent.

The Video Source Book. National Video Clearing House. Lists thousands of available videos. Excellent.

The following companies rent professional films of plays:

Contemporary Films
267 W. 25th Street
New York, New York 10001

Arthur Cantor Inc.
2112 Broadway, Suite 400
New York, New York 10023

Audio Brandon Films
737 Greenbay Road
Wilmette, Illinois 60091
(Excellent Shakespeare series)

The following companies offer videos on theatre history, Shakespeare and his plays, acting, voice training, movement, stage combat, script analysis, auditioning, characterization, makeup, lighting, set construction, etc.

Combat Video
322 NW 175th
Seattle, Washington 98177

DVC, Inc
7301 East 46th Street
Indianapolis, Indiana 46226

Films for the Humanities
P. O. Box 2053
Princeton, New Jersey 98543

First Light Video Publishing
2321 Abbot Kinney Blvd Top Floor
Venice, CA 90291

Insight Media
2161 Broadway
New York, New York 10024

Olesen Company
1535 Ivar Avenue
Hollywood, California 90028

Theatre Arts Video Library
174 Andrew Avenue
Leucadia, California 92024

THEATRE ORGANIZATIONS & PERIODICALS

Affiliation with any of the following groups will keep you abreast of new events in the profession. Membership will also entitle you to receive the organization's bulletin and to attend the conferences.

ORGANIZATIONS

Actors Equity
165 West 46Th Street
New York, New York 10036.
(212) 869-8530.
They will forward mail to members.

Alpha Psi Omega
Wabash College
P. O. Box 352
Crawfordsville, Indiana 47933
(drama honorary for college students)

American Alliance for Theatre and Education
Theatre Department
Arizona State University
P.O. Box 872002
Tempe, Arizona 85287
(480) 965-6046

American Theatre of Higher Education
P. O. Box 15282
Evansville, Indiana 47716

ASCAP
1 Lincoln Plaza
New York, New York 10023
(212) 595-3050

BMI
320 West 57Th Street
New York, New York 10019
(212) 586-2000

Delta Psi Omega
Wabash College
P. O. Box 352
Crawfordsville, Indiana 47933
(drama honorary for junior college students)

Dramatists Guild
234 West 44Th Street
New York, New York 10036
(212) 398-9366
They will forward mail to members.

Educational Theatre Association
2343 Auburn Avenue
Cincinnati, Ohio 45219
(513) 421-3900

International Theatre Institute
1860 Broadway
New York, New York 10019

International Thespian Society
3368 Central Parkway
Cincinnati, Ohio 45225
(for secondary school students)

National Collegiate Players
Box 66
Hamline University
St. Paul, Minnesota 55104

Speech Communication Association
5105 Backlick Road, Suite E
Annandale, Virginia 22003
(for high school and college students and faculty)

PERIODICALS – EDUCATIONAL

Communication Education

Speech Communication Association
5105 Backlick Road, Suite E
Annandale, Virginia 22003

Dramatics Magazine
Thespian Society & Educational Theatre Assoc.
3368 Central Parkway
Cincinnati, Ohio 45225

New Theatre Quarterly
32 East 57 Street
New York, New York 10022

Playbill
(Alpha Psi Omega & Delta Psi Omega)
71 Vanderbilt Avenue
New York, New York 10169

Stage Directions
P. O. Box 1911
Marion, OH 43306-4011
(for academic and community theatre)

PERIODICALS – COMMERCIAL

American Theatre
520 8th Ave 24th Floor
New York, New York 10018

Entertainment Design
249 W. 17th Street
New York, New York 10011
(212) 462-3600
Fax (212) 367-8345
(a 30-year-old trade publication focusing on the art and technology of show business, with coverage including design and technology)

Lighting Dimensions Magazine
5680 Greenwood Plaza Blvd.
Suite 100
Greenwood Village, CO 80111
(303) 741-2901
Fax (720) 489-3101
(trade magazine for lighting professionals, targeting designers twelve issues per year)

Plays, Inc.
120 Boylston Street
Boston, Massachusetts 02116
(monthly magazine with scripts and skits for teenagers)

Theatre Crafts
135 Fifth Avenue
New York, New York 10010
(articles on backstage work, techniques, etc.)